CONSTITUTIONAL COUNTERREVOLUTION?

In this book, Richard Funston focuses upon the Supreme Court's efforts in the areas of race relations, legislative apportionment, pornography, religion, and criminal defendants' rights. "Judicial interpretation and the criticism theory being an on-going enterprise, however, the book began to undergo a transformation while it was still in preparation."

Funston points out that what began as a critique of the Warren Court became a study of "the continuities and discontinuities in the decision-making of the Warren and Burger Courts." His chapters point up the complexity of the issues in Court cases and the author shows that "absolute" principles have a way of colliding with other "absolutes" and that the "absolute" will sooner or later "collapse under its own weight."

He shows that almost from the first day on the Supreme Court bench, Earl Warren and the Court which he led were embroiled in controversy — and that "one of the frustrations of writing about the contemporary Court is that one is shooting at a moving target." He discusses Mr. Justice Douglas's retirement (and his replacement by John Paul Stevens) and the impact of these moves. He sees that the present Justices have given evidence of a desire to apply their power sparingly, coupled with "healthy scepticism about the practical limits of the law as a vehicle for social change.

Funston summarizes in this book that we must reduce the public's expectations of the Court and that the Court must reduce its "expectations of itself." But "it is intelligence that makes the difference between judicial restraint and a do-nothing Court."

CONSTITUTIONAL COUNTERREVOLUTION?

The Warren Court And The Burger Court:
Judicial Policy Making In Modern America

RICHARD Y. FUNSTON

SCHENKMAN PUBLISHING COMPANY, INC.

Halsted Press Division

John Wiley & Sons

New York — London — Sydney — Toronto

Copyright © 1977
Schenkman Publishing Company, Inc.
Cambridge, Massachusetts 02138

Distributed solely by Halsted Press, a Division
of John Wiley & Sons, Inc., New York

Library of Congress Cataloging in Publication Data

Funston, Richard
    Constitutional counterrevolution?

  Bibliography: p.
  Includes indexes.
  1. United States. Supreme Court.   I. Title.
KP8748.F85   347'.73'26   76-49923
ISBN 0-470-99022-8
ISBN 0-470-99023-6 pbk.

Printed in the United States of America

This book is dedicated to

D.S.H.

R.P.L.

&

J.A.C.G.

*If I have seen further, it
is by standing upon the
shoulders of Giants.*
— Sir Isaac Newton

Contents

Preface

This book began, an uncomfortable number of years ago, as a critique of the work of the Supreme Court under the Chief Justiceship of the late Earl Warren. While there were already a number of commentaries on the Warren Court, I was concerned that each of them suffered from one of three deficiencies.

There were the polemical works which, regardless of their assessment of the Court, were often characterized by innuendo and half-truth and failed to present a balanced perspective because they did not try to do so. The more dispassionate scholarly works, on the other hand, tended to divide into two groups. Either they were simple catalogues of the Court's holdings, or they were written for the *cognoscenti* and assumed a broad-ranging background in constitutional law. The former group, because they did not concern themselves with the intellectual coherence of the Court's opinions, were largely uncritical, while the latter, being primarily directed at law school audiences, were too difficult for undergraduates and interested lay readers. As a consequence, beginning students and educated laypersons were denied access to the thoughtful analyses of such as Professors Bickel, Jaffe, and Kurland and thus could not grasp the burden of the scholarly complaint about the Warren Court. Because I believe that judges, and not least Justices of the Supreme Court of the United States, ought to be able to explain why they are doing what they are doing, I sought to produce a volume geared to the level of this neglected audience which would synthesize the academic criticism of the Warren Court yet not assume any prior familiarity with case law on the reader's part.

Not being able to canvass the full spectrum of Warren Court decision-making in a necessarily limited number of pages, I chose to focus upon the Court's efforts in the areas of race relations, legislative apportionment, and criminal defendants' rights, Mr. Chief Justice Warren himself having selected these as the most important aspects of the Court's work during his tenure. Again because Warren had indicated that it had presented the most intractable problems while he was Chief Justice, the obscenity litigation was chosen as an example of the Court's First Amendment interpretation. In addition, chapters have been devoted to the problem of the retroactive effect of a constitutional decision and to issues of the appropriate relationship between church

and state; the first because of its association with the criminal defendants' rights rulings, the second because of the public furor which
many of the Court's holding in this area elicited. The idea was to
summarize the substance of the Court's decisions in each area and to
suggest the questions which scholarly critics had raised about the
reasons given to justify these decisions.

Judicial interpretation and the ciriticism thereof being an on-going
enterprise, however, the book began to undergo a transformation
while it was still in preparation. After 1970, the Supreme Court was
again fully manned under a new Chief Justice and increasingly staffed
by the appointees of an unpopular and eventually discredited President. This has occasioned much hand-wringing and gnashing of teeth
which, though it now comes from the opposite side of the political
spectrum, is reminiscent of the good old days of the Warren Court.
While a few scholars, notably Leonard Levy, have contributed to this
criticism, most of it has been journalistic rather than academic and has
been based upon prognostications of what the Court *might* do rather
than informed by fact. Much of the criticism has seemed to me unfounded. What began as a critique of the Warren Court, therefore, has
become a study of the continuities and discontinuities in the
decision-making of the Warren and Burger Courts, Although the subject has changed somewhat, nevertheless, I have attempted to maintain the approach of summarizing the case law, while introducing the
reader to the scholarly criticism of that law. In the final chapter, I have
advanced my own conclusions about the relationship or, more appropriately, relationships between the Warren Court and the Burger
Court. But, precisely because of the evolutionary nature of Supreme
Court decision-making, those conclusions must be regarded as tentative indeed. Some of them may even be upset by the Court before this
book goes to press, but that is merely part of the hazard and fascination
of following and commenting upon the Supreme Court of the United
States.

As with any book, the writing of this one involved incurring certain
obligations which should now be acknowledged. Professors Douglas
S. Hobbs, J.A.C. Grant, and Leo Snowiss of U.C.L.A. and Professor
Charles Andrain of San Diego State University have all read parts of
this manuscript in a variety of guises during the past half dozen years.
Each has offered helpful comment and constructive, though some-

times harsh, criticism. Where I have incorporated their suggestions, the manuscript has been improved; where I have ignored them, I have done so at my peril. I am greatly indebted to each of these scholars, but needless to say they are not to be held responsible for my analysis and interpretation. Mrs. Veva Link and Ms. Paula Forrester typed the manuscript with speed, accuracy, and a good nature to which the author was not at all times entitled. My wife, Jan, should also be thanked for various conscripted labors which she performed. But my greatest debt is owed to my graduate assistant, Mr. Frank Eddy, now a member of the faculty at Jacksonville State College, who provided both research and editorial assistance above and beyond the call of duty. Finally, a small vote of gratitude is due to Martin, Cleo, Missy, and Two, who steadfastly refused to take this project seriously and thereby spared me from the dreaded consequences of all work and no play.

R.Y.F.

Davis, California
April, 1976

CONSTITUTIONAL COUNTERREVOLUTION?

Chapter 1
The Need for Reasons

We Americans are accustomed to think of our political history in terms of Presidential administrations.[1] Mere mention of the name Franklin Delano Roosevelt serves quickly and concisely to conjure up in most of our minds the tenor of an entire period; so does that of Jackson and Lincoln and Theodore Roosevelt. This sort of referential historical thinking is harmless enough, but, on the whole, it is not very accurate. Conditioned to think of the Presidency as the central office in the entire political system, we too often forget that the experiences of other agencies or institutions might better encapsulate, delimit, or suggest the mood of various eras in our history.

In particular this is true of the nearly two decades from the Korean War and the departure of President Truman from office to the potential political, and therefore judicial, realignment of the 1970's. No other institution of government quite so adequately reflected the central issues and concerns of American life during this period as did the Supreme Court under the leadership of Earl Warren. While it is true that the Chief Justice of the United States Supreme Court is only the first among equals,[2] it is also true that within a few months of Warren's appointment the Court, speaking through the new Chief Justice, handed down a unanimous decision outlawing school segregation.[3] Over the next fifteen years that decision was followed by literally dozens of "landmark" decisions—most of them containing unprecedented guarantees of individuals' civil liberties—involving race relations,[4] law enforcement proce-

---

[1]*See, e.g.* R. HOFSTADTER, THE AMERICAN POLITICAL TRADITION (1948).

[2]Danelski, *The Influence of the Chief Justice in the Decisional Process*, in COURTS, JUDGES, AND POLITICS: AN INTRODUCTION TO THE JUDICIAL PROCESS 497 (W. Murphy & C. Pritchett eds. 1961).

[3]Brown v. Board of Education, 347 U.S. 483 (1954); Bolling v. Sharpe, 347 U.S. 497 (1954).

[4]Cooper v. Aaron, 358 U.S. 1 (1961); Peterson v. Greenville, 373 U.S. 244 (1963); Griffin v. County School Board of Prince Edward County, 377 U.S. 218 (1964); Heart of Atlanta Motel v. United States, 379 U.S. 241 (1964); Harper v. Virginia Board of Elections, 383 U.S. 663 (1966); Reitman v. Mulkey, 387 U.S. 369 (1967); Loving v. Virginia, 388 U.S. 1 (1967).

dures,[5] religious practices,[6] and voting.[7] With courage and compassion, the Court led a transformation of the law, while the other branches of the government delayed,[8] and in so doing the "Warren Court" and Earl Warren personally became the center of a storm of controversy, the likes of which the Court had not experienced since the "bad old days" of 1937.[9] Although the Warren Court was not the central reality of the period, it will probably be remembered in the history books as its chief symbol.

That period, however, has allegedly come to an end. With the 1968 election of Richard Milhous Nixon to the Presidency, some thought that a new, if not entirely desirable, era in American politics was in the offing,[10] and this new era seemed to have a remarkably good chance to be suddenly reflected in Supreme Court decision-making. With the virtually forced resignation of Mr. Justice Fortas[11] and the retirement of Mr. Chief Justice Warren, coupled with the deaths of Hugo Lafayette Black and John Marshall Harlan, President Nixon was afforded a virtually unprecedented opportunity to remake the membership of the Supreme Court in his first term of office. Having vigorously criticized the Court in his campaign, the new President set about his task with enthusiasm. But, though he behaved no differently than any previous President in this regard,[12] Mr. Nixon was vehemently criticized for attempting to mold

[5]Mapp v. Ohio, 367 U.S. 643 (1961); Gideon v. Wainwright, 372 U.S. 335 (1963); Escobedo v. Illinois, 378 U.S. 478 (1964); Miranda v. Arizona, 384 U.S. 436 (1966); Berger v. New York, 388 U.S. 41 (1967); United States v. Wade, 388 U.S. 218 (1967); Katz v. United States, 389 U.S. 347 (1967); Terry v. Ohio, 392 U.S. 1 (1968); Chimel v. California, 395 U.S. 752 (1969).

[6]McGowan v. Maryland, 366 U.S. 420 (1961); Engel v. Vitale, 370 U.S. 421 (1962); Abington v. Schempp, 374 U.S. 203 (1963); Sherbert v. Verner, 374 U.S. 398 (1963); Board of Education v. Allen, 392 U.S. 236 (1968).

[7]Baker v. Carr, 369 U.S. 186 (1962); Wesberry v. Sanders, 376 U.S. 1 (1964); Reynolds v. Sims, 377 U.S. 533 (1964); Harper v. Virginia Board of Elections, 383 U.S. 663 (1966); Avery v. Midland County, 390 U.S. 474 (1968); Kirkpatrick v. Preisler, 394 U.S. 526 (1969).

[8]See Cox, *Chief Justice Earl Warren*, 83 HARV. L. REV. 1 (1969).

[9]See A. MASON, THE SUPREME COURT FROM TAFT TO WARREN 94-98, 113-115 (1958); J. ALSOP & T. CATLEDGE, THE 168 DAYS (1938).

[10]See, e.g., S. LUBELL, THE HIDDEN CRISIS IN AMERICAN POLITICS (1969); R. SCAMMON & B. WATTENBERG, THE REAL MAJORITY (1970); K. PHILLIPS, THE EMERGING REPUBLICAN MAJORITY (1969).

[11]R. SHOGAN, A QUESTION OF JUDGMENT: THE FORTAS CASE AND THE STRUGGLE FOR THE SUPREME COURT (1972).

[12]See G. SCHUBERT, CONSTITUTIONAL POLITICS 37-66 (1960).

the Court "in his own image."[13] While the ill-chosen nominations of Clement Haynsworth and G. Harold Carswell were rejected by the Senate,[14] liberal opinion in America was nonetheless disturbed by the successful appointments of William Rehnquist, Lewis Powell, Harry Blackmun, and Warren Earl Burger. Indeed, it has become an accepted dogma of contemporary liberalism that a new Court majority is about a wholesale reversal of that body of precedent and policy established during the Warren years. The Burger Court, it is alleged, is out to tear down the house that Earl built. The change in the Chief Justiceship which occurred in 1969 thus symbolizes for many not simply an abrupt break with previous constitutional interpretation but the end of a unique period in American political history and the beginning of another.

For a time, then, the Supreme Court has been lifted from its normal obscurity to stage center in the American political debate. This is a position which may be uncomfortable and is certainly uncustomary for an institution which has normally been characterized by a relatively low popular visibility.[15] To be sure, Americans do become aware of a few major decisions each term of Court, but very few of them know, understand, or care anything about the line of cases of which the landmark case is a part, let alone about the totality of the Court's decision-making. While the average American displays little interest in or knowledge of politics,[16] his appreciation of the Supreme Court is especially minimal.

This sharing in the public ignorance of political institutions, however, is not what scholars have in mind when they speak of the Court as a

[13]*See* J. SIMON, IN HIS OWN IMAGE: THE SUPREME COURT IN RICHARD NIXON'S AMERICA (1973).

[14]*See generally* R. HARRIS, DECISION (1971).

[15]S. WASBY, THE IMPACT OF THE UNITED STATES SUPREME COURT: SOME PERSPECTIVES 237-242 (1970); Murphy & Tanenhaus, *Public Opinion and the United States Supreme Court: Mapping Some Prerequisites for Court Legitimation of Regime Changes* in FRONTIERS OF JUDICIAL RESEARCH 273 (J. Grossman & J. Tanenhaus eds. 1969): Dolbeare, *The Public Views the Supreme Court,* in LAW, POLITICS, AND THE FEDERAL COURTS 194 (H. Jacob ed. 1967); Dolbeare & Hammond, *The Political Party Basis of Attitudes Toward the Supreme Court,* 31 PUB. OP. Q. 16 (1967): Kessel, *Public Perceptions of the Supreme Court,* 10 MIDW. J. POL. SCI. 167 (1966).

[16]*See* Stokes & Miller, *Party Government and the Saliency of Congress,* 26 PUB. OP. Q. 531 (1962); Miller, *The Political Behavior of the Electorate,* in THE AMERICAN GOVERNMENT ANNUAL: 1960-61, at 41 (E. Latham, *et. al.,* eds. 1960); B. BERELSON, P. LAZARSFELD, & W. McPHEE, VOTING 215-233 (1954).

political agency.[17] War, it has been said, is politics carried on by other means. So, too, is litigation. Politics is the resolution of conflict,[18] and law is the tangible statement of that resolution at any given point in time. Of course, in the simple-minded sense that government partakes of politics and vice versa, the Court is necessarily political, since it is an agency of government. But even under the more sophisticated definitions of "politics" advanced by modern social scientists,[19] the Supreme Court of the United States remains peculiarly political. This is so because it is both independent of and coordinate with the other branches of the national government and because it has been afforded a device through which it can protect its position. This mechanism through which the Court guards its political prerogatives is its power of constitutional inter-

[17]*See* G. SCHUBERT, *supra* note 12; R. McCLOSKEY, THE AMERICAN SU-PREME COURT (1960); J. PELTASON, FEDERAL COURTS IN THE POLITICAL PROCESS (1955).

Behaviorally oriented scholars sometimes claim that the political nature of the Court was not recognized until the invention of the Guttman scale. *See, e.g.*, H. SPAETH (ed.), THE WARREN COURT: CASES AND COMMENTARY 17, n. 1 (1966). This claim is not merely extreme; it is fatuous. That public policy considerations are a motivating factor in the Court's decision-making has been known at least since Corwin, Haines, Pound, and Holmes — if not since Marshall. *See, e.g.*, E. CORWIN, THE DOCTRINE OF JUDICIAL REVIEW (1914); E. CORWIN, COURT OVER CONSTITUTION (1938); Haines, *General Observations on the Effects of Personal, Political, and Economic Influences in the Decisions of Judges*, 17 ILL. L. REV. 96 (1922); C. HAINES, THE AMERICAN DOCTRINE OF JUDICIAL SUPREMACY (1932); Pound, *Liberty of Contract*, 18 YALE L. J. 454 (1909); Lochner v. New York, 198 U.S. 45, 75-76 (1905) (Holmes, J., dissenting); M. LERNER (ed.), THE MIND AND FAITH OF JUSTICE HOLMES (1954). Nor do traditionally oriented students of the Court deny this. *See, e.g.*, A. BICKEL, THE LEAST DANGEROUS BRANCH: THE SUPREME COURT AT THE BAR OF POLITICS (1962); R. McCLOSKEY, THE AMERICAN SUPREME COURT (1960). Rather, they question the utility of the behavioralists' methodology for adequately examining the political nature of the Court. *See* Mendelson, *The Untroubled World of Jurimetrics*, 26 J. POL. 914 (1964); Mendleson, *The Neo-Behavioral Approach to the Judicial Process: A Critique*, 57 AM. POL. SCI. REV. 593 (1963); Roche, *Political Science and Science Fiction*, 52 AM. POL. SCI. REV. 1026 (1958).

[18]*See* R. DAHL. PLURALIST DEMOCRACY IN THE UNITED STATES: CON-FLICT AND CONSENT (1967); D. NIMMO & T. UNGS, AMERICAN POLITICAL PATTERNS: CONFLICT AND CONSENSUS (1969); T. HOBBES, LEVIATHAN (1651).

[19]*See, e.g.*, H. LASSWELL, POLITICS: WHO GETS WHAT, WHEN, HOW (1936); H. LASSWELL & A. KAPLAN, POWER AND SOCIETY: A FRAMEWORK FOR POLITICAL INQUIRY (1950); D. EASTON, THE POLITICAL SYSTEM (1953); D. EASTON, A SYSTEMS ANALYSIS OF POLITICAL LIFE (1965); D. EASTON (ed.), VARIETIES OF POLITICAL THEORY (1966).

pretation. The distinguishing feature of judicial decision-making in America is the power of the federal judiciary and ultimately the Supreme Court to judge with finality the constitutionality not simply of state statutes but also of the acts of the coordinate branches of the federal government,[20] in other words, the Court's power to declare them unconstitutional. What an incredible idea! Nine men elected by nobody, qualified by nothing but senility, a law degree, and a friendship with the President exercise the power to nullify and void the pronouncements and actions of the people's elected representatives!

This would not be a particularly important power, if the Constitution were a clear, precise, and all-inclusive legal code. In that case, the Justices would merely discover the law. Indeed, many Americans seem to believe that this is exactly the case. Apparently, they conceive of the law as some sort of foreign language. (In one sense, they are not far wrong.) They do not, for example, read Russian, but they are convinced that the squiggles and swirls of the Cyrillic alphabet have meaning for those persons who have studied and mastered them. Similarly, they do not know the meaning of such phrases as "due process of law," "cruel and unusual punishment," and "unreasonable search and seizure," but they believe that anybody with a legal education does. And even the Supreme Court itself has been willing to aid and abet this conception. Thus, in *United States v. Butler*, declaring the first Agricultural Adjustment Act unconstitutional, Mr. Justice Roberts wrote:

> There should be no misunderstanding as to the function of this court in such a case. It is sometimes said that the court assumes a power to overrule or control the action of the people's representatives. This is a misconception. The Constitution is the supreme law of the land ordained and established by the people. All legislation must conform to the principles it lays down. When an act of Congress is appropriately challenged in the courts as not conforming to the constitutional mandate the judicial branch of the Government has only one duty,—to lay the article of the Constitution which is invoked beside the statute which is challenged and to decide whether the latter squares with the former. All the court does, or can do, is to announce its considered judgment upon the question. The only power it has, if

[20]The fact of finality does not mean, of course, that the Court's decision is irreversible. The Constitution may be amended; the statute might be rephrased to cure the defect; various political pressures may be brought to bear upon the Court to encourage it to reverse itself; or new Justices may be recruited who will join the minority in order to overrule the noxious precedent. What finality does mean is that the governmental body whose action has been declared unconstitutional is not viewed as having the power unilaterally to reverse the Court's decision. *See generally* S. WASBY, *supra* note 15; T. BECKER (ed.), THE IMPACT OF SUPREME COURT DECISIONS (1969).

such it may be called, is the power of judgment. This court neither approves nor condemns any legislative policy. Its delicate and difficult office is to ascertain and declare whether the legislation is in accordance with, or in contravention of, the provisions of the Constitution; and having done that, its duty ends. . . .[21]

This may be the case in trial courts. The law of murder, for example, is clear—or at least reasonably so. In a murder trial, it is the facts which need to be determined. True, the prosecution and judge enjoy some discretion, but, once the charge is brought, the facts determined, and before sentencing, the process of ascertaining guilt is largely mechanical. The role of the Supreme Court, however, comes where the law is unclear.

Constitutional law is not static. The Court plays a creative role. It is very much like a continuously sitting constitutional convention.[22] It has so often been said that the Constitution's greatest strength is its flexibility that that initially wise observation has been reduced to a cliché. But the Constitution is flexible because it is not specific, and a corollary of the Constitution's lack of specificity is that the Court, which is recognized as the document's authoritative interpreter, exercises a broad discretion over questions of public policy. Constitutional law, thus, becomes a political instrument.[23]

This is not to say that the Court plays a role in policy-making only when it is exercising its power to approve or disapprove of the constitutionality of a federal statute. It may also make policy while judging the constitutionality of state actions.[24] Similarly, its power of statutory construction is of great consequence.[25] But that function which makes the United States Supreme Court a uniquely political agency, unlike any other court in the world, is its broad power of "judicial review." In the American context, the term "judicial review" refers to the power of the Court to interpret the Constitution with respect to the acts of the President or of Congress and to set them aside if the Court concludes that they violate the fundamental charter.[26] This authority, in

[21]297 U.S. 1, 62-63 (1936).

[22]*Cf.* H. BLACK, A CONSTITUTIONAL FAITH (1968).

[23]*See* V. ROSENBLUM, LAW AS A POLITICAL INSTRUMENT (1955); J. GROSSMAN & M. GROSSMAN (eds.), LAW AND CHANGE IN MODERN AMERICA (1971).

[24]*See, e.g.,* Brown v. Board of Education, 347 U.S. 483 (1954); Engel v. Vitale, 370 U.S. 421 (1962); Reynolds v. Sims, 377 U.S. 533 (1964); Miranda v. Arizona, 384 U.S. 436 (1966).

[25]*See, e.g.,* United States v. Seeger, 380 U.S. 163 (1965); Welsh v. United States, 398 U.S. 333 (1970).

[26]While judicial review is the distinctive characteristic of the Supreme Court and while

turn, has significant implications for the democratic character of the American system of government. For, as an English bishop named Hoadly recognized more than two hundred years ago:

> Whoever hath an absolute authority to interpret any written or spoken laws, it is he who is truly the lawgiver to all intents and purposes, and not the person who first wrote or spoke them.[27]

How, then, did the Supreme Court obtain this unique, indeed incredible, power?

A good lawyer's answer would be simply to cite *Marbury v. Madison*,[28] the first case enunciating the doctrine. There is, however, a central, crucial flaw to such a response. It begs the question. If the power of the Court to act as the final arbiter of the Constitution is to be found in this decision by an earlier Court, one is entitled to ask where did that Court find the power.[29] Reliance upon precedent does not provide an answer, although it does set the question back another step.

If prior judicial interpretation is not conclusive of the matter, one must

its importance would be hard to minimize, it very well may have been over-studied by scholars. *See, e.g.*, L. LEVY (ed.). JUDICIAL REVIEW AND THE SUPREME COURT (1967). After all, we have it on good authority that the power to declare state acts unconstitutional is, in structural terms, the more important power.

> I do not think the United States would come to an end if we lost our power to declare an act of Congress void. I do think the Union would be imperiled if we could not make that declaration as to the laws of the several states.

O. W. HOLMES, *Law and the Court*, in COLLECTED LEGAL PAPERS 295-296 (1920).

[27]Bishop Hoadly's Sermon preached before the King, March 31, 1717, on "The Nature of the Kingdom or Church of Christ," *quoted in* Thayer, *The Origin and Scope of the American Doctrine of Constitutional Law*, 7 HARV. L. REV. 129, 152 (1893).

[28]1 Cranch 137 (1803).

A similar answer to the question of where the Court secures its power to authoritatively interpret the constitutionality of state acts would be to cite Cohens v. Virginia, 6 Wheat. 264 (1821). Of course, the Court had previously asserted such a power in Chisholm v. Georgia, 2 Dall. 419 (1793), and Martin v. Hunter's Lessee, 1 Wheat. 304 (1816), but the events subsequent to each of these cases raised considerable doubt about the validity of those assertions. *Cohens*, thus, was the first definitive statement by the Court of its power vis-à-vis the states. *Cf.* Ableman v. Booth, 21 How. 506 (1859). But, as the responses of certain southern states to the school desegregation decisions illustrates, the doctrine of interposition dies hard. *See* Cooper v. Aaron, 358 U.S. 1 (1958).

[29]This is not to say, even by implication, that the Court usurped this power. Rather, it seems that at worst it merely accepted an open invitation offered by the Framers. *See* C. BEARD, THE SUPREME COURT AND THE CONSTITUTION (1912); P. EIDELBERG, THE PHILOSOPHY OF THE AMERICAN CONSTITUTION (1968). *Cf.* L. BOUDIN, GOVERNMENT BY JUDICIARY (1932).

next turn to those two other guides to judicial decision-making—the text of the invoked document, in this case the Constitution itself, or history.[30] The textual evidence supporting the lodging of this power in the Court is, of course, quite weak. In *Marbury* itself the Great Chief Justice, John Marshall, outlines most of the arguments which have since been used to advance the thesis that this power can be found, at least implicitly, in the Constitution, and ever since *Marbury* even friendly critics have never tired of pointing to myriad logical weaknesses in Marshall's exegesis.[31] This does not mean, however, that the existence of the institution of judicial review in America cannot be squared with the Constitution; it merely means that it cannot be found there.[32]

If, then, one cannot explain or justify the existence of judicial review in America by resort to the Constitution or to the opinions of the Supreme Court, perhaps an examination of history may provide an answer. Indeed, many examples of something resembling judicial review may be found in the history of colonial America.[33] But upon closer inspection, these examples prove to be inadequate. The power of disallowance of colonial legislation exercised by the British Privy Council is hardly analogous, unless one is willing to argue that colonial legislatures were coordinate in power with the Privy Council. (Some colonial leaders, of course, appear to have labored under this delusion.) This practice may provide an historical precedent for the Court's power to scrutinize the constitutionality of state acts,[34] but it will not support the Court's exercise of that power as against congressional acts. Similarly the councils of revision which existed in some colonies are inapplicable as examples of early American experience with a practice analogous to judicial review. After all, unlike Supreme Court Justices, members of

[30]*See generally* B. CARDOZO, THE NATURE OF THE JUDICIAL PROCESS (1921); C. MILLER, THE SUPREME COURT AND THE USES OF HISTORY (1969).

[31]Marshall relied upon the following: U.S. CONST. art III, sec. 2; U.S. CONST. art. III, sec. 3; U.S. CONST. art VI, sec. 2; U.S. CONST. art. VI, sec. 3. For the best taken criticisms of Marshall's dialectic, *see* E. CORWIN, THE DOCTRINE OF JUDICIAL REVIEW ch. I (1914); C. BEARD, *supra* note 29; P. EIDELBERG, *supra* note 29, ch. 10.

[32]*See* P. EIDELBERG, *supra* note 29, ch. 10, for an excellent attempt to create a philosophic justification of judicial review consonant with the spirit and purpose of the Constitution.

[33]*See* A. KELLY & W. HARBISON, THE AMERICAN CONSTITUTION: ITS ORIGINS AND DEVELOPMENT 98-100 (4th ed. 1970).

[34]It also may not—at least until 1865. *See, e.g.*, the Virginia and Kentucky Resolutions of 1798; the South Carolina Exposition of 1828; Calhoun, *Disquisition on Government*, in I THE WORKS OF JOHN C. CALHOUN 52 (R. Cralle ed. 1854).

these councils of revision were elected. Finally, there are some early precedents of colonial courts claiming the power to void the acts of their own legislatures.[35] But the influence of these cases at the time of the Constitutional Convention is, at best, unclear.

Anyone familiar with Supreme Court opinions knows that there is yet one more, specialized brand of historical guidance to interpreting a given document—the intent of the framers. And some have contended that, although the Founding Fathers failed to provide explicitly for judicial review in the constitutional text itself, the evidence of their deliberations and statements made by Hamilton in *The Federalist*[36] demonstrate that they foresaw, in fact invited, the Court to assume this power. In short, this is a sort of conspiracy theory, and naturally enough the best exposition of the thesis has been provided by that master of conspiratorial history, Charles Austin Beard, in his classic *The Supreme Court and the Constitution.*[37] But in this work, as in his even more famous *An Economic Interpretation of the Constitution*, which itself propounds a conspiracy theory, Beard's evidence is weak and suffers from unsupported inference. At best, all Beard shows is that the Framers wanted judicial review, but they wanted a great many other things which never appeared in the final draft of the Constitution. On the other hand, not even a colorable showing of decisive historical evidence can be made to the contrary. No one has ever persuasively argued that the Founders would have opposed judicial review. At worst, then, it can only be said that the intentions of the Framers cannot be ascertained. They were a brilliant and, thus, contentious group of men. Some thought this, others that, and it will never be entirely clear just where the final judgment came to rest.

To say that none of the legal, textual, or historical reasons are sufficient in and of themselves to justify the existence of judicial review in America is not, however, to say that it cannot be explained. It may be accounted for in terms of what might be called functional reasons. Such an explanation is a good deal less tidy and much "softer" than any precise, factual answer, and those who demand replicable, elegant

---

[35]Trevett v. Weeden, Rhode Island (1786); Bayard v. Singleton, 1 Martin (N.C.) 5 (1787).

[36]THE FEDERALIST Nos. 49 & 78.

[37]With the emergence in recent years of a revisionist school of historians on the New Left, however, Beard may have surrendered his place as the leading example of what can happen when paranoia and a Ph.D. in history are joined together. *See, e.g.*, G. KOLKO, THE POLITICS OF WAR (1968).

"proofs" will be most unsatisfied by it. Nevertheless, the cumulative effect of certain American political institutions and the historical existence of certain characteristics of the American civic culture may suggest why the ultimate power of constitutional interpretation has been lodged in the Supreme Court. In the first place, Americans appear always to have entertained a "higher law" tradition.[38] This was probably transmitted to America by the common law, but it was the common law of Coke and Locke, not the common law of Hobbes and Blackstone with its all-powerful Parliament. In fact, Americans carried this tradition one step further and contributed to the art of government the idea of reducing the higher law to writing, placing limits on the government and guaranteeing certain rights to the individual citizen.[39] The existence of such a written higher law necessarily presupposes a final arbiter, although there is no reason why it must be a court of law. Secondly, there exists in America that device of sovereignty known as federalism, and federalism means legalism.[40] In other words, somebody must determine when one or the other jurisdiction exceeds its powers. But, here again, the question still remains why this final arbiter must be a court composed of non-elected, life-tenured judges. Thirdly, the American system of separation of powers presumes an agency able to judge the nature and extent of each department's powers. But, once again, why must that agency be the Supreme Court? Finally, account must be taken of Americans' traditional, peculiar, and totally illogical veneration of the legal profession and particularly of judges, who seem to represent the ultimate in achievement in the legal profession. Almost a century and a half ago, that sharp-eyed critic of American manners, Alexis de Tocqueville, noted that Americans had an "aristocracy of the bar" and a "cult of the robe," and neither of these customs appears to have diminished over time.[41] None of these factors is of itself a sufficient causal explanation for the existence of judicial review in America, but

[38]Corwin, *The Basic Doctrine of American Constitutional Law*, 12 MICH. L. REV. 247 (1914); E. CORWIN, THE HIGHER LAW BACKGROUND OF AMERICAN CONSTITUTIONAL LAW (1929).

[39]*See* A. McLAUGHLIN, FOUNDATIONS OF AMERICAN CONSTITUTIONALISM (1932).

[40]A. DICEY, LAW OF THE CONSTITUTION 171-180 (9th ed. 1939); F. FRANKFURTER, *Federalism and the Role of the Supreme Court*, in OF LAW AND LIFE & OTHER THINGS THAT MATTER 122 (P. Kurland ed. 1969).

[41]A. de TOCQUEVILLE, I DEMOCRACY IN AMERICA 283-286 (P. Bradley ed. 1945).

their combined effect is to thrust us in that direction. It is, in other words, somewhat like making wine. One puts sugar, yeast, and some grape pressings in a vat and allows them to sit for awhile, and what emerges is reminiscent of the ingredients but very unlike them. So, too, with judicial review in America. None of these elements is sufficient to account for its existence, and yet each of them is a necessary cause. If one takes these four elements and places them in a vat to ferment for a few years, what emerges will probably very closely resemble judicial review.

But, however one seeks to account for lodging the power of constitutional interpretation in the Supreme Court, such explanation is essentially beside the point. Today, Americans accept the Court's exercise of this power because it has stood the test of time. Over nearly two centuries, it has proven to be functional.[42] The crucial question, then, becomes not whether the power of constitutional construction should be given to the Court but rather what should be the appropriate scope of the Court's exercise of that power.[43]

In answering the question of what should be the proper scope of the Court's constitutional interpretation or, phrased more broadly, what should be the proper role of the Supreme Court as a policy-making agency, the central problem which must be kept in mind is that the Court is a counter-majoritarian institution. That is not to say that it is necessarily an "undemocratic" institution, depending upon one's understanding of democracy.[44] But, nevertheless, a small group of unelected men is empowered to interpret authoritatively the charter which establishes the framework of government, the very document which grants, defines, and limits governmental power.

The Court, of course, along with various other devices or institutions of the American constitutional system, is the product of a self-contradictory, philosophic dualism in American political thought which can be traced as far back as the Mayflower Compact.[45] One of the salient characteristics of political philosophy in America has been the conviction that man is an irrational animal and, thus, incapable of self-government. On the other hand, Americans have always desired democratic organization and have paid more than lip service to the tradition of the town

[42]*See* Dahl, *Decision-Making in a Democracy: the Supreme Court as a National Policy-Maker*, 6 J. PUB. L. 279 (1957).
[43]*See generally*, L. LEVY, *supra* note 26.
[44]*See, e.g.*, Rostow, *The Democratic Character of Judicial Review*, 56 HARV. L. REV. 193 (1952).
[45]*See generally* A. MASON (ed.), FREE GOVERNMENT IN THE MAKING (1965).

meeting. The result has been a dualism in American political thought: a desire for limited government on the one hand and for democratically responsible government on the other. Americans have never really faced up to this dualism, and thus it persists even today. A favorite slogan among the New American Left, for example, has been "Power to the People." But power for what? Power to improve the status of cértain minority groups and to protect minority rights. The New Left, then, is, at least in this respect, very much within the American tradition, a tradition which pays homage to minority rights, while at the same time voicing its commitment to majority rule, despite the fact that the two are logically and philosophically irreconcilable.

Americans are not, however, in much danger of absolute rule by the Supreme Court, even if it were a certified band of Platonic guardians—which it is not. The Constitution was designed not only to build in checks upon the democratic elements of the government but also to provide democratic checks upon oligarchic tendencies.[46] Those who speak of government by the judiciary simply overstate the case.[47] A series of devices external to the Court were provided which serve to limit its power. The Court is, as Hamilton rightly and wisely observed, the least dangerous branch. Moreover, recognizing its weaknesses and political vulnerability, the Court has developed a number of devices which serve to limit internally its policy-making and, thus, to protect it from political struggles with the other, more powerful branches of the government.

Primary among the external limitations by which the other branches exercise some degree of control over the Court's decision-making is the power of appointment and removal. The Supreme Court is not a self-perpetuating agency. Appointment to the Court is a frankly and openly political matter, and this is probably as it should be. The Supreme Court is a unique judicial agency, and criteria relevant for service on other courts are probably not applicable to the assessment of the qualifications of potential Supreme Court Justices. Suggestions have been made that Congress, by statute, set more stringent requirements for appointment to the Court, e.g., nomination by the American Bar Association, possession of a law degree (Most Justices have had one anyway.), or prior judicial experience. But the adoption of such procedures would be unfortunate, for the questions with which the Supreme Court deals require political

---

[46]*See* P. EIDELBERG, *supra* note 29.
[47]*See, e.g.,* L. BOUDIN, *supra* note 29.

judgment rather than proficiency in the technicalities of private law. For example, among those who have served on the Supreme Bench, the following would have been disqualified from consideration by a requirement of prior judicial experience: Marshall, Story, Taney, Miller, Bradley, Hughes, Brandeis, Stone, Black, and Frankfurter. Nomination by the President, who himself has been elected by the voters (usually a majority thereof), insures that a prospective Justice will be, in general terms, representative (Presidents seldom appoint their political enemies to the Court.), and the necessity of confirmation by the Senate further assures not only competence but also that the political views of the nominee will be within the mainstream of contemporary American values, as the Haynsworth-Carswell fiasco demonstrated. Congress's power to impeach, moreover, serves as a potential, albeit drastic, tool for rectifying judicial error. It is true that only eight federal judges have ever been impeached, of which only one was a Supreme Court Justice, and only four have ever been convicted. But it would be a foolhardy man indeed who would totally ignore this ultimate power of removal which the Constitution has lodged in the elected legislature.

The second external control cannot be found in the Constitution; that is precisely why it is a control. Nowhere in the Constitution is the Court's size specified. Article III provides that there shall be a Supreme Court, but, at the discretion of Congress and the President, its size may range from one to one million. This hiatus is a double-edged sword; Congress may either increase or decrease the number of Justices. Thus, with Mr. Justice Catron's death in 1865, the Congress, over President Johnson's veto, reduced the size of the Court from 10 to 8, in order to deny the President a Supreme Court nomination. But, with the retirement of Mr. Justice Grier, the Congress was equally willing to reincrease the size of the Court to nine, enabling President Grant to appoint Justices Bradley and Strong, both "greenback" men, thereby securing the demise of the short-lived *Hepburn v. Griswold.*[48] Of course Franklin Roosevelt also attempted to "pack" the Court, and, while he was tactically defeated in that effort, it would be difficult to argue that he was any less successful strategically than was the Reconstruction Congress.

Congress possesses yet one more way by which it may coerce an overly ambitious Supreme Court, and that is by its control over the Court's jurisdiction.[49] The Court's original jurisdiction, i.e., those cases which

[48] 8 Wall. 603 (1870), overruled by Knox v. Lee, 12 Wall. 457 (1871).
[49] *But see* R. BERGER, CONGRESS v. THE SUPREME COURT ch. 9 (1969). *Cf.*

the Court may hear in a trial of first instance, is specified in the Constitution and is very limited. Moreover, it cannot be expanded.[50] Its appellate jurisdiction, however, which has historically proven to be of much more importance, is not exclusive. It can be expanded by Congress. But it also may be contracted, or perhaps even cut-off entirely. This device, too, was used by the Radical Republican Congress during Reconstruction to influence judicial decision-making. One McCardle, a southern newspaperman who had written certain editorials not wholly pleasing to the commanders of the Union occupying force, was tried and convicted by a military commission. He appealed contending that the military court which had tried him and which had been established by the Reconstruction Acts had no lawful authority. The case, therefore, involved, at least by implication, the constitutionality of the Reconstruction Acts. The Court took jurisdiction and heard the case, and it appeared that it might issue a decision unfavorable to the constitutionality of Reconstruction. Fearing this outcome, Congress rescinded the statute lodging jurisdiction over such appeals in the Supreme Court. President Johnson vetoed the rescinsion bill, which was quite frankly designed to kill the *McCardle* case, but his veto was overridden. Despite the fact that the case had already been heard, than an opinion had apparently been written, and that the statute could have been construed as applying prospectively only, the Court issued a decision dismissing McCardle's appeal on the grounds that Congress had the power to rescind the Court's appellate jurisdiction, and, therefore, it no longer had jurisdiction in the case.[51] Though logically indefensible, the decision is explainable in terms of prudence, and a very wise exercise of prudence at that.

While the Congress may curtail the Court's appellate jurisdiction, the President has an even more direct mechanism for controlling judicial policy-making. The Court has no power to oversee the execution of its own decisions. This is the responsibility of the President. As with most other acts of policy in the American governmental system, at least one other branch must act before the Court's declaration of public policy is effectively implemented. Just as Congress may appropriate monies for a program which the President does not spend, or as the President may

Wechsler, *The Court and The Constitution*, 65 COLUM. L. REV. 1001, 1005 (1965). *See also* J. GOEBEL, HISTORY OF THE SUPREME COURT OF THE UNITED STATES: ANTECEDENTS AND BEGINNINGS TO 1801 240 (1971); C. FAIRMAN, RECONSTRUCTION AND REUNION 1864-88: PART ONE 514 (1971).

[50]Marbury v. Madison, 1 Cranch 137 (1803).

[51]*Ex parte* McCardle, 7 Wall. 506 (1869).

initiate a program which the Congress will not adequately fund, so too the Supreme Court must depend upon presidential execution before its will becomes law. Seemingly, only one President, Jackson, ever directly refused to carry out the Court's mandate (and that story may be apocryphal), but even reluctant or half-hearted execution by an administration is usually enough to blunt significantly any judicially policy reform, as the unhappy history of desegregation so adequately demonstrates.

Recognizing its political limits, the Court has developed for itself certain doctrines whose chief content is a generalization on the timing and scope of the exercise of the judicial function;[52] or, as the late Mr. Justice Robert Jackson put it, the Supreme Court "has a philosophy that, while it has a duty to decide constitutional questions, it must escape that duty if possible."[53] Laymen call these doctrines by which that duty is escaped "technicalities." Students and admirers of the Court tend to call them "words of art." But, whatever they are called, their function is clear—to protect the Court's public prestige (which is ultimately the source of the Court's power) by insuring that it does not expend its energies on cases which are not important enough or on cases which are of too immediate a political importance for the Court to handle. Each of these rules proceeds from a common premise: the Court's power is finite. If it expends that power in vain gestures, no matter how noble, which antagonize the public or its elected representatives, then it will not have sufficient public support when something that really counts comes along.

These doctrines or rules of decision are of two sorts. First, there are doctrines which allow the Court to refuse to hear a given case at all. Second, the Court has at its disposal a set of rules, which, if the Court must hear the case (and if it follows the rules), allow it to reach a decision on the narrowest possible grounds.

Foremost among the doctrines which allow the Court to decline jurisdiction over a case is the so-called "case and controversy" rule. If, as Chief Justice Marshall argued in *Marbury v. Madison*, the Supreme Court's power to construe the Constitution against other governmental agencies can be deduced from the Court's obligation to decide lawsuits conformably with the law, including the law of the Constitution, it must

---

[52]The finest analytic discussion of these doctrines is Bickel, *The Passive Virtues*, 75 HARV. L. REV. 40 (1961). *See also* A. BICKEL, *supra* note 17, at ch. 5.

[53]R. JACKSON, THE STRUGGLE FOR JUDICIAL SUPREMACY 305-306 (1941).

necessarily follow that that power can be exercised only in a lawsuit. Marshall offered no other coherent justification for lodging the power in the Court, and the Constitution, whatever other support it may or may not afford Marshall, extends the judicial power only to "cases and controversies."[54] The Court, in other words, must confine itself to real issues, in a real controversy, between real parties.

Some, in fact, have gone on to argue that *all* cases that are justiciable must be heard. But, of course, this argument cannot get around the sheer necessity of limiting each term's business to what nine men and their law clerks can fruitfully deal with. Given this necessary discretion over its docket, however, the Court is then free to use the case and controversy rule to duck tough questions.

What is, the layman will ask, a case and controversy? The answer is that not every argument or dispute which is presented in the form of a lawsuit will qualify for a hearing by the Supreme Court. To have a case and controversy, in the constitutional sense, there must be (a) adverse parties who (b) have a substantial legal interest (c) in a dispute arising out of real, not hypothetical, facts and (d) in which there can be an enforceable determination of the rights of the parties. No made up, collusive, or "friendly" suits in which both parties are actually seeking the same result will be heard.

There have, however, been exceptions, exceptions which, the grade school grammar teacher would say, prove the rule.[55] But all that the exceptions really prove is that the rule is flexible enough to allow the Court to interpret it with some discretion. Each of the exceptions were cases which, at the time, the Court was eager to decide. On the other hand, if the Court wishes to avoid an issue for one reasoon or another it can insist upon a strict construction of the doctrine. For example, in *United Public Workers v. Mitchell*,[56] the Court dodged a ruling on the constitutionality of the Hatch Act, which was intended to prevent political influence in the civil service, by invoking the case and controversy rule. A public employees union sought to secure a ruling against the act so that in the future its members could engage in various political activities. None of the employees, however, had yet violated the

[54]U.S. CONST. art. III, sec. 2.

[55]*See, e.g.*, Hylton v. United States, 3 Dall. 171 (1796); Bailey v. Drexel Furniture Co., 259 U.S. 20 (1922); Carter v. Carter Coal Co., 298 U.S. 238 (1936); Robinson v. California, 370 U.S. 660 (1962).

[56]330 U.S. 75 (1947). *See also* United States Civil Service Comm'n. v. National Assoc. of Letter Carriers, 413 U. S. 548 (1973).

act, and thus their claim was based upon conjecture. The Court, seeking to avoid a decision on the constitutional merits of the statute, replied that the union had not presented a justiciable case and controversy. The employees should violate the act, and then, if the sanctions which they feared were invoked against them, they would have a case, which the Court *might* hear.

Related to the case and controversy rule is the Court's self-imposed limit preventing it from issuing advisory opinions. The origin of this rule is so well-known as hardly to require retelling.[57] President Washington, seeking some legal counsel on a contemplated treaty, sent a copy of the treaty to the members of the Court asking them to advise him on a few technical points. Mr. Chief Justice John Jay curtly returned the treaty with the reply that the Court was not in the business of issuing opinions in the abstract. Since that time, despite the self-refuting nature of Jay's response, the Court has continued to adhere to the doctrine that it will not issue advisory opinions for anyone, even Presidents.

The requirement of standing to sue draws attention to yet another aspect of the case and controversy rule. To maintain a suit in the federal courts a litigant must have a personal and substantial interest which differentiates him from the general mass of the citizenry. Thus in *Tileston v. Ullman* the Court was relieved, at least for the moment, of passing upon the constitutionality of a Connecticut statute prohibiting the use by any person of any contraceptive drug or instrument.[58]Dr. Tileston, an instructor at the Yale Medical School, had filed suit on behalf of three of his patients whose lives would be endangered by conception, or at least so Tileston claimed. He alleged that the Connecticut anti-birth control statute threatened these women with the deprivation of life without due process of law in violation of the Fourteenth Amendment. The Court, however, dismissed Tileston's claim on the grounds that he had no standing to assert the constitutionmal question which he was raising. Wrote the Court:

> There is no allegation or proof that appellant's life is in danger. His patients are not party to this proceeding and there is no basis on which we can say that he has standing to secure an adjudication of his patients' right to life, which they do not assert on their own behalf.[59]

[57]The story is fully related in C. HAINES, THE ROLE OF THE SUPREME COURT IN AMERICAN GOVERNMENT AND POLITICS 1789-1835, at 144 (1944); 10 J. SPARKS, THE LIFE OF GOUVERNOUR MORRIS 359 (1832); 5 J. MARSHALL, LIFE OF GEORGE WASHINGTON 441 (1804).
[58]318 U.S. 44 (1943).
[59]*Id*. at 46.

The defect in *Tileston*, however, was remedied in *Poe v. Ullman.*[60] One Dr. Buxton sued on his own behalf seeking an injunction against the operation of the Connecticut statute on the grounds that it prevented the full, conscientious exercise of his profession, and thereby injured him in violation of the Fourteenth Amendment. In addition, two of Buxton's patients, suing under fictitious names, alleged that their health would be impaired unless conception were prevented.

During oral argument, however, counsel for the plaintiffs was forced to reply to a question from the bench that Connecticut had never enforced the law against people who used contraceptives. The entire history of the enforcement of the Connecticut statute amounted to only three prosecutions: two for vending machine sales and one against two doctors and a nurse for aiding and abetting a violation of the statute by operating a birth control clinic. Counsel for the state, on the other hand, was able to produce a letter from the state's Commissioner of Food and Drugs to the effect that there was no legal reason why a doctor could not prescribe or a drug store provide diaphragms, since they might have therapeutic, as distinguished from contraceptive, value. At this point, the Court dismissed the case on the grounds that it was not "ripe." It raised an issue which was "academic." In other words, even in a perfectly real, concrete, and fully developed case and controversy, the Supreme Court does not owe litigants an adjudication.

Constitutional challenges may also come too late as well as too early. For example, during the Second World War the United States Government brought suit to compel Montgomery Ward & Co. to comply with the government's order expropriating Montgomery Ward's property. By the time the case had wound its way through the judicial process to the Court, the war ended, and before the case could be heard, but after the Court had accepted the petition for certiorari, the property was restored to the company. The Court then dismissed the petition on the grounds that the case had become moot, refusing to resolve an issue raising questions of the highest importance concerning the relation between the Constitution, socialism, and emergency circumstances.[61]

Also related to the doctrines of ripeness and mootness is the rule of exhaustion of remedy. Petitions for certiorari, asking the Supreme Court to hear a given case, will not be considered by the Court unless all prior appeals allowed for by law have been taken. Even a real case and

[60]367 U.S. 497 (1961).
[61]Montgomery Ward & Co. v. United States, 326 U.S. 690 (1945).

controversy which is perfectly ripe and joined by litigants having standing to pose the issues cannot be taken directly from the court of first instance to the Supreme Court; all intermediate appeals must be exhausted before the Court can even be asked to hear the case.[62]

Moreover, there is no guarantee that the Court will consent to hear the case. The Court's control over its own docket, that is its power to choose those cases which it will hear, is virtually complete.[63] Thus, many cases which conform to all of these rules are, nevertheless, never heard by the Supreme Court.

Once the Court does accept a case, however, there is yet another set of rules, doctrines of self-restraint, which serve to guide the Court in arriving at its judgment. These rules have been devised and refined over the years by Justices concerned with the appropriate role of the Court within the political system in order to protect both the public and the Court. They are purely self-imposed, if imposed at all, and they function to limit the scope of the Court's decision in any case.

Many of these rules may be lumped together under what could be called the doctrine of alternative holings. The Court will not pass on a constitutional question, even if it is properly presented, if there is also some non-constitutional alternative for disposing of the case. If a case can be decided on either of two bases, one involving a constitutional question, the other a question of statutory construction, this rule would dictate a decision based on the latter ground.[64] A state act challenged as violative of the Fourteenth Amendment and as contrary to a federal statute would, for example, be struck down on the statutory infirmity.[65] A related rule is that if a state court judgment, though challenged on constitutional grounds, can be sustained on an independent state basis the Supreme Court will not consider the constitutional question.[66] Related to this rule is the canon that the Supreme Court will accept as authoritative the construction of state law rendered by the highest court in the state, no matter how foolish or irrational that interpretation may

---

[62]*See* Uveges v. Pennsylvania, 335 U.S. 437 (1948); Brown v. Allen, 344 U.S. 554 (1953); E. CORWIN, THE CONSTITUTION OF THE UNITED STATES: ANALYSIS AND INTERPRETATION 642 (1964).

[63]*See generally* H. SPAETH, AN INTRODUCTION TO SUPREME COURT DECISION-MAKING (1965).

[64]Rescue Army v. Municipal Court, 331 U.S. 549, 568-575 (1947), Ashwander v. T. V. A., 297 U.S. 288, 346 (1936) (Brandeis, J., concurring.)

[65]E. CORWIN, *supra* note 62, at 630.

[66]Berea College v. Kentucky, 211 U.S. 45, 53 (1908).

be.[67] But the Court will construe congressional statutes, and here again the doctrine of alternative holdings comes into play. If the constitutionality of an act of Congress is challenged, the Court will first inquire whether a construction of the statute is fairly possible by which the constitutional question may be avoided.[68]

If the statute cannot be otherwise construed, however, and if no alternative, non-constitutional grounds for decision are open, then the Court must address itself to the constitutional question. But, so the canons of judicial construction would have it, the Court will not formulate a rule of constitutional law broader than is required by the precise facts to which it is to be applied.[69] In fact, this rule is also recognized and adhered to in cases declaring state statutes to be unconstitutional. Thus, in voiding the New York Regents' Prayer, the Court was quite explicit in noting that its holding was confined to prayer in the public schools and did not apply to other manifestations of public piety, if that they be, such as the inscription "In God We Trust" upon our coinage.[70] Much of the public rancor which the school prayer decision occasioned might have been muted had the public understood this rule of the judicial game. (Much more, especially that of the more vocal critics, might have been silenced, had they simply read the opinion.)

If all else fails, the Supreme Court's widest and most radical avenue of escape from the adjudication of constitutional questions is to invoke the political question doctrine.[71] In truth, all questions which the Court considers are political, but this doctrine is of special application. If the Court cannot get out of taking a highly controversial case or if it wishes to positively indicate that it does not desire to adjudicate a certain category of cases,[72] the Court may label the issue a "political question," a

[67]Kedroff v. St. Nicholas Cathedral, 344 U.S. 94 (1952); Reitman v. Mulkey, 387 U.S. 369 (1967).

[68]United States v. C.I.O., 335 U.S. 106 (1948); Miller v. United States, 11 Wall. 268 (1871).

[69]Steamship Co. v. Emigration Commissioners, 113 U.S. 33, 39 (1883)); Ashwander v. T.V.A., 297 U.S. 288, 346 (1936) (Brandeis, J., concurring); Rescue Army v. Municipal Court, 331 U.S. 549, 568-575 (1947).

[70]Engel v. Vitale, 370 U.S. 421, 435 n.21 (1962).

[71]See E. CORWIN, supra note 62, at 611-615.

[72]Simply denying appeals for certiorari in a given category of cases will not suffice, since reasons are never given for such denials. Thus, litigants may continue to raise an issue, unless actively discouraged by an invocation of the political question doctrine.

question beyond the scope of judicial power to provide a satisfactory solution.

To date, one of the best examples of the use of this doctrine is the case in which it originated, *Luther v. Borden*.[73] When it was chartered by the British Crown in 1663, Rhode Island established, relative to the other colonies, a reasonably democratic political order. The charter, however, contained no provision for amendment and by 1842, in what must surely be one of the classic examples of the need for constitutional flexibility, Rhode Island, originally one of the most democratic of the colonies, had become one of the least democratic states. Dissidents demanded a long overdue expansion of the franchise to provide for universal white male suffrage. When their demands were not met, they took matters into their own hands and held their own open elections at which, not surprisingly, their leader, Thomas Dorr, was elected Governor of the state. The Governor of the charter government, however, did not jovially recognize the error of restricting the franchise and hand over the keys to the State-house to Dorr. Rather, he called out the militia, and with the help of some federal troops dispatched by President Tyler at the Governor's request, the so-called "Dorr Rebellion" was quashed.[74] During the course of the hostilities, one Borden, a member of the militia supporting the charter government, broke into the house of a Dorr supporter named Luther and arrested him. After the failure of the "rebellion", Luther filed suit against Borden for trespass. Realizing that he stood no chance to recover in a Rhode Island state court, Luther moved to Massachusetts and lodged his complaint in a federal district court on diversity of citizenship grounds. Borden's reply was, of course, that he was not personally liable, having been acting as an agent of the state. But Luther counter-claimed that the Dorr government had been the legitimate government of Rhode Island and, therefore, Borden could not rely upon the orders of an illegitimate government to protect himself. Thus, the case asked the federal courts to declare what was and was not the valid government in Rhode Island.

When, in 1849, the case finally reached the Supreme Court, the Court chose to side-step the issue by holding that the question of state government legitimacy was not a proper one for settlement by a judicial body. Why? Because such an issue was, according to Mr. Chief Justice Taney, a "political question." Taney's formulation of the new doctrine was obviously influenced by several factors. Foremost among these was

[73]7 How. 1 (1849).
[74]*See generally* A. MOWRY, THE DORR WAR (1968).

the chaos that would have resulted from a finding that the charter government had no legal existence and, consequently, that all of its actions subsequent to the rebellion, that is for the past seven years, were null and void. Moreover, the Rhode Island state courts themselves had declined to find that they had any judicial responsibility to determine the proper locus of state governmental authority, and, therefore, there was a total absence of any standards under state law which might be appealable to the Supreme Court. Finally, according to Chief Justice Taney, there existed no federal constitutional ground for determining the locus of state governmental authority, other than Article IV, section 4, which guarantees to each state a republican form of government, and this clause, Taney argued, committed the matter to Congress. Congress determined whether or not a state had a republican form of government when it admitted, or refused to admit, the state's representatives to their seats.[75]

It is clear that all of these factors influenced Taney in declaring the case to be a "political question." It is less clear from the opinion, however, how one recognizes a "political question" when he sees one. In *Luther*, Taney listed the following as contributing to making the case "political:"

1.   The fact that the Constitution committed the question to a coordinate branch of the federal government;
2.   The fact that one branch, i.e., President Tyler, had already taken decisive action, indicating that branch's view of the proper disposition of the matter;
3.   The need for finality in the executive's decisions; and
4.   The lack of any criteria or manageable standards to aid in making a judicial decision.

Taney did not, however, indicate if all of these factors were to be given the same weight in determining if a case were "political" or if some of them might be more important than others. It seems clear then that the most significant factor in influencing the Court's decision was that the case simply was impossible of satisfactory judicial resolution, and therefore the Court chose not to decide it.

Over the years, the political question doctrine has been used to get the Court out of some tight spots. In particular, it proved exceptionally useful during the Reconstruction period and during the early history of the reapportionment cases.[76] Many legal scholars have attempted to find

---

[75]This theory, of course, provided the constitutional underpinnings for the assertion of congressional prerogatives during Reconstruction.

[76]Texas v. White, 7 Wall. 700 (1869); Colegrove v. Green, 328 U.S. 549 (1946).

some sort of objective content in the doctrine, but the doctrine resists being domesticated in this way.[77] It is different from all of the other doctrines we have been discussing and is different in kind not simply in degree. It is greatly more flexible than any other. It is simply a doctrine of prudence rather than of construction. The Court alone declares questions to be "political," and it does so by the case, not by the category.

The Supreme Court, then, recognizes that its power to construe the Constitution must be exercised with restraint. Consequently, it approaches constitutional questions with reluctance and will decide a case on a constitutional issue only when there is no feasible alternative. To advance this end, the Court has imposed upon itself a comprehensive body of rules aimed at encouraging self-restraint and avoiding constitutional issues. To summarize:[78]

1. The Court will not anticipate a question of constitutional dimension in advance of the necessity of deciding it, nor is it the habit of the Court to decide questions of a constitutional nature unless absolutely necessary to the case at hand.

2. The Court will not formulate a rule of constitutional law broader than required by the precise facts of the case to which it is to be applied.

3. The Court will not pass on a constitutional question, although properly presented, if there is also some other ground on which the case may be disposed of.

4. When the validity of an act of Congress is drawn into question, and even if serious doubt of its constitutionality is raised, the Court will attempt to find another construction of the statute by which it may be saved.

5. Any question presented to the Court must be justiciable. In other words, it must meet the test of the case and controversy rule and be susceptible of judicial resolution. The Court will not issue advisory opinions, no matter how politically important the issue.

6. An important element of justiciability is standing to sue. Not everyone with enough time and money to file a suit is entitled to litigate the constitutionality of federal and state statutes. Rather, the litigant's interest must be one that is peculiar and personal to him and not one which he shares generally with all other citizens,

---

[77] *See e.g.*, Weston, *Political Questions*, 38 HARV. L. REV. 296 (1925); J. FRANK, *Political Questions*, in SUPREME COURT & SUPREME LAW 36 (E. Cahn ed. 1954); Baker v. Carr, 369 U.S. 186 (1962) (Brennan, J.); M. SHAPIRO, LAW AND POLITICS IN THE SUPREME COURT 174-215 (1964); Tollett, *Political Questions and the Law*, 42 U. DET. L.J. 439 (1965). *Cf.* Finkelstein, *Judicial Self-Limitations*, 37 HARV. L. REV. 338 (1924); Finkelstein, *Further Notes on Judicial Self-Limitation*, 39 HARV. L. REV. 221 (1925); R. JACKSON, THE SUPREME COURT IN THE AMERICAN SYSTEM OF GOVERNMENT 56 (1955): P. STROM, THE SUPREME COURT AND POLITICAL QUESTIONS: A STUDY IN JUDICIAL EVASION (1974); A. BICKEL, *supra* note 17, at 183-198. *See generally The Supreme Court, 1968 Term*, 83 HARV. L. REV. 62-77 (1969).

[78] *See also* Ashwander v. T.V.A., 297 U.S. 288, 346 (1936) (Brandeis, J., concurring).

and the interest which he is defending must be a legally recognized and protected right immediately threatened by the challenged governmental action.

7.   Controversies that otherwise meet the test of justiciability are, nevertheless, occasionally refused a hearing on the merits on the ground that they involve a "political question," i.e., a question the Court does not for some reason wish to decide.

These various self-imposed limits upon the Court are sometimes dismissed as technical. But their net effect is far from technical. For example, there is usually nobody who has standing to challenge the constitutionality of a federal expenditure.[79] A moment's thought about this rule will show what the doctrine of standing to sue does to the argument that judicial review means judicial supremacy.[80]

Others have criticized these rules as inevitably introducing accidental factors into constitutional decision-making. But, rightly understood, these doctrines should be applauded, because an insistence upon their application has a number of benefits. First, they assure that constitutional decisions of great importance will be raised by genuinely adversary parties, with the Court thus deriving the benefit of well-briefed, well-argued cases. The Court is, thus, by virtue of the rules, better informed in its policy-making. Second, these doctrines relieve the defendant, which in constitutional cases more often than not is the public, of the cost and trouble of defending in an action where the plaintiff has no substantial personal interest in the outcome. Frivolous actions, in other words, are discouraged. Third, these doctrines relieve the Court of an overwhelming burden by vastly reducing the number of cases it must consider. Finally, these rules, if followed, allow the Court to avoid without loss of face unnecessary confrontations with the politically better muscled coordinate branches of the federal government.

The Court, of course, has discretion over the application of these doctrines, and the stringency with which they are applied will vary according to the tenor of the political times and the wisdom of the members of the Court. These rules are rules of self-restraint born of a sense of prudence and institutional self-preservation, and some men will be more prudent than others or have a greater commitment to the institution of the Supreme Court than others.

Disregard of the rules will enlarge the Court's potential as a policy-maker. If the first sort of internal rules, those which limit the number of

[79]Frothingham v. Mellon, 262 U.S. 447 (1923); Massachusetts v. Laird, 400 U.S. 886 (1970). *But see* Flast v. Cohen, 392 U.S. 83 (1968).

[80]*E.g.*, L. BOUDIN, *supra* note 29.

cases the Court will hear, are modified or qualified or overlooked, the Court's opportunity to make policy will be quantitatively increased. If the Court qualifies or ignores the second set of rules, those which guide it in its decision-making, the qualitative scope of its policy-making will be expanded. However, if the Court plays fast and loose with either or both sets of rules, it will also increase its political visibility and thus invite partisan response to its policy-making.

But no matter whether a Court seeks to disregard or to bend or to modify these rules either to expand the quantitative opportunities for its policy-making or to enlarge the qualitative scope of the policy pronouncements which it does make or both, or whether it strictly adheres to these doctrines so as to restrain itself from rendering decisions in all but those cases which it simply cannot escape and then in those to limit itself to only the narrowest of grounds, all Courts, activist and not, are confronted with yet one more intangible but nonetheless real restriction, the necessity for opinion craftsmanship. Some students of the judicial process, however, dismiss this limitation as being, at best, not very important.[81] After all, no less authoritative a personage then Mr. Chief Justice Charles Evans Hughes has told us that the Constitution is what the Supreme Court says it is. Isn't it really only the results that count? Who cares whether the Court's policy-making is based upon principle or expediency? Who but a few law professors is concerned with the logical coherence of the Court's reasoning? Isn't the outcome of a given case far more important than the "rationalizations" which the Court advances to justify it?

The answer to each of these questions must be an emphatic "NO." Ultimately, all law is based upon the premise that man can use his power of reason to improve the quality of his life.[82] The ultimate interpreters of the law in the American system of government, Supreme Court Justices, appointed for life, are placed in the unique, if not always enviable, position of being able to identify and define those values which are the most fundamental in the American culture. Put somewhat differently, constitutional law could be conceived of as applied political theory. In the context of a lawsuit, the Justices are required to test the validity of our values against the reality of life and, since reality can seldom be changed, to explain the relevance of those values to the actual process of living and, if the values are found to be wanting, to modify, to improve, or if necessary to discard those values and create new ones to replace them.

[81]*E.g.*, H. SPAETH, *supra* note 17, at ch. 1.
[82]*See generally* F. FRANKFURTER, *supra* note 40.

If a humanistic education may be defined as a knowledge of the best that has been thought and written, then a study of constitutional law may be seen as one of the most humanistic efforts in the study of American government, for constitutional law is not concerned with the "technology" of American government but addresses itself to the philosophic and problematic substance. It confronts the interplay between social issues and questions of institutional structure and adaptation, and it takes as its text some of the most scholarly and philosophic statements issuing from the government itself, opinions of the United States Supreme Court. The Justices of the Court are unique not simply in that the nature of the institution allows them to consider social issues removed from the immediacy of practical politics but in that their institutional, if not psychological detachment, affords them the opportunity, which regrettably they do not always take, to think at, if not always to think through, these problems and then to express their conclusions in more or less well-reasoned opinions.

The trouble with result-oriented jurisprudence is that it ignores the basis of the Court's legitimacy. Sound reasoning serves to justify the Court's role not only as the authoritative constitutional interpreter but also as the symbol of national values which transcend politics. One of the most important functions which the Court serves is not that of declaring the law but that of providing for the United States that symbol of historical continuity which all nations apparently need.[83]

> Senior members of the Court are witnesses to the reality and validity of our present—distracted, improbable, illegitimate as it often appears—because in their persons they assure us of its link to the past which they also witnessed and in which they were themselves once the harbingers of something outrageously new. . . . When the great Holmes, who was wounded at Ball's Bluff and at Antietam, retired in 1932, being past ninety, the emotional public response was not due wholly to his undoubted greatness. It was also that his years, his years alone, fulfilled one of the functions of the Supreme Court.[84]

Americans suffer the Court to exercise the great policy-making power which it does because they perceive it to be legitimate. But faulty reasoning undermines that legitimacy. "A sense of continuity is . . . precious in a world assaulted by change. That fact makes it . . . essential . . . that the principles embraced by the court be imbued with as much

[83]*See* Mason, *The Supreme Court: Temple and Forum,* 48 YALE REV. 524 (1959); Lerner, *Constitution and Court as Symbols,* 46 YALE L. J. 1290 (1937).
[84]A. BICKEL, *supra* note 17, at 32-33.

wisdom and intelligence as possible. Every successive failure by the court to think a problem through to a durable solution will be less and less acceptable."[85]

To be sure, the Justices do and must make value judgments. But why should anybody pay any attention to the value choices of nine other individuals who simply happen to make their living by judging? It can be argued that, at least in a democracy, a citizen is obligated to abide by the value pronouncements of the legislators, even though he may disagree with them.[86] After all, they reflect the majority will; they have been elected. But Supreme Court Justices have not. Why adhere to their value choices? "The answer . . . inheres primarily in that they are—or are obliged to be—entirely principled."[87] As Professor Alexander Bickel has suggested in his brilliant book, *The Supreme Court and the Idea of Progress*, when the Court forsakes principle for expediency it becomes merely a third, unelected, chamber of the legislative branch, and it is unlikely that the populace would long tolerate such duplication of effort—and an oligarchic one at that. The only way the Court can preserve its legitimacy and the legitimacy of the value choices which it does make is to convince the public that it follows some process in arriving at its judgments which is inherently different from that followed by the legislature. Only by the application of reason and principled logic to the issues of the day can the Court convince people that its value choices are at least as legitimate as those made by elected representatives. Indeed, when the Court declares a legislative or executive act to be unconstitutional, it is asserting that its value choices have greater legitimacy than those made by elected officials. For a generation which has experienced the "credibility gap" and the corollary diminution of the presidential office, how much more important it is that the Supreme Court, given its counter-majoritarian nature, be not only candid but also *persuasive* in explaining the reasons for the policy judgments it is making. The Court's whole power to act as the final interpreter of the Constitution is necessarily based upon reason and principle.

---

[85]TIME, June 21, 1971, at 49.

[86]*See generally* J. TUSSMAN, OBLIGATION AND THE BODY POLITIC (1960); A. FORTAS, CONCERNING DISSENT & CIVIL DISOBEDIENCE (1968); D. HANSON & R. FOWLER (eds.), OBLIGATION & DISSENT: AN INTRODUCTION TO POLITICS (1971). *Cf.* H. ZINN, DISOBEDIENCE AND DEMOCRACY (1970).

[87]Wechsler, *Toward Neutral Principles of Constitutional Law*, 73 HARV. L. REV. 1, 69 (1959).

It is, of course, true that the public does not pay much attention to the Court and even less to the logic and principle of its opinions.[88] But, even though it does not read the *United States Reports*, the public becomes aware of the intellectual strengths and weaknesses of the Court's decision-making.[89] In his classic analysis of the politics of leadership within the American system, Professor Richard Neustadt has argued that one of the major sources of presidential power is the President's reputation among "professionals."[90] This thesis "has even greater validity as applied to the Court, for a large segment of public opinion looks to lawyers to appraise its performance."[91] The research of political scientists upon the formation of public opinion in America has consistently identified a process known as the "two-step flow."[92] That is, the public does not form its opinions as the result of direct observation of and thought about events; instead, an elite of experts acts as a buffer, influencing the direction and content of public opinion. Although these researches have primarily been concerned with opinions upon issues or towards electoral candidates, there is no reason to believe that the process does not operate in the formation of Americans' opinions about their governmental institutions. Expert opinion has a way of eventually pervading other strata in the society, and, if legal scholars and other intellectual taste-makers find the Court guilty of poor logic, the Court's authority will, in the long run, be seriously impaired.

Moreover, the public will viscerally recognize the vulnerability of the Court's policies if the law begins to fluctuate rapidly. So long as constitutional law remains "constitutional," it cannot be static, but so long as it remains "law" it must retain some element of certainty. Unsound logic makes for unsound law. If the Court rejects reason in favor of results, those results will prove viable only as long as the majority can command five votes. As the reasoning gets weaker, subsequent Justices will find earlier cases easier to overrule. "Landmark"

[88] *See* note 15 *supra*.

[89] *But cf.* Adamany, Book Review, 14 MIDW. J. POL. SCI. 734, 735 (1970).

[90] R. NEUSTADT, PRESIDENTIAL POWER: THE POLITICS OF LEADERSHIP (1960).

[91] A COX, THE WARREN COURT: CONSTITUTIONAL DECISION AS AN INSTRUMENT OF REFORM 48 (1968).

[92] V. O. KEY, PUBLIC OPINION AND AMERICAN DEMOCRACY 150-151, 551-558 (1961). *See also* McClosky, Hoffmann, & O'Hara, *Issue Conflict and Consensus Among Party Leaders and Followers*, 54 AM. POL. SCI. REV. 406 (1960); McClosky, *Consensus and Ideology in American Politics*, 58 AM. POL. SCI. REV. 361 (1964).

decision will shortly be overruled by "landmark" decision. Similarly, unless the Court's decisions are explained with care, lower courts will be unsure of the law, and, thus, it will fluctuate not only over time but also from jurisdiction to jurisdiction. Arbitrary decisions arrived at on the basis of snap judgments motivated by no more than personal preference are simply edicts, which are usually short-lived. "Absolute" principles have a way of colliding with other "absolutes." Failure to recognize the complexity of the issues presented in a given case and, thus, to formulate a principle capable of accommodating the competing interests in a new context will mean that sooner or later the "absolute" will collapse under its own weight.

Opinions based upon reasoned principle, therefore, are necessary to the very self-preservation of the Supreme Court. Assuming that the institution is worth preserving, Justices must sometimes sacrifice what they conceive to be a desirable result, if they cannot logically justify that result.[93] In other words, procedure may be as important as substance; means more important than ends. To what extent has the modern Court, under the leadership either of Earl Warren or Warren Burger, provided logically coherent, principled explanations for its policy-making? Has a majority of the Justices reflected a sensitivity for the Court's inherent institutional weaknesses? Have they displayed an appropriate concern for political reality? With these questions in mind, let us turn to an analysis of some of the continuities and disjunctions in modern judicial policy-making.

[93]This, of course, is where some scholars, members of the school of legal realism and especially their contemporary successors, the judicial behavioralists, are led astray by their methodology. They begin from the assumption that any man placed in a position of power must necessarily use that power to pursue his own personal preferences. They simply cannot believe—let alone accept—that men placed in positions of power can or will—on principle—refuse to exercise that power in the service of their values. *See, e.g.*, H. SPAETH, *supra* note 17, at ch. 1. *But see* West Virginia Board of Education v. Barnette, 319 U.S. 624, (1943) (Frankfurter, J., dissenting); Griswold v. Connecticut, 381 U.S. 479, 507 (1965) (Black, J., dissenting). This is not to say, however, that all behaviorally oriented scholars are insensitive to the ethical complexities of human behavior; *see, e.g.*, Grossman, *Role-Playing and the Analysis of Judicial Behavior: The Case of Mr. Justice Frankfurter*, 11 J. PUB. L. 285 (1962).

Chapter 2
With Liberty and
Justice For All

From almost his first day on the Supreme Court bench, Earl Warren and the Court which he led were embroiled in controversy. The Warren Era dawned and with it a public awareness of the Court not equalled since 1937 with the momentous decision in *Brown v. Board of Education*,[1] overturning the doctrine of "separate but equal" and mandating the desegregation of public education in America.[2] Though not his first opinion for the Court, Mr. Chief Justice Warren's opinion in *Brown* so closely followed his appointment to the Court by President Eisenhower, to fill the vacancy left by the death of Mr. Chief Justice Vinson, that it stands as a symbolic watershed in the history of the Court and its constitutional policy-making. Coming only seven months after Warren's assumption of his seat, the decision jolted the public with the realization that, at least insofar as the Court was concerned, things were going to be different in the coming years.[3] Indeed, the public and essentially southern furor which erupted following the *School Desegregation Cases* created the impression, even in many otherwise well-informed minds, that *Brown* had sprung from the Warren brain much as had Athena from Zeus's brow. Such an impression is rather at odds with the facts. While certainly a classic example of judicial policy-making, *Brown v. Board of Education* was actually the culmination of a line of policy and precedent developed over the years by the Court. It was not a revolutionary declaration of policy emerging full-blown in a single case.

To the extent that it can be determined, the original intention of the framers of the Thirteenth, Fourteenth, and Fifteenth Amendments seems to have been to ratify and legally consolidate the results of the Civil War

---

[1] 347 U.S. 483 (1954).

[2] *See generally* B. ZIEGLER, DESEGREGATION AND THE SUPREME COURT (1958); A. GRIMES, EQUALITY IN AMERICA ch. 2 (1964); D. BERMAN, IT IS SO ORDERED (1966).

[3] Concerning the post-New Deal predecessors of the Warren Court, see R. McCLOSKEY, THE MODERN SUPREME COURT chs. II & III (1972).

and to involve the federal government in a broad and intensive program of insuring the civil rights of the newly freed slaves while elevating them to a position of first-class citizenship.[4] After a decade of Reconstruction, however, with the growing realization that such a program could not be swiftly accomplished and would necessarily involve the military occupation of the South for a very long time, with all of its attendant costs, northern ardor cooled and finally subsided completely with the Hayes-Tilden Compromise of 1877.[5] Deprived of legislative and executive support, black Americans turned to the courts, but the judiciary, as mirror of the dominant political and social trends, validated the northern abandonment of the blacks. In the *Slaughter-House Cases*,[6] the Privileges and Immunities Clause of the Fourteenth Amendment was so narrowly construed as to be virtually emasculated. But the Equal Protection Clause remained as a constitutional basis for attacking racial discrimination. Indeed, Mr. Justice Miller, author of the majority opinion in *Slaughter-House*, indicated that the primary if not sole purpose of the Equal protection Clause was to insure equal rights for blacks. That clause, however, was seriously diluted in the *Civil Rights Cases*, declaring the federal Civil Rights Act of 1875 to be unconstitutional.[7]

Southern whites, taking their cue from these decisions, moved to protect their segregated social system by enacting legislation *requiring* the separation of the races in various facilities.[8] As constitutional justification for such legislation, they borrowed a doctrine developed as a legal concept, ironically enough, by Charles Sumner, a leading radical Republican, to sustain the segregation of the public schools in Boston and endorsed by one of America's most influential and respected jurists, Lemuel Shaw: the doctrine of "separate but equal."[9] This doctrine was then adopted by the Supreme Court in *Plessy v. Ferguson*.[10] Following *Plessy*, the segregation of the races became an institutionalized way of life in parts of America, and the principle of "separate but equal" was extended throughout the South to all manner of public and private

[4]*See* Slaughter-House Cases, 16 Wall. 36, 81 (1873); J. TEN BROEK, THE ANTI-SLAVERY ORIGINS OF THE FOURTEENTH AMENDMENT (1951). *See also* H. HOROWITZ & K. KARST, LAW, LAWYERS AND SOCIAL CHANGE (1969); R. BARDOLPH, THE CIVIL RIGHTS RECORD (1970).
[5]*See generally* C. WOODWARD, REUNION AND REACTION (1951).
[6]16 Wall. 36 (1873).
[7]109 U.S. 3 (1883).
[8]*See generally* C. WOODWARD, THE STRANGE CAREER OF JIM CROW (1955).
[9]Roberts v. Boston, 59 Mass. 198 (1850).
[10]163 U.S. 537 (1896).

facilities, including business, recreation, and most significantly, in view of subsequent developments, education. These extensions, though challenged as violating the Constitution, were accepted by the Supreme Court;[11] but the doctrine of "separate but equal" ceased to have any real meaning, because the Court refused to look behind lower court determinations of fact to find if the segregated facilities were actually equal, which they were not. In short, there was a good deal of separation but very little equality.

The law, however, reflects social change, and in the second third of the twentieth century events were moving in directions which would spell the end of segregation. The Great Depression, by reducing many to a common level of destitution and despair, increased appreciation for the status of blacks and the universality of the human condition. Eleanor Roosevelt's example was also significantly influential. But most important was the Second World War. The conflict with fascism and its racist ideology presented even the least thoughtful American with a disturbing paradox, particularly when many black Americans fought with valor and distinction. Thus, following the war, Harry Truman, grandson of a Confederate soldier, took steps to desegregate the armed forces and appointed a presidential commission on civil rights. The commission's report, *To Secure These Rights*, detailing the situation of blacks in America with brutal precision, struck the nation like a bombshell. At the same time, the emergence of the Cold War contributed to the collapse of segregation, for it was felt that America could not successfully compete with communism for the loyalties of the emerging African states if it, or any of its constituent states, practiced such blatant, prejudice-based discrimination against black people.

Taking stock of their position in the post-War world, leaders at the National Association for the Advancement of Colored People determined to initiate a legal campaign against racial segregation.[12] Indeed, *Brown v. Board of Education* was the culmination of a classic case of litigation as a form of pressure group activity.[13] NAACP attorneys purposely selected higher education as the most promising target for their initial attack upon segregation. By emphasizing black's desire for an education in order to better their condition, the NAACP was tapping a

[11]*E.g.*, Cummings v. Board of Education, 175 U.S. 528 (1899); Berea College v. Kentucky, 211 U.S. 45 (1908).

[12]*See* L. MILLER, THE PETITIONERS (1967).

[13]*See* Vose, *Litigation as a Form of Pressure Group Activity*, 319 THE ANNALS 28 (1958); C. VOSE, CAUCASIANS ONLY (1959).

traditional American value. At the same time, desegregating higher education facilities would not involve the emotional concerns likely to be aroused by mixing young children and adolescents. The initial victories were scored in two cases decided on the same day in 1950.[14] While these cases did not hold that segregation per se was unconstitutional, they did indicate that the trend of judicial thinking was toward the conclusion that it was impossible for the states to comply with the "separate but equal" doctrine. Although the Court simply found a lack of substantial equality in the facilities involved in these cases, it was now looking not just to physical factors in determining equality but was turning to consider intangible, psychological factors as well.

Determined to exploit this movement of the judicial mind, the NAACP attorneys brought to the Court a group of cases challenging segregation in the public secondary and elementary schools. The leading case in this group, *Brown v. Board of Education*,[15] involved the school system of Topeka, Kansas, and had been particularly selected because of the virtually complete equality of the physical facilities provided. Building upon its earlier successes, the NAACP had now determined to force the issue of the inherent legality or illegality of segregated educational facilities. The case was, of course, a *cause célèbre*. Counsel for the segregating school systems was John W. Davis, Democratic candidate for President in 1924. Appearing for the NAACP was Thurgood (later, Mr. Justice) Marshall.

Marshall filed with the Court a brief which was to be recognized in the history of Supreme Court advocacy as the equal of Louis D. Brandeis's tradition-shattering brief in *Muller v. Oregon*.[16] Particularly famous was the appendix to the brief, in which Marshall relied upon the findings of nationally and internationally renowned social scientists to support the proposition that segregation was harmful to the psyches of both black and white children and, thereby, caused irreparable damage to the development of a healthy, heterogenous community.

Although the case was initially heard in 1952, the Supreme Court adjourned that term without rendering a decision and instead called for re-argument, submitting to counsel a set of questions concerning the intent of the framers of the Fourteenth Amendment as it related to segregated schools. Obviously aware of the potential impact of its

---

[14]Sweatt v. Painter, 339 U.S. 629 (1950); McLaurin v. Oklahoma State Regents, 339 U.S. 637 (1950).

[15]347 U.S. 482 (1954).

[16]208 U.S. 412 (1908).

decision in this case, the Court was moving with extreme caution. But, after the filing of new briefs, including an *amicus* brief filed on behalf of Brown by Herbert Brownell, the new Attorney General in the Eisenhower Administration, and after more hours of oral argumentation, the Court was finally ready to render judgment.

On May 17, 1954, a unanimous Supreme Court, speaking through its new Chief Justice, rang the death knell for segregation. For a decision of such historic significance and policy importance, however, the Chief Justice's opinion in *Brown* was remarkably brief. Indeed, *Brown* was both indicator and archetypical example of that style which was to characterize Chief Justice Warren's decision-making for the next fifteen years. Even friendly critics have felt constrained to note that the opinion manages to avoid confronting virtually every one of the vast array of legal and historical complexities with which the Court had been presented. In a backhand way, it is a sort of *tour de force*. Having held the case over for new briefs and argument on the historical questions presented to counsel, Warren now dismissed these questions as impossible to resolve and essentially irrelevant in mid-twentieth century America. As concerned segregated schools, whatever may have been the intent of the Congress which framed the Fourteenth Amendment, in modern America, the Chief Justice noted, education had become the most important function of state and local government.[17] He then concluded by emphasizing that enforced segregation in such a quantitatively and qualitatively significant aspect of public policy and social life necessarily imposed an inferior status upon black children. The feeling of inferiority generated by segregation damaged the minds and hearts of these children in ways unlikely ever to be undone. Relying upon such social scientists as the Swedish sociologist Gunnar Myrdal and the black social psychologist Kenneth B. Clark,[18] Warren wrote:

> Does segregation in public schools solely on the basis of race, even though the physical facilities and other tangible factors may be equal, deprive the children of the minority group of equal educational opportunity? We believe that it does. . . . A sense of inferiority affects the motivation of a child to learn. . . . In the field of public

---

[17]Warren, however, did not go so far as to hold that the states had a constitutional duty to provide public educational facilities. In light of the Burger Court's subsequent holding in San Antonio v. Rodriguez, 411 U.S. 1 (1973), it must be borne in mind that it is one thing for the Supreme Court to take note of the empirical fact that a particular function is at a particular moment in time the most important served by the state and quite another thing for the Court to rule that the state has no option regarding the performance of that function.

[18]*See* 347 U.S. at 494 n. 11.

education the doctrine of separate but equal has no place. Separate educational facilities are inherently unequal.[19]

Such social science-based jurisprudence was subject to immediate and vigorous criticism.[20] Defenders of segregation and opponents of equality of racial opportunity attacked the decision as illegitimate fiat.[21] Judicial decision-making, they contended, must be based upon the words of the legal text, be it constitution or statute, or upon precedent, or upon a convincing showing of the intent of the law's framers. Social scientists, they argued, especially foreign sociologists, are without legal authority and, thus, are not legitimate bases for judicial decision. Such complaints, however, ignored the fact that the Supreme Court of the United States is different in kind from all other courts. As a major policy-maker in the American constitutional system, it may be desirable for the Court to take judicial notice of materials which are inappropriate for consideration by other courts. Viewing the Court in this light, however, makes even more disturbing the reservations voiced about *Brown's* social science by friendly critics. Some, such as Professor Herbert Wechsler, charged that the decision was not based upon "neutral principles" and suggested that it would have been preferable to have rested the result upon First Amendment associational freedom, thereby avoiding the social science as well as opening the way for benign racial quotas.[22] Others criticized the methodologies employed by various of the social scientists relied upon by the Court.[23] Indeed, Clark's famous "doll test" did involve a hucksterish sleight-of-hand, and anyone who has ever examined Gunnar Myrdal's *An American Dilemma* can only conclude that it is about as scientific as a seed catalogue. More recently, Professor David Armor has suggested that the sociological data used in *Brown* was perhaps seriously flawed as a legitimate basis for governmental policy decision by virtue of its time-bound nature.[24]

But even had the evidence been above contemporary reproach, social

---

[19]*Id.* at 493, 494, 495.

[20]*See* C. LYTLE, THE WARREN COURT & ITS CRITICS 20-22, 67, 94-95 (1970).

[21]*But see* Black, *The Lawfulness of the Segregation Decisions*, 69 YALE L.J. 421 (1960).

[22]*E.g.*, Wechsler, *Toward Neutral Principles of Constitutional Law*, 73 HARV. L. REV. 1 (1959). Wechsler's position is thoroughly and critically examined in A. BICKEL, THE LEAST DANGEROUS BRANCH 49-65 (1962); Miller & Howell, *The Myth of Neutrality in Constitutional Adjudication*, 27 U. CHI. L. REV. 661 (1960).

[23]*See, e.g.*, Cahn, *Jurisprudence*, 30 N.Y.U. L. REV. 150 (1955).

[24]Armor, *The Evidence on Busing*, 28 PUB. INTEREST 90 (1972).

science jurisprudence carries within itself substantial dangers, as Edmond Cahn cogently warned.

> ... (S)ince the behavioral sciences are so very young, imprecise, and changeful, their findings have an uncertain expectancy of life. Today's sanguine asseveration may be cancelled by tomorrow's new revelation—or new technical fad. It is one thing to use the current scientific findings, however ephemeral they may be, in order to ascertain whether the legislature has acted reasonably in adopting some scheme of social or economic regulation; deference here is shown not so much to the findings as to the legislature. It would be quite another thing to have our fundamental rights rise, fall, or change along with the latest fashions of psychological literature. Today the social psychologists—at least the leaders of the discipline—are liberal and egalitarian in basic approach. Suppose, a generation hence, some of their successors were to revert to the ethnic mysticism of the very recent past; suppose they were to present us with a collection of racist notions and label them "science." What then would be the state of our constitutional rights?[25]

Though not taken seriously at the time, Cahn's admonition has the ring of Cassandra in a later decade which has seen a rebirth of interest in the genetic theory of intelligence.[26] What if the Burger Court were to employ the Warren Court method, adopting as its social scientists Arthur Jensen and Richard Herrnstein? What constitutional wonders might it then fashion? Perhaps it would have been better had the Warren Court in *Brown* taken the path mapped out by the first Justice Harlan in his dissent in *Plessy v. Ferguson*,[27] striking down segregation as fastening upon black Americans a badge of slavery wholly inconsistent with the Thirteenth Amendment.

Had the Court adopted such an approach it would, in the immediate context of *Brown*, have saved itself from an anomalous situation of its own creation. Having struck down segregation under the Equal Protection Clause of the Fourteenth Amendment, the Court was faced with the existence of segregated schools in the District of Columbia, created by act of Congress. Yet there was no constitutional guarantee of equal protection applicable to Congress; the Fourteenth Amendment relates only to state action. The Court, thus, had outlawed racial segregation in the states but left it intact as far as the federal government was concerned. To remedy this illogical situation, the Court turned to the Due Process

[25]Cahn, *supra* note 23, at 167.

[26]*See* R. HERRNSTEIN, IQ IN THE MERITOCRACY (1973); Herrnstein, *On Challenging an Orthodoxy*, 55 COMMENTARY 52 (1973), Herrnstein, *IQ*, 227 ATLANTIC MONTHLY 43 (1971); Jensen, *How Much Can We Boost IQ and Scholastic Achievement?*, 39 HARV. EDUC. REV. 1 (1969). *See generally*, J. BAKER, RACE (1973).

[27]163 U.S. 537 (1896).

Clause of the Fifth Amendment and held that federally imposed segregation violated that guarantee.[28] For purposes of modern constitutional law, then, the Fifth Amendment's Due Process Clause is, as regards congressional classifications, the equivalent of the Fourteenth Amendment's Equal Protection Clause, and the federal government is prohibited from enforcing racial or irrational categorizations.

Though *Brown* had emphasized the importance of education as a governmental function, subsequent decisions modified and eventually dispensed with that emphasis, stressing only that segregated facilities were inherently unequal. As a result, state-mandated racial discrimination in recreational facilities,[29] marriage licensing,[30] and so forth were held to be unconstitutional.[31] At least until the late 1960s, it seemed that the Court had fashioned, as a subsidiary doctrine of equal protection, the rule that race was never to be considered a valid classification.[32]

Brown, of course, whatever its failures, was a momentous decision. Its impact was felt and will continue to be felt for decades. That the Court was well aware of its responsibility was demonstrated not only by its unanimity but also by its postponing a decision on the implementation of its holding until the following term. Then, after having heard further extended oral argument, the Court ruled that the federal district courts should maintain flexibility in the implementation of *Brown*, taking into consideration the particular and unique facts involved in the situation of each individual school district.[33] The transition from segregation to desegregation should take place, the Court held, in perhaps the most egregious phrase in modern constitutional law, "with all deliberate speed."[34]

As *Brown I* had reflected the social and politial realities of mid-twentieth century America,[35] so *Brown II* reflected the Court's cognizance of the limits upon its power. Compliance would depend upon

[28]Bolling v. Sharpe, 347 U.S. 497 (1954).
[29]*See, e.g.*, Baltimore v. Dawson, 350 U.S. 877 (1955) (beaches); Holmes v. Atlanta, 350 U.S. 879 (1955) (golf courses); New Orleans City Park Ass'n v. Detiege, 358 U.S. 54 (1958) (parks).
[30]Loving v. Virginia, 388 U.S. 1 (1967).
[31]*E.g.*, Gayle v. Browder, 352 U.S. 903 (1956) (buses); McLaughlin v. Florida, 379 U.S. 184 (1964) (cohabitation).
[32]*But see* United States v. Montgomery County Board of Education, 395 U.S. 225 (1969).
[33]Brown v. Board of Education, 349 U.S. 294 (1955).
[34]*Id.* at 301.
[35]*See* Cahn, *supra* note 23, at 169.

executive support, and initially there was little of this from the Eisenhower Administration. The South devised innumerable, ingenious devices for avoiding the Court's decisions. Some states attempted to close their public schools and to replace them with private all-white systems. But, since the new "private" systems continued to be operated in the same buildings as the former public schools, with the same faculty and staff, and with state financing, federal court experienced little difficulty in holding such segregation academies unconstitutional. In Prince Edward County, Virginia, when whites found sufficient private funds to operate an actually private, all-white school, the state simply closed the public schools, with the result that the black children in the county received no formal education during a five-year period from 1959 to 1964, when the Court held that a state might not shut down the schools in selected counties, although leaving open the possibility that it would be permissible for the state to close all schools state-wide.[36] Pupil placement laws were another popular device for evading *Brown*. Such plans, euphemistically called "freedom of choice programs" for public relations purposes, left students in their previously segregated schools, but permitted the student to transfer to another school, providing he could meet certain state-imposed residence and aptitude requirements. Naturally, few if any whites transferred to the previously all-black schools, and blacks were discouraged from transferring to all-white schools by transfer procedures remarkable for their consciously contrived byzantine complexity. Though the Warren Court was to hold that such pupil placement laws were not unconstitutional on their face,[37] it warned that the judiciary would closely scrutinize such "freedom of choice" programs to insure that they were not being unconstitutionally applied, as they almost always were.[38] Finally, when all else failed, many white southerners were not above resorting to violence in an effort to stay the execution of *Brown's* mandate.

Indeed, it was Governor Faubus's pathetic resurrection of the doctrine of "interposition," completely ignoring the outcome of the Civil War, which finally forced President Eisenhower to act.[39] But no real movement toward desegregation occurred until the election of President Kennedy,[40]

[36]Griffin v. County School Board of Prince Edward County, 337 U.S. 218 (1964).

[37]Shuttlesworth v. Birmingham Board of Education, 358 U.S. 101 (1958).

[38]*See, e.g.,* Green v. County School Board of New Kent County, Virginia, 391 U.S. 430 (1968).

[39]*See* Cooper v. Aaron, 358 U.S. 1 (1958).

[40]*See* J. HARVEY, CIVIL RIGHTS DURING THE KENNEDY ADMINISTRATION (1971); R. MORGAN, THE PRESIDENT AND CIVIL RIGHTS (1970).

the further use of federal troops in Mississippi, and the assassination of President Kennedy, with its consequent elevation of Lyndon Johnson to the White House and the enactment of successive Civil Rights Acts. In short, for more than a decade after the Court's pronouncement in *Brown*, the country witnessed a great deal of deliberation but very little speed in its implementation. Even at the level of higher education, it was not until 1963, with the admission of Vivian Malone and James Hood to the University of Alabama, chiefly remembered for the opportunity which it provided Governor Wallace to stand literally in the schoolhouse door, that the last public institution of higher education was officially desegregated in the United States; and the results of a study conducted by the Department of Health, Education, and Welfare in the autumn of 1968, though not reported until January, 1970, revealed that fourteen years after the *Brown* decision 61% of the nation's black students and 65.6% of its white students still attended largely segregated schools.[41]

This failure of compliance eventually led the Court to abandon the "deliberate speed" concept. Ironically enough, this was done in the first decision of the Supreme Court under the Chief Justiceship of Warren Earl Burger. Though previous opinions of the Warren Court had suggested that the "deliberate speed" formula was no longer tolerable,[42] the Court had procrastinated on the issue, stopping short of an explicit rejection. In *Alexander v. Holmes*,[43] however, the Burger Court, in a brief but unanimous *per curiam* opinion, held that the obligation of every American school district was to terminate dual school systems at once and to operate henceforward only racially unitary systems. Continued operation of segregated schools under a standard allowing "all deliberate speed" for desegregation was no longer to be constitutionally permissible. By implication, the *Alexander* decision severed the alliance of several years' standing between the federal judiciary and the Department of Health, Education, and Welfare which had been so successful in the desegregation of southern schools,[44] with the Court moving the judiciary to a position in advance of that taken by H.E.W. Of course, in subsequent application of the *Alexander* standard, the Justices were unable to agree on exactly when "now" meant "now,"[45] but *Alexander*,

[41]Los Angeles Times, January 4, 1970, § A, at l.
[42]*E.g.*, Griffin v. County School Board of Prince Edward County, 337 U.S. 218 (1964); Green v. County School Board of New Kent County, Virginia, 391 U.S. 430 (1968).
[43]396 U.S. 19 (1969).
[44]*See The Supreme Court, 1969 Term*, 84 HARV. L. REV. 1, 32-46 (1970).
[45]Carter v. West Feliciana Parish School Board, 396 U.S. 290 (1970).

by rejecting the rule of *Brown II*, had moved the focus of constitutional concern away from the question of *when* a school board must desegregate to a concern for *what* school boards must do. How much desegregation was enough?

In *Swann v. Charlotte-Mecklenburg Board of Education*, the Burger Court managed to avoid a direct answer to that question.[46] The *Swann* case presented the Court with the opportunity to rule on what remedies are proper to eliminate school segregation. The Charlotte-Mecklenburg, North Carolina, Board of Education had prior to *Brown* operated a racially segregated school system as requred by North Carolina law. Following *Brown*, the school board had proposed a "freedom of choice" desegregation program. After involved and protracted litigation, however, a federal district court had rejected the board's plan and ordered the adoption of a more far-reaching plan prepared by a court-appointed consultant. This plan aimed to increase integration in the district through a series of interrelated measures, including the prevention of student transfers whenever such transfers would contribute to segregated schools, the desegregation of the faculty, the rezoning of attendance districts, and perhaps most controversially bus transportation for all students whose reassignment was necessary to meet the plan's specifications. The district court's order was unanimously affirmed by the Supreme Court, emphasizing its long-standing commitment to desegregation and holding that, in order to remedy past *de jure* segregation, federal courts must require school authorities to make an affirmative showing that the existence of one-race schools was not the result of discrimination, past or present. Speaking for the Court, Mr. Chief Justice Burger ruled that in eradicating segregated educational facilities the judiciary might use racial quotas as guidelines (at least in a limited, flexible way),[47] rezone school attendance districts, and order bus transportation. In spite of the opportunity which *Swann* presented, however, the Chief Justice did not set definite standards for school desegregation. He suggested that the federal courts should intervene whenever school districts failed to take "acceptable" steps to desegregate, but he fell short of prescribing standards by which to measure "acceptability." *Swann*, thus, provided the lower federal judiciary with considerable discretion but did not precisely indicate how that discretion was to be exercised. Though it did approve busing as one technique for

[46]402 U.S. 1 (1971).
[47]*See also* United States v. Montgomery County Board of Education, 395 U.S. 225 (1969).

converting to a racially unitary school system, *Swann* left several questions unanswered.[48]

To a significant degree, *Swann's* shortcomings were due to the Court's continuing confusion as to the goal of desegregation. Why have desegregation? What is its purpose? Was the purpose of *Brown* to assure, insofar as possible, equal educational opportunity for all? Or was it directed toward the assimilation of ethnic minorities, in particular blacks, into America's predominant, white culture and value system? Depending upon how one reads *Brown*, he will, of course, provide quite different answers to the question of how much desegregation is enough. A minimal, equal-educational-opportunity approach to *Brown* would require minimal desegregation. A radical, assimilationist interpretation, on the other hand, would seem to require nothing short of strict racial quotas in every school, reflecting the overall racial balance in the school district. Indeed, read one way, *Brown* may appear to rest upon the implicit, racist assumption that a black child can never receive an equal education unless he sits next to a white child. In the 1970s, however, such assimilationist premises directly conflict with demands for black control of the black community and assertions of ethnic pride and cultural identity.

In fact, while it could be argued that equal educational opportunity requires a high degree of integration, racial integration may not be crucial to educational quality. The well-known Coleman Report, issued by the United States Office of Education in 1966, found that the socio-economic composition of a school, rather than its racial composition, was apparently the key factor in educational achievement,[49] and Charles Silberman has presented evidence to suggest that sudden integration may actually depress the educational attainment of black students.[50] Nor is it too difficult to understand why. Although by 1971, 97% of southern black children attended integrated school systems (Indeed, if one uses as his measure of integration the number of blacks going to schools with majority white populations, the South is considerably more integrated than the North.),[51] the experience may not be a pleasant one, bearing little if any relation to the rosy fantasies of some liberal reformers.[52]

[48]*See The Supreme Court, 1970 Term*, 85 HARV. L. REV. 3, 74-86 (1971).
[49]U.S. OFFICE OF EDUCATION, EQUALITY OF EDUCATIONAL OPPORTUNITY (1966).
[50]C. SILBERMAN, CRISIS IN BLACK AND WHITE 298 (1964).
[51]Glazer, *Is Busing Necessary?*, 53 COMMENTARY 39, 40 (1972).
[52]*See* TIME, July 13, 1970, at 32.

Instead, the "integrated" black student is likely to encounter an ugly pattern of "internal segregation," with separate classrooms, separate lunch and gym periods, and even separate bells so that white and black students will not use the halls at the same time. In De Soto Parish, Louisiana, the school buses reportedly call for the black students at 5:30 A.M.; white students ride separately at a later, more comfortable hour. Especially hard-hit by integration are middle-class black educators, who had previously provided the black South with a sense of pride and leadership; teachers and principals at formerly all black schools are subject to wholesale demotion or dismissal on the supposedly neutral ground of competence. For many black students, desegregation may simply mean schools run by hostile whites rather than by sympathetic blacks, and "a final tragic consequence of desegregation is the forfeiture of school spirit and group identity. Left behind to be stored, scattered or abandoned are trophies, pictures, plaques, and every symbol of black identity, of black students' achievemeents."[53]

Nevertheless, the public opinion polls have continued to show a high degree of support for integration among blacks.[54] There is, however, no clear consensus in favor of busing *even among blacks*. A Gallup Poll conducted in August, 1973, reported that, if given a choice of other means to achieve integration, such as rezoning school attendance districts, only 9% of black respondents still opted for busing, and an earlier *New York Times* poll found that, were busing *the only means* to integrate, 47% of black parents still opposed it, while only 45% favored the tactic.[55] (Among white parents only 15% favored busing.) Some have argued that the objection of some blacks to integration might be offset by permitting separatist black pupils to transfer from integrated schools to all-black schools, if they (or their parents) so desired.[56] But such a scheme may be unconstitutional; or, if constitutional, it would surely be necessary to allow separatist white students to transfer to all-white schools, thus in effect setting the clock back two decades or more. Moreover, any option of this sort would present possibilities for abuse through the intimidation of integrationist parents, white and black, by racial separatists.

[53]*Id.*

[54]Los Angeles Times, September 9, 1973, Part I-A, at 5; N.Y. Times, March 30, 1970, at 86; N.Y. Times, March 22, 1970, at 45.

[55]Los Angeles Times, September 9, 1973, Part I-A, at 5; N.Y. Times, September 12, 1971, at 24.

[56]*The Supreme Court, 1970 Term*, 85 HARV. L. REV. at 79 n. 30.

It may well be, as the United States Civil Rights Commission has claimed, that opposition to busing is largely based upon misinformation as to both its costs and its effects upon educational quality.[57] But, like many other cases of public opinion in American politics, the inadequacy of the informational base does not remove this massive opposition as a factor to be reckoned with in the making of public policy, including public policy made by the judiciary.[58] Moreover, it is by no means as clear as the Civil Rights Commission would apparently like to believe that the public is misinformed about the *potential* costs of busing. The Court in *Swann*, it must be remembered, failed to give the lower courts or the public any guidance as to when a desegregation plan becomes so expensive that the benefits no longer outweigh the costs. The Court would say only that busing should not be ordered if the time or distance of travel would be so great as to risk children's health or impair their education. According to Mr. Chief Justice Burger, these hazards would be greatest in the case of young children. But, given the nature of school attendance districts, unless young children are bused they will attend the most segregated schools. Because elementary school attendance districts tend to be much smaller than the attendance districts for junior and senior high schools, elementary schools are the most reflective of the demographic composition of the residential area in which the school is located. Indeed, the *Swann* Court, like many critics of busing, failed to explain exactly how busing could threaten children's health or hamper their education; and one could argue that such risks are, in fact, quite minimal, for small children have already tolerated extensive busing. Prior to desegregation, for example, in none other than the Charlotte-Mecklenburg school district, very young black children were bused as far as 79 miles per day on round trips requiring as much as four hours to complete![59]

Indeed, the Burger Court's approval in *Swann* of busing as a remedy to segregation may in the future give rise to a desegregation plan in some schol district which closes all schools with predominantly black student populations and buses only black children. Could such a program escape constitutional challenge? Before glibly answering, one should recall that in the *Swann* case itself, under the special consultant's plan, a few schools would have remained very nearly all-white. The Court's approv-

[57]Los Angeles Times, March 11, 1973, Part I, at 1.

[58]*See generally* V.O. KEY, PUBLIC OPINION AND AMERICAN DEMOCRACY (1961).

[59]*The Supreme Court, 1970 Term*, 85 HARV. L. REV. at 80 n. 37.

al of this plan invites the interpretation that all-white schools are constitutionally less objectionable than all-black schools, and, in fact, the United States Circuit Court of Appeals for the Second Circuit has already affirmed a federal district court decision holding that an integration program involving the busing of black and Puerto Rican pupils to white neighborhoods without reciprocal busing of white students and the closing of schools only in the minority neighborhoods did not violate the equal protection guarantee.[60] But such a plan clearly imposed heavier burdens upon identifiable racial minorities. Not only were minority children required to bear whatever physical inconveniences new busing would involve but also the effect of such a "one-way" busing program may be psychological injuries as severe as those produced by the segregated schools condemned in *Brown*. Yet, to what advantage?

Very little advantage is the conclusion suggested by Professor David Armor's study for the United States Civil Rights Commission of the effects of school desegregation by busing upon the educational achievements of black students.[61] The largest study ever attempted of the before and after effects of long-term busing programs, the Armor project included research on city-suburb desegregation programs in Boston, Massachusetts, Ann Arbor, Michigan, Hartford, Connecticut, Riverside, California, and White Plains, New York. It involved some 5,000 students ranging from grades one through twelve, and most importantly it followed these children's progress from 1965 to 1971. Among its more controversial findings:

> Busing had no appreciable effect, positive or negative, upon the performance of black students on standard achievement tests. Black children bused to suburban schools made no significant gains in test scores when compared with those of their brothers and sisters who had remained behind in the inner-city schools.
>
> The grades of black students, however, generally fell when they were transferred to predominantly white schools. (Armor suggests that this was due to more rigorous grading standards in the suburban schools. While plausible, this is obviously not the only possible explanation for such a phenomenon.)

[60]Norwalk CORE v. Norwalk Board of Education, 423 F.2d 121 (2d Cir. 1970), *aff'g* 298 F. Supp. 213 (D. Conn. 1969). The Congress of Racial Equality did not appeal the decision, apparently on the theory that if the decision were bad law—and CORE clearly thought it was bad law—it was better that it remain bad law for the Second Circuit only rather than for the United States as a whole. Concerning black resistance to shouldering a disproportionate share of the "costs" of integration, *see also* Coppedge v. Franklin County Board of Education, 394 F.2d 410 (4th Cir. 1968).

[61]Armor, *supra* note 24.

The career aspirations of black students in predominantly white schools were slightly lower than those of children in predominantly black schools, perhaps as a result of their poorer grades.

Black students in white schools had a greater desire for racial separatism than black students in black schools. "Integration," concluded Armor, "heightens racial identity and consciousness and enhances ideologies that promote racial segregation."[62] This finding is the converse of one of the central sociological hypotheses in integration policy, that integration should reduce racial stereotypes, increase tolerance and generally improve race relations. The effect appears to be exactly the opposite.

Finally, and perhaps most controversially, the Armor study concluded that most of the research on race and education done before the late 1960's—in other words, most of the social science research relied upon by the federal courts in their integration decisions—was seriously flawed, wrongly interpreted, or time-bound. Armor suggests that in a new era of black militancy and black pride judicial reliance upon such studies will result in decisions which will worsen rather than improve race relations in America.

The Armor study, however, carries the problem beyond the desegregation of southern school systems, and indeed *Swann* seemed to have implications for school segregation in the North as well as in the South. Though the Court had not indicated any willingness to attack the problem of *de facto* segregation, Chief Justice Burger seemed to suggest that racial imbalance in northern schools was not wholly coincidental but that previous school segregation, albeit not required by law, had to some degree caused segregated residential patterns and not vice versa.[63] By thus turning the tables on the apologists for *de facto* segregation, the Chief Justice may have been doing no more than engaging in "chicken-and-the-egg" semantics, but *Swann* had already attracted at least as much and perhaps more public attention than had any other race relations decision of the Court since *Brown v. Board of Education.* Not only in the popular press but also in the *Supreme Court Reporter Advance Sheets*, produced by the normally staid and non-alarmist West

[62]*Id.* at 102.
[63]402 U.S. 1, 21 (1971):
  . . . (B)uilding new schools in the areas of white suburban expansion farthest from Negro population centers in order to maintain the separation of the races with a minimum departure from the formal principles of "neighborhood zoning" . . . does more than simply influence the short-run composition of the student body of a new school. It may well promote segregated residential patterns which, when combined with "neighborhood zoning," further lock the school system into the mold of separation of the races.

Publishing Company, the decision was referred to as the "school-busing" case;[64] and, however parsed, *Swann* amounted to a recognition by the Court that what was once thought to be a southern issue was now a national issue.[65]

The segregation practiced in the southern states prior to *Brown* had been *de jure*, required by state law. In the North, facilities were also segregated, but this segregation tended to be the *de facto* result of racially separated housing patterns. *Brown v. Board of Education* affected only *de jure* segregation, and for ten years following *Brown* little was done to desegregate the schools of the South. During that decade the federal courts became educated in all of the techniques of avoidance, evasion, and delay, and in their slow, methodical way struck them down, one by one.[66] But little statistically measurable progress was made. Then came the passage of the Civil Rights Act of 1964.[67] Vast federal bureaucracies sprang up to enforce this law, and desegregation no longer progressed painfully from court case to court case. Now it moved forward rapidly, as every school district in the South was required to comply with federal guidelines or face the loss of federal funds. The Department of Justice, the federal judiciary, and the Department of Health, Education, and Welfare moved in lock-step. What the courts declared was segregation became what H.E.W. declared was segregation and vice versa. H.E.W. applied the screws, and each year they got tighter and tighter and tighter. Between the fall of 1968 and the opening of school for the 1970-1971 academic year, the percentage of southern black students attending segregated schools, defined as schools with enrollments of 95% or more black, declined from 85% to 3%.[68] But one major issue remained as far as statistical desegregation was concerned, the large cities of the modern South. Most of these cities had, by some federal standard, "satisfactorily" desegregated, yet they still maintained racially identifiable schools. The continued existence of such schools, however, could no longer be attributed to a legally maintained dual school system. Rather, school segregation continued because school zones were geographically determined. At issue in the *Swann* case was the question of whether almost

[64]91 S.Ct., Advance Sheet No. 14 (1971).

[65]*See* Glazer, *supra* note 51.

[66]*See* A. BLAUSTEIN & C. FERGUSON, DESEGREGATION AND THE LAW 240-68 (1957); Vines, *Federal District Judges and Race Relations Cases in the South*, 26 J. POL. 337 (1964).

[67]42 U.S.C. § 2000a-h (1964).

[68]*See* Glazer, *supra* note 51.

all-black schools can continue to exist, if they are the product of neighborhood school districting. The Burger Court, of course, ruled that they could not and approved transportation as one means to eliminate such schools.

But such a ruling had significant implications for northern-style segregation. The city of Charlotte, North Carolina, is 64 square miles larger than Washington, D.C., but it is only part of Mecklenburg County with which it forms a single school district of 550 square miles, or approximately twice the size of New York City. If Charlotte, because it was part of Mecklenburg County, could be successfully desegregated, shouldn't city boundaries be disregarded in other places and larger school districts on the scale of Mecklenburg County be created wherever such action would make desegregation possible? To this question, a federal district judge in Richmond, Virginia, rendered an affirmative answer.[69] But the Court of Appeals reversed, holding that the district court had exceeded its authority. Even though population patterns inhibited effective intradistrict integration, the Court of Appeals found it impermissible to order interdistrict remedies. The Circuit Court's holding was affirmed by an equally divided Supreme Court.[70] Because Mr. Justice Powell did not participate, however, the Court produced no opinions, thereby leaving the question of interdistrict desegregation remedies unclear and unresolved.

The following year, in *Milliken v. Bradley*, Powell joined Justices Rehnquist, Blackmun, and Stewart in an opinion by the Chief Justice rejecting an interdistrict remedy for segregation in Detroit.[71] The federal district court had endorsed a plan to desegregate Detroit's predominately black school system by merging it with suburban school districts and then requiring the busing of perhaps as many as 310,000 inner-city students to schools outside the city limits.[72] Although the Court of Appeals had vacated the judgment on other grounds, it indicated that it had no doubts about the power of federal courts to effect desegregation even if that involved the crossing of district boundary lines.[73] Mr. Chief Justice Burger disagreed. Concerned that such judicial discretion would imperil the tradition of local control of education, he ruled that the

[69]Bradley v. School Board, 338 F.Supp. 61, *rev'd,* 462 F.2d 1058 (4th Cir. 1972).
[70]School Board of Richmond v. State Board of Education, 412 U.S. 92 (1973).
[71]418 U.S. 717 (1974). *See also* Spencer v. Kugler, 404 U.S. 1027 (1972) (mem.).
[72]Bradley v. Milliken, 345 F.Supp. 914 (E. D. Mich. 1972).
[73]480 F.2d 927 (6th Cir. 1973).

interdistrict desegregation plan was improper because, whatever might be the situation in Detroit itself, the suburban districts were not guilty of and had not even been accused of unlawful racial discrimination. School district boundaries were not mere matters of political convenience to be treated casually by judges, Burger argued, because "no single tradition in public education is more deeply rooted than local control."[74] The Chief Justice, however, was equally rigorous in his insistence that *Milliken* in no way relaxed the Court's previous rulings with respect to the duty of intradistrict desegregation; within individual districts, the necessity to maintain racially unitary schools remained, and in pursuit of such schools the judiciary might employ an arsenal of weapons, including busing. *Milliken*, nevertheless, was a potentially far-reaching and certainly bitterly fought decision. In a dissenting opinion, itself a rarity for a school desegregation case, Mr. Justice Marshall opined:

> In the short run, it may seem to be the easier course to allow our great metropolitan areas to be divided up each into two cities—one white, the other black—but it is a course, I predict, our people will ultimately regret.[75]

Indeed, the Court's resolution of the Detroit case appeared to be inconsistent with its earlier ruling in *Wright v. Emporia*, enjoining a city from withdrawing from an existing county school district which had not yet completely desegregated because the effect would have been to impede that process, even though there was no evidence of segregative intent in the desire to withdraw.[76] In order to improve the quality of education for its children and to increase its citizens' control over educational policies affecting them, the city of Emporia, Virginia, sought to create its own school district by seceding from the county district to which it belonged and which was under a court order to establish a racially unitary school system. Relying upon *Palmer v. Thompson*,[77] which had held legislative motivation to be irrelevant to constitutional adjudication, the Supreme Court refused to countenance the proposed withdrawal because, although both systems would have a majority of black students, the creation of a new, city system would mean a substantial increase in the proportion of whites in the schools attended by city residents, with a concomitant decrease in the county schools.[78]

---

[74] 418 U.S. at 741.
[75] *Id.* at 815.
[76] 407 U.S. 451 (1972).
[77] 403 U.S. 217 (1971).
[78] The figures were: without withdrawal, 34% white and 66% black, if Emporia withdrew, 48% white and 52% black in city schools, and 28% white and 72% black in county schools.

But, if that were sufficient reason to prevent Emporia from withdrawing from an existing school district, would it not be sufficient reason to compel two or more existing districts to join together? To be sure, the Court stressed that racial imbalance alone did not make the plan unacceptable and sought to rely upon additional factors, such as the potential encouragement of "white flight" and the unequal quality of the physical facilities within the city and county schools, to support its holding. But in a dissenting opinion, Mr. Chief Justice Burger, joined by the other three Nixon appointees, found these factors to be so negligible as to suggest that racial imbalance itself was what the majority had found objectionable.[79]

But, were racial imbalance per se to be unconstitutional in the public schools, *Wright* would have represented a major advance upon *Swann*, which had indicated approval of desegregation plans with some racial disparities, and would have major implications for segregated education in the North. Inexorably, the Court was being forced to face the issue of northern school segregation. In *Keyes v. School District*, the Court rendered its first but surely not its last decision on that issue.[80] The petitioners in *Keyes* claimed intentional discrimination in one portion of the city-wide school district in Denver, Colorado. They charged that the school authorities, utilizing a variety of techniques, had deliberately manipulated student attendance so as to produce a heavy concentration of black students in one area. Presented with an opportunity to abandon the distinction between *de jure* and *de facto* racial discrimination, the Court majority chose instead to identify criteria permitting a finding of *de jure* segregation in an area without a tradition of state-required racial separation. Mr. Justice Brennan's majority opinion ruled that, where it could be proven that the school officials had systematically pursued a policy which produced racial separation affecting a substantial proportion of the district's students, teachers, and schools, a finding that the entire district was a dual, segregated one was authorized. "We empha-

---

[79]Indeed, in a companion case, United States v. Scotland Neck Board of Education, 407 U.S. 484 (1972), the Court relied almost exclusively on the racial imbalance of two proposed school systems to find that a division of the existing system would unconstitutionally impede the process of eliminating the racial identification of the schools. In *Scotland Neck*, had the city been permitted to withdraw, the schools in the old district would have been 89% black, while the schools in the new city district would have had populations 57% white. The four dissenters in *Wright*, however, concurred in *Scotland Neck*, because the severance would prevent meaningful desegregation in effect and was "substantially motivated by a desire to create a predominantly white system." *Id.* at 491-92.
[80]413 U.S. 189 (1973).

size," Brennan wrote, "that the differentiating factor between *de jure* segregation and so-called *de facto* segregation . . . is *purpose* or *intent* to segregate."[81] Once such a finding were made, of course, Brennan went on, the usual remedies, including bus transportation, evolved in the southern context became applicable.

Mr. Justice Powell called for the rejection of the *de jure/de facto*. Essentially he reasoned that the right originally established in *Brown* not to be compelled to attend a segregated school had over a generation of judicial decision-making now become the right to expect that local school authorities would operate racially unitary schools. In particular, he felt that *Swann*, by approving busing, had imposed an obligation to alleviate conditions not resulting from *de jure* segregation, thereby undermining the *de jure/de facto* rationale. In a separate concurrence, Mr. Justice Douglas joined Justice Powell's appeal for a consistent, coherent, national policy on racial separation in the schools. But the majority continued to adhere to the distinction between *de jure* and *de facto* segregation. The majority's emphasis upon purpose or intent as the dispositive factor distinguishing *de jure* from *de facto* discrimination, however, ran directly counter to the Burger Court's own ruling in *Palmer v. Thompson*, insisting that inquiries into governmental purpose were not proper but that the appropriate judicial focus should be upon effect.[82] Apparently, when faced with a choice between abandoning the *de jure/de facto* distinction or abandoning *Palmer*, the Court chose to abandon *Palmer*. Whether the Court can consistently maintain the *Keyes* position, however, remains to be seen.

The Burger Court's position in the Charlotte-Mecklenburg and Denver cases illustrates again the difficulties which Presidents have, first, in predicting and, later, in controlling the decision-making behavior of their appointees to the Supreme Court. Warren, after all, was an Eisenhower appointment, one which the President is reputed to have later regretted, and the ultra-conservative McReynolds was Woodrow Wilson's gift to the nation. In contemporary America, despite some rather sweeping claims to the contrary,[83] Richard Nixon has not enjoyed anything like unqualified success in liquidating the constitutional estate

---

[81]*Id.* at 208.

[82]403 U.S. 217 (1971); *see generally* Brest, Palmer v. Thompson: *An Approach to the Problem of Unconstitutional Legislative Motive*, 1971 SUP. CT. REV. 95.

[83]*See, e.g.*, J. SIMON, IN HIS OWN IMAGE: THE SUPREME COURT IN RICHARD NIXON'S AMERICA (1973).

of the Warren Court. The school-busing decisions were clearly of little comfort to him.

Busing was a political thicket which the President did not want to enter. By 1970, however, it had shot to a place of national prominence. The Gallup Poll revealed that 94% of American parents had heard of the issue, an extraordinary level of public awareness in American politics,[84] and those who had heard of the issue were opposed to busing by a margin of almost 8 to 1.[85] But, among white parents opposed to busing, only one in four said he would object to sending his child to a school in which one half of the children were black. This was either (1) an extraordinary reflection of mass hypocrisy, or (2) support for the proposition that opposition to busing was not entirely racially motivated, or (3) an indication that a 1:1 ratio of black to white pupils might be the so-called "tipping point" for white approval of integration.[86]

Confronted with such facts of political life, President Nixon began to cast about for a formulation which would enable him to question the reasoning of those who attacked *de facto* segregation and advocated busing as one means of eliminating it without at the same time placing himself irrevocably in the Wallace camp. Ironically enough, he found that position in an article in the *New Republic*, not a notably conservative journal, by Alexander Bickel, politically liberal professor of law at Yale University, campaign adviser to Eugene McCarthy and George McGovern, and articulate legal opponent of the Viet Nam war.[87] Bickel's argument was that the disestablishment of legally enforced segregation was essential but that when integration was pushed beyond the "tipping point," whites, or at least those whites who could afford it, moved away and resegregation occurred. Consequently, Bickel concluded, it was pointless to push integration to the "tipping point." Whites wouldn't accept it, and many black leaders were moving away from a concern for integration. America should, therefore, shift its policy emphasis to the improvement of the quality of education in black schools. "Massive school integration is not going to be attained in this country very soon," wrote Professor Bickel. "Let us, therefore, try to proceed with education."[88] A subsequent issue of the New Republic was devoted to

[84]*See* V.O. KEY, *supra* note 58, at 282-87.

[85]N.Y. Times, September 12, 1971, at 24, col. 3.

[86]*See* L. FREEDMAN, POWER AND POLITICS IN AMERICA 308 n. 34 (1971).

[87]Bickel, *Desegregation: Where Do We Go From Here?*, 162 NEW REPUB. 20 (February 7, 1970).

[88]*Id.* at 22.

responses to the Bickel essay.[89] Most of the authors, generally middle-class, white liberals, were horrified by the Bickelian heresy. But his thesis was defended by Charles Hamilton, professor of political science at Columbia University and, coincidentally, co-author, with Stokley Carmichael, of *Black Power*. Subsequently, Bickel's position was endorsed by Roy Innis of CORE and by John Gardner, former Secretary of H.E.W. and head of the citizen's lobby Common Cause. With so many men of different backgrounds but unquestioned brilliance and liberality endorsing the Bickel view, Mr. Nixon decided to embrace the policy himself. Thus, in a 1970 policy statement, he set forth his position on the issue.[90] *De jure* segregation must be ended *at once*. But *de facto* segregation was another matter. It was undesirable but not necessarily illegal. To correct it would involve large-scale, compulsory busing, which was unacceptable to the President. Racial balance, he stressed, was not the only principle to be protected; the neighborhood school must also be preserved. Urgent efforts, therefore, should be taken to improve the quality of education for all, with particular attention to those schools in poverty areas which fell below the prevailing standards.

The President's position was clearly aimed at pleasing the white suburbanites of the North.[91] But it was cold comfort to the South. It was a much more vehement endorsement of *Brown* than President Eisenhower had ever given, and Senator Thurmond duly expressed his disappointment. The President had rejected the southern strategy of attempting to tie *de jure* and *de facto* together, on the theory that northerners would find the legal consequences of such a marriage unacceptable and would thus relieve the pressure on the South. *Swann* and *Keyes*, however, implicitly undercut that rejection and, while they do not constitutionally marry *de facto* and *de jure* segregation, they have at least introduced the two to one another.

There was also some irony in the fact that the Nixon position resembled or paralleled in some degree the position of some radical poverty lawyers who had begun to argue that efforts to seek equal educational opportunities for ethnic minorities through integration should be abandoned in favor of concentrating upon the problem of

---

[89]Symposium, *The Debate Over School Desegregation*, 162 NEW REPUB. 31 (March 7, 1970).

[90]*See* L. FREEDMAN, *supra* note 86, at 306-11.

[91]*See generally* R. SCAMMON & B. WATTENBERG, THE REAL MAJORITY (1970); K. PHILLIPS, THE EMERGING REPUBLICAN MAJORITY (1969).

finance.[92] The central premise behind such a strategy appears to have been that efforts at integration pitted black and brown minorities against white majorities which was politically unwise. Concentrating upon the problem of economic inequality, however, would not involve this tactical difficulty, since the majority of lower middle-class and poor Americans are white. On the other hand, any court victories for the lower-middle and lower economic groups in American society would disproportionately advantage the black and the brown, since they are overrepresented in these economic strata.

Constitutionally, this effort centered in an attack upon the local property tax system for financing public education. The tradition in American school governance, a tradition pre-dating the American Revolution, has been the local school. As a corollary, American public schools were financed primarily through local property taxation.[93] Such taxes, however, had two outstanding characteristics. First, they were highly susceptible to the wishes of the local electorate, and, second, they depended heavily upon the wealth of the local area. The property tax being the product of two numbers, the assessed valuation of a piece of property times the rate at which the local authorities chose to tax it, it followed that several kinds of inequalities might arise between different communities. There might be differential services, one community choosing to devote more of its monies to services other than education than would another community. There might be differential tax rates between communities, and, given the unequal distribution of valuable property, there might be differential tax bases. The tax base in one school district, dependent upon the valuation of the real property within the borders of that district, might differ significantly from the tax base in another school district, thus resulting in differences between the school districts in the amount of money spent per pupil. In the late 1960s, such

[92]*See, e.g.,* J. COONS, W. CLUNE, & S. SUGARMAN, PRIVATE WEALTH AND PUBLIC EDUCATION (1970); Comment, *The Evolution of Equal Protection—Education, Municipal Services, and Wealth,* 7 HARV. CIV. RIGHTS—CIV. LIB. L. REV. 103 (1972); Silard & White, *Intrastate Inequalities in Public Education,* 1970 WIS. L. REV. 7; Shanks, *Equal Education and the Law,*39 AM. SCHOLAR 255 (1970).

[93]Nationally, as of 1971, less than 10% of educational revenue was provided by the federal government; state aid accounted for about 40%, and the remainder, being in excess of 50% of all educational revenue, came from local district taxation. 49 NEA RESEARCH BULL. 53 (1971). Delaware, Hawaii, and North Carolina were the only states to have unified, statewide school financing systems. DEL. CODE ANN. tit. 14, ch. 19 (1953, Supp. 1970); Hawaii Sess. Laws, Act 38, § 1 (1968); N.C. GEN. STAT. §§ 115-78 to -124 (1966, Supp. 1971).

differential educational expenditures began to come under constitutional fire.[94] The local property tax system of public school finance was challenged as violating the Equal Protection Clause in at least two ways. First, it was argued that the system resulted in inferior educational opportunities for the children in the poorer school districts in that they did not enjoy the same per pupil expenditures as the students in the relatively wealthier districts. Second, it was asserted that the parents in the poorer districts were also the victims of unconstitutional discrimination, because they had to be taxed at a higher rate than the parents in the richer districts in order to provide equal per pupil expenditures or even, in the very poorest districts, to provide a minimum level of education for their children.[95]

Initially, these attacks upon the property tax met with some success, most significantly in California.[96] The courts which struck down the property tax method of financing public education relied upon a scheme of judicial analysis borrowed from the Warren Court. Traditionally, equal protection challenges had been judged by the Court under a standard of minimal or passive review.[97] To be valid, a statutory classification need only be rationally related to some legitimate state interest.[98] In the voting rights[99] and school desegregation cases,[100] however, the Warren Court began to develop a new standard to be

[94]*E.g.*, McInnis v. Shapiro, 293 F.Supp. 327 (N.D. Ill. 1968), *aff'd sub nom.* McInnis v. Ogilvie, 394 U.S. 322 (1969). One study counted fifty-one suits involving thirty states in progress in August 1972. Browning & Lehtman, *Law Suits Challenging State School Finance Systems*, App. F. to U.S. COMM'N ON CIVIL RIGHTS, INEQUALITY IN SCHOOL FINANCING: THE ROLE OF THE LAW 52-77 (1972).

[95]*See generally* 85 HARV. L. REV. 1049 (1972).

[96]Serrano v. Priest, 5 Cal.3d 584 (1971). In many subsequent cases, many courts followed the logic of the California Supreme Court in holding the local property tax system for financing education to be unconstitutional; *e.g.*, Sweetwater County Planning Comm. v. Hinkle, 491 P.2d 1234 (Wyo. 1971); Van Dursatz v. Hatfield, 334 F.Supp. 870 (D. Minn. 1971); Robinson v. Cahill, 118 N.J. Super. 223 (1972). *See generally* Karst, Serrano v. Priest: *A State Court's Responsibilities and Opportunities in the Development of Federal Constitutional Law*, 60 CALIF. L. REV. 720 (1972); Goldstein, *Interdistrict Inequalities in School Financing: A Critical Analysis of* Serrano v. Priest *and Its Progeny*, 120 U. PA. L. REV. 504 (1972).

[97]*See Developments in the Law—Equal Protection*, 82 HARV. L. REV. 1065 (1969).

[98]*See, e.g.*, Williamson v. Lee Optical Co., 348 U.S. 483 (1955); Railway Express Agency v. New York, 336 U.S. 106 (1949); Goesaert v. Cleary, 335 U.S. 464 (1948); Kotch v. Board of River Pilot Comm'rs, 330 U.S. 552 (1947). *See generally* Tussman & tenBroek, *The Equal Protection of the Laws*, 37 CALIF. L. REV. 341 (1949).

[99]*E.g.*, Harper v. Virginia Board of Elections, 383 U.S. 663 (1966).

employed in assessing the constitutionality of legislative classifications. Under this standard of active review, to be valid, a statutory classification involving an inherently suspect category, such as race, or touching a fundamental interest, such as voting, must advance some compelling state interest. And *"the Warren Court never found a state measure sufficiently compelling to override anything it deemed fundamental!"*[101] The compelling state interest test, therefore, reminded many students of the Court of such discredited devices as the doctrines of "reasonableness"[102] and "liberty of contract."[103] The contours of fundamentality, in particular, were so vague as to allow the Court to create new rights, reading the social preferences, prejudices, and predilections of the Justices into the Constitution.[104] Consequently, the rule was criticized as reviving the behavior of the old, economic activist Court, injecting the Supreme Court into the policy-making process absent an intelligible principle of legitimacy. Despite such criticisms, some courts found that local property taxation as a system for financing the public schools was a legislative program involving a suspect classification, wealth, and touching upon a fundamental interest, education.[105] The state, therefore, was required to show a *compelling* interest in this scheme of financing, and, not surprisingly, the state could not do that. Such extensions of the compelling state interest doctrine to economic classifications, however, were highly questionable, for they ignored decisions of the Burger Court involving the rights of welfare recipients which indicated that the new

[100]*E.g.*, Brown v. Board of Education, 347 U.S. 483 (1954); Griffin v. County School Board of Prince Edward County, 337 U.S. 218 (1964); Green v. County School Board of New Kent County, Virginia, 391 U.S. 430 (1968).

[101]Mendelson, *From Warren to Burger: The Rise and Decline of Substantive Equal Protection*, 66 AM. POL. SCI. REV. 1226 (1972) (emphasis in original).

[102]*See, e.g.,* Smyth v. Ames, 169 U.S. 466 (1898).

[103]*See, e.g.,* Lochner v. New York, 198 U.S. 45 (1905); Adkins v. Children's Hospital, 261 U.S. 525 (1923).

[104]*See* Mendelson, *supra* note 101; P. KURLAND, POLITICS, THE CONSTITUTION, AND THE WARREN COURT ch. 4 (1970); A. BICKEL, THE SUPREME COURT AND THE IDEA OF PROGRESS 103ff (1970); Gunther, *In Search of Evolving Doctrine on a Changing Court: A Model for a Newer Equal Protection*, 86 HARV. L. REV. 1, 8-20 (1972). But *see* Karst & Horowitz, Reitman v. Mulkey: *A Telophase of Substantive Equal Protection*, 1967 SUP. CT. REV. 39; Karst, *Invidious Discrimination: Justice Douglas and the Return of the "Natural-Law-Due-Process Formula,"* 16 U.C.L.A. L. REV. 716 (1969); Wright, *Professor Bickel, The Scholarly Tradition and The Supreme Court*, 84 HARV. L. REV. 769 (1971).

[105]*See* note 96 *supra.*

Justices believed that some limits must be placed upon the suspect classification/fundamental interest scheme of analysis.[106]

While equal protection litigation has become so interrelated with the struggle for the constitutional rights of black Americans, this interrelation has tended to obscure the application of the Equal Protection Clause to non-racial classifications. In fact, however, the Warren Court increasingly tended to rely on equal protection arguments to justify or to support its holdings in other areas of constitutional decision, such as reapportionment[107] or criminal defendants rights,[108] and in its last term the Warren Court pushed the ambit of the Equal Protection Clause to new limits by applying it to invalidate state residency requirements for welfare benefits.

Shapiro v. Thompson held unconstitutional statutory requirements that, in order to be eligible for aid, potential welfare recipients must have lived for the immediately preceding year within the state to which they were applying for welfare.[109] Each of the three cases consolidated for appeal in *Shapiro* had been brought by indigents who had travelled interstate, had applied for public assistance in their new domiciles, and had had their applications denied solely on the basis of their failure to meet the one-year residency requirements imposed by state law. Relying upon the Court's new-found distinction between those statutory classifications meriting strict equal protection review and those worthy of only passive judicial scrutiny, Mr. Justice Brennan reasoned that the indisputable effect of the waiting period requirement was to create two groups of needy citizens indistinguishable from each other except that one group was composed of persons who had resided within the jurisdiction for one year or more and the other of citizens who had moved into the jurisdiction within the year. This, Brennan asserted, with little attempt to argue the point, was an arbitrary classification absent some "compelling" state interest. But the states involved in the case, Connecticut and Pennsylvania, had failed to demonstrate any such interest. They had claimed that various administrative or governmental interests were served by the residency classification: facilitating planning of the

[106]Dandridge v. Williams, 397 U.S. 471 (1970); James v. Valtierra, 402 U.S. 137 (1971).

[107]*See, e.g.*, Reynolds v. Sims, 377 U.S. 533 (1964).

[108]*See, e.g.*, Douglas v. California, 372 U.S. 353 (1963); Miranda v. Arizona, 384 U.S. 436 (1966).

[109]394 U.S. 618 (1969).

welfare budget, preventing collection of public assistance in more than one state, encouraging early entry into the labor force. But, when balanced against the societal interest in providing welfare benefits to all needy families, these governmental interests were not sufficiently compelling to six members of the Supreme Court. Brennan conceded that the states' argument that the residency requirement had a tendency to discourage mass migrations of the poor into states providing higher levels of welfare assistance had great force; but this was an impermissible purpose, because it impeded the exercise of the constitutional right to travel interstate. The one-year residency requirement, therefore, violated the Equal Protection Clause when imposed by the states and denied due process when applied by Congress.[110]

Dissenting, Mr. Justice Black and Mr. Chief Justice Warren viewed the welfare program as a major experiment in cooperative federalism and maintained that, while the states could not constitutionally enact residency requirements, Congress, under its interstate commerce power, could and had authorized such requirements. Mr. Justice Harlan, speaking for himself, believed that the governmental interests or objectives presented by the states were "compelling" in that they were designed to preserve the fiscal integrity of the welfare program itself, but more fundamentally Harlan objected to the Court's requirements that state governments present "compelling" justifications for their legislative programs.

Indeed, *Shapiro* presented some troubling questions to those who remembered their constitutional history. The thought processes and methods of analysis employed by the majority in *Shapiro* were strikingly similar to those which characterized the Court during the heyday of substantive due process.[111] Under what might be called a "procedural" or limited reading of the Equal Protection Clause, the Supreme Court says to a legislature, "You may do A only if the classifications which you adopt are rational." But in *Shapiro* the Court demanded that the states justify their classifications not by showing that they were rational but that they were "compelling." Moreover, the Court intimated that even some compelling interests could not be advanced, if the classifications adopted impinged upon some fundamental value, such as the right to

[110]*See* Bolling v. Sharpe, 347 U.S. 497 (1954).

[111]*See, e.g.,* Smyth v. Ames, 169 U.S. 466 (1898); Lochner v. New York, 198 U.S. 45 (1905); Adkins v. Children's Hospital, 261 U.S. 525 (1923); New State Ice Co. v. Liebmann, 285 U.S. 262 (1932). *See generally* Thayer, *The Origin and Scope of The American Doctrine of Constitutional Law,* 7 HARV. L. REV. 129 (1893).

travel interstate. What the Warren Court then was saying to legislatures was, "No matter how rational your classifications, you may not do A, if accomplishing that objective involves the sacrifice of value B." And the Supreme Court will define what are fundamental values. But this is exactly what the old laissez faire Court did.[112] The only thing that had changed were the subjective values which the respective Courts employed. Under the standard of active equal protection review, the Court was engaged in an aggressive evaluation of questions which are appropriate for elected legislators but, arguably, are not proper for consideration by non-elected, life-tenured judges.

But the implications of *Shapiro* for judicial policy-making went even farther than this, for consider the source of the fundamental interest, the right to interstate travel, which triggered active review in this case. What is the origin of this constitutional right?[113] Some specific constitutional guarantee? Obviously, no. The Equal Protection Clause? Clearly not, unless one wishes to reduce *Shapiro* to a tautology. Article IV, Section 2? *Shapiro* itself denies it. The Commerce Clause? Again, no, for if that were the case Congress could regulate it. But *Shapiro* held that Congress could not validate these residency requirements. Thus, it must be that the right to travel interstate is part of that liberty which neither Congress nor the states can deny without due process of law. In short, the right to travel is a substantive due process right wholly created by the judiciary. *Shapiro*, then, was a very sweeping statement of judicial power. On the one hand, the Court told state legislatures and Congress that any statutory classification which *touched* (Note: The residency requirements didn't prohibit the exercise of a fundamental right; they merely inhibited it.) upon a fundamental interest would be subject to active review under the Equal Protection Clause, and, on the other hand, the Court claimed the power to create new fundamental rights only loosely tied—if at all—to the constitutional text.

Even in its narrowest compass, *Shapiro* raised serious questions concerning both the validity of other welfare limitations and also the vitality of residency requirements relative to other subjects, such as voting. The latter of these questions was muted somewhat by the Voting Rights Act of 1970 which abrogated state residency requirements of

[112]*See generally* note 104 *supra*.
[113]*See* Crandall v. Nevada, 6 Wall. 35 (1868); Edwards v. California, 314 U.S. 160 (1941); Aptheker v. Secretary of State, 378 U.S. 500 (1964). *See Generally* Boudin, *The Right to Travel*, in THE RIGHTS OF AMERICANS: WHAT THEY ARE—WHAT THEY SHOULD BE 381 (N. Dorsen ed. 1971).

more than thirty days for voting in presidential elections and which an eight-man majority happily sustained in *Oregon v. Mitchell*,[114] and in *Dunn v. Blumstein* the Court, explicitly relying upon *Shapiro*, held that conditioning the right to vote in congressional, state, and county elections upon a one-year state and ninety-day county residency requirement violated the Equal Protection Clause.[115] Only Chief Justice Burger dissented, although Justices Powell and Rehnquist did not participate. Neither such unanimity nor such continuity of Warren Court policy, however, has characterized the Burger Court with respect to the constitutional issues raised by welfare regulations.

Perhaps more strongly than any other case decided in the first term of the Burger Court, *Dandridge v. Williams* suggested that the Supreme Court was moving toward a narrower conception of its appropriate role in American government and politics.[116] Retreating from the expansive reading of the Equal Protection Clause employed in *Shapiro*, *Dandridge* refused to extend the doctrine of substantive equal protection to wealth-based classifications. By a vote of five-to-three, the Court reversed a lower federal court's ruling that Maryland's $250 per month maximum limit on the amount of welfare assistance which any one family might receive under the Aid to Families with Dependent Children (AFDC) program violated the Equal Protection Clause. While the welfare ceiling did discriminate against large families, the Court majority felt that it was not an unreasonable, capricious, or arbitrary classification in that there was a rational basis for setting a maximal welfare limit, the maintenance of the fiscal integrity of the program in allocating a finite amount of funding available. For the majority, Mr. Justice Stewart concluded that the maximum grant regulation was of a "social and economic" nature and, thus, was subject to judicial review under the traditional and limited standard of rationality.[117]

Such a ruling was not without its irony, for, in invoking the so-called "double standard", Stewart was demonstrating that a tool of jurisprudence originally conceived to promote liberal ends could be used to work

[114]400 U.S. 112 (1970).
[115]405 U.S. 330 (1972).
[116]397 U.S. 471 (1970).
[117]*Id.* at 485. The appellees also contended that the maximum grant system violated § 402 (a)(10) of the Social Security Act, but Stewart reasoned that the Maryland practice was compatible with the federal statute's requirement that aid be furnished "to all eligible individuals," since the statute left to the states the power to set the level of benefits. This was the point on which Mr. Justice Douglas dissented, limiting himself to the question of statutory interpretation and not addressing the constitutional issue.

opposite results in the area of social welfare administration.[118] Given its initial expression by Mr. Justice Harlan Fiske Stone in the *Carolene Products* case,[119] the "double standard" was the precursor of substantive equal protection,[120] for it asserted a distinction of constitutional dimensions between "property" rights and "human" rights and suggested that the standards of judicial protection of each were to be different, more rigorous for the latter than for the former. In *Dandridge*, Justice Stewart explicitly recognized that, as a factual matter, there was a difference of degree between state regulation of business enterprise and state welfare assistance. But, as a constitutional matter, he could not see that there was any qualitative difference between the two sufficient to justify the use of different standards to review the constitutionality of legislation in these areas. Hoist on their own petard, the liberal Justices Marshall and Brennan could only rail against the application of differing standards of judicial review simply because the matter involved was classified as economic. Mr. Justice Stewart, however, limited those cases in which the "compelling interest" test would be used to cases involving a classification "infected with a racially discriminatory purpose or effect."[121] All other cases were to be reviewed under the standard of simple rationality.

In discussing the lessons of *Dandridge* for the relation between Burger Court and Warren Court decision-making, it bears emphasis that the majority opinion in *Dandridge*, although it limited the number of occasions in which strict scrutiny would be used, assumed the validity and existence of two different standards of equal protection review.[122] It was not a wholesale retreat from the Warren Court's position, in that it did not reject the concept of active review. *Dandridge* adopted the Warren Court's frame of analysis but drew the line on its application. Certainly there were some Warren Court precedents available to support the proposition that interests other than race were fundamental and merited vigilant judicial protection.[123] Mr. Justice Stewart's opinion in *Dandridge*, then, must be read as implicitly saying that the Warren Court erred, not in the creation of the "compelling state interest" test, but in its

[118]*See* Funston, *The Double Standard of Constitutional Protection in the Era of the Welfare State*, 90 POL. SCI. Q. 261 (1975).

[119]United States v. Carolene Products Co., 304 U.S. 144, 152 n. 4 (1938).

[120]*See* Gunther, *supra* note 104, at 37-46.

[121]397 U.S. at 485 n. 17.

[122]*See generally* Gunther, *supra* note 104, at 1-15.

[123]*See, e.g.*, Levy v. Louisiana, 391 U.S. 68 (1968); Harper v. Virginia Board of Elections, 383 U.S. 66 (1966); Reynolds v. Sims, 377 U.S. 533 (1964); Griffin v. Illinois, 351 U.S. 12 (1956).

extension of that standard beyond specific constitutional protections. In *Dandridge*, the Court was faced, as it so often is, with the task of reconciling the Fourteenth Amendment's commands of "due process" and "equal protection" with the competing notion—fostered to a large extent by the Supreme Court itself[124]—that in American society it is the legislative and executive branches, not the judiciary, which should be responsible for apportioning governmental benefits and burdens. Indeed, a corollary of the Burger Court's qualification of substantive equal protection has been a greater deference to legislative judgment than characterized the Warren Court, a greater confidence, if you will, in and reliance upon the political process. This, of course, has not been a complete reversal of form from the Warren years, but there has been a significant shift of emphasis.

This tendency was again apparent in another of the Burger Court's equal protection decisions in the area of welfare, *James v. Valtierra*.[125] Since the Progressive Era, the California Constitution has authorized repeal of legislation, whether state, county, or city, by a referendum procedure.[126] Only ten percent of the eligible electorate in the appropriate jurisdiction need petition for a measure to be placed on the ballot for voter approval or disapproval. In addition to these voter-initiated referenda, mandatory referenda are required for approval of constitutional amendments, for certain annexations by municipalities, for the issuance of general obligation bonds, and for the approval of federally financed low-income housing *after it has been authorized by the local governing body*. According to state legislation for the administration of federal housing funds, local housing authorities are appointed by the representative governing bodies of the self-governing subdivisions within the state.[127] These local housing authorities then develop low-income housing proposals which, in turn, are subject to the approval of the local representative governing body, be it city council or county board of supervisors. But, even after approval by the representative governing body, Article 34 of the state constitution requires that the low-income housing plan be submitted to a referendum of the electorate within the affected jurisdiction.

---

[124]*E.g.*, Reynolds v. Sims, 377 U.S. 533 (1964); Williamson v. Lee Optical Co. 348 U.S. 483 (1955); Nebbia v. New York, 291 U.S. 502 (1934).

[125]402 U.S. 137 (1971).

[126]CAL. CONST. art. IV, § 1.

[127]CAL. HEALTH & SAFETY CODE §§ 34200 *et seq.* (West 1967).

In *James v. Valtierra* black and Chicano indigents claimed that Article 34 violated the Equal Protection Clause of the Fourteenth Amendment. They were eligible for low-income housing, but public housing proposals in their communities had been rejected in recent referenda. Claiming that they lacked suitable shelter, they sought an injunction against the operation of Article 34 and were upheld by a federal district court.[128] In its decision, the district court relied primarily upon the Warren Court's decision in *Hunter v. Erickson*.[129] In *Hunter*, the Court had struck down a provision of the city charter of Akron, Ohio, which required that any fair- or open-housing ordinance passed by the city council be submitted to a city-wide referendum for approval. The Court reasoned that the Fourteenth Amendment barred states and their subdivisions from imposing special burdens upon legislation designed to assist racial minorities. The federal district court in *James* ruled that, by analogy, *Hunter* controlled classifications based on wealth.

The Supreme Court disagreed and . versed the district court decision. For a five-to-three majority, Mr. Justi Black held that *Hunter* was not an appropriately analogous precedent. ın *Hunter* the special burden had fallen directly and explicitly upon racial minorities which, by virtue of the Thirteenth, Fourteenth, and Fifteenth Amendments and their underlying history, warrant special constitutional protection. In *James*, however, no racial impact was apparent. Article 34 was, on its face, neutral as to race, and the appellees had failed to show that in California blacks and browns comprised so high a proportion of the poor that in operation Article 34 did discriminate against racial minorities.[130] Thus, in case anyone had missed the point in *Dandridge*, Mr. Justice Black underscored the new Court's intention to limit active equal protection review to cases in which a statute classified on the basis of race.

James v. Valtierra, then, stands as a graphic example of the Justices' increasing reluctance to adopt the Warren Court's more expansive readings of the Equal Protection Clause. Indeed, some analysts of a left-liberal persuasion have argued that it evidences outright judicial hostility to the poor—a hostility on the part not just of Nixon appointees committed to the work ethic but of Supreme Court Justices generally.[131]

---

[128]Valtierra v. Housing Authority, 313 F.Supp. 1 (N.D. Cal. 1971).

[129]393 U.S. 385 (1969)

[130]*See The Supreme Court, 1970 Term*, 85 HARV. L. REV. at 124 n. 13.

[131]*See, e.g.*, Michelman, *On Protecting the Poor Through the Fourteenth Amendment*, 83 HARV. L. REV. 7 (1969); Tigar, *Waiver of Constitutional Rights: Disquiet in the Citadel*, 84 HARV. L. REV. 1 (1970).

After all, Justices Rehnquist and Powell were not on the Court at the time of *James* and *Dandridge*, and even more interestingly the Nixon appointees, Burger and Blackmun, split in *James*. To buttress further evidence of such judicial hostility, these critics point to *Wyman v. James* in which the Supreme Court, speaking through Mr. Justic Blackmun in his first majority opinion, held that an AFDC recipient could not refuse a visit to her home by a welfare worker without risking termination of her welfare payments, even though the welfare visit was conducted without a search warrant.[132] It is certainly true that *Wyman* does seem to be a retreat from earlier rulings concerning administrative searches.[133] Even more intriguing was its attitude toward the government's ability to use the denial of benefits as a lever to regulate the conduct of its citizens. *Shapiro v. Thompson* had seemed to indicate that the state could withhold benefits only as a means of controlling conduct that was criminally punishable, but *Wyman* took a much broader view of the power of government to use the removal of benefits as a means for controlling behavior.

There was, however, an element present in *Wyman* which the critics have tended to ignore and which offered a basis—which the Court did not use—for distinguishing the welfare home visit from other administrative search cases. The novel element in the welfare home visit, assuming it to be a "search" within the meaning of the Fourth Amendment, is that the child has an interest in the visit which is separate from that of the mother.[134] *Wyman* represented the first case in which a welfare regulation, challenged by an AFDC mother, presented an issue of a potential contradiction between the interests of the child and the interests of the mother. While the welfare worker's periodic visit is in part designed to check on the mother's financial resources, its purposes are also to see if the child is receiving adequate care, to aid in securing that care, and in infrequent cases to initiate court proceedings for child neglect or abuse.

One might, of course, protest that such logic would seem to suggest that there is an equal need for warrantless visits to non-welfare homes in order to promote children's welfare. But, however much one may wish it were not so, there does seem to be a significantly greater reason to visit

[132]400 U.S. 309 (1971).

[133]*See* Camara v. Municipal Court, 387 U.S. 523 (1967), *overruling* Frank v. Maryland, 359 U.S. 360 (1959); See v. Seattle, 387 U.S. 541 (1967). *But cf.* Colonnade Catering Corp. v. United States, 397 U.S. 72 (1970).

[134]*See* Dembitz, *The Good of the Child Versus the Rights of the Parent: The Supreme Court Upholds the Welfare Home Visit*, 86 POL. SCI. Q. 389 (1971).

the homes of welfare mothers than those of any other class of parent for the purpose of protecting children and preventing their possible abuse. The majority of child neglect and abuse cases in America occur in AFDC homes.[135] To be sure, only a small percentage of the totality of AFDC cases involve neglect, but it remains true that a very small percentage of all the homes in the United States, AFDC homes, contribute disproportionately to the incidence of child maltreatment. As poignantly expressed by counsel for the State of New York in *Wyman*, Assistant Attorney General Brenda Soloff, "Children of mothers on welfare seem more likely to suffer from neglect than others. Not necessarily for want of love, but because an accumulation of adversities takes its toll on the most helpless members of the household. In the welfare mother's home, the hard life of the slums with its high incidence of crime and heroin addiction is coupled with an absent and unsupporting father, a maintenance income, and the apathy, alienation, and hopelessness arising from dependency."[136]

In its recognition of the possible opposition of interests of parent and child, the *Wyman* majority was in line with a number of Warren Court precedents which recognized and then began to expand the rights of juveniles.[137] Indeed, once the separateness of the child's interests is recognized, the home welfare visit might be upheld on the theory of the child's implicit consent. Until *Wyman*, the principle of differing interests of parent and child in relation to welfare mothers had been ignored, partly because the welfare mother had spokesmen in the National Welfare Rights Organization, other groups, and attorneys supplied through the free legal services provided by the Office of Economic Opportunity, while welfare children were inarticulate, unorganized, and unrepresented. For this reason, before *Wyman*, the legal emphasis had always been placed upon the rights of the welfare mother, as though she were a lone individual.

Critics of the Court's welfare decisions continue to place their emphasis upon the mother's rights and interests. They contend that these decisions reveal an attitude of hostility toward the welfare recipient, and some language in *Wyman* seems to support this interpretation.[138] But, regarding the judicial hostility thesis, two observations

[135]*Id.* at 391; *see also* Wyman v. James, 400 U.S. at 322 n. 9.

[136]*Quoted* in *id.* at 392-93.

[137]*E.g., In re* Gault, 387 U.S. 1 (1967); Tinker v. Des Moines, 393 U.S. 503 (1969). *See also* Rowan v. Post Office Dept., 397 U.S. 728. 741 (1970) (Brennan, J., concurring).

[138]*See* 400 U.S. at 321-22.

must be made. First, of the nineteen major welfare decisions rendered during a five year period between 1968 and 1973 the majority (12) were decided in favor of the welfare recipient.[139] Second, the critics' position is based largely upon the "new property" or "entitlement" theory of welfare, most notably propounded by Professor Charles Reich,[140] and in *Goldberg v. Kelly* the Burger Court endorsed that theory, although its endorsement was qualified to the extent that, while it assumed welfare to be "property" within the meaning of the Due Process Clause, it did not go so far as to hold that one had a right to public assistance.[141]

The Burger Court's position in the welfare cases, however, whatever it may have said about judicial attitudes toward welfare beneficiaries, had clearly manifested an unwillingness to extend strict equal protection review to wealth-based criteria.[142] In *San Antonio Independent School District v. Rodriguez,* [143] this position was squarely confronted with the issue of educational equality, itself arising from a line of Supreme Court precedent traceable back to *Brown v. Board of Education.* The Court's choice, while close, was clear. A five-man majority, consisting of the four Nixon appointees and Mr. Justic Stewart, approved the use of the local property tax as a method for financing public education, rejecting the claim that this practice discriminated against the poor in violation of the

[139]King v. Smith, 392 U.S. 309 (1968); Shapiro v. Thompson, 394 U.S. 618 (1969); Shapiro v. Solman, 396 U.S. 5 (1969); Goldberg v. Kelly, 397 U.S. 254 (1970); Rosado v. Wyman, 397 U.S. 397 (1970); Dandridge v. Williams, 397 U.S. 471 (1970); Lewis v. Martin, 397 U.S. 552 (1970); Wyman v. James, 400 U.S. 309 (1971). Boddie v. Connecticut, 401 U.S. 371 (1971); Sanks v. Georgia, 401 U.S. 144 (1971); Richardson v. Perales, 402 U.S. 389 (1971); James v. Valtierra, 402 U.S. 137 (1971); Graham v. Richardson, 403 U.S. 365 (1971); Richardson v. Belcher, 404 U.S. 78 (1971); Townsend v. Swank, 404 U.S. 282 (1972); Lindsey v. Normet, 405 U.S. 56 (19720; Jefferson v. Hackney, 406 U.S. 535 (1972); Carleson v. Remillard, 406 U.S. 598 (1972); Ortwein v. Schwab, 410 U.S. 656 (1973).

[140]Reich, *Individual Rights and Social Welfare: The Emerging Legal Issues,* 74 YALE L. J. 1245 (1965); Reich, *The New Property,* 73 YALE L. J. 733 (1964).

[141]397 U.S. 254 (1970).

[142]*But see* United States Dept. of Agriculture v. Moreno, 413 U.S. 523 (1973) (exclusion of households containing unrelated members from federal food stamp program held to be irrational), in which the Court appeared to use a stricter version of the traditional rationality test in scrutinizing a welfare benefits classification. While invoking the language of minimal scrutiny, the *Moreno* Court shifted the burden of proof from the individual to the government; while rationality remained the key, the government was required to prove the classification rationally related to a legitimate governmental interest. The complaining party was not required to demonstrate that the statute was irrational. *See generally* Gunther, *supra* note, 104; Funston, *supra* note 118.

[143]411 U.S. 1 (1973).

Equal Protection Clause.[144] In an opinion by Mr. Justice Powell, the majority expressed continued adherence to the two-level approach to equal protection analysis but concluded that the appropriate standard in the instant case was the minimal scrutiny of the "rational basis" test. Justice Powell refused to apply active equal protection review, because he found that Texas's use of local property taxes to finance its public schools involved neither a suspect classification nor a fundamental interest.

Rather than explicitly hold that wealth-based classifications were not constitutionally suspect, however, Powell attempted to evade the issue by arguing, first, that the property tax finance system involves not wealth-based but residence-based classifications and, second, by distinguishing earlier cases which had applied strict scrutiny to wealth discriminations. In order to refute the claim that the financing of education by the local property tax discriminated against the poor, Justice Powell reviewed evidence correlating the market value of taxable property per pupil in all Texas school districts with the median family incomes and the per pupil school expenditures in those districts. No general pattern emerged.[145] It was impossible, therefore, to conclude that the Texas poor were so concentrated in districts with low values of taxable property per pupil that the local property tax financing system actually effected a program of classifications based on wealth. Indeed, since poor people may live in districts with substantial amounts of taxable commercial and industrial property, the Court could not even find evidence that people with incomes below a specified poverty level were concentrated in districts with small property tax bases. Of course, Texas may have been unique, and it is possible that in other states personal wealth and per pupil taxable property valuations may be more closely related across school districts, although the Court did cite studies from other states which supported the view that the poor are not significantly concentrated in property-poor districts.[146] But, in anticipa-

---

[144]Mr. Justice Powell was joined in the majority by Mr. Chief Justice Burger, Mr. Justice Blackmun, Mr. Justice Rehnquist, and Mr. Justice Stewart. Stewart also filed a separate concurrence. Mr. Justice White wrote a dissenting opinion joined by Justice Douglas and Justice Brennan, who also filed a separate dissent. Mr. Justice Marshall also dissented, with the agreement of Justice Douglas.

[145]At the extremes, however, in the very rich and the very poor districts, there was some correlation between individual wealth, measured in terms of median family income, and the market value of taxable property per pupil. 411 U.S. at 15 n. 38.

[146]*Id.* at 27 n. 64, *citing* Davis, *Taxpaying Ability: A Study of the Relationship Between Wealth and Income in California Counties*, in NEA COMM. ON EDUC.

tion of future suits raising the issue,[147] Mr. Justice Powell pursued a second line of argument. He noted that previous decisions which had implied that wealth-based classifications might be suspect had all involved total deprivations of rights rather than merely relative deprivations.[148] In the immediate situation, however, there was no evidence that, even in its poorest school districts, Texas was not providing an at least minimally adequate education.

This piece of evidence, in turn, supported the majority's argument that no fundamental interest was damaged by the Texas property tax system. While suggesting that the states may be under a duty to provide a minimal level of education,[149] judged in an absolute sense, at least if they intend to provide public education generally, and while not disparaging the importance of education in contemporary society, the Court nevertheless emphasized the absence of an explicit constitutional recognition of a right to education.[150] For a right to be "fundamental", it would have to be "explicitly or implicitly guaranteed by the Constitution."[151] Insofar as the *Rodriguez* majority was concerned, it was not the role of the Court to create substantive rights.[152] While this apparently represented an effort by the new Justices to constrain the Court's equal protection discretion in much the same way that Mr. Justice Black sought to confine its due process discretion (and may be just as illusory),[153] the immediate

FINANCE, THE CHALLENGE OF CHANGE IN SCHOOL FINANCE: PROCEEDINGS OF THE 10th NATIONAL CONFERENCE ON SCHOOL FINANCE 199 (1967); Ridenour & Ridenour, Serrano v. Priest: *Wealth and Kansas School Finance*, 20 KAN. L. REV. 213 (1972); Note, *A Statistical Analysis of the School Finance Decisions: On Winning Battles and Losing Wars*, 81 YALE L. J. 1303 (1972) (Connecticut).

[147]*See* J. GUTHRIE, G. KLEINDORFER, H. LEVIN & R. STOUT, SCHOOLS AND INEQUALITY 32-55 (1971) (Michigan).

[148]411 U.S. at 20-22; *see, e.g.,* Griffin v. Illinois, 351 U.S. 12 (1956) (payment for transcripts); Douglas v. California, 372 U.S. 353 (1963) (payment for appellate counsel); Williams v. Illinois, 399 U.S. 235 (1970) (imprisonment for inability to pay fine); Bullock v. Carter, 405 U.S. 134 (1972) (payment of filing fee for primary election).

[149]*Id.* at 24. Presumably, Justice Powell meant that the state must provide a minimally adequate education insofar as it chose to provide public education, leaving open the possible, if not probable, option of closing the public school system. *See also* Griffin v. County School Board of Prince Edward County, 337 U.S. 218 (1964) (*selective* closing of schools by county in order to avoid desegregation held to be unconstitutional).

[150]*Id.* at 35. Many state constitutions, however, contain explicit recognitions of education as a fundamental, *state* constitutional right; *see* note 156 *infra*.

[151]*Id.* at 33-34.

[152]*Id.*

[153]*See, e.g.,* Adamson v. California, 332 U.S. 46, 68 (1947) (Black, J., dissenting); Griswold v. Connecticut, 381 U.S. 479, 507 (1965) (Black, J., dissenting).

result was to require only that Texas have some rational basis for its use of the local property tax scheme to finance public education; and, concluding that it had, the Court sustained the Texas program.[154]

The majority was quick to point out, however, that it was not endorsing the status quo but was merely holding that it was not unconstitutional. Further efforts at reform were within the proper sphere of the legislature:

> The need is apparent for reform in tax systems which may well have relied too long and too heavily on the local property tax.[155]

Essentially, the result in *Rodriguez* appears to have been motivated by two concerns. First, the Court was willing, indeed eager, to shift the decision-making burden to the sub-national level.[156] Second, the majority in *Rodriguez* was persuaded that, in this highly sensitive area, prudence, caution, and a sense of self-restraint were the appropriate virtues to be exercised. A decision against the constitutionality of the local property taxation method of financing education would necessarily involve significant costs without necessarily effecting the promised benefits.[157] First among the contemplated costs would be the further

[154]In dissent, Mr. Justice White, while acknowledging that it was inappropriate to apply the "compelling state interest" test to wealth-based classifications, urged a standard of stricter rationality. As White viewed the situation, the local property tax finance system was unconstitutional, because it was not rationally related to the state's purpose in furthering local decision-making control over education. The property poor districts had no choice but to tax at the highest possible levels in order to generate only the most minimally adequate revenues for financing their educational system. In other decisions, the Burger Court has shown a tendency toward the creation of a new, stricter rationality test, *e.g.* United States Dept. of Agriculture v. Moreno, 413 U.S. 528 (1973); Frontiero v. Richardson, 411 U.S. 677 (1973); Eisenstadt v. Baird, 405 U.S. 438 (1972); Reed v. Reed, 404 U.S. 71 (1971).

[155]411 U.S. at 58.

[156]After *Rodriguez's* interpretation of the United States Constitution as it relates to school financing, it was still possible for state legislatures to change their system of financing public education or for state courts to find that the local property tax system violated state constitutional law. *Rodriguez* did not hold that local property taxation was the constitutionally required method for funding education, nor did it rule that local property tax finance systems might not violate provisions of state law recognizing education as a fundamental right. Indeed, *Rodriguez* seemed almost to invite state courts to make such findings, and several state judiciaries have responded. *See, e.g.,* Serrano v. Priest, 5 Cal.3d 584 (1971); Milliken v. Green, 389 Mich. 1 (1972); Robinson v. Cahill, 62 N.J. 473 (1973).

[157]*See* J. PINCUS (ed.), SCHOOL FINANCE IN TRANSITION: THE COURTS AND EDUCATIONAL REFORM (1974); *The Supreme Court, 1972 Term,* 87 HARV. L. REV. 1, 115-16 (1973); Carrington, *On Egalitarian Overzeal: A Polemic Against the Local*

centralization of educational funding under a uniform, statewide revenue collection and allocation system, removing from local communities
the power to decide for themselves how much of their tax dollar to devote
to education. While such a scheme need not necessarily lead to state
control over non-financial matters of educational policy, the tendency
would be in that direction. To some extent, however, this problem may
be avoided under a system of "district power equalizing," in which
school taxes would be collected by the state but would be reallocated to
the school districts on the basis of the districts' tax rates.[158] School
revenues, then, would depend not upon the amount of revenue collected
within a given district but upon the relative sacrifice which the residents
of the district were willing to make. Local school districts would retain
the power to set their own tax rates, but districts which taxed at the same
rate would receive equal per pupil revenues, regardless of the amount of
taxable areas within the district.

"District power equalizing," however, cannot avoid the second cost of
equalizing revenues among school districts: the tremendous increase in
educational expenditures which would follow.[159] Centralized school
funding would increase educational costs for the simple reason that it is
improbable, at best, that wealthy districts would choose to decrease their
absolute levels of school spending, while poor districts would seek to
equalize their levels of spending with those of the richer districts. As
Daniel Patrick Moynihan put it in the *University of Illinois Law Forum*:

> To the degree that one insists on equal levels of expenditure, there is nothing in the
> political process as practiced in this country that suggests that government will be
> able to push some people down; instead, what one does is to push other people up
> which will make the total level of expenditure higher.[160]

Indeed, it may be legally as well as poitically impossible to maintain or
reduce educational expenditures in such a system, since teachers salaries
are the major element in school budgets.[161] To maintain or reduce overall
education costs under a uniform system of school spending would

School Property Tax Cases, 1972 U. ILL. L. F. 232; Finn & Lenkowsky, *"Serrano" vs. the
People*, 54 COMMENTARY 68 (1972).
[158]*See* J. COONS, *et al.*, *supra* note 92, at 33-35, 200-42.
[159]*See id.* at 271-72; Carrington, *supra* note 157, at 238-40; Finn & Lenkowsky, *supra*
note 157, at 70-71.
[160]Moynihann, *Solving the Equal Educational Opportunity Dilemma: Equal Dollars
Is Not Equal Opportunity*, 1972 U. ILL. L. F. 259, 260.
[161]U.S. COMM'N ON CIVIL RIGHTS, INEQUALITY IN SCHOOL FINANCING:
THE ROLE OF LAW 34 n. 304 (1972).

require reducing some teachers' salaries or discharging some teachers. But, with the increased unionization of the educational profession, this would prove extremely unlikely, and, if union contracts were involved, probably illegal.[162]

Moreover, there are serious reasons for doubting that increasing educational expenditures would have the results desired by the educational reformers. In the first place, the poorest school districts are found in rural areas.[163] Equalization of educational financing, thus, would benefit these areas but not the inner-city schools which the liberal opponents of local property taxation sought to help. "Because large cities generally have larger than average property tax bases per pupil, the net effect of breaking the property wealth-expenditure link would be to reduce the proportion of educational funds available to large cities while increasing their share of the educational tax burden. But it is precisely the schools in large cities which have the most serious problems."[164] And, in the second place, it is far from clear that increasing expenditures produces better education. As the *Rodriguez* Court itself noted, the quality-cost controversy has generated considerable heat.[165] Perhaps most notably, Christopher Jencks of the Center for Educational Policy at Harvard has concluded, on the basis of an exhaustive three-year study, that well-endowed schools do not produce better results than do schools with small budgets.[166] According to Jencks, the quality of a school's graduates depends largely upon the quality of the students themselves. Their characteristics are determined by a variety of factors, including genetics and environment, and are generally settled by the time the student enters school. Viewing education from the larger perspective of the social and economic structures of society, Jencks has argued that the equalization of educational opportunity will not be effective in improving adult status; the schools will not solve America's problems.

Jenck's conclusions, of course, have been vigorously disputed.[167] Indeed, his study will continue to be quoted—and misquoted—for some time to come. Professor Richard Herrnstein, also of Harvard, has even

---

[162]*See, e.g.,* Simon, *The School Finance Decisions: Collective Bargaining and Future Finance Systems,* 82 YALE L. J. 409 (1973).

[163]Finn & Lenkowsky, *supra* note 157, at 71.

[164]*The Supreme Court, 1972 Term,* 87 HARV. L. REV. at 116.

[165]411 U.S. at 42-43.

[166]C. JENCKS, *et al.,* INEQUALITY: A REASSESSMENT OF THE EFFECT OF FAMILY AND SCHOOLING IN AMERICA (1972).

[167]*See* H. GANS, MORE EQUALITY (1973).

argued that equalization of educational opportunity is not a necessary social good.[168] Proceeding from the premise, drawn from a review of a century of research, that intelligence is largely inherited, Herrnstein has concluded that educational equality, coupled with unrestricted social mobility, would eventually produce a rigid class structure based upon hereditary intellectual ability, an IQ caste system.[169] Jencks himself has drawn the conclusion that, if the elimination of differences between schools in per pupil expenditures will have little appreciable effect upon equalizing adult opportunities, society should look toward the redistribution of income. But, even if that is true, even if Herrnstein is correct, the important point to keep in mind is that none of these studies has offered a creditable argument against the racial desegregation of the public schools. Indeed, it was probably a mistake for the Warren Court ever to have argued the case against segregation in terms of educational achievement.[170]

For the student of constitutional interpretation and the path of the contemporary Court, however, the most significant aspect of the quality-cost debate has been that the reformist opposition to the local property tax finance system was based upon the traditional American assumption that solutions to problems can be translated into relatively simple calculations based upon money. The educational reformers had defined "equal educational opportunity" in terms of numbers: so many classrooms, so many teachers, so many textbooks, so many dollars per pupil. But, even granting that correlations between property values and per pupil expenditures may exist across districts,[171] the central assumption remained that quality could be quantified. Yet no one has demonstrated a correlation between educational expenditures and educational quality or achievement. This idea that throwing money at a problem would make it go away was hardly the radical solution it was presented as. Rather, the belief that difficult non-financial problems are susceptible of simple financial solutions has been a basic tenet of modern

[168]Herrnstein, *IQ*, 227 ATLANTIC MONTHLY 43 (1971). *See also* Herrnstein, *On Challenging an Orthodoxy*, 55 COMMENTARY 52 (1973).
[169]R. HERRNSTEIN, IQ IN THE MERITOCRACY (1973). *See also* Jensen, *supra* note 26; J. BAKER, *supra* note 26.
[170]*See* notes 20-27 *supra* and accompanying text.
[171]*See* Berke, *School Finance and Inequality of Educational Opportunity*, in J. BERKE, A. CAMPBELL & R. GOETTEL, FINANCING EQUAL EDUCATIONAL OPPORTUNITY: ALTERNATIVES FOR STATE FINANCE I, 5-10 (1972).

liberalism.[172] From the perspective of assessing the relationships between the policy-making of the Warren and Burger Courts, perhaps the most significant aspect of *Rodriguez* lay in its refusal to continue judicial endorsement of constitutional arguments flowing from that premise. One facet of *Rodriguez*, however, was familiar and spoke of continuity. As the Warren Court in *Brown v. Board of Education*, the Burger Court in *Rodriguez* took judicial notice of and was influenced by contemporary scholarship in the social sciences,[173] although in this instance that scholarship counseled judicial restraint.[174]

The Burger Court has been similarly cautious in its approach to the problem presented by conflicts between the Constitution's concern for racial equality and the constitutional solicitude for the personal liberty of private choice. The Fourteenth Amendment insures that "No State shall . . . deny to any person within its jurisdiction the equal protection of the laws." As a result of this constitutional phraseology, the Supreme Court in its decision-making affecting racial discrimination has been concerned not only with the value of equality, what constitutes it, and how it can be measured, but also with the issue, if equality has been denied, of whether the state has denied it. The Fourteenth Amendment was designed principally to insure black Americans equal treatment under the law. For years, nevertheless, the southern states utilized the doctrine of "separate but equal" to deny equal facilities to blacks, until *Brown* and its progeny swept that doctrine into the constitutional rubbish heap. But an equally, if not more, difficult problem was presented by situations in which the discrimination was the result of private actions or preferences, and the state was, at most, indirectly involved in the discriminatory practice. Here the Court and those who follow its decision-making are presented with one of the most difficult of all problems of political theory—reconciling liberty and equality.[175] On the one hand, if the Constitution is to mean anything, it must protect the liberties of the worst citizens, not merely those of the best. On the other hand, when a private citizen relies upon the state through the enforcement of its trespass

---

[172]*See generally* T. LOWI, THE END OF LIBERALISM (1969); Finn & Lenkowsky, *supra* note 157.

[173]411 U.S. at 43 n. 86.

[174]*But see* Roe v. Wade, 410 U.S. 113 (1973), and Doe v. Bolton, 410 U.S. 179 (1973), in which the Burger Court found that a lack of scientific consensus (as to when life begins *in utero*) justified its striking down state legislation restricting abortions.

[175]*See generally* A. COX, THE WARREN COURT 29, 32-40 (1968).

laws,[176] or through its zoning powers,[177] or its power and duty to probate wills and administer estates to enforce his own racial prejudices,[178] has he not involved the state in the denial of equal protection in violation of the Constitution?[179]

This problem and the Court's efforts at resolving it serve to introduce one of the most complex doctrines of constitutional interpretation, the concept of "state action." Closely related to this doctrine, moreover, has been the question of the power of the federal government to protect civil rights against either public or private discrimination. How far can Congress go, consistent with the Constitution, in an effort to achieve equality by statute?[180] Because of the close relationship between these problems, it is no mere coincidence that the decision initially developing the concept of "state action" involved a challenge to the constitutionality of the Civil Rights Act of 1875, a federal statute designed to guarantee to blacks the full and equal enjoyment of various public accommodations. In the *Civil Rights Cases* the Supreme Court, taking an exceedingly narrow view of congressional power under the Thirteenth and Fourteenth Amendments, held that statute unconstitutional, thereby ending the last serious Reconstruction efforts to establish black equality.[181]

Ever since the *Civil Rights Cases*, the fields of public accommodations and housing have been the two areas which have given rise to the major litigation elaborating and refining the concept of "state action," although there is, of course, a close relationship between racial discrimination in housing and the problem of *de facto* segregation in education. For nearly eighty years following the *Civil Rights Cases*, the Court moved with great caution, even reluctance, in finding racially discriminatory practices to be infected with state involvement. It did rule that state judicial enforcement of racially restrictive covenants in property deeds violated the Fourteenth Amendment,[182] but it made it clear that private property owners were at liberty to sign and adhere to

[176]*See, e.g.,* Garner v. Louisiana, 368 U.S. 157 (1961).
[177]*See* Note, *Exclusionary Zoning and Equal Protection,* 84 HARV. L. REV. 1645 (1971).
[178]*See* Pennsylvania v. Board of Trusts, 353 U.S. 230 (1957).
[179]*See generally* L. MORELAND, WHITE RACISM AND THE LAW (1970).
[180]*See* M. BERGER, EQUALITY BY STATUTE (1967).
[181]109 U.S. 3 (1883).
[182]Shelley v. Kraemer, 334 U.S. 1 (1948); *see also* Barrows v. Jackson, 346 U.S. 249 (1953). *See generally* Henkin, *Shelley v. Kraemer: Notes for a Revised Opinion,* 110 U. PA. L. REV. 473 (1962).

such agreements voluntarily and, presumably, to use their property as they saw fit.

Then, on February 1, 1960, four students from North Carolina A&T College, an all-black school, entered a department store lunch counter in Greensboro, North Carolina, and ordered four cups of coffee. They were refused service, because of the segregationist policy of the department store, but, rather than as expected, they did not leave but remained seated until the day's closing. Joined by more students, they returned the next day and the next and the next. Their eventual arrest did not still the protest movement. Instead a wave of sit-ins erupted across the South challenging racial discrimination in public accommodations.

The sit-in was the product of rising expectations upon the part of black Americans, expectations engendered in no small part by the decision in *Brown v. Board of Education.* As such it was a child of the Warren Court, but now it confronted its father with the troubling question of private discrimination. The Court overturned convictions in the early cases involving demonstrations protesting racial discrimination on the grounds that the demonstrators had merely been lawfully exercising their First Amendment freedoms,[183] or that the statutes under which they had been convicted were impermissibly vague,[184] or on the extraordinary (for an appellate court) grounds that the convictions lacked evidentiary support.[185] But in *Peterson v. Greenville*[186] and *Lombard v. Louisiana*[187] these escape routes were not open. It seemed that the time had come to face the issue of the conflict between the liberty of the private business operator and the right to equality of the black patron. But that time had not come, for the Court chose to avoid the central issue by treating the discrimination as state-inspired rather than privately motivated. In *Peterson,* Mr. Chief Justice Warren relied upon the existence of a local segregation ordinance to argue that the lunch-counter manager who had excluded the demonstrators had been required to do so by local law. The absence of such an ordinance in *Lombard,* however, did not stay the Court from its appointed course. Rather, the Chief Justice relied upon public statements made by local officials to

[183]Edwards v. South Carolina, 372 U.S. 229 (1963).

[184]Garner v. Louisiana, 368 U.S. 157 (1961). *See generally* Note, *The Void-For-Vagueness Doctrine in the Supreme Court,* 109 U. PA. L. REV. 67 (1960).

[185]Taylor v. Louisiana, 370 U.S. 154 (1962).

[186]373 U.S. 244 (1963). *See generally* Lewis, *The Sit-in Cases: Great Expectations,* 1963 SUP. CT. REV. 101.

[187]373 U.S. 267 (1963). *See generally* Lewis, *supra* note 186.

argue that, again, segregation was the announced policy of the state and the discriminating restaurateurs had merely been complying with that policy. In essence, the Court seemed to be saying that, facts to the contrary notwithstanding, the operators of the private facilities would not have practiced racial discrimination, had they not been required to do so by public policy. Given the significant extent to which the state directed segregated service, the discrimination protested by the sit-in demonstrators had involved state action and, thus, violated the Equal Protection Clause—a subtle if hardly candid approach to the problem of private racial discrimination.

Equally unconvincing was the tack taken in *Bell v. Maryland*.[188] Following the convictions complained of in *Bell*, the State of Maryland had enacted a public accommodations law requiring racially non-discriminatory service in business establishments providing food and lodging to the public. Thus, by the time *Bell* reached the Supreme Court, the actions which had led to the convictions of the sit-in demonstrators would no longer have been considered criminal in Maryland. Seizing upon this change of circumstance, Mr. Justice Brennan chose to ignore the difficult constitutional issues presented and, instead, merely vacated the demonstrators' trespass convictions, remanding the case to the Maryland courts for further consideration in light of the new public accommodations statute.

This circumnavigation of the equal protection problem shattered the unanimity which had characterized the Court's approach to the sit-in convictions in *Peterson* and *Lombard*. Justices Douglas and Goldberg, in separate concurrences, resting upon analogies to the common law of public carriers, urged that state enforcement of private racial prejudice violated the "common law" of the Fourteenth Amendment. Mr. Justice Black, on the other hand, joined by Harlan and White, challenged the position that subsequent changes in the law could affect the criminality of acts proscribed by law at the time of their commission. The Fourteenth Amendment, the dissenters argued, did not touch private prejudice or acts motivated by private prejudice. No matter how bigoted, every individual had a legitimate expectation that the state would protect his private choices. As for the restrictive covenant cases,[189] Justice Black distinguished state enforcement of such covenants, in which case the

---

[188]378 U.S. 226 (1964). *See generally* Paulsen, *The Sit-In Cases of 1964: "But Answer Came There None,"* 1964 SUP. CT. REV. 137.
[189]Shelley v. Kraemer, 334 U.S. 1 (1948); Barrows v. Jackson, 346 U.S. 249 (1953).

state prohibits two willing parties from executing a mutually agreeable contract, from state protection of private property, in cases where one party was unwilling to enter into a contractual relationship, as in the enforcement of trespass ordinances against sit-in demonstrators.

This lack of harmony was to characterize virtually all of the Court's subsequent decisions dealing with the sit-in problem.[190] Only where there was sufficient evidence to support reliance upon the *Peterson-Lombard* rationale that state policy itself required segregated facilities was the Court able to present a united front.[191] But, however scattered, no majority of Warren Court Justices ever squarely faced the issue presented by the sit-in cases. What is the constitutional status of private discrimination? The Court never abandoned the concept of "state action" as the necessary requirement for energizing the constitutional guarantee of equal protection. But neither did it embrace Mr. Justice Black's argument that there is no constitutional objection to state enforcement of private discrimination.

In the early 1960s, those seeking to eliminate racial discrimination from American life through political action had had two paths open to them. They might rely upon the people's elected representatives in Congress to enact appropriate legislation, or they might persuade the Supreme Court to reject the doctrine of "state action" and apply the same legal standard to both private and public conduct. Initially, the reformers chose to rely upon the Court, thus saying something no doubt about their attitudes toward democracy and the American people.

For the Court to strike at private racial discrimination, however, involved difficulties of logic and principle.[192] A small band of Platonic guardians, ruling by fiat, might have found it easy to deal with the problem, but the Court is not such a group. If the Court is to persist as a viable actor in the policy-making process of a polity committed to democracy, its policy pronouncements must rest upon some principle to be found, explicitly or implicitly, in the fundamental law. Surely the Constitution did not favor racial discrimination, but no less did it favor individual liberty, including the liberty to be racist. How could the Court overturn the trespass convictions of morally just sit-in demonstrators

[190]*See* Griffin v. Maryland, 378 U.S. 130 (1964); Bouie v. City of Columbia, 378 U.S. 347 (1964); Barr v. City of Columbia, 378 U.S. 146 (1964). *See generally* Paulsen, *supra* note 188.

[191]*See* Robinson v. Florida, 378 U.S. 153 (1964).

[192]For an excellent discussion of the legal, moral, and philosophic dimensions of the problem of private racial discrimination, *see* A. COX, *supra* note 175, at ch. 2.

without fashioning a rule of law so broad as to endanger individual liberty and personal privacy?

The Court might have resolved the dilemma by relying upon the theory, derived from the restrictive covenant cases, that private prejudice is beyond the reach of the Equal Protection Clause but that state enforcement of a private decision to discriminate automatically becomes state action. Such a constitutional principle, however, would have been too broad. Under this theory, how could one distinguish between the state's enforcement of Smith's decision to throw demonstrators out of his restaurant and state enforcement of his decision to throw them out of his living-room? Obviously there are differences between restaurants and private living-rooms, but this theory for voiding the sit-in demonstrators' convictions was incapable of making those distinctions. In each case, the state enforces private, racially motivated discrimination.

To avoid such a broad ruling with its unwanted consequences, the Court might have adopted Mr. Justice Douglas's theory that those businesses performing public services are engaged in a form of public activity so closely akin to that provided by the state that they are, in effect, instruments of the state. Thus, anyone operating book stores, cafeterias, schools, or recreational facilities are agents of the state and their discrimination constitutes governmental action. The problem with such a position is that it would, in essence, write Mussolini's theory of the corporate state into American constitutional law.[193] In pluralistic, post-industrial, interdependent American society, Douglas's theory would eliminate any legal distinction between the public and private spheres of conduct. Such a wholesale diminution of the value of personal privacy may be desirable, but it is counter to the expressed wishes of many modern American opinion leaders,[194] including the good Justice Douglas himself.[195]

---

[193]*But cf.* T. LOWI, *supra* note 172. Professor Lowi argues that the predominant decisional strain of post-New Deal jurisprudence has indeed been the delegation of public power to private groups coupled with a theory of representation which closely parallels the philosophy of the corporate state. *See generally* G. MOSCA, THE RULING CLASS (H. Kahn transl. 1939); G. SALVEMINI, THE ORIGINS OF FASCISM IN ITALY (R. Vivarelli transl. 1973).

[194]*See, e.g.*, A. WESTIN, PRIVACY AND FREEDOM (1967); R. MILLER, THE ASSAULT ON PRIVACY (1971); R. PENNOCK & J. CHAPMAN (eds.), PRIVACY (1971).

[195]*See* Griswold v. Connecticut, 381 U.S. 479, 480-86 (1965) (Douglas, J.); *see also* note 223 *infra.*

Finally, the Court might have endorsed the theory that the Equal Protection Clause imposed a positive state duty to eliminate racial discrimination. It is not enough that the state remain neutral in matters of race, the Fourteenth Amendment requires governmental authorities to take affirmative action to prevent racial discrimination in housing, employment, and public accommodations. Certainly such a theory would have been consistent with the contemporary rise of the positive state. Government is today expected to do far, far more than was expected of it only a few generations ago. Positive government involvement is accepted as a matter of course in such areas as health, education, social welfare, employment, the economy, and old-age pensions. Why not with respect to race? While an understandable, even attractive, position, the positive state duty theory, however, suffered from at least two defects. First, such a doctrine could easily become a vehicle of oppression, and, second, it was probably inappropriate for the Supreme Court to be making such a decision. In the first place, the positive state duty theory could not be confined to the problem of race. If a private club may not limit its membership to whites, why should it be able to limit its membership to Protestants? And, if that, why should a parochial school be able to exclude students not of its faith? In short, the positive state duty theory, in the wrong hands, could justify governmental elimination of the cultural heritage of various groups from Irish Catholics to Black Muslims. In the second place, while non-discriminatory policies regarding public accommodations and housing may be desirable, certainly if the effects of racism are to be eradicated, in terms of democratic theory the judicial process is not the best vehicle for initiating these policies. The judiciary is institutionally incapable of the kind of line-drawing that would be required. There are significant differences between Holiday Inns and small, private boarding houses operated by spinster sisters. It may be appropriate to prohibit discrimination in the former but tolerate it in the latter, because of the overweighing interest in personal privacy. But this is the kind of interest balancing which is best performed by and, therefore, best left to legislatures. For judges to make these kinds of expedient distinctions would be to betray the craft and function of judging. While the goal of eliminating racial discrimination in housing, employment, and public accommodations is a worthy one, in a nation committed to the republican principle it makes a great deal of difference which governmental institution initiates and effectuates that policy.

The sit-in cases, however, presented the Warren Court with a peculiarly difficult dilemma. While legal logic and principle may have augured against bringing private discrimination within the prohibitions of the Fourteenth Amendment, decisions affirming the demonstrators' convictions would have appeared to be a judicial legitimation of racial prejudice. The Court was, thus, faced with the task of finding some grounds on which to free those who had protested raical injustice, while at the same time avoiding a sweeping statement of constitutional policy which might at some future date work to the detriment of individual freedom and privacy. In view of this situation, the sit-in decisions of 1963 and 1964, though strained, may be viewed, even applauded, as a *tour de force.*[196] They steered a brilliant, if not candid, course between undesirable consequences, endorsing neither constitutional extreme, yet leaving the way open for, even encouraging, congressional action on the issue. Perhaps this jucidial path was somewhat smoothed by the manifest reality that Congress was beginning to bestir itself in this area and, at the very time the Court was releasing sit-in demonstrators, was moving toward the passage of the Civil Rights Act of 1964.[197]

Title II of the Civil Rights Act of 1964 provided for injunctive relief against racial discrimination in hotels, motels, gas stations, restaurants, theatres and other public accommodations affecting interstate commerce. The constitutionality of Title II was challenged almost immediately upon its enactment. Although Congress had based the act upon the Equal Protection Clause and its power under Section 5 of the Fourteenth Amendment to enforce that amendment through appropriate legislation, as well as on its power to regulate interstate commerce, the Supreme Court did not reach the equal protecion question in its decisions sustaining the act, preferring to rest its case upon the commerce power alone. In *Heart of Atlanta Motel v. United States,*[198] the Court reasoned that racial discrimination in public accommodations impaired interstate commerce by discouraging travel on the part of a substantial portion of the black community, resulting in an artificial restriction of the national market. Discrimination against blacks discouraged them from travelling; this resulted in their loss to American business as customers; thus, businesses such as motels or restaurants, having fewer customers, sold less than if there were no discrimination; and, in turn, these businesses themselves bought less from their suppliers. Racial discrimination,

[196]*But see* Lewis, *supra* note 186; Paulsen, *supra* note 188; *cf.* A. COX, *supra* note 175, at 39-40.
[197]78 Stat. 241.
[198]379 U.S. 241 (1964).

therefore, created a vicious circle with a depressant effect upon commerce.

Having found the public accommodations section of the Civil Rights Act to have been within Congress's commerce power, the Court then turned to its application to the Heart of Atlanta Motel. It had little trouble in showing that the motel was subject to Congress's commerce power. It was readily accessible to interstate highways. It solicited business through advertisements in various magazines having interstate circulations, and approximately 75% of its clientele was engaged in interstate travel. The Court rejected the motel's contention that Congress's commerce power was restricted by the fact that the evil against which it was legislating was a moral one.[199] According to the Court, the only question was whether Congress could have had a rational basis for finding that racial discrimination affected interstate commerce and whether the means which it selected to eliminate the evil were reasonable and appropriate. The answer in both cases was in the affirmative.

But, in *Heart of Atlanta's* companion case, *Katzenbach v. McClung*,[200] the Court was faced with a more difficult problem, for it was not so easy to show that Ollie's Barbecue, the discriminating facility in question, was subject to the national commerce power. The diner, after all, was not located on or near interstate highways, nor was it readily accessible to bus, rail, or air terminals. It did not solicit business from interstate travellers, and there was no claim that a substantial portion of its patrons were interstate travellers. Ollie's was essentially a local restaurant, engaged in the white collar (and white skin) family trade. Indeed, it bought less than one half of its foodstuffs from a supplier who purchased the produce from outside the state; Ollie's transactions, however, were entirely intra-state. Nevertheless, the Court found that it was subject to the commerce power. Relying upon precedent from the New Deal era,[201] dealing with the regulation of agriculture, the Court ruled that, even though Ollie's drew an insignificant amount of its supplies from out of state, its contribution to interstate commerce, when taken together with that of all others similarly situated, was far from trivial. Rejecting the contention that the United States Government must prove in each case that discrimination in a particular restaurant affected interstate commerce, the Court held: "Where we find that the legislators, in light of the facts and testimony before them, have a rational basis for

[199]*See* Hoke v. United States, 227 U.S. 308 (1913).
[200]379 U.S. 294 (1964).
[201]Wickard v. Filburn, 317 U.S. 111 (1942).

finding a chosen regulatory scheme necessary to the protection of commerce, our investigation is at an end."[202]

Race, being a national problem, required a national solution. The Warren Court had vigorously, if not always successfully, attacked governmental discrimination. But, because so many activities of such vast importance are conducted by private initiative in American society, the Court's racial pronouncements did not have the vast consequences which some had anticipated. Legislation was necessary, and state legislation was unlikely. Congress, thus, was confronted with and responded to the need to provide some restructuring of American race relations.[203] But, in sustaining Congress's power to deal with the problem, the Warren Court further altered the balance of power in the American federal system.[204] Other legislation directed against private racial prejudice could be advanced on *Katzenbach's* reading of the commerce clause. The Warren Court's expansion of the commerce power was so broad that it could be argued that Congress has the power to insure equal access for all to the products of interstate commerce, even in the ultimate stages of distribution. Very stringent federal consumer protection statutes could, for example, be sustained under the rationale of *Katzenbach*. Such laws, like anti-discrimination laws, might be desirable. But it is ironic that only a few years after the Warren Court went to such lengths to expand Congress's potential power, and thus ultimately the power of the federal bureaucracy, America began to experience a rebirth of interest in the principle of federalism,[205] a re-emphasis upon decentralization,[206] and a heightened concern for the protection of personal privacy.[207]

Such shifting concerns and their concomitant reordering of values have been reflected in Burger Court decision-making. In 1957, the Warren Court had ruled upon the constitutional issue raised by the will

[202]379 U.S. at 303-04.

[203]*See also* South Carolina v. Katzenbach, 383 U.S. 301 (1966).

[204]*See* P. KURLAND, *supra* note 104, at ch. 3 (1970).

[205]*See* A. MACMAHON, ADMINISTERING FEDERALISM IN A DEMOCRACY (1972); R. LEACH, AMERICAN FEDERALISM (1970); J. SUNDQUIST & D. DAVIS, MAKING FEDERALISM WORK (1969). *See also* R. DAHL, AFTER THE REVOLUTION? (1970).

[206]*See* I. SHARKANSKY, THE MALIGNED STATES (1972); M. REAGAN, THE NEW FEDERALISM (1972); D. LOCKHARD, THE PERVERTED PRIORITIES OF AMERICAN POLITICS ch. 9 (1971).

[207]*See* note 194 *supra*.

of Stephen Girard, a Philadelphia philanthropist.[208] By the terms of his will, Girard had established an educational trust to support Girard College; admission to the institution was to be restricted to "poor white male orphans." Officials of the City of Philadelphia were appointed administrators of the trust, as provided in Girard's will, but several decades later the Warren Court ruled that the trustees' refusal to admit two black applicants constituted racial discrimination on the part of the state. An attempt was then made to substitute private trustees for the city administrators of the trust, but this action was blocked by the Third Circuit Court of Appeals, an action which the Supreme Court chose not to review.[209]

Similarly, the attempt by Macon, Georgia, to withdraw in 1964 as trustee of a park bequeathed to the city by United States Senator Augustus Bacon in 1914 for the use of "white women and children" proved unsuccessful. In *Evans v. Newton*, the Warren Court decided that the public nature of parks, and the long period for which the Macon park had been under public control, made it reasonable to treat it as a public institution.[210] Bacon's Park, therefore, could not be operated as a segregated facility. Even under private management, the park remained within the reach of the Fourteenth Amendment's prohibition against discriminatory "state action."

Following the decision in *Evans v. Newton*, the case was remanded to the Georgia courts for a decision on the issue of whether, under state law, operating the park on an integrated basis was so inconsistent with Senator Bacon's intent in willing the park to the city that the property must revert to his heirs. In *Evans v. Abney*, the Burger Court upheld the decision of the Georgia Supreme Court returning the property to the heirs.[211] As a matter of state law, the Georgia court's decision had not been inevitable.[212] A long-established rule of interpreting wills provides that, if a charitable trust would fail because of an impossible or illegal condition in the will, a court can save the trust by applying the doctrine of *cy pres*. This doctrine, which Georgia had adopted by statute, allows a court to authorize a deviation from the strict letter of a bequest in order to achieve the donor's general charitable intention, unless, of course, the

[208]Pennsylvania v. Board of Trusts, 353 U.S. 230 (1957).
[209]Pennsylvania v. Brown, 342 F.2d 120 (3d Cir. 1968), *cert. denied*, 391 U.S. 921 (1968).
[210]382 U.S. 296 (1966).
[211]396 U.S. 435 (1970).
[212]*See The Supreme Court, 1969 Term*, 84 HARV. L. REV. at 54-60.

will specifically provides that, if its conditions cannot be met, the trust property is to revert to the heirs. Bacon's will contained no such reverter clause, but the Georgia court concluded that Bacon's desire to exclude black's was inseparable from his charitable intention in donating the park. The court, therefore, refused to delete the "whites only" condition from the will, thus requiring the city to return the property to Bacon's estate. Speaking for a five-man majority, Mr. Justice Black, finding no racial motivation in the Georgia court's decision, concluded that the state court had made a constitutionally permissible use of its discretion in interpreting wills. Dissenting from the opinion, Mr. Justice Douglas argued that the continued use of the property as a municipal park would carry out a larger share of Senator Bacon's purpose than the complete destruction of the park which the Court had affirmed. He also pointed out that conveying the property to the Senator's heirs would not necessarily preserve Bacon's segregationist purpose, since many private uses of the land, such as establishing a theatre or a restaurant, would require the owners to admit blacks as well as whites under the federal civil rights statutes.[213]

Indeed, the Court's decision to uphold the reversion of the property does seem harsh. The heirs received a valuable piece of real estate, improved by the city at taxpayer expense, on which they had paid no taxes and expended no capital. They enjoyed this windfall at the expense of the citizens of Macon, both white and black, who were deprived of the park's benefits. The black citizens of Macon, moreover, paid an additional price by being made the scapegoats for the closing. At the same time, they may have seen but one interpretation of the incident: The city preferred to close the park rather than to integrate it. The blacks, thus, were potentially required to bear the wrath of the white community and the stigma of seeming state discrimination.

Despite Mr. Justice Douglas, however, it is not clear that any other result could have been reached. While there were, to be sure, a number of arguments which pointed toward an opposite result, each of them fell short of providing a defensible basis for reversing the state court decision. First, it might have been argued that the Georgia Supreme Court's refusal to apply the *cy pres* doctrine amounted to a discriminatory state action.[214] But the failure of the court to apply *cy pres* was not conclusive proof of discriminatory state intent. After all, the

[213]*See* Daniel v. Paul, 395 U.S. 298 (1969).
[214]*See, e.g.*, Shelley v. Kraemer, 334 U.S. 1 (1948).

application of the *cy pres* doctrine depends not on the intent of the state but upon the intention of the person who made the bequest, and, as Mr. Justice Black pointed out, Sen. Bacon's will could plausibly be read to say that he would have found an integrated park less desirable than no park at all. A second method by which the Court might have invalidated the reversion of the property to the heirs was suggested by the reasoning of *Reitman v. Mulkey.*[215] In *Reitman*, the Supreme Court had concluded that state encouragement of private acts of discrimination itself constituted unconstitutional "state action." Six years before Sen. Bacon drafted his will, the Georgia legislature had enacted a statute explicitly authorizing the establishment of charitable trusts with racially restrictive conditions. But this argument would have been applicable only to *Evans v. Newton.* There the city was attempting to implement the Senator's racially discriminatory private action, an act which the state had encouraged. In *Evans v. Abney*, on the other hand, the private act involved was not one which the state had encouraged, but rather the decision by Sen. Bacon's heirs to seek reversion of the property to themselves. Thirdly, Justice Douglas argued that the Georgia Supreme Court decision could be reversed on the basis of *Griffin v. Prince Edward County School Board*, in which the Supreme Court had invalidated an effort to avoid integration by shutting down the public schools.[216] But in *Evans* the park was closed because of a private civil lawsuit to enforce the terms of a will and not because of a voluntary action on the part of public officials. In fact, the state attorney general had intervened in the case to argue that the park should be kept open by application of the *cy pres* doctrine. The decision of the Georgia Supreme Court to return the property to the heirs, therefore, may have been unfortunate, or unwise, or—viewed from a perspective other than that of Sen. Bacon and his heirs—even unjust. But Mr. Justice Black would appear to have been correct in his conclusion that it was not unconstitutional.

Though the factual situations to which the *Evans* precedent would be applicable were limited, the decision stood as a graphic example of the Burger Court's reluctance to extend the scope of the Equal Protection Clause through an expansive conception of state involvement in racial discrimination. This was underscored by the result in *Moose Lodge No. 107 v. Irvis*,[217] in which the Court rejected a finding of "state action"

[215]387 U.S. 369 (1967). *See generally* Black, *"State Action," Equal Protection, and California's Proposition 14*, 81 HARV. L. REV. 69 (1967).
[216]377 U.S. 218 (1964).
[217]407 U.S. 163 (1972).

despite the existence of several grounds on which the racially discriminatory acts in question might plausibly have been construed as having involved the public authorities.[218] Moreover, as a practical matter, the *Irvis* holding was of greater significance than the *Evans* decision, for the discrimination practiced in *Irvis* occurs much more commonly than do private bequests to the state. Leroy Irvis, a Pennsylvania state legislator, visited the Moose Lodge in Harrisburrg, the state capital, as the guest of a member. He was refused service at the bar solely because he was black. Irvis then brought suit under a federal civil rights statute,[219] seeking an injunction against the Harrisburg Moose Lodge preventing it from discriminating on the basis of race. The civil rights statute involved had been passed during the Reconstruction Era under Congress's power to enforce the Fourteenth Amendment through appropriate legislation, hence the necessity of showing "state action." Irvis argued that, because the state liquor authority had issued the Moose Lodge a private club license authorizing the sale of alcoholic beverages on the premises, the refusal of service constituted discriminatory state action in violation of the Equal Protection Clause.

This claim was sustained by the lower federal courts,[220] but the Supreme Court, speaking through its newest member, Mr. Justice Rehnquist, reversed. The grant of a state liquor license to a racially discriminatory private club and the subsequent regulation of that club by the state liquor control board did not constitute sufficient state involvement for the six-man majority in *Moose Lodge* to bring the Fourteenth Amendment into operation. Mr. Justice Rehnquist was careful, however, not to break with earlier precedents defining the scope of "state action." Rather, he applied the formula adopted in *Reitman v. Mulkey*,[221] the case which had nullified California's so-called "Proposition 14:" A state may not significantly involve itself with invidious discrimination. Distinguishing prior cases involving discrimination in public eating places,[222] Rehnquist stressed that Pennsylvania had not placed the power, property, or prestige of the state behind the racial discrimination of Moose Lodge No. 107. The state had played no part in establishing or enforcing the discriminatory members and guests policies of the lodge, nor had the state encouraged the adoption of such policies.

---

[218]*See The Supreme Court, 1971 Term*, 86 HARV. L. REV. 1, 70-75 (1972).
[219]42 U.S.C. § 1983.
[220]Irvis v. Scott, 318 F. Supp. 1246 (M.D. Pa. 1970).
[221]387 U.S. 369 (1967). *See generally* Black, *supra* note 215.
[222]*E.g.*, Peterson v. Greenville, 3773 U.S. 244 (1963).

Neverthelesss, as Mr. Justice Douglas pointed out in dissent,[223] there were factual bases for finding that "state action" was involved in the Moose Lodge's discrimination. Pennsylvania's scheme of liquor licensing, after all, involved extensive regulation of the licensee's hours of operation, premises, and entertainment. Not every involvement of the state with a private person or association should, of course, automatically make the actions of that person or group "state action." The state, for example, confers numerous benefits such as fire and police protection or drivers' licenses, none of which could reasonably be thought to bring the Fourteenth Amendment into play. But these benefits are available to everyone or at least to those who meet some well-defined minimum standards of competence. Pennsylvania, however, strictly limited the number of liquor licenses available and retained broad discretion over their award. Such a process actively involved the state in selecting one applicant over another. It could be argued, therefore, that the activities of a state-selected beneficiary were sufficiently an extension of the activities of the state to invoke the guarantees and restrictions of the Fourteenth Amendment.

Mr. Justice Rehnquist thought not, though he was less than clear on the question of how great a connection must exist between the state and a private enterprise to convert the actions of the enterprise into "state action." Rehnquist suggested that there would be sufficient state involvement were the state to play a role similar to that of a partner in the discriminatory enterprise or were the state to grant a monopoly to such an enterprise. While he did not define "partnership" with any degree of precision, what Mr. Justice Rehnquist apparently had in mind would be a relationship between the state and the private enterprise in which there were some kind of mutual benefit, as, for example, in *Burton v. Wilmington Parking Authority*,[224] one of the Warren Court's leading "state action" precedents. In *Burton* the state had built a public parking garage in which was located a restaurant. This restaurant was leased to an

---

[223]407 U.S. at 179. *But see* Mr. Justice Douglas's concurrence in Columbia Broadcasting System, Inc. v. Democratic National Committee, 412 U.S. 94 (1973), in which he voted to sustain discriminatory editorial broadcast policies on the grounds that the broadcasters, as members of the press, were protected by the First Amendment against governmental action infringing upon their control over the allocation of broadcast time. Since the broadcasters are licensed by the Federal Communications Commission, however, it is unclear why, under Douglas's earlier reasoning in the private racial discrimination cases, the broadcasters' policies did not constitute governmental action.

[224]365 U.S. 715 (1961).

operator who subsequently engaged in racially discriminatory practices. The Court found that the private actions of this restaurateur were sufficiently clothed with a public character to constitute "state action." For one thing, the public nature of the building guaranteed the restaurant a tax exemption. On the other hand, the state enjoyed a substantial benefit from the relationship, because the restaurant's rental payments were essential to the successful financing of the parking facility. Justice Rehnquist argued that the relation in *Moose Lodge* did not approach the public/private intimacy present in *Burton*. But both Pennsylvania and its liquor licensees enjoyed benefits from their relationship. Pennsylvania monopolized the sale of liquor within that state; those establishments which retail liquor in Pennsylvania were compelled to buy it from the only wholesale distributor available, the State of Pennsylvania. The licensee, thus, received from the state permission to operate a lucrative business and a valuable property in the license itself; the state, on the other hand, was provided with a distribution system for its liquor from which it derived a significant revenue. There was, then, a mutually beneficial relationship of substantial degree.

As for Mr. Justice Rehnquist's suggestion that the discrimination of a private enterprise which is the holder of a state-granted monoploy would be "state action," the theory apparently is that by making a monopolistic grant to a racial discriminator the state thereby deprives the victims of the discrimination of goods or services which they would otherwise have been able to obtain. But, again as noted by Douglas, Pennsylvania had a severely restricted state-wide quota system for the issuance of liquor licenses, and that license quota had been filled for several years. Therefore, at least theoretically, it was possible that, if a significant number of liquor licensees practiced racial discrimination, blacks in Pennsylvania could be effectively foreclosed from the opportunity to purchase liquor. Since the majority in *Moose Lodge* did not consider this a relevant argument, it would seem that only a state grant of an exclusive franchise to a single operator would amount to "state action" under Rehnquist's monopoly theory.[225]

The fact that the Court did not take advantage of these opportunities in *Moose Lodge* to declare the challenged conduct to be "state action," suggests either (1) that the expansion of the Equal Protection Clause

[225]*See* Gilmore v. Montgomery, 417 U.S. 556 (1974) (city's allocation of exclusive possession of its recreational facilities to all-white schools and groups violates equal protection).

which had taken place during the preceding decade has come to a halt[226] or (2) that privacy is becoming a more important constitutional value than equality. This second possible interpretation is strengthened if *Moose Lodge* is read in light of *Eisenstadt v. Baird*,[227] in which the Burger Court overturned a state ban on the distribution of contraceptives to the unmarried, and by the abortion decisions.[228] But whichever interpretation is correct, the practical consequences will be essentially the same: A wide range of more or less private racial discrimination is going to remain beyond the scope of the Fourteenth Amendment.

What the Burger Court seems to be saying—and this constitutes one of the real and major differences between the Burger Court and the Warren Court—is that further implementation of social policies against racial injustice must be accomplished through state and federal legislation. Pennsylvania, for example, could compel its liquor licensees to provide non-discriminatory service. Several other states have already done this.[229] Indeed, following the Burger Court's constitutional decision in *Moose Lodge*, the Pennsylvania Supreme Court found that Moose Lodge No. 107 was a "place of public accommodation" within the meaning of the Pennsylvania Human Relations Act, prohibiting racial discrimination in service in such public accommodations.[230] The initial reaction of the Moose Lodge was to close its facilities to all except members, rather than serve non-white guests.

More stringent legislation, however, prohibiting private social clubs from discriminating on the basis of race, for example in membership requirements, may encounter serious constitutional problems of privacy and freedom of association. Privacy is becoming a major legal and political concern,[231] and the Court might fashion a constitutional right to privacy broad enough to protect private social clubs from anti-discrimination statutes. An even stronger constitutional argument against such legislation, however, could be based upon the infringement of freedom of association.[232] While the Court's freedom of association cases

[226]*Cf.* 2 BLACK L. J. 195-254 (1972).

[227]405 U.S. 438 (1972).

[228]Roe v. Wade, 410 U.S. 113 (1973); Doe v. Bolton, 410 U.S. 179 (1973).

[229]*See, e.g.*, ILL. ANN. STAT. ch. 43, § 133 (1944); ME. REV. STAT. ANN. tit. 17, § 1301-A (1964); N.M. STAT. § 46-10-13.1 (Supp. 1971).

[230]Pennsylvania Human Relations Comm'n v. Moose Lodge No. 107, 294 A.2d 594 (Pa. 1972).

[231]*See* note 194 *supra*.

[232]*See generally* D. FELLMAN, THE CONSTITUTIONAL RIGHT OF ASSOCIATION (1963).

have involved political association,[233] the freedom of association is derived from the First Amendment's guarantees of freedom of speech and assembly and these guarantees protect non-political speech and non-political assembly. Having refused to draw a constitutional line between political and social speech,[234] the Court would probably have to refuse to recognize a distinction between political association and social association. Moreover, if private social clubs do have a constitutional right to discriminate on the basis of race, the denial of state benefits, such as the denial of liquor licenses, to such clubs because of their discrimination could arguably be construed as infringing upon a constitutional right by placing a state-imposed penalty upon its exerise.[235]

For a decade and a half, the Warren Court struggled to eradicate racial discrimination, both public and private, from American society. On its own, the Court was largely unsuccessful.[236] The significant advances in racial justice were the results of actions taken not by the Court but by the President and Congress: the sending of troops to Little Rock by President Eisenhower, the moral tone of President Kennedy's leadership, the legislative manipulation of President Johnson, and the Civil Rights Acts of 1964, 1965, and 1968. But it could be argued that none of these would have occurred had it not been for the Warren Court. While it was ineffectual in an immediate sense, the Warren Court did succeed by indirection. By forcing the issue of racial injustice, the Court required the President and Congress to make some kind of positive response.

But, today, in view of black demands for cultural autonomy, one must

[233]*E.g.*, United States v. Robel, 389 U.S. 258 (1967); Gibson v. Florida Legislative Investigation Committee, 372 U.S. 539 (1963); Shelton v. Tucker, 364 U.S. 479 (1960); NAACP. v. Alabama, 357 U.S. 449 (1958).

[234]Stanley v. Georgia, 394 U.S. 557 (1969).

[235]*See* Sherbert v. Verner, 374 U.S. 398 (1962). Interestingly, Justices Brennan and Marshall, who dissented in *Moose Lodge*, subsequently argued in California v. La Rue, 409 U.S. 109, 123 (1972) (dissenting opinions), that California regulations prohibiting nude dancing in bars, insofar as those regulations affected some non-obscene entertainment within the limits of protected free expression, were an unconstitutional condition attached to the grant of a liquor license. Would the Justices take the same attitude toward a requirement that a liquor licensee, such as a private club, abstain from discrimination on the basis of race or sex? Could such a license applicant claim a First Amendment right to freedom of association? *But see* Gilmore v. Montgomery, 417 U.S. 556 (1974).

[236]*See generally* H. RODGERS, JR., & C. BULLOCK, LAW AND SOCIAL CHANGE: CIVIL RIGHTS LAWS AND THEIR CONSEQUENCES (1972); S. WASBY, THE IMPACT OF THE UNITED STATES SUPREME COURT 169-186 (1970); R. BARDOLPH, *supra* note 4, at 311-537 (1970).

ask, as Professor Bickel asked,[237] whether the desegregation decisions were really based upon a viable, just principle. Given the assimilationist premise of *Brown*, given the social psychological statistics on which it was based, would the government be justified in forcing blacks to attend integrated schools, even if the majority of blacks in a particular community might prefer to maintain, operate, and attend their own schools? Was the Warren Court's concern for the hearts and minds of black children an example of high idealism? Or was it a case of white patronization? Can a black child not secure a decent education lest he sit next to a white? Under the rationale of *Brown*, are all-black dorms lawful? If so, what about all-white classes? And, if that, why not all-black schools? Are *Brown* and its progeny relevant to the racial problems of the '70's? Is the value of a racially unified society still important? Or will the principle that race is never a valid classification prove unsatisfactory, even inoperative, in an era of increasing ethnic consciousness?

In its efforts to eliminate inequality, economic as well as racial, the Warren Court, particularly in its last years, seemed to push the value of equality beyond all reasonable limits. Equality was the Court's primary value, a concern for discrimination its chief characteristic. But, towards the end, equality became a value unto itself, superior to all other values under all circumstances. Just as an earlier Court had subordinated all other values to that of private property, so too the Warren Court in its concern for equality became insensitive to the legitimate claims of other, competing values. But constitutional history has taught that that sort of judicial decision-making is not, in the long run, the best way for the Court to behave.

What began as a simple crusade to rectify an admitted social injustice, racial segregation in the South, became an enormously complex legal, political, and social problem. By the early 1970s, many Americans had come to feel, rightly or wrongly, that *Brown* and its progeny had gotten out of hand.[238] Constitutional law being a reflection of time, place, and circumstance, this mood began to appear on the Supreme Court. There has been no manifest intention on the part of the Burger Court to reverse *Brown*. It would be difficult indeed to argue that a Court which has insisted upon immediate school desegregation,[239] approved busing,[240] and refused to allow a city to withdraw from a county school district,

[237]Bickel, *supra* note 87; A. BICKEL, *supra* note 104, at ch. 4.

[238]*See, e.g.*, Glazer, *supra* note 51.

[239]Alexander v. Holmes, 396 U.S. 19 (1969).

[240]Swann v. Charlotte-Mecklenburg Board of Education, 402 U.S. 1 (1971).

even though for non-racial reasons, because it would inhibit desegregation,[241] has any intention of retreating from *Brown*.[242] But, on the other
hand, decisions such as *Milliken, Moose Lodge,* and *Rodriguez* are
examples of a judicial desire to transfer the burden for solving America's
racial problems from constitutional adjudication to the political process.
They evince a determination to draw the line, to say "This far and no
farther," to refuse to continue extending the logic of *Brown ad infinitum.*

[241]Wright v. Emporia, 407 U.S. 451 (1972).
[242]*But see* note 226 *supra.*

Chapter 3
The New Math

The Burger Court's respect for and confidence in the traditional political processes has also been evident in its handling of the Warren Court's precedents relating to the apportionment of electoral districts. Here again, however, there has been no manifest abandonment of Warren Court doctrine but a more flexible application of standards.

For purposes of analytic clarity, the Supreme Court's handling of the issue of legislative apportionment can best be discussed historically, and that history may be divided into three periods.[1] The first of these periods, while difficult to specify its beginning, terminated with the decision in *Baker v. Carr*.[2] The second extended from *Baker* to the landmark decisions of 1964.[3] The third period commenced with those decisions but outlived the Warren Court, carrying over into the 1970's to confront a somewhat different Court.[4]

[1]The literature on the Court and reapportionment is voluminous. Among the better studies are: R. DIXON, DEMOCRATIC REPRESENTATION: REAPPORTIONMENT IN LAW AND POLITICS (1968); G. BAKER, THE REAPPORTIONMENT REVOLUTION: REPRESENTATION, POLITICAL POWER AND THE SUPREME COURT (1967); R. McKAY, REAPPORTIONMENT: THE LAW AND POLITICS OF EQUAL REPRESENTATION (1965); M. SHAPIRO, LAW AND POLITICS IN THE SUPREME COURT ch. 5 (1964); Dixon, *The Warren Court Crusade for the Holy Grail of "One Man, One Vote,"*1969 SUP. CT. REV. 219; Irwin, *Representation and Election: The Reapportionment Cases in Retrospect*, 67 MICH. L. REV. 729 (1969); McKay, *Reapportionment: Success Story of the Warren Court*, 67 MICH. L. REV. 223 (1968); McKay, *Reapportionment and Local Government*, 36 GEO. WASH. L. REV. 713 (1968); McKay, *Court, Congress, and Reapportionment*, 63 MICH. L. REV. 255 (1964); Auerbach, *The Reapportionment Cases: One Person, One Vote—One Vote, One Value*, 1964 SUP. CT. REV. 1; McKay, *Political Thickets and Crazy Quilts: Reapportionment and Equal Protection*, 61 MICH. L. REV. 645 (1963); McKay, *The Federal Analogy And State Apportionment Standards*, 38 NOTRE D. LAW. 487 (1963); Neal, *Baker v. Carr: Politics in Search of Law*, 1962 SUP. CT. REV. 252.

[2]369 U.S. 186 (1962).

[3]Wesberry v. Sanders, 376 U.S. 1 (1964); Reynolds v. Sims, 377 U.S. 533 (1964); Lucas v. Forty-fourth General Assembly of Colorado, 377 U.S. 713 (1964).

[4]*See, e.g.*, Hadley v. Junior College District of Metropolitan Kansas City, 397 U.S. 50 (1970); Gordon v. Lance, 403 U.S. 1 (1971); Whitcomb v. Chavis, 403 U.S. 124 (1971); Abate v. Mundt, 403 U.S. 182 (1971); Mahan v. Howell, 410 U.S. 315 (1973).

The first era of the apportionment litigation was inextricably bound up with the "political question" doctrine.[5] During this period, the paramount issue was the justiciability of apportionment cases, and the Court's approach to that problem was classically demonstrated by Mr. Justice Frankfurter's opinion in *Colegrove v. Green.*[6] In *Colegrove*, three Illinois voters brought suit to restrain the conducting of the forthcoming Illinois congressional elections under the then existing apportionment, an apportionment which had been drawn in 1901 and had remained unchanged for forty-five years. Mr. Justice Frankfurter dismissed the suit on several grounds. First, the legal merits of the appellants' resort to a federal apportionment statute had already been settled, adversely to the appellants' case, in *Wood v. Broom.*[7] Second, the Court had no power to grant equitable relief in such a matter. "The appellants," wrote Frankfurter, "ask of this Court what is beyond its competence to grant . . . No court can affirmatively re-map [congressional] districts . . . At best [it] could only declare the existing electoral system invalid..."[8] The remedy in such a case, Justice Frankfurter intimated, lay with the political rather than the judicial process. Third, the appellants lacked standing to raise the issue. This was not, according to Frankfurter, an action brought to recover damages suffered by virtue of discrimination which set the appellants apart from other citizens. Rather, he observed, "the basis for the suit is not a private wrong, but a wrong suffered by Illinois as a polity."[9] Fourth, and most importantly, the suit did not present a justiciable case and controversy. Instead, it was a "political question."

In Frankfurter's opinion, *Colegrove* presented a "political question" for at least three different reasons. The Court could afford no remedy in the matter. The issue involved party contests. And, finally, the matter was already committed to Congress by sections two, four and five of Article I of the Constitution.

Because of the criticism, much of it based upon misinterpretation, which Frankfurter's opinion in *Colegrove* received in the succeeding generation, it is important to emphasize what he did not say in this opinion. He did not argue that the Court might never interfere with the electoral process. In the face of the Fifteenth Amendment, such a contention would have been fatuous. Neither did he assert that Congress

[5] *See* ch. I *supra* at pp. 20-23.
[6] 328 U.S. 549 (1946).
[7] 287 U.S. 1 (1932).
[8] 328 U.S. at 552-553.
[9] *Id.* at 552.

had exclusive control over congressional elections. Nor did he say that a voter would never have standing, *qua* voter, to sue. Rather, the key to the opinion lay in its last paragraph in which Mr. Justice Frankfurter called for extreme judicial restraint in this area and warned the Court against entering "the political thicket."[10] Given the absence of judicially manageable standards in this area, Frankfurter cautioned, the issue of apportionment was simply one insusceptible of judicial resolution.

Mr. Justice Black, joined by two others, dissented on the grounds that the case was justiciable in that it presented an equal protection claim.[11] The petitioners had, in Black's view, been injured and as such had standing to sue. It was but a hollow mockery, he thought, for Mr. Justice Frankfurter to tell the appellants to rely upon the political process in a malapportioned state. Since there was no other remedy open to a citizen deprived of his right to vote, the appellants, Black argued, should have been granted the judicial relief which they requested, and he went on to note that the only relief which they sought was an injunction restraining the forthcoming election. Justice Frankfurter's fears were groundless, Justice Black contended; no judicial supervision of elections was asked for. The appellants sought only that state officials be enjoined from enforcing an inequitable state apportionment law.

Only seven Justices presided in *Colegrove*, and Mr. Justice Frankfurter's holding on the justiciability of apportionment cases was acceptable to only three of the four members of the majority. Mr. Justice Rutledge, who provided the decisive fourth vote, assumed the case to be justiciable but concurred in the dismissal of the appeal on the grounds of a lack of power on the part of the Court to grant a remedy. The Court should decline jurisdiction, as Rutledge saw it, because the case was of "so delicate a character."[12] In one of his few moments of prophetic vision, Justice Rutledge observed, "The right here is not absolute. And the cure sought may be worse than the disease."[13]

Over the course of the following years, however, the Court tacitly acquiesced in Justice Frankfurter's opinion as to the justiciability of apportionment cases. In the fourteen years after *Colegrove*, thirteen different apportionment suits were dismissed *per curiam* on the basis of *Colegrove*.[14]

[10]*Id*. at 556.
[11]*Id*. at 566.
[12]*Id*. at 565.
[13]*Id*. at 566.
[14]*See* MacDougall v. Green, 335 U.S. 281 (1948), South v. Peters, 399 U.S. 276 (1950), and cases discussed and distinguished in Baker v. Carr, 369 U.S. 186, 208-237 (1962).

But in 1960 the Court declared an Alabama statute redrawing the boundary lines of the city of Tuskeegee to be unconstitutional, because it was a "racial gerrymander." The Alabama state legislature had redrawn Tuskeegee in such a way as to exclude all but a small fraction of the black residents. These residents then brought suit to enjoin the conducting of city elections under this apportionment, contending that they had been deprived of their right to vote in violation of the Fifteenth Amendment. In *Gomillion v. Lightfoot*, the Court sustained their claim.[15] Speaking for the Court, none other than the author of *Colegrove v. Green*, Mr. Justice Frankfurter himself, distinguished the case from *Colegrove* on two different grounds. First, in this case the voters had been entirely deprived of their right to vote by an affirmative state action, whereas in *Colegrove* the petitioners had merely had their vote diluted by inaction on the part of the state. Second, the Alabama legislature had isolated a racial minority for discriminatory purposes,[16] whereas in *Colegrove* and the subsequent apportionment appeals race had had no bearing. The case, thus, was justiciable. Despite Justice Frankfurter's qualifications, however, *Gomillion* opened the door to a reconsideration of the *Colegrove* doctrine concerning the justiciability of legislative apportionment cases.

Baker v. Carr was the vehicle which, two years after *Gomillion*, announced a new trend in the Supreme Court's approach to decision-making in apportionment cases.[17] The suit challenged the apportionment of the lower house of the Tennessee state legislature. Speaking for the majority of the Court, Mr. Justice Brennan held:

> 1. The Court had jurisdiction, because the "complaint sets forth a case arising under the Constitution, the subject matter is within the federal judicial power...;"[18]
> 2. *Colegrove* notwithstanding, the appellants had standing, because the facts showed that they had been disadvantaged as individuals; and
> 3. the suit was justiciable, because it did not fall within the purview of the "political question" doctrine.

The central problem in *Baker* was, of course, justiciability. In support of his conclusion that the case did not present a political question, Justice Brennan argued that political question cases concerned only the relation-

[15] 364 U.S. 339 (1960).

[16] By the time of the *Gomillion* decision, it had become clear that Brown v. Board of Education, 347 U.S. 483 (1954), and its progeny stood for the principle that race was an invidious and inherently suspect classification.

[17] 369 U.S. 186 (1962). *See generally* McCloskey, *The Reapportionment Case,* 76 HARV. L. REV. 54 (1962); Neal, *supra* note 1.

[18] *Id.* at 200.

ship between the Court and the coordinate branches of the federal government. It did not affect the federal judiciary's relations with the states.

> The non-justiciability of a political question is primarily a function of the separation of powers.[19]

Not all separation of powers cases presented political questions. But all political question cases involved questions of the separation of powers. To buttress this argument, Brennan listed a number of areas of litigation in which, he contended, political questions had always been considered to arise:

1. foreign relations[20]
2. dates of duration of hostilities[21]
3. status of the Indian tribes[22]
4. guaranty clause cases.[23]

But, in the last instance, Brennan was quick to point out that Guaranty Clause cases were considered to present political questions, not because they concerned the validity of state governmental arrangements, but because they were constitutionally committed to another branch of the federal government. Cases arising in these areas were, for Brennan, political questions; because they had been specifically assigned by the Constitution to another branch of the federal government; or because, if the Court were to consider such cases, there existed the possibility of embarrassment to the United States government from conflicting pronouncements by different branches; or because judicial resolution of such a problem would involve a lack of due respect for a coordinate branch of the government; or because judicially discoverable and manageable standards were lacking.[24] *Baker*, therefore, was justiciable since none of these elements was present.

[19]*Id.* at 210.
[20]*Id.* at 211-213, *citing* Oetjen v. Central Leather Co., 246 U.S. 297 (1918), *and* Doe v. Braden, 16 How. 636 (1853).
[21]*Id.* at 213-214, *citing* Commercial Trust Co. v. Miller, 262 U.S. 51 (1923), *and* Martin v. Mott, 12 Wheat. 19 (1827).
[22]*Id.* at 215-218, *citing* United States v. Holliday, 3 Wall. 407 (1866).
[23]*Id.* at 218-226, *citing* Luther v. Borden, 7 How. 1 (1849).
[24]Under Brennan's analysis in *Baker* it would seem that the Warren Court should have declined to hear Powell v. McCormack, 395 U.S. 486 (1969) (denying Congress power to exclude a member-elect), on the grounds that it presented a political question. What *Powell* demonstrates, of course, is the fatuousness of attempts such as Brennan's to reduce the

One might have thought that the Court lacked manageable standards to apply to such a case, but Brennan denied this. The case was brought under the Equal Protection Clause of the Fourteenth Amendment whose standards were, he claimed, well-developed and familiar. But what were those standards? Against what standard was the districting compared, so that the majority might conclude that votes were "debased?"[25] The Court held that apportionment in Tennessee was "arbitrary and capricious."[26] But arbitrary and capricious relative to what? This sort of language implies some kind of standard by which legislative apportionments may be measured. But, despite this implication, and despite Brennan's statement that the standards were well-developed and familiar, the majority in *Baker* failed to indicate what those standards were.[27] Instead, having held the suit to be justiciable, the appellants to have standing, and the federal courts to have jurisdiction in such cases, the Court then remanded the suit to the federal district court for further proceedings.

This cavalier approach occasioned a vigorous concurrence from Mr. Justice Clark, who felt that the Court should itself have granted the appellants judicial relief. Unlike Brennan, Clark thus faced the issue of standards. For Clark, the constitutional standard against which apportionments should be measured was rationality. If an apportionment were irrational, it was unconstitutional, and Clark could discern no rational policy behind Tennessee's apportionment, characterizing it as "a crazy quilt" of discrimination.[28] But what about deliberately contrived malapportionment? Wouldn't that be rational? And if so, would it not meet Clark's standard and, thus, be constitutional?

Baker also provoked some equally vigorous (bitter?) dissents; so vigorous in fact that Mr. Justice Stewart felt it necessary to pen a separate concurrence in an effort simply to calm the troubled waters. Mr. Justice Harlan took the position that no constitutional right had been violated. Inequality, he pointed out, is not precluded by the Fourteenth Amendment—only inequality based upon impermissible standards such as race.

political question doctrine to some sort of functional categories. *See generally The Supreme Court, 1968 Term*, 83 HARV. L. REV. 7, 63-68 (1969).

[25]369 U.S. at 188, 194. *See also* McCloskey, *supra* note 17.

[26]*Id.* at 226.

[27]Brennan's strongest point for holding that *Baker* was justiciable was not his argument that it did not present a political question. Rather, his best support was to rely upon precedent and to point out, as he eventually did at the end of this section of his opinion, that *Colegrove* was, in fact, four-to-three in favor of the view that apportionment cases were justiciable.

[28]369 U.S. at 254.

In answer to Justice Clark, Harlan contended that there might be any number of rational bases for the Tennessee apportionment scheme. The most powerful dissent, however, indeed the most powerful opinion in the entire case was that of Mr. Justice Frankfurter. He dissented on the grounds that *Baker* presented a Guaranty Clause case "masquerading" as an equal protection claim and, therefore, was non-justiciable. In discussing justiciability, Frankfurter sought to avoid judicial intervention into areas historically committed to other governmental agencies. But, unlike Brennan, he would have included in this category cases involving the political institutions of the states. Whereas Brennan was concerned with the separation of powers, Frankfurter, no less concerned with preservation of that separation than Brennan, was also concerned for federalism. Alone among all of the Justices, Frankfurter addressed himself to the implied question of institutional ability: What functions can the Supreme Court perform, and which can it perform well? He would have avoided political controversy in order to harbor the Court's prestige which is the ultimate base of its limited power. Because apportionment cases, of necessity, involve the allocation of raw political power, Frankfurter would have avoided them. In *Baker*, only he faced the theoretical problem of defining "republican government," and he concluded that it was a problem, like slavery,[29] which ultimately was insusceptible of judicial resolution.

In spite of the nearly wholesale reversal of *Colegrove* in approach if not in fact, *Baker* failed to do two very important things. First, it did not indicate what standards were to be applied in examining the constitutional validity of a challenged legislative apportionment; nor, second, did it specify what forms of relief might be granted by a lower federal court if it found that, in fact, a challenged apportionment was unconstitutional. The lower courts were simply cut adrift, told that they could, indeed should, hear apportionment suits but not told what they were to do with them after they had heard them. The second period of the Court's handling of apportionment cases, then, can be seen as one in which the Warren Court was attempting to answer these questions, especially the first.

This second period commenced as soon as the first had ended. The term following *Baker*, the Court considered *Gray v. Sanders*.[30] In *Gray*, the Court, speaking through Mr. Justice Douglas, rejected the so-called

---

[29]*See* Dred Scott v. Sandford, 19 How. 393 (1857).
[30]372 U.S. 368 (1963).

"federal analogy" in striking down the Georgia County Unit System, an electoral scheme modelled on the federal electoral college by which Georgia elected its Governor. The Court held that, while the electoral college was justified by historical compromise, that compromise had in no way implied the acceptability of a similar system in the states. Although *Gray* involved only the weighting of votes in statewide elections, it was significantly and prophetically the initial expression of the phrase "one man, one vote." Voters, held Douglas, could not constitutionally be classified on the basis of residence. Rather, it was the requirement of the Equal Protection Clause that, once the geographic unit was chosen, all who participated must be given an equal vote. In an effort to substantiate this conclusion, Justice Douglas relied upon not only the Fourteenth, Fifteenth, Seventeenth, and Nineteenth Amendments to the Constitution but also the Preamble, the Declaration of Independence, and the Gettysburg Address, providing the American public with yet one more example of his "everything-but-the-kitchen-sink" school of jurisprudence.[31]

The following year, Georgia was again before the Supreme Court, defending in a challenge to the apportionment of its congressional districts. In *Wesberry v. Sanders* that congressional districting was held to grossly discriminate against certain voters and to contravene sections two and four of Article I.[32] Although *Wesberry* was decided under Article I, rather than under the Equal Protection Clause, it was becoming apparent that equality of population was evolving as the constitutional standard for apportionment cases.

For the majority in *Wesberry*, the basic principle of justice in a republican regime is equality of election. But, despite Mr. Justice Black's historical assertions, were the Framers really concerned with mere equality?[33] In other words, isn't the fundamental problem in the apportionment cases to understand the elements of good government? Representation undoubtedly is a part of good government. But it is only a part. As Mr. Justice Harlan demonstrated in his *Wesberry* dissent, the Framers were not concerned with the intrinsic right of popular representation.[34] Rather, they viewed representation, *and a mixed system of*

[31]*See also* Griswold v. Connecticut, 381 U.S. 479 (1965).
[32]376 U.S. 1 (1964).
[33]Concerning Mr. Justice Black's rather radical revision of the American past,. see Kelly, *Clio and the Court: An Illicit Love Affair,* 1965 SUP. CT. REV. 119. *See generally* C. MILLER, THE SUPREME COURT AND THE USES OF HISTORY ch. VII (1969).
[34]376 U.S. at 24-42.

representation, as a means conducive to the end of good governent and not as an end of itself.[35]

The central problem of all political organization is the regulation of conflict. A legislature is merely a particular type of political institution for the adjustment of societal conflict. This task of conflict adjustment is performed through the medium of representation. Within itself the legislature reflects the various cleavages within the larger society. The legislature then attempts to modulate these divisions through legislation. If this legislation is to be a successful mechanism for conflict resolution, the legislature must fairly accurately reflect the conflicts, at least the major conflicts, within society. If it does, we say it is representative. But this raises the question of what conflicts it is that the legislature is supposed to reflect. What is it, in other words, that a legislature should represent? Individuals or interests? Since the interests which give rise to political conflicts—wealth, intellectual ability, race, religious conviction—are unevenly distributed throughout society, if individuals are equally represented, interests cannot be given equal representation.[36]

One, of course, may ask what difference it makes. Why should interests be represented? The answer is to be found in *Federalist Number 10* and in Madison's fear of the tyranny of the majority. Unless certain interests are given extra numbers in the legislature, they may be unjustly treated by the legislative majority.[37] For example, let us take a Protestant minority in a Catholic country. History has shown that, at least in our hypothetical country, Catholic majorities have from time to time had a tendency to deal harshly, even unjustly, with Protestant minorities. Would it be unfair, therefore, in order to give the Protestants at least some protection, to allocate one-third of the seats in the upper house of

[35]See THE FEDERALIST Nos. 10, 14, 35, 39, 49, 52, 54, 56, 57, 63, and 84. *See also* G. WOOD, THE CREATION OF THE AMERICAN REPUBLIC, 1776-1787, chs. I, II, V, VI, XI, XIII, XV (1969); P. EIDELBERG, THE PHILOSOPHY OF THE AMERICAN CONSTITUTION chs. 4-8 (1968).

[36]See R. DAHL, PLURALIST DEMOCRACY IN THE UNITED STATES: CONFLICT AND CONSENT (1967); M. SHAPIRO (ed.), THE SUPREME COURT AND CONSTITUTIONAL RIGHTS at 80-83 (1967); R. DAHL, A PREFACE TO DEMOCRATIC THEORY (1956).

[37]A different, but no less interesting, defense of the functional representation proposal has emerged from the contemporary American Left. To wit:

The *Observer* suggests that Texas cut the cant about legislators representing people and redistrict the Senate according to special interests. That way the oil industry, for example, will have only one senator, rather than a piece of 15 or 20 senators. THE TEXAS OBSERVER, June 18, 1971, at 1.

the legislature to them, even though they compromise only ten percent of the total population, and perhaps to require that any bill affecting religion be passed by a two-thirds majority?

But there are problems with functional representation, as this concept is called. If a minority interest is given special weight what is to prevent it from using its added power unjustly toward the majority? If a minority has enough power to prevent a majority from acting unjustly, it will by definition have enough representation to prevent the majority from acting justly. When the philosophic question of what, interests or individuals, is to be represented is boiled down to a practical political problem, it comes out something like this: Is it possible to protect certain minorities by giving them a larger share of representatives in the legislature than they would be entitled to simply by their numbers, without at the same time creating a potential injustice either to other minorities or to the majority?[38]

It was in an effort to solve this problem that the Framers hit upon the idea of bicameralism.[39] To be sure, there are practical, political reasons for the existence of two houses in the Congress, but those two houses were also the product of philosophic principle. The reasons for the adoption of bicameralism in America are not only historical but also rational. In attempting to provide both representation of individuals and of interests, the Framers created two co-equal legislative houses. Election to each would have different bases. The popular majority would be represented in one house; interests would be represented in the other. The Senate represents an effort on the part of the Framers (and, in all honesty, a not entirely successful effort, but a good faith effort nonetheless) to provide for interest articulation and representation.

It may seem somewhat ludicrous today, but in the formative era it was generally assumed that the most dynamic institution in the federal government, the driving force within the system, would be the House of Representatives.[40] The House would be popularly elected. It would

---

[38]Yet another practical problem of the first order is how does one recognize those minorities which should be given additional representation. How are they to be distinguished from other minorities? Clearly not all minorities can be given additional representative strength. For a more detailed discussion of these and other problems with functional representation, see R. DAHL, PLURALIST DEMOCRACY IN THE UNITED STATES at ch. 5; T. LOWI, THE END OF LIBERALISM 53-54 (1969).

[39]See G. WOOD, supra note 35; P. EIDELBERG, supra note 35; R. DAHL, supra note 38, at 109-125. See generally Rae, Political Democracy as a Property of Political Institutions, 65 AM. POL. SCI. REV. 111, 116 & n. 15 (1971).

[40]THE FEDERALIST Nos. 52-61, 66.

represent people as individuals. It would represent the popular majority; and as such it would be that branch which was most subject to popular passion, to sudden changes of public opinion; and it would be the House which would be most dangerous to the rights of minorities.

Like Acton, the Framers believed very strongly in the corrupting tendencies of power. Their fear of unchecked power led them to construct a system in which every agency of government would function so as to constrain every other. It followed that the House of Representatives, like every other branch of the government, must be restricted in its exercise of power. It would be restricted by the Constitution, by the President, by the Supreme Court, and very importantly by the Senate. Since the House would be the most likely to commit injustices upon minorities, the Senate was to be constituted in such a manner as to overrepresent minority interests and, thus, to check the House's tendency to deal ignorantly or unjustly with minority rights.

But, as already noted, the Senate also represents a not particularly successful effort to institutionalize interest representation in the national legislature. What happened to the Framers' idea of representing interests? Many things, but most crucially the question of the composition of the Senate, originally proposed as an abstract philosophic problem of the overrepresentation of special class or economic interests, became inextricably linked with the far more mundane but more immediate problem of placating the smaller states. States were and are far too heterogenous for state residence to serve as a viable indicator of a single, predominant interest of many, cumulative interests. Once this concession was made to the smaller states, the Senate's potential to serve as a functionally representative body was irreparably undermined.

However, while the Senate never in practice functioned as a functionally representative body, might not bicameral legislatures with each house apportioned on a different basis work fairly well within state legislatures? Given American housing patterns, the single family dwelling, the societal tendency to settle in economically and ethnically homogenous enclaves, doesn't geography, at the sub-state level, serve as a rough indicator of other interests? In view of Americans' tendency to segregate themselves not only by race but also by age and income, don't neighborhoods suggest, not absolutely accurately but not absolutely inaccurately either, the cumulative interests of their residents?[41] Might

[41]*See* P. BACHRACH & M. BARATZ, POWER & POVERTY: THEORY & PRACTICE (1970); W. CONNOLLY (ed.), THE BIAS OF PLURALISM (1969); R. WARREN (ed.), POLITICS AND THE GHETTOS (1969); R. WOOD, SUBURBIA: ITS

not residence serve as an admittedly imprecise but not altogether irrelevant basis for the apportionment of one house of a state legislature to insure interest representation?

Whether it may or may not in reality, it may not in constitutional law. For it was this very question which Mr. Chief Justice Warren dismissed out of hand in *Reynolds v. Sims*.[42] In *Reynolds*, the Chief Justice, applying the "one man, one vote" principle, ruled that both houses of a bicameral state legislature must be apportioned on a population basis. Warren, however, unlike Black in *Wesberry*, sought to justify this standard by an appeal to political philosophy rather than to history. Warren did, initially, turn to history in order to dispose of the federal analogy. He concluded that historically the fundamental principle of representation in America had been equal representation for equal numbers of citizens. The federal analogy was inapposite, the Chief Justice argued, because the subdivisions of the states, i.e., the counties, were never sovereign entities like the states themselves. But, how many states ever were sovereign entities?[43] The fragility of this argument necessitated Warren's shift to political philosophy. According to Chief Justice Warren, the proper judicial focus is upon individual rights.[44] By thus focusing upon the individual, Warren excluded from his consideration the problem of the ends of representation. All concerns foreign to individual representation became, at best, mere qualifications of the problem. Good government, therefore, and the institutional elements necessary to its realization were subordinated to the problem of representation, rather than vice versa.

Since the individual was seen as the fundamental concern of representative government, the Chief Justice was able to distinguish between individuals and interests. But what is it, then, about individuals which is to be represented? Warren ignored this problem.

> Legislators represent people, not trees or acres. Legislators are elected by voters, not farms or cities or economic interests. As long as ours is a representative form of government, and our legislatures are those instruments of government elected

PEOPLE AND THEIR POLITICS (1958); Bell, *A New Suburban Politics*, 47 SOC. FORCES 280 (1969); Zikmund, *A Comparison of Political Attitude and Activity Patterns in Central Cities and Suburbs*, 31 PUB. OP. Q. 69 (1967); Wirt, *The Political Sociology of American Suburbia*, 27 J. POL. 647 (1965). *See also* note 37 *supra*.

[42] 377 U.S. 533 (1964).

[43] Answer: Fourteen or fifteen, depending upon how one treats the Bear Flag Republic of California.

[44] 377 U.S. at 567.

directly by and directly representative of the people, the right to elect legislators in a free and unimpaired fashion is a bedrock of our political system.[45]

But how can one know a man politically, divorced from his interests? The politically naked man, the individual *qua* individual, is virtually unrepresentable. It is only as he puts on his political clothes, i.e., his interests, that his representative can recognize him.

For Warren, however, democracy, ideally, would be directly participatory. Representative government is merely self-government through the medium of representation. Wrote Warren:

> ... (E)ach and every citizen has an inalienable right to full and effective participation in the political processes of his State's legislative bodies. Most citizens can achieve this participation only as qualified voters through the election of legislators to represent them. Full and effective participation by all citizens in state government requires, therefore, that each citizen have an equally effective voice in the election of members of his state legislature.[46]

Representative government in this very Rousseauean concept is an imperfect substitute for ideal government, i.e., direct, participatory, popular democracy. Given this minimal, almost disparaging concept of representative government, it was not difficult for the Chief Justice to conclude voting must always be equal and unweighted. But the Burkean concept of the representative function was entirely missing from Warren's majority opinion,[47] and this constitutes a fundamental difference between the Court's majority in *Reynolds* and the Founding Fathers. For the Court, representative government is merely a practical solution to a practical problem. For the Framers, it was a means to an end—good government.[48]

Having justified to his own satisfaction the one man, one vote standard, Mr. Chief Justice Warren then applied his standard to both houses of a bicameral state legislature. The Constitution, according to the Chief Justice, required that both houses be apportioned on a population

[45]*Id.* at 562. *Cf.* note 37 *supra*.
[46]*Id.* at 565.
[47]*But see* Burke, *Speech to the Electors of Bristol*, in LEGISLATIVE POLITICS U.S.A. 150 (T. Lowi ed. 1962).
[48]*See* G. WOOD, *supra* note 35, at 553-562; P. EIDELBERG, *supra* note 35, at chs. 5, 7, & 8.

Perhaps the most disingenuous portion of Mr. Chief Justice' Warren's *Reynolds* opinion was his effort to expropriate the Founding Fathers with a little juggling in the footnotes. Thus, the text of the opinion spoke of "the Founding Fathers", but the notes cited Thomas Jefferson, who, whatever else might be said about him, can hardly be regarded as one of the Constitution's framers. *See* 377 U.S. 533, 573 & n. 53.

basis only, because "ours is a representative form of government."[49] But this begs the crucial question. To be sure, we have a representative form of government. But what is it that our form of government was designed to represent? Chief Justice Warren ignored the fact that in the history of political thought there have been several theories of representation, some quite divergent from his own.

Warren's approach also begged the question of why, if numbers are to be the only standard, an upper house is necessary at all. The Chief Justice spoke of the upper house as providing mature reflection, but this raises the problem of what the purpose of a legislature is. With the constitutional spotlight focused solely on the individual voter rather than the group dynamics of American politics,[50] there is no reason for treating an individual differently in one house than in the other. Thus, despite Warren's protestations about varying the lengths of terms and the sizes of districts between the two houses, bicameralism, under the *Reynolds* approach, becomes a sort of political appendicitis rather than an instrument for tempering majoritarianism with the requirements of a broader consensus. But, for the authors of *The Federalist*, the Senate was more than an historical accident; it was organized in the way it was in order to provide the interest representation necessary to a good regime.[51]

Some might respond that, whatever the Framers' ideas regarding the Senate, they are irrelevant to the composition of the upper houses of state legislative chambers. But, if the concept of a bicameral legislature incorporating a mixed system of representation was wise at the national level, where due to geographic apportionment it has not in fact worked, how much wiser would it be at the state level, where due to society's housing patterns it would have a chance to work reasonably well?[52] (Lest I am criticized for ignoring a logical hiatus, let me state clearly that I recognize the assumption being here made. What is wise should be

[49]377 U.S. at 562.

[50]*See* D. TRUMAN, THE GOVERNMENTAL PROCESS (1951); A. HOLTZMAN, INTEREST GROUPS AND LOBBYING (1966); F. MUNGER & D. PRICE (eds.), READINGS IN POLITICAL PARTIES AND PRESSURE GROUPS (1964); R. BAUER, I. POOL, & A. DEXTER, AMERICAN BUSINESS AND PUBLIC POLICY (1963); Weinstein, *The Group Approach: Arthur F. Bentley*, in ESSAYS ON THE SCIENTIFIC STUDY OF POLITICS (H. Storing ed. 1962). *But cf.* T. LOWI, *supra* note 38; W. Connolly, *supra* note 41; Rothman, *Systematic Political Theory*, 54 AM. POL. SCI. REV. 15 (1960).

[51]*See* note 48 *supra*; *cf.* G. BAKER, *supra* note 1, at 19. *See generally* Rae, *supra* note 39.

[52]*See* note 37 *supra*; *cf.* Reynolds v. Sims, 377 U.S. 533, 573.

constitutional. On the other hand, what is unwise need not necessarily be unconstitutional.)[53] Surely most of the drafters of state constitutions did not think in these terms when they established bicameral legislatures with senates elected on a geographic basis. Rather, they most likely adopted the pattern of the national Congress in the tacit belief that there was something good to be said for it. And there was! Anyone familiar with Merton's distinction between latent and manifest functions must realize that an institution can serve other and more important purposes than those for which it was consciously designed.[54] That those men who created state legislatures did not explicitly recognize the importance of functional representation is no reason for condemning the latent good sense of their product.

Dissenting in *Reynolds*, Mr. Justice Harlan accused the Court of reducing people to ciphers. But, in the main, Harlan's dissent was occasioned by a much different view of the Court and its appropriate function in the American political system than that which motivated the majority.

> These decisions give support to a current mistaken view of the Constitution and the constitutional function of this Court. This view, in a nutshell, is that every major social ill in this country can find its cure in some constitutional "principle," and that this Court should "take the lead" in promoting reform when other branches of government fail to act. The Constitution is not a panacea for every blot upon the public welfare, nor should this Court, ordained as a judicial body, be thought of as a general haven for reform movements.[55]

Like Mr. Justice Holmes before him, Justice Harlan was unwilling to countenance the Court's acceptance of a role as "necessary corrective" to the "errors," active or passive, of the democratic process.[56]

Mr. Chief Justice Warren was directly met on his own grounds by Mr. Justice Stewart in *Lucas v. Forty-Fourth General Assembly of Colorado*.[57] In *Lucas*, the voters of Colorado had, in 1962, by a margin of greater

[53]Note also that to favor interest representation is not necessarily to defend the particular malapportionment present in *Reynolds*. But the wisdom of the particular apportionment adopted was not—or at least should not have been—the appropriate question in *Reynolds*. The question before the Court was whether it was constitutionally permissible to apportion one house of a bicameral state legislature on some basis other than straight population.

[54]R. MERTON, SOCIAL THEORY AND SOCIAL STRUCTURE 61-66 (1957). *See also* Rae, *supra* note 39.

[55]377 U.S. at 624-625.

[56]*See, e.g.*, Lochner v. New York, 198 U.S. 45, 75 (1905) (Holmes, J., dissenting).

[57]377 U.S. 713 (1964).

than two-to-one, rejected a plan which would have apportioned seats in both houses of the state legislature on a population basis, and by a margin of roughly two-to-one the same voters had approved an apportionment plan whereby the lower house was apportioned on a population basis and the upper house was to be apportioned on a complex formula which took into consideration a number of factors among which was population. In effect, then, the voters of Colorado had in a referendum indicated *by a landslide* that they did not wish to apportion their legislature on the basis which *Reynolds*, two years later, was to hold that they must.

On the same day it decided *Reynolds*, the Warren Court held that the plan approved by a vast majority of Colorado's voters was unconstitutional and that the plan rejected, or one similar to it, must be instituted. Both houses, in other words, must be apportioned on a population basis only. Chief Justice Warren, who again wrote the majority opinion, followed his reasoning in *Reynolds*, continuing to emphasize individual rights to the exclusion of all other considerations. The people, he argued, cannot deprive themselves of their own rights, nor can a majority deprive a minority of their personal rights. In other words, Warren asked only the very low level question: Can a majority ever override a constitutional right? Phrased thus, the answer is obviously "No."

But the answer would not have been so easy if Mr. Chief Justice Warren had asked himself the more appropriate question. In a state in which eight per cent of the voters can initiate change via the initiative process, in a state with a popularly elected executive leader, in a state in which one branch of the legislature is apportioned on a population basis, in a state with only a single metropolitan center containing 53% of the state's total population, is it constitutionally unfair or unreasonable to base one-half of one-third of the law-making process on some foundation other than straight population? This is the question which Mr. Justice Stewart approached. Stewart saw the issues presented in *Lucas* as ultimately far more complex than did Warren. For Stewart the proper focus was overall fairness and reasonableness. No apportionment can be reasonable or fair which does not assure ultimate effective majority rule, Stewart argued.[58] But, if a system does insure such ultimate effective majority rule, may it not also then be responsive to the adequate

[58]Stewart appears to have in mind what the Framers referred to as "the republican prinicple." *See* P. EIDELBERG, *supra* note 35, at 92, 196–197; R. DAHL, A PREFACE TO DEMOCRATIC THEORY 27 (1956). *See also* McCloskey, *supra* note 17.

articulation of minority interests and allow them some voice in the law-making chambers? For Stewart, who adopted a very Lockean approach, political man can not be separated from his interests.[59] Tactly Stewart stood for the proposition that individuals have not merely a right to vote but also a right to have their interests articulated in the legislature. Whereas the right to lose at an election, the right to vote and perpetually to be in the minority, would satisfy Chief Justice's Warren's standard, Stewart implied that individuals have a greater right, the right to be effectively represented. Therefore, the standard for apportionment must not only consider population but also take into account group interests. The Court, Stewart cryptically noted, had made one political theory, majoritarian democracy, a constitutional requirement.[60]

The second period of the history of the apportionment cases, then, saw the Court extend the "one man, one vote" standard to every legislature in the United States with the exception of the United States Senate—which was reasonably safe from the Court's onslaught. *Reynolds*, however, failed to spell out any precise constitutional tests to determine when that standard was satisfied. It merely recognized that districts could not be drawn with "mathematical exactness."[61] It is doubtful, however, that the Court majority ever gave adequate thought to the ramifications of its reapportionment decisions. The slogan "one man, one vote" proved extremely deceptive in its simplicity. Like the sirens' song it lured the judicial sailors ever closer. The third period of the Court's handling of apportionment cases, thus, was marked by an evolution of subsidiary doctrines to govern apportionment cases and by a plethora of continually more complex problems.[62]

Foremost among these problems was the elaboration of the constitutionally proper basis of population for purposes of apportionment. The Warren Court ruled that state legislatures and the House of Representatives must be apportioned on a population basis, but it was not particularly precise in its definition of "population." Did it mean

[59]This is also the tacit premise of much contemporary political behavior research; *e.g.*, S. LIPSET, POLITICAL MAN: THE SOCIAL BASES OF POLITICS (1960).

[60]*Compare* Lucas v. Forty-fourth General Assembly of Colorado, 377 U.S. 713, 744 (1964) (Stewart, J. dissenting), *with* Lochner v. New York, 198 U.S. 45, 75 (1905) (Holmes, J., dissenting).

[61]377 U.S. at 577.

[62]*See* R. DIXON, *supra* note 1; CALIF. ASS'Y COMM. ON ELECTIONS AND REAPPORTIONMENT REP., REAPPORTIONMENT IN CALIFORNIA: CONSULTANTS' REPORT TO THE ASSEMBLY, vol. 7, no. 9 (April, 1965); Dixon, *Reapportionment Perspectives: What Is Fair Representation?*, 51 A.B.A. J. 319 (1965).

inhabitants, or residents, or registered voters, or what? In his *Reynolds* opinion, Mr. Chief Justice Warren spoke of each of these terms in different places as though they were (1) synonymous and (2) distinguishable.[63] Each of these measures of population, if adopted as the basis for apportionment, would involve its own peculiar inequalities.

Until 1966, all of the cases which the Court had considered used the inhabitant measure, but in each the disparities under any measure of population were so great that the Court was not faced with the difficult problem of considering particular definitions of population. Then, in *Burns v. Richardson*, the Court was forced to consider the question of whether a state might use at its base for apportioning legislative seats a population other than total inhabitants.[64] In Hawaii, due to the concentration of significant numbers of non-resident servicemen and their families, who were themselves ineligible to vote, the use of total population figures in apportioning seats produced results substantially different than if another basis, such as registered voters, were used. For this reason, Hawaii chose to apportion its legislative seats on the basis of registered voters rather than total inhabitants. The Court held that

> ... neither in Reynolds v. Sims nor in any other decision has this Court suggested that the States are required to include aliens, transients, short-term or temporary residents, or persons denied the right to vote for conviction of crime in an apportionment base ... We hold that the present apportionment satisfies the Equal Protection Clause .... [65]

This, however, does not entirely settle the matter. Suppose that a state, such as Hawaii, elected to apportion legislative seats on the basis of registered voters and suppose that in certain districts there arises a substantial difference between registered and actual voters. In certain districts, the ratio of actual voters to registered voters is substantially higher than in other districts. Do the residents of the districts where the voter turn-outs are substantially higher have a constitutional claim that their votes are diluted? After all, if a hundred thousand people in one district elect only one representative while but a few thousand in a different district elect another have not the former had their votes "debased?" This is the arithmetic logic of the "one man, one vote" decisions of 1964 which simply and erroneously assumed equality of voting participation rates across districts. It might, of course, be argued that the non-voters had simply waived their rights. But might not the

---

[63]377 U.S. at 560, 561, 562, 565, 577.
[64]384 U.S. 73 (1966). *Cf.* Carrington v. Rash, 380 U.S. 89 (1965).
[65]*Id.* at 92-93.

same logic apply to the voters in *Lucas*? In either case, the waiver of some affects the voting power of others.

On the other hand, consider the practical political impact of accepting actual voters as a constitutionally proper population base for apportioning legislative seats. Such a scheme would tend to favor upper- and upper-middle class, white districts over districts comprised primarily of ethnic and economic minorities, due to the differential rates of political participation characteristic of these areas.[66] Moreover, if a court were to validate the use of actual voters as the population base on which to apportion a legislature, the issue would then become which election should serve as the apportionment base. The type of election, we know, affects the volume of voter turn-out in different areas. And what would be the result if it could be shown that at a particular election, which was later selected by the state legislature as the apportionment base, large numbers of eligible voters in certain areas were unable to vote not because of ignorance or apathy but because of a flood or other natural disaster? Finally, if actual voters are accepted as a constitutionally sufficient measure of population, how many years back might a legislature go in selecting an election to serve as the apportionment base? Two years? Four years? Eight? Ten? Twenty? One hundred?

This is not to imply that these questions are unanswerable. But it is to say that whoever adopts the standard "one man, one vote" had better be prepared to answer them. There is no indication that the Warren Court was so prepared, for, except for its rather lame effort in *Burns*, it studiously failed to confront them.

The Court did, however, face up to the second of the major problems created by its 1964 reapportionment decisions. In those decisions, the majority had vehemently and explicitly asserted that equality of population was to be the standard to govern the apportionment of legislative representation. But, assuming an acceptable definition of population, the problem still remained to indicate what constituted a substantial equality thereof. How equal was equal? *Reynolds* had held that mathematical nicety was not mandatory in the drawing of legislative districts, but for several terms following that decision the permissible limits of deviation

[66]*See* L. MILBRATH, POLITICAL PARTICIPATION (1965); A. CAMPBELL, P. CONVERSE, W. MILLER, & D. STOKES, THE AMERICAN VOTER (1960); B. BERELSON, P. LAZARSFELD, & W. McPHEE, VOTING (1954); Jennings & Ziegler, *Class, Party, and Race in Four Types of Elections: The Case of Atlanta,* 28 J. POL. 391 (1966). *See also* Andrews, *American Voting Participation,* 19 W. POL. Q. 639 (1966).

from mathematical exactness were not indicated by the Court in any manner intelligible to those other than seers or divines.

Initially, the Court had open to it three indices to measure the equality of a districting arrangement. The first of these was the ratio of the most populous district to the least populous district. For example, in a state in which the largest district contained 15,000 persons and the smallest contained 5,000, the ratio would be 3:1. Alternatively, the Court might, in assessing the relative equality of a districting scheme, have looked at the relative value of the vote. That is, it might have established a maximum permissible deviation from the electoral mean. Taking the example again, assume that our two districts were in a state in which the ideal district would contain 10,000 persons. The state's apportionment scheme would, thus, be characterized by a deviation of ±50%. This particular measure had been advocated by the American Political Science Association, which in a 1951 report had suggested that a reasonable standard for insuring apportionment fairness would be ±15%.[67] Finally, there was the Dauer-Kelsay Index.[68] Under this measure, the equity of a given apportionment was to be examined not by concentration upon gross disparities but by determining the minimum percentage of the population capable of electing a simple majority of the legislative body. Again consider the above example; while the population disparity between the largest and smallest districts is indeed great, if the other districts are all of nearly equal size, it would require almost 50% of the state's population to elect 50% of this legislature. In other words, if our two hypothetical districts are state senate districts in a state with a population of 1,000,000 and an upper-house of 100 seats, and if the ninety-eight other districts each have populations of exactly 10,000, then, although the apportionment will be characterized by a deviation of ±50% and although the largest district will be three times greater than the smallest, it will still require districts representing 50.5% of the states population to control a majority in the senate.

Quite clearly, the least accurate, grossest, and most insensitive measure of apportionment equality is the population ratio between largest and smallest district. Equally clearly, this was the measure the Warren Court adopted in examining the constitutionality of challenged

[67]Committee on the Reapp. of Cong., Am. Pol. Sci. Assoc., *The Reapportionment of Congress*, 45 AM. POL. SCI. REV. 153 (1951).

[68]Dauer & Kelsay, *Unrepresentative States*, 44 NAT'L MUN. REV. 571 (1955). *See generally* Schubert & Press, *Measuring Malapportionment*, 58 AM. POL. SCI. REV. 302 (1964); Alker & Russett, *On Measuring Inequality*, 9 BEHAV. SCI. 207 (1964).

apportionments. The Court tended to concern itself with extreme deviations rather than with overall patterns of apportionmnent. Thus, congressional apportionments involving a ratio between the largest and smallest districts of 1.2 to 1 or greater and state legislative apportionments which involved maximum population variances of 1.7 to 1 or more were declared to be unconstitutional.[69]

Then, in Mr. Chief Justice Warren's last term, the Court performed what amounted to a double about-face. It not only adopted a new standard for determining permissible deviations from mathematical exactness in apportionment suits but also it moved to limit the definition of permissible deviation. In *Kirkpatrick v. Preisler*, the Warren Court found unsatisfactory a Missouri congressional districting plan in which the largest and smallest districts differed from one another by only six per cent, i.e., $\pm 3\%$![70] While looking at the relative value of the vote, as suggested by the American Political Science Association, is probably a better standard to use than focusing on the extremes, the Court's application of this standard in *Kirkpatrick* seems so dogmatic as to be unreasonable. Speaking for the Court, Mr. Justice Brennan explained that the "one man, one vote" principle

> requires that the state make a good faith effort to achieve *precise mathematical equality* . . . [and] justify each variance, *no matter how small* . . . We can see no . . . cutoff point at which population variances suddenly become [too small to matter][71]

Apparently, every district must have exactly the same population.

The only appropriate reply to Brennan must be that the entire history of the Supreme Court stands for the proposition that no constitutional principle can be an absolute.[72] No inflexible principle has ever proven

[69]Kirkpatrick v. Preisler, 385 U.S. 450 (1967), *aff'g per curiam* Preisler v. Secretary of State, 257 F. Supp. 953 (1966) (involving Missouri congressional districts), Lucas v. Forty-fourth General Assembly of Colorado, 377 U.S. 713 (1965) (involving state legislative districting).

[70]394 U.S. 526 (1969). *But see* Abate v. Mundt, 403 U.S. 182 (1972) (accepting a population variance of 12% for local governmental units); Mahan v. Howell, 410 U.S. 315 (1973) (validating 16% difference in state legislative districting). *See also* Connor v. Williams, 404 U.S. 549 (1972).

[71]*Id.* at 530-31 (emphasis added).

[72]*E.g., compare* United States v. Carolene Products Co., 304 U.S. 144, 152 n. 4, *with* Sheppard v. Maxwell, 384 U.S. 333 (1966); *compare* Sturges v. Crowninshield, 4 Wheat. 122 (1819), *with* City of El Paso v. Simmons, 370 U.S. 497 (1965); *compare* Champion v. Ames, 188 U.S. 321 (1903), *with* Brooks v. United States, 267 U.S. 432 (1925); *compare* Allgeyer v. Louisiana 165 U.S. 578 (1897), *with* West Coast Hotel v. Parrish, 300 U.S. 379 (1937).

capable of satisfactory application. If the law is not tempered with realism and common sense, it soon ceases to be the law. *Kirkpatrick's* dogmatic application of "one man, one vote" gives rise to potentially absurd consequences. People living in the same building, even in the same family, would be required to vote in different districts. It is legitimate to wonder if the social, political, and fiscal costs of creating and administering such a romantic electoral system might not outweigh whatever benefits might be gained.

But, if the problems of defining population and mathematical equality were both difficult for and not entirely satisfactorily settled by the Warren Court, its contribution to the law of partisan contrived malapportionment, i.e., gerrymandering, was surprisingly even less clear. The problem of gerrymandering is, of course, well understood and easily illustrated. Assume a state with a population for apportionment purposes of one million persons and a lower house in its legislature whose size is constitutionally fixed at one hundred seats. Clearly, the ideal district in this state would have a population of 10,000 persons. Now, examine county X:

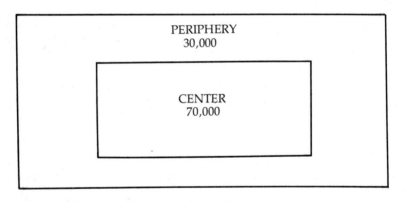

PERIPHERY
30,000

CENTER
70,000

The central area of county X with a population of 70,000 is urban in nature, largely inhabited by low-income families of ethnic minorities, and overwhelmingly Democratic. The peripheral area, with a population of only 30,000, is rural and suburban, populated almost exclusively by upper-middle class whites, most of whom are Republicans. Apportioning county X would seem to be simplicity itself; the central area should be carved into seven districts, while the periphery would receive three seats. Not necessarily! Without stepping over the county line, districts can be drawn in such a way as to give the peripheral population the potential of electing a majority of the county's legislators. For example,

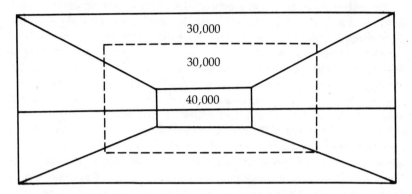

Conceding the central area four solid seats, the legislature may pair the remaining 30,000 central area residents with their equal number in the suburbs in six districts each of 10,000 population. To be sure, the district lines will not be nearly so neat as in the diagram, but each of these six districts could be drawn to comprise 5,000 urban residents and 5,000 peripheral area residents. In practical terms, this would probably accord six legislative seats to the suburbs, since upper-middle class whites participate in the electoral process at far greater rates than do urban ghetto dwellers. In other words, an apparent electoral majority can be converted into a legislative minority by that time-honored technique of American politics, "cracking" districts. But this hypothetical apportionment would admirably satisfy the arithmetic requirements of "one man, one vote," although one viscerally feels that its constitutionality is questionable.[73]

The Warren Court did confront the problem of gerrymandering, but the ambiguity of its decisions left the constitutional status of the practice far from clear. *Gomillion*, of course, dealt with the problem, but because the discrimination involved in that case was so manifest and grotesque it provided a singularly narrow precedent. It is by no means clear, then, that the reapportionment decisions affect gerrymandering. Besides, even if gerrymanders do run afoul of the Equal Protection Clause, the reapportionment decisions have further complicated rather than clari-

[73]*See generally* Baker, *Gerrymandering: Privileged Sanctuary or Next Judicial Target?*, in REAPPORTIONMENT IN THE 1970s, at 121 (N. Polsby ed. 1971).

fied the problem. If gerrymanders are unconstitutional denials of equal protection, how are they to be identified? In the old days, *circa* 1960, one of the easiest ways to recognize potential partisan gerrymanders was to examine if a newly adopted districting departed from natural geographic or traditional political boundaries.[74] But the reapportionment decisions have actually encouraged this sort of legislative behavior by stressing the importance of mathematical precision and denigrating traditional districting schemes. In particular, this is true of *Kirkpatrick* which, in its obsession with arithmetic exactness, rejected such other districting values as compactness and contiguity. Thus, even if they do make gerrymandering unconstitutional, and it is not clear that they do, the apportionment decisions make it far more difficult for voters disadvantaged by a gerrymander to prove that that is what has taken place. Counsel for the gerrymandering legislature can cite *Reynolds* for the proposition that the legislature was under a constitutional mandate to redistrict and, further, can rely on that mandate to explain some rather oddly shaped, but equally populated, districts.

Yet another aspect of the gerrymandering problem involves the question of intent. Are all gerrymanders unconstitutional? What about a gerrymander motivated not by partisan greed but by the beneficent intent to give an identifiable minority at least some representation? Illustrative of this problem, though not particularly helpful in resolving it, was the case of *Wright v. Rockefeller*, involving congressional districts in New York.[75] The size of the districts was not at issue; rather, the appellant challenged the constitutionality of the recently reapportioned 18th Congressional District, a strange eleven-sided figure with a population 83.6% black and Puerto Rican. It was claimed that this district was the product of a gerrymander by which the state had transferred a racially identifiable population out of the so-called "Silk Stocking" district, then represented by John Lindsay, where it was regularly outvoted and into the Harlem bailiwick of Adam Clayton Powell where it might be better represented. The Court majority, speaking through Mr. Justice Black, avoided the merits of the issue and relied upon the lower

[74]For example, in the hypothetical example *supra* at pp. 114-15, if the central city were bounded on three sides by a river which had historically been regarded as a natural and inviolable boundary, any apportionment which involved disregarding that boundary would have been suspect. But not so under *Kirkpatrick*, for the legislature can claim that creating districts which straddle the river is necessary to achieve population equality. *See generally* Reynolds v. Sims, 377 U.S. 533, 622-623 (1964) (Harlan, J., dissenting).

[75]376 U.S. 52 (1964).

court's determination that discrimination had not been proven. This, however, was highly questionable, as the dissenters pointed out, since it was not at all clear from the lower court opinion exactly what the court had decided.[76] Dissenting, Mr. Justice Douglas, joined by Justice Goldberg, stressed the point that race is never a valid classification, even if its effect is beneficent. Consistent with the Court's opinion in *Reynolds*, Douglas continued to reject the contention that interests might be a constitutional basis for representation and to insist that the individual, *qua* individual, is all important. The apportionment in this case arguably was designed to facilitate the articulation of certain interests in the national political arena. For Douglas, however, interest articulation was irrelevant. Individual participation was all. Interests were to be considered, for purposes of apportionment, as standardized. Thus, in Douglas's opinion in *Wright*, Harlan's prophecy of *Reynolds* came to pass; individuals were reduced to ciphers, beings with no interests. The crucial question, however, remained unanswered. Is the consideration of racial or, by implication, other factors in districting constitutionally permissible? Clearly it would be impermissible when, as in *Gomillion*, it disadvantaged a racial minority. But what if the purpose were to guarantee a minority at least some representation? Douglas gave his answer, but the majority of the Warren Court ignored the issue.

Yet a fourth problem which the Warren Court failed to adequately answer in the apportionment litigation was the question of the type of district which would be found permissible. Dicta in *Reynolds* suggested that a state might choose other districting forms than the single member plurality district which has been traditional in America. But subsequent litigation implied that the type of district chosen might have con-stitutional significance. Multi-member districts, for example, were upheld in *Fortson v. Dorsey;*[77] but Mr. Justice Brennan seriously qualified the Court's approval of such districts, and Mr. Justice Douglas thought them to be unconstitutional per se. The case involved the apportionment of Georgia senate seats. The fifty-four seats were apportioned by counties, with each county electing at least one senator, and the seven most populous counties electing twenty-one senators. These legislators were to be elected at large from within the county, although each elected was then assigned to a subdistrict, in effect turning the populous counties into multi-member senate districts. A federal

[76] *See* Wright v. Rockefeller, 211 F Supp. 460 (1962).
[77] 379 U.S. 433 (1965).

district court held that this scheme unconstitutionally discriminated against the voters in the populous counties, but the Warren Court reversed. "Every Fulton County [Atlanta] voter . . . ," wrote Mr. Justice Brennan, "may vote for seven senators to represent [himself] in the legislature . . . ."[78]

But here again the "representation" question was overlooked because interests were denigrated. At-large, winner-take-all electoral systems make it more difficult for identifiable minorities, such as blacks and Republicans in Atlanta, to elect legislators in proportion to their strength. Such a scheme as that employed in *Fortson* might very well result in the nullification of the unanimous choice of the voters in a subdistrict, thrusting upon them a senator for whom no one in the subdistrict had voted. The *Fortson* majority thought not.

> It is not accurate to treat a senator from a multi-district county as the representative of only that district within the county wherein he resides.[79]

But why not? Again the representation question is begged. To paraphrase Justice Brennan: It is not accurate to treat a Senator from a multi-state nation as the representative of the state within the nation wherein he resides. But that of course is exactly accurate! Single member districts appear to be more desirable than multi-member districts because they (1) keep the representative closer and more directly responsible to his constituents, (2) increase the likelihood that divergent viewpoints and minority interests will receive at least some representation, and (3) strengthen the two-party system by avoiding the winner-take-all result of at-large elections. Put differently, multi-member districting could (1) permit a larger city in a two-city district to elect all of the representatives from that district and (2) deprive ethnic minorities of the opportunity to elect members of their own race to represent them.[80] Nor would this situation necessarily be corrected by a requirement that the representative of the district reside within it.[81] "Uncle Toms" are not hard to find.

Nevertheless, multi-member districting passed a major test in *Whitcomb v. Chavis* in which the districting of Marion County, Indiana, including the City of Indianapolis, was challenged as depriving an identifiable racial minority of the representation to which its numerical

[78]*Id.* at 437.

[79]*Id.* at 438.

[80]*E.g.*, Mann v. Davis, 245 F. Supp. 241 (E.D. Va.), *aff'd*, 383 U.S. 42 (1965). *See generally* Rae, *supra* note 39.

[81]*But cf.* Dusch v. Davis, 387 U.S. 112 (1967).

strength would appear to have entitled it.[82] Patrick Chavis and other black residents of Indianapolis's Center Township ghetto claimed that the multi-member district in Marion County from which eight state senators and fifteen state assemblymen were elected at large, denied them effective representation, since, under the multi-member district scheme, the ghetto minority was incapable of electing legislators responsive to ghetto interests.[83] The black plaintiffs, however, were forced to admit that, unlike the *Gomillion* case, there was no evidence of a legislative attempt to discriminate against black voters,[84] and they conceded that the Indiana apportionment, including the Marion County multi-member district, satisfied the standards for population equality that had been required in 1965, the last time the Indiana apportionment had been constitutionally challenged.[85]

Declining the opportunity to extend the Warren Court's reapportionment precedents beyond the requirement of simple mathematical equality, the Burger Court sustained the multi-member districting plan. For the Court, Mr. Justice White concluded that, since the plan had not been created to discriminate against Center Township residents and since those residents enjoyed the opportunity to participate in the political process, including the opportunity to vote, the mandate of the reapportionment decisions had not been violated. The fact that there was little if

[82]403 U.S. 124 (1971).

[83]In the same case, a black resident of Lake County, also a multi-member district but a smaller one, alleged that his vote had been diluted by the multi-member districting plan, on the grounds that he had fewer opportunities than a Marion county voter to cast critical, tie-breaking votes in elections and that, because Marion County's legislators tended to vote as a bloc, Marion County voters enjoyed more and better representation. His argument reduced itself to the claim that equal protection requires that all legislative districts within a state must have the same number of representatives, because any deviation from such uniform districting debases the votes of the voters in the smaller districts. *See generally* Banzhaf, *Multi-Member Electoral Districts—Do they Violate the "One Man, One Vote" Principle*, 75 YALE L.J. 1309 (1966). The Court rejected the argument.

[84]*But see* White v. Regester, 412 U.S. 755 (1973) (invalidating use of multi-member districting as part of a demonstrable pattern to deny political representation to identifiable racial minorities).

[85]Stout v. Bottorff, 249 F. Supp. 488 (S.D. Ind. 1965). On its own initiative, however, the Court held that prior judicial approval did not insulate the apportionment from consideration under more recently developed standards. The Court then found the overall districting plan to be unconstitutional due to population variances of 28.20% between the largest and smallest senate districts and of 24.78% between the largest and smallest assembly districts. But, in remanding the case, the Court rebuked the district court for having eliminated *all* multi-member districts without adequate justification. 403 U.S. at 60-63.

any correspondence between the black population of Marion County and its share of Marion County's legislative delegation was dismissed by White as simply a case of an interest group's being out-voted.

And so it was. But such a consideration merited more careful analysis than Mr. Justice White's out-of-hand rejection accorded it. American politics is fundamentally based upon interest groups.[86] The individual right to vote is meaningful primarily, if not exclusively, insofar as it assures that the groups, social or categoric, to which one belongs or with which one identifies will be represented in the political process. If a group with an identifiable interest is deprived of the opportunity to elect representatives within a reasonable proportion to its numbers, that group may be as effectively foreclosed from meaningful political participation as it would have been had it been entirely deprived of the right to vote.[87] In denigrating such considerations, however, the result in *Whitcomb* was firmly founded upon the underlying assumptions of the earlier reapportionment decisions.

The *Whitcomb* decision may, however, be applauded on the minimal ground that it was at least better than the alternative open to the Court. As Justice White observed, a losing minority, no matter how substantial, receives no representation in either multi-member or single-member districts. Had the Court attempted to resolve the problem of effective representation by establishing permissible ratios between number of ballots cast and number of representatives elected, the result would have been—contrary to American constitutional history, philosophy, and intent—to establish proportional representation as a constitutional principle.[88] Given the tendency of proportional representation to encourage

---

[86]*See* note 50 *supra;* R. DAHL, *supra* note 58, at ch. 5; Comment, *Effective Representation and Multimember Districts,* 68 MICH. L. REV. 1577, 1588 (1970) ("interest groups, and not individuals, are the real electors of representatives...."). *See also* note 37 *supra.*

There are, of course, alternative theories on which to base an argument for the constitutional protection of voting rights. *See* Kirby, *The Right to Vote,* in THE RIGHTS OF AMERICANS 175 (Dorsen ed. 1971).

[87]*Cf.* R. DIXON, *supra* note 1, at 17.

[88]The Court would also have placed upon itself the burden of identifying those interest groups which merit such constitutional protection. *See generally* R. DAHL, *supra* note 38, at chs. 1 & 5. It might, of course, be argued that the Fifteenth Amendment accords special constitutional solicitude to the voting rights of black Americans. *See generally* W. GILLETTE, THE RIGHT TO VOTE (1969). Indeed, dissenting from the holding in *Whitcomb,* Justices Douglas, Marshall, and Brennan argued (1) that the voting rights of blacks do enjoy a special constitutional protection and (2) that the Marion County districting did in fact dilute black votes and, thus, concluded (3) that the Indiana

the proliferation of political parties and, thus, to result in coalition governments, one may wonder if its adoption at the state level would be wise.[89] But proportional representation appears to be the only way to facilitate interest representation without abandoning the "one man, one vote" principle.[90]

The final problem raised by the "one man, one vote" decisions of 1964 was their applicability to local government units. In its first case to consider the problem, *Sailors v. Board of Education*, the Warren Court hesitated.[91] At issue was the districting of county school boards in Michigan. Members of these county boards were elected not by direct popular vote but by the local school boards which were themselves elected by popular vote within each school district. The composition of these local boards gave rise to no constitutional problems; but the apportionment of the county boards did, for on the county board the representative of each local board had one and only one vote, regardless of the fact that some local school districts were far more populous than

apportionment was unconstitutional. Such a conclusion, however, is singularly inconsistent with the position taken by Justices Douglas, Marshall, and Brennan in James v. Valtierra, 402 U.S. 137, 144 (1971), where they asserted that the equal protection clause of the Fourteenth Amendment extends to interest groups other than blacks.

[89]Or even possible. Since none of the states utilize a parliamentary form of government with the executive elected from within the legislature (Rather, one is compelled to add, all of the states rely upon a "federal analogy" in the selection of their governors.), the adoption of proportional representation in a state legislature would possibly lead not to coalition government but to gubernatorial autocracy. *See generally* J. HERMANS, DEMOCRACY OR ANARCHY? A STUDY OF PROPORTIONAL REPRESENTATION (1941); Rae, *supra* note 39.

[90]A second, alternative form of districting is weighted or fractional voting. This scheme is the mirror image of multi-member districting. Rather than electing seven senators from one county, weighted voting proposes to elect one senator and give him seven votes. Although it avoids some of the problems of multi-member districting, it creates others unique to itself. For example, it wreaks havoc with the committee system. A senator with seven votes renders a five-man committee superfluous. Moreover, the weighted voting arrangement renders representatives from the more populous districts less accessible to their constituents by sheer dint of numbers. Weighted voting has been upheld at the lower court level in two cases and found violative of the Constitution in another. Maryland Committee for Fair Representation v. Tawes, 180 A.2d 656 (Md. 1962); Thigpen v. Meyers, 231 F.Supp. 938 (D.D.C. 1964); WMCA v. Lomenzo, 238 F.Supp. 916 (S.D.N.Y. 1965). This type of districting has also been voided in other suits on state statutory or constitutional grounds. Jackman v. Bodine, 205 A.2d 713 (N.J. 1964). The Supreme Court, however, has failed to confront the problem, and as yet it remains exactly that—a problem.

[91]387 U.S. 105 (1967). *See generally* R. DIXON, *supra* note 1, at 544-559; McKay, *Reapportionment and Local Government*, 36 GEO. WASH. L. REV. 713 (1968).

others. The Court, however, unanimously ruled that this was of no constitutional significance. Members of the county school boards need not come from districts which were equal in population, because the functions of the county boards were not "legislative" in character. For the Court, Mr. Justice Douglas viewed the method of selection of the county school board as essentially appointive rather than elective and concluded that there was no constitutional reason why non-legislative officers might not be chosen by some means other than election, even if this were to involve inequities in the apportionemnt of seats. But Justice Douglas's avoidance of the issue by distinguishing between legislative and administrative functions raised the question of why, then, the "one man, one vote" concept had been applied to governors who surely also performed non-legislative, administrative functions.[92]

The inadequacy of the *Sailors'* attempt to limit the scope of "one man, one vote" by distinguishing between "legislative" and "non-legislative" officials led the Court to abandon that distinction within a year.[93] *Avery v. Midland County* represented the first case in which a local governmental apportionment was found unconstitutional.[94] The suit involved the apportionment of seats on the county board of supervisors, called the County Commissioners Court, in Midland County, Texas. One of the five members of the court was elected at large from the entire county, but voted only in the event of tied ballots. The other four Commissioners were elected from districts. Three of these districts had populations of 852, 414, and 828, while the fourth district, encompassing the entire city of Midland-Odessa, contained a population of 67,906. This unequal districting was defended on the grounds that (1) the Commissioners Court's functions were not legislative in character; (2) the city of Midland-Odessa was not sufficiently governed by the county body but, rather, exercised home-rule through its own city council over most matters of concern to the inhabitants of the city; and (3) the County Commissioners' powers disproportionately affected the rural areas of Midland County. The Court rejected these contentions on the theory that the County Commissioners exercised "general governmental pow-

[92]The distinction was probably motivated in part by a desire to avoid the problems of elective judiciaries. But even there it is specious.

[93]*But see* Salyer Land Co. v. Tulare Lake Basin Water Storage Dist., 410 U.S. 719 (1973) (upholding use of preferential voting in local elections if necessary to meet a compelling state interest and if the local unit performs only special, limited functions).

[94]390 U.S. 474 (1968).

[95]*Id.* at 482.

ers" over the county. While the majority admitted that the County Commissioners exercised negligible legislative functions, they felt, nonetheless, that this standard, which the Court itself had used only a yea before, was an inadequate one to guide the judiciary in applying the "one man, one vote" principle. "As the brief description of the court's functions . . . amply demonstrates," wrote Mr. Justice White, "this unit of local government cannot be easily classified in the neat categories favored by civics texts."[95]

In applying the rule of "one man, one vote" to local governments, however, the Court lost Mr. Justice Fortas by the wayside. While Mr. Justice Harlan's dissent was predictable, the defection of Fortas was a cause for some eyebrow-raising among Court watchers. Harlan, as was his wont, dissented on the grounds of prudence and practice. First, he continued to advance the claim that the Court had exceeded its appropriate constitutional role by entering the "political thicket" against the advice of Mr. Justice Frankfurter.[96] Second, Harlan argued, even had the Court been correct in its disposition of the 1964 apportionment cases, it would be wise to wait before forging ahead into the "dark continent" of American government.[97] *Reynolds* had raised more questions than it had answered, and Harlan thought it would be wise to answer them first. If, in the long run, "one man, one vote" were to prove incapable of application to the fifty state legislatures, why make matters worse by precipitously inflicting that principle upon the more than 80,000 subunits of American local government?[98] Moreover, Harlan argued that there might be some crucial distinctions, in terms of functions, between general and local governments which would make the "one man, one vote" principle, even if wise for larger units, inapplicable to local agencies. These agencies, Harlan contended, should be allowed greater flexibility in order to adapt to changing social conditions and to experiment with alternative arrangements for meeting those changed conditions.[99] Mr. Justice Fortas was harsher even than Harlan. He accused the Court of adopting an overly simplistic approach to the

[96]Colegrove v. Green, 328 U.S. 549, 556 (1946).

[97]*See* H. GILBERTSON, THE COUNTY: THE "DARK CONTINENT" OF AMERICAN POLITICS (1917).

[98]390 U.S. 474, 490 (1968) (Harlan, J., dissenting); 390 U.S. at 499 (Fortas, J., dissenting). *See generally* J. BOLLENS, SPECIAL DISTRICT GOVERNMENTS IN THE UNITED STATES (1957); J. BOLLENS & H. SCHMANDT, THE METROPOLIS: ITS PEOPLE, POLITICS, AND ECONOMIC LIFE (1965).

[99]Indeed, *Avery* might be interpreted as an attempt by Mr. Justice Harlan to burn his bridges behind him and retreat to new defensive positions. Throughout the "in-

problem. It had not, in Fortas's view, recognized that the interests of all citizens in a particular elected body are not necessarily the same. Certain governing bodies may have only a slight or remote impact on some of their constituents and a vast and direct impact on others. Ghetto dwellers, for example, may have a crucial, overriding interest in the policies of a metropolitan housing authority, while rural residents may have little or none. Similarly, central city inhabitants may have almost no interest in a county irrigation district whose decisions are of virtually immeasurable consequence for local farmers. Moreover, Fortas argued, the Court had neglected to take into account the fact that single executives, elected by the constitutency at large, might exercise sufficient independent power to check imprudent or unjust actions taken by a malapportioned body. This was certainly the case in Midland County, where any effort by the rural-dominated County Commissioners Court to tax unfairly the city's residents could have been and probably would have been blocked by the county tax assessor, who, given that he was elected at large from within the county, could reasonably have been anticipated to be highly responsive to the interests of the Midland-Odessa voters. The apportionment of the County Commissioners Court on a basis of population equality would, felt Fortas, result in the representation of one interest only, that of the urban dwellers, while depriving that group which had the greatest interest in the County Court and was most affectd by its decisions, i.e., rural residents, of a significant voice in their own government.

Paradoxically, Fortas's dissent continued to declaim his allegiance to *Reynolds v. Sims,* despite the fact that nearly everything he said in *Avery* was at variance with the reasoning of *Reynolds.* Interest representation was crucial to Fortas's position. The sum of his argument was that the majoritarian fixation of the "one man, one vote" rule would probably result in the denial of legislative access and representation for small groups with distinct interests. Yet that would be true of state legislatures as much as of the Midland County Commissioners Court.[100]

corporation" decisions, he continuously argued against a "carbon copy" rule on the grounds that the state governments should be allowed greater flexibility in their responses to evolving social problems. In *Avery,* he may have been abandoning the states, at least for apportionment purposes, to champion the cause, without changing his rationale, of the sub-state units of government.

[100]Both of the dissents in *Avery* actually appear to have been motivated by a concern for the applicability of the "one man, one vote" rule to special district governments, those literally tens of thousands of local governments, such as water districts, irrigation districts,

In contrast, the Burger Court, while not abandoning the application of the "one man, one vote" standard to agencies of local government, has demonstrated greater flexibility in applying the principle. In *Abate v. Mundt*,[101] decided the same day as *Whitcomb v. Chavis*,[102] the Court accepted as constitutionally permissible a population variance of 12% in the apportionment of the Rockland County, New York, Board of Supervisors. While *Abate's* statement that "slightly greater percentage deviations may be tolerable for local government apportionment schemes"[103] was read by some as indicating only that the Court was "developing distinct apportionment standards for local government,"[104] while continuing to insist on zero deviation in state legislative and congressional districting, *Abate* actually was the signal of a growing disquietude within the Court concerning the wisdom of the preceding reapportionment decisions. By sustaining Rockland County's desire to preserve the integrity of its own political subdivisions as a constitutionally sufficient justification for deviating from mathematical exactness in the apportionment of districts, the Burger Court opened the door for a reappraisal of *Reynolds* and its progeny.[105]

housing districts, and so forth, which are organized to perform special, limited functions. *See generally* J. BOLLENS, *supra* note 98. Both Fortas and Harlan apparently doubted both the wisdom and practicability of applying the *Reynolds* standard to these governments. *But see* Hadley v. Junior College District of Metropolitan Kansas City, 397 U.S. 50 (1970) ("one man, one vote" principle applicable to special district as well as general governments); *but cf.* Salyer Land Co. v. Tulare Lake Basin Water Storage Dist., 410 U.S. 719 (1973).

[101]403 U.S. 182 (1971).

[102]Also decided on the same day, Gordon v. Lance, 403 U.S. 1 (1971), held that West Virginia's extraordinary majority requirement that 60% of the voters in a referendum election must approve of the assumption of a bonded indebtedness or a tax increase before it could become law did not constitute a debasement of the vote in violation of the "one man, one vote" principle. As Mr. Justice Harlan commented:

> Today the Court sustains a provision that gives opponents of school bond issues half again the voting power of proponents.
>
> The Court justifies the wondrous results . . . [by relying] heavily on the "federal analogy" and the prevalence of similar anti-majoritarian elements in the constitutions of the several states.
>
> To my mind the relevance of such considerations . . . is undeniable and their cumulative effect is unanswerable. I can only marvel, therefore, that they were dismissed singly and in combination, in a line of cases which began with Gray v. Sanders . . . and ended with Hadley v. Junior College District. . . .

403 U.S. at 166

[103]403 U.S. at 185.

[104]*The Supreme Court, 1970 Term*, 85 HARV. L. REV. 3, 149 (1971).

[105]Whether consciously intended or not, *Abate* was also a constitutional shot in the arm for urban government reformers. One popular proposal for the reform of government

This relaxation of the standards for the determination of population equality across districts was continued in *Mahan v. Howell.*[106] Although the districting of the Virgina House of Delegates involved a maximum deviation of 16.4%,[107] the Court found the apportionment to be constitutionally permissible. The deviation was not regarded as excessive, since it was necessary to rational state policy objectives. Virginia had sought to draw its legislative districts in conformity, insofar as possible, with county and city boundaries, thereby providing for the representation of local communities within the House of Delegates. The Court was persuaded that the preservation of the integrity of political subdivisions was rational, because it furthered the purpose of facilitating enactment of statutes of purely local concern. Therefore, the apportionment plan was sustained, even though Virginia had departed from its policy of respecting local political subdivision boundaries by splitting Fairfax County into two five-member districts.[108] The proper judicial concern, held Mr. Justice Rehnquist, should be with the rationality of the overall districting scheme. Indeed, four months after the decision in *Mahan*, the Court held in *Gaffney v. Cummings*[109] and its companion case, *White v. Regester*,[110] that population disparities of less than 10% between state

in metropolitan areas has been the adoption of a regional government embracing several smaller, though not necessarily small, cities and perhaps cutting across county lines. *See* J. BOLLENS & H. SCHMANDT, *supra* note 98, at chs. 12-16. It has been suggested, however, that for such proposals to succeed the populous but poor central city will have to accord the affluent suburbs a disproportionate voting power in the apportionment of such a federated local government scheme in exchange for the suburbs' disproportionate contribution to the regional government's tax base. But until *Abate*, Hadley v. Junior College District, 397 U.S. 50 (1970), and Avery v. Midland County, 390 U.S. 474 (1968), seemed to prohibit the adoption of such a plan through legislation, and Lucas v. Colorado, 377 U.S. 713 (1964), appeared to preclude urban voters from opting for their own underrepresentation. *See generally* Dixon, *Local Representation: Constitutional Mandates and Apportionment Options*, 36 GEO. WASH. L. REV. 693 (1968).

[106]410 U.S. 315 (1973).

[107]Actually, the deviation may have been as great as 23.6%, depending upon the method of computation used. *See* Howell v. Mahan, 330 F.Supp. 1138, 1139-40 n. 1 (E.D. Va. 1971). The district court seemed to have favored the method which produced the larger disparity but found it unnecessary to calculate the exact deviation, since it viewed even 16.4% as excessive. The Supreme Court, however, proceeded as if the district court had made a finding of fact that the deviation was 16.4%.

[108]The Court reasoned that the overall apportionment plan should not be condemned merely because Virginia had sought to avoid extremely large multi-member districts by bisecting its most populous county.

[109]412 U.S. 735 (1973).

[110]412 U.S. 755 (1973).

legislative districts were constitutionally *de minimis*.[111] Speaking for the Court, Mr. Justice White evoked memories of Stewart's dissent in *Lucas* by reasoning that the goal of the Court's apportionment policy was not mathematical precision but the realization of fair and effective representation which was threatened only by gross malapportionment.

In *Mahan*, Justice Rehnquist had argued that prior decisions imposing more stringent standards of population equality were distinguishable, because they had dealt with congressional districting and, thus, were decided under Article I, Section 2, rather than under the Equal Protection Clause. Textually, such a distinction seems specious, for the language of Section 2 of Article I appears to be no more rigorous in its application to legislative districting problems than does the phraseology of the Fourteenth Amendment. As for precendent, *Wesberry v. Sanders*, dealing with congressional districting, and *Reynolds v. Sims*, dealing with state apportionment, as well as subsequent apportionment cases, seemed to employ virtually identical goals and standards to measure the acceptability of districting schemes. The standards articulated in state districting cases appeared to define the measure to be applied to congressional apportionment and vice versa. Nevertheless, on the same day as *Gaffney* and *Regester*, the Burger Court struck down a congressional districting scheme with a maximum population difference of a mere 4.1%![112]

It may, of course, be argued that the new majority has been persuaded that countervailing state interests, insignificant in the congressional context, are of sufficient importance at the state and sub-state level to justify more lenient standards of population equality in legislative districting. But, if that is the case, the holdings in *Gaffney* and *Regester* rest upon a fundamental inconsistency.[113] On the one hand, the Court has relied upon the proposition that certain interests, such as the preservation of the integrity of local political subdivisions, are suf-

[111]Six Justices joined in the opinion of the Court. Justices Douglas and Marshall joined in a single opinion written by Justice Brennan dissenting from the holding in *Gaffney* and dissenting in part and concurring in part in *Regester*.

[112]White v. Weiser, 412 U.S. 783 (1973). It remains possible, however, that the reapportionment field will yet see a process of reverse extension of constitutional standards similar to that which has taken place in the area of "incorporation," by which more flexible standards at the state level are extended to the federal level. *See, e.g.*, Williams v. Florida, 399 U.S. 78 (1970) (upholding the use of less than twelve-member juries as consistent with the Sixth Amendment); and Apodaca v. Oregon, 406 U.S. 404 (1972) (sustaining the use of non-unanimous jury verdicts).

[113]*See The Supreme Court, 1972 Term*, 87 HARV. L. REV. 1, 91 (1973).

ficiently important at the state level to justify differential treatment for state and congressional apportionments. But, on the other hand, *Gaffney* and *Regester* have then held that *no* countervailing interest need be advanced to justify population disparities of less than 10% in state districting.

While *Gaffney* and *Regester* have permitted deviations of less than 10% without justification, however, they do not stand for the counter proposition that districting schemes with such *de minimis* disparities are immune to constitutional challenge. Even a mathematically precise districting plan which effected a racial discrimination, for example, could be invalidated on equal protection grounds. Thus, *Regester* itself overturned Texas's multi-member districting scheme, because it had the effect of invidiously discriminating against blacks and Chicanos. In *Gaffney*, however, the Court spurned the claim that the Connecticut apportionment plan was unconstitutional because based upon improper political motives.[114] The state conceded that the plan adopted had been intended to perpetuate the relative strengths of Republicans and Democrats as reflected in recent elections, but the mere fact that partisan considerations had played a role in the formulation of the districting was insufficient for the Court to label it unconstitutional.[115]

Taken as a whole, the Burger Court's reapportionment decisions are another reflection of the new majority's disenchantment with the Warren Court's two-level equal protection analysis.[116] At a more specific level, they evidence a growing judicial disillusionment with the pursuit of that will-o-the-wisp, mathematical exactness. "Underlying the Court's modification of state legislative districting standards is a reassessment of the nature of the right to an equally weighted vote and of the courts' role in the apportionment process."[117] In this area, the price for decreasing the federal judiciary's interference with the political process is the toleration of more flexible standards for the definition of population equality across districts. It is a price the Burger Court appears willing to pay.

Ultimately, however, this position may be no candidate for acclaim. The Burger Court has chosen to follow a balancing approach to

[114]*See also* Palmer v. Thompson, 403 U.S. 217 (1971).

[115]*Gaffney*, thus, suggests that the Court remains reluctant in the extreme to enter the "political thicket" of gerrymandering, despite the urging of reapportionment partisans that his be the next target for judicial attack. *See* Baker, *supra* note 73, at 140-42.

[116]*See* ch. II, pp. 61 & 66-69.

[117]*The Supreme Court, 1972 Term*, 87 HARV. L. REV. at 93.

governmental apportionment, indicating that it will weigh the deviation from mathematical exactness against the justification for it. Non-population based apportionments must be justified by policy considerations which are reasonable, as defined by a majority of the Court. Such a situation seems incredibly unacceptable to anyone familiar with the halcyon days of substantive due process. Yet just such an analysis is "the only means available to reconcile the competing values of 'one man, one vote' with flexibility in . . . government,"[118] suggesting once again that there was something wrong with the adoption of the "one man, one vote" standard.

That "something" has been the failure of the Supreme Court during the past decade—with the exceptions of Harlan, Stewart, and Fortas—to think long and deeply about the fundamental problem of democratic theory that underlies the reapportionment decisions. That problem is suggested by the following example:

> Let us say that the citizens of a community, one hundred in number, unanimously vote in favor of some government decision that benefits them all equally. Here we have the ideal type of democracy—all the citizens participated equally in making a political decision that benefited them all equally. Now let us suppose a vote that was not unanimous. Sixty citizens wanted policy X, which benefited them. Forty wanted policy Y, which benefited *them*. We normally solve such a problem by resorting to majority rule. But majority rule is a practical expedient for handling disagreements and is only partially compatible with the basic principles of a democracy. We may argue that equality was maintained because each man cast one vote. But there was not equality in making the governmental decision. The sixty made the decision; the forty did not. Nor was there equality of benefits from the decision. The sixty got something they wanted; the forty got nothing. In short, it is easy to talk glibly about majority rule and government by the "people"; but the person who always casts his one equal vote, and always finds himself in the minority, and never gets anything he wants, may not think of himself as quite equal to the person whose vote is always in the majority and who always gets what he wants.[119]

Approximation of the ideal of democratic equality depends not only upon the protection of individual rights but also upon the construction of appropriate institutions, designed to prevent the creation of permanent minorites. This is both a moral and a practical imperative, for, if a group consistently loses at the polls, it will sooner or later—and more likely sooner than later—lose all confidence in the electoral process and resort to some other probably more violent means for the protection of its interests. While population-based apportionment may contribute to

[118]*The Supreme Court, 1970 Term,* 85 HARV. L. REV. at 152.
[119]M. SHAPIRO, *supra* note 36, at 81.

democratic equality by preventing certain minorities from consistently
thwarting certain majorities, it can also, as Mr. Justice Stewart pointed
out in his *Lucas* dissent, inhibit democratic equality by permanently
isolating certain minorities and depriving them of a representative voice
in the legislative chamber.[120] The object should be, as Stewart observed in
Lucas, to assure ultimate, effective majority control, while allowing
minorities sufficient political strength to secure concession and compromise.[121]

> The majoritarian will argue that any such arrangement is a betrayal of democracy
> because any "concession" to a minority is in fact a substitution of what the minority
> wanted for what the majority wanted no matter what nice language you dress it up
> in; but . . . majoritarianism is not synonymous with democracy and a betrayal of
> majoritarianism not necessarily a betrayal of democracy.
> The Supreme Court's decisions on reapportionment prevent us from giving
> certain minorities an extra margin of representation that would insure their real
> participation in policy-making. As a result, these decisions have deprived us of one
> means of overcoming the dilemmas that arise when we realize that rule by the
> majority is not the same as rule by the people.[122]

In spite of such considerations, however, the reapportionment decisions must surely be regarded as the Warren Court's great success
story.[123] One may suspect that this was so because the decisions tapped
what was already a widely held value. The complex wisdom of the system
of checks and balances is little understood or appreciated by most
Americans.[124] At the level of popular thinking, "democracy" is generally
conceived as being the central, fundamental value of the systemic
arrangements of American government, although understanding of
what is represented by the term "democracy" may vary widely.[125] As
with the "incorporation" decisions, so too with the apportionment cases.

[120]377 U.S. 713, 744 (1964).

[121]*But see* Reynolds v. Sims, 377 U.S. 533, 576 (Warren, C. J.) ("If such a scheme were
permissible, . . . (d)eadlock between the two [legislative houses] might result in compromise
and concession. . . ").

[122]M. SHAPIRO, *supra* note 36, at 82.

[123]*See* McKay, *Reapportionment: Success Story of the Warren Court*, 67 MICH. L.
REV. 223 (1968).

[124]*See* McCloskey, *Consensus and Ideology in American Politics*, 58 AM. POL. SCL
REV. 361 (1964); McClosky, Hoffman, and O'Hara, *Issue Conflict and Consensus Among
Party Leaders and Followers*, 54 AM. POL. SCI. REV. 406 (1960).

[125]*Id.; see also* Prothro & Grigg, *Fundamental Principles of Democracy: Bases of
Agreement and Disagreement*, 22 J. POL. 276 (1960); Lane, *The Fear of Equality*, 53 AM.
POL. SCI. REV. 35 (1959).

They merely wrote into the Constitution rights which the people already believed they had.

But, if the rate of compliance with the apportionment decisions has been such as to render them an empirical success, it is worth speculating on the potential practical political effect of "one man, one vote" before mourning the demise of the Warren Court. At the time of the decisions, many laudatory commentators conjured up a model of rural dominated legislatures consistently thwarting the will of the urban majority.[126] But this model was made of whole cloth. What studies have been done indicate that "cow county" representativies were not inimical to pro-urban policies.[127] If they dealt unfairly with urban problems, it was almost always out of ignorance rather than malice. However, one might dismiss these inherently erroneous models as simply harmless partisan rhetorical devices, if their prescription—"one man, one vote"—were likely to result in the predicted benefits. But would it? In the 1970s population based apportionment will result in the transfer of political power from "cow counties" not to urban areas but to the suburbs, and given what we know about the politics of suburbia one may reasonably suspect that the policy outputs brought on by what were hailed as Supreme Court victories for liberalism will be anything but.[128] Rather, the efffect of a rigorous insistence upon simplistic numerology will be to accord suburban residents yet more power, power to keep ethnic minorities in their place—urban ghettos—, power to prevent black encroachment on white suburbs, and at the same time power to insure the continued exapnsion of suburban blight yet further into the rural areas, power to continue to engage in the practice of "terricide," power to force, as in California, rural areas to export their natural resources for suburban use, power to pollute, power to destroy. This may, of course, be an overly bleak picture. Education on the subjects of both race and ecology may result in suburban voters using their power in an enlightened fashion, but a pessimistic view seems more suitable. Ironically, due to the

---

[126]Two of the leading examples of this exercise in fantasy are G. BAKER, *supra* note 1, and Fribourg, *The Reapportionment Crisis* (Public Affairs Pamphlet No. 411 1967).

[127]S. WASBY, THE IMPACT OF THE UNITED STATES SUPREME COURT: SOME PERSPECTIVES 124-26 (1970). *See also* E. BUSHNELL (ed.), IMPACT OF REAPPORTIONMENT ON THE THIRTEEN WESTERN STATES (1970); N. POLSBY (ed.), REAPPORTIONMENT IN THE 1970s. (1971).

[128]*Id.*: *see also* note 41 *supra*; P. KURLAND, POLITICS, THE CONSTITUTION, AND THE WARREN COURT xix (1970); T. LIPPMAN, SPIRO AGNEW'S AMERICA: THE VICE PRESIDENT AND THE POLITICS OF SUBURBIA (1972).

apportionment decisions, the Warren Court may in some part be held responsible for any further deterioration in America's environment and its race relations in the 1970s.

It is at least equally ironic that the Burger Court, purportedly the judicial vanguard of the "emerging Republican majority," should be withdrawing from the more advanced positions of reapportionment doctrine. But it has refused to abandon either the standard or the field entirely. It has continued to insist that electoral districts be apportioned substantially on the basis of population, in order to insure "fair and effective representation."[129] Such a redefinition of the citizen's voting right "does not repudiate *Reynolds'* basic conern,"[130] though it might have been achieved without *Reynolds'* blow at the principle of bicameralism.

[129]Gaffney v. Cummings, 412 U.S. 735, 748 (1973).
[130]*The Supreme Court, 1972 Term*, 87 HARV. L. REV. at 94.

Chapter 4
Courthouse & Station House

As students of the Supreme Court are fond of noting, Alexis de Tocqueville, that shrewd nineteenth century observer of American political folkways, astutely observed that no major issue arises in American politics that does not eventually resolve itself into a judicial controversy.[1] In mid-twentieth century America crime certainly has become a political issue.[2] Whether it was so before it reached the Supreme Court or whether its conversion into a political issue was a Warren Court contribution to American society is a matter subject to debate. Suffice it to say that the influence has been reciprocal, and the public reaction mixed. For every adulatory praise of the Warren Court's liberalization of the process by which criminal convictions are secured in this country there has been at least one vehemently indignant charge that the Court has been "coddling" criminals. Indeed, if there has been any single area of Warren Court decision-making on which the Nixon appointees have been expected to cut back, it has been the criminal defendants' rights decisions.[3]

By their very nature, however, these decisions would necessarily be subject to reinterpretation and readjustment over the years, no matter by whom the Justices were appointed. Far more significant for the long run will be the decisions which laid the constitutional foundation for the "criminal coddling" cases, those decisions which, in the lawyer's parlance, "incorporated" the Bill of Rights into the Fourteenth Amendment or, in the layman's language, made the Bill of Rights applicable against the states. These decisions may well prove to have been the most

[1]A. de TOCQUEVILLE, DEMOCRACY IN AMERICA ch. VI (P. Bradley transl. 1945).

[2]*See generally* R. HARRIS, THE FEAR OF CRIME (1968); R. CLARK, CRIME IN AMERICA (1970); R. SCAMMON & B. WATTENBERG, THE REAL MAJORITY 17, 21, 37ff., 40-41, 180, 207-08 (1971); CONGRESSIONAL QUARTERLY, CRIME AND THE LAW (1971).

[3]*See, e.g.*, Kurland, *1970 Term: Notes on the Emergence of the Burger Court*, 1971 SUP. CT. REV. 265, 298-308; *The Supreme Court, 1970 Term*, 85 HARV. L. REV. 3, 40-44 (1971).

important area of Warren Court creativity, and there appears to be no Burger Court sentiment to reverse this trend.[4]

Simple numbers demonstrate how completely this process was the work of the Warren Court. Prior to 1961, only eight of the twenty-six provisions of the Bill of Rights had been applied to the states:[5] all of the First Amendment,[6] the Fifth Amendment's eminent domain provision,[7] and the Sixth Amendment's guarantee of a public trial.[8] Two other provisions, the Fourth Amendment and the Eighth Amendment's ban on cruel and unusual punishments, were questionably applicable. But the Vinson Court had not found that a second attempt by the State of Louisiana to electrocute Willie Francis, after the first attempt had failed due to a mechanical defect, would constitute cruel and unusual punishment;[9] nor had it concluded that, even though the core values of the Fourth Amendment were protected against state violation, the Constitution required the exclusion of evidence at trial which had been secured in violation of the amendment.[10] By the 1969 retirement of Mr. Chief Justice Warren, however, only seven Bill of Rights guarantees remained inapplicable against the states.[11]

In 1960, the average American, usually bored by the "technicalities" of criminal procedure, probably believed that, were the state to charge him with a non-capital felony, the Constitution would require that he be accorded the right to counsel, a jury trial, and the right to confront the

---

[4]*E.g.*, Schilb v. Kuebel, 404 U.S. 357 (1971); *In re* Winship, 397 U.S. 358 (1970).

[5]It must be borne in mind that, when speaking of the "incorporation" of the Bill of Rights into the Fourteenth Amendment, that only the first eight amendments are referred to. The Tenth Amendment, obviously, cannot apply against the states themselves, and until recently the Court never mentioned the Ninth Amendment. Manifestly, it refers either to unenumerated, inspecific natural law rights or to the theory that certain rights flow from the nature of the social compact. Therefore, though for different reasons of course, it was unacceptable to both "incorporationists", such as Mr. Justice Black, and to the "judicial restrainists" such as Mr. Justice Frankfurter. That their analyses were correct was demonstrated by the Court's decision in Griswold v. Connecticut, 381 U.S. 479 (1965).

[6]Gitlow v. New York, 268 U.S. 652 (1925) (speech and press); Grossjean v. American Press Co., 297 U.S. 233 (1933) (press); DeJonge v. Oregon, 299 U.S. 353 (1937) (assembly); Lovell v. Griffin, 303 U.S. 444 (1938) (speech and press); Cantwell v. Connecticut, 310 U.S. 296 (1940) (religion); Shelton v. Tucker, 364 U.S. 479 (1960) (association); NAACP v. Button, 371 U.S. 415 (1962) (association and speech).

[7]Chicago, Burlington, & Quincy R. Co. v. Chicago, 166 U.S. 226 (1897).

[8]*In re* Oliver, 333 U.S. 257 (1948).

[9]Louisiana *ex rel.* Francis v. Resweber, 329 U.S. 459 (1947).

[10]Wolf v. Colorado, 338 U.S. 25 (1949).

[11]*See* Table I *infra* at pp. 154-56.

witnesses against him and that the Constitution would prevent the state from placing him in a second jeopardy were the first prosecution unsuccessful. In all of these beliefs, the average American *circa* 1960 would have been wrong. That is not to say that the citizen might not have been protected by state law or that a state could have systematically and arbitrarily denied all of these rights in a single prosecution. But it is to say that, as of 1960, the average American's belief that he was protected by the Bill of Rights in that forum where most criminal trials occur, the state court, was incorrect.

The Bill of Rights was designed primarily not as a great civil libertarian measure but as a protection against an all-powerful national government.[12] The concern of many Anti-Federalists for a Bill of Rights proceeded from their states' rights biases rather than from any civil libertarianism on their part.[13] They were, for example, concerned to prevent the federal government from establishing a national religion but were perfectly willing to countenance established churches in the several states. And in 1833 the Great Chief Justice, John Marshall, ruled on the basis of the explicit wording of the Constitution as well as his own familiarity with the historical circumstances and expectations attending the adoption of the Bill of Rights that the states were not limited in their actions by the provisions of the first eight amendments.[14]

So things remained until the Civil War and the ratification of the Fourteenth Amendment which prohibits the states from making or enforcing "any law which shall abridge the privileges and immunities of citizens of the United States" or from denying any person "life, liberty, or property, without due process of law. . . ." It might be thought that either or both of these provisions would make the Bill of Rights applicable to the states. In the *Slaughter-House Cases*, however, Mr. Justice Miller so narrowly construed the Privileges and Immunities Clause as to render it a virtual nullity, a status which it has continued to enjoy to the present day,[15] and several subsequent cases rejected the idea

---

[12]*See* I. BRANDT, THE BILL OF RIGHTS (1965); L. LEVY, THOMAS JEFFERSON AND CIVIL LIBERTIES: THE DARKER SIDE (1963); Berns, *Freedom of the Press and the Alien and Sedition Laws: A Reappraisal*, 1970 SUP. CT. REV. 109.

[13]*See* Kenyoun, *Men of Little Faith: The Anti-Federalists on The Nature of Representative Government*, 12 WILLIAM & MARY Q. 3 (1955). Berns, *supra* note 12.

[14]Barron v. Baltimore, 7 Pet. 243 (1833).

[15]16 Wall.36, 71, 77-79 (1873). *Cf.* Twining v. New Jersey, 211 U.S. 78, 97 (1908); Hague v. C.I.O., 307 U.S. 496 (1939); Madden v. Kentucky, 309 U.S. 83 (1940); Edwards v. California, 314 U.S. 160 (1941).

that the Due Process Clause was a shorthand version of the Bill of Rights.[16] Thus, the "total incorporation" theory never commanded a majority of the Supreme Court, though it fell but one vote short of becoming constitutional law in *Adamson v. California.*[17] Indeed, the Court on several occasions expressed itself as opposed to the doctrine.[18]

No such expressions, however, have been heard since *Adamson.* In fact, the Court increasingly followed a program of " 'selective' incorporation or 'absorption' [which] amounts to little more than a diluted form of the full incorporation theory."[19] By circumventing or reversing earlier opinions that particular Bill of Rights guarantees were not safeguarded against state action by the Privileges and Immunities Clause or other provision of the Fourteenth Amendment,[20] the Court extended these guarantees against the states by virtue of the Due Process Clause of

[16]*E.g.* Hurtado v. California, 110 U.S. 516 (1884); Twining v. New Jersey, 211 U.S. 78 (1908); Palko v. Connecticut, 302 U.S. 319 (1937); Adamson v. California, 332 U.S. 46 (1947).

[17]332 U.S. 46 (1947).

[18]*In re* Kemmler, 136 U.S. 436 (1890); McElvaine v. Brush, 142 U.S. 155 (1892); Maxwell v. Dow, 176 U.S. 581 (1900).

[19]Pointer v. Texas, 380 U.S. 400, 410 (1965) (Harlan, J., concurring). Justice Harlan continued by castigating his brethren for "[ignoring] the possibility that not all phases of any given guaranty described in the Bill of Rights are necessarily fundamental."

Note also that Mr. Justice Harlan appears to have regarded the terms "incorporation" and "absorption" as interchangeable. *But see* Frankfurter, *Memorandum on "Incorporation" of the Bill of Rights in the Due Process Clause of the Fourteenth Amendment,* 78 HARV. L. REV. 746 (1965).

[20]U.S. v. Cruikshank, 92 U.S. 542 (1875); Prudential Insurance Co. v. Cheek, 259 U.S. 530 (1922) (First Amendment).

Presser v. Illinois, 116 U.S. 252 (1886) (Second Amendment).

Weeks v. United States, 232 U.S. 383 (1914) (Fourth Amendment).

Davidson v. New Orleans, 96 U.S. 97 (1877) (Fifth Amendment, just compensation); Hurtado v. California, 110 U.S. 516 (1884) (Fifth Amendment, grand jury); Palko v. Connecticut, 302 U.S. 319 (1937) (Fifth Amendment, double jeopardy); Twining v. New Jersey, 211 U.S. 78 (1908); Snyder v. Massachusetts, 291 U.S. 97 (1933); Adamson v. California, 332 U.S. 46 (1947); Cohen v. Hurley, 366 U.S. 117 (1961) (Fifth Amendment, self-incrimination).

Maxwell v. Dow, 176 U.S. 581 (1900) (Sixth Amendment, jury trial); Betts v. Brady, 316 U.S. 455 (1942) (Sixth Amendment, right to counsel); West v. Louisiana, 194 U.S. 258 (1904) (Sixth Amendment, confrontation of witnesses).

Walker v. Sauvinet, 92 U.S. 90 (1876) (Seventh Amendment).

In re Kemmler, 136 U.S. 436 (1890); McElvaine v. Brush, 142 U.S. 155 (1892); O'Neil v. Vermont, 144 U.S. 323 (1892) (Eighth Amendment, cruel and unusual punishment).

that amendment, often by the same standards as applicable to the federal government.[21]

The technical constitutional means for this enlargement of the Fourteenth Amendment was initially provided by the Court's decision in *Palko v. Connecticut*.[22] In *Palko*, the Court faced the question of whether the Fourteenth Amendment embraced the protection against double jeopardy contained in the Fifth Amendment. Justice Cardozo, speaking for the Court, answered in the negative. The Fourteenth Amendment, Cardozo said, did not automatically protect all the rights extended by the Bill of Rights, but instead guaranteed only those "implicit in the concept of ordered liberty" and those principles of justice "so rooted in the traditions and conscience of our people as to be ranked as fundamental." This interpretation, though immediately restrictive, opened the way for judicial development of a whole series of constitutional rights to be guaranteed by the Court as against the states, for now all that needed to be done to open the Pandora's box of "selective incorporation" was to expand the domain of "implicit in the concept of ordered liberty."

Out of *Palko*, in respect to the question of the application of the Bill of Rights guarantees against the states, four different schools of judicial thought arose. The first, represented by such figures as Mr. Justice Frankfurter and Mr. Justice Harlan, emphasized the flexible nature of the Constitution and the wisdom of allowing for legal growth and change. "Due process of law . . .," Frankfurter once observed from the

[21]First Amendment: Gitlow v. New York, 268 U.S. 652 (1925) (speech and press); Grossjean v. American Press Co., 297 U.S. 233 (1936) (press); DeJonge v. Oregon, 299 U.S. 353 (1937) (assembly); Lovell v. Griffin, 303 U.S. 444 (1938) (speech and press); Cantwell v. Connecticut, 310 U.S. 296 (1940) (religion); Shelton v. Tucker, 364 U.S. 479 (1960) (association); NAACP v. Button, 371 U.S. 415 (1962) (association and speech).

Fourth Amendment: Wolf v. Colorado, 338 U.S. 25 (1949); Mapp v. Ohio, 367 U.S. 643 (1961); Ker v. California, 374 U.S. 23 (1963).

Fifth Amendment: Chicago, Burlington, & Quincy R. Co. v. Chicago, 166 U.S. 226 (1897) (eminent domain); Malloy v. Hogan, 378 U.S. 1 (1964) (self-incrimination); Murphy v. Waterfront Comm'n, 378 U.S. 52 (1964) (self-incrimination); Griffin v. California, 380 U.S. 609 (1965) (self-incrimination).

Sixth Amendment: *In re* Oliver, 333 U.S. 257 (1948) (public trial); Gideon v. Wainwright, 372 U.S. 335 (1963) (right to counsel); Pointer v. Texas, 380 U.S. 400 (1965) (confrontation of witnesses).

Eighth Amendment: Louisiana *ex rel.* Francis v. Resweber, 329 U.S. 459 (1947) (cruel and unusual punishment); Robinson v. California, 370 U.S. 660 (1962) (cruel and unusual punishment).

[22]302 U.S. 319 (1937).

bench, "expresses a demand for civilized standards of law. It is thus not a stagnant formulation of what has been achieved in the past but a standard for judgment in the progressive evolution of the institutions of a free society."[23] Justices of this bent would test the constitutionality of state criminal procedures by what they called the standard of "fundamental fairness."

The second school adhered to a policy of "selective incorporation," generally under the *Palko* standard, applying selected provisions of the Bill of Rights to the states, though not all of the first eight amendments. The "selective incorporationist" school also emphasized the necessity of constitutional growth and change, but they would subject that growth to the limits of the Bill of Rights guarantees rather than utilize the more open-ended Frankfurterian test. Perhaps the flavor of this judicial approach was best captured by Mr. Justice Brennan in an address replying to those scholars who had objected that selective incorporation violated the principle of *stare decisis*.

> When a decision finds that a specific not deemed sixty or seventy years ago to be a "fundamental right" now has that character, has the Court really overruled the old precedent or, rather, has the Court appraised the specific in today's context of the necessity for restraining arbitrary actions by governments more powerful and more pervasive than in our ancestor's day? In other words, does not the common thread of the holdings extending the restrictions against the states—none arrived at until after a long series of decisions grappling with the pros and cons of the issues—simply enforce the conclusion that in today's America the guarantees in question are essential to the preservation and furtherance of the constitutional structure of government for a free society? For the genius of the Constitution resides not in any static meaning that it has in a world that is dead and gone, but in its adaptability of its great principles to cope with current problems and current needs.[24]

Now one might ask what was the difference between the "fundamental fairness" position and the "selective incorporation" approach. The difference lay in the standards by which they would apply the Bill of Rights guarantees to the states. The selective incorporationists would apply a Bill of Rights provision to the states "carbon copy." That is, they would require the states to meet the same standards under a given provision of the Bill of Rights as were required of the federal government. When a particular provision was incorporated into the Fourteenth Amendment, all of the previous judicial interpretations as to the meaning of that provision were to go along with it—bag and baggage. Those of the

[23]Malinski v. New York, 324 U.S. 401, 414 (1945).
[24]Brennan, *Extension of the Bill of Rights to the States*, 44 J. URB. L. 11, 18-19 (1966).

"fundamental fairness" school, on the other hand, while perhaps finding the substance of a particular Bill of Rights protection to be part of "fundamental fairness," would argue for lower standards under the Fourteenth Amendment than were required of the national government by the Bill of Rights.[25] This position sprang, first, from a concern for federalism. "It is one of the happy incidents of a federal system," wrote Mr. Justice Brandeis, "that a state may serve as a laboratory, and try novel . . . experiments."[26] Second, Frankfurter and Harlan often expressed a concern for the implication for the Bill of Rights guarantees of applying them to the states by the same standards as they apply to the federal government. It was, they argued, unrealistic to require the states with their more limited resources to live up to the same standards as were required of the federal government. If this were done, they predicted, the consequence in the long run would be not to raise the standards which the states must meet but rather to lower the standards required of the federal government. The Court might well have to "water down" the Bill of Rights in order to apply it realistically to the states.

Over and against these two schools of thought stood Mr. Justice Black and his "total incorporation" thesis. For Black the crucial factors in interpreting the Constitution were language and history, not reasonableness or desirability.[27] As Black read history, of course, this meant that the Bill of Rights was intended by the framers of the Fourteenth Amendment to have been applied *in toto* to the states.[28] For Black, the "fundamental fairness" test and to a lesser degree "selective incorporation" vested judges with a tyrannical discretion they should not have.

Finally, there was a position, originally taken in *Adamson* by Justices Murphy and Rutledge but later endorsed by Justices Goldberg and Douglas during the Warren years[29] which might be characterized as "the Bill of Rights and more," a position which attempted to have the best of both worlds, Black's literalism and Frankfurter's expanding Constitution. According to this school of interpretation, the Fourteenth Amendment did indeed apply the entire Bill of Rights to the states,

[25]*See, e.g.,* Jacobellis v. Ohio, 378 U.S. 184, 203 (1964) (Harlan, J., dissenting); Pointer v. Texas, 380 U.S. 400, 408 (1965) (Harlan, J., concurring).
[26]New State Ice Co. v. Liebmann, 285 U.S. 262, 280, 311 (1934) (dissenting opinion).
[27]*See* H. BLACK, A CONSTITUTIONAL FAITH (1968), *reviewed,* Frank, 85 POL. SCI. Q. 640 (1970).
[28]*See* Adamson v. California, 326 U.S. 46, 68, 92-123 (1947) (Black, J., dissenting).
[29]*Id.* at 123; Griswold v. Connecticut, 381 U.S. 479 (1965).

perhaps even including the Ninth Amendment,[30] but these were not the only limitations upon state power. Others might be found in the future, depending upon society's evolving sense of fairness.

To both the "fundamental fairness" school and "the Bill of Rights and more" thinkers, the "incorporationists," both selective and total, charged that neither approach amounted to anything more than a revival of natural law, substantive due process, and the errors of the old laissez-faire Court.[31] They rested, in short, upon a mistaken conception of the judicial function. To this charge, Frankfurter and Harlan replied that due process of law could not and should not be confined to a particular set of existing procedures, because due process speaks for the future as well as to the present and at any given time may include those procedures that are fair and feasible in light of then existing values and capabilities. In particular, the Black theory of total incorporation would strike at the very strength of the Constitution, its flexiblility. Black's formula, or so Frankfurter charged, would reduce the Constitution to a rigid, dogmatic, and largely antiquated document.[32] Incorporation, especially "carbon copy" incorporation, would trap the country in a constitutional strait jacket. To which the incorporationists retorted that the definition of due process in terms of social values must invite the question of who would determine the values; and, since in a practical sense it would be the Supreme Court, the other tests invited the Court to impose its own value preferences upon the country behind a smoke screen of constitutional rhetoric. It would be better to rely upon the specificity of the Bill of Rights, and if the American people wanted to change the specifics they have resort to the amending process. But the specificity of the Bill of Rights, replied Frankfurter and Harlan, is largely illusory.[33] The so-called literal language of the Bill of Rights in no way directs or confines judicial interpretation along specific lines. Rather, it shifts the focus and begs the question. How specific is "unreasonable" within the meaning of the Fourth Amendment?[34] When does the Sixth Amendment right to counsel begin?[35] At arrest? At the preliminary hearing? At arraignment?

[30]Griswold v. Connecticut, 381 U.S. 479, 486 (1965) (Goldberg, J., concurring).

[31]*Id.* at 507 (Black, J., dissenting).

[32]*See* Adamson v. California, 326 U.S. 46, 59 (1947) (Frankfurter, J., concurring).

[33]*See, e.g.,* Griswold v. Connecticut, 381 U.S. 479, 499 (1965) (Harlan, J., concurring).

[34]*E.g., compare* Chimel v. California, 395 U.S. 752 (1969), *with* United States v. Rabinowitz, 339 U.S. 56 (1950).

[35]*Compare* Miranda v. Arizona, 384 U.S. 436 (1966), *with* Crooker v. California, 357 U.S. 433 (1958).

Or at the trial itself? And when does it end? At sentencing? After the first appeal? The first petition for habeas corpus? Does it include probation and parole hearings? Do indigent defendants have a right to counsel at state expense?[36] If so, only in capital cases? Felony cases? Or even simple misdemeanors? In resolving these problems is the Bill of Rights significantly more specific than the Due Process Clause of the Fourteenth Amendment?

Despite such difficulties, the doctrine of selective incorporation was to carry the day. But to such an extent that, by the time of his retirement in 1971, Mr. Justice Black could be said to have lost the doctrinal battle but won the war of results.[37] The first wave in the Black Tide broke in 1961, in the case of Mrs. Dolly Mapp.[38] Although previous Courts had found it relatively easy to apply the Fifth Amendment's "just compensation" clause to the states by virtue of a substantive reading of the Due Process Clause[39] and to incorporate the First Amendment protections into the Fourteenth Amendment by virtue of a selective incorporation,[40] reading the remaining guarantees into the Fourteenth Amendment had proven to be a slower and more difficult job. In part, this seems to have stemmed from the fact that Amendments I through III refer implicitly to the actions of the executive and legislative branches of government, while Amendments V through VIII are directed toward judicial procedures, with Amendment IV falling somewhere in between, and until the 1960s the Supreme Court was reticent to bind state judiciaries. Put differently, the High Court had no reluctance to limit legislators and executives but was moved by a sort of judicial *esprit de corps* when it came to restraining judges. This was in all probability a subconscious rather than a conscious factor in judicial decision-making, but its presence was nonetheless real and significant. Thus, in *Wolf v. Colorado*,[41] the Court had found that the "core" of the values protected by the Fourth Amendment were "implicit in the concept of ordered liberty," but had refused to hold that a state conviction must be reversed because evidence admitted at the trial had been obtained under circumstances which would have required its exclusion in a federal court as an infraction of the Fourth Amendment.[42]

---

[36]*Compare* Gideon v. Wainwright, 372 U.S. 335 (1963), *and* Argersinger v. Hamlin, 407 U.S. 25 (1972), *with* Betts v. Brady, 316 U.S. 455 (1942).

[37]*See generally* Duncan v. Louisiana, 391 U.S. 145, 162 (1968) (Black, J., concurring).

[38]Mapp v. Ohio, 367 U.S. 643 (1961).

[39]Chicago, Burlington, & Quincy R. Co., v. Chicago, 166 U.S. 226 (1897).

[40]*See* note 6 *supra*.

[41]338 U.S. 25 (1949).

[42]Boyd v. United States, 116 U.S. 616 (1886).

Mr. Justice Frankfurter, author of the *Wolf* opinion, subsequently moved the Court to a median position in which the exclusion of evidence was required in state cases, if it were obtained in a manner "shocking to the conscience."[43] This rule, however, had the unfortunate consequence in application by a divided Court of some Justices implicitly charging that their brethren were so manifestly hard-hearted that their consciences would not be shocked by the Saint Bartholomew's Day massacre and their brethren responding by implication that their colleagues were weak-kneed, lily-livered and unnecessarily squeamish.[44] Such an unfortunate rule of judicial decision-making had to be abandoned, and it was, in *Mapp v. Ohio.*

Miss Mapp's home had been forcibly entered by police officers, without a search warrant, on the basis of information that a "wanted" person was hiding there. Although the ensuing search failed to produce the culprit, the officers did find—in a trunk in the basement—a number of obscene books and pictures for the possession of which Miss Mapp was tried and convicted. Although she appealed her conviction on First Amendment grounds, arguing that the state could not make it illegal merely to possess obscenity,[45] the Warren Court majority, much to the annoyance of Mr. Justice Harlan, chose to dispense with the case on the basis of the Fourth Amendment. The search by which the materials had been procured, wrote Mr. Justice Clark, had violated the Fourth Amendment's ban on unreasonable searches and seizures and that Amendment, being enforceable against the states through the Due Process Clause of the Fourteenth Amendment, must be enforceable against them by the same sanction of exclusion as is used against the federal government. Were it otherwise, the protection of the Fourth Amendment against state action would be valueless.

There have been those, of course, who have argued that the exclusionary rule is totally illogical, that it serves to set the guilty free merely because the constable has blundered.[46]

> Titus, you have been found guilty of conducting a lottery; Flavius, you have confessedly violated the Constitution. Titus ought to suffer imprisonment for crime, and Flavius for contempt. But no! We shall let you *both* go free. We shall not punish Flavius directly, but shall do so by reversing Titus' conviction. This is our

[43]Rochin v. California, 342 U.S. 165 (1952).

[44]*E.g.*, Irvine v. California, 347 U.S. 128 (1954).

[45]*But see* Stanley v. Georgia, 394 U.S. 557 (1969) (possession of pornographic materials, absent intent to distribute, is protected by First Amendment).

[46]*See, e.g.*, People v. Defore, 150 N.E. 584 (N.Y. 1923) (Cardozo, J.).

way of teaching people like Flavius to behave, and of teaching people like Titus to behave, and incidentally of securing respect for the Constitution. Our way of upholding the Constitution is not to strike at the man who breaks it, but to let off somebody else who broke something else.[47]

But Clark could not agree. The experience of the dozen years since *Wolf* had shown that the states could not create effective deterrents to unlawful police search activities other than exclusion,[48] and those states which continued to admit unlawfully seized evidence simply were encouraging disobedience of the Constitution which they were bound to support.

The public and particularly the police reaction to the *Mapp* decision was intense and largely negative.[49] But the Warren Court had, for the first but not the last time, taken a significant step toward injecting the Constitution and, thus, the Supreme Court into the process of the administration of criminal justice. Two years later, they took another, even larger stride, though it was largely at the invitation of the states.[50]

Clarence Earl Gideon had been charged with a non-capital felony in a Florida state court. He appeared without funds and without an attorney and requested that the court appoint counsel for him. This request was denied, and he was convicted. Subsequently, however, Gideon sought release on a federal writ of habeas corpus, arguing that his conviction had been secured in violation of his Sixth Amendment right to counsel. Some thirty-one years earlier, in *Powell v. Alabama*,[51] the Supreme Court had reversed the rape convictions of the so-called "Scottsboro Boys," convictions secured in one of the major perversions of procedural fairness in America's legal history, holding that in capital cases involving exceptional circumstances the states were required by the Due Process Clause to appoint counsel for indigent defendants. Ten years later, in *Betts v. Brady*,[52] the Court adjusted its rule to require the appointment of counsel at state expense for indigent defendants in all capital cases *and* in non-capital felonies involving exceptional circumstances. Gideon's trial, however, had not involved either a capital offense or exceptional circumstances. Nevertheless, the Court unanimously reversed *Betts*.

[47] 8 J. WIGMORE, EVIDENCE, § 2180, at 4 (1940).
[48] *E.g.*, People v. Cahan, 44 Cal. 2d 434 (1955).
[49] *See* C. LYTLE, THE WARREN COURT & ITS CRITICS ch. 6 (1968).
[50] Gideon v. Wainwright, 372 U.S. 335 (1963). Gideon v. Wainwright is perhaps the best known decision in modern Supreme Court history thanks to the best-selling case study by Anthony Lewis, GIDEON'S TRUMPET (1964).
[51] 287 U.S. 45 (1932).
[52] 316 U.S. 455 (1942).

Exultantly and triumphantly, Mr. Justice Black delivered the opinion for the Court, holding that, while the *Betts* majority had correctly assumed that a provision of the Bill of Rights which was fundamental and essential to a fair trial was applicable to the states by virtue of the Fourteenth Amendment, that majority had incorrectly concluded that the Sixth Amendment's right to counsel, including the right to appointed counsel, was not such a right. Mr. Justice Harlan, forced to "eat crow," concurred, apparently greatly influenced by the fact that twenty-three states had filed a brief *amicus curiae* on behalf, not of Florida, but of Gideon.[53] The "exceptional circumstances" rule in non-capital cases, concluded Harlan, had proven incapable of application.

The following term the Court abandoned a similar rule which it had created to determine the admissibility of confessions in state criminal proceedings. This rule, as with the "exceptional circumstances" standard for defining the ambit of the right to counsel in state trials, had developed out of a Depression era case involving a peculiarly gross violation of due process, *Brown v. Mississippi*.[54] In *Brown*, the Court had voided the murder convictions of three black youths, convictions based solely upon confessions obtained by physical brutality and torture. *Brown*, however, clearly demonstrated the reluctance of the Court to fasten Bill of Rights standards on state criminal trials, for the confessions were excluded because the manner in which they had been obtained was revolting to the Court's sense of justice and fundamental fairness not because that procedure had been violative of the Fifth Amendment's privilege against self-incrimination. As a consequence, for the next three decades the question of what constituted coercion became a crucial, albeit difficult, one for the Court. While physical violence clearly amounted to coercion, it was not necessarily apparent that psychological pressures short of violence might also be coercive. In *Chambers v. Florida*, however, the Court did exclude a confession on the grounds that it had been obtained by methods which, though short of physical abuse, had been so calculated to "break" the suspect as to amount to psychological coercion.[55] Again, however, the fact situation presented by *Chambers* had been an extreme one. As yet more prisoners appealed their convictions, arguing that their confessions had also been coerced, the Court was forced to formulate, reformulate, and modify a rule based

[53]The entire story of the conception, development, and filing of the influential *amicus* brief is recounted in A. LEWIS, *supra* note 50, at 141-150.

[54]297 U.S. 278 (1936).

[55]309 U.S. 227 (1940).

upon the totality of the situation involved.[56] According to this rule the admissibility in state criminal trials of allegedly coerced confessions was to be determined by the examination of such factors as the maturity, sophistication, and intelligence of the defendant, the length of his interrogation, the behavior of the questioning officers, and so forth. Almost by definition such a "totality of the circumstances" rule was open-ended and vague in the extreme, leaving almost all touched by it in a position of uncertainty as to what the law of the Constitution was. Then, in *Malloy v. Hogan*, the Warren Court elected to move beyond the "totality of the circumstances" doctrine to apply the Fifth Amendment's self-incrimination privilege to the states.[57]

According to Mr. Justice Brennan, who wrote the opinion for the majority in *Malloy*, the earlier precedent denying the application of the self-incrimination privilege to the states had been eroded by two lines of cases, the first being the coerced confession cases which had prohibited imprisonment as a method of coercion. The second line of cases undermining precedent had been those involving the Fourth Amendment's prohibition against unreasonable searches and seizures.[58] There was, or so Brennan claimed, a parallel between the privilege and the Fourth Amendment's exclusionary rule. *Mapp*, argued Brennan, relying heavily if implicitly upon Mr. Justice Black's concurrence in that case,[59] had applied the exclusionary rule to the states on the basis of the intimate relationship between the Fourth Amendment's prohibition and the Fifth Amendment's guarantee against self-incrimination. Since the Fourth Amendment had now been made applicable to the states, it made sense to apply the intimately related self-incrimination privilege to them also.

For Mr. Justice Harlan, dissenting, all of this made very little sense at all. He could not understand how a line of decision which had explicitly avowed a lack of any intention to apply the Fifth Amendment's self-incrimination provision to the states could, nevertheless, have done so. Nor could a man who had dissented in *Mapp* on the grounds that the exclusionary rule was a judge-made rule of evidence applicable to federal proceedings only agree that that decision had augured the "in-

---

[56]*E.g.*, Lisenba v. California, 314 U.S. 219 (1941); Ashcraft v. Tennessee, 322 U.S. 143 (1944); Haley v. Ohio, 332 U.S. 596 (1948); Watts v. Indiana, 338 U.S. 49 (1949); Thomas v. Arizona, 356 U.S. 390 (1958).

[57]378 U.S. 1 (1964). On the same day, the Court held that one jurisdiction in the federal system could not compel a witness to give testimony which might incriminate him under the laws of the other jurisdiction. Murphy v. Waterfront Comm'n, 378 U.S. 52 (1964).

[58]*E.g.*, Mapp v. Ohio, 367 U.S. 643 (1961).

[59]*Id.* at 661.

corporation" of the self-incrimination privilege. But Harlan, as was so often true during the Warren years, remained a voice crying in the wilderness for logic and craftsmanship.

Holmes, however, reminded us that a page of history is worth a volume of logic, and there is a discernible similarity in the Court's development of the Fourth Amendment, the self-incrimination privilege of the Fifth Amendment, and the Sixth Amendment's right to counsel, leading to their "incorporation" into the Fourteenth Amendment. In each case, the Court began cautiously, applying a fundamental fairness test, rather than employing the particular Bill of Rights guarantee invoked by the appellant. This test, however, proved to be so vague that its application and effect depended upon the unique facts of the individual case. The Court was, thus, vested with a tremendous amount of discretion in the review of state criminal convictions. But this vast discretion was burdensome both to the Court and to the states. The Court's case load was increased, and, as the Court proceeded on a case-by-case resolution of the problem, the law became ever more complicated, shot through with exceptions, and difficult to understand. The states, on the other hand, found this situation onerous, because they could never be certain of the validity of their own criminal procedures or, thus, of the finality of their criminal convictions. The states, therefore, began to move to adopt on their own initiative some procedure which more or less approximated the federal practice. By the time of the *Mapp* decision, for example, nineteen states had adopted, either by statute or by state court decision, the exclusionary rule, and twenty-three states filed an *amicus* brief on behalf of Gideon. At this point, the Warren Court, persuaded by the experience of those states adopting these procedures that the states could live with the Bill of Rights guarantees and by their own failure to develop workable rules of constitutional law of general applicability under the case-by-case approach, incorporated the constitutional rule into the Fourteenth Amendment.

It was, however, with the incorporation of the Fifth Amendment's self-incrimination privilege and the Sixth Amendment's right to counsel, with the decisions in *Malloy* and *Gideon*, themselves both relatively popular, that the Court began to get into trouble in the criminal defendant's rights area. The problem lay not with the application of these provisions to the states but with their interpretation. What did they mean? The Warren Court, however, rather than take time to consolidate its advances, rather than gain some experience with the application of "incorporated" rights to state procedures, continued to forge ahead and eventually, in order to overrule *Palko* in fact as well as in approach, created an entirely new standard of "incorporation."

As a practical matter, the issue in *Duncan v. Louisiana* was not whether a state could deny a defendant a jury trial.[60] Since every state guaranteed a jury trial for more serious crimes, the issue presented in *Duncan* was a narrow one. The Sixth Amendment requires a jury trial in all criminal prosecutions, but this has been interpreted by the Supreme Court to except the trial of petty offenses on the grounds that the Framers had in mind the common law practice at the time they wrote the amendment.[61] The question in *Duncan*, then, was whether the federal distinction between serious and petty offenses, between jury and non-jury crimes, was a constitutional requirement.[62] The Court held that it was, requiring a jury trial in all state cases which, if tried in a federal court, would necessarily be tried by a jury.

After paying homage to the great sanction accorded jury trial by history and usage, Mr. Justice White turned to a discussion of the inapplicability or desuetude of precedents suggesting that the federal jury trial right was not and should not be a right guaranteed against state infringement by the Due Process Clause of the Fourteenth Amendment.[63] Among the fundamental purposes of the jury, White argued, was the prevention of government oppression. While an independent judiciary significantly contributes to lessening the possibilities of arbitrary government, the judiciary remains part of the government. Jury trial, then, represents a further step in the campaign of liberty by protecting the criminally accused against corrupt, biased, or eccentric judges. By involving the private citizen in the judical process as juror, the Sixth Amendment manifests an extreme reluctance to entrust plenary power over life and liberty to the government alone.

White, then proceeded to add something new to "incorporation" theory by rejecting Cardozo's test for whether a given Bill of Rights protection was incorporated into the Fourteenth Amendment. According to Cardozo, writing for the majority in *Palko*, the test for inclusion or exclusion was whether a given procedure were "implicit in the concept of ordered liberty." White, however, narrowed the test to whether a given criminal procedure were "fundamental to the American scheme of

[60] 391 U.S. 145 (1968).
[61] *See* Schick v. United States, 195 U.S. 65 (1904).
[62] *See also* Baldwin v. New York, 399 U.S. 66 (1970).
[63] Maxwell v. Dow, 176 U.S. 581 (1900); Palko v. Connecticut, 302 U.S. 319, 325 (1937).

justice." In other words, according to the *Duncan* majority, the test was not, as Cardozo's test would have it, whether a fair and equitable system of criminal justice could be imagined in which a given protection of the Bill of Rights was absent. In the case of jury trial, for example, a fair and just system of criminal procedure, a system of ordered liberty, could easily be conceived in which there were no jury trials. One need look no farther than western Europe.[64] Rather, the test for White was whether, given the American system of criminal justice, a particular procedure were fundamental. According to White, jury trial was such a fundamental, because the entire structure and style of criminal proceedings in American courts had been developed in connection with and were designed to complement jury trial. "The deep commitment of the Nation to the right of jury trial in serious criminal cases . . . must therefore be respected by the States."[65]

Such a standard may not, however, have been as great a repudiation of Cardozo as it might seem, for the *Palko* opinion also spoke of another test for incorporation which Cardozo seemed to equate with "implicit in the concept of ordered liberty." That is, he also spoke of whether a given procedure were "so rooted in the traditions and conscience of our people as to be ranked as fundamental."[66] This sounds very much like White's test and, thus, may have rendered Mr. Justice White's lengthy footnote number fourteen in *Duncan* not merely less important than White apparently thought it but unnecessary. On the other hand, White seems to have been laying the groundwork for the ultimate overruling of *Palko's* immediate holding that the double jeopardy provision of the Fifth Amendment was not applicable against the states. If this is so, then Justice White may be deemed to have been imminently successful, for the year following *Duncan* the Warren Court, relying upon the *Duncan* test of incorporation, ruled that the result in *Palko* was no longer good law.[67]

Duncan, however, was a doubly significant holding because, for the first time in the long and inconsistent history of "incorporation," it apparently took the Court farther than it wanted to go. By "carbon copy" application of the Sixth Amendment's jury trial provision to the states, the Court had fastened upon the states the requirements of

---

[64]*See* J. MERRYMAN, THE CIVIL LAW TRADITION (1969); H. ABRAHAM, THE JUDICIAL PROCESS ch. 3 (1968). *See generally*, S. BEDFORD, THE FACES OF JUSTICE (1961).

[65]391 U.S. at 156.

[66]302 U.S. at 325, quoting Snyder v. Massachusetts, 291 U.S. 97, 105 (1934).

[67]Benton v. Maryland, 395 U.S. 784 (1969).

twelve-member juries and unanimous verdicts. But in the history of the common law the number twelve is not sacrosanct,[68] and the unanimity rule is not necessarily self-evident from the constitutional text. All that Mr. Justice White would say to the problem was to note cryptically in a footnote that the Court's interpretations were always "subject to reconsideration."[69] This, however, moved Mr. Justice Fortas to write a separate concurrence, objecting not to the majority's immediate holding but to the "carbon copy" application of the ancillary judicial doctrines which had grown up around the Sixth Amendment. While jury trial in all but petty offenses might be fundamental to due process in the American scheme of justice, Fortas could see no reason to impose such federal requirements as a unanimous verdict of twelve jurors upon the states. As an example, at the time of the decision in *Duncan*, at least ten states had begun to experiment with the practice of holding criminal trials of first instance before a judge only with a right of appeal to a *de novo* trial by a jury in a different court.[70] Such a practice decreased both the costs and delays of criminal trials, since juries were used only in the cases of those persons convicted.

Mr. Justice Harlan, dissenting, also objected to the application of the jury trial to state criminal proceedings, since a fundamentally fair trial could be conducted without a jury. Although the jury was not without its virtues, Harlan admitted, he could find no reasons, constitutional or otherwise, for preventing the states from limiting jury trial to promote the efficient administration of justice. Juries were, Harlan noted, cumbersome, slow, and costly. Jury trial often placed complex issues in the hands of untrained laymen, and as such it might be argued jury trials decreased public respect for the law. Just as the Warren majority had often relied upon social science in other of its landmark cases,[71] so Harlan concluded by taking judicial notice of recent empirical studies of the illogic of jury decision-making and of the decreasing use of both civil and criminal juries throughout the common law world.[72] Such impressive statistics demonstrated, for Harlan, that *Duncan* marked a step backwards in American legal development, fastening a given procedure upon

[68]*See* J. THAYER, A PRELIMINARY TREATISE ON EVIDENCE AT THE COMMON LAW 1-182 (1896); R. von MOSCHZISKER, TRIAL BY JURY 5-62 (1922).
[69]391 U.S. at 158 n. 30.
[70]*Id.*
[71]*See, e.g.*, Brown v. Board of Education, 347 U.S. 483 (1954); Miranda v. Arizona, 384 U.S. 436 (1966).
[72]*See, e.g.*, H. KALVEN & H. ZEISEL, THE AMERICAN JURY (1966).

the states rather than encouraging them to develop new, more desirable, and more effective means for the trial of criminal cases.

Before, Harlan had argued that the application of Bill of Rights guarantees to the states would eventually result in the erosion of the standards by which those guarantees applied to the federal government.[73] Though he would probably have enjoyed little feeling of exultation, *Duncan* and its progeny have borne out Harlan's reservations. In *Williams v. Florida*,[74] the Burger Court, impressed by the differences between state and federal jurisdictions in terms of kinds and quantities of crimes with which they dealt,[75] validated Florida's use of six-member juries in all but capital cases, and in *Apodaca v. Oregon* the Burger Court sustained the use of non-unanimous jury verdicts in state criminal trials.[76] Several questions must now await resolution by the Court. For example, if Oregon may use a ten-to-two verdict for conviction, may some other state use a three-fourths or a two-thirds rule? What about a simple majority? If six-man juries are constitutionally sufficient, are five-man juries? Four? Three? May a state combine *Williams* and *Apodaca* and use five-man juries with a simple majority to convict? Or will the Court draw a line, based upon considerations of policy if not the constitutional text, below which no state may go? Is there a constitutionally required minimum number of jurors? Or a minimum percentage thereof for conviction? It is important to remember, as Harlan's ghost rides triumphant, that wherever the Court draws the line, by virtue of "carbon copy incorporation," that line is applicable to federal as well as state proceedings. While Congress may maintain twelve-member juries and unanimous verdicts for conviction, there is no constitutional duty that it do so. Some civil libertarians have complained bitterly about "the Court's recent departure from our traditional concept of jury trial."[77] But it should always be borne in mind that the forefather of that departure, if not its necessary cause, was *Duncan*, the doctrine of incorporation, and the Warren Court.

[73]*See* note 25 *supra*.

[74]399 U.S. 78 (1970). *See also* Colgrove v. Battin, 413 U.S. 149 (1973) (6-person jury permissible in federal civil cases under Seventh Amendment).

[75]*See, e.g.*, Friendly, *The Bill of Rights as a Code of Criminal Procedure*, 53 CALIF. L. REV. 929 (1965), citing statistics showing that in 1963 the Supreme Court and County Courts of New York handled 19,888 criminal cases, and the state's lower courts handled 452,271 felonies and misdemeanors. During approximately the same period, the federal district courts for New York disposed of a mere 1,816 criminal cases.

[76]406 U.S. 404 (1972).

[77]*The Supreme Court, 1971 Term*, 86 HARV. L. REV. 1, 156 (1972).

Of the Nixon appointees, only Mr. Justice Powell apparently has drawn the Harlanesque conclusion that incorporation may be a double-edged sword, the price of whose services may come exorbitantly high.[78] The other new members of the Court have plunged ahead to extend the Warren Court's incorporation crusade, perhaps most notably in *Argersinger v. Hamlin*.[79] *Argersinger* amplified the effective scope of *Gideon v. Wainwright* by following the lead of Warren Court precedents rejecting the argument that the law's distinction between felonious offenses and misdemeanors was of constitutional significance.[80] While *Gideon* had been applauded as one of the greatest liberal precedents of the Warren era,[81] that decision had established a constitutional right to appointed counsel for the indigent only in serious cases. The *Gideon* Court did not deal with the problem of misdemeanors. Thus, despite a general recognition of the principle that the poor were entitled to fair and equal treatment in the courts, the right to legal assistance in misdemeanor cases was not guaranteed by the Sixth Amendment. The problem was left to the states, and their treatment of the problem differed widely.[82] Many persons, concerned with the efficient administration of criminal justice, opposed the extension of the right to counsel to misdemeanors on the ground that it was administratively infeasible. Others, favoring such an extension, argued that fairness and equality were more important values than administrative efficiency and could be achieved only by the extension of *Gideon* to misdemeanor trials. Moreover, they contended, judicial administration could be streamlined and the congestion of the courts lessened through the adoption of various reforms, such as the decriminalization of such actions as public drunkenness or the smoking of marijuana. Confronted with these conflicting positions, each meritorious, the Burger Court in *Argersinger* chose to avoid a forthright

[78]Johnson v. Louisiana, 406 U.S. 356, 371 (1972) (concurring opinion). Justice Powell asserted that, while the Sixth Amendment did require the unanimity rule in federal cases, the Fourteenth Amendment did not require the states to apply the jury trial right with all its judicial gloss. Application of identical jury trial rights to both the states and the federal judicial system, when coupled with the Court's unwillingness to set rigid standards for the states, resulted in the "dilution of federal right" much to Powell's unhappiness. *Id.* at 375.

[79]407 U.S. 25 (1972).

[80]*See, e.g.*, Duncan v. Louisiana, 391 U.S. 145 (1968); Kinsella v. Singleton, 361 U.S. 234 (1960); McElroy v. Guagliardo, 361 U.S. 281 (1960).

[81]*See generally* A. LEWIS, *supra* note 50; Israel, *Gideon v. Wainwright: The "Art" of Overruling*, 1963 SUP. CT. REV. 211.

[82]*See* L. HERMAN, THE RIGHT TO COUNSEL IN MISDEMEANOR COURT (1973).

holding that a right to appointed counsel was applicable in misdemeanor cases. Nevertheless, it did extend *Gideon* to the extent that it held that no person might be imprisoned for any offense, whether classified as petty, misdemeanor, or felony, unless he was represented by counsel.[83]

The Burger Court has even attempted some incorporation of its own, giving explicit recognition in *Schilb v. Kuebel* to the long-standing assumption that the Eighth Amendment's prohibition of excessive bail was applicable to the states through the Fourteenth Amendment.[84] But, as Tables I and II show, there is not much, if any, of this road left to travel. By the time of Mr. Chief Justice Warren's retirement virtually every significant guarantee in the first eight amendments had been applied to the states. Perhaps the only important Bill of Rights protections left unincorporated are the Fifth Amendment's grand jury provision and the Seventh Amendment's guarantee of a jury trial in civil suits. But it is most unlikely that a Court, even one that has expressed such great confidence in grand juries,[85] headed by a Chief Justice who has been a crusader for the reform of judicial administration would fasten these restrictions upon state criminal and civil processes.[86] As for the

[83]The previous term, the Burger Court had held, Tate v. Short, 401 U.S. 395 (1971), it was a denial of equal protection to limit punishment to payment of a fine for those able to pay it but to convert the fine to imprisonment for those who were unable to pay it. *Tate*, thus, struck at the traditional sentencing practice of "fine *or* imprisonment," but it left available the option of confining everyone guilty of a particular misdemeanor offense to jail. If a state had adopted such a solution, however, *Argersinger* would seem to have given the poor an advantage over the rich, unless the state adopted the practice of providing indigents charged with the particular offense with counsel. Since it could not compel a state to provide appointed counsel, the only option available for the Court in such a situation, were a wealthy convict to challenge his incarceration, would be to hold that no one within the affected state might be sentenced to imprisonment for the particular offense, unless all are accorded counsel.

Having ruled it constitutionally impermissible to imprison for non-payment of a fine, the *Tate* Court indicated that the states might, rather than imprison all convicted of a particular offense, employ fines as a sentencing method but allow the indigent to satisfy their fine on an installment basis. Having held that the states may not imprison those indigents convicted of misdemeanors whom they have not provided with counsel, the Burger Court would seem to have, in *Argersinger*, established it as a rule of law that one may pay for his lesser crimes much the way one purchases a washing machine.

[84]403 U.S. 357, 365 (1971).

[85]*E.g.*, Branzburg v. Hayes, 408 U.S. 665 (1972); United States v. Calandra, 414 U.S. 338 (1974).

[86]*See, e.g.*, Address by Chief Justice Burger to Nat'l Conf. on the Judiciary, Mar. 12, 1971, in 54 JUDICATURE 410 (1971). *See generally* Swindler, *The Chief Justice and Law Reform, 1921-1971,* 1971 SUP. CT. REV. 241.

remaining, unincorporated provisions, the Second and Third Amendments, neither have proven to be significant bulwarks of American liberties; indeed, the Third Amendment has never even been litigated in either a federal or state case![87]

Comparisons between the Burger and Warren Courts, then, must not be sought in the application to the states of a dwindling number of available protections but in expressions of a willingness on the part of the Burger Court to reverse this trend, statements of a judicial intention to release the states from restrictions placed upon them by the Warren Court through the process of selective incorporation. To date, there has been only one such expression, in *Coolidge v. New Hampshire*, in which three, and possibly four, Justices indicated their willingness to overrule *Mapp v. Ohio*.[88] Decided before the appointment of Justices Powell and Rehnquist, *Coolidge* may be an augury of future developments in the law of search and seizure, but as a datum from which conclusions may be drawn about divergences between the Burger and Warren Courts in the area of "incorporation" its significance lies in its uniqueness. In fact, while a state case, *Coolidge* may indicate disagreement between the dominant majorities of the two Courts not over the issue of federalism but as regards the substance of the constitutional provision itself. If this is so, *Coolidge* portends the overruling not only of *Mapp* but also of *Weeks v. United States*,[89] the expression of a judicial desire to do away with the exclusionary rule at the federal as well as the state level.[90]

[87]E. CORWIN, THE CONSTITUTION OF THE UNITED STATES: ANALYSIS AND INTERPRETATION 923 (1964).

[88]403 U.S. 443 (1971). The difficulty in the count is caused by the fact that Mr. Justice Black, while questioning the basis for the exclusionary rule under the Fourth Amendment, thought that some unlawfully seized evidence might be excluded under a Fifth Amendment rationale, 403 U.S. at 496-500. Justices Harlan, *id.* at 490-91, Blackmun, *id.* at 510, and Chief Justice Burger, *id.* at 493, however, were quite outspoken in their condemnation of the rule. *See also* pp. 209-10 *infra*.

[89]232 U.S. 383 (1914).

[90]In this respect, Chief Justice Burger's remarks concerning the "monstrous price we pay for the Exclusionary Rule in which we seem to have imprisoned ourselves" are particularly suggestive. 403 U.S. at 493. *See also* United States v. Calandra, 414 U.S. 338 (1974) (illegally seized evidence may be used as a basis for questioning in grand jury hearings).

TABLE I

SELECTIVE INCORPORATION BY SUBSTANTIVE PROVISION

Bill of Rights Provision	Case In Which Provision Was "Incorporated" Into the Fourteenth Amendment
First Amendment:	
freedom of speech	Fiske v. Kansas, 274 U.S. 380 (1927) [see also Gitlow v. New York, 268 U.S. 652 (1925)]
freedom of press	Near v. Minnesota, 283 U.S. 697 (1931)
freedom of assembly	DeJonge v. Oregon, 299 U.S. 353 (1937)
freedom of religion	Cantwell v. Connecticut, 310 U.S. 296 (1940) [free exercise]
	Everson v. Board of Education, 330 U.S. 1 (1947) [establishment]
freedom of association+	N.A.A.C.P. v. Alabama, 357 U.S. 449 (1958) [see also Shelton v. Tucker, 364 U.S. 479 (1960)]
*Second Amendment:**	
never considered	[but see Presser v. Illinois, 116 U.S. 252 (1886)]
*Third Amendment:**	
never litigated in either a federal or a state case	
Fourth Amendment:	
search and seizure	Wolf v. Colorado 338 U.S. 25 (1949) [see also Mapp v. Ohio, 367 U.S. 643 (1961)]

Fifth Amendment:*
grand jury*

double jeopardy   Benton v. Maryland, 395 U.S. 784 (1969)
                         [see also Louisiana *ex rel.* Francis v. Reswe-
                         ber, 329 U.S. 459 (1949)]

self-incrimination   Malloy v. Hogan, 378 U.S. 1 (1964)

due process*#

eminent domain   Chicago, B. & Q. R. Co. v. Chicago, 166 U.S.
                         226 (1897)

Sixth Amendment:*
speedy trial   Klopfer v. North Carolina, 386 U.S. 213
                         (1967)

public trial   *In re* Oliver, 333 U.S. 257 (1948)

jury trial (criminal)   Duncan v. Louisiana, 391 U.S. 145 (1968)

be informed of charges*@

confront adverse
  witnesses   Pointer v. Texas, 380 U.S. 400 (1965)

compulsory process   Washington v. Texas, 388 U.S. 14 (1967)

counsel   Gideon v. Wainwright, 372 U.S. 335 (1963).

Seventh Amendment:*
jury trial (civil)*

Eighth Amendment:
excessive bail   Schilb v. Kuebel, 404 U.S. 357 (1972)

cruel and unusual
  punishment   Robinson v. California, 370 U.S. 660 (1962)
                         [see also Louisiana *ex rel.* Francis v. Reswe-
                         ber, 329 U.S. 459 (1947)]

   *Provision of or complete amendment not applicable against the states
through the Fourteenth Amendment.
   +The freedom of association is not specifically mentioned in the

constitutional text but is a judicially created right, implied from the conjunction of the freedoms of speech and assembly.

#Obviously, the Due Process Clause of the Fifth Amendment could not be incorporated into the Fourteenth Amendment; nor need it be, since the Fourteenth Amendment contains its own Due Process Clause.

@Since all states presently provide for this, it could not be challenged as a constitutional matter.

TABLE II

THE CHRONOLOGY OF SELECTIVE INCORPORATION

Date   Bill of Rights Provision "Incorporated" [Case]

1897   Fifth Amendment, eminent domain [Chicago, B. & Q. R. Co. v. Chicago, 166 U.S. 226]

1927   First Amendment, freedom of speech [Fiske v. Kansas, 274 U.S. 380 (see also Gitlow v. New York, 268 U.S. 652 (1925)]

1931   First Amendment, freedom of press [Near v. Minnesota, 283 U.S. 697]

1937   First Amendment, freedom of assembly [DeJonge v. Oregon, 299 U.S. 353)]

1940   First Amendment, free exercise of religion [Cantwell v. Connecticut, 310 U.S. 296]

1947   First Amendment, establishment of religion [Everson v. Board of Education, 330 U.S. 1]

1948   Sixth Amendment, public trial [*In re* Oliver, 333 U.S. 257]

1949   Fourth Amendment [Wolf v. Colorado, 338 U.S. 25 (see also Mapp v. Ohio, 367 U.S. 643 (1961)]

1958   First Amendment, freedom of association [N.A.A.C.P. v. Alabama, 357 U.S. 449 (see also Shelton v. Tucker, 364 U.S. 479 (1960)]

1962   Eighth Amendment, cruel and unusual punishment [Robinson v. California, 370 U.S. 660 (see also Louisiana *ex rel.* Francis v. Resweber, 329 U.S. 459 (1947)]

1963   Sixth Amendment, counsel [Gideon v. Wainwright, 372 U.S. 335]

1964   Fifth Amendment, self-incrimination [Malloy v. Hogan, 378 U.S. 1]

1965   Sixth Amendment, confrontation [Pointer v. Texas, 380 U.S. 400]

1967   Sixth Amendment, speedy trial [Klopfer v. North Carolina, 386 U.S. 213]

    Sixth Amendment, compulsory process [Washington v. Texas, 388 U.S. 14]

1968   Sixth Amendment, jury trial [Duncan v. Louisiana, 391 U.S. 145]

1969   Fifth Amendment, double jeopardy [Benton v. Maryland, 395 U.S. 784 (see also Louisiana *ex rel.* Francis v. Resweber, 329 U.S. 459 (1947)]

1972   Eighth Amendment, excessive bail [Schilb v. Kuebel, 404 U.S. 357]

Indeed, in the area of criminal defendants' rights, the striking differences between the Burger Court and the Warren majority have not been in the application of the Bill of Rights guarantees to the states, but rather in their interpretation. With virtually all of the Bill of Rights incorporated into the Fourteenth Amendment the Warren Court was faced with the task of explaining what these protections meant in the context of real criminal investigations, and it has been these decisions which have been the source of the "law and order" debate.[91] Whereas the incorporation decisions, to the extent that the public was aware of them, were relatively well-received, no doubt because they confirmed the American citizen in rights he already believed he possessed, the subsequent cases interpreting the Bill of Rights provisions, particularly those which affected the police, sparked charges of "criminal coddling."[92]

Before considering the logical strengths and weaknesses of those decisions, therefore, it should be remembered that all members of the Supreme Court, men who have made a life-long personal and professional commitment to the rule of law, abhor crime. Whatever objections, in terms both of law and policy, to which the Warren Court's criminal defendants' rights decisions may be open (and there are several), the Court did not open the jailhouse doors to turn thousands of convicted felons loose upon society. In the first place, one who ponders for a moment the Supreme Court's rule of standing—to maintain an action in the federal courts one must have suffered some injury which sets him apart for the great mass of the citizenry—will perceive that the law-abiding citizen will seldom, if ever, be in a position to litigate the meaning of the constitutional limits upon the criminal process. No matter how flagrantly one's constitutional rights may have been abused by police misconduct, he will not possess standing to raise the issue, unless he has been convicted. Of course, he may have recourse to a suit under a federal civil rights statute, but that is another matter.[93] In the second place, one must also realize that victory for a convicted criminal does not necessarily mean release; the usual practice is to remand for retrial, excluding

---

[91]*E.g.*, Miranda v. Arizona, 384 U.S. 436 (1966); United States v. Wade, 388 U.S. 218 (1967); Gilbert v. California, 388 U.S. 263 (1967); Chimel v. California, 395 U.S. 752 (1969). *See generally* J. GALLOWAY (ed)., THE SUPREME COURT AND THE RIGHTS OF THE ACCUSED (1974).

[92]*See* F. GRAHAM, THE DUE PROCESS REVOLUTION (1970); R. HARRIS, *supra* note 2; C. LYTLE, *supra* note 49.

[93]*See* 42 U.S.C. § 1983 (1964).

the evidence obtained in violation of the Constitution. But even then the state is normally successful on retrial; so, for example, Ernesto Miranda made constitutional law but remained in the Arizona State Penitentiary.[94]

There is, however, another facet of the charges against the Warren Court's decisions affecting the administration of criminal justice which is not so easily dealt with. This is the argument that the constitutional policies created by the Court during the Sixties, while they did not secure the release of many from the jails, made it vastly more difficult to put "known" perpetrators of crime in the jails in the first place.[95] This allegation needs to be examined in greater detail.

Surely the most hotly debated decisions of the Supreme Court recently have been those which relate to the interrogation process. The basic fear in this area, of course, has been that of the third degree. For decades the third degree, physically and/or psychologically coercive interrogation practices, had aroused concern, and, while sharp differences had arisen over the cure, no one had ever ventured to defend the disease. Taken together as a whole, the Supreme Court's confession cases,[96] going as far back as *Brown v. Mississippi*,[97] tend to form a pattern.

> Following the commission of a crime the police take the accused into custody. During the course of his detention he is not permitted access to counsel and he is interrogated about the crime. The period of detention varies in length, but it is almost always longer than the local law allows. The interrogation terminates with his confession. He is then brought before a magistrate and formally charged with the offense. When the confession is offered at the trial the defendant does not usually deny having made it, but he repudiates it. Violence and threats on the part of the interrogating officers are alleged. These allegations are almost always denied. On rare occasions there will be objective evidence that the prisoner suffered injuries while in custody; in such cases there will be conflicting testimony as to how they were incurred. There will also be allegations as to the length and intensity of the interrogation. Unlike the charge of physical abuse, the length and frequency of interrogation is generally not disputed.[98]

[94]State v. Miranda, 104 Ariz. 174 (1969).

[95]*See generally* Symposium, *Interrogation of Criminal Defendants—Some Views on Miranda v. Arizona,* 35 FORD. L. REV. 169 (1966). *See also* note 92 *supra.*

[96]*See, e.g.,* Brown v. Mississippi, 297 U.S. 278 (1936); Chambers v. Florida, 309 U.S. 227 (1940); Lisenba v. California, 314 U.S. 219 (1941); Ashcraft v. Tennessee, 322 U.S. 143 (1944); Haley v. Ohio, 332 U.S. 596 (1948); Watts v. Indiana, 338 U.S. 49 (1949); Thomas v. Arizona, 356 U.S. 390 (1958). *See generally,* O. STEPHENS, THE SUPREME COURT AND CONFESSIONS OF GUILT (1974).

[97]297 U.S. 278 (1936).

[98]Schaefer, *Federalism and State Criminal Procedure,* 70 HARV. L. REV. 1, 11 (1956). *See also* O. STEPHENS, *supra* note 96.

By the early Sixties, however, two constitutional protections were beginning to flow together, by virtue of Supreme Court interpretation, in such a way as to affect police interrogation practices. The first of these was the Sixth Amendment's right to counsel. Even before *Gideon* one of the most crucial questions surrounding the Sixth Amendment right was the problem of when, at what stage of the criminal case, should a lawyer be allowed to consult with his suspect client.[99] Some legal authorities felt that a defendant needed a lawyer immediately after arrest more acutely than he did later.[100] But the police were strongly opposed to that idea, reasoning that early access to counsel would discourage defendants from confessing, and in 1958 the Warren Court had rejected the claim of a man with adequate funds to retain a lawyer that he should have been allowed to phone his attorney before being questioned by the police.[101] In his dissenting opinion, Mr. Justice Douglas opined,

> The right to have counsel at the pre-trial stage is often necessary to give meaning to the right to be heard at the trial itself. It may also be necessary as a restraint on the coercive power of the police. ... The third degree flourishes only in secrecy.[102]

Douglas's voice, however, went unheeded until *Malloy v. Hogan* performed what could only be described as a shot-gun wedding of the self-incrimination privilege to the coerced confession cases.[103] In *Malloy* Mr. Justice Brennan's approach, as Justice Harlan pointed out in dissent, constituted very questionable logic and very questionable history. In none of the confession cases had the self-incrimination privilege been applied as a standard to determine admissibility. Rather, the Court had reasoned that the compulsion to testify against oneself, against which the Fifth Amendment protected, meant *legal* compulsion. Since the police had no legal right to make a suspect answer, i.e., they could not charge a suspect with perjury or contempt, there was no legal obligation to respond to police questioning, and thus there was nothing to which the self-incrimination privilege could attach. But *Malloy's* history and logic were not as important as its prophecy. Whatever one may have thought of the reasoning and result in *Malloy*, one could not treat lightly the way it anticipated the near future.

---

[99]*See, e.g.*, Hamilton v. Alabama, 368 U.S. 52 (1961); White v. Maryland, 373 U.S. 59 (1963).

[100]*See, e.g.*, Powell v. Alabama, 287 U.S. 45, 57 (1937) (Sutherland, J.)

[101]Crooker v. California, 357 U.S. 433 (1958).

[102]*Id.* at 443.

[103]378 U.S. 1 (1964).

The pregnant meaning of the conjunction of the Sixth Amendment's right to counsel and the Fifth Amendment's self-incrimination privilege began to become apparent in the case of Danny Escobedo.[104] Arrested in connection with the murder of his brother-in-law, Escobedo made no statement to police and was released after fourteen hours in custody, when his lawyer obtained a writ of habeas corpus. Some ten days later, Escobedo's accomplice, one DiGerlando, who was being held by the police on another matter, told the officers that Escobedo had in fact been the murderer. Danny and his sister were again arrested. At the station house, Escobedo requested to see his lawyer, but the request was denied. In the meantime, his lawyer, having learned of Escobedo's arrest from the mother of another client, had gone to the station house and requested to see Danny. He was, of course, denied permission to see Escobedo until after the interrogation was finished, but he did spy Danny through a partially open door and waived to him, a gesture which Escobedo later testified he interpreted to mean that he should not say anything. The police, however, told Escobedo of DiGerlando's charge and asked if he would like to confront his accuser, to which he replied that he would. When DiGerlando entered the interrogation room, Escobedo uttered the fatal statement: "I didn't shoot Manuel; you did it." But, unbeknownst to Escobedo, under Illinois law his admission of complicity in the crime was as damaging as if he had confessed to having fired the shots himself.

On appeal, however, the Warren Court, divided five-to-four as it so often was in the major criminal defendants' rights cases, reversed Escobedo's conviction, holding that when a police inquiry into an unsolved crime shifts from the investigatory to the accusatory stage the police must warn the suspect of his absolute right to remain silent and must honor his request for counsel. Statements made in the absence of such warnings were to be inadmissible at trial. Speaking for the majority, in a typically poorly organized opinion, Mr. Justice Goldberg initially addressed himself to the question of why counsel should be necessary at the accusatory stage. Because, replied Goldberg, ours is an adversary system. It is a system of competition between prosecution and defense, and that system begins to operate as soon as the process shifts from the investigatory to the accusatory. It is as crucial to have counsel at this stage as at the trial itself. In fact, argued Goldberg, there is a direct relation between the importance to the prosecution of a given stage in the criminal process and the suspect's need for counsel at that stage.

---

[104]Escobedo v. Illinois, 378 U.S. 478 (1964).

Earlier in the same term the Court had held that the Sixth Amendment prohibited the use of incriminating statements elicited by federal officials from the suspect after he had been indicted and in the absence of counsel.[105] Clearly, an indicted person could not be questioned by the police, except in the presence of his lawyer. But Escobedo had not been indicted at the time he committed his slip-of-the-tongue. Was this crucial? No, thought Goldberg. When Escobedo had made his request for counsel the crucial stage of the proceeding had been reached; the process had already shifted from the investigatory to the accusatory stage. To make the right to counsel depend upon the existence of a formal indictment would have been, for Goldberg, to elevate form over substance. But, while the *Escobedo* majority was clear that a police investigation of a crime might shift from the investigatory to the accusatory before the suspect were officially indicted, it was less than clear as to when, in fact, that transformation did take place. How was a police officer, operating in good faith and seeking to comply with the Constitution, to know that this important change in the character of the proceeding had occurred? The Court provided no answer.

Significantly for future constitutional development, *Escobedo* was, even when not opaque, a complex holding based upon a unique fact situation. In a sentence, *Escobedo* had held that where a police investigation was no longer a general inquiry into an unsolved crime but had begun to focus upon a particular suspect, the suspect had been taken into police custody, the police had begun to carry out a process of interrogation designed to elicit incriminating statements, the suspect had requested and been denied the opportunity to consult with counsel, and the police had not effectively warned him of his right to remain silent, the Sixth Amendment's right to counsel, as made applicable to the states via the Fourteenth Amendment, had been violated and no statement elicited during the interrogation might be used against the suspect at trial. But note the number of elements involved in this ruling: (1) focus, (2) custody, (3) a process of interrogation designed to elicit incriminating statements, (4) a request for counsel, and (5) the absence of a warning of a right to silence. Was it necessary that all of these elements be present before *Escobedo's* exclusionary rule became operative? In particular, must the accused request counsel? Danny Escobedo, due to long and repeated contacts with the police, had had sufficient experience to ask to see his attorney. But most criminal suspects lack such sophistication.

[105]Massiah v. United States, 377 U.S. 201 (1964).

This fact led many state and some federal judges, who were opposed to the thrust of *Escobedo*, to fasten upon the element of request as a vehicle to narrow *Escobedo* to its immediate facts and, thus, deny its application to the vast majority of confession cases.[106] This niggardly reading of *Escobedo* led the Warren Court to "clarify" that holding two years later in *Miranda v. Arizona.*[107]

Miranda, arguably, represents an object lesson to states' rights theorists of interposition, judicial or otherwise, for the attempts by the intermediate appellate judiciary to limit *Escobedo* provoked the Warren Court to execute a quantum jump in the constitutional law of interrogation procedures. Whereas *Escobedo* had required but a one-part warning of the right to remain silent, the five-man majority in *Miranda* held that, when a suspect is to be subjected to a process of custodial interrogation, the police must issue a far more detailed four-part warning: The suspect must be advised (1) that he has a right to remain silent, (2) that if he does make a statement it may be used against him at trial, (3) that he has the right to consult with counsel, and (4) that if he cannot afford an attorney one will be provided for him. Once the warnings have been given, the subsequent procedure is clear. If the suspect chooses to exercise his right to remain silent, the interrogation must cease. If he indicates a desire to have counsel present, the interrogation must be suspended until the attorney arrives or, in the case of the indigent suspect, until a lawyer has been supplied for him. And, if the interrogation does continue without the presence of counsel and a statement is taken, "a heavy burden rests on the government to demonstrate that the defendant knowingly and intelligently waived" the rights conferred upon him.[108] While waiver is, thus, still possible, it will be difficult to prove. Only if the warnings are fully and completely given, followed by a constitutionally effective waiver, will any statement made in the custodial interrogation be admissible at trial.

---

[106]*See, e.g.*, Bichell v. State, 235 Md. 395 (1964); People v. Hartgraves, 31 Ill.2d 375 (1965); Sturgis v. State, 235 Md. 343 (1965). *See also* Edwards v. Holman, 342 F.2d 679 (5th Cir. 1964); United States v. Pate, 240 F.Supp. 237 (N.D. Ill. 1965); Davidson v. United States, 236 F.Supp. 264 (W.D. Okla. 1964); State v. Fox, 131 N.W.2d 684 (Iowa 1964); Commonwealth v. Tracy, 207 N.E.2d 16 (Mass. 1965), *cert. denied*, 384 U.S. 1022 (1966); King v. Delaware, 212 A.2d 772 (Del. 1965).

But see People v. Dorado, 62 Cal.2d 338 (1965), *cert. denied*, 381 U.S. 937 (1965).
[107]383 U.S. 436 (1966).
[108]*Id.* at 475.

What *Miranda* really represented was an advisory opinion to the nation's police forces, for the *Miranda* majority indicated that their prescribed warnings were not the only procedure by which the rights of the suspect might be protected. The states were left free to adopt other procedures, if they were equally rigorous. But, absent procedural safeguards effective to protect the self-incrimination privilege at the interrogation, the prosecution was to be prevented from using any statements, either inculpatory or exculpatory, made to the police.

Speaking for the majority, Mr. Chief Justice Warren denied that the Court had any intention of hampering the traditional functions of law enforcement in the investigating of crimes and the bringing of criminals to trial. Just as Justice Goldberg in *Escobedo* had claimed that that decision had been motivated by a concern not only for the justice of law enforcement but also for its efficiency, Warren straight-facedly argued that *Miranda* would ultimately improve law enforcement by encouraging it to rely upon scientific investigative practices and, thereby, improving its public image.

To support the ruling, the Chief Justice relied upon a discussion of the nature of custodial interrogation. After briefly cataloguing the physical abuses to which secret, in-custody questioning may lead, buttressed by specific examples of the third degree drawn from the Court's own prior cases, Warren shifted to the psychological factors involved in custodial interrogation. Just as the Court had relied upon social science findings and amateur psychology to sustain its findings in *Brown v. Board of Education*,[109] so now the *Miranda* majority concluded that custodial interrogation was inherently coercive by surveying a number of police manuals and texts.[110] These manuals and texts, used in police science courses as well as police department in-service training programs, advocated a number of psychological tactics to be used by police interrogators. Among these were an emphasis upon secrecy and unfamiliar surroundings, displaying an air of confidence in the suspect's guilt, minimizing the moral seriousness of the offense, encouraging the suspect by telling him that it really hadn't been his fault but that society

[109] 347 U.S. 483 (1954).
[110] *E.g*, F. INBAU & J. REID, CRIMINAL INTERROGATION AND CONFESSIONS (1962); C. O'HARA, FUNDAMENTALS OF CRIMINAL INVESTIGATION (1956); W. DIENSTEIN, TECHNICS FOR THE CRIME INVESTIGATOR (1952); H. MULBAR, INTERROGATION (1951); R. KIDD, POLICE INTERROGATION (1940).

or the victim was responsible, the "Mutt and Jeff" act, and, finally, some manuals even advocated inducing confessions by trickery. The lesson regarding custodial interrogation which Warren urged be drawn from these manuals was that, even in the absence of physical brutality, custodial interrogation trades on the weaknesses of individuals. Alone, in unfamiliar surroundings, cut-off from any outside support, the criminal suspect is confronted by patient, persistent officers who appear confident of his guilt and seek him merely to confirm the facts of their already preconceived account of the crime. They seek to keep him psychologically off balance and insecure, and when all else fails they may resort to outright deception, such as offering false legal advice. In essence, the police persuade, cajole, or trick the suspect into abandoning his constitutional rights.

The question, then, was whether the scope of the self-incrimination privilege could be expanded to encompass non-judicial statements. In Warren's view, it could. Noting that the privilege had consistently been accorded a liberal construction by the Supreme Court, Warren suggested that the essence of the privilege was the protection of individual privacy and dignity. The voluntariness doctrine, developed in the coerced confession cases,[111] had prohibited all practices which exerted such pressure upon the individual as to disable him from making a free and rational choice. The very nature of custodial interrogation, Warren argued, as demonstrated by the police manuals, was to put the individual in such an emotional state as to impair his capacity for rational judgment. The suspect's abdication of his constitutional rights could not be made knowingly in such an atmosphere of compulsion. The one protective device which would be effective in offsetting such compulsion and in insuring that decisions to waive the privilege against self-incrimination were knowing and voluntary would be the presence of counsel. Then, in case anyone had missed the point, the Chief Justice again set forth at length the four-part warning procedure which the Court was suggesting the states follow to insure the voluntariness of confessions.

Mr. Justice Clark objected that the majority had moved too far too fast on too little evidence and chided the majority for having misrepresented law enforcement's overall performance. Mr. Justice Harlan attacked the majority opinion as utopian, unfounded, one-sided, and impolitic. It was, he complained, an unjustified and unreasonable departure from precedent. But, even were the Court's reading of precedent correct,

---

[111]*See* note 96 *supra.*

Harlan contended the results produced by *Miranda* would be unsuppor-table on public policy grounds. The Court had made no showing that confessions were not an essential element in the prosecution of a substantial percentage of American criminal convictions, and, Harlan assumed, the *Miranda* ruling would substantially decrease the number of confessions.

The most hard-hitting dissent, however, was penned by the Kennedy appointee, Mr. Justice Byron White. As he had in *Escobedo*, White charged that the decision was unwise and would unduly hamper legitimate law enforcement efforts. He attacked the majority opinion as unsupported by the history of the self-incrimination privilege. But, unlike Harrlan, White did not argue that this rendered the decision necessarily incorrect. It merely pointed out that the Court was departing from precedent to impart a new meaning to the words of the Con-stitution. While White did not argue that the Court should not make public policy, he did insist that, as an unelected, unrepresentative institution, its policy-making activities must be well-founded, and this is where Justice White parted company with the majority. The basis of the ruling in *Miranda* was, he felt, inadequate.

The self-incrimination privilege dictates the rejection of statements only if they are the product of compulsion. The *Miranda* majority, of course, argued that custodial interrogation was always compelling. But had the majority produced any evidence to support this assertion? Seventy years of judicial experience stood for the proposition that police interrogation was not sufficiently compelling to be legally significant. Now the *Miranda* majority found that it was. But on what basis? A series of manuals, at least five years out-of-date, which the Court had assumed had some influence upon or correlation with police practice. But the majority had produced no evidence to support that assumption. The Court had not examined a single transcript of any actual interrogation; indeed, the majority had refused to examine the transcripts of the interrogations involved in *Miranda* and its companion cases.[112] Yet, upon this evidence, the majority had concluded that custodial inter-rogation was inherently coercive. The Court's opinion purported to be based upon social science evidence, but judged by any of the standards for empirical investigation in the social sciences the factual bases for the Court's premises were inadequate.

---

[112]Vignera v. New York, Westover v. United States, and California v. Stewart, all raising similar issues, were consolidated with Miranda v. Arizona on appeal.

Moreover, as Justice White observed, the *Miranda* decision was illogical. If the Court's concern was that some confessions were coerced, while others were not, the old voluntariness test, under the Due Process Clause, would have been adequate. But, if the Court's conclusion that all confessions obtained by custodial interrogation are coerced were accepted as true, how could a suspect ever waive his right to counsel? If a suspect in an inherently coercive situation is asked if he wants to invoke his right to counsel and he replies in the negative, why wasn't his waiver coerced and, thus, ineffective?[113] If he had confessed at that point, according to *Miranda*, his confession would have been inadmissible as coerced. How, then, could his waiver be accepted as voluntary? And why, if counsel were present and told the accused merely to tell the truth, would the situation be any less coercive?

Given the manifest shortcomings of *Miranda*, Mr. Justice White felt compelled to disclaim with some emotion any personal responsibility for the consequences of *Miranda*.

> There is, in my view, every reason to believe that a good many criminal defendants, who otherwise would have been convicted on what this Court has previously thought to be the most satisfactory kind of evidence, will . . . either not be tried at all or acquitted. . . .
>
> In some unknown number of cases the Court's rule will return a killer, a rapist or other criminal to the streets and to the environment which produced him, to repeat his crime whenever it pleases him. As a consequence there will not be a gain, but a loss, in human dignity. The real concern is not the unfortunate consequences of this new decision on the criminal law as an abstract, disembodied series of authoritative proscriptions, but the impact on those who rely on the public authority for protection and who without it can only engage in violent self-help with guns, knives and the help of their neighbors similarly inclined. There is, of course, a saving factor: the next victims are uncertain, unnamed and unrepresented in this case.[114]

Mr. Justice White's Pontius Pilate-like position and (perhaps) excessively harsh words aside, *Miranda* was not without its opacity. The *Miranda* guarantees became operative, according to the Chief Justice, only when the police intended to carry out a process of custodial interrogation. But what is a process of "custodial interrogation?" What is custody? Could the police stop a person on the street, in a "stop and frisk" situation, and address questions to him without first providing the *Miranda* warnings? Chief Justice Warren treated the custody question in

[113]*See* Von Moltke v. Gillies, 332 U.S. 708 (1948). *See also* Kuh, *Some Views on Miranda v. Arizona,* 35 FORD L. REV. 233, 234-35 (1966).
[114]384 U.S. at 542.

contradictory fashion. At one point in his *Miranda* opinion, he spoke of custody as deprivation "of freedom of movement in any significant way."[115] But later in the opinion he emphasized that on-scene police investigation was not to be discouraged and noted that it was an act of responsible citizenship to cooperate with the police.[116] Did this mean that one must be in a police facility, either station house or patrol car, to be in custody? Obviously, the consequence of such a position would be to encourage police avoidance of *Miranda* by conducting on-street interrogations, and the Warren Court refused to countenance such evasion.[117] But the problem of the on-street viability of *Miranda* remains unresolved. Moreover, even if the suspect is admittedly in custody, need the police give the *Miranda* warnings unless they commence a process of interrogation? *Escobedo* spoke of "interrogation designed to elicit incriminating statements."[118] But clearly not all police questioning is designed to elicit incriminating statements. What is the operative effect of *Miranda* upon such police questioning? And, once the warnings are given, what is their life span? Need a suspect be warned only once and then be presumed informed, even though he may be held in custody and interrogated over a period of several days? Or must he be warned before each interrogation? If so, would a faulty sixth warning obviate a confession following it, although the preceding five had been constitutionally sufficient?[119]

Finally, how great an advance upon the previous constitutional law of confessions does *Miranda* really represent? *Miranda* said that the state must bear a heavy burden of proof when claiming that the defendant waived his rights during interrogation. But how heavy? What will suffice? Suppose four or five officers testify that the defendant was emphatically and unequivocally given the full *Miranda* warnings just before he confessed but the defendant denies this? Has the state met its heavy burden of proof? If so, did *Miranda* really advance the law of confessions or merely shift the focus of the old "swearing contest" from

[115]*Id.* at 444.
[116]*Id.* at 477-78.
[117]*See* Orozco v. Texas, 394 U.S. 424 (1969).
[118]378 U.S. at 491.
[119]Such a rule would, of course, work to the advantage only of the experienced criminal. While legal sophistication is not generally prevalent among arrested suspects, at least one of the "impact" studies of *Miranda* reported finding defendants who did not request counsel on the grounds that "That's the *worst* place to have a lawyer because the police play it straight then. I wanted them to make a mistake." Medalie, *et al., infra* note 122, at 1378.

the voluntariness of the confession to the validity of the waiver? If not, why believe one criminal defendant against four or five policemen? Even assuming that the majority of policemen are given to lying under oath, have criminal defendants shown themselves to be more trustworthy than police officers generally?

In answering such questions, it bears emphasis that the central premise of the *Miranda* opinion was not that no confession could ever be constitutionally obtained but that no confession obtained by virtue of the suspect's ignorance of his rights could ever be constitutionally sufficient. In order to make a constitutionally sufficient confession, one must waive his privilege against self-incrimination, and, in order to waive rights, one must know what rights he has. Philosophically, then, the *Miranda* majority's thinking was closely related to that of the nineteenth century Utilitarians, such as Jeremy Bentham and John Stuart Mill, who argued that people (and governments) should act in accordance with their self-interest rightly understood.[120] Wrong action, according to Utilitarianism, was the product of an improper or inadequate knowledge of one's self-interest. There is a certain similarity between this position and the *Miranda* majority's argument that only when a suspect is fully appraised of his rights can he make an intelligent choice to confess or not. The *Miranda* opinion, thus, was based upon two interrelated assumptions: (1) The police will give adequate and effective warnings to suspects of their rights and will honor invocations of those rights, and; (2) a suspect will understand the warnings and their importance for him.

A number of studies have been done since *Miranda* to test the effects of the decision upon the actual operation of law enforcement and, thus, indirectly to throw some light upon the adequacy of the Court's assumptions.[121] Perhaps the two best-known of these have been studies conducted by the Yale and Georgetown Law Schools.[122] The Yale study, based upon the observation of police behavior in interrogations con-

[120]*See* J. MILL, UTILITARIANISM (1863); J. BENTHAM, A FRAGMENT ON GOVERNMENT (1776).

[121]*E.g.,* Younger, *Results of a Survey Conducted in The District Attorney's Office of Los Angeles County Regarding The Effects of The* Dorado *and* Miranda *Decisions Upon The Prosecutions of Felony Cases,* 5 AM. CRIM. L. Q. 32 (1966); Reiss & Black, *Interrogations and The Criminal Process,* 374 ANNALS 47 (1967); Seeburger & Wettick, *Miranda in Pittsburgh,* 29 U. PITT L. REV. 1 (1967).

[122]Note, *Interrogations in New Haven,* 76 YALE L.J. 1521 (1967); Medalie, Zeitz & Alexander, *Custodial Police Interrogations in Our Nation's Capital,* 66 MICH. L. REV. 1347 (1968). *See also* Griffiths & Ayres, *A Postscript to The Miranda Project,* 77 YALE L.J. 300 (1967).

ducted in New Haven, Connecticut, during the summer of 1966, immediately following *Miranda*, sought to evaluate two propositions.[123] First, the study attempted to examine the validity of the contentions of the *Miranda* critics that the decision would seriously hamper law enforcement. Second, the Yale project examined the *Miranda* majority's contention that custodial interrogations were inherently coercive.

Respecting the first proposition, the Yale researchers found that there had been little complete adherence to *Miranda*, although they observed that most interrogated suspects had been given some advice of their rights, if not a full, four-part *Miranda* warning. The adequacy of the warnings, however, had increased over time, and it may have been somewhat unrealistic to expect full compliance by the police in the days immediately following the Court's decision in *Miranda*, particularly since the New Haven Police Department's in-service training program did not even begin to include lectures fully explaining *Miranda* until the end of the summer. (New Haven having had at this time a relatively enlightened Chief of Police, it is perhaps not idle speculation that many jurisdictions were even slower in making their officers aware of the *Miranda* requirements than was New Haven.) More interestingly, the Yale observers found that police compliance with *Miranda* was dependent upon the nature of the case. Circumstances, in particular the seriousness of the crime and the sufficiency of the evidence, influenced compliance. Of those charged with serious crimes,[124] the suspect most likely to receive a full *Miranda* warning was the one against whom the

[123]One of the major methodological difficulties encountered, of course, was the possibility that the presence of the observers would consciously or unconsciously influence the police to adjust their behavior. To test the effect, if any, which the observers' presence had upon the police, a group of persons who had been interrogated by the New Haven police prior to the commencement of the study and after its completion were interviewed. To compare these informants' perceptions of the interrogation process with that which the students actually witnessed, a second group of persons, whose interrogations the observers had seen, were interviewed, and their accounts were compared with those given by the unobserved group. No significant differences were found in the perceptions of the two groups, leading the researchers to conclude that the presence of the observers had not had any appreciable effect upon the officers. Note, *supra* note 122, at 1530-32.

[124]"Seriousness" was defined by police perception rather than by legislative categorization. Police interrogators were given cards each containing the name of a particular offense and told to sort them into two piles, one for serious crimes and the other representing non-serious violations. Not surprisingly, the police tended to regard certain misdemeanors, particularly those involving violence or the threat of violence, as serious, while viewing some felonies, such as so-called "white collar" crimes, as not serious. *Id.* at 1551 n. 88.

police had sufficient evidence to go to trial but not sufficient evidence to convict. The suspect least likely to receive warnings was the one against whom the officers had not only insufficient evidence to convict but also, short of the suspect's own statements, inadequate evidence to bring the case to trial. In such cases, the officers were forced to take a chance on the admissibility of statements procured in interrogation, in order simply to get the case to trial. Whatever one's normative evaluation of such police conduct may be, it seems to represent highly rational behavior, given the police role.[125]

The Yale observers also found, as they might have expected, that adherence to the spirit of *Miranda* was even 'ess than compliance with the letter of its law. Indeed, police interrogators had created a number of tactics to incorporate the *Miranda* warnings into their own interrogation repetoire. They might change the wording slightly or fail to give the warnings until after extensive questioning. Even more popular was the practice of giving the warnings in such a tone or manner as to imply that the suspect had better not exercise his rights or reading the warnings in such a way as to imply that they were mere bureaucratic routine, meaningless formalisms.

As concerned the question of whether interrogations were inherently coercive, the Yale study found no undue use of physical force by the police. Indeed, informal conversations between the Yale law students and the officers indicated that the police had no desire to engage in any "rough stuff." The researchers then attempted to measure psychological coercion by isolating a number of elements or indices of such coercion, such as the length of the interrogation or the demeanor of the officers, but they found that few of the interrogations which they witnessed contained more than one of these elements. Indeed, some interrogations were completely free of any of the measures of psychological coercion. In other words, not all of the interrogations were coercive, physically or psychologically, Mr. Chief Justice Warren to the contrary notwithstanding. Interestingly enough, however, when the researchers attempted to identify those cases in which the interrogation exhibited the greatest degree of coercion, they found that those situations in which the full

[125]*See generally* J. SKOLNICK, JUSTICE WITHOUT TRIAL (1966); J. WILSON, VARIETIES OF POLICE BEHAVIOR (1968); Muir, The Development of Policemen (unpublished paper delivered at the Sixty-sixth Annual Meeting of the American Political Science Assoc., Los Angeles, Calif., Sept. 8-12, 1970); Muir, The Moral Growth of Policemen (unpublished paper delivered at the Twenty-seventh Annual Meeting of the Western Political Science Assoc., San Diego, Calif., April 5-7, 1973).

Miranda warnings were most likely to be given were also the very cases in which the police were most likely to utilize coercive interrogation tactics. Perhaps for this reason, the police were no less successful in those interrogations in which they complied with *Miranda* than in those in which they did not. In short, the Yale analysis indicated that, while the Court's fears that interrogations were necessarily coercive were not groundless, coercion was less prevalent than expected. But, on the other hand, the critics' claims that *Miranda* would drastically reduce the effectiveness of law enforcement proved to be essentially without foundation.

This, however, raises the problem of why the critics were wrong. Why did the police receive no less a percentage of statements, admissions, or confessions from those who received the *Miranda* warnings than from those who did not? After all, whether they thought it desirable or not, most reasonable and intelligent Americans had believed that that would be the result of the *Miranda* decision. Certainly all of the members of the Supreme Court, both the majority Justices and the *Miranda* dissenters, proceeded from the assumption that the decision would reduce the number of confessions, statements, and admissions.

Clues to the answer of why *Miranda's* impact was more limited than anticipated are provided by several of the subsequent studies of its implementation and effect,[126] most significantly and directly by the project of the Institute of Criminal Law and Procedure at Georgetown University Law School.[127] Unlike the New Haven study, which focused on post-*Miranda* police behavior, the Georgetown research concentrated on the criminal suspect and his perceptions of the interrogation process and of the warnings. More extensive than the Yale project, the Georgetown study is based upon a series of intensive, administered interviews of criminal suspects interrogated in Washington, D.C., following *Miranda*. While these interviews were designed to gather a wide variety of data concerning a number of issues, the study's central finding must be that the percentage of those arrested in the post-*Miranda* period who gave statements to the police was only slightly less than that which gave statements in pre-*Miranda* interrogations. How can this be explained? Well, to be sure, if no warnings were given, there was little assertion of rights. But, even if the warnings were given, a significantly high percentage of interrogated suspects chose not to assert their rights.

[126]*See* note 121 *supra.*
[127]Medalie, Zeitz & Alexander, *supra* note 122.

This failure on the part of suspects was related, the Georgetown researchers found, to the individual suspect's understanding, or lack thereof, of the substance of the warnings and their significance for him. In order to test the suspect's understanding, the Georgetown interviewer would read the warning to the suspect and then ask him to explain what it meant. The suspects' responses were categorized as "understanding" and "non-understanding," and the conclusion drawn was that the average criminal suspect was not characterized by great legal sensitivity. Approximately one in six failed to understand that he had a right to silence, even when explicitly told he had such a right. One out of five could not comprehend that he might have counsel present during the interrogation, and one in four failed to grasp that, if he could not afford counsel, counsel would be provided free of charge and might be present during the interrogation. Among the typical responses:

> —The police "had some lawyer of their own who was working with them."
> —It means that "I would have to pay for a lawyer."
> —They planned to "appoint someone at court."
> —"I just have to write for one and wait for him to answer."
> —"I don't know why one would need a lawyer in a station house; it's never done."
> —The warning "means I would answer [questions by the police] if a lawyer is present."[128]

And, if such findings are disheartening, it should be borne in mind that the Georgetown study, if anything, *understates* the degree of suspect ignorance, for the interviewers gave the suspects the *Miranda* warnings in a relatively neutral manner in a non-custodial situation. Confronted by an actual arrest situation with its attendant fears and pressures, the average suspect is probably even less likely to comprehend the purport of the *Miranda* warnings than the Georgetown study estimated. The suspect's understanding of the *Miranda* admonitions, of course, was closely correlated with his behavior. Two-thirds of those who understood the warning of the right to station house counsel requested counsel, and approximately sixty percent of those who grasped the meaning of the right to silence gave no statements.

But, *even when the warnings were given and understood*, 34% of the suspects did not request counsel, and 41% chose to make a statement to the police. Why? At least three explanations are offered by the Georgetown study. The first, and least prevalent, reason for not invoking one's rights was criminal sophistication. Some habitual crimi-

[128]*Id.* at 1375.

nals told the researchers that they did not request counsel in the hope that the police would make a mistake at which point the suspect would "spill his guts," confident that he would have his conviction reversed on appeal.[129] A second and more significant influence was the hope of leniency. Many suspects indicated that, feeling that there was no way to bamboozle the officers, they had cooperated hoping that this would be taken into consideration when they were charged, tried, or sentenced. But the most important factor explaining the continued existence of statements and admissions made during interrogation appears to be the psychology of confession.[130] Many of the suspects told the interviewers that they had felt a virtual compulsion to tell someone of their transgressions, even if that someone was a police officer. This desire to "get things off your chest," a phenomenon upon which the Roman Catholic church has astutely traded for centuries, appears to be a widespread (universal?) factor in human behavior beyond the power of the Supreme Court of the United States to control.

The prosecution-police oriented critics of *Miranda*, who contended that the decision would automatically reduce to zero the number of confessions, statements, and admissions given to the police, have thus proven to be wrong; but so too have the civil libertarians who contend that the fact that confessions, admissions, and statements have not dried-up can only prove that the police are not complying with *Miranda*. In fact, the continued existence of confessions and other statements given during interrogation is a much more complex matter than these people are willing to grant. The explanation for a suspect's providing the interrogating officers with information or even a confession must depend upon the facts of the individual case not wholesale explanations. If a suspect makes a statement, admission, or confession, it may be because (1) the police did not warn him pursuant to *Miranda*; or (2) they did warn him, but he did not understand the warnings; or (3) the warnings were given and understood, but for some reason the suspect chose to talk anyway.

Given *Miranda's* apparent lack of practical impact, then, it was and is absurd for "law and order" advocates to be too upset by it. For exactly the same reason, however, it was and is probably equally pointless for

[129]*Id*. at 1378.

[130]*See* Sterling, *Police Interrogation and the Psychology of Confession*, 14 J. PUB. L. 25 (1965); Driver, *Confessions and the Social Psychology of Coercion*, 82 HARV. L. REV. 42 (1968).

self-styled civil libertarians to become overwrought by the Burger
Court's efforts at limiting, restricting, or retrenching upon the Warren
Court precedent. Nevertheless, *Harris v. New York*[131] has been seen as
"the clearest evidence of hostility"[132] to Warren Court criminal defendants' rights decisions on the part of Nixon appointees. *Harris*, having
been indicted on two counts of selling heroin, testified in his own behalf.
He categorically denied having made the first alleged sale but admitted
making the second. He claimed, however, that the substance dealt in the
second transaction had been only baking soda and, in an apparent effort
to escape conviction on the theory of entrapment,[133] that the sale had
been made at the instigation of a police officer. On cross-examination,
the prosecution sought to impeach the credibility of Harris by reading a
statement which he had made immediately after his arrest, admitting
both sales. But this statement had been taken as part of an interrogation
occurring before the *Miranda* decision, hence no *Miranda* warnings had
been given. The trial, however, took place after the *Miranda* decision
and, according to *Johnson v. New Jersey*,[134] *Miranda* had thus been
applicable at the trial. For that reason Harris's unwarned statement could
not have been used as evidence of his guilt, but, over defense objection,
the trial judge allowed the prosecutor to read the statement, instructing
the jury to consider it only in assessing Harris's credibility. And the
Supreme Court affirmed the conviction! In an opinion joined by Mr.
Justice Blackmun and three members of the *Miranda* minority (Harlan,
White, and Stewart), the new Chief Justice held that a defendant's
statement, procured without the proper *Miranda* warnings, could be
admitted to impeach his contradictory testimony at the trial.

Chief Justice Burger's position rested upon the presumption that the
need for the jury to accurately assess the defendant's credibility and the
necessity of preventing perjury outweighed the "speculative possibility"
that the police would be encouraged to avoid *Miranda*. Dismissing as
dicta language in *Miranda* which had indicated that statements taken in
the absence of warnings were to be inadmissible for all purposes, Burger

[131]401 U.S. 222 (1971).

[132]*The Supreme Court, 1970 Term*, 85 HARV. L. REV. at 44; *see also* Dershowitz &
Ely, Harris v. New York: *Some Anxious Observations on the Candor and Logic of the
Emerging Nixon Majority*, 80 YALE L.J. 1198 (1971).

[133]*But see* United States v. Russell, 411 U.S. 423 (1973) (rejecting entrapment defense
where officer did not commit crime himself but merely contributed means for criminal
enterprise which had begun before his infiltration and continued after it).

[134]383 U.S. 719 (1966). *See also* ch. V. *infra* at pp. 220-22.

argued that *Miranda* barred only the use of unwarned statements as direct evidence of guilt and not as collateral evidence of truthfulness, at least where the jury was given precautionary instructions. The Chief Justice's position relied heavily upon *Walder v. United States*,[135] which allowed the prosecution to introduce evidence procured in an unreasonable search and seizure conducted two years before to impeach Walder's testimony that he had never possessed narcotics, although the Fourth Amendment's exclusionary rule would have barred the use of the unconstitutionally seized evidence as direct proof of guilt. Chief Justice Burger found no significant differences between *Harris* and *Walder*.

Dissenting, Mr. Justice Brennan thought there were indeed significant differences of principle between *Walder* and *Harris*. The evidence admitted in *Walder* had been unrelated to the charge on which Walder was being tried, while the statements in *Harris* were directly connected with the crime for which Harris was on trial. The evidence used for impeachment in *Walder*, indicating that Walder had possessed heroin two years earlier, could only have been used by the jury to assess Walder's credibility; it could not have been misused by the jury as evidence of guilt, for it proved nothing about the later acts of which he was accused. But the statements in *Harris* provided information about the very actions for which Harris was being prosecuted.

At the very least, *Harris* will probably give rise to a rash of cases testing the adequacy of limiting instructions.[136] The majority in *Harris* felt that instructing the jury not to consider the statement as proof of Harris's guilt was a sufficient safeguard. But grave doubts exist about the ability of jurors to perform such mental gymnastics.[137] While the Chief Justice did not suggest that even a full confession would be inadmissible for impeachment purposes, it is difficult to believe that a jury, even if instructed to do so, could ignore such conclusive evidence in arriving at its verdict. The Court, thus, might stop short of allowing full confessions to be introduced for purposes of impeachment. But where should the line be drawn?

Harris, moreover, did raise questions about the continued vitality of *Miranda*. The two cases were not necessarily incompatible. They could

[135]347 U.S. 62 (1954).

[136]The Warren Court had increasingly evidenced a disquietude with the adequacy of limiting instructions as a prophylactic device to prevent constitutional errors. *See, e.g.*, Burton v. United States, 391 U.S. 123 (1968). The Burger Court apparently has greater confidence in jurors' powers to discriminate.

[137]*See* H. KALVEN & H. ZEISEL, *supra* note 72.

be reconciled logically, were *Miranda* read as establishing a rule designed to deter police misconduct but which could be set aside when other social policies, such as protecting the integrity of the fact-finding process at trial, outweigh the societal interest in deterring certain forms of police behavior. And the two cases were possibly reconcilable in terms of actual effect on the theory that it was unlikely that the police, who want statements for direct evidence, would be encouraged to evade *Miranda* on the "speculative possibility"[138] that (1) the suspect would make incriminating statements were he not warned pursuant to *Miranda*, (2) defense counsel, aware of his client's previous incriminating statements, would nevertheless put the defendant on the stand, where (3) he would testify contrary to his earlier statements.[139] It could be argued, on the other hand, that *Harris* substantially undercut *Miranda's* deterrent effect.[140] Before *Harris*, it was generally thought that an unwarned statement could not be used by the prosecution in any manner. After *Harris*, police disregard of *Miranda* might give the prosecution an advantage. If the prosecution can produce enough independently obtained evidence to present to the jury, the defendant who has made an unwarned statement to the police will be placed in an extremely difficult position.[141] If he does not take the stand, he runs a substantial risk of being convicted; the jury will be suspicious of his failure to attempt to refute the evidence against him and may draw inferences of guilt. But, if he does testify, he risks introduction of the unwarned statement for impeachment purposes. In either event, conviction is likely. *Harris*, thus, might encourage the police to ignore *Miranda*. But whether *Harris* would or would not encourage law enforcement to disregard *Miranda* the question remained "Would it make any difference?". And from what was known about the actual impact of *Miranda*, the answer was probably "Not much."

This process of blunting or qualifying *Miranda* was continued in *Michigan v. Tucker*, refusing to apply the doctrine of "the fruit of the poisonous tree" to the testimony of a witness to whom the prosecution

---

[138]401 U.S. at 225.

[139]*See* Blake, *Miranda Revision—Not Much Impact*, Los Angeles Times, March 7, 1971, §G, at 2.

[140]*See The Supreme Court, 1970 Term*, 85 HARV. L. REV. at 44-53. *See also* Dillard v. State, 274 N.E.2d 387 (Ind. 1971) (denial of mistrial after receiving confession inadmissible under *Miranda* held to be harmless error).

[141]*Cf.* Griffin v. California, 380 U.S. 609 (1965); Adamson v. California, 332 U.S. 46 (1947).

had been led only as the result of an improper interrogation.[142] At his interrogation, Tucker had been fully advised of his rights, except that he was not told he could have a court-appointed lawyer were he unable to afford counsel, his interrogation having taken place prior to *Miranda's* obliging police to advise a suspect of his right to free counsel. Tucker's trial, however, occurred after the announcement of *Miranda* which was, thus, applicable at the trial, and his statements made at the time of his arrest were properly excluded. But damaging evidence came from a witness who, Tucker had told the police, was a friend who would corroborate his alibi. Despite Tucker's appeal, the Supreme Court held the friend's testimony to have been admissible. *Tucker* likely was a narrow holding, being one of those relatively few, albeit difficult, cases in which the interrogation preceded but the trial followed *Miranda;* that undoubtedly accounted for why the result was reached over the dissent of only Mr. Justice Douglas, although Mr. Justice Brennan's concurrence contained, as Mr. Justice Stewart observed, "a couple of argumentative footnotes."[143] Certainly, a contrary result would have been unlikely to deter similar police misconduct. But, as in *Harris*, the Court emphasized that the dispositive value was the protection of the integrity of the fact-finding process. The testimony of the witness was properly admitted because it served the trial purpose of discovering the truth. Significantly, however, the Court again declined an opportunity to overturn *Miranda*.

The Burger Court's erosion of *Miranda* has been paralleled by its restriction of the ambit of the Warren Court's precedents affecting the conduct of the identification procedure known as "the lineup." *United States v. Wade*[144] and *Gilbert v. California*[145] announced that any in-court identification of a defendant by a prosecution witness would have to be excluded, had it been "tainted" by a pretrial lineup conducted in the absence of defense counsel. As in *Miranda*, Justices White, Harlan, and Stewart argued that the Court's exclusion of relevant evidence rested upon unsupported assumptions. But the majority insisted that the Sixth and Fourteenth Amendments entitled a person accused of either a federal or a state crime to have his attorney present during any pretrial lineup. Like *Miranda*, *Wade* and *Gilbert* were subjected to vigorous criticism by the public, the police, and Congress. The ultimate congres-

[142]417 U.S. 433 (1974).
[143]*Id*. at 453.
[144]388 U.S. 218 (1967).
[145]388 U.S. 263 (1967).

sional response, however, was the surprisingly modest provision of the
1968 Crime Control Act that the "testimony of a witness that he saw the
accused commit or participate in the commission of the crime . . . shall be
admissible in evidence" in any federal criminal prosecution.[146] By
comparison, the Burger Court's reply in *Kirby v. Illinois* was strong
indeed.[147]

In *Kirby*, a five-man majority limited the application of the *Wade-
Gilbert* requirements, in both federal and state cases, to lineups conducted *after* the indictment of the defendants. Following the *Wade* and
Gilbert decisions, many lower courts, in marked contrast to the intermediate appellate judiciary's response to the *Escobedo* ruling and
perhaps chastened by the lesson of *Miranda*,[148] had read the Warren
Court's identification cases as applying to *all* pretrial lineups.[149] But the
Kirby majority refused to extend the per se exclusionary rule of *Wade*
and *Gilbert* to preindictment identifications conducted in the absence of
defense counsel. Mr. Justice Stewart, announcing the judgment of the
Court, adopted the position which he had urged in dissent in *Escobedo*.[150] Stewart agreed that the right to counsel attached when the
criminal process shifted from the investigatory to the accusatory, but he
took the view that that transformation occurs when the accused is
formally charged with the crime, *not before*. Only then has the state
committed itself to prosecute; only then have adversary proceedings
been initiated. In our criminal justice system, as it has evolved over time,
such proceedings as indictment, arraignment, and trial are not arbitrary,
meaningless formalities, Stewart argued, but important, meaningful
proceedings, each marking a new point in the criminal process. It is, then,
at the time of indictment that the right to counsel becomes operative. In
contrast, Mr. Justice Brennan, joined by Justices Douglas and Marshall,
insisted that Stewart's distinctions were mere formalisms, unrelated to
the real functioning of the criminal process. The dangers of unfairness,
suggestion, and mistaken identity against which the *Wade-Gilbert*
requirement of counsel had been directed were, Brennan contended, as
present before indictment as after. More difficult to understand was the
dissent of Mr. Justice White, who had vigorously criticized the results in

[146]18 U.S.C. § 3502.
[147]406 U.S. 682 (1972).
[148]*See* note 106 *supra*.
[149]*See* G. GUNTHER & N. DOWLING, INDIVIDUAL RIGHTS IN CON-
STITUTIONAL LAW: 1973 SUPPLEMENT 96 (1973).
[150]378 U.S. 478, 493 (1964).

Wade and *Gilbert* but now took the view that those decisions governed *Kirby* and compelled reversal.

Mr. Justice Stewart, however, did stress that *Kirby* did not stand for the proposition that all police identification procedures were beyond the reach of constitutional protection. Due process would still be available to attack police lineups that were "unnecessarily suggestive and conducive to irreparable mistaken identity."[151] But, for the *Kirby* majority, the Sixth Amendment's guarantee would not attach until a criminal prosecution was commenced.

The major problem with this approach is that it was so literal as to beg the question. By its express provisions, the Sixth Amendment does not become operative until the commencement of a criminal prosecution.[152] But this does not take us very far; the issue is when does that commencement take place. By emphasizing the concept of "focus," Mr. Justice Goldberg had attempted a functional approach to the problem in *Escobedo* and, quite frankly, had failed to provide any very clear or workable answer to the question.[153] In *Kirby*, Mr. Justice Stewart seems to have resolved the problem by not trying to answer the question at all. To be sure, the right to counsel is applicable "only at or after the time that adversary judicial proceedings have been initiated,"[154] but *Escobedo* had already held that this transformation of the process could occur before indictment.

Stewart's response in *Kirby* was not to refine the *Escobedo* approach, qualifying it, clarifying it, explaining where it had gone wrong, but rather was to distinguish *Escobedo* away as an inapplicable precedent. Relying upon *Miranda's* use of *Escobedo* as a foundation for the erection of a Fifth Amendment right to counsel, Stewart concluded that *Escobedo* had been primarily concerned with the vindication of the self-incrimination privilege and not with the protection of the Sixth Amendment. Since the opinion in *Wade* had explicitly rejected the contention

[151]406 U.S. at 691.

[152]The Sixth Amendment reads as follows:

In all criminal prosecutions, the accused shall enjoy the right to a speedy and public trial, by an impartial jury of the State and district wherein the crime shall have been committed, which district shall have been previously ascertained by law, and to be informed of the nature and cause of the accusation; to be confronted with the Witnesses against him; to have compulsory process for obtaining witnesses in his favor, and to have the Assistance of Council for his defense.

[153]*See* pp. 162-64 *supra. See generally The Supreme Court, 1971 Term*, 86 HARV. L. REV. at 159-64.

[154]406 U.S. at 688.

that the self-incrimination privilege was violated by requiring a defendant to exhibit himself for identification purposes, it followed that *Kirby*
was not controlled by *Miranda* nor, by process of logical extension, by
Escobedo.[155] But this left unexplained why the Warren Court had relied
upon *Escobedo* and *Miranda* in reaching the results in *Wade* and
Gilbert.[156] In those cases, the Court had attempted to identify those
"critical confrontations" at which the presence of the defense counsel
would advance the cause of a fair trial. Whether the Court succeeded in
doing so is a separate question; in *Wade* and *Gilbert*, at least the attempt
was made. No such effort was expended in *Kirby*.

This was unfortunate, for *Kirby* presented the Court with an excellent
opportunity to articulate the balance between procedural fairness and
the benefits of prompt identification of criminal suspects.[157] On the one
hand, a defendant in a police lineup is in a particularly poor position to
challenge unfairness in the conduct of the lineup. He cannot know what
conversations may have transpired between the witness and the police
before or after his appearance, or perhaps even during his appearance,
due to the blinding intensity of the lights used for these exercises. The
opportunity to employ the power of suggestion is great and may be
abused by the police, as in a lineup in which the defendant is the only
individual who resembles the suspect's description. In such circumstances, the presence of counsel may be necessary to maintain the
accused's right to a fair trial. On the other hand, *prompt* identification
may have several benefits which outweigh the potential for unfairness
and, thus, argue against the requirement of the presence of counsel under
certain circumstances, as when an individual is apprehended shortly
after the commission of a crime and is immediately shown to witnesses.
The arrested suspect may not be the person sought. A requirement that
the identification must wait until a defense counsel appears may result in
the lengthy incarceration of an innocent suspect, while at the same time
giving the actual criminal more time to perfect his escape. A prompt but
counsel-less identification might have permitted the early release of the
individual and helped the police to determine whether to continue their
search of the area. Moreover, it would be desirable for the suspect to be
exhibited to the witnesses as soon as possible, while the criminal's
appearance is still fresh in their minds. In circumstances such as *Wade*

[155]*Id.* at 689.
[156]388 U.S. 218, 226; *see also* Kirby v. Illinois, 406 U.S. 682, 693 n. 3 (Brennan, J.,
dissenting).
[157]*See generally The Supreme Court, 1971 Term*, 86 HARV. L. REV. at 161-64.

and *Gilbert*, the benefits of prompt identification had already been lost. In *Wade*, the lineup occurred seven months after the commission of the crime, a month after the defendant's arrest, and two weeks after the appointment of counsel. In *Gilbert*, the lineup had been conducted eleven weeks after the crime, sixteen days after Gilbert's indictment, and following the appointment of a defense counsel. *Wade* and *Gilbert*, thus, might be seen at one end of a continuum representing the identification process at the other end of which are identification confrontations conducted minutes after the crime has been committed. *Kirby* fell between these two extremes and, thus, might have served as the vehicle for reasoned clarification of the law. The majority of the Burger Court eschewed the opportunity.

The following term, however, the Court did indicate that even some post-indictment stages might not be critical, were the accused not physically present. In *United States v. Ash*, a six-man majority ruled that a pre-trial display of photographs to a prosecution witness for purposes of identifying the accused did not involve the pernicious dangers of a lineup and, thus, the presence of defense counsel was not constitutionally required.[158] While Justices Brennan, Marshall, and Douglas again protested this "evisceration" of the principles of *Wade* and *Gilbert*, the *Wade* opinion itself had held that such preparatory steps in the gathering of evidence for the prosecution as the scientific analyses of fingerprints, blood samples, and so forth were not critical stages entitling the accused to the presence of counsel.[159]

As *Ash* itself suggests, interrogation and lineup procedures may be conceptualized as facets of a larger police function, the detection or gathering of evidence of crime.[160] Obviously, there are ways other than interrogation and lineups to go about gathering evidence. As both an historical and a practical matter, the most important of these has been an actual, physical search by the police for and the seizure of evidence.[161] In the United States, of course, the practice of search and seizure has been associated with the constitutional law of the Fourth Amendment, which

[158]413 U.S. 300 (1973).
[159]388 U.S. at 222.
[160]*See* L. TIFFANY, D. McINTYRE & D. ROTENBERG, DETECTION OF CRIME (1967).
[161]*See generally* H. KERPER, INTRODUCTION TO THE CRIMINAL JUSTICE SYSTEM 235-270 (1972); D. KARLEN, ANGLO-AMERICAN CRIMINAL JUSTICE 129-132 (1967).

prohibits "unreasonable" searches and seizures.[162] The Supreme Court's interpretation of that amendment, however, has not been noted for its consistency.

The Fourth Amendment provides that

> The right of the people to be secure in their persons, houses, papers, and effects, against unreasonable searches and seizures, shall not be violated, and no Warrants shall issue, but upon probable cause, supported by Oath or affirmation, and particularly describing the place to be searched, and the persons or things to be seized.

The amendment clearly possesses both the virtue of brevity and the vice of ambiguity. Neither is the critical term "unreasonable" defined, nor is the relationship between the reasonableness requirement and the warrant provision clarified. Given the conjunction of the two clauses, at least three interpretations are possible on the face of the text. First, the warrant provision and the reasonableness requirement might be conceived of as synonymous. Any search conducted with a search warrant would be constitutionally reasonable; any search conducted without such a warrant would be constitutionally unreasonable. Or, secondly, the reasonableness requirement might be interpreted as providing an additional restriction on the warrant provision, implying that some searches are unreasonable, even when conducted under the authority of a search warrant. Any search conducted in the absence of a warrant would be unreasonable, but the reasonableness of a search conducted under a warrant would turn on the validity of the warrant. Or, thirdly, the first clause might be read as providing an additional search power. Any search conducted with a warrant would be reasonable, but so too might be a search conducted without a warrant. The reasonableness of a police search perpetrated in the absence of a warrant would turn upon the facts of the particular case. In practice, the Supreme Court has adopted an amalgam of the second and third possible readings of the Fourth Amendment. Some searches, even if conducted with a warrant, are unreasonable, if the affidavits upon which the warrant was issued were insufficient, untruthful, or did not establish probable cause.[163] On the other hand, some searches have been declared reasonable, even though conducted in the absence of a warrant.[164]

---

[162]*See generally* N. LASSON, THE FOURTH AMENDMENT (1937); J. LANDYNSKI, SEARCH AND SEIZURE AND THE SUPREME COURT (1966).

[163]E.g., Aguilar v. Texas, 378 U. S. 108 (1964); Spinelli v. United States, 393 U.S. 410 (1969).

[164]E.g., Carroll v. United States, 267 U.S. 132 (1925); Marron v. United States, 275

To the extent that the exceptions to the warrant requirement are broadened, obviously, the potential protection to privacy afforded by the Fourth Amendment is narrowed. Constitutional searches without a warrant, however, are subject to at least one important limitation. Before any of these searches may be carried out, probable cause must exist. Probable cause is a flexible concept which does not lend itself to precise definition. Perhaps the Court's most quoted definition has been "facts or circumstances . . . such as to warrant a man of prudence and caution in believing that the offense has been [or is being] committed. . . ."[165] Under this interpretation of the Fourth Amendment, with its attendant limitation, the two most traditional exceptions to the warrant requirement have been searches of movable vehicles and searches incident to arrest.[166]

The power of the police to search a movable vehicle was, of course, much broadened as a practical matter by the invention of the automobile.[167] The right to search incident to a valid arrest, however, while related to the vehicular search differs from it in at least two respects. First, it is a much more ancient practice, being almost as old as professional police forces, and is, thus, well-rooted in the common law tradition. Second, while the automobile search has been justified on the grounds that it is usually impractical to obtain a warrant before the vehicle has moved from the officer's jurisdiction, the Supreme Court has on several occasions, in approving searches incident to arrest, disclaimed the need to obtain a warrant, even when the police had had sufficient time to do so.[168] This question of whether the reasonableness standard of the Fourth Amendment requires police to secure a search warrant, if they have sufficient time to get one, has been one of the two key problems in the Court's development of the law of search incident to arrest. The second has been the problem of the constitutionally permissible scope of the search conducted without benefit of a warrant.[169] With respect to the

U.S. 192 (1927); Harris v. United States, 331 U.S. 145 (1947); Brinegar v. United States, 338 U.S. 160 (1949).

[165]Stacey v. Emery, 97 U.S. 642 (1878).

[166]*See* J. LANDYNSKI, *supra* note 162, at ch. IV. For recent judicial discussions of the exceptions to the warrant requirement, *see* Almeida-Sanchez v. United States, 413 U.S. 266 (1973), and Cady v. Dombrowski, 413 U.S. 433 (1973).

[167]*See, e.g.*, Carroll v. United States, 267 U.S. 132 (1925); Brinegar v. United States, 338 U.S. 160 (1949); Coolidge v. New Hampshire, 402 U.S. 443 (1971).

[168]*E.g.*, Rabinowitz v. United States, 339 U.S. 56 (1950).

[169]*E.g.*, Harris v. United States, 331 U.S. 145 (1947); Kremen v. United States, 353 U.S. 346 (1957); Preston v. United States, 376 U.S. 364 (1964); Cooper v. California, 386 U.S. 58 (1967).

problem of obtaining a warrant, the Vinson Court had, in *Trupiano v. United States*, stressed the necessity of securing a warrant, were there adequate time, in order for an arrest search to meet the Fourth Amendment standard.[170] But only two years later in *Rabinowitz v. United States* the Court reversed itself, overruling *Trupiano* and emphasizing that the key factor in determining the constitutionality of a search was the "reasonableness" of the search and not the feasibility of securing a warrant.[171] As for the issue of how extensive a search might be conducted incident to an arrest, earlier Courts had, over the decades, dealt with the problem with varying degrees of strictness.[172]

Confronted with these confusing and often contradictory precedents, the Warren Court, having extended the exclusionary rule to all American police jurisdictions in *Mapp* and having manifested a rigorous attitude toward police conduct affected by the Fourth Amendment,[173] made its contribution to the resolution of these problems in *Chimel v. California*,[174] involving a series of numismatic robberies of a bizarre nature. Chimel, a coin collector himself, had burglarized the home of a friend, another numismatist, and the coin shop owned by a second acquaintance, but only after determining by conversation that both friends were adequately insured. His bragging, however, led to his arrest. At the time of his arrest and over Chimel's objections, the police conducted a one hour search of his entire three-bedroom home, including the attic and garage. The evidence secured by virtue of this extensive arrest search was admitted at trial, and Chimel was convicted. The Warren Court, however reversed the conviction, holding that a search incident to a valid arrest should not go beyond the area from which the arrested person might obtain weapons or evidentiary items. Stressing the crucial part which warrants play in the constitutional scheme of search and seizure, the majority reaffirmed its preference for search warrants as the means to prevent unlawful searches which might otherwise be conducted by overzealous officers. But the Court did not question the power of the police to search without a warrant contemporaneous to a valid arrest. The interests of law enforcement in the protection of the lives of the officers and the prevention of the destruction of evidence must also be

----

[170]334 U.S. 699 (1948).
[171]339 U.S. 56 (1950).
[172]*See* note 169 *supra*.
[173]*E.g.*, Mapp v. Ohio, 367 U.S. 643 (1961); Preston v. United States, 376 U.S. 364; Cooper v. California, 386 U.S. 58 (1967); Spinelli v. United States, 393 U.S. 410 (1969).
[174]395 U.S. 752 (1969).

recognized. It is enough to satisfy the constitutional standard of reasonableness that such a search be confined to the area within the arrestee's immediate control, and that area was strictly defined by the *Chimel* Court. The Court, however, did not go as far as Chimel urged and revive the *Trupiano* doctrine, requiring that search warrants be obtained whenever the officers have sufficient time to do so, and this was the point upon which Mr. Justice White's dissent turned.[175]

Joined by Justice Black, White agreed that in the absence of a warrant the search of the area within the arrestee's reach was reasonable. But White would have held that a search of the entire premises within which the arrest took place, as in Chimel, might also be reasonable, if the officers had probable cause to arrest and it had been impracticable to obtain a search warrant. In other words, White urged the position that, if the police had had time to get a warrant but did not, then the search incident to the arrest must be confined to the area within the arrestee's immediate control; the police should be penalized for their own lethargy and incompetence. But, if the police did not have time to secure a warrant, then the search conducted incident to the arrest might be of greater scope.

While Mr. Justice White's argument has a good deal of force and logic, it is difficult to understand how he could apply it to the fact situation in *Chimel* and dissent. Chimel's arrest had been planned long beforehand; the police had had adequate time and evidence to obtain a search warrant. Since the *Chimel* Court was not faced with an emergency situation in which the arrest had not been planned for some time before its execution, a subsequent Court might still adopt White's position, reviving *Trupiano* and limiting *Chimel* to circumstances in which the police have had time to secure a warrant but failed to, thus permitting warrantless searches beyond the "immediate control" of the arrestee when there was no time to procure a search warrant in advance. In such circumstances, a more extensive search without benefit of a warrant could be justified by the potential danger either to the arresting officers or to the evidence presented, either at the time of the arrest or later, by bystanders friendly to the arrestee. Indeed, Mr. Justice White argued that the *Chimel* search should have been valid, given that, absent such an extensive search, Mrs. Chimel, who presumably knew the whereabouts of the incriminating evidence, could reasonably be expected to destroy the evidence before the officers returned with a warrant. *Chimel*, then, was not the final word in this area of the law; perhaps there are no "final" words in constitutional

[175]*Id*. at 770.

law. It was but a stage in the continuous process of constitutional formulation. Even at the time of its announcement, however, *Chimel's* emphasis upon the importance of search warrants collided with the Warren Court's own expansion of the "emergency" exception to the warrant requirement in *Schmerber v. California.*[176]

The destruction of the evidence rationale presents a third exception to the warrant requirement of the Fourth Amendment which, given modern technology, has been particularly closely related with the development of a rather specialized area of the law dealing with searches of the body. *Schmerber v. California,* decided but one week after *Miranda,* upheld the taking of a blood sample from a conscious person and in spite of his objection by a physician at the direction of the police. The sample thus taken led to Schmerber's conviction for drunken driving. The Supreme Court had earlier held that the person of the suspect might constitutionally be used for identification purposes, but in *Rochin v. California* the Court had held that the officers had gone too far in their zeal to secure evidence from the person of Mr. Rochin.[177] In his *Rochin* concurrence, Mr. Justice Douglas had in dicta equated blood taken from the veins with substances secured from the defendant's stomach.[178] In either case, Douglas contended, the evidence would be inadmissible unless taken with the consent of the accused.

Five years after *Rochin,* the Warren Court was faced with this exact problem in *Breithaupt v. Abram.*[179] Differences in approach among the Justices resulted in a sharp split in the vote, but the majority affirmed a manslaughter conviction based in part upon a blood sample taken from an unconscious defendant who had been involved in a fatal automobile accident. Breithaupt had rested his defense upon the Fourth, Fifth, and Fourteenth Amendments, but at the time neither the exclusionary rule nor the self-incrimination privilege applied to the states.[180] The case, therefore, was decided under the *Rochin* rule, and the majority did not find that the police conduct in the instant case had been sufficiently shocking to require reversal of the conviction.

Prior to *Schmerber, Rochin* and *Breithaupt* constituted the law of intra-corporeal searches. But in the interim between *Breithaupt* and *Schmerber Mapp, Malloy,* and *Gideon* were all decided, as well as

[176]384 U.S. 757 (1966).
[177]342 U.S. 165 (1952).
[178]*Id.* at 177 n. l.
[179]352 U.S. 432 (1957).
[180]*See* Adamson v. California, 332 U.S. 46 (1947); Wolf v. Colorado, 338 U.S. 25 (1949).

Escobedo. All of these developments led Schmerber to hope that the Court might reconsider *Breithaupt* or at least distinguish his case from it.

On appeal, Schmerber raised four issues. First, he relied upon *Rochin*, seeking to distinquish *Rochin* and his own case from *Breithaupt* on the grounds that Breithaupt had been unconscious. The Court, however, summarily dismissed this argument, finding no constitutionally significant difference between conscious and unconscious citizens. Schmerber secondly argued that his privilege against self-incrimination had been violated. The majority, however rejected this contention by distinguishing between evidence of a "testimonial" or "communicative" nature and evidence of a "physical" nature. The Fifth Amendment, they indicated, applied only to the former kind of evidence; the amendment prohibited only the compulsion of "testimonial" evidence. The self-incrimination privilege, therefore, did not apply to fingerprints, photographs, voice identifications, court appearances, physical measurements, or blood tests.[181] The Court did, however, note that a prosecution comment upon a defendant's refusal to submit to a test or his request for an alternative test, especially where such request was the result of religious conviction, would be inadmissible.[182] Third, Schmerber argued that he had been denied the right to counsel. Since the case had arisen in California where, due to the State Supreme Court's holding in *People v. Dorado*,[183] interpreting *Escobedo*, Schmerber had been warned of his right to counsel, had consulted with an attorney, and had been advised that he need not submit to the test. Compelling him to submit to the test, Schmerber contended, had amounted to a deprivation of the right to counsel. The *Schmerber* majority responded by noting its preceding construction of the Fifth Amendment. Since Schmerber had not had a

---

[181]The Court, however, balked at including lie detector tests, not because polygraph tests measure physiological responses, but because those responses are elicited by interrogation. But the opinion is unclear as to whether it is condemning polygraph tests per se or is limiting its condemnation to compulsion to submit to a lie detector test.

The position taken by *Schmerber* is essentially that advocated by Wigmore. 8 J. WIGMORE, *supra* note 47 at §§ 2263-64. *See also* United States v. Wade, 388 U.S. 218 (1968) (lineups); United States v. Dionisio, 410 U.S. 1 (1973) (voice exemplars); United States v. Mara, 410 U.S. 19 (1973) (handwriting exemplars); United States v. Ash, 413 U.S. 300 (1973) (photographs).

See generally Comment, *Constitutional Law: The Supreme Court Delineates the Relationship Between the Fourth and Fifth Amendments*, 1967 DUKE L. J. 366; Comment, *Blood-Alcohol Tests: Some Constitutional Aspects*, 35 U. of MO. at K.C. L. REV. 175 (1967); Ruffin, *Intoxication Tests and the Bill of Rights: A New Look*, 2 CAL. W. L. REV. 1 (1966); Note, *Forcible Administration of Blood Tests*, 14 U.C.L.A. L. REV. 680 (1967).

[182]384 U.S. at 765 n. 9 & 771 n.13; *see also* Griffin v. California, 380 U.S. 609 (1965).

[183]62 Cal.2d 338 (1965), *cert. denied*, 381 U.S. 937 (1965).

right to refuse the blood test, the erroneous advice of counsel could not and did not give him a greater right. Fourthly and lastly, Schmerber claimed that the blood test constituted a search in violation of the Fourth Amendment, and, thus, the evidence should have been excluded at trial. The Court responded, however, that the officers had plainly had probable cause to arrest Schmerber and to conduct a search incident to the arrest. The officers had been confronted with the potential destruction of the evidence by virtue of bodily absorption, and the test chosen, administered by a physician in a hospital, had been reasonable.

Mr. Justice Black in dissent contended that the majority's distinction between "testimonial" or "communicative" evidence, on the one hand, and "physical" evidence, on the other, was specious.[184] Schmerber had, in Black's literalistic view, been compelled to provide evidence which communicated incriminating facts to the police. The majority, however, pointed out that, if the words "testimonial" and "communicative" were used as consistently and literally as Mr. Justice Black urged, the result would be that all evidence would be "testimonial," and, thus, the introduction of any evidence at trial which the defendant did not freely consent to have introduced would amount to a violation of the Fifth Amendment.

The *Schmerber* majority, however, was quite clear that a blood test was a search and seizure within the meaning of the Fourth Amendment and as such must meet the constitutional standard of reasonableness. In the absence of a search warrant, there must be a valid arrest. Indeed, *Schmerber* indicated that circumstances above and beyond probable cause to arrest would be necessary to justify a blood test subsequent to the arrest. The police, in other words, must not only arrest but also have a "clear indication" that the suspect is intoxicated.[185] But such a holding lacks logic, for the more certain the officers are that the suspect is intoxicated the less they will need a blood test.

Any critical analysis of the *Schmerber* result, however, must be tempered with the recognition that *Schmerber* confronted the Warren Court with a conundrum of its own making. In part, *Miranda* had rested upon the argument that reliance upon confessions alone was ultimately damaging to law enforcement. Therefore, the *Miranda* majority had explicitly encouraged the police to rely upon more sophisticated and scientific methods for the detection and prosecution of crime. To have then ruled in favor of Schmerber would have penalized such reliance and

[184]384 U.S. at 773.
[185]*Id.* at 770.

would have added fuel to the "criminal coddling" charges. The *Schmerber* dissenters absolutely failed to recognize this difficulty.

Schmerber, thus, like *Miranda*, may be seen as an advisory opinion to the nation's police forces, telling them what methods could and could not be used in the enforcement of the criminal law. *Schmerber*, in fact, was not necessarily incompatible with *Miranda*. The Warren Court used the existence of a process of custodial interrogation as a standard for determining when the *Miranda* requirements applied. A necessary corollary would be that law enforcement practices not involving custodial interrogation do not bring the Fifth Amendment's self-incrimination privilege, as interpreted by *Miranda*, into play, and the underlying purpose of *Miranda* would not be violated by requiring an accused suspect to cooperate in a process involving the identification of physical characteristics, so long as the process did not violate the reasonableness provision of the Fourth Amendement or the "fundamental fairness" required by the due process clauses, as for example requiring the suspect to disrobe in order to administer a breathalyzer test. The Court's opinion in *Schmerber* clearly suggests that it is necessary that blood tests be administered by medical personnel in a medical environment according to accepted medical practices and that alternative tests be made available to avoid violation of First Amendment religious freedom.

While the Warren Court was willing to approve blood testing, however, it was unwilling to countenance other types of warrantless searches made possible by modern technology. The development of the telephone and the discovery of electricity were technological advances with legal consequences of the greatest import, for they introduced into the police arsenal of detection methods the wiretap and, later, the electronic "bug." The constitutional status of these methods, however, was not clear, for the term "search" in the Fourth Amendment is no more self-defining than the term "reasonable."[186] The search with which the Framers had been familiar was composed of two elements: (1) entry into the dwelling (2) for purposes of securing tangible evidence of crime. Obviously, neither of these elements was present in the wire tap. Was it then a search within the meaning of the Fourth Amendment? Whether the Constitution prohibited the warrantless interception of phone conversations for the gathering of criminal evidence was the dilemma the Supreme Court was first called upon to resolve in *Olmstead v. United States*.[187] Speaking for a five-man majority, Mr. Chief Justice Taft

---

[186]*See generally* J. LANDYNSKI, *supra* note 162, at ch. VIII.
[187]277 U.S. 438 (1928).

viewed the Fourth Amendment guarantee in its narrowest possible terms. In effect, the majority looked upon the Fourth Amendment as a guarantee against only a particular method of invasion of privacy—as a ban on physical intrusion into the home and the seizure of material objects—rather than as a protection for the right to privacy itself. Since there was no trespass in the tapping of Olmstead's phone, there had been no search, and, furthermore, an immaterial object, conversation, could not have been "seized." The *Olmstead* majority made it quite clear, however, that Congress could provide for the privacy of the telephone by statute, and in 1934 Congress passed legislation creating the Federal Commerce Commission. Section 605 of the act provided that "no person not being authorized by the sender shall intercept any communication and divulge or publish the existence, contents, substance, purport, effect or meaning of such intercepted communication. . . ."[188] There was no evidence that this language represented an effort to respond to *Olmstead's* invitation, but the Court soon began interpreting Section 605 as though it were.[189] In essence the Court was attempting to "overrule" *Olmstead* by analogizing Section 605 to the Fourth Amendment. But the section did not apply to electronic eavesdropping, and advances in the miniaturization of electronic components were increasingly rendering the wiretap obsolete. Yet the Court refused to extend the Fourth Amendment to cover electronic eavesdropping.[190] Only an actual physical trespass would bring the amendment into play, though the trespass might be small indeed.[191] Then, in 1967, in *Katz v. United States*, the Warren Court for the first time brought non-trespassory eavesdropping within the scope of the protection of the Fourth Amendment.[192] In addition to rejecting the trespass rule, the Court abandoned the old formula of "constitutionally protected areas"[193] and firmly established the application of the Fourth Amendment to intangibles.[194]

---

[188]47 U.S.C. § 605 (1964), *as amended*, Pub. L. No. 90-351, §§ 801-04, 82 Stat. 211 (1968).

[189]*See, e.g.*, Nardone v. United States, 302 U.S. 379 (1937); Nardone v. United States, 308 U.S. 338 (1939); Benanti v. United States, 355 U.S. 96 (1957); Lee v. Florida, 392 U.S. 378 (1968).

[190]*See, e.g.*, Goldman v. United States, 316 U.S. 129 (1942); On Lee v. United States, 343 U.S. 747 (1952).

[191]*See* Silverman v. United States, 365 U.S. 505 (1961).

[192]389 U.S. 347 (1967).

[193]*See* Goldman v. United States, 316 U.S. 129 (1942); Silverman v. United States, 365 U.S. 505 (1961).

[194]*See also* Warden v. Hayden, 387 U.S. 294 (1967).

Katz had been convicted of transmitting wagering information in interstate commerce. This conviction was based upon six tape recordings, averaging three minutes each, of Katz's end of telephone conversations placed from three different public telephone booths. These recordings were obtained by the FBI through the use of an electronic listening device attached to the outside of the booths. There had been no physical penetration of the enclosed booths themselves. The devices had been activated only while Katz was using the phone and were turned off as soon as he left the booths. The eavesdropping had been conducted only after an investigation had indicated that Katz regularly used these phones to call a known gambler. No effort, however, had been made to secure judicial authorization for the eavesdropping.

Speaking for all but Justice Black, Mr. Justice Stewart reversed Katz's conviction, holding *Olmstead* to be good law no longer. The protection of the Fourth Amendment could not, for Stewart, be limited only to material objects and police actions involving actual trespass. He refused, moreover, to deal with the case in terms of "constitutionally protected areas." Since the Fourth Amendment speaks of "persons, papers, houses, and effects," the Supreme Court had, prior to *Katz*, always asked itself if the area occupied by the defendant was sufficiently similar to the privacy of the home to justify the protection of the amendment.[195] Both Katz and the government, therefore, had placed heavy emphasis in argument on the issue of whether a phone booth was a "constitutionally protected area." Stewart, however, dismissed this whole line of reasoning with the terse but common sense observation that the Fourth Amendment "protects people, not places."[196] The critical question for Mr. Justice Stewart was whether the government's activities violated a justifiable expectation of private use of the booth. Essentially, Stewart took a functional approach to the interpretation of the Constitution, in contrast to Mr. Justice Black's literalist approach.[197] Black, as usual,[198] relied upon words, while Stewart examined the Fourth Amendment to determine its underlying purpose, which he took to be the protection of personal privacy. He then balanced the relative public and private interests and struck the balance against the government practice in this case, holding the search to have been "unreasonable." "Unreasonable"

[195]*E.g.* On Lee v. United States, 343 U.S. 427 (1963).

[196]389 U.S. at 351.

[197]*Id.* at 364.

[198]*See, e.g.*, Griswold v. Connecticut, 381 U.S. 479, 507 (1965) (Black, J., dissenting); Tinker v. Des Moines, 393 U.S. 503, 515 (1969) (Black, J., dissenting). *See generally* H. BLACK, *supra* note 27.

because, although the eavesdropping was properly limited in scope, it had not been authorized by a judicial warrant. Therefore, the evidence obtained against Katz should not have been admitted at his trial.

Although, in view of modern technological advances, Mr. Justice Stewart's liberal reading of the scope of the Fourth Amendment and his rejection of the old trespass doctrine were probably justified, his new standard for determining when the Fourth Amendment applied was and is certain to spawn a plethora of litigation. Stewart's standard was that the Fourth Amendment comes into play whenever the person has a justifiable expectation of privacy. Government invasions of such justifiable expectations must be reasonable within the meaning of the Fourth Amendment. But when does a person have a justifiable expectation of privacy? Suppose Katz had gone to a public park to conduct his wagering activities or to a restaurant. Would he there have had a justifiable expectation of privacy? Or, to take another example, does one have a justifiable expectation of privacy when conversing in a jail visiting room? None other than the author of *Katz*, Mr. Justice Stewart himself, has told us that he does not.[199]

Perhaps Mr. Justice Harlan, concurring in *Katz*, has made the best effort thus far by a Supreme Court Justice to elaborate Stewart's test.[200] For Harlan, the Fourth Amendment came into play if two requirements were met:

> First that a person have exhibited an actual (subjective) expectation of privacy and, second, that the expectation be one that society is prepared to recognize as "reasonable."[201]

In other words, a person cannot claim an invasion of privacy if his earlier actions indicated an open indifference to the fact that he might be observed. Normally, however, this requirement will always be met in an electronic eavesdropping case, since eavesdropping by its very nature is meant to be secret. The effectiveness of the "bug" depends upon the fact that it violates the normal expectation that one can rely upon his senses to tell him that someone is within earshot. Mr. Justice Harlan's second requirement, however, would appear to mean that the government can invade conversational privacy, if it can show that society can no longer reasonably be required to honor the expectation of privacy in a particular case or a particular category of cases.

[199]*See* Lanza v. New York, 370 U.S. 139 (1962). *But cf.* North v. Superior Court, 104 Cal. Rptr. 833 (1972).
[200]389 U.S. at 361.
[201]*Id.*

Once an invasion of privacy has occurred, however, there remains the question of its reasonableness, for the Fourth Amendment prevents only unreasonable invasions of citizens' privacy. In *Katz*, the government did not argue, because the facts would not have supported the argument, that the evidence would have been lost due to any delay which might have been involved in obtaining a warrant. There was no fear for the lives of the officers. The destruction of the evidence rationale did not apply. Katz was not under arrest, nor was he a movable vehicle. Thus, none of the exceptions to the warrant requirement were applicable. Absent a warrant, then, the search was unreasonable.

However, this, in turn, raises the problem of whether a warrant permitting technological searches could ever be designed which would comply with the Fourth Amendment. The Warren Court's contribution, if it can be called that, to the resolution of this problem was contained in *Berger v. New York*,[202] striking down New York State's permissive eavesdropping/wiretapping statute.[203] The *Berger* majority felt that the New York statute was unconstitutional on its face, because it did not contain adequate judicial supervision of police utilization of such technological searches and, thus, resembled the general warrants found so objectionable by the American Revolutionists and Framers of the Constitution.[204] The law simply required an officer petitioning for a warrant to eavesdrop or wiretap to appear before a judge and describe the intended subject of the surveillance. It did not require a specification of the crime suspected or the conversation sought, and, if a warrant were issued, it remained in force for sixty days. There was, however, no provision for a prompt execution of the warrant nor for its prompt termination once the conversation sought had been seized. The statute failed to provide for the return of the warrant, after termination of the surveillance, and it did not require a new showing of probable cause for

[202]388 U.S. 41 (1967).

[203]N.Y. CODE CRIM. PROC § 813-a (McKinney 1958), *as amended* (McKinney Supp. 1967).

An ex parte order for eavesdropping ✱✱✱ may be issued by any justice of the Supreme Court or judge of a county court or of the court of general sessions of the County of New York upon oath or affirmation of a district attorney, or of the attorney general or of an officer above the rank of sergeant ✱✱✱ that there is reasonable ground to believe that evidence of crime may be thus obtained, and particularly describing the person or persons whose communications ✱✱✱ are to be overheard or recorded and the person thereof. ✱✱✱ Any such order shall be effective for the time specified therein but not for a period of more than two months unless extended or renewed by the justice or judge who signed and issued the original order upon satisfying himself that such extension or renewal is in the public interest.

[204]*See* J. LANDYNSKI, *supra* note 162, at 21 ff.

the renewal of the warrant. For all of these reasons, the *Berger* majority felt that New York statute ran afoul of the Fourth Amendment.

But, as Mr. Justice White pointed out in dissent,[205] *Berger* may be read so stringently as to imply that any permissive wiretapping/ eavesdropping statute would necessarily be unconstitutional. On the other hand, of course, Mr. Justice Stewart stated in *Katz* that a properly limited warrant could be obtained,[206] and all of the Justices save Black, who didn't think warrants were necessary anyway, signed that opinion. But how could a conversation ever be described with sufficient particularity? The Fourth Amendment, recall, requires warrants supported by oaths or affirmations *"particularly describing* the place to be searched and the persons or things to be seized."[207] But how can the police ever know the time and precise content of a conversation? It may, however, be countered that if "papers," "effects," and "search" are to be broadly construed, so as to bring tapping and "bugging" within the Fourth Amendment, "particularly" should also be relaxed. But, even if that were done, the technological search warrant encounters problems of overbreadth. Though the wiretap may differ from the electronic eavesdropper, in that the former is more discriminating, both continue over time and actually resemble a series of searches. Yet under a warrant procedure to permit wiretapping and electronic eavesdropping, this series of searches would be conducted on the basis of only a single showing of probable cause. Finally, it has been a requirement of the common law for several centuries that an officer intent upon conducting a search, except under those circumstances where he reasonably believes that his life would be endangered or where he is in "hot pursuit," must give notice of his intention and authority before entering the premises to be searched. A requirement of prior notice, however, would obviously defeat the purpose of wiretapping and electronic eavesdropping.[208]

Further clarification of the permissible scope, if any, of the technological search warrant is likely to result from the almost certain challenges to the constitutionality of the Omnibus Crime Control and Safe Streets Act of 1968.[209] Title III of the act prohibits the interception and disclosure of nearly all wire or oral communications, unless consented to by one of the parties to the communication or authorized by

[205] 388 U.S. at 107.
[206] 389 U.S. at 355 & n. 16.
[207] Emphasis added.
[208] *Cf.* Alderman v. United States, 394 U.S. 165 (1969).
[209] 18 U.S.C. §§ 2510-20 (1968).

a judicial order. But Title III also provides for court-authorized "bugging" and wiretapping on a showing by federal officers that particular communications concerning particular offenses are likely to be intercepted.[210] The law allows continuous electronic surveillance for up to thirty days on a single court order and provides for an unlimited number of thirty-day extensions. While the breadth of the search thus permitted may be objectionable, it must be remembered that society has an interest in the detection and prosecution of crime, and in an age in which the criminal makes use of the telephone and the sophistication of electronic gadgetry it is probably unrealistic to prohibit police reliance upon tapping and "bugging." Indeed, the President's Commission on Law Enforcement and the Administration of Justice recommended the legalization of such practices, under carefully drafted warrant procedures, as the only effective way to combat organized crime.[211] Moreover, permitting the use of listening devices under carefully supervised conditions may more effectively safeguard privacy than an absolute bar which might encourage uncontrolled official lawlessness and perjury, such as the use and subsequent denial of telephone taps to secure leads. As of this writing, however, the constitutionality of Title III of the crime control bill has not been passed upon by the Supreme Court, although in *United States v. White*[212] the Burger Court did confine the impact of *Katz*, ruling that it had not destroyed the vitality of *On Lee v. United States*[213] and, thus, sustaining a conviction based upon incriminating statements transmitted to government agents by a listening device concealed upon the person of an informer.[214] And, in *United States v. Kahn*, a six-man majority held that, although Title III requires the naming in the application and interception order of the person whom the authorities have probable cause to believe is committing an offense, since the government had no reason to believe that Kahn's wife was implicated in his bookmaking operations, neither the language of the wiretap order nor of Title III required the supression at trial of intercepted conversations revealing her complicity, though her husband but not herself had

[210]*Id.* at § 2518.
[211]PRES. COMM'N ON LAW ENFORCEMENT AND ADMIN. OF JUSTICE, THE CHALLENGE OF CRIME IN A FREE SOCIETY 201-04 (1967).
[212]401 U.S. 745 (1971).
[213]343 U.S. 747 (1952).
[214]The decision in *White*, however, was not entirely clear-cut, owing to the fact that the result turned in large part upon the question of the retroactive effect of *Katz*, a question discussed at greater length in ch. V *infra*.

been named in the application and order.[215] *Kahn* may have been simply an extension to electronic surveillance of the traditional maxim that, once an officer is legally upon the premises, he need not close his eyes to the commission of an offense. It failed, however, to address the fundamental question of whether the officers were *legally* upon the premises, i.e., whether Title III met the constitutional requirements, although its implications were hard to ignore.

But whatever the constitutional status of judicially authorized electronic surveillance, the Burger Court has made it perfectly clear that exceptions to the rule of *judicial* control of searches, including electronic searches, will be construed quite narrowly. The Crime Control Act of 1968 asserts that warrantless eavesdropping authorized by the President for national security purposes is legal.[216] The Nixon Administration then attempted to expand this exception, contending that national security affairs might include domestic matters. The administration's argument, however, was unanimously rebuffed by the Burger Court, speaking through the most recent of President Nixon's own appointees! Mr. Justice Powell was quite careful, to the point of redundancy, in emphasizing that the issue before the Court in *United States v. United States District Court for the Eastern District of Michigan* and, thus, the Court's holding was a narrow one.[217] The Court did not decide the question of the constitutionality of Title III's authorization of judicially warranted eavesdropping for certain domestic crimes, nor was it concerned with the power of the President to authorize warrantless electronic surveillance in national security cases involving foreign

---

[215] 415 U.S. 143 (1974).

[216] 18 U.S.C. § 2511 (3).

[217] 407 U.S. 297 (1972). The Burger Court has persisted in a strict construction of Title III as it relates to executive authorization. Thus, in United States v. Giordano, 416 U.S. 505 (1974), the Court held that Congress, being careful to insure that the mature judgment of a particular, responsible official would be involved in any wiretapping decision, had empowered *only* the Attorney General or an Assistant Attorney General specially designated by him to authorize applications for wire tap orders; authorization by the Executive Assistant to the Attorney General was statutorily insufficient. The sloppy and blatantly illegal practices under the Attorney Generalship of John Mitchell, therefore, had fatally imperiled dozens of cases involving literally hundreds of racketeers, gamblers, and narcotics pushers. See TIME, May 27, 1974, at 57. But, in United States v. Chavez, 416 U.S. 562 (1974), the Court ruled that, where the Attorney General had actually authorized wire tap applications, the fact that the applications and court orders incorrectly identified an Assistant Attorney General as the authorizing officer did not require suppression of evidence obtained. The decisions in both *Giordano* and *Chavez* were 5-4, Mr. Justice White providing the majority in each case.

affairs. Rather, it was confronted only with the question of the President's power, either under statutory or constitutional provisions, to authorize warrantless wiretapping and "bugging" in national security cases involving domestic matters. Powell could find no support for the view that the statute authorized this type of presidential conduct. Both the words of the statute and its legislative history indicated that the national security exception to the warrant provisions was essentially neutral. It simply emphasized that nothing in the act was to be construed as expanding or contracting the President's powers under the Constitution. The only remaining question then was whether warrantless electronic searches conducted on presidential authority alone violated the Fourth Amendment. In Powell's view they did. The Justice's approach was to balance the government's interest in conducting such searches, which he admitted had a certain pragmatic force, against the societal and individual interests in protecting personal privacy and especially the *privacy of speech*. Indeed, although it never explicitly entered the opinion, the First Amendment and the implications of this kind of "bugging" for the exercise of First Amendment freedoms appear to have played a crucial role in the Court's resolution of this case. Mr. Justice Powell examined the various exceptions which had been created to the Fourth Amendment's requirement of a search warrant and concluded that in each of these instances the exception had been created because securing a warrant could have defeated the purpose of the search, such as protecting the lives of officers involved in the execution of an arrest. But, in the case of domestic national security electronic surveillance, securing a warrant from a neutral and detached magistrate would not frustrate any legitimate purpose which the government might have. Hence, the balance was struck in favor of the individual interest and against the reasonableness of the government practice. The only disturbing portion of the opinion lay in its last section, where Justice Powell intimated that the standards controlling the issuance of electronic surveillance warrants might be less stringent for domestic *national security* cases than for the investigation of ordinary crimes, thus leaving open the door for the possible creation of a sort of electronic "stop and frisk."

And the Burger majority has demonstrated a willingness to give a broad construction to the Warren Court's authorization of "stop and frisk" practices. This practice has gained salience in recent years, because it gives rise not only to constitutional issues but also to political and social problems, especially when employed by predominantly white law enforcement agencies in black neighborhoods.[218] Common law doctrines permitting the detaining of persons on grounds less than those necessary to justify an arrest are a couple of hundred years old,[219] but recently some states have taken the added precaution of statutorily authorizing the practice.[220] Such "stop and frisk" legislation has been recommended by both the President's Commission on Law Enforcement and the Administration of Justice and the American Law Institute.[221] In part, the rationale underlying these recommendations has been that such legislation actually would serve to protect privacy by forestalling the invalid arrest of innocent persons.[222]

There would, of course, have been no doubt about the constitutionality of the "stop and frisk" practice, whether authorized by statute or not, if the police were required to meet the standard of probable cause to arrest in order to justify stopping and frisking a suspect. But, on the other hand, such a requirement would obviously defeat the purpose of the practice. Therefore, in seeking to justify stopping and frisking on grounds less than probable cause to arrest, some advocates of the practice and some lower courts distinguished between a stop and frisk and an arrest and search.[223] A stop and frisk, the argument went, was only a brief detention accompanied by a cursory pat down of the outer clothing. Being less intrusive than an arrest and search, a stop and frisk, thus, did not have to meet the full standard for probable cause to arrest in order to be constitutionally justifiable.

[218]*See generally* Souris, *Stop and Frisk or Arrest and Search—The Use and Misuse of Euphemisms,* 57 J. CRIM. L. C. & P.S. 251 (1966); Reich, *Police Questioning of Law Abiding Citizens,* 75 YALE L.J. 1161 (1966); Vorenberg, *Police Detention and Interrogation of Uncounselled Suspects,* 44 BOSTON U. L. REV. 423 (1964).

[219]*See* 2 HAWKINS, PLEAS OF THE CROWN 128-29 (8th ed. 1824).

[220]*See, e.g.,* N.Y. CODE CRIM. PROC. § 180(a) (McKinney Supp. 1967); R.I. GEN. LAWS ANN. §§ 12-7-1-17 (1956); N.H. REV. STAT. ANN. §§ 594:1-23 (1955); HAWAII REV. LAWS §§ 255-4, -5, -8, -9 (1955); DEL. CODE ANN. tit. 11, §§ 1901-12 (1953).

[221]PRES. COMM'N, *supra* note 211, at 94-5 (1967); AMERICAN LAW INSTITUTE, MODEL CODE OF PRE-ARRAIGNMENT PROCEDURE 2.02 (Tent. Draft No. 1, 1966).

[222]*See* Traynor, *Mapp v. Ohio at Large in the Fifty States,* 1962 DUKE L.J. 319, 333-34. *See also* Younger, *Stop and Frisk: "Say It Like It Is,"* 58 J. CRIM. L.C. & P.S. 293, 300 (1967).

[223]*See* People v. Peters, 18 N.Y.2d 238 (1966), *aff'd on other grounds,* 392 U.S. 40 (1968); People v. Sibron, 18 N.Y.2d 603 (1966), *rev'd on other grounds,* 392 U.S. 40 (1968); People v. Rivera, 14 N.Y.2d 441 (1964); Kuh, *Reflections on New York's "Stop and Frisk" Law and Its Claimed Unconstitutionality,* 56 J. CRIM. L.C. & P.S. 32 (1965).

This distinction was rejected by the Warren Court in *Terry v. Ohio*.[224] In *Terry*, the Court held the practice of "stop and frisk" to be controlled by the Fourth Amendment; then, balancing the individual interest in immunity from police interference against the community interest in the prevention of crime and the protection of the lives of law encorcement officers, the Court concluded that the practice was constitutional where reasonable. The Court, thus, resolved the debate over the constitutionality of "stop and frisk" in favor of the practice but, at the same time, sought to establish a constitutional standard to govern its exercise. In *Terry*, the Court approved a warrantless frisk in the absence of probable cause to arrest as being reasonable "under all of the circumstances of the on-street encounter."[225] But, in a companion case, *Sibron v. New York*, the Court held that the frisk had been unreasonable given the circumstances.[226]

In *Terry*, a police officer with thirty-nine years experience observed two men repeatedly walking past a store window. They then returned to the street corner, where they were briefly joined by a third man. After the third man left, the two resumed their pacing ritual, finally leaving to rejoin the third man. Suspecting that the men were "casing" the store for an armed robbery, the policeman approached them, identified himself, and asked their names. In response, the men only mumbled something between themselves. At this point, the officer grabbed Terry, spun him around so as to place him between the other two suspects and himself, and patted down the outside of Terry's clothing, finding a pistol. Disarming Terry, the officer then placed all three men against a wall, patted them down, and found another weapon. Terry and one of the others were then arrested and subsequently convicted of carrying concealed weapons.

The Supreme Court affirmed the conviction over Terry's objection that it had been procured by means of an unreasonable search. Speaking for the majority, Mr. Chief Justice Warren rejected the theory that, because a stop and frisk involved a lesser restraint than an arrest and search, it fell outside the limits of the Fourth Amendment protection. But the Chief Justice recognized that the Fourth Amendment's standard was not an inflexible absolute. Rather, he argued, there can be different kinds

[224]392 U.S. 1 (1968).
[225]*Id*. at 9.
[226]392 U.S. 40 (1968). Peters v. New York, 392 U.S. 40 (1968), another companion case, was not applicable to the problem, since the Court found that probable cause to arrest had been present.

of searches and seizures, each involving varying degrees of intrusion upon personal privacy, and, therefore, different balances could be stuck under the "reasonableness" test. The standard of evidence necessary under the Fourth Amendment to justify a given police intrusion upon individual privacy might vary depending upon the relative strengths of the government's interest in initiating the search and the individual's interest in being protected from a particular intrusion. Applying this flexible standard, the Chief Justice decided that the on-the-spot police response which is involved in a "stop and frisk" situation is not the type of police activity which is governed by the probable cause standard of the second clause of the Fourth Amendment. Instead, the constitutional test would be whether in each case the particular type of search was a "reasonable" one. Warren concluded that the governmental interest in the prevention of crime, especially crimes of violence with their attendant danger to innocent bystanders, coupled with the interest of the individual police officer in protection from attack by possibly armed individuals whose conduct he is legitimately investigating was sufficient to justify a limited search. But the officer must be warranted in the belief that, in carrying out his investigation, he or others may be in danger, and the frisk must be no more extensive than is necessary to assure the officer that the suspect is not carrying a concealed weapon. Only Mr. Justice Douglas dissented, insisting that a search and seizure cannot be reasonable under the Fourth Amendment unless based upon probable cause.

While the Court, using its new, flexible standard, found the frisk in *Terry* to have been a reasonable search, it reversed Sibron's conviction on the grounds that the circumstances involved in the frisk of his person had been insufficient to justify the officer in the belief that he was in danger. In *Sibron*, a policeman had, over a period of eight hours, observed Sibron talking with a number of known narcotics addicts. On the basis of these actions alone, the officer accosted Sibron and demanded an explanation of his actions. When Sibron only mumbled a reply, the officer said, "You know what I'm after." Sibron then began to reach into his pocket. The officer caught his hand, reached into the same pocket himself, and discovered envelopes containing heroin. The Supreme Court, however, in a second opinion by the Chief Justice, reversed Sibron's conviction for the unauthorized possession of narcotics. With only Mr. Justice Black dissenting, the majority found that the evidence should have been excluded at trial, because the frisk had been unreasonable, the officer not having sufficient facts to warrant a belief that Sibron was armed and dangerous.

Terry and *Sibron*, however, raised as many questions as they answered. Arguably, the suspect's behavior in *Sibron*, reaching into his pocket, had called for quick action on the officer's part to an even greater degree than the suspects' behavior in *Terry*, mumbling amongst themselves. Yet the Court thought not and produced different results in the two cases. Why? What factors, present in *Terry*, had been absent in *Sibron*? How could one distinguish the two cases? It seems that a combination of three factors account for the differing judgments: (1) the experience of the officers involved, (2) the greater extent of the search in *Sibron* vis-à-vis the purely protective pat down in *Terry*, and (3) the Court's own subjective judgment as to the degree of the suspicious nature of the behavior involved in each case. But, were this so, the problem with *Terry* was that the circumstances involved were so extreme. Most instances in which the police seek to detain a suspect do not and will not involve such experienced officers investigating such incredibly suspicious conduct. As such, *Terry* did not serve as a particularly illuminating guideline for the police. Did they have the power to require the suspect's cooperation? Or would a refusal to cooperate serve as a factor in establishing probable cause to arrest? Must the officer be acting upon his own observation? Or might he act on the basis of information garnered solely from an informer's tip? Was the nature of the crime suspected crucial in determining whether there was a power to stop and frisk? Did the differing results in *Sibron* and *Terry* support the proposition that the power was limited to crimes of violence or against property but did not extend to so-called "possessory" crimes, such as narcotics offenses? Even friendly critics of *Terry* recognized that eventually the Court would have to face these and other, related questions.[227]

And they were faced, by the Burger Court, in *Adams v. Williams*.[228] A policeman, acting on the tip of a nearby anonymous informer allegedly known to the officer, approached Williams's parked automobile in the middle of the night in a high crime neighborhood. Told by the informant that Williams had narcotics in the car and a gun at his waist, the officer

---

[227]E.g., LaFave, *"Street Encounters" and the Constitution*: Terry, Sibron, Peters, *and Beyond*, 67 MICH. L. REV. 40 (1968).

[228]407 U.S. 143 (1972).

requested Williams to open the door. Instead, he rolled down the window. Without further preliminaries, the officer thrust his hand into the car and removed a loaded pistol from the waistband of Williams's pants, exactly where the informant had predicted it would be. Williams was then arrested for the unlawful possession of the gun, and a subsequent search of the automobile incident to the arrest produced more weapons and a substantial quantity of heroin. Convicted for the possession of the gun and the heroin, Williams successfully sought a federal writ of habeas corpus,[229] but the Supreme Court, in an opinion by Mr. Justice Rehnquist, remarkable for its brevity, reversed.

Justice Rehnquist analyzed the constitutional reasonableness of the stop and frisk to which Williams had been subjected in two steps. First, the Justice examined the reasonableness of the stop, reading *Terry* to have held that a police officer may, short of arrest, require a person to cooperate with him where the officer, on the basis of a reasonable suspicion, believes the individual may be engaged in or is about to be engaged in some form of criminal conduct. The *Williams* majority, thus, recognized a stop itself, absent a frisk, may, by freezing the status quo, promote certain law enforcement interests. As such, the *Williams* majority rejected by implication the apparent assumption of Mr. Chief Justice Warren in *Terry* that an on-the-street stop for questioning was not of itself coercive, at least insofar as the suspect did not resist.[230] Rather, the Burger Court adopted the more realistic approach urged by Mr. Justice Harlan's *Terry* concurrence that the ordinary police stop for questioning restrains the suspect's freedom of movement and, thus, constitutes a "seizure" within the meaning of the Fourth Amendment.[231] Having brought the investigatory stop within the Consititution's limits, Rehnquist then inquired if the stop in *Williams* had met the Fourth Amendment's standard of reasonableness and explicitly rejected the argument that reasonable cause for a stop could be based only upon the officer's personal observation. Instead, the officer's reasonable belief could be based upon an informer's tip, Justice Rehnquist held, if that tip carried sufficient "indicia of realiability."[232] In Justice Rehnquist's view the tip in *Williams* had carried enough indicia of reliability to warrant the officer's forcible stop. The informant had been known to the officer personally and had furnished him with information in the past. The

[229] 441 F.2d 395 (2d Cir. 1971) (per curiam).
[230] 392 U.S. at 19, n. 16.
[231] *Id.* at 32-33.
[232] 407 U.S. at 147.

informer had come forward on his own initiative and had given information which was immediately verifiable, and the informer could have been held criminally liable for giving false information. While these indicia would have been insufficient to support either an arrest or a search warrant under the Warren Court's ruling regarding when an informant's tip might support probable cause,[233] Justice Rehnquist, adopting Chief Justice Warren's own flexible approach from *Terry*, found them adequate for the "stop and frisk" situation.

Finding the stop reasonable, Rehnquist then inquired into the reasonableness of the frisk. The standard articulated by the *Williams* majority for determining when a frisk was reasonably incident to a stop was whether the officer had reasonable cause to believe the suspect was presently armed and might be dangerous, either to the officer or to others. Mr. Justice Rehnquist found this standard to have been satisfied in *Williams*. Having found all of the acts preceding the discovery of the revolver to have been constitutionally justifiable, the *Williams* majority concluded that, following its discovery, probable cause existed to support Williams's arrest, which in turn rendered lawful the search of his vehicle incident to that arrest. The weapons and narcotics thus unearthed had, therefore, been properly admitted into evidence at Williams's trial. Almost without comment, Mr. Justice Rehnquist refused to limit the officer's power to frisk to those situations in which the crime under suspicion was one of violence. This seems to be both consistent with *Terry* and "wholly acceptable,"[234] for once the officer's right to stop is upheld, it is unreasonable to require the officer to engage in a further, thorough consideration of the danger to his safety.[235] Even those wrongly suspected of relatively minor crimes have been known to panic and to assault police officers with or without firearms.

The critical aspect of *Williams*, then, lay not in its refusal to condiditon the power to stop or to frisk upon the nature of the crime under suspicion nor in the Court's realistic approach to the coercive nature of an investigatory stop. But, in its articulation of the standard for determining the reasonableness of such stops, the Burger Court gave every impression that, while it would continue to engage, as did the *Terry* Court, in a

[233]Spinelli v. United States, 393 U.S. 410 (1969); Aguilar v. Texas, 378 U.S. 108 (1964).

[234]*The Supreme Court, 1971 Term*, 86 HARV. L. REV. at 175, n. 17.

[235]*But cf.* Kuh, *In-field Interrogation: Stop, Question, Detention and Frisk*, 3 CRIM. L. BULL. 597 (1967). *See generally* Younger, *The Perjury Routine*, 3 CRIM. L. BULL. 551 (1967).

balancing of the individual interest in privacy as against the competing government interest in the investigation of crime, that balance has now swung decisively in favor of the latter.

Indeed, in *United States v. Dionisio*, the Court reasoned that a grand jury subpoena is not a seizure within the meaning of the Fourth Amendment.[236] Since it is not a constitutional seizure, therefore, there is no necessity that reasonableness be shown. This approach was quite in contrast with *Williams* which, even though it found the frisk to be reasonable, did view the essence of a seizure to be the restraint of the freedom to walk away. It is, however, perfectly in harmony with the Burger Court's consistent approval of wide-ranging investigatory powers for grand juries.[237] Thus in *United States v. Calandra* the Court held that, while evidence obtained from unlawful searches and seizures may still be barred at actual trials, a witness summoned to appear and testify before a grand jury has no Fourth Amendment right to refuse to answer questions based upon such evidence.[238] *Calandra* can hardly be expected to prompt more care on the part of police in conducting searches, and *Dionisio* may invite the routine subpoenaing of the "usual suspects."[239] Similarly, the companion decisions in *United States v. Robinson*[240] and *Gustafson v. Florida*,[241] allowing full-custody arrest searches of persons stopped for simple traffic offenses, while not logically inconsistent with *Chimel*, did at least seem to represent a minor expansion of the Warren Court's understanding of the permissible scope of searches incident to arrest.

This trend on the part of the Burger Court, manifesting a greater solicitousness for the interests of law enforcement than did the Warren Court, has not been limited to tha area of search and seizure but has characterized the entire spectrum of the Court's decisions affecting police procedures and delimiting the constitutional rights of the criminally accused. In this area of Burger Court policy-making, unlike the

[236]410 U.S. 1 (1973). Relying upon Gilbert v. California, 388 U.S. 263 (1967), and United States v. Wade, 388 U.S. 218 (1967), the Court, speaking through Mr. Justice Stewart, first rejected Dionisio's claim that a required appearance before the grand jury to participate in a voice identification test violated the self-incrimination privilege. Again, the Court reiterated that the compelled provision of "physical" evidence does not violate the Fifth Amendment. *See* note 181 *supra*.

[237]*E.g.*, Branzburg v. Hayes, 408 U.S. 665 (1972).

[238]414 U.S. 338 (1974).

[239]*See The Supreme Court, 1972 Term*, 87 HARV. L. REV. 1, 204-13 (1973).

[240]414 U.S. 218 (1973).

[241]414 U.S. 260 (1973).

racial cases, there has been no effort to hold the line of Warren precedents;[242] unlike the reapportionment decisions, no adherence to a Warren Court principle, though applied with greater flexibility; but, instead, a conscious attempt to reverse the direction of judicial decision-making established during the preceding decade. *Harris* has qualified *Miranda's* restrictions upon the interrogation process; the identification procedure decisions have cut-back on *Wade* and *Gilbert*. *Calandra*, permitting the introduction of illegally seized evidence to a grand jury, might also be extended to statements secured in the absence of *Miranda* warnings, given the Burger Court's disquietude with *Miranda* and its apparent confidence in grand juries.[243] The court might even extend the *Kirk* rule to cover interrogations as well as lineups. The *Miranda* warnings would be retained but would become applicable only after indictment, arriving essentially at Mr. Justice Stewart's position in *Escobedo*.[244]

In part, this change of form seems to stem from the differing perspectives from which the two Court's majorities have viewed the problems of criminal defendants' rights. On the Burger Court, the Nixon appointees, joined often by Potter Stewart and consistently by Byron White, have taken the approach urged by Mr. Justice White's dissent in *Miranda*; they have viewed the situation systemically, from the top down. The Burger Court has placed its emphasis upon the legitimate interest of the law-abiding majority. To the extent that individual considerations have entered the Burger majority's thinking on these issues, the individual has been seen as victim or potential victim, whose interests coincide with those of law enforcement. The Warren Court, conversely, chose to view the situation from the bottom up, emphasizing the parts rather than the whole. The individual was central, and he was seen as criminal suspect or potential criminal suspect, the possibly innocent actor at the mercy of large, impersonal, bureaucratic forces

---

[242]In a somewhat limited sphere, however, the Burger Court's holding in United States v. Russell, 411 U.S. 423 (1973), that the defense of entrapment is a narrow one, though viewed with alarm in some quarters, is perfectly consistent with Warren Court rulings. While the result in *Russell* was undoubtedly based upon a policy judgment made by the majority that infiltration is a necessary means of apprehending members of narcotics rings, the Warren Court itself had validated the use of deceit where necessary to law enforcement success. Lewis v. United States, 385 U.S. 206 (1966). In light of *Lewis*, "*Russell* was a very clear case." 87 HARV. L. REV. at 250.

[243]*E.g.*, Branzburg v. Hayes, 408 U.S. 665 (1972); United States v. Dionisio, 410 U.S. 1 (1973).

[244]378 U.S. 478, 493 (1964) (dissenting opinion).

interested only in convictions but not in justice. In such a con-
ceptualization, individual interests did not coincide with the interests of
law enforcement but were seen as largely, if not exclusively, opposed to
the interests of the police, and the Warren majority placed its emphasis
upon the individual interests, as it conceived them. If the rights of each
were protected, the rights of all would be secure.

The liberalism of the Warren Court, however, should not be over-
emphasized. Many of its constitutional pronouncements affecting the
administration of criminal justice were reached by only the barest of
majorities. What we know of the impact of its most controversial
decision in this area, *Miranda*, does not support the "criminal coddling"
charges, whatever may have been the intentions of the Justices. The
Court did not rule that technological surveillance was per se unconstitutional, and in *Schmerber* and *Terry* it rendered two major decisions
favorable to law enforcement. But, on balance, it is correct that the
Warren Court did seek to liberalize the criminal law or at least the
procedures for its administration. Some of the policy changes which it
mandated probably would not have occurred without the Court. But how
effectively can five Justices in Washington, D.C., oversee the day-to-day
enforcement of the criminal law throughout America? Whatever else the
studies of the impact of *Miranda* and the continuing number of cases
involving confession and search-and-seizure problems may demonstrate, they certainly very clearly illustrate how naive it was and is to
believe that appellate courts and especially the Supreme Court of the
United States can ever effectively control on-street police behavior. As
one moves from the streets and into the courts and then through the
process of judicial administration of the criminal law, the Court, of
course, becomes increasingly effective. But the job of policing the police
must, in large measure, be left to other agencies: to legislatures, to
administrative officers, to politically active and concerned citizens, and
to a free press. Appellate courts are slow; they can consider only a small
percentage of all criminal cases; and they can correct violations of
constitutional rights only *ex post facto*.

The Burger Court seems to have recognized this, and here, again, the
differences between the Burger majority and the Warren majority may
stem not so much, or at least not entirely, from a postulated simple
dichotomy between conservative and liberal values but from a greater
preference on the part of the Burger majority for legislation as the vehicle
for policy reform. The exclusionary rule, for example, is a very crude

tool.[245] It serves the interest only of those who have been found in possession of worthwhile and objective evidence, such as weapons or contraband. It does nothing for the citizen whose privacy has been invaded by the police in an unlawful but fruitless search. The exclusion of evidence at trial does not punish the offending officers, and the continued incidence of unlawful searches severly undercuts the argument that it deters such objectionable police behavior.[246] The votes are not yet present on the Burger Court, if they will ever be, to abandon the exclusionary rule, but in *Coolidge v. New Hampshire*, a case in which only a four-man plurality continued to adhere to the basic approach of *Chimel*, narrowly construing the exceptions to the Fourth Amendment's warrant requirement, that suggestion was raised by more than one Justice, and the tenor of some of the dissenting opinions was unusually sharp.[247]

In fact, in another case decided on the same day as *Coolidge*, *Bivens v. Six Unknown Named Agents*, Mr. Chief Justice Burger traced the evolution, criticisms, and weaknesses of the exclusionary rule and, in what can only be viewed as an advisory opinion directed to Congress, set forth his own remedial recommendations.[248] Specifically at issue in *Bivens* was the judicial creation of a cause for action for damages against federal agents who had acted unlawfully. The majority opinion, authored by Justice Brennan, found no constitutional bar to the creation by the Court rather than by Congress of such a remedy for Fourth Amendment violations. Justices Black, Blackmun, and the Chief Justice objected to this assumption of judicial power. But Chief Justice Burger, going far beyond the immediate issues, took the occasion to spell out his views on the deficiencies of the exclusionary rule, to urge legislative reform, and to suggest a model statute for Congress's consideration. Rejecting private damage actions against individual officers as inadequate to vindicate constitutional rights, Burger's plan encompassed a waiver of sovereign immunity to suit, the creation of a remedy against the government itself to afford compensation to those whose rights have been violated, and the establishing of a quasi-judicial tribunal patterned after the United States Court of Claims to hear such cases. Congress, of course, has not yet

[245]*See* the discussion of Mapp v. Ohio, 367 U.S. 643 (1961), pp. 142-43 *supra*.
[246]*See* Oaks, *Studying the Exclusionary Rule in Search and Seizure*, 37 U. CHI. L. REV. 665 (1970).
[247]403 U.S. 443 (1971). *See also* p. 153 & note 88 *supra*.
[248]403 U.S. 388 (1971).

accepted the Chief Justice's invitation, although three years after *Bivens* and *Coolidge* Mr. Chief Justice Burger and Justices Powell and Rehnquist again voiced strong reservations about the exclusionary rule;[249] and *Calandra* has further eviscerated it.

In the final analysis, it would seem that Mr. Justice Rehnquist's observation in *Cady v. Dombrowski*, though directed at Fourth Amendment interpretation, could legitimately be extended to the whole compass of criminal defendants' rights decisions: "(T)his branch of the law is something less than a seamless web."[250] The Court can, of course, make some contribution to the development of criminal law policy in this country. It can set the limits within which legislation operates. This is what was done in the "incorporation" decisions, and the application of Bill of Rights guarantees to the states appears to be a legacy of the Warren Court which is destined to last. These decisions have been accepted by the public and continued by the Nixon appointees. But in the interpretation of the substantive content of those guarantees applied to the states, the Warren inheritance seems much more tenuous. The revision, reversal, or qualification of these decisions should come as little surprise, however. Majorities of the public and of the executive agencies affected by these decisions, whether rightly or wrongly, were opposed to the course which the Warren Court had set for itself.

In the long run, of course, the only way to get both effective and just enforcement of the criminal law is to recruit and support good policemen. That will be expensive, but anyone who thinks that bullets are cheaper than police officers with college degrees, carefully screened by both mental and emotional testing, simply doesn't understand the problem.[251] Such a policy reform, however, cannot be accomplished by judicial fiat. In this area, any Court, whether liberally or conservatively oriented, suffers as a policy-making agency from several critical inadequacies.

[249]Schneckloth v. Bustamonte, 412 U.S. 218, 250 (1973) (concurring opinion).
[250]413 U.S. 433, 440 (1973).
[251]*See generally*, R. CLARK, *supra* note 2.

Chapter 5
Of Chimeras and Court
and Consternations

An innovative court must eventually confront the question of what, if any, responsibility it owes to those who have relied upon previous law. Prior to *Mapp v. Ohio*,[1] for instance, state police conducted constitutionally deficient searches in the good faith belief that whatever they seized would be admissible as evidence. The Supreme Court had told them that it would be.[2] When that position was reversed and the exclusionary rule applied to the states, were not those persons convicted as a result of such searches imprisoned in violation of their constitutional rights and, thus, entitled to be released? On the other hand, would not such a holding work an unacceptable and irrational penalization of the public generally and in particular the police who had relied, not upon their own judgment, but the judgment of the highest court in the land?[3] Although by no means a novel problem,[4] the difficulties involved in

---

[1]367 U.S. 643 (1961).

[2]Wolf v. Colorado, 338 U.S. 25 (1949).

[3]In fact, the retroactive application of *Mapp* could have worked an even more irrational penalization of the police and public by forcing the reversal of convictions of persons whose constitutional rights had *not* been violated. Searches conducted prior to *Mapp* may have been constitutionally sufficient, but state trial courts were not required to examine their sufficiency. Consequently, state law enforcement agencies would probably not have kept evidence regarding the "reasonableness" of the searches which they conducted. If *Mapp* had been accorded retroactive effect, a criminal convicted by evidence gained in a police search and seizure might still have challenged the search, and the state would have had difficulty proving its legality—the police would have no evidence on the question and the trial record would have no statement on the subject. Appellate courts would then have to balance a convict's testimony contesting the legality of the search which convicted him against the testimony of the officers who conducted the search or that of the trial judge. If, however, the officers or judge had died or were otherwise unable to testify, the state would probably have no way of contesting the defendant's claim, and he would go free.

[4]*See, e.g.*, Goller v. White, 20 Wis.2d 402 (1963) (judicial abolition of parental immunity rule in negligence actions made prospective only except as applicable to instant case); Parker v. Port Huron Hospital, 361 Mich. 1 (1960) (prospective abrogation of

developing a coherent theory of retrospective effect were accentuated by the Warren Court's enlargement of the rights enjoyed by the criminally accused. The prospect of public reaction to a mass, legalized exodus from the prisons caused the court to re-evaluate the usual rule of absolute retroactivity for constitutional decisions.[5]

This question of the retroactive effect of the new constitutional procedures in the area of criminal law raised the perennial problem of what is the law, and what is the relationship of the judiciary to the law—a source of continuing debate among legal scholars for centuries. The declaratory theory, most notably expressed in the writings of Blackstone, contends that the law is an objectively determinable entity which magistrates, free from personal inclination or predilection, apply as it is revealed to them through litigation; rather than being the creator of the law, the judge is but its discoverer.[6] If the law were, in fact, eternal,

charitable hospital from liability to patients for negligence); Naftalin v. King, 257 Minn. 498 (1960) (declaration of statute creating state indebtedness to be unconstitutional not to be considered prospectively binding on similar laws which might be passed in the future); Molitor v. Kaneland Community Unit Dist., 18 Ill.2d 11 (1959) (abolition of school districts' tort immunity restricted to the instant case and to cases subsequently arising); Dooling v. Overholser, 243 F.2d 825 (D.C. Cir. 1957) (construction of mental health commitment statute restricted to prospective application); Hare v. General Contract Purchase Corporation, 220 Ark. 601 (1952) (all *future* "time price differential" transactions held to violate state constitutional mandate against usury); Baker v. St. Louis, 340 Mo. 986 (1937) (where overruled decisions deal with a rule of procedure, the effect of subsequent overruling decisions is prospective only); Great Northern Ry. Co. v. Sunburst Oil & Refining Co., 287 U.S. 358 (1932) (administrative rate changes apply prospectively only and do not affect intermediate transactions); Gelpke v. Dubuque, 68 U.S. (1 Wall.) 175 (1873) (state supreme court decision declaring statute authorizing a certain municipal bond issuance to be unconstitutional held to have prospective effect only and not to affect the rights of parties already having purchased such bonds.).

[5]*See, e.g.*, Linkletter v. Walker, 381 U.S. 618, 628 (1965), *citing* McNerlin v. Denno, 378 U.S. 575 (1964); Jackson v. Denno, 378 U.S. 368 (1964); Doughty v. Maxwell, 376 U.S. 202 (1964); Gideon v. Wainwright, 372 U.S. 335 (1963); Reck v. Pate, 367 U.S. 433 (1961); Eskridge v. Washington Prison Board, 357 U.S. 214 (1958); Griffin v. Illinois, 351 U.S. 12 (1956).

Linkletter was the first case in which the United States Supreme Court held a constitutional right to be nonretroactive. The need for such a limitation did not become apparent until the Warren Court extended the Bill of Rights guarantees to the states, while simultaneously expanding the availability of both direct and collateral attack. Fay v. Noia, 372 U.S. 391 (1963); Douglas v. California, 372 U.S. 353 (1963).

[6]*E.g.*, "There should be no misunderstanding as to the function of this court in such a case. It is sometimes said that the court assumes a power to overrule or control the action of the people's representatives. This is a misconception. The Constitution is the supreme law of the land ordained and established by the people. All legislation must conform to the

abiding, and unchanging, the answer to the retroactivity question would have been obvious.[7] When *Mapp*, for example, "discovered" that the exclusionary rule was required of the states, its discovery meant that, since the adoption of the Fourteenth Amendment, that had *always* been the law. By accepting the fruits of unreasonable searches the states had indeed been following unconstitutional practices, albeit unconsciously, and those persons whose rights were violated by these practices were illegally jailed.

Others, however, have maintained that judges do in fact do something more than discover law; they make it interstitially by filling in with judicial interpretation the vague, indefinite, or generic terms of the statutory or constitutional law. Implicit in this conception is the admission, when a case is overruled, that the earlier decision, rather than having been incorrect, was simply a judicial determination which later judges, of different opinions, think to be inapplicable to contemporary realities. Rather than being erased by the later, overruling decision, the previous case is considered to have been an existing juridical fact, and intermediate cases decided under it are not to be disturbed. In the words of Mr. Chief Justice Hughes, "The past cannot always be erased by a new judicial declaration."[8] The absolute retroactivity of any court decision, therefore, is not logically compelled.[9] Since courts, and particularly the

principles it lays down. When an act of Congress is appropriately challenged in the courts as not conforming to the constitutional mandate the judicial branch of the government has only one duty—to lay the article of the Constitution which is invoked beside the statute which is challenged and to decide whether the latter squares with the former." United States v. Butler, 297 U.S. 1, 62 (1936) (Roberts, J.). *See also* Norton v. Shelby County Taxing District, 118 U.S. 425 (1886).

The declaratory theory, i.e., the judge rather than being the creator of the law is but its discoverer, was first expounded by Sir Matthew Hale in his *History of the Common Law* and attained it foremost expression in the writings of Blackstone, who stated the maxim that the duty of a court was not to "pronounce a new law, but to maintain and expound the old one." J. GRAY, NATURE AND SOURCES OF THE COMMON LAW 206-222 (1st ed. 1909); W. BLACKSTONE, COMMENTARIES 69 (15th ed. 1809).

[7]Partly as a palliative to the logical determinism of the declaratory theory, the common law developed the doctrine of *res judicata* in order to preclude the reopening of previously decided cases, particularly those involving economic matters. *See generally* BLACK'S LAW DICTIONARY 1470 (4th ed. 1951).

[8]Chicot County Drainage District v. Baxter State Bank, 308 U.S. 371, 374 (1940.)

[9]If a power of prospective application exists, it cannot be confined solely to overruling situations. It is perforce applicable to *any* holding which involves a significant change from what had previously been considered to be the law. Significantly, most of the appeals by Supreme Court Justices for prospective application of the Court's decisions came in the context of opinions which did not involve the overruling of precedent. *See, e.g.*, Eskridge v.

United States Supreme Court, do at times make new law, the modern view "admits of some exceptions to the usual retroactive operation of judicial decisions."[10]

But prospectivity is not easily accepted on psychological grounds. Many scholarly arguments have been advanced against prospective application of Court decisions for precisely this reason.[11] But these arguments invariably proceed from the premise that, despite its short-comings, Blackstone's symbolic concept of the judicial process is the central pillar of judicial power and prestige. This symbolic view of the Supreme Court as bound by fixed, overriding law, which it applies impersonally and impartially, is supposed to constitute a major factor in securing respect for and obedience to its decisions. Prospective limitation of decisions, it is argued, will destroy this symbol, by heightening public consciousness of the element of judicial choice.[12] The destruction of the symbol will, in turn, result in the destruction of the emotional loyalties which it commands, with a subsequent decline in the prestige of the Court.

But judicial prestige and particularly public respect for the rule of law might suffer greater damage if retroactive application of the new constitutional rules of criminal procedure were to free criminals who subsequently committed new crimes. If the opening of the jailhouse doors were followed by an increase in the incidence of murder, rape, and theft, the public would not remain neutral to the Court, Blackstone to the contrary notwithstanding. Recognizing this fact, the Warren Court advanced the proposition that it had the power to limit the retroactive

Washington Prison Board, 357 U.S. 214, 216 (1958) (Harlan and Wittaker, JJ. dissenting); Griffin v. Illinois, 351 U.S. 12, 25 (1956) (Frankfurter, J., concurring); Mosser v. Darrow, 341 U.S. 267, 276 (1951) (Black, J., dissenting).

[10]Traynor, *The Judges and Law Reform*, 5 TRIAL 37 (April/May 1969).

[11]*See, e.g,* Schwartz, *Retroactivity, Reliability, and Due Process: A Reply to Professor Mishkin*, 33 U. CHI. L. REV. 719 (1966); Currier, *Time and Change in Judge-Made Law: Prospective Overruling*, 51 VA. L. REV. 201 (1965); Meador, *Habeas Corpus and the "Retroactivity" Illusion*, 50 VA. L. REV. 1115 (1964); Morris, *The End of an Experiment in Federalism—A Note on Mapp v. Ohio*, 36 WASH. L. REV. 407 (1961); Torcia & King, *The Mirage of Retroactivity and Changing Constitutional Concepts*, 66 DICK. L. REV. (1962). But *cf.* Mishkin, *The High Court, the Great Writ, and the Due Process of Time and Law*, 79 HARV. L. REV. 56 (1965); Bender, *The Retroactive Effect of an Overruling Constitutional Decision: Mapp v. Ohio*, 110 U. PA. L. REV. 650 (1962); Note, *Prospective Overruling and Retroactive Application in Federal Courts*, 71 YALE L.J. 907 (1962); Note, *Collateral Attack of Pre-Mapp v. Ohio Convictions Based on Illegally Obtained Evidence in State Courts*, 16 RUTGERS L. REV. 587 (1962).

[12]*Cf.* Spanel v. Mounds View School District, 118 N.W. 2d 795, 796 (Minn. 1962).

effect of its decisions. Having asserted that it had such a power, however, the Court was then faced with the question of the extent to which it wished to exercise it.

In the abstract, a court has a number of alternatives open to it in resolving the question of the retroactive effect of a newly recognized right. It may decide that no limitation on retroactivity is justified. But, for reasons already discussed, absolute retroactivity for many of the criminal defendants' rights decisions was unacceptable to all but the most libertarian of legal analysts. It is doubtful that the Court could survive the practical consequences of this theoretical approach. Absolute prospectivity, however, was equally unworkable. The effective operation of the judicial process depends upon parties raising issues for judicial decision and presenting, through adversary argument, the considerations relevant to a wise resolution of those issues. Litigation is encouraged only by the possibility of winning a rewarding judgment. If a new rule is given absolutely prospective effect, it obviously does not determine even the judgment awarded in the case in which it is announced. The result would be a stultification of the law. A purely prospective opinion is mere dictum; the court is reduced to issuing advisory opinions, and litigants' incentive to argue for changes in the law is destroyed.[13] If, then, a court determines that a new right should not be applied to *all* proceedings, the question becomes where to draw the line.

In drawing that line, a court must determine what particular form of limitation would be appropriate. The Warren Court suggested three possible approaches: (1) It might decide to apply the new rule to all cases which had not been "finalized," i.e., to all cases still open to direct appellate review; (2) It might adopt a rule stipulating that the new procedural guarantee applied only to trials commencing after the date of the announcement of the new right; or, (3) It might grant relief only in

---

[13]*See* Stovall v. Denno, 388 U.S. 293, 301 (1967); Mishkin, *supra* note 11, at 61. *Contra* A. BICKEL, THE SUPREME COURT & THE IDEA OF PROGRESS 54-57 (1970); Johnson, *Retroactivity in Retrospect*, 56 CALIF. L. REV. 1612, 1631 (1968). *See also* People v. Bandhauer, 66 Cal. 2d 536 (1967), *cert. denied*, 390 U.S. 911 (1968) (change in rules of argumentation at penalty trials in death penalty cases given purely prospective effect and not accorded to instant parties in case announcing change).

It is sometimes pointed out that certain litigants may have recurring problems in a specific area of the law and, thus, adequate incentive for litigating issues of change in the law even if a new holding would be given prospective effect only. Although this is correct, it is not an adequate excuse for absolute prospective limitation in that, while such a rule will not deter these institutional litigants, it will have that effect on all others.

See also von Moschzisker, *Stare Decisis in Courts of Last Resort*, 37 HARV. L. REV. 409 (1924).

those cases in which an alleged violation of the new right had occurred after the date of the case announcing it. These three standards may be characterized as (1) the final-judgment rule, (2) the trial-date rule, and (3) the violation-date rule.[14]

Initially the Warren Court adopted a final-judgment rule to govern the retrospective application of certain of its decisions increasing the scope of criminal defendants' rights. In *Linkletter v. Walker*[15] the Court denied federal habeas corpus relief from a state conviction based upon unconstitutionally seized evidence, because the prisoner's conviction had become final before the *Mapp* decision. The *Linkletter* ruling depended upon: (1) the past reliance of the states upon the rule which had been reversed in *Mapp*; (2) the purpose of the new rule of criminal procedure advanced in *Mapp*; and (3) the effect on the administration of justice of a retrospective application of the *Mapp* holding.

Mr. Justice Clark's opinion in *Linkletter* admitted that "heretofore, without discussion, we have applied new constitutional rules to cases finalized before the promulgation of the rule."[16] Clark, however, distinguished the standard under litigation, i.e., the exclusion in state courts of evidence obtained by illegal searches and seizures, from those maxims given retroactive effect on the basis of the purpose of the rule. The intent of the exclusionary rule, according to Clark, was to deter lawless police action, whereas the rules given retroactive effect had been applied to improve the reliability of the guilt determining process. The purpose of *Mapp*, Clark reasoned, would not be served by making it retrospective, since the illegal search had already taken place. Moreover, Clark argued, despite "flags in the wind,"[17] the states had continued to rely upon the Court's earlier holding in *Wolf v. Colorado* that the rule of exclusion did not apply in state courts.[18] The acceptance of the *Wolf*

[14]For a particularly lucid analysis of the strengths and weaknesses of each of these rules, *see* Johnson, *supra* note 13.

There are, of course, other logical possibilities. A trial-date rule, for example, applies a constitutional change only to trials begun after the date of the decision announcing the change and does not apply the change to trials begun before the date of the change. But it could be argued that this penalizes those few defendants whose trials are in progress at the time of the announcement of the change. Logically, thus, one could imagine two different trial-date rules, which would depend upon the nature of the rule changed by the Supreme Court: (1) a trial-commencement-date rule, or (2) a trial-conclusion-date rule.

[15]381 U.S. 618 (1965).

[16]*Id.* at 621. *See generally* note 5 *supra*.

[17]*E.g.*, Irvine v. California, 347 U.S. 128 (1954).

[18]338 U.S. 25 (1949).

doctrine prior to the *Mapp* decision was an operative and at least partially controlling fact: "The thousands of cases that were finally decided on *Wolf* cannot be obliterated."[19] Indeed, "public policy . . . must be given its proper weight."[20] Neither the intent of *Mapp*, nor the interest of society, nor the preservation of justice would be served by making *Mapp* retroactive. "There is," the *Linkletter* opinion pointed out, "no likelihood of unreliability or coercion present in a search and seizure case."[21] The evidence, though unlawfully obtained, was of itself objective. Moreover, the Court itself had, prior to *Mapp*, specifically authorized the use of such evidence in state trials. Turning to the question of its power to make decisions prospective only, the Court, after reviewing nine quite disparate Supreme Court decisions and two state cases,[22] concluded that it was the "accepted rule" that the Court did possess that power. The *Mapp* rule, thus, should be and could be and, therefore, was applied only to those cases not finalized at the time of the decision in *Mapp* and to all cases subsequently arising.

Despite some merit, the *Linkletter* decision deserved (and received) much criticism.[23] In the first place, all of the cases cited as support for the general theory of prospective limitation could have been distinguished. The basic difficulty with these cases was that none of them involved the effect of a change by a court in its own doctrines; all dealt with changes in applicable law made by other lawmaking authorities while a case was pending. Thus, the *Linkletter* opinion cited cases involving intervening changes of federal law by treaty, by act of Congress, and by constitutional amendment, and modification of state common law by a state supreme court during pendency of a diversity action in a federal court. Secondly, it is difficult to conceive of any circumstance involving establishment of a new rule in which past reliance would not be a factor. But the idea that such reliance should have been respected in *Linkletter* was particularly hard to maintain. It must contend with the Court's explicit declaration in *Wolf v. Colorado* that

[19]381 U.S. at 636.
[20]*Id.*
[21]*Id.* at 638.
[22]United States v. Schooner Peggy, 1 Cranch 103 (1801); Gelpke v. Dubuque, 68 U.S. 175 (1863); Dinsmore v. Southern Express Co., 183 U.S. 115 (1901); Crozier v. Fried, 224 U.S. 290 (1912); Great N. Ry. Co. v. Sunburst Oil & Refining Co., 287 U.S. 358 (1932); United States v. Chambers, 291 U.S. 218 (1934); Carpenter v. Wabash R. Co., 309 U.S. 23 (1940); Vandenbark v. Owens-Illinois Glass Co., 311 U.S. 538 (1941); James v. United States, 366 U.S. 213 (1961); Bingham v. Miller, 17 Ohio 445 (1848); State v. Jones, 44 N.M. 623 (1940).
[23]*See, e.g.*, works cited at note 11 *supra*.

The security of one's privacy against arbitrary intrusion by the police—which is at the core of the Fourth Amendment—is basic to a free society. It is therefore "implicit in the concept of ordered liberty" and as such enforceable against the States by virtue of the Due Process Clause.[24]

Of course, *Wolf* also explicitly held that state convictions would not be reversed because evidence obtained in violation of these constitutional restrictions was presented at the trial, and state officials did, in fact, rely upon this aspect of the decision. But the extent to which such reliance was justifiable is certainly questionable. Even if state prosecutors acted legitimately in introducing such evidence, and if state courts were correct in accepting it, the unconstitutional actions of the state police in obtaining it were hardly the kind of conduct *Wolf* intended to encourage.[25]

But, if the reliance factor were a legitimate consideration, the retroactive extension of *Mapp* to those cases not finalized at the time of its decision was illogical. The application of the *Mapp* rule, it would seem, should have been limited to those cases subsequently arising, the relevant issue being the time of the trial of first instance. If the purpose of *Mapp* was deterrent only and yet the states' reliance on *Wolf* was justifiable, according the *Mapp* rule to cases initially tried before the promulgation of that standard was an illogical penalization of the police.

Most seriously, *Linkletter's* scheme of analysis proved inadequate in its very first application. *Tehan v. United States ex rel. Shott*[26] denied retrospective application of the Court's previous holding in *Griffin v. California* that adverse comment by a prosecutor or trial judge upon a defendant's failure to testify in a state criminal trial violates the privilege against compulsory self-incrimination.[27] Ostensibly, *Tehan* rested upon

---

[24]338 U.S. 25, 27-28 (1949).

[25]Indeed, the *Linkletter* opinion recognized as much when, in reviewing the history of the *Mapp* rule, it said:

> Only a few States had made any changes in their rule of admissibility since *Wolf* and many of those not following the federal exclusionary rule were, in effect, using *Wolf* as a license to violate the Fourteenth Amendment's proscription of unreasonable searches and seizures as applied to the States by the *Wolf* case itself. As we noted in *Mapp* "further delay in [applying the exclusionary rule to the States] could have no effect other than to compound the difficulties"; a definitive continuance of *Wolf* might have increased the number of cases involving illegal searches in non-exclusionary States and also enticed those in the exclusionary column to reverse their position, as some States had done prior to *Mapp*.

381 U.S. 618, 635 (1965) (brackets in original). *But see* note 3 *supra*.

[26]382 U.S. 406 (1966).

[27]380 U.S. 609 (1965).

the reasoning of *Linkletter*. But, once again, it would seem that that reasoning would have better supported a violation-date rule, reversing convictions only if the proscribed comment was made after the *Griffin* decision, than a final-judgment rule as was adopted.[28] More crucially, assuming the *Linkletter* arguments of state reliance and policy considerations applied in the *Tehan* case (an assumption which this author believes invalid but, nevertheless, makes for the sake of brevity), was the purpose of the *Griffin* rule synonymous with that of *Mapp*? Mr. Justice Stewart, in his opinion for the Court, unequivocally held that it was:

> The basic purposes that lie behind the privilege against self-incrimination do not relate to protecting the innocent from conviction.[29]

Yet, in the very footnote supporting this statement, Mr. Justice Stewart cited Mr. Justice Goldberg's opinion in *Murphy v. Waterfront Comm'n* which read in part:

> The privilege, while sometimes a shelter to the guilty, is often a protection to the innocent.[30]

If the basis of the privilege is accurately reflected in this passage, then one intended effect of the privilege is, indeed, to insure the reliability of the guilt-determining process. Moreover the *Griffin* opinion expressly invalidated comment on failure to take the stand on the ground that juries may more readily draw an inference of guilt "when the court solemnizes the silence of the accused into evidence against him."[31] It is apparent that the *Linkletter* rationale was subverted in *Tehan* by the felt need to support a desirable result, seen by the Court as inconsistent with that approach. In other words, although the *Linkletter* rule purported to weigh a number of factors relevant to retroactive application of a new procedural guarantee, it became apparent from *Tehan* that one of those

---

[28]The application of a trial-date rule, applying *Griffin* only to cases begun after that decision, would have allowed prosecutors and judges participating in trials which were in progress at the time *Griffin* was announced but which had not yet reached the stage of prosecution summation or judicial charge to the jury to have commented upon any defendant's failure to testify in such a trial. This would seem as illogical in one direction as *Tehan* was in the other. The purpose of the no-comment rule was deterrent, and neither the prosecutor nor the judge who commented upon an accused's failure to testify after *Griffin* could have justified his comment on the grounds of past reliance upon the old practice. Moreover, it is doubtful that the impact upon the administration of justice would have been so significant as to justify the refusal to apply *Griffin* to trials in progress at the time of its announcement.

[29]382 U.S. at 415.

[30]378 U.S. 52, 55 (1964).

[31]380 U.S. at 614.

factors—not forcing the release of convicted criminals—was significantly weightier than all of the others combined.

Whatever its shortcomings, however, the *Tehan* result seemed to indicate that the Warren Court favored the final-judgment rule as a retroactivity standard and that a similar approach would be adopted to determine the retrospective effect on other of its criminal defendants' rights decisions. Consequently, the decision in *Johnson v. New Jersey*[32] came as a great surprise, for in *Johnson* the Court applied a trial-date rather than a final-judgment rule to govern the retroactivity of its decisions affecting police interrogation procedures.[33]

Johnson represented an attempt to reply to a very valid point raised by Mr. Justice Black in *Linkletter*. Black had dissented on the grounds that the final-judgment rule was capricious in the extreme; a prisoner who was tried and convicted in a state whose appellate courts were up on their docket would remain imprisoned, having exhausted his direct review, while a comparable defendant in a less efficient jurisdiction would probably go free. In *Johnson*, the Court very neatly solved this problem, although not quite in the way Mr. Justice Black had in mind. Relying on *Linkletter* for the proposition that the Court possesses a general power of prospective limitation, a seven-man majority, speaking through the Chief Justice, went beyond *Linkletter* to hold that the requirements of *Escobedo v. Illinois* and *Miranda v. Arizona* would apply only to trials begun after the dates of the respective decisions. The majority explicitly recognized that the purpose of the rules which the Court had laid down in *Escobedo* and *Miranda* had been to protect the innocent from conviction, as well as to deter coercive police practices, but they reasoned that the extent to which a given constitutional rule of criminal procedure did or did not improve the reliability of the guilt determining process was a matter of degree. Although statements obtained in violation of *Escobedo* and *Miranda* might under certain circumstances be unreliable, this possibility was not as great as when the accused was subjected to overt physical or psychological coercion, and convictions based upon such coercive tactics were still subject to challenge under the involuntariness test, which had itself been significantly broadened in recent years.[34] Chief Justice Warren noted that, had the Court been

[32]384 U.S. 719 (1966).
[33]Escobedo v. Illinois, 378 U.S. 478 (1964); Miranda v. Arizona, 384 U.S. 436 (1966).
[34]*See, e.g.*, Haynes v. Washington, 373 U.S. 503 (1963); Lynumn v. Illinois, 372 U.S. 528 (1963); Townsend v. Sain, 372 U.S. 293 (1961); Spano v. New York, 360 U.S. 315 (1959); Mallory v. United States, 354 U.S. 449 (1957); McNabb v. United States, 318 U.S. 332 (1943).

persuaded that *Miranda* could have been "fully anticipated" from the *Escobedo* holding, it might have applied *Miranda* to trials begun after the date of the *Escobedo* decision. But the Court was unconvinced of this and was significantly impressed by the burden which a final-judgment rule of retroactivity for *Escobedo* and *Miranda* would place upon the administration of justice. Undoubtedly, these practical considerations rather than legal tradition dictated the result.[35]

But, granting the legitimacy of practicality as a controlling factor in judicial decision-making, the *Johnson* decision remains questionable. In the first place, the Court did not explain why police reliance on *Escobedo* required a trial-date rule to determine the retroactive effect of *Miranda*. If the reliance of law enforcement agencies upon *Escobedo* were to be the determinative factor, clearly the significant date was not the date of trial but the date at which the confession had been obtained. Thus, a violation-date rule would appear to have been appropriate, since the trial-date rule adopted in *Johnson* still required the reversal of convictions in cases in which an interrogation pursuant to the *Escobedo* rule produced a confession but *Miranda* was decided before the case came to trial. A trial-date rule determining the retroactivity of *Miranda* seems to be appropriate only if the Court were concerned with the reliance upon *Escobedo*, not of the police, but of prosecutors. In other words, if the Court were concerned with protecting convictions for prosecutors who, having a confession which they reasonably believed to be admissible, failed either to obtain or to introduce other evidence of guilt, the date of the trial is the date of primary importance. But the Court nowhere mentioned in *Johnson* the reliance of prosecutors as a factor and, instead, spoke only of the reliance of law enforcement agencies upon *Escobedo* in interrogations in the two years preceding *Miranda*.

Moreover, *Johnson*, because it merely refined rather than rejected the *Linkletter* reasoning, created its own capriciousness. *Johnson* made it clear that persons whose convictions had been attained by the use of coerced confessions could still challange those convictions under a due process-fundamental fairness rationale. But *Johnson* also made plain that the coercion standard to be applied in such challenges would be the one existing in 1966, even if the person's confession were coerced in 1936. Although it was unlikely that many such cases would arise, that was certainly an anomalous piece of logic.

Most seriously, *Johnson* manifested, in the extreme, a tendency the Warren Court exhibited in all of its retroactivity holdings: that is to

---

[35]*See The Supreme Court, 1965 Term,* 80 HARV. L. REV. 91, 141 (1966).

modify the reasoning of the original decisions whenever that reasoning would seem to indicate the necessity of retrospective application. Thus, the purpose of *Griffin*, which emphasized the many reasons why an otherwise innocent person might see fit not to testify in his own behalf, was reduced in *Tehan* to the protection of some vaguely defined interest in individual dignity. In *Johnson*, the extent to which *Miranda* had been designed to protect the innocent from conviction was even more drastically discounted in an attempt to keep the jailhouse doors closed. The consequence of this sleight of hand manipulation of the purposes behind the original decisions was that those decisions, being deprived of compelling reasons for their announcement, were made to appear to have been unsound. Thus, for example, *Johnson* dismissed *Miranda* as a substantial improvement of the guilt-determining process with the extraordinary statement that "nonretroactivity...will not preclude persons whose trials have already been completed from invoking the same safeguards as part of an involuntariness claim."[36] But, if the ever-evolving voluntariness test were an adequate protection of the rights of criminal defendants, it would seem that *Escobedo* and *Miranda* were wrongly decided![37]

Nevertheless, the Court had apparently become infatuated with its newly discovered ability to even more closely resemble a legislature; or, if it had not become infatuated, it was at least having some good fun confounding law review commentators, because it next went beyond even its holding in *Johnson*. In *Stovall v. Denno*,[38] the Court adopted a violation-date rule to deny any retroactive vitality whatsoever to its decisions in *United States v. Wade*[39] and *Gilbert v. California*.[40] In

[36] 384 U.S. at 730.

[37] *Johnson* did not confront the somewhat specialized problem of the applicability of the *Miranda* standards to retrials occasioned by the reversals of convictions on other grounds. In Jenkins v. Delaware, 395 U.S. 213 (1969), the Court ruled that *Miranda* did not apply, as a constitutional requirement, to post-*Miranda* retrials of cases originally tried before the *Miranda* decision. Reviewing the various tests which the Court had advanced to determine retroactivity, Mr. Chief Justice Warren, for a six-man majority, reasoned that, although the issue of the application of *Miranda* to retrials had not been presented in *Johnson*,

> because of the increased evidentiary burden that would be placed unreasonably upon law enforcement officials by insisting that *Miranda* be applied to retrials, and for all of the reasons we gave in *Johnson* for not applying *Miranda* retroactively,

Johnson should not be read as encompassing retrials. *Id*. at 221.

[38] 388 U.S. 293 (1967).

[39] 388 U.S. 218 (1967).

[40] 388 U.S. 263 (1967).

refusing to apply either *Wade* or *Gilbert* retroactively, the Court held these decisions, entitling an accused to the presence of his counsel at police lineups, controlled only lineups occurring after the date of the decisions in *Wade* and *Gilbert*. The Court concluded that

> no distinction is justified between convictions now final . . . and convictions at various stages of trial and direct review. We regard the factors of reliance and burden on the administration of justice as entitled to such overriding significance as to make that distinction unsupportable.[41]

Again the Court in its retroactivity decision noticeably undermined the foundation of its decisions changing the earlier procedures. The majority in *Stovall* thought that the extent to which the *Wade-Gilbert* requirements would improve the reliability of the determination of guilt was merely a question of probabilities and that that probability was so slight as not to justify its retroactive application, despite the same Court's own argument in *Wade* that the lineup is replete with "hazards of unfairness to the criminally accused."[42] As in *Johnson*, the Court indicated that relief was still open to defendants convicted in the past who could demonstrate that a particular lineup, conducted without the presence of counsel, had been so unfair as to deny them due process. But again, if due process rules were adequate to safeguard the rights of defendants in lineups, there would appear to have been no need for providing them with a right to counsel at such procedures. Indeed, it would seem to be more difficult to show that a lineup without the presence of counsel actually prejudiced the defendant than to demonstrate that a confession had been coerced. The Court itself noted that suspects are often unable to assist counsel with the sort of information requisite to show prejudice.

Stovall's adoption of a violation-date rule, however, signalled the wave of the future. In its last years the Warren Court evinced a growing disenchantment with the final-judgment rule and increasingly favored a violation-date standard for limiting the retroactive effect of its criminal defendants' rights decision.[43] For example, remarking that it saw "no basis for a distinction between convictions that have become final and cases at various stages of trial and appeal,"[44] the Court held that its decision in *Duncan v. Louisiana*[45] was to have only prospective

[41]388 U.S. at 300-01.
[42]388 U.S. 218, 234.
[43]*See* Jenkins v. Delaware, 395 U.S. 213 (1969); Desist v. United States 394 U.S. 244 (1969); Fuller v. Alaska, 393 U.S. 80 (1968); DeStefano v. Woods, 392 U.S. 631 (1968).
[44]DeStefano v. Woods, 392 U.S. 631, 635 n.2.
[45]391 U.S. 145 (1968); *see also* Bloom v. Illinois, 391 U.S. 194 (1968).

application for the following reasons: (1) The values implemented by the right to trial by jury would not be measurably served by requiring retrial of all persons convicted in the past by procedures not consistent with the right to trial by jury; (2) good faith reliance upon past opinions of the Court to the effect that the jury trial requirement was not applicable to the states;[46] and (3) the significantly adverse effect of a holding of general retroactivity on the administration of criminal justice.[47] While certain rules of limited significance were accorded absolute retroactivity after 1967,[48] all major changes in the constitutional law applicable to criminal detection practices were limited to prospective application only by the adoption of a violation-date standard.[49]

On the whole, the Warren Court's abandonment of the final-judgment rule was a wise step.

> A final-judgment rule is an uneasy and unsatisfactory compromise between full retroactivity and pure prospectivity that satisfies neither the interests of the state nor those of defendants.[50]

What is more difficult to applaud is the length of time which it took a majority to recognize this fact. As a consequence of the Court's failure to exercise intellectual rigor, the rules of retroactivity which the Court applied to its constitutional changes in criminal procedure were a

[46]*E.g.*, Maxwell v. Dow, 176 U.S. 581 (1900).

[47]DeStefano v. Woods, 392 U.S. 631 (1968). Given the nature of the constitutional guarantee involved, i.e., the right to trial by jury, this was, of course, a case where trial-date and violation-date rules produced synonymous results.

[48]Berger v. California, 393 U.S. 314 (1969), *applying* Barber v. Page, 390 U.S. 719 (1968) (use of preliminary hearing testimony in absence of witness inadmissible unless state made good faith effort to secure witness's presence); Arsenault v. Massachusetts, 393 U.S. 5 (1969), *applying* White v. Maryland, 373 U.S. 59 (1964) (preliminary arraignment constitutes critical stage of criminal proceeding necessitating right to counsel); McConnell v. Rhay, 393 U.S. 2 (1968), *applying* Mempa v. Rhay, 389 U.S. 128 (1967) (right to counsel applicable to proceedings for revocation of probation); Roberts v. Russell, 392 U.S. 293 (1968), *applying* Bruton v. United States, 391 U.S. 123 (1968) (excluding inculpatory confession of codefendant as violation of Sixth Amendment right to confrontation).

[49]*E.g.*, Stovall v. Denno, 388 U.S. 293 (1967), *applying* Wade v. United States, 388 U.S. 213 (1967), *and* Gilbert v. California, 388 U.S. 263 (1967) (excluding identifications based upon lineups conducted in absence of defense counsel); DeStefano v. Woods, 392 U.S. 631 (1968), *applying* Duncan v. Louisiana, 391 U.S. 145 (1968), (jury trial in serious criminal cases required of states by Due Process Clause of 14th Amendment); Fuller v. Alaska, 393 U.S. 80 (1969), *applying* Lee v. Florida, 392 U.S. 378 (1968) (holding wiretap evidence inadmissisble in state courts); Desist v. United States, 394 U.S. 244 (1969), *applying* Katz v. United States, 389 U.S. 407 (1967) (ruling that use of wiretap and electronic eavesdrop evidence covered by reasonableness standard of Fourth Amendment).

[50]Johnson, *supra* note 13, at 1631.

melange of final-judgment, trial-date, and violation-date standards. Certainly logic—as well as liberalism—was severly taxed by the retroactivity decisions.[51] There was no consistency in what the Court did on this subject. No general principle was announced which would clearly indicate whether criminal law decisions were to be retroactive or prospective. Rather, the Court preferred to leave the matter to be determined issue by issue. Any criticism of the Court for lack of logical consistency must be tempered, of course, not only by Holmes's aphorism that logic is not the life of the law but also by the realization that the retroactivity cases confronted the Court with the necessity of steering a middle course between the logical implications of its constitutionally based pronouncements on criminal procedure and the political reality of public reaction.

But, on the other hand, there did exist a consistent principle which would have achieved the desired results while at the same time being compatible with the Warren Court's legislative inclinations. Given its predisposition for turning the Bill of Rights into a code of criminal procedure,[52] it would seem that the next logical step for the Court to have taken would have been for it to have frankly and candidly admitted its lawmaking functions. The doctrine that a final judgment entered under a given rule of law may withstand subsequent judicial change in that rule is long established,[53] and though that doctrine is perhaps more firmly settled in the context of civil litigation the underlying considerations of finality find significant parallels in the criminal field.[54] If the Due Process Clause of the Fourteenth Amendment be a procedural guarantee only, the validity of any conviction is to be determined by the constitutional standards applicable to the criminal justice process at the time at which it was obtained. So long as the extant standards were observed, the conviction would be valid. Any new rules of law would be given purely prospective application *with the exception of the parties in the particular case in which the new rule is announced.*[55]

---

[51]*See generally* People v. Feggans, 67 Cal.2d 444, 451-452 (1967) (Peters, J., dissenting); Mishkin, *supra* note 11.

[52]*See* Friendly, *The Bill of Rights as a Code of Criminal Procedure,* 53 CALIF. L. REV. 929 (1965).

[53]The leading case, heavily relied upon in *Linkletter,* is Chicot County Drainage District v. Baxter State Bank, 308 U.S. 371 (1940). Nor is the process unique to the United States, being practiced in Germany, Austria, and Italy.

[54]Amsterdam, *Search, Seizure and Section 2255; A Comment,* 112 U. PA. L. REV. 378 (1964).

[55]Such an approach has already been judicially suggested in Goller V. White, 20

Such an approach would have fully supported the results which the Warren Court eventually produced in its retroactivity decisions, while avoiding many, if not all, of the problems raised thereby. The Court, moreover, would have had a sound basis for such activisim in its legal expertise and experience. Yet, judicial prestige need not have suffered serious diminution.[56] At the same time, many of the more serious objections to the "general power" theory expressed in the retroactivity decisions would have been met. By according an exception to the party or parties arguing for a particular change in the law, while judging the legitimacy of all other convictions by the constitutional standards applicable at the time, this rule would not have the effect of discouraging parties from arguing for legal change and advancement. It would, in fact, embrace the Cardozo-Frankfurter concept of an expanding due process.[57] The way would, thus, be left open for a continuing progress in and civilization of the law without condemnation of our fathers. Furthermore, such an approach would have automatically confronted the issue of prospective effect at the time of the decision.[58] Otherwise, the Court, so long as it continues to act like a Court, being confined to "Cases . . . [and] Controversies,"[59] is forced either into *post hoc* resolutions of the retroactivity problem or into the issuance of advisory opinions.[60] Unless the Court changes its role and becomes an administrative agency, a

---

Wis.2d 402 (1963), and Molitor v. Kaneland Community Unit District, 18 Ill.2d 11 (1959). *But cf.* note 13 *supra*.

[56]*But cf.* P. MISHKIN & C. MORRIS, ON LAW IN COURTS 308-314 (1965); Bender, *supra* note 11.

[57]"Due process of law . . . expresses a demand for civilized standards of law. It is thus not a stagnant formulation of what has been achieved but a standard for judgment in the progressive evolution of a free society." Malinski v. New York, 324 U.S. 401, 414 (1945) (Frankfurter, J., concurring). *See also* Haley v. Ohio, 332 U.S. 596, 603 (1948) (Frankfurter, J., concurring); Palko v. Connecticut, 302 U.S. 319 (1937) (Cardozo, J.); B. CARDOZO, THE NATURE OF THE JUDICIAL PROCESS (1925).

[58]It was a necessary implication of the general prospectivity approach of the Warren Court that the question of prospective limitation should have been raised and faced in each of the decisions announcing a significant change in the constitutional law of criminal procedure. Indeed, the opinion in *Linkletter* recognized as much, though perhaps unwittingly, declaring that "once the premise is accepted that we are neither required to, nor prohibited from applying a decision retrospectively, we must then weigh the merits and demerits in each case. . . . " 381 U.S. 618, 629 (1965). Perhaps no other aspect of the Warren Court's retroactivity decisions was as severely criticized as its *post hoc* approach to the problem. *See, e.g.,* Friendly, *Reactions of a Lawyer—Newly Become Judge,* 71 YALE L.J. 218, 235 n. 105 (1961); Friendly, *supra* note 52, at 940 n. 64; Mishkin, *supra* note 11.

[59]U.S. CONST. art. III, sec. 2.

[60]*See* note 13 *supra*.

procedural due process scheme is the only way to confront the issue in the decision initially changing the constitutional standard.[61] Finally, by limiting the retroactive effect of any new rule to the instant parties only, this rule would have avoided the potential chaos inherent in the Warren Court's rationale that courts have the power to accord absolute prospectivity, absolute retroactivity, or some intermediate variant to procedural changes in the criminal law. One need only consider the difficulties inherent in the application of a general theory of prospective limitation in intermediate appellate courts or in state supreme courts on federal questions to perceive that the adoption of such a general practice might create problems beyond the effective capacity of the regular judicial machinery.[62]

While one does not wish to sound like Goldilocks (" . . . but this porridge is *just right!*"), let alone Pollyanna, it would seem that this approach would have combined the best of both judicial activism and judicial self-restraint. The Court could have made an extremely strong case for activism in this area on the basis of its unique expertise. Who knows better about judicial proceedings than a judge? By this reasoning, the Court would not have been caught in the tautology of Mr. Justice Stewart's logic in *Tehan*. They would simply have had recourse to their own magisterial experience. Yet, this approach would have been based upon one of the keystones of judicial self-restraint, opposition to a substantive reading of the Due Process Clause. Judicial restraint, moreover, might still have been preserved in areas such as legislative apportionment, where the Court had no claim to special expertise.

Nor need the Court's prestige have suffered from such a blatant admission of judicial policy-making. If the power of Blackstonian symbolism and the loyalties which it commands remain undiminished and are still central to the Court's prestige, this approach would have

---

[61]*See generally* M. SHAPIRO, THE SUPREME COURT AND ADMINISTRATIVE AGENCIES ch. 1 (1968); M. SHAPIRO, LAW AND POLITICS IN THE SUPREME COURT 24-29 (1964); Mishkin, *Prophecy, Realism, and the Supreme Court: The Development of Institutional Unity*, 40 .A.B.A. J. 680 (1954).

This is not to deny, of course, that there may be some significant parallels between courts and administrative agencies; *e.g., compare* Shapiro, *Stability and Change in Judicial Decision-Making: Incrementalism or Stare Decisis?*, 2 LAW IN TRANS. Q. 134 (1965), *with* Lindblom, *The Science of "Muddling Through,"* 19 PUB. ADMIN. REV. 79 (1959).

[62]These difficulties, of course, might be avoided by limiting the power to the Supreme Court only, but it would be difficult to find a rationale for such a power which would not apply to all courts equally. Certainly the justification advanced in *Linkletter* was not uniquely suited to the Supreme Court. *See* Johnson, *supra* note 13.

rested upon one of the central pillars of the Blackstonian concept—legal expertise. On the other hand, if, as some have claimed, the symbolic concept of the Court has been dying in recent years, at least among the enlightened, then such a candid admission might even have possibly gained respect for the Court. Finally, Blackstonian symbolism aside, this due process rule would not have resulted in the public outcry incident to the wholesale release of criminals under a rule of absolute retroactivity. Since, according to the basic presumption of the Anglo-American legal system, the innocent are never convicted, the courts cannot use their cases to change the criminal law. Thus, any change under any rule short of absolute prospectivity must potentially involve the release of criminals. The due process appraoch would limit the retrospective effect of any change to the party before the Court.

Essentially the same result was reached by the Warren Court's adoption of a violation-date rule as the constitutionally preferred standard in *Stovall* and the subsequent retroactivity cases. However, due to the fact that in adopting the violation-date rule the Court continued to rely upon the underlying rationale of *Linkletter*, it created certain anomalies. First, unlike the due process rule, it allowed for the attack of previously obtained convictions under contemporary due process standards. Second, and as a consequence, it undermined the legitimacy of the very changes which it had mandated. The due process scheme would not have allowed for such a retrospective application of evolving standards. Nor need it have undermined the rationale of particular changes in the law, if those changes were compelled by changed contemporary conditions.

But this, of course, raises the problem of whether the Warren Court ever sufficiently justified its criminal defendants' rights decisions as something other than the personal preferences of five individuals who happen to have found themselves on the Supreme Court at a particular moment. The Court's rough-and-ready, even slipshod, approach to the retroactivity issue was but a mirror reflection of its criminal defendants' rights decision-making. In fact, the Court's discovery of its power to limit its pronouncements, like a legislature, to something less than full retroactivity may well have encouraged it to legislate still further. With the specter of necessary retroactivity abolished, the Warren Court could write brave words to justify its decisions effecting procedural changes in the administration of the criminal law yet later seriously hedge those words by cautiously limiting their retrospective status.

The Burger Court, too, has found this power of the Court to limit the retroactivity of its holdings to be a desirable judicial tool. Ironically enough, however, it has found this power, first discovered by the Warren Court, desirable because it allows the new Justices to limit certain of the criminal defendants' rights holdings which they find to be objectionable. Rather than reject the power or creatively adopt a new and consistent theory of prospective effect, the Burger Court has endorsed the Warren Court's approach to the problem of retroactivity but has done so in order to confine or mitigate the impact of Warren Court precedents.[63] For example, in *Williams v. United States,*[64] the Burger Court adopted a violation-date rule to govern the retrospective effect of *Chimel v. California.*[65] *Chimel's* rule, narrowing the permissible scope of searches incident to arrest to the person of the arrestee and the area within his immediate control,[66] was held to be inapplicable to searches antedating that decision. In announcing the judgment of the Court in *Williams,*[67] Mr Justice White adhered to the Warren Court's post-*Linkletter* approach. Since the purpose of the new constitutional standard embraced in *Chimel* had not been to reform an aspect of the criminal process which might substantially impair the truth-finding function, earlier violations of that standard raised no serious questions about the accuracy of guilty verdicts in past trials. The *Chimel* rule, therefore, did not require retroactive application. Moreover, in *William's* companion case, *Elkanich v. United States,* Justice White could find no constitutional difference between the applicability of *Chimel* to convictions before the Court on direct appeal and those involving collateral proceedings.[68]

[63]Concerning the Burger Court's approach to the retroactive effect of legislative, rather than judicial, changes in the law, *see* Bryson v. United States, 396 U.S. 64 (1969) (subsequent repeal of statute irrelevant to validity of perjury conviction under statute as applicable at time of false swearing).

[64]401 U.S. 646 (1971); *see also* Hill v. California, 401 U.S. 797 (1971).

[65]395 U.S. 752 (1969).

[66]*See* ch. IV *supra* at pp. 186-87.

[67]Mr. Justice White's plurality opinion was joined by Mr. Chief Justice Burger and Justices Stewart and Blackmun. Mr. Justice Brennan filed a separate concurrence, in which he sought to disassociate himself from any reference to the issue of guilt. Mr. Justice Harlan, distinguishing between direct and collateral attack, dissented but concurred in the companion decision in *Elkanich.* Mr. Justice Marshall, concurring in part and dissenting in part, agreed substantially with Mr. Justice Harlan. Mr. Justice Black concurred on the grounds that *Chimel* had been wrongly decided. Mr. Justice Douglas took no part in the decision, but in Mackey v. United States, 401 U.S. 667, 713 (1971) (dissenting opinion), emphasized his commitment to the traditional rule of absolute and necessary retroactivity.

[68]401 U.S. 646 (1971).

On the contrary, Mr. Justice Harlan, concurring in part and dissenting in part, purported to find great constitutional significance in the distinction between direct appellate review and collateral review in habeas corpus cases.[69] Although he had played a major role in influencing the Court to rethink the rule of necessary retroactivity for constitutional changes,[70] Harlan now despaired of its handiwork. He was bothered both by the tortured logic and the inconsistent results produced in a half decade's retroactivity decisions, but he was most concerned with the legislative character which those decisions had increasingly manifested. The scope of retroactivity, he insisted, "must be determined upon principles that comport with the judicial function, and not upon considerations which are appropriate . . . for a legislative body."[71] For Harlan, the judicial function mandated that the Court "apply the law as it is at the time, not as it once was;"[72] therefore, he urged the according of full retroactivity to new procedural due process rulings in all direct review cases, but he would deny retrospective effect in habeas procedings. However, in view of the well-founded criticisms which *Linkletter's* final-judgment rule had received,[73] Harlan's argument, while its motivation was surely understandable, was less than persuasive. Indeed, he weakened his own case by stating that there might be some exceptions which would call for retroactivity even on collateral review.[74]

Nevertheless, Mr. Justice Harlan's approach carried the day. But, quite literally, that is all that it carried. On the same day that it decided *Williams* and *Elkanich*, April 5, 1971, the Burger Court addressed the question of the retroactive effect of *Marchetti v. United States*[75] and *Grosso v. United States*,[76] precluding the criminal conviction of gamblers who had properly asserted their privilege against self-incrimination as a ground for their failure to comply with the gambling tax laws' registration requirements.[77] *United States v. United States Coin and Currency* involved a direct review of a forfeiture proceeding;[78] *Mackey v. United*

[69]*Id.* at 675.

[70]*See* Eskridge v. Washington Prison Bd., 357 U.S. 214, 216 (1958) (Harlan, J., dissenting); Jackson v. Denno, 378 U.S. 368, 439 (1964) (Harlan, J., dissenting).

[71]401 U.S. at 677.

[72]*Id.* at 681.

[73]*See* notes 11 and 13 *supra*.

[74]401 U.S. at 692-95.

[75]390 U.S. 39 (1968).

[76]390 U.S. 62 (1968). *See also* Haynes v. United States, 390 U.S. 85 (1968); Leary v. United States, 395 U.S. 6 (1969); United States v. Freed, 401 U.S. 601 (1971).

[77]U.S.C. §§ 4411, 4412, 4901.

[78]401 U.S. 715 (1971).

States entailed a collateral challenge to a conviction for income tax evasion.[79] Mr. Chief Justice Burger and Justices White, Stewart, and Blackmun supported non-retroactivity for *Marcchetti* and *Grosso*; Justices Black, Douglas, Brennan, and Marshall urged complete retroactivity. Mr Justice Harlan, espousing his distinction between direct appeals and collateral attacks, cast the deciding vote in both cases. He would apply *Marchetti* and *Grosso* to the forfeiture proceeding in *United States Coin and Currency* but not to the tax evasion conviction in *Mackey*. Presumably, this result was pleasing to no one, except Mr. Justice Harlan and Donald Angelini, the proprietor of United States Coin and Currency.

The Harlan triumph, however, was short-lived, for the Court has since reaffirmed its continued adherence to the *Linkletter-Stovall* approach to retroactivity. Thus, in *Adams v. Illinois*,[80] a plurality invoked a violation-date rule to govern the retroactive effect of the Burger Court's own rule in *Coleman v. Alabama* that the preliminary hearing is a critical stage of the criminal process at which the accused is constitutionally entitled to the assistance of counsel,[81] while in *Ivan V. v. New York* a unanimous Court,[82] employing the *Linkletter* rationale, found that the requirement of proof beyond a reasonable doubt at the adjudicatory phase of a juvenile proceeding, announced in *In re Winship*,[83] was to be given absolutely retroactive application. But, within a year, a nearly unanimous Court,[84] again relying on *Linkletter* and *Stovall*, held that the "prophylactic" due process limitations established by *North Carolina v. Pearce*[85] to guard against the possibility of vindictiveness in cases where a judge imposes a more severe sentence upon a defendant after a new trial were not to be retroactively applicable to resentencing proceedings that occured prior to the date of the *Pearce* decision.

In part, this fluid approach to the retroactivity problem has been embraced and continued by the Burger Court, because it has allowed the

[79]401 U.S. 667 (1971).

[80]405 U.S. 278 (1972).

[81]399 U.S. 1 (1970). Justices Brennan, Stewart, and White concluded in *Adams* that *Coleman* should not apply retroactively. Mr. Chief Justice Burger and Mr. Justice Blackmun each filed separate concurrences, arguing that *Coleman* had been wrongly decided. Mr. Justice Douglas and Justice Marshall dissented. Justices Rehnquist and Powell took no part in the decision.

[82]407 U.S. 203 (1972).

[83]397 U.S. 358 (1970).

[84]Michigan v. Payne, 412 U.S. 47 (1973). The decision was 8 to 1, Marshall dissenting.

[85]395 U.S. 711 (1969).

Court to avoid some difficult questions, at least for a time. In *DeBacker v. Brainard*, for example, the Court was able to dismiss the claim that jury trials are required in juvenile proceedings by invoking the holding in *DeStefano v. Woods* that *Duncan v. Louisiana* was not retroactive.[86] The reliance upon the Warren Court's retroactivity aspproach, however, has created some stunning anomalies. *In re Winship*, for example, may be absolutely retroactive; but in *Lego v. Twomey* the Court found that determining the admissibility of a confession by a preponderance-of-the-evidence test was permissible, since the hearing on the voluntariness of confessions was not designed to implement the presumption of innocence or enhance the reliability of jury verdicts.[87] Shades of *Johnson v. New Jersey*! Similarly, in *United States v. White*, a widely divided Court discussed the prescience of federal appellate judges.[88] White had been convicted in 1966 on the basis of statements made to an informant wearing an electronic eavesdropping device; these statements were transmitted to listening federal officers who testified at White's trial. *On Lee v. United States* had, of course, sustained such "third-party bugging," but *On Lee* had been decided in 1952.[89] In 1967, the Supreme Court had rendered its decision in *Katz v. United States*, holding electronic surveillance to be subject to the requirements of the Fourth Amendment without regard to physical trespass.[90] While *Katz* had been decided after the events and trial in White's case, the Circuit Court of Appeals in 1968 reasoned that *Katz* must have overruled *On Lee sub silentio* and, therefore, held the agents' testimony to have been barred by the Fourth Amendment.[91] The following year, however, the Supreme Court issued its decision in *Desist*, ruling *Katz* to have been non-retroactive. In *White*, the Court found that *Desist* was controlling and that the Court of Appeals had erred in not reviewing the case on the basis of *On Lee*. In short, as Mr. Justice Harlan bitterly complained in dissent, the Court of Appeals was told that in 1968 it should have ignored the 1967 decision in *Katz* because in 1969 the Supreme Court was going to hold *Katz* non-retroactive! Such rulings make it difficult not to concur with Mr. Justice Marshall's complaint in *Michigan v. Payne* that the retroactivity decisions have become a "charade."[92]

[86]396 U.S. 28 (1969).
[87]404 U.S. 477 (1972).
[88]401 U.S. 745 (1971).
[89]343 U.S. 747 (1952).
[90]393 U.S. 347 (1967).
[91]405 F.2d 838 (7th Cir. 1969).
[92]Michigan v. Payne, 412 U.S. 47, 61 (1973) (dissenting opinion).

Earlier in the same term, however, Mr. Justice Rehnquist, speaking for the Court in *Robinson v. Neil*,[93] had indicated an appreciation that the retroactivity rationale of *Linkletter* and its progeny, whatever its strengths and weaknesses may have been with respect to constitutional interpretations bearing on the use of evidence or on a particular mode of trial, was not necessarily appropriate for determining the retroactivity of non-procedural constitutional decisions, such as those bearing on the double jeopardy provision.[94] A guarantee like that against double jeopardy differs from the procedural guarantees held to have prospective effect only in the *Linkletter* line of cases in that, rather than being concerned with the procedures which shall be followed at the trial, double jeopardy prevents a trial from taking place at all. Accordingly, the *Robinson* Court held that the decision in *Waller v. Florida*, barring on double jeopardy grounds two prosecutions, municipal and state, based on the same offense, was to be given fully retroactive effect.[95] But the exact significance and continued, future vitality of *Robinson* has been obscured by the subsequent decision in *Gosa v. Mayden* and its companion case, *Warner v. Fleming*.[96] In *Gosa* and *Warner* the Court was very badly split by the question of the retroactivity of the holding in *O'Callahan v. Parker* that armed forces personnel charged with crimes that are not "service connected" are constitutionally entitled to indictment by grand jury and trial in a civilian court.[97] Only eight Justices reached the retroactivity issue, and they divided four to four over whether *O'Callahan's* ruling involved procedural constitutional rights,

---

[93]409 U.S. 505 (1973).

[94]U.S. CONST. amend. V. For anyone concerned with the candor of contemporary governmental policy-making, the Court's treatment of the question of the retroactivity of its double jeopardy decisions must surely be counted a disgrace. In Price v. Georgia, 398 U.S. 323, 331 n. 9 (1970), the Court noted, in passing, in a footnote that the decision in Benton v. Maryland, 395 U.S. 784 (1969), overruling Palko v. Connecticut, 302 U.S. 319 (1937), and applying the double jeopardy provision of the Fifth Amendment to the states via a process of "incorporation" into the Fourteenth Amendment had been made fully retroactive. The reader was referred to Waller v. Florida, 397 U.S. 387, 391 n. 2 (1970). Were the careful reader to turn to *Waller*, however, he would find that in n.2 the Court expressly abjured decision on the retroactivity of *Benton* noting instead that "when this Court granted certiorari in Price v. Georgia, it requested that counsel 'brief and argue [the] question of retroactivity of Benton v. Maryland'.... By our decision in [this] case ... we do not resolve ... the question. ... " 397 U.S. at 391 n. 2. *Price's* reliance upon *Waller*, thus, would seem circular in the extreme.

[95]397 U.S. 387 (1970); *but see* Bartkus v. Illinois, 359 U.S. 121 (1959); Abbate v. United States, 359 U.S. 187 (1959).

[96]413 U.S. 665 (1973).

[97]395 U.S. 258 (1969).

the retroactivity of which was to be determined by *Linkletter's* scheme of analysis, or non-procedural rights, to which the *Robinson* approach should apply.[98]

Such difference of judicial opinion, however, has been characteristic of the retroactivity-prospectivity debate since before *Linkletter*.[99] In that sense, the Burger Court has but carried on the tradition of the Warren Court. Indeed, in perhaps no other area of constitutional decision-making have the rationale and results of the Burger Court been so consistent with those of the Warren Court. The results, in particular, have been consistently chaotic. While it may continue to experience difficulties in defining the contours of prospectivity, however, the Burger Court has seen fit to extend the principle of a judicial power to limit the retroactivity of decisions into areas other than the constitutional law of criminal procedure. In *Lemon v. Kurtzman*,[100] a plurality, significantly composed of the four Nixon appointees,[101] ruled that, while the Pennsylvania "purchase of services" program to aid parochial schools had been earlier declared unconstitutional as a violation of the First Amendment,[102] Pennsylvania was not prohibited from reimbursing parochial schools for services performed prior to that decision. Thus has the logical conundrum of retroactivity been introduced to the equally difficult problem of church-state relations. Can such a confluence bode well for judicial logic in the future?

[98]Justice Blackmun, joined by Mr. Chief Justice Burger and Justices White and Powell, felt that *O'Callahan* should be prospective only. Justices Douglas, Marshall, Brennan, and Stewart believed it should be retroactive, although Stewart felt that the crime in *Warner* had been "service connected" and, as such, had been properly tried before a court martial. Mr. Justice Rehnquist simply concurred in the judgment on the grounds that *O'Callahan* had been wrongly decided.

[99]*See* note 9 *supra.*

[100]411 U.S. 192 (1973).

[101]Mr. Chief Justice Burger's opinion was joined only by Justices Blackmun, Powell, and Rehnquist. Mr. Justice White concurred in the result. Justices Brennan, Douglas, and Stewart dissented. Justice Marshall did not participate.

[102]403 U.S. 602 (1971).

Chapter 6
Much Ado About Nothing

In 1951, the New York Board of Regents were made

> aware of the dire need, in these days of concentrated attacks by an atheistic way of life upon our world and in these times of rising juvenile delinquency, of crime increasing both numerically and in gravity of offense, with an ever-swelling number of criminals being counted in the younger age groups, of finding ways to pass on America's Moral and Spiritual Heritage to our youth through the public school system.[1]

The instrument chosen to counter this erosion of America's moral fiber was, given the alleged gravity of the situation, surprisingly modest. It was a twenty-two word, nondenominational prayer authored by the Board: "Almighty God, we acknowledge our dependence upon Thee, and we beg Thy blessings upon us, our parents, our teachers and our country." This prayer, in conjunction with the flag salute, was to be recited in the public schools of the State of New York at the beginning of each school day. Recital of the prayer was to be voluntary, and any comment upon a student's failure to participate was strictly prohibited. Nevertheless, the parents of ten students, including both sectarians who objected to the particular form of worship prescribed and secularists who opposed any public sponsorship of religious devotions, brought an action to have the regulation authorizing the prayer declared unconstitutional as an establishment of religion. Thus was the stage set for one of the Warren Court's most controversial, most bitterly debated, and least important declarations of public policy, the school prayer cases.[2]

While students of the Court, including the former Chief Justice himself, may point to such cases as *Brown v. Board of Education*, *Reynolds v. Sims*, or *Miranda v. Arizona* as being among the most significant of the Warren Court's pronouncements, for sheer quantity and violence of adverse public reaction, it would be hard to deny a place

---

[1]Brief for the Board of Regents of the University of the State of New York as Amicus Curiae at 14, Engel v. Vitale, 370 U.S. 421 (1962) (capitalization in the original).

[2]*See generally* C. LYTLE, THE WARREN COURT & ITS CRITICS 47, 62-69, 91, 109 (1968); G. MITAU, DECADE OF DECISION ch. IV (1967).

in that pantheon to the school prayer decisions, *Engel v. Vitale*[3] and *Abington School District v. Schempp.*[4] But, in terms of their actual effect upon American behavior or for their contribution to a clarification of the law, *Engel* and *Schempp* must recieve low marks.[5] They were, however, prophetic indicators of a shift in judicial concern which was to accelerate in the late '60's and to continue into the Burger Era. Previously, the Supreme Court's interpretation of the religion clauses of the First Amendment had dealt almost exclusively with the Free Exercise Clause; cases treating with the Establishment Clause were notable for their scarcity.[6] But the Warren Era was to see an almost total reversal of this pattern. Decisions dealing with the constitutional prohibition against an established religion were to proliferate, while free exercise interpretation was to decline precipitately in quantity and significance. The Warren Court was to issue only five opinions dealing with the free exercise of religion,[7] and at least three of these were primarily important because of

---

[3] 370 U.S. 421 (1962).

[4] 374 U.S. 203 (1963).

[5] Regarding the impact of *Engel* and *Schempp*, see S. WASBY, THE IMPACT OF THE UNITED STATES SUPREME COURT 126-35 (1970); Birkby, *The Supreme Court and the Bible Belt: Tennessee Reaction to the "Schempp" Decision,* 10 MIDW. J. POL. SCI. 304 (1966); Beaney and Beiser, *Prayer in Politics: The Impact of Engel and Schempp on the Political Process,* 13 J. PUB. L. 475 (1964). For commentary upon the adequacy of *Engel's* and *Schempp's* enunciation of the law, *see* Brown, *Quis Custodiet Ipsos Custodes?—The School Prayer Cases,* 1963 SUP. CT. REV. 1; Choper, *Religion in the Public Schools: A Proposed Constitutional Standard,* 47 MINN. L. REV. 329 (1963); Kurland, *The Regents' Prayer Case: "Full of Sound and Fury, Signifying . . . ,"* 1962 SUP. CT. REV. 1; Sutherland, *Establishment According to Engel,* 76 HARV. L. REV. 25 (1962).

[6] The First Amendment provides that

> Congress shall make no law respecting an establishment of religion, or prohibiting the free exercise thereof; . . . .

Among the best scholarly studies of the First Amendment's religion clauses are L. PFEFFER, CHURCH, STATE AND FREEDOM (1967); P. KAUPER, RELIGION AND THE CONSTITUTION (1964); P. KURLAND, RELIGION AND THE LAW (1962); *see also* H. ABRAHAM, FREEDOM AND THE COURT ch. VI (2d ed. 1972). M.D. W. HOWE, THE GARDEN AND THE WILDERNESS (1965) and W. MARNELL, THE FIRST AMENDMENT (1964) provide useful historical background concerning the original intention and development of the amendment.

[7] Kreshik v. St. Nicholas Cathedral of the Russian Orthodox Church, 363 U.S. 190 (1960); Torcaso v. Watkins, 367 U.S. 488 (1961); Braunfield v. Brown, 366 U.S. 599 (1961); Gallagher v. Crown Kosher Super Market, 366 U.S. 611 (1961); Sherbert v. Verner, 374 U.S. 398 (1963) *See also* United States v. Seeger, 380 U.S. 163 (1965). *See generally* Kauper, *The Warren Court: Religious Liberty and Church-State Relations,* 67 MICH. L. REV. 269 (1968).

their implications for the Establishment Clause.[8] Indeed, the result in *Engel v. Vitale* may have been unanticipated, and this may perhaps have contributed to the storm of public indignation; since only the year before the Court had upheld, in part against free exercise challenges, the constitutionality of several states' so-called "Blue Laws," requiring business closure on Sundays.[9] The decision in the *Sunday Closing Cases*, moreover, seemed to have been perfectly consistent with the decision a decade earlier in one of the first religion-in-the-schools cases, *Zorach v. Clauson*.[10] Not only the result in *Zorach*, approving released time programs for off-campus religious instruction, but also the rhetoric seemed to suggest that the Court would permit state programs supportive of religion, so long as no religion received preferential treatment and there were no coercion of dissenters.[11] "We are," wrote Mr. Justice Douglas for the majority, "a religious people whose institutions presuppose a Supreme Being. . . . When the state encourages religious instruction or cooperates with religious authorities . . ., it follows the best of our traditions."[12] Surely the New York Board of Regents had done no more.

The Warren Court, however, thought otherwise, and in *Engel* declared the Regents' Prayer to have violated the First Amendment. Mr. Justice Black's opinion for the majority was particularly remarkable in that, except for a passing footnote reference to *Everson v. Board of Education*,[13] it completely lacked legal documentation.[14] Instead, as had been his went in other cases,[15] Black chose to rely upon a recitation of American history. The Establishment Clause, he argued, had been aimed at just this type of governmental action—action from which the early colonists had fled to America. Once government enters the business of prescribing prayers, it invites the pressures of various groups as to the

[8]Torcaso v. Watkins, 367 U.S. 488 (1961); Braunfield v. Brown, 366 U.S. 599 (1961); Sherbert v. Verner, 374 U.S. 398 (1963).

[9]McGowan v. Maryland, 366 U.S. 420 (1961); Two Guys From Harrison-Allentown, Inc. v. McGinley, 366 U.S. 582 (1961); Braunfield v. Brown, 366 U.S. 599 (1961); Gallagher v. Crown Kosher Super Market, 366 U.S. 611 (1961).

[10]343 U.S. 306 (1952). *See also* Everson v. Board of Education, 330 U.S. 1 (1947); McCollum v. Board of Education, 333 U.S. 203 (1948).

[11]*See generally* Sorauf, *Zorach v. Clauson: The Impact of a Supreme Court Decision*, 53 AM. POL. SCI. REV. 777 (1959).

[12]343 U.S. at 313.

[13]330 U.S. 1 (1947).

[14]*See* Kauper, *supra* note 7; Kurland, *supra* note 5.

[15]*E.g.*, Wesberry v. Sanders, 376 U.S. 1 (1964). *See generally* Kelly, *Clio and the Court: An Illicit Love Affair*, 1965 SUP. CT. REV. 119.

content of those prayers, and this kind of activity has historically proven destructive of the public peace.[16] Rejecting attempts by the state to save the prayer ceremony on the rationale that the absence of compulsion eliminated any constitutional problem, Mr. Justice Black found the Establishment Clause to clearly indicate that government might not compose official prayers as part of a religious program even were the prayer nondenominational and participation voluntary.

The clause spoke with no such clarity to Mr. Justice Stewart, the lone dissenter in the case. For him the Establishment Clause had not been violated, since there was no establishment of an official religion. Resting upon the tenor of *Zorach*, Stewart suggested that neither hostility nor neutrality but cooperation was the function of government in the area of religion. The Court's decision, Stewart felt, had denied to those who so desired the opportunity to share in the nation's spiritual heritage. The problem with this approach, however, is that it seems to have rested on the implicit assumption that the prayer cerememony had been initiated by the children or by their parents rather than imposed by the state.

Mr. Justice Douglas contributed a gratuitous concurrence. Gratuitous, first, because the good Justice, like many of the Court's critics, was more concerned with the problem of federal aid to parochial education than with the facts of the case before him. Thus, he took the much broader position that government could not finance a religious exercise of any kind.[17] Gratuitious, second, because Douglas either ignored or was unaware of the fact that it was his own touching dictum in *Zorach* on the place of religion in American life which had greatly contributed to the embarrassing position in which the Court now found itself.

Various *post hoc* prescriptions, directed toward the alleviation of that embarrassment, were subsequently advanced by professional Court-watchers. Actually, *Engel* had involved several issues. The petition for certiorari had kept open the possibility of urging a violation of the Free Exercise Clause, on the theory that nonconforming children were coerced. When granting a hearing on the merits, however, the court had chosen to hear the establishment argument only. Now, some legal scholars argued that it would have been desirable to have rested the *Engel* result on the Free Exercise rather than the Establishment Clause.[18] The

[16]*See generally* R. MORGAN, THE POLITICS OF RELIGIOUS CONFLICT (1968).
[17]370 U.S. at 437.
[18]*See, e.g.*, Kauper, *Prayer, Public Schools, and the Supreme Court*, 61 MICH. L. REV. 1031 (1963).

Court could have found coercion present, or so the reasoning went, by stressing the psychological dynamics of the classroom situation, as the Warren Court had earlier done in *Brown*.[19] But the constitutional protection of one's free exercise of his religion is different from the protection against racial discrimination, for the elementary reason that one has some modicum of choice over his religion but not over his race. Arguably, the Free Exercise Clause merely protects one's freedom of conscience. It cannot and was not intended to relieve the dissenter of the social onus arising from his dissent. The right to dissent does not involve the right to be spared occasions for dissenting. To call a choice a "cruel dilemma" should not obscure the fact that, in America, one remains free to choose.[20]

But a second and more subtle reason for resting *Engel* upon the Free Exercise Clause was advanced by a few, including the more thoughtful religious leaders. This was the argument that the prayer decision actually promoted the freedom of religious commitment of those who held the favored belief from the potential compromise of that freedom involved in government sponsorship.[21] Indeed, one of the arguments advanced by the defenders of the Regents' Prayer was that its validity should be sustained, because its content reflected the *lowest common denominator* of all religious groups in the United States![22]

Whatever the wisdom of preferring a free exercise rationale, the Warren Court chose to rely upon the Esablishment Clause in *Engel*. Mr. Justice Black, therefore, stressed several times that the Regents' Prayer had been composed and instituted by the government. The response of those in favor of religious programs in the public schools was, of course, to adopt a program free of official authorship. The following year, in *School District of Abington v. Schempp* and its companion case, *Murray v. Curlett*, the Warren Court found this ruse to be constitutionally irrelevant.[23] The *Schempp* case originated in Pennsylvania, where a state law required that each school day be opened with a reading of at least ten verses from the Bible, without comment. Upon the written request of a parent or guardian, any student was to be excused from the exercise, but the Schempp family, Unitarians, brought suit to enjoin the practice

[19] *But see* Pollack, *Public Prayers in Public Schools*, 77 HARV. L. REV. 62 (1963).

[20] *See* Griswold, *Absolute is in the Dark—A Discussion of the Approach of the Supreme Court to Constitutional Questions*, 8 UTAH L. REV. 167 (1963).

[21] *See* Katz & Southerland, *Religious Pluralism and the Supreme Court*, DAEDALUS 180 (Winter 1967).

[22] *See* P. BERGER, THE NOISE OF SOLEMN ASSEMBLIES (1961).

[23] 374 U.S. 203 (1963).

entirely. The *Murray* case arose in Baltimore, where the school board had adopted opening exercises in the public schools consisting primarily of the recitation of the Lord's Prayer. This practice incurred the wrath of Mrs. Madelyn Murray, Jean d'Arc of American atheism, who found it highly objectionable. Others found her to be, but the Supreme Court ruled the exercises in both cases to violate the First Amendment's prohibition against established religions. Mr. Justice Clark's opinion for an eight-man majority amounted to a repetition of the *Engel* reasoning as applied to publicly sanctioned, as opposed to publicly written, religious devotions. As such, it added little, if anything, to what had been said and not said in *Engel*.[24]

But, nevertheless, *Schempp* and *Engel*, when taken together and considered in the light of *Tocaso v. Watkins*,[25] one of the few Warren free exercise precendents, do raise a moral problem of constitutional dimensions for the 1970s—the secularization of the public schools.[26] On the one hand, after *Torcaso*, we know that for constitutional purposes some non-theistic moral codes are religions.[27] On the other hand, we have the increasing demands of students and advocates of radical school reform that the schools concern themselves not only with the intellectual but also with the moral, ethical, and emotional growth of the student.[28] What, then, is the effect of *Engel* and *Schempp* on the teaching of secular ethical codes in the public schools? If *Engel* and *Schempp* forbid the teaching of religions founded upon a belief in the existence of a God but permit the teaching of some humanist ethical code, is not the result to prefer one religion, secular humanism, over other, theistic religions?

Even at the time they were announced, *Engel* and *Schempp* seemed uniquely at odds with the recent decisions of the very same Court sustaining the constitutionality of "Blue Laws," which prohibited a great variety of Sunday retail business activities but made numerous exceptions for resort and entertainment activities.[29] In his opinion for the

[24]*See* Brown, *supra* note 5.

[25]367 U.S. 488 (1961).

[26]*See* M. KONVITZ, RELIGIOUS LIBERTY AND CONSCIENCE (1969); Katz & Southerland, *supra* note 21.

[27]"Among religions in this country which do not teach what would generally be considered a belief in the existence of God are Buddhism, Taoism, Ethical Culture, Secular Humanism, and others." 367 U.S. at 495 n. 11 (Black, J.). *See also* United States v. Seeger, 380 U.S. 163 (1965).

[28]*See, e.g.*, P. GOODMAN, GROWING UP ABSURD (1960), and NEW REFORMATION (1970).

[29]McGowan v. Maryland, 366 U.S. 420 (1961); Two Guys From Harrison-Allentown,

Court in the *Sunday Closing Cases*, Mr. Chief Justice Warren had addressed himself to two central questions: equal protection and church-state separation. The equal protection argument he had dismissed out-of-hand, but the separation issue was more serious and was treated accordingly. After examining at length the history of "Blue Laws," the Chief Justice concluded that, although originally religious in intent, Sunday closing was now required as a means to achieve a valid secular purpose, the provision of a uniform day of rest, relaxation, and family togetherness. The legislature might have chosen any day of the week for such required closures but had opted for Sunday. That this happened to be the day commonly celebrated by Christians as the Sabbath was, for Warren, a mere coincidence, of no more constitutional significance than if the legislature had chosen Saturday, the Sabbath for some other religions, or Tuesday. In contemporary America, Sunday retail closing laws were motivated by primarily temporal considerations and, there-fore, did not involve an unconstitutional attempt to establish a religion. The problem presented by two of the four *Sunday Closing Cases*, however, was more difficult in that they involved application of the "Blue Laws" to orthodox Jewish establishments which, under rabbinical law, were obliged to close on Saturdays.[30] As a consequence, proprietors of these stores in states which did not exempt them from the Sunday closing requirement suffered a severe competitive hardship. They argued, therefore, that this constituted a state imposed penalty incurred by and inhibiting the free exercise of their religion. Mr. Chief Justice Warren, however, swept aside this objection with the observation that the statutes simply regulated "secular activity" and imposed "only an indirect burden on religion."[31]

The rationale of the School Prayer and Bible-reading decisions seemed manifestly at odds with the softer position embraced by the *Sunday Closing Cases*, and the reversal seemed complete with the decision, delivered the same day as *Schempp*, in *Sherbert v. Verner*.[32] Mrs. Sherbert, a Seventh Day Adventist, had applied for and received unemployment compensation in the State of South Carolina. The state then sought and did find for Mrs. Sherbert "acceptable" employment, with the exception that this would have required her to work on

---

Inc. v. McGinley, 366 U.S. 582 (1961); Braunfield v. Brown, 366 U.S. 599 (1961); Gallagher v. Crown Kosher Super Market, 366 U.S. 611 (1961).

[30]Braunfield v. Brown, *id.*; Gallagher v. Crown Kosher Super Market, *id.*

[31]*Id.* at 605-06.

[32]374 U.S. 398 (1963).

Saturdays. Mrs. Sherbert refused the job, and the state, pursuant to its statutory provisions, terminated her unemployment compenstion. The Supreme Court, however, found South Carolina to have inhibited Mrs. Sherbert's free exercise of her religion by denying her unemployment benefits on the basis of her refusal to labor on her Sabbath. Superficial contraditions notwithstanding, however, there were differences both of kind and of degree between the situation in *Sherbert* and the circumstances involved in the *Sunday Closing Cases*. First, the two might be distinguished on the grounds that the retailers in the *Sunday Closing Cases* suffered only a partial loss, one day's revenue, but Mrs. Sherbert's loss was plenary, the termination of her unemployment benefits *in toto*. Second, the Jewish merchants in the *Sunday Closing Cases* were not compelled by the state to violate the tenets of their religion. They were not required to remain open on Saturdays, and any financial loss which they did suffer was purely the result of voluntary choice, whereas Mrs. Sherbert suffered not only economic injury but was compelled by the state, if she desired to relieve that injury, to violate the tenets of her religion. This element of state coercion had not been present in the same form or with the same force in the *Sunday Closing Cases*. Moreover, in those cases the secular interest, to provide a uniform day of rest, had been met, while in *Sherbert* the secular interest, to relieve the onus of unemployment, had actually been thwarted by the state's own action.

Even if the *Sunday Closing Cases* might, however, be distinquised, *Sherbert* presented a number of interesting problems for Establishment Clause exegesis. First, didn't the result in *Sherbert* violate the Establishment Clause?[33] A state government was told that it must sanction otherwise prohibited activity because that activity was religiously inspired. But the same activity was forbidden to non-Sabbatarians (non-religionists). Did this not amount to preferential treatment of particular religions? But, for the Court to have provided an affirmative answer resolving *Sherbert* in the opposite direction would have brought it face-to-face with the conscientious objector exemption to the draft. For doesn't the granting of exemptions from military service to those who are conscientiously opposed to war "on the basis of their religious training and belief"[34] amount to government encouragement of certain religious

[33]*But cf.* Moore, *The Supreme Court and the Relationship Between the "Establishment" and "Free Exercise" Clauses*, 42 TEX. L. REV. 142 (1963).

[34]50 U.S.C.App. § 456(j). *See generally* Donnici, *Governmental Encouragement of Religious Ideology: A Study of the Current Conscientious Objector Exemption from Military Service*, 13 J. PUB. L. 16 (1964); Note, *The Conscientious Objector and the First Amendment*, 34 U. CHI. L. REV. 79 (1966).

ideologies? Second, just as Mrs. Sherbert's faith imposed upon her the very grave obligation of keeping the Sabbath on Saturday, other religions require their adherents to send their children to parochial schools, and in *Pierce v. Society of Sisters* the Court had held that parents have a constitutional right to send their children to religious schools.[35] Might these parents, then, relying upon *Sherbert*, argue that, since they must pay public school taxes, the failure of the state to give financial support to parochial as well as public schools and, thus, to defray their parochial school tuition costs imposed a serious financial burden upon their exercise of religious freedom? Or, put differently, following the majority's reasoning in *Sherbert*, might not parochial school parents argue that their ineligibility for state financial benefits derived solely from the practice of their religion and that the withholding of state aid forced them to choose between the precepts of their religion and the forfeiting of benefits? Lastly, in his *Sherbert* concurrence, Mr. Justice Douglas, totally ignoring his admonition in *Engel* that government might not constitutionally finance any kind of religious exercise, wrote, "If appellant is otherwise qualified for unemployment benefits, payments will be made to her not as a Seventh-day Adventist, but as an unemployed worker."[36] What was the difference between this and saying that payments could be made to parochial schools, not as religious institutions, but as educational establishments?

None, apparently, for in *Board of Education v. Allen* the Warren Court revived the "child benefit" theory first enunciated in *Everson* to sustain New York's practice of providing free textbooks to parochial school students.[37] School districts within the State of New York were required by statute to buy textbooks and loan them without charge to all junior and senior high school students who lived within the district, including students enrolled in parochial schools as well as those attending public or private non-sectarian institutions. Against a challenge that this program contravened the First Amendment, a six-man majority, speaking through Mr. Justice White, found the practice to be

[35] 268 U.S. 510 (1925).

[36] 374 U.S. at 412.

[37] 392 U.S. 236 (1968); *see also* Everson v. Board of Education, 330 U.S. 1 (1947). *See generally* La Noue, *The Child Benefit Theory Revisited: Textbooks, Transportation and Medical Care*, 13 J. PUB. L. 76 (1964); Note, *The Elementary and Secondary Education Act of 1965 and the First Amendment*, 41 IND. L. J. 302 (1966).

[38] *See generally* Valente, *Aid to Church Related Education—New Directions Without Dogma*, 55 VA. L. REV. 579 (1969); Freund, *Public Aid to Parochial Schools*, 82 HARV. L. REV. 1680 (1969).

religiously neutral.[38] Admitting the difficulty of inscribing a precise line between religious neutrality and state aid to religion, White argued that the primary goal toward which the New York program was directed was the provision of an adequate education for all of the children in the state, a valid secular purpose. Furnishing the benefits of a general program to parochial school students amounted only to an incidental assistance to religion. The books were provided upon request of the pupil, not the school, and, since the books were merely loaned to the student, the state retained ownership of them. No public money or property, thus, was transferred to the parochial school; the financial benefits of the program accrued only to the children or their parents.

Justices Black, Douglas, and Fortas each filed a separate dissent, but all were concerned with the fact that the initiative for text selection, under the New York program, lay with the schools themselves. Most blunt of the three dissenters, Justice Douglas, insisted that there could not be the slightest doubt that parochial schools would use this opportunity to select those texts which best promoted their particular sectarian creeds.[39] The state would, then, be furnishing books promoting specific religious doctrines or dogmas, and this, for Douglas, violated the non-estab-lishment principle. Each of the dissenters was concerned, justifiably so, that the revivification of the "child benefit" theory would invite yet further efforts to assist parochial education.

But, for the long run, the Warren precedent which was to have the greatest significance for the law of church-state relations was one in which the Court did not even reach the merits. *Flast v. Cohen* involved a constitutional challenge to the 1965 Elementary and Secondary Educa-tion Act brought by several federal taxpayers.[40] This federal law provided for the establishing of special education centers to provide remedial instruction, laboratories, and special teachers which were to be available to both public and non-public, including parochial, school students. Funds were also provided for the purchase of textbooks to be made available to both public and non-public school students, though ownership of the books was to remain in the public school districts.

In *Flast*, the Court limited its consideration to the issue of standing. In *Frothingham v. Mellon* an earlier Court had held unanimously that a

[39]Cf. Note, *Sectarian Books, The Supreme Court and the Establishment Clause,* 79 YALE L.J. 111 (1969).

[40]392 U.S. 83 (1965). The background, politics, provisions, and constitutional problems of the Education Act are variously discussed in H. ABRAHAM, *supra* note 6, at 282-87; R. MORGAN, *supra* note 16, at 102-09; Note, *supra* note 37.

federal taxpayer's interest, *qua* taxpayer, in any federal spending program was so remote, minute, and conjectural as to be insufficient to sustain a court action challenging such a program.[41] In effect, the *Frothingham* decision, thus, rendered any federal spending program, such as the 1965 Elementary and Secondary Education Act, immune from judicial attack.[42] While the *Frothingham* rule strictly applied only to *federal* taxpayers, the decisions in *Engel* and *Schempp* had already suggested a judicial disquietude with the standing rule in Establishment Clause cases,[43] and this was made manifest in *Flast*. Speaking for the Court, Mr. Chief Justice Warren modified the *Frothingham* rule to allow for federal taxpayers' suits challenging federal spending programs under certain, limited conditions. Specifically, the Chief Justice held that a taxpayer might maintain such a suit, if he could allege that the spending program violated a specific constitutional limitation, such as the First Amendment, rather than merely exceeded the powers delegated to Congress. Since the taxpayers in *Flast* had claimed that the 1965 Elementary and Secondary Education Act contravened the Establishment Clause, they satisfied this new rule of standing, but, having resolved the standing issue in their favor, the Court declined to pass on the merits of the suit and remanded the case to a lower court.

In *Allen*, of course, the Warren Court subsequently validated public provision of textbooks to parochial students. But the Court avoided opportunities to pass upon the constitutional validity of tax exemptions granted to property used for religious purposes or the permissibility of straightforward, monetary grants to church-related colleges.[44] The

[41]262 U.S. 447 (1923).

[42]Since the passage of the Elementary and Secondary Education Act, Senator Sam Ervin had repeatedly urged legislation expressly vesting the federal judiciary with jurisdiction to hear taxpayers' suits challenging the constitutionality of federal grants or loans on First Amendment grounds. *See Hearings on S. 2097 Before the Subcomm. on Constitutional Rights of the Senate Comm. on the Judiciary*, 89th Cong., 2d Sess. (1968); *see generally* Note, *The Insular Status of the Religion Clauses: The Dilemma of Standing*, 36 GEO. WASH. L. REV. 648 (1968). Senator Ervin's proposals, however, were consistently defeated. The Senator then turned to the Court; it was he who successfully argued the *Flast* case for the qualification, if not the reversal, of the *Frothingham* rule.

[43]*See* Abington School Dist. v. Schempp, 374 U.S. 203, 224 n. 9 (Clark, J.); *id.* at 266 n. 30 (Brennan, J., concurring).

[44]*See* Lundberg v. Alameda County, 46 Cal.2d 644, *appeal dismissed sub. nom.* Heisey v. Alameda County, 352 U.S. 921 (1956); General Finance Corp. v. Archetto, 176 A.2d 73 (R.I. 1961), *appeal dismissed*, 369 U.S. 423 (1962); Horace Mann League v. Board of Public Works, 242 645, *cert. denied*, 385 U.S. 97 (1966); Murray v. Comptroller, 241 Md. 383, *cert. denied*, 385 U.S. 816 (1966).

resolution of these issues would depend upon a systematic analysis of the benefits inherent in such programs and of the values implicit in the religion clauses of the First Amendment and then a ranking of the social priorities involved. But this task the Warren Court foreswore. By virtue of its decision in *Flast*, however, it had made certain that its successor would have the opportunity to perform it, for taxpayers, both federal and state, were now able to avail themselves of access to the federal judiciary.

Indeed, Warren Earl Burger's first majority opinion in a constitutional case was to come in an Establishment Clause litigation.[45] In the term immediately following Mr. Chief Justice Warren's retirement, the new Chief Justice, speaking for five members of the Court, upheld New York's granting of a property tax exemption to real property owned by religious organizations and used solely for a religious purpose, worship. The result in *Walz v. Tax Commission* was rendered a virtual certainty by the interplay of two factors.[46] The first was history; church property had consistently been exempted from taxation since the eighteenth century, and this practice had been upheld by an unbroken line of judicial precedent.[47] The second factor was considerations of public policy. Given the long-standing nature of church tax exemptions, an abrupt outlawing of these exemptions might quite probably have had several undesirable consequences, including the drastic reduction of church welfare programs.[48] Given these considerations, then, the Court sustained the exemptions, reasoning that the purpose of the exemptions was neither to advance nor to inhibit religion. Church property was granted a tax exemption only as part of a general scheme of exemptions granted to non-profit organizations which the state found to be "beneficial . . . , stabilizing influences in community life."[49] Moreover,

---

[45]Walz v. Tax Commission, 397 U.S. 664 (1970). The Chief Justice's very first "opinion of the Court" had come in First National Bank in Plant City, Florida v. Dickinson, 396 U.S. 122 (1969). He had also, prior to *Walz*, expressed the majority's opinion in United States v. Interstate Commerce Commission, 396 U.S. 491 (1970), and Tooahnippah v. Hickel, 397 U.S. 598 (1970). None of these cases, however, had involved issues of constitutional dimensions, although in *Interstate Commerce Commission* there had been a claim of deprivation of property without due process; but this claim and the Court's disposition of it had been quite peripheral to the central issues of monopoly and the interpretation of the Interstate Commerce Act.

[46]See Katz, *Radiations from Church Tax Exemptions*, 1970 SUP. CT. REV. 93.

[47]Id. at 93-97; *see also* M. HOWE, *supra* note 6.

[48]*The Supreme Court, 1969 Term*, 84 HARV. L. REV. 1, 127-33 (1970).

[49]397 U.S. at 673.

the Chief Justice relied upon the ingenious argument that the exemption should be valid because the taxation of church-owned property would actually involve the government in a closer relationship with religion than would an exemption. The tax exemption, therefore, was viewed by the majority as an essentially neutral device which avoided excessive government entanglement with religion.

Despite the almost foregone nature of the result, *Walz* represented a major departure from the Warren Court's establishment decisions, because Chief Justice Burger accepted the proposition that a grant of tax exemptions to churches *was* a grant of an economic benefit.[50] But this necessitated abandoning the indirect benefit theory on which *Allen* had been based. In *Allen*, of course, the Warren Court had invoked *Everson's* "no aid" fiction to approve a state program which had benefited religious instruction, theorizing that any benefit to religion was merely an incidental consequence of a general public program the primary purpose and effect of which was secular in nature. The public purchase and provision of school books for all schools had been seen as a means to raise the general education level within the state. But, in *Walz*, any secular purpose which might have been achieved by the exemption policy was qualitatively different from that involved in *Allen*, since the aid went directly to the churches. There was, in short, no "child benefit," only "church benefit."

Having agreed that the tax exemption provided a direct benefit to the churches, Mr. Chief Justice Burger tried to show that it did not amount to constitutionally impermissible establishment of religion. To make such a showing, the Chief Justice sought to rely upon three different lines of argument: the valid secular purpose or "good works" theory; the theory that the tax exemption actually promoted separation; and history. To begin, the Chief Justice reasoned that the exemption was part of a valid secular program of general application which granted tax exemptions to a broad class of property owned by non-profit organizations having beneficent and positive effects upon the stability of community life. Interestingly enough, a similar argument had been advanced in *Schempp*. The school districts had argued that their prayer services were held for the purpose of promoting moral values and perpetuating American institutions. And, of course, the *Schempp* Court had rejected this argument. Even more interesting was that nowhere in Chief Justice Burger's opinion in *Walz* was *Schempp* mentioned! Having tried to use

[50]*See generally* Bittker, *Churches, Taxes and the Constitution*, 78 YALE L.J. 1285 (1969).

the "good works" theory, however, the Chief Justice abandoned that line of reasoning as unnecessary and tried to turn the tables on the critics of the tax exemption by arguing that the exemption actually served to minimize church-state contact. But the Chief Justice eventually rejected this line of argument too and finally fell back upon the history of the First Amendment. According to the Chief Justice's understanding of the Establishment Clause, "establishment" equalled "sponsorship."[51] Anything less than public *sponsorship* of religion or particular religious ideologies is constitutional. This, of course, had been the exact position taken by Mr. Justice Stewart in his dissent in *Engel*.

Mr. Justice Douglas, himself the very author of the "neutrality" concept, was the lone dissenter in *Walz*. He began with an outrageous misstatement of the issue presented. "The question in this case . . . is whether believers—organized in church groups—can be exempted from real estate taxes merely because they are believers, while non-believers, whether organized or not, must pay the real estate taxes."[52] That, of course, was *not* the question. Under the New York statute, organized non-believers might qualify for the exemption, while unorganized believers were not exempted. Mr. Justice Douglas, nevertheless, pushed on. The principal thrust of his dissent was that tax exemptions were indistinguishable from grants of public funds; the words "subsidize" and "subsidy" run throughout the opinion.

Mr. Justice Harlan, concurring, agreed with Justice Douglas that tax exemptions did not, as an economic matter, differ from subsidies. But, he noted, that subsidies invite more political controversy because, unlike exemptions, they require periodic extension. Direct aid, moreover, is usually granted on the basis of enumerated and complex qualifications, rather than being granted generally as are exemptions, and, thus, subsidies involve a higher degree of state administration than do exemptions.

The majority, however, found a difference between grants of tax funds and tax exemptions. "The grant of a tax exemption," argued Mr. Chief Justice Burger, "is not sponsorship [of religious activity] since the government does not transfer part of its revenues to churches but simply

[51]397 U.S. at 668, 669, 672.
    "Sponsorship," as the Chief Justice uses the word, has something of the connotation that it has when we say a local merchant "sponsors" a little league baseball team; the boys not only use the bats which the merchant bought for them but wear his name on their backs.
84 HARV. L. REV. at 129.

abstains from demanding that the church support the state."[52] But the
Chief Justice also accepted Mr. Justice Harlan's distinction between
grants and exemptions based upon the extent to which they resulted in
church-state involvement in the program's administration. "Obviously," he wrote, "a direct money subsidy would be a relationship
pregnant with involvement."[53]

The primary significance of the *Walz* decision, then, lay in its effort to
provide a standard by which the Court could measure whether the effect
of a particular statute was to further an impermissible establishment of
religion. The Chief Justice's answer was that only those programs which
entailed an "excessive entanglement" of government with religion were
unconstitutional under the First Amendment.[54] This interpretation of
the Establishment Clause was, somewhat surprisingly, applauded by
such liberal commentators upon the Court's policy-making as the
Harvard Law Review.[55] The Chief Justice's approach was seen as being
superior to the old indirect benefit theory in at least three ways. First, it
was consonant with the historical purpose of the Establishment Clause.
Second, the indirect benefit theory kept bringing up one conflict after
another between the Establishment Clause and the Free Exercise Clause.
When a government program of general application, such as unemployment compensation or the draft, interfered in some substantial way with
an individual's pursuit of his religious convictions, it could be argued
either that (1) the Free Exercise Clause compelled an exemption be made
or that (2) the Establishment Clause prohibited any such exemption.
That conflict could only be resolved by viewing one clause as superior to
the other or by, as the *Walz* court did, balancing the interests protected
by the two clauses against one another in light of the facts of the
individual case.

While Mr. Chief Justice Burger's approach did not eliminate the
potential for confict between the Establishment and Free Exercise
Clauses, his very limited understanding of what would constitute
establishment certainly would tend to minimize the opportunities for
such conflict. According to the *Walz* analysis, the values protected by the
First Amendment's religion clauses would be served best by a policy of
governmental neutrality toward religion. In the pursuit of such neutrality, government would remain free to adopt many policies affecting

[52]397 U.S. at 675.
[53]*Id*. at 675.
[54]*Id*. at 674.
[55]84 HARV. L. REV. at 129-30. *See also* Katz, *supra* note 46.

religion, including provisions designed to neutralize what might otherwise be considered restrictive effects on the freedom of religious choice arising out of government action. Under the Chief Justice's interpretation of the Establishment Clause, it would presumably be permissible for government to adopt so-called "neutralizing aids" to counteract restrictions upon religious freedom which would otherwise result from a government policy. The classic example of such a neutralizing aid would be the chaplaincy program in the armed forces. The constitutionality of this program would not be debatable, under Burger's approach in *Walz*, since the chaplaincy program is intended to promote religious freedom not to sponsor religion. Having separated men from their ordinary opportunities for worship, government may constitutionally substitute alternative opportunities. Such a program would be consistent with a policy of governmental religious neutrality and, therefore, would not be forbidden by the Establishment Cluase.

Walz, then, might be read as (1) rejecting *sub silentio* the reasoning of the school prayer cases, (2) seriously undermining the authority of *Everson*, and (3) establishing *Zorach v. Clauson* as the leading establishment case.[56] Indeed, although it did not mention *Schempp*, Mr. Chief Justice Burger's opinion in *Walz* did quote approvingly from *Zorach*, perhaps to the great chagrin of Mr. Justice Douglas: "We are a religious people . . . and we make room for as wide a variety of beliefs and creeds as the spiritual needs of man deem necessary. . . . *When the state encourages religious instruction, . . . it follows the best of our traditions*. For it then respects the religious nature of our people and accommodates the public service to their spiritual needs."[57]

The third advantage which commentators claimed for Burger's approach over the old "no aid" theory was closely related to the second. If the "no aid" or "wall of separation" theory were strictly carried to its logical conclusion, too many desirable programs would have been invalidated. The Court, therefore, had created the primary purpose and effect doctrine; if a program could be classified as primarily secular in purpose and effect, the lending of textbooks in *Allen*, for example, its assistance to religion would be dismissed as an incidental side effect. But the primary purpose and effect test suffered from the same problem as the variable obscenity rule.[58] How does one ascertain the primary effect

[56]343 U.S. 306 (1952).

[57]*Id.* at 313-14, *quoted* at 397 U.S. at 672 (emphasis added by Burger, C. J.).

[58]*See, e.g.*, Ginzburg v. United States, 383 U.S. 463 (1966). *Ginzburg* and the difficulties with the variable obscenity rule are discussed in ch. VIII *infra*.

of a program which has several? A statute which provides aid to Catholic colleges may have the effects of (1) improving higher education standards nationally and (2) saving Catholic colleges from extinction so that they may be used for the further inculcation of Catholicism. Which of these two effects is primary depends upon the values against which the effects are judged. Mr. Chief Justice Burger's standard abandoned the effort to specify the primary effect in favor of a Holmesian approach, assessing on the basis of empirical reality the extent to which a particular public policy introduces religion into politics and vice versa. The Chief Justice used the term "benevolent neutrality" to characterize the difficult course which government policy-makers must steer between the religion clauses of the First Amendment,[59] either of which, if extended to its logical extreme, would defeat the purposes of the other. In pursuing a policy of "benevolent neutrality," all that the state must avoid is "excessive entanglement" with religion.

Nevertheless, despite the praise which the Chief Justice's opinion in *Walz* received, his "excessive entanglement" test left many, many questions open. The long-term impact of *Walz* would, of course, depend upon how liberally the Court would define "excessive." The specific holding in *Walz*, limited to tax exemptions, was exceptionally narrow, because such exemptions had been recognized for so many years. Over the course of nearly two centuries, churches had acquired property and constructed buildings in reliance upon their property tax exemption. If those exemptions were suddenly to be invalidated, religious strife in politics would probably have been increased rather than diminished. The exemption under attack in *Walz*, moreover, included not only church property but also property owned by a broad spectrum of charitable, educational, and other non-profit institutions. As the Chief Justice noted, the exemption did not single out churches for aid; to have excluded churches from the class of non-profit, charitable organizations that were thus exempted might have been viewed as discrimination *against* religion. Abstaining from taxing church property involved little or no continuing administrative relationship between the churches and the state. To remove the exemption would have involved state and church in disputes over tax assessments and tax foreclosures and could have resulted in many churches being forced to move out of the inner-cities where property values are high. But what about an historically new program of broad-scale subsidies to religiously affiliated educational institutions? In modern America, without public subsidy, many church-

[59] 397 U.S. 668.

affiliated schools and colleges might be forced to close. Could not such a result, societally detrimental for a number of reasons, be viewed as similar to that averted in *Walz*? And, thus, could not the *Walz* principle, sustaining the granting of admitted economic benefits to churches, be extended to validate such a subsidy program?

Lemon v. Kurtzman[60] and *Tilton v. Richardson*[61] provided the first opportunity after *Walz* to articulate the "excessive entanglement" standard for determining whether legislation violated the Establishment Clause.[62] *Lemon* and its companion cases overturned two comprehensive state schemes for the financial assistance of nonpublic elementary and secondary schools. But *Tilton* upheld federal construction grants to both religious and non-sectarian colleges. While the two decisions failed to furnish very precise criteria for judging when a statute did or did not contravene the First Amendment, there was every probability that they would at least result in a very severe limitation on public aid to parochial education.

In *Lemon*, the Court struck down statutes from Pennsylvania and Rhode Island which attempted to provide state assistance in the paying of the salaries of teachers in parochial schools who taught secular subjects.[63] For the Court, Mr. Chief Justice Burger thought that the purpose behind the two statutes, the enhancement of secular education for *all* students within the state, was a valid one, but he found that the means which the two states had adopted to further this purpose involved an excessive entanglement of church and state.[64] For one thing, Burger argued, the atmosphere of parochial schools is so pervasively religious that, even in good faith, parochial school teachers would be likely to inject religious doctrine into their secular teaching. Moreover, were the state rigorously to enforce the statutes' requirements that secular and religious instruction be kept separate, this would require close and

[60]403 U.S. 602 (1971), decided together with Earley v. DiCenso and Robinson v. DiCenso.

[61]403 U.S. 672 (1971).

[62]*See generally* Giannella, *Lemon and Tilton: The Bitter and the Sweet of Church-State Entanglement*, 1971 SUP. CT. REV. 147.

[63]PA. STAT. ANN. tit. 24, §§ 5601-09 (Supp. 1971); R.I. GEN. LAWS ANN §§ 16-51-1 to -51-9 (Supp. 1970). Under the Rhode Island program, the aid went directly to the teachers rather than to the schools. But both state programs were directed toward enhancing the competitive position of the private schools vis-à-vis the public schools.

[64]Perhaps because he found the entanglement excessive, the Chief Justice did not reach the question of the statutes' effects; in any case, the *Lemon* majority did not consider the effect test.

continuous governmental policing of the parochial school classsroom. Additionally, both state programs challenged in *Lemon* required the state to audit regularly the books of the parochial schools in order to determine which expenditures had been made for religious and which for secular instruction. This, of course, contrasted sharply with the "one time" nature of the tax exemption sustained in *Walz*. Lastly, the Chief Justice predicted that, given the annual nature of appropriations and in view of the on-going financial pressures on parochial education, it was reasonable to believe that the Rhode Island and Pennsylvania programs would invite lobbying along religious lines to maintain, if not to increase, the level of state aid.[65] This, of course, had been the very position taken by Mr. Justice Harlan in his *Walz* concurrence and was not dissimilar to Mr. Justice Black's reasoning in *Engel*. The two state plans, thus, felt the Chief Justice, might very well result in religious partisanship intruding into the political arena and in the public invasion of religious instruction, neither of which could be permitted by the Establishment Clause.

In *Tilton*, however, a five-man majority upheld the constitutionality of the federal Higher Education Act of 1963.[66] This act provides federal funds to colleges for building construction and makes no distinctions between church-related colleges and secular institutions of higher learning, although it does forbid grants to schools of divinity or for the construction of buildings to be used for worship.[67] This direct granting of federal money to colleges affiliated with religious bodies had been challenged as a violation of the Establishment Clause by fifteen Connecticut taxpayers,[68] joined by the Connecticut Civil Liberties Union and

[65]The Chief Justice emphasized, however, that the Court was not condemning all political controversy generated by the conflicting views of religious groups. Indeed, he predicted that American churches would frequently "take strong positions on public issues," for "religious values pervade the fabric of our national life." 403 U.S. at 623.

[66]20 U.S.C. §§ 701-89 (1964), as amended, 20 U.S.C. §§ 711-89 (1965-69 Supp. V).

[67]As originally passed, the federal funds were limited to use for the construction of library facilities or of buildings which would be devoted to research in or the teaching of mathematics, modern foreign languages, engineering, or the sciences. In 1965, the act was amended to remove this restriction, although the prohibition on the granting of funds to divinity schools or for the construction of facilities for worship or religious instruction was retained. 20 U.S.C. § 751(a) (2) (C), (D) (1965-69 Supp. V). All restrictions upon the use of the subsidized facilities, however, were to terminate twenty years after the completion of the construction. 20 U.S.C. §§ 754 (1965-69 Supp. V). In *Tilton*, the court did strike down this termination provision, on the grounds that it would allow for an impermissible effect: ultimately permitting religious institutions to use federally-funded facilties for religious activities. 403 U.S. at 682-84.

[68]The case had been initiated after the Warren Court's relaxation of the standing rule

the American Jewish Congress, in a suit against the Secretary of Health, Education and Welfare, the State of Connecticut, and four Catholic colleges.[69] Although the case involved only construction grants to four small schools under one federal law, the implications of the Court's decision ultimately would affect the eligibility of every church-related college under any present or future program of direct, federal aid to institutions of higher education. Many observers had predicted that the federal government must eventually provide a major amount of direct, financial support to colleges and universities,[70] and it seemed likely that a favorable decision in *Tilton* would encourage the proposal of legislation, at both the state and federal levels, to make funds available to private, sectarian and non-sectarian, colleges and universities. On the other hand, a decision against the colleges in *Tilton* might very well signal the death knell for church-supported colleges in this country, given the financially depressed state of parochial higher education. For that reason, much of higher education rallied to the support of the four colleges; five major educational associations—the Association of American Colleges, the American Council on Education, the National Association of State Universities and Land Grant Colleges, the Association of American Universities, and the Council for the Advancement of Small Colleges—filed an *amicus curiae* brief on behalf of the appellees.

For the Court, Mr. Chief Justice Burger measured the act against three criteria. And behold, it was good! The three criteria which the Chief Justice used were:

1. Did the act advance a valid secular prupose?
2. Did it achieve any constitutionally impermissible result?
3. What was the degree of government supervision?

In the first place, the Chief Justice found that increasing the enrollment capacities of America's colleges was a valid secular goal. Because the act explicitly prohibited the direct funding of any religious activity, it fostered no impermissible effect; and, finally, the Chief Justice argued that for three different reasons the act could be enforced with only a minimal amount of contact between the church and public authorities. The maturity and attendant skepticism of the average college student,

for First Amendment litigation in Flast v. Cohen, 392 U.S. 83 (1968). *Lemon* and its companion cases were also taxpayers' suits.

[69] Albertus Magnus, Annhurst, Fairfield, and Sacred Heart.

[70] *See* 109 CONG. REC. 19492-96 (1963) (debate of United States Senate at time of passage of Higher Education Facilities Act); N.Y. Times, Aug. 22, 1971, 4, at 7 (remarks of President Nixon, citing statistic that parochial schools are closing at the rate of one a day).

the internal discipline of the college-level course, and the general principles of academic freedom made it less likely that a religious atmosphere would as seriously pervade college-level instruction than it would at the elementary and secondary levels; the subsidized facilities, buildings, unlike the teachers in Rhode Island and Pennsylvania, would be religiously neutral; and the subsidy was a one-time rather than a continuing grant.

Walz, of course, had set forth the "excessive entanglement" test as a standard to guide the Court in First Amendment establishment cases. But, because *Walz* involved such a unique situation, it had not indicated the permissible limits of entanglement. How much was too much? *Tilton* and *Lemon* both faced that question, but their apparently contradictory rulings that the entanglement resulting from the federal statute was not excessive but that resulting from the state programs was provided precious little guidance to the resolution of the quantitative question of degree. *Tilton*, in particular, found the Court relying upon a number of questionable arguments.[71] For example, the Chief Justice's opinion ignored the economic reality that every public grant of money, goods, or services, to the extent that it replaces what would otherwise be an inevitable expense, increases the parochial colleges' discretionary spending powers.[72] Nor is the Court's distinction between aid to buildings and aid to teachers as convincing as it might at first appear. Even a science building, while religiously neutral, is not necessarily religiously sterile. Each class in the new, federally financed science building could, for example, be opened with prayer. The Court emphasized the one-time nature of the payment, but the federal policing of the use of the building continues for the life of the facility. Furthermore, although individual grants are separate and unique, the federal program itself is an on-going one and may invite religious lobbying efforts.

Lemon, on the other hand, was perhaps most important for its translation into headlines: AID TO PAROCHIAL SCHOOLS HELD UNCONSTITUTIONAL. And, indeed, it did seem to have created an insoluble paradox for programs of financial assistance to parochial schools, at least at the elementary and secondary levels. On the one hand, the Chief Justice told the schools that their secular and religious teaching must be completely separated. But, on the other hand, he then held that the enforcement of such separation would require excessive government

---

[71]*See The Supreme Court, 1970 Term*, 85 HARV. L. REV. 3, 167-79 (1971).

[72]*See* Choper, *The Establishment Clause and Aid to Parochial Schools*, 56 CALIF. L. REV. 260 (1968).

regulation. As such, the *Lemon* decision did seem to doom all forms of so-called "purchase of services" programs, whereby the state contracted with parochial schools and paid them for their provision of secular instruction.[73]

But, in view of the fiscal distress of parochial education,[74] it seemed virtually certain that some other relief plans would be devised. Among the more popular proposals, though there were several variants of this scheme, was the granting of tax deductions against property or income tax payments to the parents of private school students.[75] Another possibility, again with several alternative forms, was the provision of tuition grants to the parents of students enrolled in non-public schools.[76] But, in a series of decisions at the end of the 1972 Term, the Court refused to allow these financial aids to pass constitutional muster.[77]

In the leading case, *Committee for Public Education v. Nyquist,* the Court struck down a comprehensive New York program for furnishing public assistance to non-public elementary and secondary schools.[78] This program involved (1) direct money grants to non-public schools, both secular and sectarian, in low-income areas for the "maintenance and repair" of facilities, (2) tuition reimbursement grants to low-income parents of students attending private schools, and (3) income tax relief for the middle-income parents of non-public school pupils. By retreating

---

[73]*See The Supreme Court, 1970 Term,* 85 HARV. L. REV. at 175; *cf.* Giannella, *supra* note 62, at 196-97.

[74]*See, e.g.,* Brief for the National Catholic Education Association *et al.* as Amici Curiae at 14-17, Lemon v. Kurtzman, 403 U.S. 602 (1971).

[75]*See* Giannella, *supra* note 62, at 198-99; *The Supreme Court, 1970 Term,* 85 HARV. L. REV. at 177-78.

[76]*Id.* at 195-98.

[77]Levitt v. Committee for Public Education and Religious Liberty, 413 U.S. 472 (1973); Hunt v. McNair, 413 U.S. 734 (1973); Committee for Public Education and Religious Liberty v. Nyquist, 413 U.S. 756 (1973); Sloan v. Lemon, 413 U.S. 825 (1973).

[78]N.Y. Laws 1972, ch. 414, §§ 1-5, amending N.Y. Educ. Law, Art. 12, §§549-553 (McKinney's Consol. Laws, ch. 16, Supp. 1972), and N. Y. Tax Law §§ 612 (c), 612(j) (McKinney's Consol. Laws, ch. 60, Supp. 1972).

One of the companion cases, Sloan v. Lemon, 413 U.S. 825 (1973), involving a Pennsylvania tuition reimbursement program enacted following the decision in Lemon v. Kurtzman, 403 U.S. 602 (1971), was easily disposed of on the basis of *Nyquist,* there being no significant differences between the Pennsylvania and New York programs. Levitt v. Committee for Public Education and Religious Liberty, 413 U.S. 472 (1973), concerning another New York scheme for the reimbursement of non-public schools for certain costs of testing and record-keeping, was resolved adversely to the state program on the same reasoning as applied by *Nyquist* to the "maintenance and repair" program.

again to the primary purpose and effect test, the Court invalidated the entire program.

In *Lemon*, Mr. Chief Justice Burger had not even reached the question of effect,[79] and his treatment of the issue in *Tilton* had certainly seemed to indicate that, under the "excessive entanglement" test, the Court would rigorously confine the scope of its inquiry into the effect of a statutory plan which might aid religious instruction and would cease attempting to define or divine which of many effects might be "primary."[80] But, in *Nyquist*, Mr. Justice Powell, speaking for the Court, contended that the entanglement rule had not been meant to supersede the primary purpose and effect standard but was instead intended to supplement it, thereby creating a three-part test by which to measure the constitutionality of a statutory scheme challenged as violating the Establishment Clause. Mr. Chief Justice Burger, however, insisted in dissent that, under the principles established in *Everson* and *Allen*, an assistance program of general application which distributed benefits to individuals, "even though many of those individuals may elect to use those benefits in ways that 'aid' religious instruction or worship,"[81] did not involve a sufficiently intimate relation between church and state to be proscribed by the First Amendment.

Mr. Justice Powell, however, choosing to concentrate upon the effect of the New York program rather than the degree of entanglement which it produced, found the tuition reimbursement scheme "an incentive to parents to send their children to sectarian schools."[82] Distinguishing *Everson* and *Allen* on the grounds that, in those cases, "the class of beneficiaries included *all* school children, those in pubilc as well as those in private schools,"[83] Justice Powell unmistakably indicated that the channel for indirect aid would be "a narrow one."[84] For similar reasons, the income tax relief provision for middle-income parents failed the "effect" test. The Court thought that the provision, although formally a tax deduction, was actually a tax credit, since the deduction permitted was not related to the amount spent for tuition but had been designed to yield a predetermined amount of tax forgiveness. In effect, then, there was no significant difference between the tax benefit and the tuition

[79] 403 U.S. at 613-14; *see also* note 64 *supra*.
[80] 403 U.S. at 679-80.
[81] 413 U.S. at 799.
[82] *Id*. at 786.
[83] *Id*. at 782 n. 38 (emphasis in original).
[84] *Id*. at 775.

reimbursement. New York had, of course, relied upon the result in *Walz*, but Mr. Justice Powell had little trouble in turning *Walz* back upon the state (and the Chief Justice), arguing that the tax exemption in *Walz* had had the effect of minimizing church-state involvement, while the tax benefit would serve to increase that involvement. The "maintenance and repair" provision was also viewed as producing an unconstitutional effect, since there was nothing in the statute to prevent parochial schools from using the funds to maintain or repair facilities used for religious purposes.

Only Mr. Justice White objected to the invalidation of the "maintenance and repair" section of the New York program.[85] He insisted that the test was "one of 'primary' effect, not *any* effect" and charged the Court with having abdicated the duty of making that judgment.[86] Mr. Justice Powell's reply was to note,

> We do not think that such metaphysical judgments are either possible or necessary. Our cases simply do not support the notion that a law found to have a "primary" effect to promote some legitimate end under the State's police power is immune from further examination to ascertain whether it also has the direct and immediate effect of advancing religion.[87]

While Powell's position in this debate was probably the correct one, it still remains to ask whether, after *Walz, Lemon,* and *Tilton,* his—and Mr. Justice White's—reliance upon the primary purpose and effect test was an appropriate one. The dissent in *Nyquist* by the author of the "excessive entanglement" standard, Mr. Chief Justice Burger, when considered in conjunction with the scholarly praise which that standard had received, suggests that it was not.

Nevertheless, the only program to survive this revivification of the primary purpose and effect rule was South Carolina's Educational Facilities Act,[88] a plan designed to allow private colleges, including church-related institutions, to rely upon the state's ability to borrow money at low interest rates, an ability resting upon the federal income tax exemption for interest income derived from government bonds. The Educational Facilities Authority, established by the act, was to assist

---

[85]*Id.* at 813. Mr. Chief Justice Burger and Mr. Justice Rehnquist each filed separate dissents, in which the other joined, as regarded the tuition reimbursement and tax benefit schemes, but they, too found the "maintenance and repair" provisions to be beyond the constitutional pale.

[86]*Id.* at 823 (emphasis in original).

[87]*Id.* at 783 n. 39.

[88]S.C. Code Ann. §§ 22-41 *et seq.* (Cum. Supp. 1971).

private colleges in construction projects through the issuance of state revenue bonds. The funds generated by the bonds would be made available to the college, which would, in return, convey title to the project to the Authority but would continue to maintain and operate the facility under a lease-back arrangement. No state tax revenues were involved in the program in any way, since all of the Authority's operating expenses were to be derived solely from the revenues of the projects which it financed. No assistance, moreover, was to be made available for the construction of any facility to be used for a religious purpose. Applying the "effect" test, but relying heavily upon *Tilton*, *Hunt v. McNair* held that the First Amendment did not prohibit financial aid to education simply because "aid to one aspect of an institution frees it to spend its other resources on religious ends."[89] Mr. Justice Powell, again the majority's spokesman, was somewhat more disturbed by the potential entanglement inherent in the Authority's powers to inspect the facilities constructed under its auspices to insure that they were not being used for religious purposes, as well as by the sweeping powers apparently granted by the statute to the Authority to participate in management decisions regarding the projects it financed. But the inspection provision was found to be no more entangling than that involved in *Tilton*. The Authority's power to participate in management, Mr. Justice Powell admitted, presented a closer issue, but, as he read the statute, this power was limited to instances in which a college had defaulted on its lease agreement. Since that was not the situation before the Court, the *McNair* majority reserved judgment.

An examination of the disparate results produced by *Lemon* and *Nyquist*, on the one hand, and *Tilton* and *McNair*, on the other, might suggest that the Burger Court is implicitly drawing a distinction between colleges and the lower levels of education for purposes of First Amendment adjudication. All efforts to aid education below the college level have run afoul of the Establishment Clause, but not public assistance to private higher education. Moreover, there is language in both *Tilton* and *McNair* to the effect that church-related colleges and universities are not necessarily pervasively sectarian, though parochial elementary and secondary schools may be.[90] But, on the face of the constitutional text, this hardly seems a legitimate distinction. The Establishment Clause is not worded in the language of gradation.

[89] 413 U.S. 734, 743 (1973). *But cf.* Choper, *supra* note 72.
[90] Tilton v. Richardson, 403 U.S. at 682, Hunt v. McNair, 413 U.S. at 743.

Nyquist and *McNair*, therefore, cannot be viewed as the final word on the subject. Given the financial situation of sectarian education in America,[91] coupled with the zeal of its advocates, other programs of aid are sure to be attempted. Indeed, Mr. Justice Powell seemed to go out of his way to leave open invitations strewn throughout his opinion in *Nyquist*. The program of grants for the maintenance and repair of facilities, for example, could be redrafted to exclude religious facilities, thereby paralleling the construction grants sustained in *Tilton* and *McNair*. Similarly, income tax benefit programs might be recast in such a way as to survive constitutional challenge. In a footnote to his *Nyquist* opinion, Justice Powell wrote:

> Since the program here does not have the elements of a genuine tax deduction, such as for charitable contributions, we do not have before us, and do not decide, whether that form of tax benefit is constitutionally acceptable under the "neutrality" test in *Walz*.[92]

The legislative champions of public assistance to parochial education can hardly be expected to ignore such language.

Beyond this, wholly new alternatives might be tried. One possibility would be shared-time arrangements.[93] This might involve some kind of dual enrollment plan, by which parochial and public school students would receive simultaneous instruction in secular subjects with the parochial students released for part of the day to attend sectarian instruction; or, it could involve sending public school teachers into private schools. Yet another proposal is a voucher plan.[94] Government would issue to the parents of all school children vouchers redeemable in cash by the school the children attend. Any school, public or private, sectarian or non-sectarian, which could establish through such means as standardized tests that it provided an acceptable quantity and quality of education would qualify for participation. Such a plan, by hypothesis, would pursue a valid secular purpose, the education of all children; yet, government regulation and entanglement would be minimal. Supporters of this type of program claim that it would promote the quality of all schools by increasing the vigor with which they would compete with one

[91]*See* notes 70 & 74 *supra.*

[92]413 U.S. at 790 n. 49.

[93]*See* Giannella, *supra* note 62 at 194-95; *The Supreme Court, 1970 Term*, 85 HARV. L. REV. at 178.

[94]*See* Areen, *Educational Vouchers*, 6 HARV. CIV. RIGHTS—CIV. LIB. L. REV. 466 (1971); King, *Rebuilding the "Fallen House"—State Tuition Grants for Elementary and Secondary Education*, 84 HARV. L. REV. 1057 (1971); Giannella, *supra* note 62, at 195-98.

another, that it would widen the range of educational choice open to parents, and that it would, thus, increase parental control over their children's education.[95] On the other hand, a proliferation of private schools might arguably destroy the political cohesiveness promoted by a unitary school system,[96] and the voucher system could also be subject to abuse as a device for evading the mandate of the school desegregation decisions.[97]

The Burger Court, thus, will be kept busy in this area for some time to come, unless it chooses to abandon the field, which might not be an altogether bad idea. The Court itself has, with pleasing if uncommon candor, admitted that it "can only dimly perceive the lines of demarcation in this extraordinarily sensitive area of constitutional law,"[98] and it may be argued that, in the final analysis, the establishment of religion decisions of both the Warren and Burger Courts, especially the "religion in the schools" cases, have been unfortunate. Unfortunate not in that the Court was right or wrong in any given case but in that the whole issue was and is of such negligible importance. It is interesting, perhaps even instructive, to examine the contrast between the public's reaction to the school prayer decisions and the state aid to private schools cases with its greetings for the reapportionment holdings of the past decade.[99] Criticism of the reapportionment decisions, both those of the Warren Court and those of the Burger Court, has been, at worst, moderate, and there has been strong support for the Court from many quarters. It is ironic that the religion cases, which have so much less potential for real change in this country's social and political structure, have provoked so much greater outcry. The defenders of the faiths loudly assert that the Court is out to destroy religion and will not be satisfied until it has struck "In God

[95]CENTER FOR THE STUDY OF PUBLIC POLICY, EDUCATION VOUCHERS 1-6 (1970); M. FRIEDMAN, CAPITALISM AND FREEDOM 89-98 (1962).

[96]Gordon, *The Unconstitutionality of Public Aid to Parochial Schools*, in THE WALL BETWEEN CHURCH AND STATE 73, 74-78 (D. Oaks ed. 1963).

[97]*But see* Norwood v. Harrison, 413 U.S. 455 (1973), invalidating a Mississippi textbook loan program which included students in private schools with racially discriminatory policies; the Court indicated that, although narrow, the channel for indirect aid to parochial schools was broader than that for permissible public aid to racially discriminatory schools. Moreover, direct state tuition grants to support private "segregation academies" have invariably been overturned by the Court. *See* Griffin v. County School Bd., 377 U.S. 218 (1964); Hall v. St. Helena Parish, 368 U.S. 515 (1962); Wallace v. United States, 389 U.S. 215 (1967); Poindexter v. Louisiana Fin. Ass. Comm., 389 U.S. 571 (1968); Brown v. South Carolina, 393 U.S. 222 (1968).

[98]Lemon v. Kurtzman, 403 U.S. 602, 612 (1971).

[99]*See* C. LYTLE, *supra* note 2, at 45-47, 62-69, 91, 109.

We Trust" from our coinage.[100] The zealots of atheism and separation no less vehemently proffer their own *argumentum ad horrendum*, the truest believers among them apparently willing to deny to parochial schools even the public provision of sewage service. Both sides are willing to carry the debate to absurd lengths, and the Court finds itself caught in the middle, the tool of one group, the whipping boy of the other. Not for the first or only time, Robert McCloskey appears to have been prescient when, more than a decade ago, looking at the cases from a political perspective, he concluded that it would be better for the Court to avoid decisions in this area.

> On the basis of power and value considerations taken together, a strong case could be made for judicial avoidance of the whole issue of state aid to religion. . . . The subject seems peculiarly well calculated to generate resistance and backlash and peculiarly ill calculated to enlist adequate countervailing support. . . . If the evil aimed at by the Court were a great one, this expenditure of judicial power might not be excessive. But the evil in its present manifestations is fairly moderate. Even so, judicial correction of it might be warranted, if there were not other, graver wrongs simultaneously pressing for judicial attention and also taxing the power capacities of the Court. But when we take into account that there are those other wrongs, the price of dealing with this one may seem very dear indeed.[101]

[100]*But see* Engel v. Vitale, 370 U.S. 421, 435 n. 21.

[101]McCloskey, *Principles, Powers, and Values: The Establishment Clause and the Supreme Court,* 1964 RELIGION AND THE PUBLIC ORDER 3, 28.

Chapter 7
Nine Old Men and a
Few Dirty Books

No area of constitutional law was so wholly the creation of the Warren Court as was the law of obscenity regulation. During the first century and a half of its history, the Supreme Court had never confronted the First Amendment issue presented by the censorship of allegedly pornographic expression. During its tenure, however, the Warren Court rendered several significant decisions in this area of First Amendment freedom, developing constitutional doctrines of both interest and importance not merely for the bar but for the general public as well.[1] The Court's efforts, however, were less than satisfactory; in an interview shortly after his retirement Mr. Chief Justice Warren characterized obscenity as the Court's "most difficult area."[2] It has continued to be a difficult area for the Burger Court, largely due to the fact that the "new" Court has continued to adhere to the decisional approach of the "old" Court. But the results produced in obscenity cases during the Burger era have been more agreeable to the would-be censors than was the case during the Warren years. In view of this apparent disjunction in modern constitutional policy-making, it may be of profit to reconsider this body of judge-made law and to analyze its philosophic and political implications.

A systematic examination of the obscenity decisions reveals two central or generic constitutional issues.[3] The first of these derives from

---

[1]For general discussions of obscenity and the law, see Alpert, *Judicial Censorship of Obscene Literature*, 52 HARV. L. REV. 40 (1937); Lockhart & McClure, *Literature, the Law of Obscenity and the Constitution*, 38 MINN. L. REV. 295 (1954); Symposium, *Obscenity and the Arts*, 20 LAW & CONTEMP. PROB. 531 (1955); Kalven, *The Metaphysics of the Law of Obscenity*, 1960 SUP. CT. REV. 1; Lockhart & McClure, *Censorship of Obscenity: The Developing Constitutional Standards*, 45 MINN. L. REV. 5 (1960)); M. ERNST & A. SCHWARTZ, CENSORSHIP: THE SEARCH FOR THE OBSCENE (1966); Gagnon & Simon, *Pornography—Raging Menace or Paper Tiger?*, in THE SEXUAL SCENE 137 (J. Gagnon & W. Simon eds. 1970); Funston, *Pornography and Politics: The Court, the Constitution, and the Commission*, 24 W. POL. Q. 635 (1971).

[2]N.Y. Times, June 27, 1969, at 17.

[3]Others have seen the problems as involving matters of state procedures for enforcing

the imprecision of the term "obscenity." In its efforts to define the obscene, the Court has promulgated several different standards. Briefly, they are:

1. the "social value" test;
2. the American Law Institute test, i.e. "Whether to the average person, applying contemporary community standards, the dominant theme of the material taken as a whole appeals to prurient interest;"[4]
3. the "hard-core pornography" test;
4. the "contextual" or "variable obscenity" test.

The second set of constitutional difficulties involves, at least implicitly, the "clear and present danger" doctrine which is normally applied by the Court in free speech cases.[5] What is the potential "danger" which obscenity regulation seeks to avert? At one time or another, it has been suggested that obscenity must be censored because of its tendency to:

1. stimulate or provoke the commission of anti-social sexual acts;
2. excite psychological arousal;
3. contribute to the development of an aversion toward normal sexuality;
4. advance improper sexual mores;
5. erode character with long-term consequences for conduct.[6]

The Court first attempted to define "obscenity" in *Butler v. Michigan*, in which it unanimously invalidated a state statute prohibiting the sale of printed matter "tending to incite minors to violent or depraved or immoral acts."[7] Mr. Justice Frankfurter interpreted the statute as

obscenity regulation and the difficulties of prior censorship. *See, e.g.,* D. FELLMAN, THE CENSORSHIP OF BOOKS (1957); Nimmer, *The Consitutionality of Official Censorship of Movies,* 25 U. CHI. L. REV. 625 (1958); Monaghan, *First Amendment "Due Process,"* 83 HARV. L. REV. 518 (1970); A. KELLY & W. HARBISON, THE AMERICAN CONSTITUTION: ITS ORIGINS & DEVELOPMENT 1045-1053 (1970). Although these problems are both real and difficult, I consider them to be peripheral to a general discussion of obscenity regulation per se. Therefore, major decisions such as Kingsley Books v. Brown, 354 U.S. 436 (1957), and Times Film Corp. v. Chicago, 365 U.S. 43 (1961), dealing with the constitutionality of prior restraints, and Marcus v. Search Warrants, 367 U.S. 717 (1961), Bantam Books v. Sullivan, 372 U.S. 58 (1963), and Freedman v. Maryland, 380 U.S. 51 (1965), dealing with state procedures for enforcing obscenity statutes, are beyond the scope of this chapter.
    [4]MODEL PENAL CODE 207.10 (Tent. Draft No. 6, 1957).
    [5]*See* Schenck v. U.S., 249 U.S. 47 (1919); Bradenburg v. Ohio, 395 U.S. 444 (1969). *See generally* Strong, *Fifty Years of "Clear and Present Danger": From Schenck to Brandenburg—And Beyond,* 1969 SUP. CT. REV. 41.
    [6]For an elaboration of the possibility of this evil, *see* Roth v. U.S., 354 U.S. 476, 502 (1957) (Harlan, J., concurring in part and dissenting in part).
    [7]352 U.S. 380 (1957).

preventing the sale to the general public of literature which might injuriously affect the young. To his mind this was "to burn the house to roast the pig."[8] Thus, by implication, *Butler* rejected the traditional test for obscenity, i.e., the effect of isolated passages upon the susceptible.[9] Adults became not merely the preferred but the constitutionally required audience by which to test the obscenity of materials distributed to the general public. Moreover, by holding that the impact upon children was an impermissible standard for judging the obscenity of materials generally distributed, the Court seemed to imply that neither could the young serve as a justification for the generalized censorship of obscenity.

The following term, in *Roth v. United States* and its companion case, *Alberts v. California*, the Court explicitly discarded the long-standing English definition of obscenity, while simultaneously changing the constitutionally required test audience from "adults" to the *"average adult."*[10] *Roth* upheld federal postal censorship of pornographic materials, and *Alberts* sustained a California statute imposing criminal sanctions upon the distribution of obscene literature.

Mr. Justice Brennan, for the Court, began his opinion in a manner clearly presaging his conclusion.

> The dispositive question is whether obscenity is utterance within the area of protected speech and press.[11]

The question could, of course, be framed otherwise. For Mr. Justice Harlan the issue was the constitutional permissibility of censoring the materials actually before the Court. Justices Black and Douglas, on the other hand, inquired as to the constitutionality of the utilization of the criminal law to regulate expression in order to prevent the alleged evils of obscenity. The objection to Mr. Justice Brennan's metaphysical statement of the "dispositive question," as both Mr. Chief Justice Warren and Mr. Justice Harlan noted, is that the Court was thus cutting itself off from the empirical environment to decide an abstract question in a vacuum. Indeed, Brennan seems to have assumed that the only argument against the constitutionality of obscenity regulation rests on the premise that the First Amendment is an absolute, protecting all speech, and that

[8]*Id.* at 383.

[9]Regina v. Hicklin, L.R. 3 Q.B. 360 (1868). The famous test of obscenity as "pornographic matter having influence upon particularly susceptible persons" appears in the opinion of Lord Cockburn at 371.

[10]354 U.S. 476 (1957).

[11]*Id.* at 481.

all that was necessary to support obscenity censorship was to refute this premise.

Having stated the issue, Mr. Justice Brennan cut directly through to its heart. "All ideas having even the slightest redeeming social importance," he stated, are protected against governmental restraint. Obscenity, on the other hand, is, said Brennan, "utterly without redeeming social importance." Brennan then considered the assertion that there must be a clear and present danger of some social evil to justify the regulation of speech, and the great dilemma predicted for the Court when it encountered this problem miraculously evaporated. Obscenity being external to the realm of constitutionally protected speech, wrote Justice Brennan, relying on *Beauharnais v. Illinois*,[12] "it is unnecessary... to consider the issues behind the phrase 'clear and present danger.'"

The *Roth* Court, thus, utilized the two-level free speech theory which first appeared in the *Chaplinsky* case and became accepted constitutional doctrine in *Beauharnais*.[13] On the first level are expressions which, while anathema to the majority, may constitutionally be censored only if they present a "clear and present danger" of the realization of some social evil. On the second level are expressions so superfluous as to present little or no difficulty in determining the legality of their prohibition. In judging the constitutionality of any regulation of expression, the Court must first examine the social utility of the communication. If it has none, it may be curtailed. If it has some, the Court must then ascertain the clarity, proximity, and gravity of the danger which might result from it. Obscenity, thus, may be banned not because it is dangerous but because it is worthless.

But how are we to recognize this communication which is so worthless that it can be regulated without justification? What is the test for determining that a certain book is obscene? Here Justice Brennan had recourse to the words of the A.L.I.'s Model Penal Code: "Whether to the average person, applying contemporary community standards, the dominant theme of the material taken as a whole appeals to prurient interest."

In his dissent Mr. Justice Douglas attacked the two-level theory, calling instead for a uniform free speech theory applicable to both artistic and political expression. He objected to the *Roth* trial judge's use of offensiveness to "the common conscience of the community" as an evidentiary standard. Such a legal rule would be clearly unconstitutional,

[12] 343 U.S. 250 (1952).
[13] *Id.*; Chaplinsky v. New Hampshire, 315 U.S. 568 (1942).

Douglas contended, "if religion, economics, politics, or philosophy were involved. How does it become a constitutional standard when literature treating with sex is concerned?"[14]

Mr. Justice Harlan, opposing Brennan's all-encompassing approach, advocated independent judicial review of obscenity findings. But another point in Mr. Justice Harlan's opinion was of even greater interest. As in the criminal defendants' rights cases,[15] Justice Harlan's concern for the federal system led him to urge a lower standard under the Fourteenth Amendment than is imposed on the national government by the Bill of Rights. He did not, however, deny the validity of the two-level free speech theory, thus creating in essence a four-level theory. Nonetheless, Justice Harlan labored manfully to employ his complex standard, while limiting his decision to the materials actually involved in the instant cases. Because the states' interest in the control of obscene expression was to be subjected to a less severe constitutional test, he concurred in the *Alberts* holding. In Harlan's view, however, the federal government had not demonstrated a sufficiently acute interest in the subject, and, therefore, he dissented in *Roth*.

The censors were encouraged by their victories in *Roth* and *Alberts*, but the social value test actually resulted in a stringent limitation on what might constitutionally be censored, as was evidenced by three per curiam decisions the following term.[16] These three decisions, giving no explanation of their basis other than a citation of *Roth* as precedent, seemed to indicate that the Court was moving toward the acceptance of something similar to the hard-core pornography standard. At the very least, they demonstrated that the Court had begun to recognize the logically tenuous underpinnings of the two-level theory.

In *Kingsley Pictures Corp. v. Regents*, the Court unanimously invalidated an action of the New York Board of Regents censoring the film version of D. H. Lawrence's *Lady Chatterley's Lover*.[17] The Regents'

[14]354 U.S. at 512.

[15]*See, e.g.*, Duncan v. Louisiana, 391 U.S. 145, 171 (1968) (Harlan & Stewart, JJ., dissenting); Pointer v. Texas, 380 U.S. 400, 408 (1965) (Harlan, J., concurring); Jacobellis v. Ohio, 378 U.S. 184, 203 (Harlan, J., dissenting).

[16]One, the Homosexual Magazine, Inc. v. Oelsen, 355 U.S. 371 (1958), *reversing* 241 F.2d 772 (9th Cir. 1957); Sunshine Book Co. v. Summerfield, 355 U.S. 372 (1958), *reversing* 249 F.2d 114 (D.C. Cir. 1957); Times Film Corp. v. Chicago, 355 U.S. 35 (1958), *reversing* 244 F.2d 432 (7th Cir. 1957).

[17]360 U.S. 684 (1959). Motion pictures were included in the press whose freedom is guaranteed by the First Amendment in United States v. Paramount Pictures, 334 U.S. 131 (1948), and granted an immunity from state censorship identical to that of newspapers in Burstyn v. Wilson, 343 U.S. 495 (1952). *See generally* Klein, *Film Censorship: The*

action presented an issue of prior restraint, but only Justices Black and Douglas, concurring, considered the question. The other Justices nullified the Regents' decision on narrower grounds. Mr. Justice Stewart, for the Court, interpreted the Regents' efforts at bowdlerization as based on the rationale that the film endorsed immoral behavior, adultery, as desirable, appropriate, or proper under certain circumstances. Without considering whether the film was in fact obscene, Justice Stewart rejected regulation of so-called "ideological obscenity." He explicitly held that the advocacy of improper sexual values was an insufficient justification for the suppression of expression.

At the same term, in *Smith v. California*, a unanimous Court struck down a Los Angeles ordinance which made punishable mere possession of obscene literature by a bookseller.[18] Smith had challenged his conviction on various grounds. He argued that the ordinance, because it waived proof of *scienter*, was unconstitutional; he objected to the trial judge's refusal to admit the testimony of two expert witnesses regarding the community's contemporary literary and moral standards; he contended that the ordinance applied unconstitutionally restrictive standards; and, finally, he argued that, even were the ordinance constitutional, the literature in his possession had not been obscene. Although Mr. Justice Brennan's opinion for the Court suggested that full *scienter* might not constitutionally be required to sustain a conviction, he found the Los Angeles ordinance unconstitutional on its face, because it completely eliminated all mental factors from its definition of the crime. A statute entirely dispensing with any requirement of knowledge of the contents of the books on the part of the seller could not help but impose a

---

American and British Experience, 12 VILL. L. REV. 419 (1967); I. CARMEN, MOVIES, CENSORSHIP, AND THE LAW (1966); Note, 69 YALE L.J. 141 (1959); Nimmer *supra* note 3.

The *Kingsley* case illustrated yet another characteristic of obscenity decisions—the profusion of opinions. The nine Justices wrote six opinions in *Kingsley* and *Jacobellis*, five in *Roth*, and fourteen in *Ginzburg* and *Mishkin*.

Similarly, *Kingsley* manifested the unique ability of the obscenity cases to open up basic issues transcending the problems of obscenity. In *Kingsley*, Mr. Justice Clark, like Mr. Justice Stewart, found the New York statute unconstitutional on its face. Justices Frankfurter and Harlan each filed opinions with different points of departure, but each contended that the statute was not *prima facie* unconstitutional but only as applied in the particular case. Frankfurter analogized the Court's function in obscenity cases to that found in the confession cases. The *Kingsley* decision, then, disclosed even more explicitly than did *Roth* a major tension between those Justices who favored a clear statement of ruling principle and those who favored a particularized balancing.

[18] 361 U.S. 147 (1959).

severe limitation on the public's access to constitutionally protected materials, as book sellers would tend to restrict their inventories to materials with which they were personally familiar.[19]

Three years later, the Court set up a new and somewhat more restrictive definition of obscenity, the so-called "hard-core pornography" test. *Manual Enterprises v. Day*[20] marked the first time since *Roth* that the Court had, in a full opinion, addressed the constitutional problems of *federal* censorship. At issue was the power of the Post Office Department to withhold from the mails three magazines directed toward male homosexuals and consisting almost entirely of photographs of nude boys. For the Court,[21] Mr. Justice Harlan reversed, without remanding, the district court's judgment that the magazines were obscene and, thus, non-mailable. The lower court had, in Harlan's view, incorrectly applied *Roth*. An important test of obscenity which, according to Justice Harlan, was implicit in *Roth* was whether the material in question was, on its face, characterized by " 'patent offensiveness' or 'indecency.' "[22] Since the photographs involved in the instant case displayed no greater nudity than was commonly tolerated in photographs of nude females and since nudity per se was not obscene, Mr. Justice Harlan concluded that the three magazines did not represent hard-core pornography.

Though the Court had advanced numerous tests for and definitions of obscenity, it was still having trouble applying any of them in actual practice. This difficulty was demonstrated with vigor in *Jacobellis v. Ohio*.[23] The defendant, the manager of a motion picture theater, was convicted of violating a state statute which outlawed the exhibition of obscene motion pictures. The obscenity charge was based on a single, brief love scene from the French film *Les Amants*. In reversing the

[19]This would, indeed, have constituted a severe restriction in Smith's own personal case, for he admitted at trial it usually took him three months to read an average book.

For an analysis of the logical implications of this argument of restraint by consequence for cases involving the constitutionality of loyalty programs or the procedures of legislative investigating committees, *see* Kalven, *supra* note l.

[20]370 U.S. 478 (1962).

[21]While Mr. Justice Harlan's opinion is identified as the opinion of the Court, it was joined only by Mr. Justice Stewart. Justices Frankfurter and White did not participate, but the seven Justices who did managed to produce 3 opinions. Mr. Justice Brennan, joined by Mr. Chief Justice Warren and Mr. Justice Douglas, found the Post Office Department's action to be without statutory authorization. Mr. Justice Black concurred without opinion, and Mr. Justice Clark dissented.

[22]370 U.S. at 482

[23]378 U.S. 184 (1964). But see Miller v. California, 413 U.S. 15 (1973), discussed *infra* at pp. 289-93.

conviction, the nine Justices produced six opinions based upon four different definitions of obscenity. Mr. Justice Brennan, speaking for the Court, relied on the A.L.I. test. Mr. Justice Stewart advocated the hard-core pornography standard. Mr. Justice Goldberg had recourse to the variable obscenity rule, first suggested by Chief Justice Warren in *Roth* and *Alberts*. The Chief Justice, on the other hand, dissented. Mr. Justice Harlan once again expounded his four-level theory, while Justices Black and Douglas, joined by Mr. Justice White, in separate concurrences continued to advance their dissenting view in *Roth* that the regulation of obscenity by criminal sanctions is unconstitutional.

Although it established little more than a general statement incapable of precise meaning, the majority in *Jacobellis* did take some step toward making the test for obscenity less enigmatic. Since the protection of free expression is found in the Constitution, the Court held, the community standard by which the allegedly obscene material is to be judged cannot be limited to local communities but rather indicated the nation at large. It was on this point that Chief Justice Warren dissented. Of perhaps equal importance was the Court's explicit recognition of its *Butler* decision; the state's interest in preventing dissemination of material harmful to children, the Court held, does not justify total suppression of material which would not meet the test it had established.[24]

Shortly, however, the Court moved toward yet another test for obscenity. In *Ginzburg v. United States* it laid down the variable obscenity rule.[25] The majority in *Ginzburg* held that, at least in borderline cases, the manner in which material is displayed and merchandized may be important in determining the obscenity of its content. "Where the purveyor's sole emphasis is on the sexually provocative aspects of his publications," Mr. Justice Brennan wrote for the Court, "that fact may be decisive in the determination of obscenity... (E)vidence

[24]Perhaps the most significant aspect of *Jacobellis* had very little to do with obscenity regulation but carried important implications for state criminal procedures, and the process of "selective incorporation" in which the Warren Court engaged in relation to those procedures. In his dissent, Mr. Chief Justice Warren observed:

If the proceeding involved is criminal there must be a right to a jury trial, a right to counsel, and all other safeguards necessary to assure due process of law.

384 U.S. 184, 201. The Chief Justice's contention regarding the right to counsel had, of course, already borne fruit in Gideon v. Wainwright, 372 U.S. 335 (1963). His prophetic vision with respect to jury trial came to pass in Duncan v. Louisiana, 391 U.S. 145 (1968).

[25]383 U.S. 563 (1966). *See also* A Book Named "John Cleland's Memoirs of a Woman of Pleasure" v. Attorney General of Massachusetts, 383 U.S. 413 (1966). *See Generally* Magrath, *The Obscenity Cases: Grapes of Roth*, 1966 SUP. CT. REV. 7.

of pandering may be probative with respect to the nature of the material."

In dissent, Justices Black and Douglas continued to urge that obscenity regulation contravenes the First Amendment. More surprising, and more scathing, were the dissents of the usually restrained Justices Harlan and Stewart. Harlan saw the variable obscenity test as "an astonishing piece of judicial improvisation" that might inspire new censorship attacks upon long permissible classics. Stewart was especially incensed by what he viewed as the Court's sustaining of the defendant's conviction for reasons other than the charges against him. "Ginzburg was not charged with 'commercial exploitation,' " the Justice wrote. "He was not charged with 'pandering'; he was not charged with 'titillation.' " The Court had, thus, contended Stewart, denied the defendant due process of law, by upholding his conviction for crimes against which there was no federal statute.

In *Ginzburg's* companion case, *Mishkin v. New York*,[26] Mr. Justice Brennan revised the prurient-appeal test he had himself postulated in *Roth*. Mishkin argued that his books, consisting of so-called "bondage photos" of naked girls whipping each other, were not legally obscene because they excited only sick rather than normal people. Justice Brennan, for the six-man majority, agreed — and duly adjusted the prurient interest test from the "average adult" to the average member of any "probable recipient group." Thus, a book or film need not have a prurient appeal to society at large to be declared obscene. It can be judged obscene if it "panders" to a "clearly defined deviant sexual group," such as lesbians or masochists.[27]

In this area of First Amendment litigation, then, the Warren Court established several standards by which obscenity is to be judged. These tests were variously applied, usually with limited success. Indeed, one might contend that in its later years the Warren Court virtually "threw in the towel." *Redrup v. New York* overturned three state obscenity convictions.[28] In none of the cases had certiorari originally been granted to determine whether the questioned materials were in fact obscene. Each had been accepted for review on other grounds, limited to particularized questions. But, seven months after oral argument, the Court issued a brief per curiam opinion which stated that it was unnecessary to decide

[26]383 U.S. 502 (1966). *See also* Magrath, *supra* note 25.
[27]*But see In re* Klor, 64 Cal.2d 199 (1966) (preparation of obscene materials for artist's personal growth without intent to distribute cannot be made a crime).
[28]386 U.S. 767 (1967).

the cases on the grounds for which they had been granted certiorari, for the Court had determined that the materials were not obscene. But under what standard? The opinion did not specify.

One month after *Redrup* the Court reversed thirteen state and federal obscenity convictions without waiting for briefs or arguments on the merits.[29] On the basis of only the short briefs filed in petitioning for certiorari, the Court granted certiorari and reversed, merely citing *Redrup*. The exact significance of these per curiam reversals was difficult to assay. Did they indicate a victory for Justices Black and Douglas, or did they stand for the triumph of the hard-core pornography — "I know it when I see it." — approach?

Students of the Supreme Court and its constitutional doctrines, however, do not enjoy the luxury of unexplained per curiam opinions. To understand the constitutional issues involved in this area of increasing public concern, it is necessary to analyze the validity of each of these tests for or definitions of obscenity.

The "social value" test, at base, is the theory that obscenity is "filth for filth's sake," communication so bereft of intellectual or artistic quality as to possess no redeeming merit whatsoever. As such, this test is closely allied with the justification for obscenity regulation which contends that obscene material has as its sole *raison d'etre* the excitation of lustful thoughts and desires. However, not only pornography but also erotic expression of unquestioned aesthetic value may have as its sole or principal object the sexual arousal of the reader or viewer. Is there, possibly, a genus, "privileged obscenity," encompassing such classics as the writings of Chaucer, Rabelais, Boccaccio, Shakespeare, Swift, Zola, Aristophanes, and perhaps even the Bible, which, while arguably obscene, may have some small redeeming social worth? Even more fundamental is the question: Why has it been uncritically assumed that erotically stimulating expression has no "redeeming social value" per se?

The "redeeming social value" test, as generally applied, however, places the burden of proof on the defendant in obscenity cases. That is, in order to save the work, the defense must prove that it has some

[29]Kenney v. New York, 288 U.S. 440 (1967); Friedman v. New York, 388 U.S. 441 (1967); Ratner v. California, 388 U.S. 442 (1967); Cobert v. New York, 388 U.S. 443 (1967); Shepherd v. New York, 388 U.S. 444 (1967); Avansino v. New York, 388 U.S. 446 (1967); Aday v. United States, 388 U.S. 447 (1967); Corinth Publication, Inc. v. Wesberry, 388 U.S. 448 (1967); Books, Inc. v. United States, 388 U.S. 449 (1967); Rosenbloom v. Virginia, 388 U.S. 450 (1967); Quantities of Copies of Books v. Kansas, 388 U.S. 452 (1967); Mazes v. Ohio, 388 U.S. 453 (1967); Shackman v. California, 388 U.S. 454 (1967).

"redeeming social value;" the prosecution is not required to prove it has none. Rather, the prosecution must prove only that "to the average person, applying contemporary community standards, the dominant theme of the material taken as a whole appeals to prurient interest." This system of burden of proof is unfortunate, at least for the defendant, for the A.L.I. test is open to even more numerous and basic criticisms than the "social value" test.

This is not to deny that, when postulated in *Roth*, the American Law Institute standard represented an advance over any test which had preceded it. It insisted on the *average* person, on the material considered *as a whole*, and on the *dominant* theme. But it shared the central weakness of all prior definitions of obscenity; the word is still defined in terms of itself. Indeed, the Court and the American Law Institute could not agree on the definition of the all-important phrase "prurient interest."[30] On the one hand, the A.L.I. rejected "the prevailing tests of tendency to arouse lustful thoughts or desires because it is unrealistically broad."[31] But, after borrowing the phrase from the Model Penal Code, the Court stated that "material which deals with sex in a manner appealing to prurient interest [is] material having a tendency to excite lustful thoughts."[32] The Court's definition of the phrase appears to be in consonance with the dictionary. The key word, "prurient," is defined by Mr. Webster in terms of "lascivious longings" and "lewd". The obscene, then, is whatever appeals to an interest in the obscene.

The audience problem introduced by the word "average" was even greater than the definitional problem presented by "prurient". The obvious question was whether the prurient interest of an imaginarily average individual is the most desirable yardstick against which to measure the appeal of materials in all cases? *Mishkin*, of course, answered this in part by informing us that material not prurient for the average person may nevertheless be obscene if intended for a group for whom it is highly prurient. But what about the opposite situation? Is material, directed to an audience for whom it lacks prurient allurement, still to be legally obscene simply because it would appeal to the prurient

[30] As noted *supra* note 4, this test was borrowed by the Court from the American Law Institute's Model Penal Code. The phrase "prurient interest," which one must candidly admit is somewhat less than common, even in legal parlance, was itself borrowed by the A.L.I. from Mr. Justice McKenna's opinion in Mutual Film Co. v. Industrial Comm'n of Ohio, 236 U.S. 230 (1915).

[31] *See* note 4 *supra*.

[32] Roth v. United States, 354 U.S. 476, 490 (1957).

interest of the average person were it to fall into his hands? Who, in fact, is this "average person"? Does he represent a hypothetical compound of all groups within society, including children? Or is he the man in the street? Or is he society's sensual mean, obscenity's counterpart to negligence's "reasonable man"? Perhaps the most serious defect in the "average person" section of the A.L.I.. test is that the average person may be attracted to a particular material solely by its risqué reputation with no concern for its aesthetic value. How are we to regard art or literature of merit which the average person inspects only for its eroticism?

The "contemporary community standards" portion of the test was subject to numerous and related criticisms. The most obvious questions were: What is to be the community? And what are to be the standards? *Jacobellis* purported to answer the first question, but, according to psychologists and sociologists, it answered it in a manner directly contrary to the facts. These scientists claim that there is no such thing as a national community standard of sexual mores. Rather, they have found an immensely wide variety of commonly accepted attitudes, practices, and experiences, e.g., between urban and rural sections as relates to bestiality.[33]

The second question was even more serious. What is to be the standard? Expounded principles or actual actions? What we say or what we do? It remains the principle in America that premarital sexual intercourse is undesirable or wrong. That principle to the contrary notwithstanding, our practices reveal a virtually universal hypocrisy.[34] This is vital, for the members of a jury in an obscenity case will have a tendency to regard as "indecent", "impure", or "pornographic" whatever conflicts with their individual sexual prejudices. The community attitude toward coital positions may, for example, be decisive in a given trial. This, of course, raises the entire problem of whether the jury or experts should have primacy in the trying of obscenity cases. Presumably, though not necessarily, the jury will be the better judge of the community standard, but will have little or no ability to judge the social value of a given work. The judiciary is then left in the highly unenviable, and subjective, position of balancing the two.

Finally, strict application of the A.L.I. test would probably result in

---

[33]*See, e.g.*, E. KRONHAUSEN & P. KRONHAUSEN, PORNOGRAPHY AND THE LAW 175-94 (1964). *See also Miller v. California*, 413 U.S. 15 (1973), discussed *infra* at pp. 289-93.

[34]*See generally* A. KINSEY, SEXUAL BEHAVIOR IN THE HUMAN MALE (1948) and SEXUAL BEHAVIOR IN THE HUMAN FEMALE (1953).

cultural homogeneity, mediocrity, and sterility. *Avant garde* art and literature are by definition ahead of their times. On the other hand, those who will be charged with the administration of a public program for the control of sexual expression—our police, judges, and attorneys—are generally from the more conservative and more sexually repressed segments of society and have relatively little expertise in such highly specialized disciplines as literary criticism, art history, or the psychology of sexual response.[35]

Ironically, these difficulties with the A.L.I. test were acknowledged by the Warren Court itself. In *Interstate Circuit, Inc. v. City of Dallas*, the appellant, a film exhibitor and distributor, challenged the action of the Motion Picture Classification Board of Dallas, classifying the motion picture *Viva Maria* as "not suitable for young persons."[36] Under a Dallas city ordinance, a picture so classified could be shown only by theaters licensed to show "not suitable" films. Interstate did not possess such a license and, thus, was enjoined from exhibiting the film. On appeal from the injunction, Interstate claimed that the standards which governed the classification of films by the Board were unconstitutionally vague. Those standards were:

"Not suitable for young persons" means: (1) Describing or portraying brutality, criminal violence or depravity in such a manner as to be, in the judgment of the Board, likely to incite or encourage crime or delinquency on the part of young persons; or

(2) Describing or portraying nudity beyond the customary limits of candor in the community, or sexual promiscuity or extra-marital or abnormal sexual relations in such a manner as to be, in the judgment of the Board, likely to incite or encourage delinquency or sexual promiscuity on the part of young persons or to appeal to their prurient interest.

A film shall be considered "likely to incite or encourage" crime or delinquency or sexual promiscuity on the part of young persons, if, in the judgment of the Board, there is a substantial probability that it will create the impression on young persons, that such conduct is profitable, desirable, acceptable, respectable, praiseworthy or commonly accepted. A film shall be considered as appealing to "prurient interest" of young persons if in the judgment of the Board, its calculated or dominant effect on young persons is substantially to arouse sexual desire. In determining whether a film is "not suitable for young persons," the Board shall consider the film as a whole,

[35]See notes 33 and 34 *supra*.
Indeed, the reasoning of the Court in contradiction to the sociological facts, the ensuing criticism of social scientists, the Court's lack of expertise due to its class origin, and the role played by public opinion in the "contemporary community standards" test should remind the constitutional scholar of no historical analogy more strongly than the "liberty of contract" decisions.
[36]390 U.S. 676 (1968)

> rather than isolated portions, and shall determine whether its harmful effects outweigh artistic or educational values such film may have for young persons.[37]

In other words, the Board was to be guided in its classifications, i.e., its determination of obscenity, by a test identical to the A.L.I. test as modified by *Mishkin*. The Board was to label a film "not suitable" if, in its judgment, the dominant theme of the film taken as a whole appealed to the prurient interest of a clearly defined probable recipient group — persons under 18. In applying this standard, it was to consider the customary limits of candor of the community, and we may assume *arguendo* that the Board is composed of average adults.

Yet the Court struck down the Board's action on the grounds that the standards which the ordinance established to guide the Board in the exercise of its discretion were unconstitutionally vague! The Court found first that the ordinance did not include a definition of sexual promiscuity. "It could extend," wrote the majority's spokesman, Mr. Justice Marshall, "depending upon one's moral judgment, from the obvious to any sexual contacts outside a marital relationship." Second, relying on *Kingsley Pictures*, the majority held that allowing the Board to classify pictures on the basis of its own judgment of what was desirable, acceptable, or respectable conduct was an overbroad interference with the right to express and advocate one's own ideas as to what are appropriate values, morals, or life styles. The Court did not discuss that section of the ordinance modeled on the A.L.I. test which empowered the Board to classify a film as "unsuitable" if it found the film to appeal to young persons' prurient interests. But the implication is, as Mr. Justice Harlan pointedly criticized in dissent, that the A.L.I. test itself is impermissibly vague. "The truth is," wrote Justice Harlan, "that the Court has demanded greater precision of language from the City of Dallas than the Court can itself give. . . ."

Disturbed by the difficulties inherent in the foregoing definitions of obscenity, many jurists and legal analysts have urged the Court to explicitly narrow the legal definition of obscenity to "hard-core pornography." Most of those writing about hard-core pornography, however, treat it as though it were so simple to recognize that any discussion of its nature and characteristics is completely unnecessary.[38] While these

---

[37]*Id.* at 681-2, *quoting* DALLAS, TEX., REV. CODE OF CIV. & CRIM. ORDINANCES ch. 46A (1960).

[38]*See, e.g.,* Bromberg, *Five Tests for Obscenity*, 41 CHI. B.REC. 416, 418-19 (1960); H. ELLIS, *The Revaluation of Obscenity*, in MORE ESSAYS ON LOVE AND VIRTUE

scholars have exaggerated the ease with which hard-core pornography can be identified, certainly one of its qualities must be that it performs a masturbatory function. The detailed content analysis of works of erotic realism and hard-core pornography conducted by Drs. Phyllis and Eberhard Kronhausen has adduced support for Dr. Margaret Mead's argument that pornography is essentially an appeal to the autoerotic fantasies of the sexually immature. The Kronhausens found that erotic realism, while dealing with sexual subjects in a specific and direct manner, was based upon both physiological and psychological reality. On the other hand, hard-core pornography manifested the characteristics of a wish-fulfillment daydream. These books invariably consisted of a succession of increasingly erotic scenes, deliberately omitting nonerotic passages, and typically describing, as scatologically as possible, seduction, defloration, incest, permissive-seductive parent figures, supersexed males, nymphomaniac females, blacks and Asiatics as sex symbols, homosexuality (particularly lesbianism), mass orgies, and flagellation.[39]

The Kronhausens' research and the hard-core pornography test, however, are virtually worthless when applied to *pictorial*, as opposed to written, representations. What, for example, is to be done with art books, destined for the coffee tables of the rich, which present in color photographs the amatory temple sculpture of India, or the erotic art of the Greeks and Etruscans, or the frescoes of Pompeii? It is precisely in this situation that the hard-core pornography test fails, for a single picture or *objet d'art* is not susceptible of the detailed content analysis this test requires. In the case of pictorial representations, the courts would simply have to rely on arbitrary judgments of quality.[40]

Hard-core pornography tests, moreover, do not cover people like Roth, Alberts, and Ginzburg, who marketed non-pornographic material as if it were pornography. To attempt to meet the question, is obscenity

130 (1931); Brief for Respondent-Appellant in Vermont v. Verham News Corp. (Windsor County Court, Docket 2779, Supreme Court, Docket 1305) 22 (1959).

[39]M. MEAD, *Sex and Censorship in Contemporary Society*, in NEW WORLD WRITINGS 7, 18 (1953); E. KRONHAUSEN & P. KRONHAUSEN, *supra* note 33, at 178-243.

Concerning the psychodynamics of pornography, *see also* Abse, *Psychodynamic Aspects of the Problem of the Definition of Obscenity*, 20 LAW & COMTEMP. PROB. 572 (1955); Eliasberg, *Art: Immoral or Immortal?*, 45 J. CRIM. L. & P.S. 224 (1955).

[40]It might also be argued that to define obscenity as hard-core pornography is to beg the question by requiring a definition of "pornography." Thus, as with "prurient interest," the definition is circular.

an inherent characteristic of obscene material, the Warren Court adopted the "variable" or "contextual" obscenity test first proposed by Mr. Chief Justice Warren in *Roth* and *Alberts* and explicitly rejected by Mr. Justice Harlan in the same cases. But the closeness of the decision in *Ginzburg* and the depth of division between the majority and minority Justices speak eloquently of the problems involved with this standard. Under this test, material is judged by "its appeal to and effect upon the audience to which the material is primarily directed. In this view, material is never inherently obscene; instead, its obscenity varies with the circumstances of its dissemination."[41] Thus, under the contextual obscenity standard, if material of even great social value lacked redeeming importance for its primary audience, it might appropriately be declared to be obscene. It was apparently this result that Justice Harlan had in mind in his *Ginzburg* dissent, when he suggested that the variable obscenity rule might encourage new attacks on such works as James Joyce's *Ulysses*. Moreover, when applied in state courts, the contextual obscenity rule makes possible the anomalous situation of a book or film being banned in some jurisdictions and being found not obscene in others, depending upon how the material was directed, displayed, or advertised and at or to whom.

But the central difficulty with the variable obscenity test remains its audience problem. If the test is to work in practice, satisfactorily distinguishing the obscene and censorable from the constitutionally protected expression, the material's primary audience must first be defined with extreme precision. Then the nature of the material's appeal to and effect upon that audience must be rigorously analyzed. But how is the primary audience, as distinguished from the peripheral audiences, to be measured? Quantitatively? Indeed, may not material be directed equally and simultaneously to two or more groups?

Perhaps the most difficult aspect of the audience problem under the contextual obscenity test is the situation presented by peripheral audiences of adolescents. Can material, pornographic for adolescents but not for adults, be kept from the young without unconstitutionally abridging their elders' access to the material? Constitutionally, at least, it can be. *Ginsberg v. New York* upheld the constitutionality on its face of a state criminal obscenity statute which prohibited the sale to minors of material defined to be obscene on the basis of its appeal to them,

---

[41]Lockhart & McClure, *supra* note 1, at 77.

regardless of its obscenity or non-obscenity for adults.[42] Since the statute did not prohibit the sale of these materials to persons seventeen or older, no *Butler* problem was raised. In appealing his conviction, Ginsberg did not argue that the magazines, for the sale of which he had been prosecuted, were not obscene nor did he challenge the statutory definition of obscenity. Rather, he directly contended that the constitutional freedom of expression and its corollary freedom to read, see, or hear these expressions could not be made dependent upon age. The case, thus, presented the question whether state legislatures could constitutionally accord to minors a more restricted right than that accorded to adults to determine for themselves what material, including material dealing with sex, they would read and see. The Court concluded that, even where there may be an invasion of protected freedom, the power of the state to control the conduct of children extends beyond the scope of its authority over adults.[43]

In the majority's view two interests justified this extended power. First, Mr. Justice Brennan, the majority's spokesman, observed that constitutional interpretation has consistently held that supervison of children is best left to the parents. It is not irrational, then, to believe that parents are entitled to the support of the state in the discharge of their parental responsibilities. If a parent wished his children to read materials such as those sold by Ginsberg, Brennan noted, he could, under the New York statute, purchase them for his child. Second, the state itself has an independent interest in the well-being of its youth. Although the

---

[42]390 U.S. 629 (1968). *See generally* Krislov, *From Ginzburg to Ginsberg: The Unhurried Children's Hour in Obscenity Litigation,* 1968 SUP. CT.REV. 153.

[43]*See* Prince v. Massachusetts, 321 U.S. 158 (1944). *See also* New Jersey v. Perricone, 181 A.2d 751 (N.J. 1962); Morrison v. Missouri, 252 S.W.2d 97 (Mo. 1952); Arnold v. Arnold, 18 S.2d 130 (Ala. 1944); Gardner v. Hall, 26 A.2d 799 (N.J. 1942).

Several commentators, including some who believe that general censorship of obscenity is irreconcilable with the First Amendment, have suggested that it would be constitutionally permissible for legislation to deal with the problem of the exposure of children to pornographic works. On age classifications with regard to obscenity laws, *see generally* Dibble, *Obscenity: A State Quarantine to Protect Children,* 39 SO. CAL. L. REV. 345 (1960); Kalven, *supra* note 1, at 7; Magrath, *supra* note 25, at 75; Emerson, *Toward a General Theory of the First Amendment,* 72 YALE L.J. 877 938-39 (1963); Henkin, *Morals and the Constitution: The Sin of Obscenity,* 63 COLUM. L. REV. 391, 413, n. 68 (1963); Note, *Constitutional Problems in Obscenity Legislation Protecting Children,* 54 GEO. L.J., 1379 (1966); I. CARMEN, *supra* note 17, at 247-60; Wall, *Obscenity and Youth: The Problem and a Possible Solution,* 1 CRIM. L. BULL 28 (1965); Comment, *Exclusion of Children from Violent Movies,* 67 COLUM. L. REV. 1149 (1967).

supervision of children is best left to parents, this supervision is not always provided, either because the child is orphaned or because the parents prove to be unfit. Then, society's interest in protecting the welfare of the child transcends the parental interest and justifies reasonable regulations upon the conduct of the children.[44]

The only question then remaining for the Court was whether a state legislature might reasonably conclude that exposure to obscene materials was detrimental to youth. Again invoking the two-level theory, Justice Brennan argued that, since obscene material was beyond the protection of the First Amendment, it was necessary only to determine if it was irrational to believe that exposure to obscenity is harmful to minors. Brennan admitted that no evidence had been adduced to show that such exposure basically impaired ethical or moral development, but, in a gratuitous display of judicial restraint, he continued that it was not necessary for the legislation in the present case to be correct. It need only be rational. The majority opinion then concluded that, in view of the imprecise state of knowledge concerning the effects of obscenity, it was not irrational for a legislature to believe that moral damage might result from exposure to pornography. Hence, the legislative judgment, embodied in the New York anti-obscenity statute, was neither irrational nor constitutionally impermissible.

Dissenting, Justices Black and Douglas agreed that the statute was not irrational. But that, they contended, was an appropriate test only in due process litigation, where the question was whether the legislature, in the absence of any constitutional prohibition, had the power to pass a given statute. The instant case, they felt, was quite different since a constitutional prohibition, the First Amendment, did exist. Here the question was not the rationality of the statute but whether it transgressed upon constitutionally protected freedoms, which, they felt, it did.

The *Ginsberg* decision to the contrary notwithstanding, one is still driven to wonder if it is possible to keep material away from minors without infringing upon the constitutional rights of adults. Obviously it is possible to do so with at least reasonable success where the material is motion pictures or theatrical performances, but where it is books and magazines confidence appears less warranted. The *Smith* rule would seem to preclude requiring the seller to determine at his own risk which books or magazines must not be sold to youths. Forbidding the public display of material not fit for adolescents, though available to adults,

---

[44]*See* note 43 *supra. But see In re* Gault, 387 U.S. 1 (1967); Tinker v. Des Moines School District, 393 U.S. 503 (1969); *In re* Winship, 397 U.S. 358 (1970).

would present problems of undue interference with the material's primary audience. On the other hand, "adults only" counters at book stores or newsstands would actually be a powerful attraction for the young and would probably create an additional problem of adolescent shoplifting.[45]

To define obscenity, however, assuming such a feat to be possible, is not to justify its regulation. Why should obscenity be censored? Five possible dangers, the prevention of which might justify obscenity censorship, were noted at the outset. In *Kingsley Pictures*, the Court rejected one of these, thematic obscenity, as an unconstitutional predicate for governmental regulation. (Indeed, it is difficult to understand how, for purposes of First Amendment interpretation, the advocacy of a particular code of sexual morals differs from the advocacy of political or economic philosophies or ideas.) Otherwise, the Court, as exemplified by the use of the two-level theory in *Roth* and *Ginsberg*, has studiously avoided rendering an opinion upon the other possible justifications for the censorship of obscenity.

The argument most commonly advanced by the proponents of obscenity regulation is that pornography effects anti-social sexual conduct either immediately or in the future through its impact on character. But, as the presidential obscenity commission demonstrated and as Mr. Justice Brennan admitted in *Ginsberg*, these justifications evaporate in the light of an absence of evidence to show any causal connection between exposure to pornographic books or films or photos and overt sexual behavior.[46] Candor, of course, compels the admission that there is an equal lack of evidence to disprove the thesis that there is a causal link between exposure to obscenity and overt, anti-social sexual conduct. And it bears emphasis that intelligent, rational, responsible

[45]The "variable obscenity" test presents other practical difficulties for law enforcement. Variable obscenity would often require evidence beyond the material itself. Thus, a police officer could not always make the necessary preliminary judgments from a book or picture itself to warrant an arrest.

[46]The evidence is summarized in M. JAHODA, THE IMPACT OF LITERATURE (1954); Lockhart & McClure, *supra* note 1, at 373-385; Dibble, *supra* note 43; Wall, *supra* note 43, at 30; Cairns, Paul, & Wishner, *Sex Censorship: The Assumptions of Anti-Obscenity Laws and the Evidence*, 46 MINN. L. REV. 1009 (1962); Elias, *Sex Publications & Moral Corruption: The Supreme Court Dilemma*, 9 W. & M. L. REV. 302 (1967); Note, 52 KY. L.J. 429 (1964); Note, 34 FORD. L. REV. 692 (1966); Note, 55 CAL. L. REV. 926 (1967).

See also United States v. Roth, 237 F.2d 796, 812-817 (C.A. 2d Cir. 1956) (Frank J., concurring).

But see Gaylin, Book Review, 77 YALE L.J. 579, 5911-95 (1968).

men, including some members of the United States Supreme Court, believe that such a connection may exist. But, while the possibility of harmful effects from pornography should not be dismissed as frivolous, it must be recognized that, at present, that possibility remains essentially speculative.[47]

As for the evil of arousing sexual thoughts short of action, there is no doubt that the written word or the cinematic image can excite the imagination; that is what they are designed to do. But one must admit that there is a certain comic aspect to the idea that the Law in all its majesty should be so solemnly concerned with individuals' sexual fantasies.[48]

The only possible evil remaining then is the offending, shocking, or disgusting of a non-captive audience.[49] Arousing disgust and revulsion in a voluntary audience, however, would seem to be a constitutionally inadequate basis for the governmental curtailment of speech. But, more importantly, if this supposed evil is an evil, it must by definition destroy the other possible justifications for obscenity regulation, for it suggests an effect of obscenity that is the diametric opposite of that on which the other four are predicated: Obscenity is socially injurious, not because it is attractive, but because it is repugnant.

In light of these serious problems with each of the legal tests for obscenity and with each of the constitutional justifications advanced for its regulation, one may wonder about the wisdom either of enacting new anti-obscenity legislation or of continued enforcement of the largely antiquated obscenity regulatory statutes already on the books. In the absence of any evidence suggesting the existence of a "clear and present danger" with regard to exposure to erotica, should we not abolish all obscenity legislation? In spite of the objections of some, the Supreme Court, even in civil liberties cases, is engaged in the balancing of interests.[50] But, in this area of constitutional litigation, neither history nor precedent nor policy nor even the sociological data, upon which the

[47]*But see* Henkin, *supra* note 43, arguing that obscenity legislation advances absolutely no legitimate state interest but is predicated upon a puritanical sense of sin and morality and, thus, is unconstitutional as a violation of due process.

[48]*See* Kalven, Book Review, 24 U. CHI. L. REV. 769 (1957).

[49]Note that, except for *Ginsberg* which involved a sixteen year-old "plant," these are the only kind of audiences which have been the object of the Supreme Court's obscenity litigation.

[50]*Compare* Frantz, *The First Amendment in the Balance,* 71 YALE L.J. 1424 (1962) *and* Frantz, *Is the First Amendment Law? A Reply to Professor Mendelson,* 51 CALIF. L. REV. 729 (1963); *with* Mendelson, *On the Meaning of the First Amendment: Absolutes in the*

Warren Court was so fond of relying, has provided any clear guide. Therefore, in striking the balance, why, where there is no evidence of an actual, proximate danger of social or individual injury arising from pornography, should the Court not be guided by the First Amendment's preference for freedom of expression?

In part, the difficulties experienced by the Court in this area have been the result of an inadequacy in our classical free speech theory. Neither Mill nor Meiklejohn provide much assistance in discovering why artistic expression should be protected by the First Amendment.[51] Similarly, the famous First Amendment opinions of Hand, Holmes, and Brandeis have emphasized the interrelationship of freedom of communication and the democratic process. But it makes little sense to consider artistic expression in this framework. Politics has little or nothing to do with the social importance of painting, sculpture, drama, the cinema, or the literary arts. These things are necessary to civilization for reasons quite apart from the electoral process. Therefore, the Court or those commentators who follow its doctrinal developments, must attempt to provide a rationale for the constitutional guarantee of freedom of speech that will be equally applicable to both political and artistic expression.[52]

In *Stanley v. Georgia*, the Warren Court appeared to have taken a step in this direction.[53] Armed with a search warrant to investigate alleged bookmaking activities, police entered and searched Stanley's home. In the course of the search, while looking through a desk drawer in an upstairs bedroom, they discovered a roll of 8 mm. film. Using a projector and screen which they also found, the police viewed the film, determined it was obscene, and arrested Stanley under a Georgia statute proscribing the possession of pornographic material. Stanley was convicted, but upon appeal the Supreme Court reversed on the grounds that mere private possession of obscene matter, without intent to distribute or sell, cannot constitutionally be made a crime.[54]

Balance, 50 CALIF. L. REV. 821 (1962), and Mendelson, *The First Amendment and the Judicial Process: A Reply to Mr. Frantz,* 17 VAND. L. REV. 479 (1964).

[51] J.S. MILL, ON LIBERTY; A. MEIKLEJOHN, POLITICAL FREEDOM (1960).

[52] This, of course, is more easily advocated than effectuated. For a not very successful attempt at creating such a free speech doctrine, *see* A. MEIKLEJOHN, *supra* note 51, a revision of his earlier FREE SPEECH AND ITS RELATION TO SELF-GOVERNMENT (1948); *cf.* Professor Chaffee's review of Mr. Meiklejohn's first book, 62 HARV. L. REV. 891 (1949).

[53] 394 U.S. 557 (1969). *See generally* Katz, *Privacy and Pornography: Stanley v. Georgia,* 1969 SUP. CT. REV. 203.

[54] *See also In re* Klor, 64 Cal.2d 199 (1966).

Georgia contended that, since obscenity, under *Roth*, was not within the area of constitutionally protected speech, the states were free to deal with it in any way deemed necessary, just as they might deal with the possession of harmful, dangerous, or addictive drugs. In essence, Georgia argued, "If the state can protect the body of the citizen, may it not protect his mind?" The Court thought not. No matter how noble a purpose the moral uplifting of the citizenry, the Justices declared, the power of thought control was contrary to our constitutional heritage. For the Court, Mr. Justice Marshall admitted that *Roth* had held that pornography was not protected by the First Amendment, but he distinguished *Roth* and all the other obscenity cases on the grounds that they dealt with distribution. Although the state has a valid interest in dealing with the problem of obscenity, Marshall argued, that interest was not sufficient to make private possession of pornography, absent any intent to distribute, a crime. This for two reasons: (1) It is now well established that the Constitution protects the right to receive information and ideas; this right is fundamental to a free society and is not predicated on the social worth of the information or ideas received; (2) also fundamental to a free society is the right, except in very limited circumstances, to be free from governmental intrusion upon one's privacy. The Georgia statute violated, in the Court's opinion, both of these rights. Stanley was merely "asserting the right to read or observe what he pleases—the right to satisfy his intellectual and emotional needs in the privacy of his own home. . . . If the First Amendment means anything, it means that a State has no business telling a man, sitting alone in his own home, what books he may read or what films he may watch."[55]

Although the Court concluded by stating that its holding in *Stanley* in no way impaired its previous obscenity decisions, it was difficult to maintain that *Stanley* did not seriously undermine the rationale of those rulings. First, to hold that one has a right to receive ideas and information regardless of their social worth and then to reiterate those decisions upholding the regulation, predicated upon redeeming social value, of the distribution of certain ideas or information, seriously begs the quesiton. To say that the government cannot tell a man what he may read in his own home has critical implications for the regulation of dissemination. To be sure, the government retains the power to regulate public exhibitions or to control the acquisitions of the public library. But, if the state may not interfere with a man's right to receive information, how is

[55] 394 U.S. at 565. *See generally* Griswold v. Connecticut, 381 U.S. 479 (1965).

he to receive the information, at least in his own home, unless he has a right to acquire it? And the only way to acquire it is to purchase it.[56]

Secondly, when adults were involved, the Court retreated from its *Ginsberg* holding. The thrust of *Ginsberg* was to the effect that the absence of evidence with respect to the effect of obscenity might justify its regulation. But in *Stanley* the Court stated explicitly that the absence of any empirical basis for the proposition that exposure to obscenity leads to deviant sexual behavior or crimes of sexual violence could not serve as a justification for obscenity regulation. "Given the present state of knowledge," wrote Justice Marshall, "the State may no more prohibit mere possession of obscenity on the ground that it may lead to antisocial conduct than it may prohibit the possession of chemistry books on the ground that they may lead to the manufacture of homemade spirits."[57] The Court did observe that there might be other justifications for the prohibition of obscene literature, for example, the danger that obscenity might fall into the hands of children. But this still leaves open the question of whether there can be any controls placed upon the distribution of literautre to adults. A second possible justification for the regulation of the distribution of obscenity, which the Court noted, was the danger that obscene material might intrude upon the sensibilities or privacy of the general public. But at most this potential danger can justify only limited statutes controlling the unsolicited advertising either publicly or through the mails of films, books, and magazines.[58]

Finally, the *Stanley* Court refused to draw a line between the transmission of ideas and mere entertainment. The implications of this for bringing obscene expression within the protection of the First Amendment were enormous. If entertainment, though for no other purpose than diversion or escape from the complex pressures of the modern world, could not be declared to utterly lack redeeming social value, the two-level theory could no longer be validly applied to pornography. Under *Stanley's* reasoning, an adult's entertainment even if by pornographic pictures or literature, would possess a redeeming social value. If that were the case, the controls over sales of pornography to adults must then be measured by the standards of the First Amendment.[59]

[56]Ah! There's the rub. The *Stanley* holding considered in the light of the egalitarian tendency of the Warren Court's opinions raised the equal protection question: How can the state prevent the poor John Doe from paying his few dollars to view a film in the voluntary privacy of the movie theater, while the rich Stanley, who can afford to make his own films, is beyond the state's authority?

See United States v. Langford, 315 F.Supp. 472 (D. Minn. 1970) (using the mails to send

The Burger Court, however, has seriously and significantly recoiled from these logical imperatives of *Stanley*. In *United States v. Reidel*[60] and its companion case, *United States v. Thirty-Seven Photographs*,[61] the Burger Court chastised two lower federal courts which had indeed read *Stanley* to the effect that, if a citizen had a right to possess obscene matter in the privacy of his home, he must have the right to receive it voluntarily. While the major concern in *Thirty-Seven Photographs* was apparently not with obscenity regulation per se but rather with the Pandora's box affecting custom searches which would have been opened by extending *Stanley* beyond the border, *Reidel*, holding that a federal obscenity statute which prohibits mailing of obscene material was not unconstitutional as applied to willing adult recipients, represented an incredible judicial about-face. Speaking through Mr. Justice White, the *Reidel* majority chose to emphasize that *Stanley* had explicitly reaffirmed *Roth* and, thus, insisted that the trial courts had misread *Stanley*. But, as Mr. Justice Black pointed out in an excellent, though cryptic, dissent, the Court's opinion never satisfactorily explained exactly how or why the trial courts' interpretations of *Stanley* had been incorrect. Mr. Justice Marshall, concurring, made a valiant, albeit lame, effort to reconcile *Stanley* with *Reidel*, thereby saving his own handiwork in the former case. Marshall argued that the mail order distribution of pornography presented the possibility that the material might be received by children, a justification for obscenity censorship noted in *Stanley*, and, thus, that the two cases were compatible. Justice Marshall's

obscene matter cannot constitutionally be made an offense within the logical extension of the *Stanley* decision); United States v. Lethe, 312 F.Supp. 421 (S. D. Cal. 1970) (the right to possess implies the right to buy or receive obscene materials and the right to buy is meaningless unless someone has the right to sell).

See generally Brown v. Board of Education, 347 U.S. 483 (1954); Gideon v. Wainwright, 372 U.S. 335 (1963); Douglas v. California, 372 U.S. 352 (1963); Anders v. California, 386 U.S. 738 (1967).

See also A. BICKEL, THE SUPREME COURT AND THE IDEA OF PROGRESS (1970).

[57] 394 U.S. at 567.

[58] *See* Rowan v. U.S. Post Office Dept., 397 U.S. 728 (1970) (upholding private citizen's statutory right to terminate mailings from specified senders). *But cf.* Cohen v. California, 403 U.S. 15 (1971) (disturbance of the peace conviction for walking through corridor of public building wearing jacket bearing words "Fuck the Draft" could not be sustained consistent with First and Fourteenth Amendments).

[59] *See* Katz, *supra* note 53.

[60] 402 U.S. 351 (1971).

[61] 402 U.S. 363 (1971).

attempt to limit the *Reidel* holding to mail order distribution, however, did not appear to be warranted in light of Mr. Justice White's statement that

> The District Court gave *Stanley* too wide a sweep. To extrapolate from Stanley's right to have and peruse obscene material in the privacy of his own home a First Amendment right in Reidel to sell it to him would effectively scuttle *Roth*, the precise result that the *Stanley* opinion abjured. . . . The focus of [*Stanley*] was on freedom of mind and thought and on the privacy of one's home. It does not require that we fashion or recognize a constitutional right. . . to distribute or sell obscene materials.[62]

And, indeed, in *Paris Adult Theatre I v. Slaton*, the Burger majority forcefully reiterated its rejection of the proposition that *Stanley* had created either a First Amendment right to receive information or a general privacy right to the possession and use of obscene material by consenting adults.[63]

To reach its result in *Paris* the Court sought to distinguish between privacy in a place and privacy in a protected intimate relationship. The privacy right created in *Stanley* was, the Court argued, strictly limited to the private possession of obscene material in the home and was not to be extended to public accommodations, such as bars and theaters, where there could be no reasonable expectation of privacy.[64] In addition, the majority opinion,[65] authored by Mr. Chief Justice Burger, flatly rejected the contention that the state has no interest in telling adults what they

[62]*Id.* at 355-56.

[63]413 U.S. 49 (1973). In companion cases, the Court further strengthened the government's regulatory power. United States v. Orito, 413 U.S. 139 (1973), upheld a federal statute, 18 U.S.C. §1462 (1970), making it a crime to transport pornography across state lines on public carriers, even though the transporter intends to keep the material strictly for his private use. In United States v. Twelve 200-Ft. Reels of Super 8mm. Film, 413 U.S. 123 (1973), the Court decided that federal officials may constitutionally prohibit the importation of obscene matter, even if the importer claims that it is for his purely personal use, thereby sustaining 19 U.S.C. § 1305(a) (1970).

[64]The previous term in California v. LaRue, 409 U.S. 109 (1972), the Court had upheld a state administrative order banning live and filmed nudity and the simulation of sex acts in bars, even though the prohibited entertainment might have included expression protected by the First Amendment. In reaching this result, the Court based its decision upon state power to regulate liquor under the Twenty-First Amendment. But the critical, if only implicit, factor would appear to have been the Burger majority's attitude toward sexually explicit expression, not its attitude toward liquor regulation. The existence of the Twenty-First Amendment proved to be merely a fortuitous coincidence in *LaRue*.

[65]Mr Chief Justice Burger and Justices White, Blackmun, Powell, and Rehnquist formed the majority in *Paris* and in Miller v. California, 413 U.S. 15 (1973). Justices

may see or read. The abortion decisions, rendered only six months earlier, however, had recognized that certain private choices were constitutionally protected.[66] In order to confine the thrust of those cases, Mr. Chief Justice Burger argued that the constitutional right to privacy there recognized had been predicated upon the degree of intimacy of the relationship; the privacy protection extended to certain kinds of intimate personal relations such as familial, maternal, marital, procreative, and parental. But the private possession and use of obscene matter was not one of these constitutionally protected relationships. Government, therefore, might make morally neutral judgments about the effect of obscenity upon society and prohibit it, just as prostitution and drug use are prohibited, in the interest of maintaining order, morality, and "a decent society."[67]

The Chief Justice was not bothered by the argument that, because there is no proof that obscenity generates harmful societal effects, the government has no power to prohibit it. Rather, resorting to the approach taken in *Ginsberg*, he noted that, while no conclusive evidence existed demonstrating an actual and proximate connection between obscenity and anti-social sexual behavior, it could not be argued that it was irrational for a legislature to decide that the prohibition of obscenity was necessary to the realization of legitimate state interests. Burger, then, sought to canvass the various legitimate state interests which might be served by the regulation of pornography. The state might, the Chief Justice argued, be concerned for the tone and quality of life, particularly in the central city. It might wish to prevent the exposure of juveniles and unwilling adults to sexually explicit materials. It might wish to prevent the debasement and distortion of a "sensitive, key relationship of human existence, central to family life;"[68] or it might desire to prevent crimes of sexual violence.

Brennan, Marshall, and Stewart dissented in opinions by Mr. Justice Brennan. Mr. Justice Douglas filed a separate dissent in both cases.

[66]Roe v. Wade, 410 U.S. 113 (1973); Doe v. Bolton, 410 U.S. 179 (1973).

[67]413 U.S. at 69 & n. 13.

It remained unclear, however, whether acts between consenting adults, while not protected as part of intimate personal relationships, might not be constitutionally protected from governmental regulation if carried on within the private home. The result in *Paris* on this issue manifested a reluctance on the part of the Court to recognize a general right to sexual privacy, under which so-called "victimless crimes" involving consenting adults, such as prostitution or homosexuality, would be declared constitutionally beyond the power of the states to regulate, a reluctance also exhibited in Eisenstadt v. Baird, 405 U.S. 438 (1972).

[68]*Id.* at 63.

Two problems arise from Chief Justice Burger's discussion of legitimate state interests involved in the regulation of obscenity. First, many of these very same interests were explicitly rejected in *Stanley* as inappropriate bases for governmental regulation of expression, absent a showing of a causal linkage between obscenity and crime.[69] Yet *Paris* did not purport to overrule *Stanley*. Second, if obscene material is not protected by the First Amendment, why should there by any discussion of the legitimacy of the state's interests in its regulation? Such a discussion is relevant only when the Court is balancing a constitutionally protected private interest, such as the freedom of expression, against a postulated societal interest embodied in some statutory scheme. Burger's *Paris* opinion, thus, implicitly suggested that obscene expression was constitutionally protected expression. But, on the same day that it announced its decision in *Paris*, the Court reaffirmed its commitment to the two-level theory of the First Amendment. In *Miller v. California*, the Court explicitly noted that under *Roth* obscenity was to be presumed devoid of social merit and, thus, beyond the purview of the First Amendment.[70]

Despite its apparent contradiction of *Paris*, however, *Miller* thoroughly re-examined the tests which had been developed to define the obscene and concluded that they needed revision in favor of stricter but more concrete standards. Again speaking for the Court, Mr. Chief Justice Burger began by conceding that many state anti-obscenity statutes were so imprecisely drawn as to be constitutionally void for vagueness.[71] Nevertheless, he insisted that the requisite specificity could be obtained and even went so far as to make some suggestions of how a statute might be framed in order to appropriately describe the kinds of depictions of sexual conduct which were to be proscribed. He could offer, however, only two concrete examples of such precisely drawn statutes.[72] Ironically enough, in view of the *Miller* Court's more conservative approach to obscenity censorship, one of these two statutes was an Oregon law which limits criminal obscenity offenses to pandering and the sale of pornography to children and permits virtually anything else. The Court, however, indicated that in the future a work might be found obscene if

[69]*See The Supreme Court, 1972 Term*, 87 HARV. L. REV. 1, 173 (1973).
[70]413 U.S. 15 (1973).
[71]*See generally* Note, *The Void-For-Vagueness Doctrine in the Supreme Court*, 109 U. PA. L. REV. 67 (1960).
[72]ORE. LAWS ch. 743, art. 29, §§ 255-62 (1971); Hawaii Session Laws act 9, ch. 12, pt. 2, §§ 1210-16 (1972).

(a) . . . "the average person applying contemporary community standards" would find that the work, taken as a whole, appeals to the prurient interest . . . (b) . . . the work depicts or describes, in a patently offensive way, sexual conduct specifically defined by the applicable state law, and (c) . . . the work, taken as a whole, lacks serious literary, artistic, political, or scientific value.[73]

Each of these elements represented an alteration of or departure from previous standards for the determination of obscenity. Particularly in its acceptance of the idea that the trier of fact might apply standards of candor and offensiveness other than national standards in deciding if a given work is obscene, the Burger Court appeared to be motivated by a desire to relinquish its role as national censor. Given the posture in which *Miller* reached the Court, however, the majority held only that national standards were not required. Did this mean that the states were free to permit localities and municipalities to adopt their own community standards? Or would the Court require that each state adopt a uniform standard, in order to prevent an undesirable proliferation of local standards? The latter course would be almost as illogical as the national standard approach embraced in *Jacobellis*. Except for very small or relatively unpopulated states, state-wide standards of sexual morality are no more likely to exist than national standards. Indeed, in such demographically heterogenous states as California or New York, even different neighborhoods within a city may have different standards. For that reason, when he counselled in *Jacobellis* against the Court's becoming the ultimate censor, Mr. Chief Justice Warren urged local standards be the rule.[74] But a local-standard rule would be a nightmare

[73]413 U.S. at 24.
[74]387 U.S. 184, 202 (1964) (dissenting opinion).

[T]his Court [should] not establish itself as an ultimate censor, in each case . . . making an independent *de novo* judgment on the question of obscenity.

See generally Comment, *The Scope of Supreme Court Review in Obscenity Cases*, 1965 DUKE L.J. 596; Note, *The Application of a Local Standard or National Standard of Decency in the Use of the Roth-Memoirs Test*, 1971 WASH. U. L. Q. 691; Note, *The Geography of Obscenity's "Contemporary Community Standard,"* 8 WAKE FOREST L. REV. 81 (1971).

The decision in *Miller* had been anticipated by Mr. Justice Blackmun's first expression of opinion as a Supreme Court Justice. On the last day of the 1969 Term, Mr. Justice Blackmun went out of his way to dissent from the Court's per curiam reversal of a Minnesota obscenity conviction. Joined by Mr. Chief Justice Burger and Mr. Justice Harlan, Mr. Justice Blackmun wrote

I am not persuaded that the First and Fourteenth Amendments necessarily

for publishers, art exhibitors, and motion picture producers, a nightmare which could have seriously chilling effects upon expressive freedoms. Clearly, some works will be acceptable in some parts of a state—or of the nation—but unacceptable in others. A local variability rule would very probably force distributors to choose between circulating various versions of a given work, forfeiting part of their business, or tailoring their materials so as to be acceptable under the most regressive anti-obscenity law in the country. Any of these options would be expensive, and certain of the costs would be borne by society as well as by the distributors.

Sensitive to these difficulties, Justices Brennan, Stewart, and Marshall urged that virtually all pornography bans be scrapped as constitutionally unworkable. These dissenters, like the *Miller* majority, seemed to desire that the Court abandon its ultimate censorial role, but they differed with the majority over how this might best and most effectively be accomplished. Speaking for the dissenters, Mr. Justice Brennan, himself the chief architect of the constitutional law of obscenity regulation, candidly confessed that his handiwork had been largely a failure.[75] Undoubtedly this was so because Brennan and the Court had taken a wrong turn at the very beginning. By invoking the two-level theory in *Roth*, the Court had chosen to treat obscenity censorship as a definitional problem, rather than confronting the fundamental question of what empirical evidence justified such censorship. But the definition of obscenity had proven incredibly elusive and had necessarily involved the use of extremely vague concepts. Brennan now argued in *Miller* that, because they rested upon such indefinite terms, the various obscenity standards had themselves been unconstitutionally vague. They had failed to give those contemplating sexually explicit expression adequate notice of exactly what was and was not permissible. As a consequence, they had potentially had a chilling effect upon individual freedom. But, too, they had damaged the Court as an institution by undermining the predictability of judicial decision-making, while disproportionately increasing the Court's workload through the docketing of numerous and complex obscenity appeals. The only way out of this self-created conundrum, or so the *Miller* dissenters would have it, was to strike down all obscenity censorship laws as applied to willing adult audiences,

prescribe a national and uniform standard . . . of what each of our several states constitutionally may do to regulate obscene products within its borders.
Hoyt v. Minnesota, 399 U.S. 524 (1970).

[75]Mr. Justice Douglas also dissented, in a separate opinion, in which he continued to adhere to the notion that the First Amendment "absolutely" protects expression.

absent a showing of some clear and present social danger arising from
exposure to pornographic expression.

Sardonically, then, *Miller* represented that rarity in obscenity cases,
unanimous agreement among the Justices. Every member of the Court
agreed on one point: The Supreme Court's handing of obscenity cases
during the preceding decade and a half had been abysmally bankrupt.
The majority, however, continued to express confidence in the definitional approach to the problem. It was not, for Mr. Chief Justice Burger,
that the approach adopted in *Roth* and its progeny had been wrong but
that the definitions developed had not been sufficiently precise.

But, for a man so careful to tell the states to be precise in drawing up
their laws on obscenity, the Chief Justice was remarkably imprecise in
his own definition. The most significant departure from previous
obscenity law worked by the *Miller* opinion lay in its rejection of the
doctrine evolved by the Warren Court that a work must be "utterly
without redeeming social value" to be considered obscene.[76] Characterizing this doctrine as a "sharp break" with *Roth*,[77] which had assumed
obscenity beyond the constitutional pale, Chief Justice Burger held that
even materials with some redeeming social value might permissibly be
labelled obscene, if they were found to lack "serious literary, artistic,
political, or scientific value."[78] But in its efforts to provide basic
guidelines in the search for the serious the *Miller* majority was singularly
unenlightening. On the one hand, it appeared that, in its effort to
abdicate the office of national censor, the Court intended to defer to
juries in their determinations of offensiveness and pruriency. Thus, the
Court held that expert testimony would be unnecessary when the
allegedly obscene materials were introduced into evidence, since "hard
core pornography... can and does speak for itself."[79] On the other hand,
some measure of appellate review must be maintained, lest works of
serious value be proscribed under excessively prudish local standards. If
pruriency and offensiveness are to be determined under local standards,
however, is seriousness? Or should the serious value of a work be judged
by national standards? The Court offered no reply, other than to
emphasize that its ruling was directed at hard-core pornography and to

[76]*See* A Book Named "John Cleland's Memoirs of a Woman of Pleasure" v. Attorney
General of Massachusetts, 383 U.S. 413 (1966).

[77]413 U.S. at 21. *But see* Magrath, *supra* note 25, at 10 (*Memoirs* test implicit in *Roth's*
logic).

[78]*Id.* at 24.

[79]*Id.* at 56 n. 6.

urge that appellate courts broadly interpret the "serious value" test.[80] But the examples advanced by Mr. Chief Justice Burger were not especially lucid indicators of how the test should work. "A quotation from Voltaire in the flyleaf of a book will not constitutionally redeem an otherwise obscene publication," he wrote.[81] Yet the only example of an otherwise obscene publication which the Court cited as having serious value was a medical text![82] In between these two extremes, however, there lies a vast grey area. What, for example, is to be the legal status of Masters' and Johnson's *Human Sexual Response?* Immediately following, and no doubt encouraged by the ruling in *Miller,* Utah officials sought to prevent the exhibition of Bernardo Bertolucci's *Last Tango in Paris,* and Georgia authorities moved against the film *Carnal Knowledge.*[83] To be sure, a work need not be a classic or a textbook to have "serious literary, artistic, political, or scientific value." But, from the day it issued *Miller,* it was clear that, despite its best intentions to withdraw from the field, the Burger Court would not be able to rest upon that decision, for ambiguities in the majority opinion, as with so many other majority opinions in this area, assured that there would be new appeals.

In *Jenkins v. Georgia,* the Court refused to contenance the effort to prosecute the exhibition of *Carnal Knowledge.*[84] In essence, the Court told Americans that this was not the kind of film it had had in mind when it had drafted the *Miller* guidelines, but it could not tell them why. *Jenkins* did establish what had been only implicit in *Miller;* the standards by which the obscenity of a given work was to be judged need not be the standards of a hypothetical statewide community. Indeed, Mr. Justice Rehnquist, delivering the opinion of the Court, indicated that it was constitutionally permissible to instruct jurors to apply "contemporary community standards" without precisely defining the community. Each juror might rely upon his own understanding of the appropriate "community" whose contemporary standards of sexual discussion were to be the measure of the licit and the illicit. But, having so deferred to jurors' descretion and even though admitting that questions of offensiveness and pruriency were essentially questions of fact, the *Jenkins* Court held that the Georgia jury could not have found *Carnal Knowledge* to be pornographic, whatever standard it had employed. The fact

[80]*Id.* at 30.
[81]*Id.* at 25 n. 7.
[82]*Id.* at 26.
[83]*See* TIME, July 2, 1973, at 42.
[84]418 U.S. 153 (1974).

that this was exactly what the jury had found did not seem to trouble Mr. Justice Rehnquist. So, although the Court in *Miller* had been confident that hard-core pornography could and would speak for itself, in *Jenkins* the material in question spoke in a different tongue to the trial jury than to the Justices of the Supreme Court. However, in a companion case, *Hamling v. United States*,[85] the Burger majority recognized the obscene in an advertising brochure intended to promote *The Illustrated Presidential Report of the Commission on Obscenity and Pornography*, a cheap attempt to capitalize on the serious efforts of the Lockhart Commission, and sustained convictions for mailing and conspiring to mail pornography in violation of federal postal regulations.[86] The only readily manifest difference between *Carnal Knowledge* and the advertising brochure would appear to have been the exhibition of human genitalia in the latter.[87] By continuing case-by-case determinations of obscenity, second-guessing juries' findings of fact, the Court was admitting that it had not yet escaped from its role as the country's chief censor. Merely deciding *Jenkins* and *Hamling* constituted a concession by the Burger Court that *Miller's* attempt to clarify the law had failed.

Indeed, *Miller*, by uncritically endorsing *Roth*, rested upon and continued a basic logical confusion in the law of obscenity regulation. *Roth* (and *Miller*) proceeded from the premise that obscenity might be censored because it was without any redeeming social value. Yet *Roth* defined obscenity in such a way that obscene works might still be protected by the First Amendment, if they possessed "even the slightest redeeming social importance."[88] Similarly, in *Paris*, as already discussed, the same Court which rendered *Miller* discussed the social interests involved in censorship of the obscene. But the view that obscenity is unprotected by the First Amendment because possessed of no possible redemptive social value is inconsistent with such a discussion. A consideration of the societal interests justifying obscenity censorship is appropriate only if one assumes that obscenity is a First Amendment problem involving the weighing of the value of the speech against a potential societal harm. The approach taken in *Paris* was disingenuous in the extraordinary, for its refusal to recognize the First Amendment basis

---

[85]__U.S.__, 94 S.Ct. 2887 (1974).

[86]Justices White, Blackmun, and Powell and Chief Justice Burger joined an opinion by Mr. Justice Rehnquist. Mr. Justice Brennan, joined by Justices Stewart and Marshall, dissented. Mr. Justice Douglas dissented separately.

[87]*Compare* 94 S.Ct. at 2755 *with id.* at 2895.

[88]354 U.S. 476, 484 (1957).

of *Stanley* directly conflicted with the abortion decisions' mainifest acknowledgement that the right to privacy sustained in *Stanley* had been based upon a First Amendment rationale. [89]

Perhaps more than any other line of precedent the obscenity decisions argue that an abrupt change has taken place on the Supreme Court. Doctrinally, however, the Burger Court's approach is not necessarily inconsistent with that of the Warren Court, which never explicitly brought obscene expression within the protection of the First Amendment and which continued to treat the problem as definitional in nature. *Reidel*, *Thirty-Seven Photographs*, *Paris*, and *Miller* may at the most stand for the proposition that the "new" Court will be more tolerant of governmental actions aimed at the suppression of obscenity than was the "old" Court. Certainly, the Nixon appointees have replaced man who were in the majority in *Stanley*, and Mr. Chief Justice Burger's opinions in *Paris* and *Miller* produced those unique occurrences in obscenity cases, majority opinions for the Court. More than simple changes of personnel, however, may lie behind the intellectually incoherent shift from *Stanley* to *Miller*. Despite Mr. Justice Black's disclaimer in *Reidel* that he could not "believe [the Court] is bowing to popular passions and what it perceives to be the temper of the times,"[90] the Justices could hardly have been unaware of the public outcry which had greeted the recommendation of the President's Commission on Obscenity and Pornography that all governmental regulation of erotic expression be abolished.[91] The holdings in the Burger Court's obscenity decisions, then, may be better explained in terms of political prudence than of legal logic. But, while these decisions may indicate that obscenity is one subject area in which the Burger Court will differ from the Warren Court, they also suggest that there is no reason to believe that the Burger Court will provide any more rationally convincing or craftsmanlike opinions in this area than did the much criticized Warren Court.

[89]Roe v. Wade, 410 U.S. 113, 152 (1973).

[90]402 U.S. at 388.

[91]THE REPORT OF THE COMMISSION OF OBSCENITY AND PORNO-GRAPHY (1970).

On October 24, 1970, President Nixon, at the urging of 34 of the 43 Republican members of the United States Senate, totally repudiated the recommendations of the Commission on Obscenity and Pornography. The President labelled the Commission's Report as "morally bankrupt" and called upon every state in the Union to enact anti-obscenity legislation. *See* Los Angeles Times, Oct. 11, 1970, sec. A. at 8, col. 1; Los Angeles Times, Oct. 25, 1970, sec. A. at 1, col. 6.

Chapter 8
The Warren Court
in Retrospect

The late Professor Edward S. Corwin, dean of American constitutional scholars, once observed that "constitutional law has always a central interest to guard."[1] This central interest might change as Courts changed, but always, or so Corwin argued, the process remained the same—a particular value was elevated to a place of preeminence and militantly protected from popular interference by the Supreme Court through its power of constitutional interpretation. The Warren Court, far from being an exception to Corwin's rule, was virtually its archetype. Underlying the Court's policy-making were two dominant themes.[2]

The first of these was the centralization or nationalization of political problems and processes. The nationalization of the Bill of Rights,[3] the nationalization of the electoral process,[4] the nationalization of the legal standards for the determination of obscenity,[5] all of these were realized during the nearly two decades of the Warren Court's

---

[1]*Quoted in* Moreland, Book Review, 65 AM. POL. SCI. REV. 208 (1971).

[2]*See generally* P. KURLAND, POLITICS, THE CONSTITUTION, AND THE WARREN COURT (1970); L. JAFFE, ENGLISH AND AMERICAN JUDGES AS LAWMAKERS (1969); A. COX, THE WARREN COURT: CONSTITUTIONAL DECISION AS AN INSTRUMENT OF REFORM (1968).

[3]*See, e.g.,* Duncan v. Louisiana, 391 U.S. 145 (1968); Griffin v. California, 380 U.S. 609 (1965); Pointer v. Texas, 380 U.S. 400 (1965); Murphy v. Waterfront Comm'n, 378 U.S. 52 (1964); Malloy v. Hogan, 378 U.S. 1 (1964); Gideon v. Wainwright, 372 U.S. 335 (1963); Ker v. California, 374 U.S. 23 (1963); Mapp v. Ohio, 367 U.S. 643 (1961).

[4]*See, e.g.,* Reynolds v. Sims, 377 U.S. 533 (1964); Wesberry v. Sanders, 376 U.S. 1 (1964); Baker v. Carr, 369 U.S. 186 (1962). *See generally* R. CLAUDE, THE SUPREME COURT AND THE ELECTORAL PROCESS (1970).

[5]Jacobellis v. Ohio, 378 U.S. 184 (1964).

tenure. "To what extent the Supreme Court . . . caused [this] centralization rather than acquiesced in it is a question that does not produce a
ready answer."[6] Indeed, the evolution of the American business corporation has probably had more to do with the nationalization of political
issues, the centralization of governmental power, and the decline of
federalism than all of the Supreme Court decisions of the last forty years
wrapped together and multiplied to the *nth* power.[7] But, for purposes of
analyzing the Warren Court, what is more important about this
particular aspect of the Court's decision-making is that it was not unique
to the Warren Court. Over its history, the Court's tendency has been to
be a nationalizing agency. The Warren Court may have moved farther
and faster in that process than some prior Courts, but in this regard it
may merely have been mirroring the effects of rapid technological
advances in mid-twentieth century America, such as the development of
television, which had a distinctly nationalizing impact upon the character of American life. Whatever its acceleration rate, the Warren Court's
nationalist tendencies did not differentiate it from earlier Courts.

What did distinguish the Warren Court was a second characteristic
common to its decisions—a vigorous concern for, almost an obsession
with, the value of equality. The desegregation cases, the reapportionment decisions, the criminal defendants' rights cases all removed from
the ambit of state power matters which previously had been considered
to be peculiarly within the jurisdiction of the states. But, in doing so, each
of these lines of cases proceeded from a militant egalitarianism.[8]

---

[6]P. KURLAND, *supra* note 2, at 56.

[7]*See* A. MILLER, THE SUPREME COURT AND AMERICAN CAPITALISM
(1968).

[8]The Warren Court, however, was curiously partisan, arbitrary, and inequitable in its
application of the principle of equality as a constitutional standard by which to measure
governmental actions. The old, laissez-faire Court's invocation of the Due Process Clauses,
of course, had done little to avail groups, such as criminal defendants, with whom the
Justices did not identify; *see, e.g.,* Twining v. New Jersey, 211 U.S. 78 (1908); West v.
Louisiana, 194 U.S. 258 (1904); Maxwell v. Dow, 176 U.S. 581 (1900); O'Neil v. Vermont,
144 U.S. 323 (1892); Hurtado v. California, 110 U.S. 516 (1884). So, too, the Warren Court
was unmoved by pleas for equal treatment emanating from business concerns; *see, e.g.,*
Two Guys v. McGinley, 366 U.S. 582 (1961); McGowan v. Maryland, 366 U.S. 420 (1961).
"In the area of economic regulation and taxation, the Court almost invariably sustained the
state regulation." P. KURLAND, *supra* note 2, at 163. *See* Walters v. St. Louis, 347 U.S.
231 (1954); Allied Stores v. Bowers, 358 U.S. 522 (1959); Youngstown Sheet & Tube Co. v.
Bowers, 358 U.S. 534 (1959); Safeway Stores, Inc. v. Oklahoma Retail Grocers Ass'n, 360
U.S. 344 (1959); Ferguson v. Skrupa, 372 U.S. 726 (1963); Florida Avocado Growers v.
Paul, 373 U.S. 132 (1963); Fireman v. Chicago, R.I. & P.R. Co., 393 U.S. 129 (1968). In only

Problems and processes had been nationalized by previous Courts, but never in the pursuit of this value. Almost from its very first decision, however, the Warren Court's attention revolved around equality and its realization in American society. From *Brown v. Board of Education*[9] through *Daniel v. Paul*,[10] the civil rights cases were always, explicitly, uncomprisingly directed toward the goal of equality.

> Never in the Court's history—not in Marshall's day or any other—did the Court establish its objectives and march so steadfastly toward them as did the Warren Court in its civil rights litigation.[11]

Much the same could be said about the economic discrimination cases[12] and the reapportionment decisions.[13] Less readily perceived but no less real was the egalitarian concern underlying the criminal defendants' rights decisions.

> The Court's concern with criminal procedure can be understood only in the context of the struggle for civil rights. ... Concern with civil rights almost inevitably required attention to the rights of defendants in criminal cases. It is hard to conceive of a Court that would accept the challenge of guaranteeing the rights of Negroes and other disadvantaged groups to equality before the law and at the same time do nothing to ameliorate the invidious discrimination between rich and poor which existed in the criminal process. It would have been equally anomalous for such a Court to ignore the clear evidence that members of disadvantaged groups generally bore the brunt of most unlawful police activity.

> If the Court's espousal of equality before the law was to be credible, it required not only that the poor Negro be permitted to vote and to attend a school with whites, but also that he and other disadvantaged individuals be able to exercise, as well as possess, the same rights as the affluent white when suspected of crime.[14]

Similarly, the decisions under the religion clauses of the First Amendment sought to compel equality. Certain of the free exercise decisions "may be viewed as resting on the simple proposition that no person may

a single major tax case did the corporate taxpayer prevail, WHYY, Inc. v. Glassboro, 393 U.S. 117 (1968).

[9]347 U.S. 483 (1954).

[10]395 U.S. 298 (1969).

[11]P. KURLAND, *supra* note 2, at 73.

[12]*E.g.*, Shapiro v. Thompson, 394 U.S. 618 (1969); Sniadach v. Family Finance Corp., 395 U.S. 337 (1969).

[13]*E.g.*, Reynolds v. Sims, 377 U.S. 533 (1964); Wesberry v. Sanders, 376 U.S. 1 (1964); Baker v. Carr, 369 U.S. 186 (1962).

[14]Pye, *The Warren Court and Criminal Procedure*, 67 MICH. L. REV. 249, 256-57 (1968).

be discriminated against on religious grounds,"[15] and the school prayer cases in particular were based upon the tacit premise that the First Amendment guarantees not simply religious tolerance but rather equality of religious freedom.[16]

In pursuit of these egalitarian values, the Warren Court increasingly came to view the Constitution not simply as a prophylactic, limiting governmental injustice and discrimination, but as a mandate, requiring positive state action to prevent discrimination and injustice. "The sense that government has affirmative responsibilities for human rights and especially for the elimination of inequalities, whether racial or otherwise, [was] one of the dominant forces" in the Warren Court's constitutional interpretation.[17] It was, however, a force reflective of a more thoroughgoing change in American social philosophy.

> Contemporary society accepts the political principle that the modern State owes its citizens various obligations—a growing economy, jobs, education, medical care, old-age assistance and so forth. That the principle has been extended to human rights is hardly surprising. Since human rights are secured by the Constitution, it [was only] natural to import that part of the political principle into constitutional law.[18]

As part of its efforts to create a doctrine of affirmative state responsibility, the Warren Court came very close to establishing the principle that every socially perceived wrong should have a legal remedy.[19] Perhaps no other facet of the Warren Court's policy-making so simply and clearly illustrated the advances which have been made in Anglo-American jurisprudence as did this developing principle of American law. It was certainly a far cry from the medieval English legal maxim, "No writ; no remedy."[20]

One small problem, however, did confront the Warren Court in its campaign for equality. Its egalitarian bent could not "find specific justification in the language or history of the Constitution as originally framed. . . ."[21] The Founding Fathers had some—but little—equalitarian intent. Rather, it appears that they intended that mobility, both social

---

[15]Abington v. Schemp, 374 U.S. 203 (1963); Engel v. Vitale, 370 U.S. 421 (1962). *See* P. Kurland, *supra* note 2, at 166 & n. 214; Katz & Southerland, *Religious Pluralism and the Supreme Court*, 96 DAEDALUS 180, 183 (1967).

[16]Kauper, *The Warren Court: Religious Liberty and Church-State Relations*, in THE WARREN COURT: A CRITICAL ANALYSIS 82 (Sayler, Boyer, & Gooding eds. 1969).

[17]A. COX, *supra* note 2, at 35.

[18]*Id.* at 35-36.

[19]*See* Reynolds v. Sims, 377 U.S. 533, 624 (1964) (Harlan, J., dissenting).

[20]*See* F. MAITLAND, THE FORMS OF ACTION AT COMMON LAW (1909).

[21]P. KURLAND, *supra* note 2 at 105.

and geographic, should be the dominant principle of liberty in America.[22] All men were to be free, free to be unequal. Subsequently, of course, the Framers of the Fourteenth Amendment did indeed place the doctrine of equality within the Constitution. But the Warren Court itself found the history and intent of that provision too ambiguous to serve as an appropriate guide for judicial decision.[23] Nevertheless, within a decade the Court increasingly purported to find authoritative guidance in the words or history of the Equal Protection Clause, the way literary scholars claim to find identity clues in Shakespearean anagrams.[24]

1964, in fact, may be viewed as a constitutional watershed, marking a transition from the early, reformist Warren Court to the later, radical Warren Court. It was a year which saw the Court move beyond the logical imperatives of *Baker* to the adoption of the "one man, one vote" standard and its dogmatic application to bicameral legislatures.[25] It was the year in which *Escobedo* was decided, moving the Court more deeply than ever before into the processes of criminal investigation. And it was a year which witnessed the collapse of the Court's previous unanimity in the handling of the convictions of civil rights demonstrators.[26] After

---

[22]*See* 1 M. FARRAND, THE RECORDS OF THE FEDERAL CONVENTION OF 1787, at 398 (1966 ed.) (remarks of Charles Pinckney). *See also* Roche, *Equality in America: The Expansion of a Concept,* 43 N.C.L. REV. 249 (1965); Roche, *American Liberty: An Examination of the "Tradition" of Freedom,* in ORIGINS OF AMERICAN POLITICAL THOUGHT 15 (J. Roche, ed. 1967).

[23]Brown v. Board of Education, 347 U.S. 483 (1954). *See also* Bickel, *The Original Understanding and the Segregation Decision,* 69 HARV. L. REV. 1 (1955).

[24]*See e.g.,* Lewis, *The Sit-In Cases: Great Expectations,* 1963 SUP. CT. REV. 101; Paulsen, *The Sit-In Cases of 1964: "But Answer Came There None,"* 1964 SUP. CT. REV. 137; Van Alstyne, *The Fourteenth Amendment, the "Right" to Vote, and the Understanding of the Thirty-ninth Congress,* 1965 SUP. CT. REV. 33; Kelly, *Clio and the Court: An Illicit Love Affair,* 1965 Sup. Ct. REV. 119; Casper, *Jones v. Mayer: Clio, Bemused and Confused Muse,* 1968 SUP. CT. REV. 89.

[25]Reynolds v. Sims, 377 U.S. 533 (1964).

[26]Bell v. Maryland, 378 U.S. 226 (1964).

In the succeeding years, Mr. Justice Black was to take vigorous exception to some of the Court's more libertarian assaults upon precedent, leading to charges that in his later years Black "switched" and became a conservative. *See e.g.,* Bell v. Maryland, 378 U.S. 226, 318 (1964) (Black, J., dissenting); Griswold v. Connecticut, 381 U.S. 479, 507 (1965) (Black, J., dissenting); Tinker v. DesMoines School District, 393 U.S. 503, 515 (1969) (Black, J., dissenting); Shapiro v. Thompson, 394 U.S. 618, 644 (1969) (Warren, C.J., & Black, J., dissenting). More careful analysis, however, suggests that for better or worse Mr. Justice Black remained consistent to the end; it was the court majority which shifted. *See generally* Yarbrough, *Justices Black and Douglas: The Judicial Function and the Scope of Constitutional Liberties,* 1973 DUKE L.J. 441; Snowiss, *The Legacy of Justice Black,* 1973 SUP. CT. REV. 187.

1964, equality became a constitutional first freedom, "a goal—a value—in itself that . . . [needed] little or no justification."[27] For many, "equality" became perhaps as great a shibboleth as "private property" had once been. And, as in the heyday of William Graham Sumner and Stephen Field, the Supreme Court was the Knight Protector of this dominant value.[28] To attack the Warren Court was to invite opprobrium in many circles, because criticism of the Court was equated with criticism of the value it pursued.

But the wisdom or unwisdom of the principle of equality was not necessarily at issue.[29] What was disturbing for many thoughtful Americans was not the Warren Court's dominant value but the process by which it sought to protect and extend that value. While the Warren Court's commitment to equality was unique in the history of American judicial politics, the Court's thought processes and methods of decision were uncomfortably familiar. Just as the laissez-faire Court, the Warren Court adopted a constitutional generalization and fashioned it into a rigid, substantive bar to legislation. Although the old Court had used the Due Process Clause and the Warren Court relied, for the most part, upon the Equal Protection Clause, the process remained the same, for as Professor Louis Jaffe has pointed out both clauses share a common characteristic. They "are as expansible as a giant accordion," and the Warren Court played "upon the instrument with startling virtuosity."[30] The creation of a double standard of equal protection review,[31] requiring "compelling" considerations of public policy to justify legislative classifications touching upon "fundamental" interests, could only be

[27]P. KURLAND, *supra* note 2, at 99.

[28]*See generally* R. McCLOSKEY, AMERICAN CONSERVATISM IN THE AGE OF ENTERPRISE, 1865-1910 (1951).

[29]*See generally* A. GRIMES, EQUALITY IN AMERICA (1964).

[30]L. JAFFE, *supra* note 2, at 2. *See also* Schaefer, Book Review, 84 HARV. L. REV. 1558 (1971).

The musical metaphor has been a popular one with Warren Court critics, although they have differed in their assessments of the Court's ability. Kurland, for example, finds the Court to have been less of a virtuoso than does Professor Jaffe.

It behooves any critic of the Court's performance to close on a note reminiscent of the wall plaque of frontier times: "Don't shoot the piano player. He's doing his best." It is still possible, however, to wish that he would stick to the piano and not try to be a one-man band. It is too much to ask that he take piano lessons.

Kurland, *Equal in Origin and Equal in Title to the Legislative and Executive Branches of the Government*, 78 HARV. L. REV. 143, 176 (1964).

[31]*See Developments in the Law—Equal Protection*, 82 HARV. L. REV. 1065 (1969).

characterized as "substantive equal protection."[32] But, as a standard for judicial policy-making, the "equality" of substantive equal protection shared the defect of the "due process" of substantive due process; fundamentality, like beauty, is very much in the eye of the beholder. The *ad hoc* nature of judicial determinations of which among various interests are fundamental was precisely the problem raised by substantive due process.[33] Such a standard is only as ascertainable as are the sensibilities of the Justices of the Supreme Court—and only as constant. Nevertheless, the decisional premise that in order to justify certain of its regulations or classifications a state must demonstrate a "compelling interest" was a continuing theme of the Warren Court. Often present in the anti-discrimination cases,[34] the doctrine reached a zenith of sorts in *Shapiro v. Thompson.*[35] But the "compelling interest" rationale had a way of appearing in cases not ostensibly involving equal protection issues. In *Sherbert v. Verner,*[36] for example,

> the Court emphasized that only a *compelling interest* warrants a restriction on religious liberty, and the case [made] clear that this standard [was] equally applicable to so-called indirect restraints on religious liberty.[37]

Clearly, though, the compelling state interest doctrine conflicted with the traditional presumption of statutory constitutionality. Equally clearly it vested the Court with a super-legislative power to settle questions of degree. Under the doctrine, a challenged statute might be constitutionally valid only if justified by a "compelling" interest. But compelling to whom? Presumably, when legislatures pass bills and executives sign them into law, they express their own opinion as to the "compelling" nature of the public interest involved, and the lesson of 1937 was that that expression should be given great, if not dispositive, weight. As a judicial vehicle for invalidating legislative restraints which a majority of the Justices find personally odious, the "compelling state

[32]*See* Karst & Horowitz, Reitman v. Mulkey: *A Telphase of Substantive Equal Protection,* 1967 SUP. CT. REV. 39; Mendelson, *From Warren to Burger: The Rise and Decline of Substantive Equal Protection,* 66 AM. POL. SCI. REV. 1226 (1972); A. BICKEL, THE SUPREME COURT AND THE IDEA OF PROGRESS (1970).

[33]*See* Meltzer v. C. Buck LeCraw & Co., 402 U.S. 954, 957-58 (1971) (Black, J., dissenting from denial of certiorari).

[34]*E.g.,* Harper v. Virginia State Board of Elections, 383 U.S. 663 (1966); McLaughlin v. Florida, 379 U.S. 184 (1964). *See generally* note 31 *supra.*

[35]394 U.S. 618 (1969).

[36]374 U.S. 398 (1963).

[37]Kauper, *supra,* note 16, at 84 (emphasis added).

interest" doctrine may in time take its place alongside the laissez-faire Court's efforts to distinguish between "direct" and "indirect" effects upon commerce or to identify "noxious products."[38]

Many years ago, at the height of substantive due process, James Bradley Thayer, borrowing from the Great Chief Justice,[39] argued that the Constitution does not impose any one specific option upon a legislature but leaves open a range of choices. Whatever is rational, contended Thayer, is constitutional.[40] The two-tier approach to equal protection review did not absolutely reject Thayer's test, but it did add a rather serious qualification to it. Under "active" review, even rational choices, such as the apportionment plan in *Lucas*,[41] might be barred by the Equal Protection Clause, if they restricted certain favored freedoms. It is, of course, true that Thayer himself excepted legislative choices which, though rational, were explicitly prohibited by the Constitution. But what is specific about the Equal Protection Clause? Surely, it is as imprecise, open-ended, and vague as the Due Process Clauses,[42] and the fundamentality of interests or the suspect nature of classifications still largely turns upon the Justices' subjective judgments.[43] It was in an effort to circumvent the decisions of a Court which regarded the Due Process Clauses, much as the Warren Court regarded the Equal Protection Clause, as a specific, substantive bar to legislation that Thayer formulated his rule of rationality. Moreover, if the Equal Protection Clause requires something more than mere rationality, how could it be interpreted to permit irrationality, as it surely was in *Fortson v. Morris*, where the Warren Court found it constitutional for an admittedly malapportioned Georgia legislature to bypass the popular choice for governor and choose Lester Maddox?[44] And, if the Equal Protection Clause constitutes a specific prohibition upon otherwise rational legisla-

---

[38]*E.g., compare* United States v. E. C. Knight Co., 156 U.S. 1 (1895), *with In re* Debs, 158 U.S. 564 (1895); *compare* Hammer v. Dagenhart, 247 U.S. 251 (1918), *with* Brooks v. United States, 267 U.S. 432 (1925).

[39]*See* McCulloch v. Maryland, 4 Wheat. 316 (1819).

[40]Thayer, *The Origin and Scope of the American Doctrine of Constitutional Law*, 7 HARV. L. REV. 129 (1893).

[41]Lucas v. Forty-fourth General Ass'y of Colorado, 377 U.S. 713 (1964).

[42]*See* L. Jaffe, *supra* note 2, at 2; A. BICKEL, *supra* note 32; P. KURLAND, *supra* note 2.

[43]*But cf. The Supreme Court, 1972 Term*, 87 HARV. L. REV. 1, 114 n. 52 (1973).

[44]385 U.S. 231 (1966).

tion, why doesn't the more specific First Amendment? Yet, this was not the view expressed in *Ginsberg*.[45]

What seems to have been a thread running throughout the Warren Court's decisions was a profound contempt for legislative agencies of government. Indeed, perhaps the most important characteristic of the Warren Court's decisions as a whole was a general disparagement not of liberal, democratic results but of the democratic process, especially as represented by the legislative process. The Court apparently had little or no confidence that legislatures and the legislative process would produce "right" results.[46] In this context, Mr. Chief Justice Warren's opinion in *Reynolds v. Sims* is revealing. Representative government was seen there as merely the best of a bad bargain, the least noxious of a number of repellent alternatives. Any concept of legislative leadership was completely disparaged. In its disregard of group interests, the opinion implicitly manifested a distaste for group interest politics—the stuff of the American legislative process. Equality was achieved by reducing people to the lowest common denominator, faceless ciphers.[47]

It is of no small significance that, as Professor Philip Kurland has observed, the Warren Court's decisions centralizing political power largely meant centralizing power in the Court.[48] When it took power from the states over racial relations, legislative apportionment, or criminal justice procedures, the Warren Court assumed that power for itself. Even when it was willing to share power with the Congress, as in civil rights, the Court tendered "power under the enabling clauses of the Thirteenth, Fourteenth, and Fifteenth Amendments, as if it were the Court's to grant...."[49] Nor did it quail, in *Wesberry v. Sanders*, at raising serious doubts concerning the constitutional validity of one house of the Congress of the United States.[50] Only the Presidency escaped this arrogation of power to the judiciary. In fact, the Warren Court assisted to

[45]Ginsberg v. New York, 390 U.S. 629 (1968).

[46]This tendency of distrust was carried over into the Burger era and applied to administrative agencies in Alexander v. Holmes County Board of Education, 396 U.S. 19 (1969), in which the Court in essence severed its alliance with the Department of Health, Education and Welfare in the cause of desegregation. *See The Supreme Court, 1969 Term*, 84 HARV. L. REV. 1, 34 (1970).

[47]*See* Reynolds v. Sims, 377 U.S. 533, 624 (1964) (Harlan, J. dissenting).

[48]*See* P. KURLAND, *supra* note 2, at 86.

[49]*Id.* at 87.

[50]376 U.S. 1, 20 (1964) (Harland, J., dissenting).

a very great degree in the continued expansion of the powers of the modern President.

> The . . . Court in its civil rights rulings and its requirement of a wholesale revision of the districts of the House of Representatives, . . . clearly befriended the cause of the continuously strong Presidency.[51]

This outcome may not have been foreseen, but perhaps aiding the President was not a wholly unwelcome consequence for the Warren Court either.

Similarly, the possible ultimate effect of *Avery v. Midland County* was consistent with a perceived distrust of legislatures. Extension of the "one man, one vote" standard to local governments might encourage the removal of these agencies from the electoral process altogether and the establishment of some sort of appointive system, converting the selection process in these units into something approximating federal judicial recruitment. It is hard to suppress the feeling that something more than the electoral principle lay behind the apportionment decisions when none of them concerned elective *judiciaries*.

Fundamental to this suspicion of legislatures as governing agencies was the Warren Court's revival of the doctrine of fundamental, unenumerated rights. Whether employed as substantive due process or as substantive equal protection, the doctrine of unenumerated rights, when co-opted by the Court and joined to its position as authoritative constitutional interpreter, has always proven to vest the Justices with unlimited and ultimately unhealthy discretion in their decisions concerning American social and political problems. During the first third of this century, the doctrine, as revealed through the vagaries of the Due Process Clauses, was used by an economically conservative Court to thwart any efforts at the public regulation of property and labor.[52] After 1937, this scheme of judicial analysis was repudiated insofar as economic regulation was concerned and for a brief while with respect to other areas as well.[53] Indeed, it was in an effort to confine the ambit of judicial choice that Mr. Justice Black espoused his theory of the "incorporation" of the

---

[51]L. KOENIG, THE CHIEF EXECUTIVE 406 (1964). *See also* P. KURLAND, *supra* note 2, at ch. 2.

[52]*See* Tyson v. Banton, 273 U.S. 418 (1927); Adkins v. Children's Hospital, 261 U.S. 525 (1923); Coppage v. Kansas, 236 U.S. 1 (1915); Lochner v. New York, 198 U.S. 45 (1905).

[53]*See* Nebbia v. New York, 291 U.S. 502 (1934); West Coast Hotel v. Parrish, 300 U.S. 379 (1937). *See generally* McCloskey, *Economic Due Process and The Supreme Court: An Exhumation and Reburial*, 1962 SUP. CT. REV. 34.

Bill of Rights into the Fourteenth Amendment.[54] But, although he was successful in applying most of the Bill's guarantees to the states,[55] Black's victory was ultimately an illusory one, for virtually total "incorporation" still failed to confine judicial discretion. This was amply illustrated by the result in *Griswold v. Connecticut.*[56] *Griswold* was the last in a series of cases attempting to challenge Connecticut's statute prohibiting the use of contraceptives. Griswold, as Executive Director of the Planned Parenthood League of Connecticut, had been convicted, along with a physician, as an accessory in abetting a violation of the anti-use statute by having counselled married couples in the use of birth control devices. Although it had avoided earlier opportunities to pass on the merits of the Connecticut legislation by invoking the doctrines of standing and ripeness,[57] the Court now found the anti-contraceptive statute to intrude upon constitutionally protected rights. The case, however, is a classic of intra-Court dissension, hostility, and innuendo. All of the Justices, including the two dissenters,[58] found the Connecticut statute to be objectionable, and all agreed that the Fourteenth Amendment protected those rights and only those rights which are fundamental. But they differed sharply as to how one goes about discovering fundamental rights.

The seven-man majority split four ways, with no opinion commanding the signatures of more than three members. Mr. Justice Douglas, whose opinion, though labelled the opinion of the Court, was joined only by Justice Clark, suggested that the Fourteenth Amendment embodied the Bill of Rights plus some cognate rights not explicitly mentioned in the Constitution.[59] For Douglas, the specific guarantees of the Bill of Rights had penumbrae, formed by emantions from those guarantees, which help to give them life and substance. Constitutional rights could not, Mr. Justice Douglas argued, be confined to constitutional specifics. In view of the increasing necessity of privacy, the enforcement of the Connecticut statute, at least against married couples, would infringe upon a right to privacy protected by penumbrae of the First, Third, Fourth, and Fifth Amendments. In concurrence, Mr. Justice Harlan objected to the assumption that the statute could not be prohibited by the Fourteenth

[54]*E.g.*, Adamson v. California, 322 U.S. 46, 68 (1947) (Black, J., dissenting).

[55]*See* ch. IV *supra* at pp. 134-53.

[56]381 U.S. 479 (1965).

[57]Poe v. Ullman, 367 U.S. 497 (1961); Tileston v. Ullman, 318 U.S. 44 (1943). *See generally* ch. I *supra* at pp. 17-18.

[58]Justices Black and Stewart filed dissents.

[59]381 U.S. 479.

Amendment unless it were found to violate some specific or penumbral right assured by the Bill of Rights.[60] The Due Process Clause of the Fourteenth Amendment, he asserted, was robust, vigorous and capable of standing on its own constitutional two feet. The proper question presented by the case was whether the Connecticut statute infringed upon basic values implicit in the concept of ordered liberty, and the proper answer to that question was, for Harlan, "Yes." Therefore, the statute was unconstitutional. While both Douglas's "penumbra" theory and Harlan's "order liberty" approach had some basis in precedent, however, it was Mr. Justice Goldberg's rather awkward injection of the Ninth Amendment into the controversy that was most interesting.[61] That amendment's language seems clearly to indicate that the rights of the people are not to be found solely within the specifics of the constitutional text.[62]

But what is to be the guide to discovering the substantive content of these unenumerated but fundamental rights? As Mr. Justice Black opined in dissent, if the Ninth Amendment means anything, it must mean natural law.[63] For Black, the use of any such approach would allow Supreme Court Justices to strike down legislation enacted by the people's elected representatives which a majority of the Justices found to be offensive, uncivilized, unreasonable, or unwise. But these qualities, argued Black, noting that he too was shocked by the Connecticut statute and its enforcement implications, should not be confused with unconstitutionality. The use of Douglas's penumbral approach, Goldberg's Ninth Amendment reasoning, or Harlan's due process theory would turn the Supreme Court into a band of Platonic guardians, having an ultimate veto power over the democratic process. Mr. Justice Black's concern, however, was not shared by many members of the Warren majority. Rather, as the *Harvard Law Review* observed, "The prime importance of *Griswold* . . . is as evidence that, despite all the attacks that have been leveled at fundamental rights-due process as a method of judicial review, hydra-like it has always reappeared."[64]

Increasingly during Mr. Chief Justice Warren's tenure, the Court was unwilling to be bound by the specific enumerations of the Bill of Rights.

[60]*Id.* at 499.
[61]*Id.* at 486.
[62]"The enumeration in the Constitution, of certain rights, shall not be construed to deny or disparage others retained by the people." U.S. CONST. amend. IX.
[63]381 U.S. at 507.
[64]84 HARV. L. REV. 1525, 1529 (1971).

Among the unenumerated but "fundamental" rights discovered by the Warren Court to be constitutional bars to legislative policy-making were the right to travel abroad,[65] the right to travel interstate,[66] and the freedom to marry.[67] Nor were the Justices circumspect about what they were doing. Mr. Justice Brennan, for example, speaking of the role of the Supreme Court as a protector of individual rights, uttered this immortal note of Warren Court self-congratulation:

> . . . (L)aw is again coming alive as a living process responsive to changing human needs . . . Perhaps some of you may detect, as I think I do, the philosophy of St. Thomas Aquinas in the New Jurisprudence. Call it a resurgence if you will of concepts of natural law—but no matter.[68]

But no matter?!?!?! That is certainly a cavalier way to deal with a major issue in the history of American constitutional jurisprudence. It dismisses out-of-hand the most thoughtful criticisms of Hand, Holmes, Brandeis, and Pound—to name but the dead. Nevertheless, it is indicative of the manner in which the Warren Court majority's thought processes operated.

Adoption of the doctrine of unenumerated constitutional rights, however, involves a special judicial burden. "Because the fundamental rights-due process technique potentially allows courts so much discretion, judges who use it must take care to set self-imposed limits in the form of reasoned and clear statements of the interests that are being protected."[69] While opinion craftsmanship is to be desired of all Supreme Court pronouncements,[70] it is particularly important that a Court which embraces the natural law concept of unenumerated, fundamental rights produce opinions of *exceptional* clarity, candor, and persuasiveness. Yet it is generally conceded that this was the Warren Court's greatest weakness.[71] Its opinions do not parse well.[72] "Indeed, one can be among the ardent admirers of the Court and still concede the defects of its opinion writing."[73] Thus, Professor Kauper, a friendly critic, was moved to lament:

[65]*See* Aptheker v. Secretary of State, 378 U.S. 500 (1964); Kent v. Dulles, 357 U.S. 116 (1958).
[66]Shapiro v. Thompson, 394 U.S. 618 (1969).
[67]Loving v. Virginia, 338 U.S. 1 (1967).
[68]Brennan, *Extension of the Bill of Rights to the States*, 44 J. URB. L. 11, 22-23 (1966).
[69]84 HARV. L. REV. at 1531.
[70]*See* ch. I *supra* at pp. 25-29.
[71]*See* notes 2 and 24 *supra*.
[72]*See* A. BICKEL, *supra* note 32, at ch. 3.
[73]P. KURLAND, *supra* note 2, at 91.

> Leaving aside the results, one may venture criticism of the way in which the Court handled some of the cases.[74]

Although Kauper was speaking of the religion cases, his sentiment could apply across the entire spectrum of the Warren Court's decision-making. One of the characteristics shared by the reapportionment, desegregation, obscenity, and criminal defendants' rights rulings was the absence of an adequate rationale for the conclusions reached.

For a jurisprudence of reason and reflection, the Warren Court substituted a jurisprudence of words and slogans. The style of legal argument adopted by many members of the Court often seemed to be one of a search for quotable words and phrases.[75]

> These hyperbolic images, these appeals to the ultimates of free government, this substitution of wholesale dogmatic assertion for a reasoned consideration of the opposing interests illustrate a disturbing aspect of the activist mentality. It is as if the invoked concepts were completely released from their moorings in the soil either of historic or current reality. The slightest invasion of an interest is confounded with the worst. The most emotive sentiments are evoked by the most trivial occasions. The sense of proportion is forgotten.[76]

Even such a staunch supporter of the Warren Court as Professor Kalven has recognized, perhaps unwittingly, the Court's tendency toward the creation of a jurisprudence of words.

> What catches the eye is the daring, unconventional selection of adjectives. . . The Court is interested enough to be minting contemporary epigrams. . .[77]

Unfortunately, that seems to be about as far as the Court's interest went. When the highest praise the Supreme Court can evoke from a sympathetic critic is occasioned not by the logical consistency of its opinions or the intellectual rigor of its principles but by its choice of adjectives, something would seem to be amiss.

It might be asked why the Court should be persuasive, or at least candid, in its opinions. But the ready answer is that the Court is an agency of government and an oligarchic one at that. Modern Americans have been increasingly demanding from their Presidents frank, logical, persuasive accounts of the reasons for our policies, both foreign and domestic. Absent such justifications, many Americans are unwilling to

[74]Kauper, *supra* note 16, at 96.
[75]*See* Schaefer, *supra* note 30, at 1559.
[76]L. JAFFE, *supra* note 2, at 101.
[77]Kalven, *"Uninhibited, Robust, and Wide-Open"—A Note on Free Speech and the Warren Court,* in THE WARREN COURT: A CRITICAL ANALYSIS 98 (Sayler, Boyer, & Gooding eds. 1969).

consider the policies of their government as legitimate, refuse to cooperate with them, and protest any continued pursuit of them. Legislators, too, have been subjected to these demands. Each congressional election produces persistent appeals for the candidates to speak to the issues rather than to engage in political sloganeering and also produces dangerous disenchantment and alienation if the candidates fail to comply. So, too, the Supreme Court of the United States is under a mandate to provide compelling explanations for its policy adoptions. Were it not for this fact, exegetical analysis of Supreme Court opinions would be of little value except as a sort of twentieth century scholastic game to keep a few idiosyncratic law professors employed and off the streets. But craftsmanship in the writing of opinions is essential to the legitimation of the Court's role in our mixed governmental system and to the legitimation of the policies which it produces.[78] Even among behaviorally oriented students of the judicial process,[79] who tend to minimize the significance of dialectical analysis, those who have approached their subject with a cybernetic model have concluded that clear and comprehensible opinions are important for the generation of positive feedback, public compliance, and diffuse support for the Court.[80] Each and every judicial statement which fails to meet the test of craftsmanship may well contribute to a "general cynicism which springs inevitably from decisions that pronounce rather than persuade."[81]

Judicially created public policy can be legitimate if supported by rational, logically coherent opinions consistent with the philosophy of the Constitution and based upon the wording of the statutory or constitutional text, or upon the intent of the Framers of the provision, or upon our national history, or upon prior judicial interpretation, or upon a convincing demonstration of changed social conditions.[82] But the

[78]*See generally* P. EIDELBERG, THE PHILOSOPHY OF THE AMERICAN CONSTITUTION ch. 10 (1968); A. BICKEL, THE LEAST DANGEROUS BRANCH: THE SUPREME COURT AT THE BAR OF POLITICS (1962); A. BICKEL, *supra* note 32.

[79]Concerning the differences between behavioral and traditional approaches to the study of law and courts, see Schubert, *Academic Ideology and the Study of Adjudication,* 61 AM. POL. SCI. REV. 106 (1967); *but cf.* Dixon, *Who Is Listening? Political Science Research in Public Law,* 4 P.S. 19 (1971).

[80]*See* S. GOLDMAN & T. JAHNIGE, THE FEDERAL COURTS AS A POLITICAL SYSTEM ch. 7 (1971).

[81]*The Supreme Court, 1971 Term,* 86 HARV. L. REV. 1, 164 (1972).

[82]*See* B. CARDOZO, THE NATURE OF THE JUDICIAL PROCESS (1921); *see also* P. EIDELBERG, *supra* note 78. An excellent example of the way in which the Court, adhering to these decisional guidelines, can nevertheless keep a constitutional provision abreast of changed circumstances without violating the underlying constituional philoso-

Warren Court's major decisions,[83] especially the substantive equal protection cases,[84] found little support in the language of the Constitution. Its history has repeatedly been criticized.[85] Its reliance upon social science was not only questionable but also inconsistent.[86] And its disregard for precedent was truly amazing. Consider for example, the Court's opinion in *Miranda*, a decision which purported to be based upon the Fifth Amendment but could cite not a single Fifth Amendment precedent to support itself.[87] Similarly, "Justice Black's opinion [in *Engel v. Vitale*] was notable because, except for one brief reference to the *Everson* case in a footnote, it completely lacked documentation."[88] This type of policy-making behavior is legitimate for a legislature, given the electoral principle. But an unelected body must seek legitimation for its policy statements somewhere else. An appeal to the Law of Nature is not enough.[89]

A judge, Mr. Justice Brandeis once counseled, "may advise; he may not command or coerce. He does coerce when without convincing the judgment he overcomes the will by the weight of his authority."[90] Most who have examined the Warren Court's opinions, even those who have applauded the results effected, have found them unpersuasive.[91] According to Brandeis's test, then, the Warren Court was engaged in

phy is provided by the evolution of the Contract Clause. *Compare* Sturges v. Crowinshield, 4 Wheat. 122 (1819), *with* City of El Paso v. Simmons, 379 U.S. 497 (1965). While the two decisions exhibit a marked difference in interpretation of the Contract Clause, the determinative factor underlying both appears to be the contemporary economic situation. Thus, the two decisions, though inconsistent on one level, are both consistent with the Founding Fathers' purpose in creating the clause, i.e., to achieve and insure economic stability. *See generally* C. MILLER, THE SUPREME COURT AND THE USES OF HISTORY (1969); Funston, Requiescat in Pace: *A Memorial to the Contract Clause*, 31 FED. B.J. 350 (1972).

[83]*E.g.*, Brown v. Board of Education, 347 U.S. 436 (1954); Reynolds v. Sims, 377 U.S. 533 (1964); Miranda v. Arizona, 384 U.S. 436 (1966).

[84]*E.g.*, Shapiro v. Thompson, 394 U.S. 618 (1969).

[85]*See* Kelly, *supra* note 24; Casper, *supra* note 24.

[86]*See* Cahn, *Jurisprudence*, 30 N.Y.U. L. REV. 150 (1955); Miranda v. Arizona, 384 U.S. 436, 526 (1966) (White, J., dissenting). *See also* Ginsberg v. New York, 390 U.S. 629 (1968).

[87]Miranda v. Arizona, 384 U.S. at 510-513 (Harlan, J., dissenting).

[88]Kauper, *supra* note 16, at 89.

[89]*See* Kurland, *The Court Should Decide Less and Explain More*, N. Y. Times Magazine, June 9, 1968, at 34.

[90]Horning v. District of Columbia, 254 U.S. 135, 139 (1920).

[91]*See* notes 2 and 24 *supra*.

coercion. The nature of the judicial process at the Supreme Court level during these years was inherently coercive.

The shortcomings of Warren Court opinion drafting, however, were but one manifestation of its larger tendency to disregard both the internal and the external limits upon judicial power.[92] One of the foremost institutional restraints upon any Supreme Court policy-making is the doctrine of *stare decisis*, the legal precept that a court is to be guided in its decision-making by previously decided cases. The Warren Court, however, when it was not disregarding precedent entirely, as in *Miranda* or *Engel*, launched an all-out attack upon it.

> Congress is, of course, not bound to adhere to decisions that it has made at earlier times. It can reverse itself as often as a majority thinks it appropriate to do so, without being called to account for its inconsistency. So, too, apparently with the Warren Court. It . . . paid less heed to stare decisis—one of the features that Cardozo pointed out as distinguishing legislative legislation from judicial legislation—than any Supreme Court in history. . . . The list of opinions destroyed by the Warren Court reads like a table of contents from an old constitutional law casebook. The willingness to disregard stare decisis . . . has a worthy pedigree. But the volume and speed of the Warren Court as it engaged in this enterprise have never been witnessed before. . . . It started by overruling *Plessy v. Ferguson* and ended by destroying *Palko v. Connecticut*. And between these, a very large number of constitutional landmarks that once were "the law of the land" were made into artifacts for the study of historians.[93]

When not laying previous decisions to rest, the Court busied itself with broadening the rule of standing and narrowing the political question doctrine. Both the rejection of the political question argument in *Baker v.*

[92]The poor quality of many Warren Court opinions was also a factor further contributing to centralization of power in the Court. As Professor Lowi points out:

> A strong and clear ruling . . . leads to significant decentralization of caseload and a good deal of self-administration by lower courts and counsel. . . . (A)n area with good leading opinions is an area of "easy law" in which there are few appeals to the top; nonetheless the area is centralized too, in the sense that each decision in each lower judicial unit becomes more consistent with all other comparable decisions, because the clear rule is a good criterion, departures from which are easily detectible by higher courts and clients. In contrast, the Supreme Court can inundate itself in areas of "hard law" where it cannot or will not enunciate a leading opinion expressing good governing rules. In such an area there is even greater centralization, but in the worse sense of the word because responsibility can be maintained only through regular, bureaucratic supervision. . . .

T. LOWI, THE END OF LIBERALISM: IDEOLOGY, POLICY, AND THE CRISIS OF PUBLIC AUTHORITY 302 (1969).
[93]P. KURLAND, *supra* note 2, at 186-187, 90-91 (footnotes omitted).

Carr[94] and the expansion of the grounds for standing to raise constitutional issues in *Flast v. Cohen*[95] evidence the Court's thirst for policy-making. Both decisions had the effect of opening up areas which had previously been thought closed to the exercise of judicial power. It is perhaps not too dramatic to say that in these decisions the Court resembled a hunter tearing down previously posted "No Hunting" signs and then proceeding to blast away at the terrified rabbits with no small amount of carnage. *Flast*, moreover, may serve as yet another example of the Warren Court's congenital impatience with the legislative process. An incidental result of that decision was to put an end to various proposals pending in the Congress which would have vested the federal courts with jurisdiction to hear federal taxpayer's suits raising First Amendment challenges to federal appropriations programs. Perhaps not trusting Congress to pass one of those measures, the Court in one quick gesture preempted the field.[96]

The response, both popular and legislative, to many of the Court's major policy statements, responses which should not have been wholly unanticipated, raises the intriguing question of whether the Warren Court forgot not only the internal rules of limitation but also the prior history of the Supreme Court which taught that there can be external restraints upon its power. Do the Fortas fiasco and the proposals to impeach Mr. Justice Douglas stand for the proposition that the Warren Court Justices came to feel too smug and self-secure? Did the continued announcement of desegregation and criminal justice decisions in the face of reluctant enforcement and non-compliance represent an effort to ignore or a failure to perceive the Court's inherent weaknesses?

What the decisions of the Warren Court certainly seem to indicate is the absence of a sense of political reality. A bit of the politician's sense of the climate of popular opinion is an invaluable element for a Supreme Court Justice.[97] But few of the Justices of the Warren Court seem to have possessed such an appreciation. This may, in part, account for the Court's failure to produce better opinions. Professor Kauper has noted:

[94]369 U.S. 186 (1962).
[95]392 U.S. 83 (1968).
[96]*See* Hearings on S.2097 Before the Subcomm. on Constitutional Rights of the Senate Comm. on the Judiciary, 89th Cong., 2d Sess, (1966). *See also* H. ABRAHAM, FREEDOM AND THE COURT: CIVIL RIGHTS AND LIBERTIES IN THE UNITED STATES 239 n. 2 (1967); Note, *The Insular Status of the Religion Clauses: The Dilemma of Standing*, 36 GEO. WASH. L. REV. 648 (1968); Kauper, *supra* note 16, at 88.
[97]*But cf.* Wright, *Professor Bickel, the Scholarly Tradition, and the Supreme Court*, 84 HARV. L. REV. 769, 797 (1971).

> A large part of the public furor aroused by Justice's Black's . . . opinion in *Engel*
> might well have been avoided if the Court had given thought to the public impact of
> the decision and dealt more discreetly with the issue. . . .[98]

Again, although Kauper is speaking only of the religion cases, his criticism could have applied across the board.[99]

The Court's failure of political sensitivity, however, was a function of its majority's lack of appreciation for the nature of the institution. Professor Kurland has set forth what he finds to have been the three basic failings of the Warren Court:[100]

> 1. an inability "to adhere to the step-by-step process that has long characterized the common-law and constitutional forms of adjudication;"
> 2. a failure to "recognize the incapacities that inhere in its structure;"
> 3. a failure of judicial temperament.

All of these defects were, of course, interrelated. The Court's failure of perception coupled with its non-judicial temperament rendered its inability to abide by established forms and processes virtually inevitable. There seems to have been little recognition among the Justices of the Warren Court that the Supreme Court of the United States, while a policy-making body, also remains, must remain, a court,[101] judging limited, real disputes between real persons in real cases, and for that reason "is required to behave differently from the purely political branches of government."[102] Or, more succinctly, and with appropriate apologies to Robert Burns, a court's a court for all that.

The Court, so long as it remains a court, and not a legislature, operates under certain crucial handicaps in its policy-making.

> The adversary process brings with it . . . burdens. The Court's decisions have to rest
> on the evidence and materials brought before it by the litigants or such similar
> information as may be garnered by its very small staff from already existing
> published data. The Court, because it is a court, lacks machinery for gathering the
> wide range of facts and opinions that should inform the judgment of a prime
> policymaker.[103]

The Warren Court, of course, attempted to rectify some of these

[98]Kauper, *supra* note 16, at 97.

[99]*See, e.g.*, Mishkin, *The High Court, the Great Writ, and the Due Process of Time and Law*, 79 HARV. L. REV. 56 (1965).

[100]P. KURLAND, *supra* note 2, at xx-xxi.

[101]*See* R. JACKSON, THE SUPREME COURT IN THE AMERICAN SYSTEM OF GOVERNMENT (1955).

[102]P. KURLAND, *supra* note 2, at 4.

[103]*Id.* at 196.

institutional deficiencies. Despite its apparent distrust of legislatures, it found certain advantages of the legislative process appealing. Thus, it sought, where convenient, to take cognizanze of social science knowledge and to adopt this information as a legitimate basis for judicial decision.[104] Similarly, it relaxed the requirements for the filing of *amicus curiae* briefs and sought to use this new source of information much as a legislature uses committee hearings.[105] Nevertheless, the Court, *qua* Court, suffers from limitations of personnel, of resources of budget, and of the homogeneity of experience of its membership which seriously cripple it as an agency for the formulation of public policy.[106] These mechanical shortcomings of the litigation process, arising from the case-by-case approach, moved no less formidable an advocate than Professor Bickel to conclude that

> in dealing with problems of great magnitude and pervasive ramifications, problems with complex roots and unpredictably multiplying complex offshoots . . . the judicial process is . . . too remote from the conditions and deals . . . with too narrow a slice of reality.[107]

For these and other reasons, Bickel concluded that the Court is unsuitable to serve as an initiator of social and political change. As a legitimator, yes. As a contributor, maybe. As an initiator, no.

The Court's pronouncements, however, seldom constitute the final word.[108] Congress, the President, the public respond. Congress, for example, may reply positively to a Supreme Court decision, as it did with the Civil Rights Act of 1968 in answer to *United States v. Guest;*[109] or it may respond negatively, as it did to *Miranda* and other of the criminal

---

[104]*E.g.*, Brown v. Board of Education, 347 U.S. 436 (1954); Miranda v. Arizona, 384 U.S. 436 (1966). *But see* Ginsberg v. New York, 390 U.S. 629 (1968). *See generally* A. DAVIS, THE UNITED STATES SUPREME COURT AND THE USES OF SOCIAL SCIENCE DATA (1974).

[105]*See generally* Vose, *Litigation as a Form of Pressure Group Activity*, 319 THE ANNALS 28 (1958).

[106]*See* Schmidhauser, *The Justices of the Supreme Court: A Collective Portrait*, 3 MIDW. J. POL. SCI. 2 (1959); Frankfurter, *The Supreme Court in the Mirror of the Justices*, 105 U. PA. L. REV. 785 (1957); Grossman, *Judicial Selection and the Socialization of Judges*, in THE FEDERAL JUDICIAL SYSTEM: READINGS IN PROCESS AND BEHAVIOR (T. Jahnige & S. Goldman eds. 1968).

[107]A. BICKEL, *supra* note 32, at 175.

[108]*See* S. WASBY, THE IMPACT OF THE UNITED STATES SUPREME COURT: SOME PERSPECTIVES (1970); T. BECKER (ed.), THE IMPACT OF SUPREME COURT DECISIONS (2d ed. 1973).

[109]383 U.S. 745 (1966).

defendants' rights decisions with the Omnibus Crime Control and Safe Streets Act of 1968. None other than Holmes adjured us to think things not words—a dictum which the Warren Court might profitably have taken to heart.

> Both the Court's admirers and its detractors equate the Court's pronouncements with obedience to them. . . . However bad some of the decisions, we might be better off if those were the facts. They are not.[110]

The weaknesses of the Warren majority's opinions aside, its misperception of the institution notwithstanding, might not one applaud the Court for its success? The answer is clearly, if unfortunately, "No."[111] Seventeen years after *Brown v. Board of Education*, schools remained largely segregated and unequal.[112] And children still prayed in them.[113] The obscenity decisions did not serve to educate the people to a broader view of the First Amendment.[114] Police procedures had generally been unaffected.[115] The Court's symbolic impact may have been great, but at the end of the Warren era the pages of the *United States Reports*, volumes 346-395, bore but a slight resemblance to the actual situation in contemporary American life. Where the Court's policy judgments had coincided with public acceptance, where the decisions tapped popularized preconceptions, where opinions were translated into statutes, where there was fresh and vigorous executive enforcement, there is evidence that the Court was capable of effective action. But without powerful and continuous administrative and legislative initiatives, the Court did not and could not accomplish a great deal. The systematic design and administration of a code of criminal procedure, for example, could not and was not effectively accomplished by the Court. And much the same could be said of school district regulations or legislative districting.

In spite of its immediate shortcomings, however, the claim has been advanced that the Warren Court will ultimately triumph.[116] In the long

[110]P. KURLAND, *supra* note 2, at xix.

[111]*See generally* S. WASBY, *supra* note 108; T. BECKER, *supra* note 108.

[112]*See, e.g.*, N.Y. Times, Jan. 4, 1970, at 78 (87.6% of black students in five southern states still attended schools with enrollment which was 95% or more from minority groups).

[113]*See, e.g.*, Birkby, *The Supreme Court and the Bible Belt: Tennessee Reaction to the "Schempp" Decision*, 10 MIDW. J. POL. SCI. 304 (1966).

[114]*See* ch. VII *supra* at n. 91.

[115]*See, e.g.*, Medalie, Zeitz, & Alexander, *Custodial Interrogation in Our Nation's Capital: The Attempt to Implement Miranda*, 66 MICH. L. 1347 (1968): Note, *Interrogations in New Haven: The Impact of Miranda*, 76 YALE L. J. 1521 (1967).

[116]*See, e.g.*, Wright, *supra* note 97; Black, *The Unfinished Business of the Warren*

run, it is argued, the Warren Court moved with the tide of history, and history will be its judge. Indeed, not only admirers but also critics seem united in their acceptance of historical vindication as the appropriate measure of a Court's success.[117] Even Professor Bickel, a critic, has written:

> If the [Warren Court's] bet [on the future course of events] pays off, whatever their analytic failings, the Justices will have won everything.[118]

Following the same line of reasoning, defenders of the Court have relied heavily, often explicitly, upon an analogy between the Warren Court and the Marshall Court.[119] Just as the Warren Court, it is argued, the Marshall Court was result-oriented and suffered from lapses of craftsmanship, but time has been on Marshall's side.[120] The Marshall Court was ultimately justified by the judgment of history; and so too, it is implied, will be the Warren Court. But this analogy is worth a moment's consideration. It is of no small interest that those who call upon the shade of Marshall to justify decision-making of the Warren era call upon a symbol, not upon a reality.

> One expects that those who today applaud the Warren Court's decisions would, if they lived then and were of the same persuasion, be drawn more to Marshall's critics, to Thomas Jefferson and Spencer Roane, than to his defenders.[121]

Any anology between the Warren and Marshall epochs, moreover, is hard to square with Marshall's sense of the politic. In this regard, Marshall more closely resembles Lenin than Warren. His jurisprudence was characterized by "two steps forward, one step back,"[122] not by "quantum jumps."[123] Finally, what exactly of Marshall's jurisprudence has been vindicated by history? His rabid respect for private property?[124]

Court, 46 WASH. L. REV. 3 (1970); Cox, *Chief Justice Earl Warren*, 83 HARV. L. REV. 1 (1969); Pye, *supra* note 14.

[117]*E.g.*, A. BICKEL, *supra* note 32; P. KURLAND, *supra* note 2.

[118]A. BICKEL, *supra* note 32, at 99.

[119]*E.g.*, Black, *supra* note 116, at 10-12. *See generally* P. KURLAND, *supra* note 2, at 10-15.

[120]*See* O. W. HOLMES, COLLECTED LEGAL PAPERS 269-271 (1920).

[121]P. KURLAND, *supra* note 2, at 11.

[122]*E.g.*, Cohens v. Virginia, 6 Wheat. 264 (1821); Marbury v. Madison, 1 Cranch 137 (1803).

[123]*See* Miranda v. Arizona, 384 U.S. 436, 499 (1966) (Clark, J., dissenting in part and concurring in part).

[124]*See, e.g.*, Ogden v. Saunders, 12 Wheat. 213 (1827); Dartmouth College v. Woodward, 4 Wheat. 518 (1819); Fletcher v. Peck, 6 Cranch 87 (1810).

His Contract Clause interpretations?[125] The "original package" doctrine?[126] His nationalism? Perhaps. But remember that the Civil War, which it is claimed vindicated Marshall, involved not only the nature of the Union, about which Marshall had much to say,[127] but also the question of slavery, about which he had very little to say.[128] To debate the merits of the analogy, however, is really beside the point. Whether or not Marshall has been vindicated by history is inapposite to the fate of the Warren Court. Assuming that result-orientation buttressed by hindsight is a proper posture from which to evaluate Supreme Court decision-making, does the tide of history seem to be moving in the Warren Court's direction?

Criticism of the Warren Court has often been dismissed as tradition-bound and as grounded in a fundamentally incorrect view of the Supreme Court's role in American government.[129] Critics of the Warren majority have been accused of advocating the outmoded idea that the Court should not legislate but should interpret the Constitution to mean exactly what the Founding Fathers intended regardless of social, economic, or political changes and that the Court should not seek to lead or educate the American people. Such a model is essentially a straw man. Most critics of the Warren Court have recognized the necessity of judicial policy-making.[130] What has concerned them has been the wisdom and scope of the Court's policy initiatives. Nor need one believe that the Court should not keep the Constitution abreast of genuine societal changes or should not educate the people in order to be critical of the Warren Court. One may believe these things, may share with the Warren Court's defenders many of their central premises and still wonder about the staying power of the Warren Court's policies.

Granting that the Court, if it is to succeed, will do so through its influence on changing attitudes, how successful an educator was the

[125]*Compare* Sturges v. Crowinshield, 4 Wheat. 122 (1819), *with* City of El Paso v. Simmons, 379 U.S. 497 (1965).

[126]*Compare* Brown v. Maryland, 12 Wheat. 419 (1827), *with* Youngstown Co. v. Bowers, 358 U.S. 534, 552-553, 561 (1959).

[127]McCulloch v. Maryland, 4 Wheat. 316 (1819).

[128]For the Marshall Court's only significant handling of the slavery issue, *see* The Antelope, 10 Wheat. 66 (1825). *See generally* D. DUMOND, ANTISLAVERY ORIGINS OF THE CIVIL WAR IN THE UNITED STATES (1963); Schlesinger, *The Causes of the American Civil War: A Note on Historical Sentimentalism*, 16 PARTISAN REV. 968 (1949).

[129]*E.g.*, Wright, *supra* note 97; Pye, *supra* note 14.

[130]*E.g.*, A. BICKEL, *supra* note 78; P. KURLAND, *supra* note 2.

Warren Court? None other than Judge Wright has already given it high marks.

> I speak of an identifiable new generation of lawyers because I believe that one of the greatest legacies of the Warren Court has been its revolutionary influence on the thinking of law students. The students of the 1960's were educated in a new "tradition," albeit an incipient one and perhaps only a brief, shining moment. Most of their teachers had first come to see and understand the Court and the Constitution during the New Deal years—an experience which could only serve to corroborate the positions taken by the progressive realists. Thus they generally sought to school their students of the 1960's in a mode of criticism surely appropriate to the Old Court, but of doubtful relevance to the Warren Court. The students could not help but feel the tension since, for them, the Supreme Court *was* the Warren Court. For them, there was no theoretical gulf between the law and morality; and, for them, the Court was the one institution in the society that seemed to be speaking most consistently the language of idealism which we all recited in grade school. Just as they had not lived through the Stalin era and so could not accept the conventional wisdom of the Cold War, so their coming to consciousness in the 1960's left them unscarred by worries of Court packing and judicial obstructionism. Instead, they were inspired by the dignity and moral courage of a man and an institution that was prepared to act on the ideals to which America is theoretically and rhetorically dedicated.[131]

But how truly this might have been said of the relationship between the old, laissez-faire Court,[132] an institution that was prepared to act on the ideals to which academicians such as William Graham Sumner claimed America was dedicated.[133] And, for a time, that Court was immensely successful. But in the end, its education of lawyers did not save it. A Court must educate more than the bar; it must educate the public. And in doing that, it must recognize, as must all teachers, that pedagogy has its limits. Few six year olds can be taught calculus; nor can the public be taught lessons contrary or irrelevant to the dominant values of the era. The Gallup Polls tell us that at the time of Mr. Chief Justice Warren's retirement, the American public held the Supreme Court in extremely low esteem, believing it responsible for a too rapid integration and a burgeoning crime rate.[134] The Warren Court's pedagogy would seem to have left something to be desired. Moral it may have been, but morality is not enough. The Supreme Court must convince or fail.

[131]Wright, *supra* note 97, at 804.

[132]*See* A. PAUL, CONSERVATIVE CRISIS AND THE RULE OF LAW: ATTITUDES OF BAR AND BENCH, 1887-1895 (1960).

[133]*Id. See also* W. SUMNER, WHAT SOCIAL CLASSES OWE TO EACH OTHER (1883); R. McCLOSKEY, *supra* note 28.

[134]*See* N. Y. Times, August 17, 1969, sec. 1, at 80; *id.*, August 10, 1969, sec. 1, at 42; *id.*, June 15, 1969, sec. 1, at 43.

In retrospect it may appear that many of the Warren Court's difficulties, particularly in the late '60's, arose from its failure to perceive and to accommodate itself to social and political changes which were then occurring. Rather than the vanguard of a new era, the Warren Court may have been the rear-guard of an old cause.[135] The values of New Deal liberalism were among the motive forces in Warren Court decision-making. But a vision of a new period in American political life, a period dominated by values different than those which the Warren Court expressed, is certainly possible.

Foremost among the new trends which have raised doubts that the tide of history will, at any time in the reasonably near future, vindicate the Warren Court has been a rebirth of interest in the principle of federalism.[136] This is not to say that there is a reinvigoration of concern for state government. There is not.[137] But there has been increasing demand for "decentralization" and "community," demands which have reflected a desire to return control over political decision-making to geographically smaller and less populous areas.[138] These may be ecologically defined areas, such as river basins, or man-made areas, such as metropolitan areas, or they may be even smaller areas, such as neighborhoods. But the principle is the same, and it is a principle contradictory of much of the underlying direction of Warren Court decision-making. In particular, the Warren Court's reapportionment decisions conflicted with the new demands for decentralization "for the simple reason that arithmetic has no sense of community."[139] The three most important decisions of the Warren Court, in the opinion of the former Chief Justice,[140] were *Baker v. Carr*,[141] *Brown v. Board of Education*,[142] and

[135]*See generally* T. LOWI, *supra* note 92. *See also* Schaar, Book Review, 64 AM. POL. SCI. REV. 1258 (1970).

[136]*See generally* V. EARLE (ed.), FEDERALISM: INFINITE VARIETY IN THEORY AND PRACTICE (1968); J. SUNDQUIST & D. DAVIS, MAKING FEDERALISM WORK (1969); R. LEACH, AMERICAN FEDERALISM (1970); C. PATEMAN, PARTICIPATION AND DEMOCRATIC THEORY (1970); R. DAHL, AFTER THE REVOLUTION? AUTHORITY IN A GOOD SOCIETY (1970); H. WHEELER, DEMOCRACY IN A REVOLUTIONARY ERA (1970); I. SHARKANSKY, REGIONALISM IN AMERICAN POLITICS (1970); Bell, *Federalism in Current Perspective*, 1 GA. L. REV. 586 (1967); Bingham, Book Review, 86 POL. SCI. Q. 297 (1971); Peel, Book Review, 395 THE ANNALS 229 (1971); Clarke, Book Review, 64 AM. POL. SCI. REV. 1261 (1970).

[137]*See* P. KURLAND, *supra* note 2, at ch. 3, and note 136 *supra*.

[138]*See* R. DAHL, *supra* note 136, at 59-103; A. BICKEL, *supra* note 32, at 112-151. *See generally* R. DAHL & E. TUFTE, SIZE AND DEMOCRACY (1973).

[139]P. KURLAND, *supra* note 2, at 162.

[140]TIME, July 4, 1969, at 62.

Gideon v. Wainwright.[143] Yet each of these decisions was characterized by a nationalization of rights once solely under local protection and, as a corollary, by an enlargement of the powers of the central government. Thus while the policy-making of the Warren Court may superficially have won the approval of the young and the liberal, it proceeded from premises potentially at odds with their underlying values.

Also, *Baker, Brown,* and *Gideon* were each characterized by a concern for equality, and that value too has been called into question recently. The demands for decentralization have often been linked to demands for racial, religious, social, or cultural divergence.[144] To be sure, there is no necessary inconsistency between diversity and equality as a philosophic matter, but at the level of practical implementation coupling egalitarianism with nationalism has had a tendency to produce uniformity and conformity. How enduring will Supreme Court decisions directed toward these ends be in an age of renewed emphasis upon and pride in differences? Here, too, one encounters the demands of various groups, such as blacks and women, for members of their own to represent them. How compatible is the reapportionment decisions' disparagement of interest representation with these demands and the principles upon which they are based? Equality, moreover, may be an oppressive as much as a liberating value, as the residents of *Animal Farm* discovered. Consider the type of government action which might be justified on the basis of *Brown's* social psychology and the doctrine of "affirmative state duty." Would such actions be tolerated by ethnic groups in the 1970's? If not, will the decisions which suggest them remain viable?

For many of the same reasons, the Warren Court's criminal defendants' rights decisions have begun to appear to some as a self-inflicted wound, unintentionally inflicted to be sure, but nonetheless damaging.[145] If the Court's pedagogy is to be measured by its success in winning public support for the view that due process guarantees need to be applied uniformly if equality before the law is to be meaningful, it must be acknowledged a poor teacher, for it certainly failed to gain acceptance for its view.

[141]396 U.S. 186 (1962).

[142]347 U.S. 436 (1954).

[143]372 U.S. 335 (1963).

[144]*See* A. BICKEL, *supra* note 32, at 112-151, and note 136 *supra. Cf. The Supreme Court, 1969 Term,* 84 HARV. L. REV. at 32-46.

[145]*See* F. GRAHAM, THE SELF-INFLICTED WOUND (1970).

> A system of criminal justice that can guarantee neither a speedy trial nor a safe community cannot excuse its failure by pointing to an elaborate system of safeguards for the accused. Justice dictates not only that the innocent man go free, but that the guilty be punished for his crimes.[146]

By virtue of its lack of appreciation for the institutional limitations of the judicial system, sans legislative support, the Court contributed to what may yet be one of the major issues of the '70's, the congestion of American trial and appellate courts.[147] Increased opportunities for retrial and appeal, fostered by the Warren Court, have contributed to the alarming backlog of criminal cases. But, it should not be forgotten that the Sixth Amendment guarantee of "a speedy trial" cuts both ways; the public too has an interest in a speedy trial. Justice may be subverted by the accused as much as by the state.[148]

Finally, the Court's contribution, albeit indirect, to the enhancement of the power of the President and its denigration of the Congress has seemed particularly out of line with the trend of thinking in post-Viet Nam America.[149] The Court and the Presidency, however, shared much in common during the years immediately preceding Mr. Chief Justice Warren's retirement. Perhaps a more apposite analogy would be one between the Warren Court and the Johnson Presidency rather than one between the Warren Court and the Marshall Court. (Are those who argue that history will vindicate the Warren Court prepared to argue that it will also vindicate Lyndon Johnson?) Such an analogy is again called to mind by the Court's opinions.

> The Warren Court accepted with vengeance the task of protector of the individual against government and of minorities against the tyranny of majorities. But it . . . failed abysmally to persuade the people that its judgments were made for sound reasons. Its failures on this score were due to many causes. . . . One . . . , if I may

---

[146]Address by President Richard M. Nixon, March 11, 1971, in 54 JUDICATURE 404, 405 (1971).

[147]*See* H. JAMES, CRISIS IN THE COURTS (1971); Carrington, *Crowded Dockets and the Courts of Appeals: The Threat to The Function of Review of The National Law,* 82 HARV. L. REV. 542 (1969); Shapiro, *Federal Habeas Corpus: A Study in Massachusetts,* 87 HARV. L. REV. 321 (1973); Address by Shirley M. Hufstedler, Judge, United States Court of Appeals (9th Cir.). The Fellows of the American Bar Foundation and the National Conference of Bar Presidents Annual Luncheon, Feb. 3, 1974.

[148]*See* Address by Edward Bennett Williams, Chairman of the American Bar Association Committee on Crime Prevention and Control, March 13, 1971, in 54 JUDICATURE 418 (1971).

[149]*See* L. KOENIG, *supra* note 51; P. KURLAND, *supra* note 2, at ch. 2.

say so, was a judicial arrogance that . . . refused to believe that the public should be told the truth instead of being fed on slogans and platitudes.[150]

The result, of course, was a "credibility gap," similar to that which President Johnson created for himself. The public's increasing alienation from such policy-making was then manifested in the actions of its elected representatives in Congress. For the Court, this took the form of rejection of the nomination of Mr. Justice Fortas to the Chief Justiceship and finally of his forced resignation.[151]

The Fortas fiasco may ultimately be viewed as a symbolically significant turning point in American political history. Fortas's legal and intellectual qualifications notwithstanding, no less apt person could have been chosen to succeed Mr. Chief Justice Warren than Abe Fortas. As a member of the liberal, egalitarian majority of the Court, as a personal friend and confidant of Lyndon Baines Johnson, Fortas was virtually certain to rouse the anger of a Congress which was beginning to recognize that it had been insulted and ignored by the other two branches for a very long time. It is somewhat ironic that many who applauded when the Warren Court called into question the very constitutional validity of the House of Representatives should have been so aghast when the Senate raised its own questions about the legitimacy of policies the Supreme Court had been following for a decade. The controversy surrounding Fortas's appointment was far more directed at the Warren Court than at Fortas personally.

> The Fortas affair was not the cause for the weakening confidence in the Court. It was the weakened confidence in the Court that made possible the Fortas affair.[152]

In its hearings on confirmation of the nomination, "the Senate was presumably providing its own commentary on the work of the Warren Court."[153]

During the 1960's, increasingly so after 1964, neither the Court nor the President seemed willing or able to explain candidly, let alone to justify, the policies which they sought to pursue. Such attitudes generated a crisis of public confidence questioning the legitimacy of many American institutions. That crisis of confidence clearly extended o the Supreme Court.[154] Restoration of confidence will be the major task

[150]P. KURLAND, *supra* note 2, at 204-205.
[151]R. SHOGAN, A QUESTION OF JUDGMENT: THE FORTAS CASE AND THE STRUGGLE FOR THE SUPREME COURT (1972).
[152]P. KURLAND, *supra* note 2, at xxiii.
[153]Kalven, *supra* note 77, at 103.
[154]*See* Fish, Book Review, 65 AM. POL. SCI. REV. 208, 210 (1971).

confronting the Justices who, in the 1970's have succeeded the Warren Court majority.

> The restoration of that confidence is vital to the continuance of the rule of law in this country. For above everything else, the Supreme Court is symbolic of America's preference for law over force as the ruling mechanism in a democratic society.[155]

---

[155]P. KURLAND, *supra* note 2, at 206.

Chapter 9
The Burger Court
in Perspective

Political science research has identified a pattern in American presidential and party politics which, given the mechanism of judicial recruitment, is of great significance for the Supreme Court.[1] Approximately every forty years the electorate experiences a major partisan realignment. The old party coalitions disintegrate, and new ones are formed. The previously dominant party may become the new minority party; or it may remain the dominant party, but in a vastly altered form; or entirely new parties may appear to replace the old parties.[2] In any event, a single party eventually emerges as dominant and, except for deviant elections occasioned by a peculiarly personable minority party candidate, proceeds to control the White House and Capitol Hill until the next realignment. It is during these realigning periods that the Supreme Court experiences its greatest political difficulties, for most of the Justices were appointed by and represent the values of the old and now repudiated dominant party.[3] After a few years, when the newly dominant coalition has had time enough to secure a majority of seats on the Court for its own appointees, the Court adjusts to the new alignment. But, during the transition period, the Court must often sail some rough waters indeed.

This particular pattern of partisan realignment, however, does not permit of prediction. Realignments are easily identified after the fact but are hard for contemporaries to recognize. Nevertheless, there is some evidence to suggest that America is in the throes of a realigning period,[4]

[1]See W. BURNHAM, CRITICAL ELECTIONS AND THE MAINSPRINGS OF AMERICAN POLITICS (1970); A. CAMPBELL, P. CONVERSE, W. MILLER, & D. STOKES, ELECTIONS AND THE POLITICAL ORDER (1966); Key, A Theory of Critical Elections, 17 J. POL. 3 (1955).
[2]See W. CHAMBERS & W. BURNHAM (eds.), THE AMERICAN PARTY SYSTEMS: STAGES OF DEVELOPMENT (1967).
[3]See Dahl, Decision-Making in a Democracy: The Supreme Court as a National Policy-Maker, 6 J. PUB. L. 279 (1957).
[4]See, e.g., J. SUNDQUIST, DYNAMICS OF THE PARTY SYSTEM: ALIGNMENT

and this may account in no small measure for the difficulties which the Warren Court, composed largely of Roosevelt and Eisenhower appointees, experienced toward the end of its tenure. Of course, such a realignment, if it is actually occurring, would also have consequences for Supreme Court policy-making. It appears already to have had. That many of the judicial attitudes which dominated the Warren years are no longer prevalent upon the bench is beyond question. But even a major realignment need not mean that the new judicial era would not fulfill the policy goals established by the Warren Court. In the transition from the Warren to the Burger Court there has been a change. But of what magnitude?

The common knowledge has been that the differences have been very great, that the Nixon appointments have turned the Court around. This has been a view advanced by journalists,[5] civil liberties lawyers,[6] and even relatively dispassionate scholarly critics.[7] The Burger Court has taken a more jaundiced view than its predecessor of the lewd,[8] the nude,[9] and the scurrilous.[10] Several of its free speech and press decisions, if taken as a whole, suggest a dominant theme of "imposing additional burdens upon claimants in first amendment cases,"[11] and it has restricted the power of federal courts to intervene in state court proceedings to protect these rights.[12] The similarity of results produced in *Evans v. Abney* and the Jackson, Mississippi, swimming pool closure case have represented, at the very least, a blunting of the Warren Court's thrust in

AND REALIGNMENT OF POLITICAL PARTIES IN THE UNITED STATES (1973); R. SCAMMON & B. WATTENBERG, THE REAL MAJORITY (1970); S. LUBELL, THE HIDDEN CRISIS IN AMERICAN POLITICS (1970); K. PHILLIPS, THE EMERGING REPUBLICAN MAJORITY (1969); Weisberg & Rusk, *Dimensions of Candidate Evaluation*, 64 AM. POL. SCI. REV. 1167 (1970).

[5]*E.g.*, J. SIMON, IN HIS OWN IMAGE: THE SUPREME COURT IN RICHARD NIXON'S AMERICA (1973); Stone, *The Fastest Track to a Repressive Era*, I.F. Stone's Bi-Weekly, Nov. 1, 1971.

[6]*E.g.*, Dorsen, *The Court of Some Resort*, 1 CIV. LIBERTIES REV. 82 (1974).

[7]*E.g.*, *The Supreme Court, 1970 Term*, 85 HARV. L. REV. 3, 40-44 (1971).

[8]*E.g.*, Paris Adult Theatre I v. Slaton, 413 U.S. 49 (1973); Miller v. California, 413 U.S. 15 (1973); Rabe v. Washington, 405 U.S. 313 (1972).

[9]California v. La Rue, 409 U.S. 109 (1972).

[10]*E.g.*, Lewis v. New Orleans, 408 U.S. 913 (1972) (Powell, J., concurring); Gooding v. Wilson, 405 U.S. 518 (1972).

[11]*The Supreme Court, 1972 Term*, 87 HARV. L. REV. 1, 152 (1973).

[12]Samuels v. Mackell, 401 U.S. 66 (1971); Younger v. Harris, 401 U.S. 37 (1971).

the area of race relations.[13] In its refusal to extend *Brown*,[14] the new majority has been reluctant to find racial discrimination where it arguably existed,[15] and even if racial discrimination can be shown it must significantly involve the state before the Burger Court will act.[16]

At a more fundamental level, the Burger Court's more restricted view of the proper ambit of the Equal Protection Clause has manifested a growing disquietude with the doctrinal instrument used to fashion much Warren Court policy, the two-level approach to equal protection analysis.[17] The Burger years have already witnessed the beginning of the decline of substantive equal protection.[18] In its effort to confine active equal protection review, without openly repudiating *Shapiro*,[19] the Burger Court has been unwilling to create new suspect categories[20] and has sought to define "fundamental" interests more rigidly. Ironically enough, the vehicle for this has been that staple of liberal jurisprudence the "double standard" distinction between "human" rights and "property" rights.[21] Not only *Rodriguez*[22] but also its antecedent, *Dandridge*,[23] has enunciated the rule that, where the classification is nonracial, only those interests guaranteed by the Bill of Rights merit strict scrutiny;

[13]Palmer v. Thompson, 403 U.S. 217 (1971); Evans v. Abney, 396 U.S. 435 (1970). *But see* Gilmore v. Montgomery, 417 U.S. 556 (1974).

[14]Brown v. Board of Education, 347 U.S. 483 (1954).

[15]*E.g.*, San Antonio Independent School Dist. v. Rodriguez, 411 U.S. 1 (1973); Jefferson v. Hackney, 406 U.S. 435 (1972); Donaldson v. California, 404 U.S. 968 (1971); Whitcomb v. Chavis, 403 U.S. 124 (1971); James v. Valtierra, 402 U.S. 137 (1971). *But see* White v. Regester, 412 U.S. 755 (1973) (sustaining claim that multi-member districting underrepresented identifiable racial minority).

The Warren Court, of course, was not invariably eager to find discrimination on the basis of race even though a colorable showing could be made that such discrimination existed, particularly were the discrimination's results "benign;" *see* Wright v. Rockefeller, 376 U.S. 52 (1964).

[16]*E.g.*, Moose Lodge No. 107 v. Irvis, 407 U.S. 163 (1972).

[17]*See generally Developments in the Law—Equal Protection*, 82 HARV. L. REV. 1065 (1969).

[18]*See*, Mendelson, *From Warren to Burger: The Rise and Decline of Substantive Equal Protection*, 66 AM. POL. SCI. REV. 1226 (1972).

[19]Shapiro v. Thompson, 394 U.S. 618 (1969).

[20]*See, e.g.*, Frontiero v. Richardson, 411 U.S. 677 (1973); Reed v. Reed, 404 U.S. 71 (1971); Labine v. Vincent, 401 U.S. 532 (1971).

[21]*See generally* Funston, *The Double Standard of Constitutional Protection in The Era of The Welfare State*, 90 POL. SCI. Q. 261 (1975).

[22]San Antonio Independent School Dist. v. Rodriguez, 411 U.S. 1 (1973).

[23]Dandridge v. Williams, 397 U.S. 471 (1970).

interests of an economic or social nature do not.[24] The Court, of course, has indicated that the right to travel interstate will continue to be protected,[25] but it seems that that right "will receive less deference than it has,"[26] particularly "when the benefit conditioned upon residence is not explicitly safeguarded by the Constitution."[27]

"Yet in no area is the trend of the Burger Court's decision more clear than in its criminal law rulings."[28] The Court has freed police to conduct extensive searches of suspects arrested for mere traffic offenses,[29] and it has ruled that even when evidence has been illegally secured by the police it may still be used in grand jury proceedings.[30] It has brought to a halt the process of extending to the juvenile court those procedural requirements applicable in other criminal proceedings.[31] It has ended the steady expansion of the law governing the right of confrontation.[32] It has approved the warrantless use of bugged informers.[33] It has, in short, rather severely limited the emerging constitutional doctrines affecting criminal procedure, and perhaps most notably in the *Harris* twins it has evidenced a desire to reverse the trend of Warren Court decisions.[34]

The "numberless variations of fact"[35] in the area of criminal procedure will contine to present the Burger Court with opportunities to retreat. Its response to the constitutional problems of crime and law enforcement, differing as it has from that of the Warren Court, seems attributable to a difference in perspective. The Burger majority has focused upon the overall, systemic problem, viewing it from the top down; the Warren Court viewed problems from the bottom up, focusing up the individual. This difference in approach has been apparent not only in the Burger

[24]*But cf.* United States Dept. of Agriculture v. Moreno, 413 U.S. 528 (1973).
[25]Dandridge v. Williams, 397 U.S. at 484 n. 16.
[26]*The Supreme Court, 1972 Term,* 87 HARV. L. REV. at 75.
[27]*Id.; see, e.g.,* Vlandis v. Kline, 412 U.S. 441 (1973).
[28]*The Supreme Court, 1970 Term,* 85 HARV. L. REV. at 43.
[29]United States v. Robinson, 414 U.S. 218 (1973); Gustafson v. Florida, 414 U.S. 260 (1973).
[30]United States v. Calandra, 414 U.S. 338 (1974).
[31]McKeiver v. Pennsylvania, 403 U.S. 528 (1971).
[32]*E.g.,* Mancusi v. Stubbs, 408 U.S. 204 (1972); Schneble v. Florida, 405 U.S. 427 (1972); Dutton v. Evans, 400 U.S. 74 (1970).
[33]United States v. White, 401 U.S. 745 (1971).
[34]United States v. Harris, 403 U.S. 573 (1971) (proof of informer's reliability in probable cause affidavit); Harris v. New York, 401 U.S. 222 (1971) (unlawfully obtained statement admissible for impeachment purposes).
[35]Kurland, *1971 Term: The Year of the Stewart-White Court,* 1972 SUP. CT. REV. 181, 263.

Court's criminal defendants' rights decisions but in its apportionment rulings as well. In the apportionment cases, moreover, the Burger majority's new perspective has coincided with its discontent over two-level equal protectionism to produce results which have seemed difficult to reconcile with Warren precedent.[36]

"It is obvious," then, as Professor Norman Dorsen has told us, "that the halcyon days of the Warren Court are over."[37] On the other hand, we should be mindful of Professor Kurland's counsel that "only for the simpleminded are all things simple."[38] The Burger Court's decisions on race relations, reapportionment, criminal defendants' rights, and First Amendment freedoms do not form neat patterns. Moreover, the real-life situations which give rise to those decisions do not present unambiguous choices between good and bad. When, for example, the Burger Court affirmed an order of the Pittsburgh Commission on Human Relations directing a newspaper to classify its help-wanted advertisements without regard to sex, was that a liberal blow for sexual equality or a conservative attack upon freedom of the press?[39] When the Court upheld the Moose Lodge in its discriminatory treatment of Leroy Irvis, was that a fascist manifesto for racism or a libertarian recognition of the right to private choice on the part of even the most odious and benighted of the citizenry?[40]

Upon closer inspection one discovers that many of the Burger Court's " 'retreats' were more typically refusals to extend Warren Court tendencies . . . :not firm strides to the rear but sidesteps and refusals to step forward. . . ."[41] The critics of the Burger Court have often displayed a conceptual confusion between retreating and not advancing.[42] Warren Court precedents have not been reversed wholesale; the new majority has simply refused to extend many of them yet one more step. Despite dire predictions from liberal quarters, even the landmark criminal rulings of the Warren era remain intact, albeit confined. Both in *Harris v. New*

---

[36]*E.g.*, Mahan v. Howell, 410 U.S. 315 (1973); Gaffney v. Cummings, 412 U.S. 735 (1973).

[37]Dorsen, *supra* note 6, at 89.

[38]Kurland, *1970 Term: Notes on the Emergence of the Burger Court*, 1971 SUP. CT. REV. 265, 267.

[39]Pittsburgh Press Co. v. Pittsburgh Comm'n on Human Relations, 413 U.S. 376 (1973).

[40]Moose Lodge No. 107 v. Irvis, 407 U.S. 163 (1972).

[41]Gunther, *In Search of Evolving Doctrine on a Changing Court: A Model for a Newer Equal Protection*, 86 HARV. L. REV. 1, 2 (1972).

[42]*E.g.*, J. SIMON, *supra* note 5.

York[43] and *Michigan v. Tucker*,[44] the Burger Court declined opportunities to overrule *Miranda* outright.[45] This may simply have represented the absence of sufficient votes to overturn *Miranda*. But, with two members of the *Miranda* minority plus four Nixon appointees sitting, it more probably signalled a willingness to adhere to *Miranda* but not to expand it. Similarly, when the Burger Court refused to prevent the conviction of an illicit drug manufacturer, even though a government agent had furnished him with some of his raw materials, it was doing no more and no less than adhering to a rule of law which was forty-one years old.[46] The Court has struck a blow at those who would declare plea bargaining to be unconstitutional by refusing to embrace the idea that a difficult choice must necessarily be an involuntary one,[47] but it has also insisted that once a bargain is struck the prosecution must keep its word.[48] While its First Amendment interpretations have been more traditional and less expansive than those of the Warren Court, the Burger majority has shown no inclination to depart from established doctrines or to overturn earlier decisions. In the civil rights area, the worst that can be said is that the new Justices have changed the Court's attitude "from one of commitment to give black litigants what they want to one perhaps more consonant with the concept of the equality of the races."[49] Even Professor Dorsen has been forced to concede that the Burger Court has "treated this area of civil liberties relatively well."[50] A "list of non-steps may be the best measure of the difference between the Warren Court and the Burger Court,"[51] but it must always be borne in mind that it is a highly speculatively yardstick. One cannot know for certain that the Warren Court itself would have taken the next step, and it is possible that many of the decisions rendered by the Burger Court would have been no different had they been resolved by the Warren majority.

The transition from the Warren to the Burger era, then, has not involved changes "as pervasive as some mourners for the immediate past

[43]401 U.S. 222 (1971).

[44]417 U.S. 433 (1974).

[45]Miranda v. Arizona, 384 U.S. 436 (1966).

[46]United States v. Russell, 411 U.S. 423 (1973); Sorrells v. United States, 287 U.S. 435 (1932).

[47]North Carolina v. Alford, 400 U.S. 25 (1970). *See generally* Note, *The Unconstitutionality of Plea Bargaining*, 83 HARV. L. REV. 1387 (1970).

[48]Santobello v. New York, 404 U.S. 257 (1971).

[49]Kurland, *supra* note 35, at 187.

[50]Dorsen, *supra* note 6, at 89.

[51]Kalven, *Even When a Nation Is at War*, 85 HARV. L. REV. 3, 14 (1971).

would have it."[52] Indeed, in many ways the decision-making of the Burger Court has revealed some striking similarites to that of the Warren Court. In the first place, there has been the sheer volume of judicial business transacted. Each successive term of the Burger Court, with the minor exception of the 1970 Term,[53] has broken the previous record for the busiest session since the passage of the Judiciary Act of 1925.[54] And each year the backlog of cases remaining on the docket awaiting final disposition has grown.[55] Whether this has been a favorable development[56] or whether it argues that the Justices are now in danger of being taxed beyond human capabilities and require radical remedial assistance is not a matter in point to the discussion.[57] It does, however, belie charges that the Court has now paused for a brief period of relative inaction. Each term, moreover, has involved not simply a large number of decisions but "a spate of cases of more than moderate importance."[58]

The results produced have hardly constituted an erasure of the Warren legacy. In civil rights, the Burger Court has, if not always unanimously, approved the use of busing and other controversial devices for eradicating racially dual school systems both north and south of the Mason-Dixon Line,[59] and there appears to be no inclination to cut back on *Brown*. The Court's ardor for finding "state action" in discriminatory situations has cooled,[60] but the Court has been "pretty well unanimous in insisting that all clearly governmental action must be cleansed of any racial bias against minorities."[61]

Neither have the Burger Court's decisions affecting the electoral process differed "from those that would have been brought about by the

[52]Kurland, *supra* note 38, at 265.

[53]In the 1970 Term, the number of cases disposed of declined from 3357 in the 1969 Term to 3318.

[54]*The Supreme Court, 1972 Term*, 87 HARV. L. REV. at 310-14.

[55]*Id.*

[56]*See* Kalven, *supra* note 51, at 6.

[57]*See* A. BICKEL, THE CASELOAD OF THE SUPREME COURT—AND WHAT, IF ANTHING, TO DO ABOUT IT (1973).

[58]Kurland, *supra* note 38, at 272.

[59]*E.g.,* Keyes v. School Dist., 413 U.S. 189 (1973); North Carolina State Board of Education v. Swann, 402 U.S. 43 (1971); Swann v. Charlotte-Mecklenburg Board of Education, 402 U.S. 1 (1971).

[60]*E.g.,* Moose Lodge No. 107 v. Irvis, 407 U.S. 163 (1972); Evans v. Abney, 396 U.S. 435 (1970).

[61] Kurland, *Enter the Burger Court: The Constitutional Business of the Supreme Court, O.T. 1969,* 1970 SUP. CT. REV. 1, 19.

Warren Court."[62] "One man, one vote" has continued to be the official dogma; a majority of the Justices have remained convinced of their mission to protect the majority from the minority; and the Court has continued to flounder in the problems thus created, apparently trying to find some way to remove partisanship from the electoral process while leaving the party system intact.[63] "The Court is certainly not yet out of the political thicket. It is certainly not likely to come out at the place it went in. But it hasn't yet worked its way through to the other side. . . . The Burger Court will not want for thorny problems so long as it remains in the bramble bushes."[64]

Even the Court's mounting discontent with two-level equal protection analysis has produced a sort of grotesque continuity. In the first place it should be noted that it has been not only the new appointees, such as Mr. Justice Powell, who have attempted to enunciate a single standard applicable to all cases raising equal protection claims;[65] former members of the Warren majority have also tried to fashion such a doctrine, though such efforts have yet to achieve fruition.[66] But, although the Justices have grown increasingly uncomfortable with two-level equal protection review, they have not jettisoned it. "Its best established ingredients retain vitality."[67] In *Rodriguez*, for example, while the court refused to extend the scope of active review, it did acknowledge and approve its existence. The result has been that the Burger Court has now not one, not two, *but three* equal protection tests!

The new court has proven similarly incapable of cleanly and abruptly abandoning the doctrine of unenumerated fundamental rights. It has found the standard of proof beyond a reasonable doubt in criminal prosecutions to be implicit in the content of due process,[68] and in *Eisenstadt v. Baird*,[69] despite a yeomanly effort to avoid *Griswold* like the

[62]Kurland, *supra* note 38, at 279; *see, e.g.*, Perkins v. Matthews, 400 U.S. 379 (1971); Oregon v. Mitchell, 400 U.S. 112 (1970).

[63]*E.g.*, Gaffney v. Cummings, 412 U.S. 735 (1973); Mahan v. Howell, 410 U.S. 315 (1973); Abate v. Mundt, 403 U.S. 182 (1971); Whitcomb v. Chavis, 403 U.S. 124 (1971); Hadley v. Junior College Dist., 397 U.S. 50 (1970).

[64]Kurland, *supra* note 61, at 23.

[65]*E.g.*, Fronteiro v. Richardson, 411 U.S. 677, 691 (1973) (Powell, J., concurring); Weber v. Aetna Casulty & Surety Co., 406 U.S. 164 (1972) (Powell, J.).

[66]*E.g.*, Chicago Police Dept. v. Mosley, 408 U.S. 92 (1972) (Marshall, J.).

[67]Gunther, *supra* note 41, at 12.

[68]*In re* Winship, 397 U.S. 358 (1970).

[69]405 U.S. 438 (1972).

plague,[70] the majority actually wound up expanding the right to privacy recognized in *Griswold*.[71] The result was that a Court which had only two years earlier rejected a void-for-vagueness challenge to a statute making abortions criminal unless necessary for the preservation of the mother's life or health[72] then struck down all such legislation as interfering with a constitutionally protected, albeit inexplicit, freedom of personal choice in matters of procreation,[73] a right subsequently even further expanded to prevent school boards from requiring pregnant teachers to take "long" maternity leaves.[74] Such an approach to the judicial protection of privacy, at least in sexual matters, can only be viewed as a return of substantive due process.[75]

The Court rendered essentially the same performance in *Furman v. Georgia*, declaring the death penalty to be cruel and unusual punishment.[76] In *McGautha v. California*, the Burger Court had declined to find capital punishment unconstitutional even though imposed by a jury unguided by any standards for deciding the question.[77] But in *Furman* five members of the Court found the penalty to violate the Eighth Amendment. To be sure, three members of the *Furman* majority thought capital punishment unconstitutional only as applied, because arbitrary—to which the popular response has been to remove the arbitrary quality of its application rather than to abandon the penalty—but two Justices declared the penalty to be unconstitutional per se on the basis of what public morality would be if the public knew as much as the Justices knew![78]

Even in the area of criminal procedure, seen by many as the area of

---

[70]Griswold v. Connecticut, 381 U.S. 479 (1965).

[71]"If the right to privacy means anything, it is the right of the individual, married or single, to be free from unwarranted governmental intrusion into matters so fundamentally affecting a person as the decision whether to bear or beget a child." 405 U.S. at 453.

[72]United States v. Vuitch, 402 U.S. 62 (1971).

[73]Doe v. Bolton, 410 U.S. 179 (1973); Roe v. Wade, 410 U.S. 113 (1973).

[74]Cleveland Board of Education v. LaFleur, 414 U.S. 632 (1974). The parameters of "long" were not traversed.

[75]*See* Epstein, *Substantive Due Process by Any Other Name: The Abortion Cases*, 1973 SUP. CT. REV. 159; Tribe, *Toward a Model of Roles in the Due Process of Life and Law*, 87 HARV. L. REV. 1 (1973).

[76]408 U.S. 238 (1972).

[77]402 U.S. 183 (1971).

[78]Justices Douglas, Stewart, and White relied upon the selective application theory. Following *Furman*, more than half of the states have enacted statutes either setting standards for the application of the penalty or making its application mandatory for certain

greatest discontinuity between Warren and Burger Court decision-making, the record has been mixed, with principles established by the Warren Court being broadened as well as qualified. The expansion of the self-incrimination privilege may have come to a stop, but decisions such as *United States v. Knox*,[79] *Bryson v. United States*,[80] and *United States v. Kordel*[81] "afford no evidence that a rollback is forthcoming."[82] In its double jeopardy holdings, by virtue of creating another "special circumstances" rule, the Burger Court has started down the same path that earlier Courts travelled in the right-to-counsel cases.[83] And, as for the right to counsel, while *Miranda* may be distinguished to death, the Court has remained firmly committed to the right to counsel at trial, having taken the logical next step and extended the rule of *Gideon v. Wainwright*[84] to include misdemeanors.[85] So, too, *Griffin v. Illinois*[86] was expanded to provide free transcripts for indigent defendants appealing misdemeanor convictions.[87] Indeed, by providing free transcripts for appeals from cases in which the maximum punishment was a fine with no possibility of imprisonment, the Burger Court went even further in its free transcript decision than it had in the right-to-counsel ruling. In short, the Court has been "neither so hard-nosed nor so soft-headed about this part of its business as its critics would have it."[88]

Such a record, if it does not entirely undermine the claim that the Burger Court has been little more than the Nixon Court, surely suggests that such allegations must be rather seriously qualified. President Nixon's success in "reforming" Supreme Court policy-making has been a mixed bag, and indeed he suffered some grievous losses at the hands of the Burger Court. The result in *United States v. Richard M. Nixon*, of course, contributed to the termination of his presidency.[89] But even

---

types of offenses; *see generally* Note, *Discretion and the Constitutionality of the New Death Penalty Statutes*, 87 HARV. L. REV. 1690 (1974).

Justices Brennan and Marshall relied upon the offensiveness to enlightened public morality—as defined by themselves.

[79] 396 U.S. 77 (1969).
[80] 396 U.S. 64 (1969).
[81] 397 U.S. 1 (1970).
[82] Kurland, *supra* note 61, at 55. *But see* California v. Byers, 402 U.S. 424 (1971).
[83] *E.g.*, Ashe v. Swenson, 397 U.S. 436 (1970); Waller v. Florida, 397 U.S. 387 (1970).
[84] 372 U.S. 335 (1963).
[85] Argersinger v. Hamlin, 407 U.S. 25 (1972).
[86] 351 U.S. 12 (1956).
[87] Mayer v. Chicago, 404 U.S. 189 (1971).
[88] Kurland, *supra* note 35, at 307.
[89] 418 U.S. 683 (1974).

leaving that decision aside on the rationale that, while a significant declaration concerning presidential power, it enunciates a rule of law which (hopefully) will not be subject to frequent application, the Nixon Administration did not exactly enjoy unqualified success before the Court. Most notably in the *Pentagon Papers Case* the administration failed to obtain a judicial certification of its policies;[90] and, although the vote was six-to-three, Mr. Chief Justice Burger, one of the dissenters, later confided to an interviewer that on the substantive issue the Justices had actually been unanimous![91] Similarly, on two different occasions, a unanimous Burger Court rebuked the Nixon position on electronic surveillance.[92] Even when the executive was not directly involved in the litigation before the Court, its decisions did not rubber stamp presidential preference. In education, the Burger Court forced the busing issue and denied aid to parochial schools, in spite of Mr. Nixon's assurances to the Knights of Columbus.[93] The former President may have found the somewhat more conservative tone of the police procedure and obscenity decisions to his liking. But the abortion and death penalty cases can hardly have been pleasing; Mr. Nixon is on record as an opponent of the killing of fetuses[94] and a proponent of the killing of criminals.[95]

Mr. Nixon's effort to redirect the Supreme Court was certainly not an illegitimate one, although it must be conceded that more than most other Presidents his nominations were "made with an eye to politics and ideology rather than to merit or professional distinction."[96] But nomination is not the end of the recruitment process; senatorial conformation is required, and a vigilant Senate and an aroused legal profession turned aside President Nixon's more politically extreme or intellectually mediocre choices.[97] The result has been that a Court even with four Nixon appointees has hardly been his handmaiden. "The three major pillars in the Warren Court's constitutional edifice—Race Relations, Reapportion-

[90]New York Times Co. v. United States, 403 U.S. 713 (1971).

[91]N.Y. Times, July 6, 1971, § 1, at 15, col. 2.

[92]United States v. Giordano, 416 U.S. 505, (1974); United States v. United States District Court, 407 U.S. 297 (1972).

[93]N.Y. Times, Aug. 22, 1971, § 4, at 7, col. 5.

[94]*See* Mason, *The Burger Court in Historical Perspective*, 89 POL. SCI. Q. 27, 38 (1974).

[95]Los Angeles Times, Mar. 11, 1973, § I, at 1, col. 5.

[96]Mason, *supra* note 94, at 28 n. 3.

[97]*See* R. HARRIS, DECISION (1971). *See generally* H. ABRAHAM, JUSTICES & PRESIDENTS: A POLITICAL HISTORY OF APPOINTMENTS TO THE SUPREME COURT (1974).

ment, and Rules of Criminal Procedure—though somewhat eroded are
still virtually intact."[98] In obscenity the approach has continued to be
definitional; and, as a consequence, obscenity law remains a muddle.[99]
The Burger Court has continued to assert a judicial power to limit
decisional retroactivity and a judicial ability to recognize fundamental,
unenumerated rights. The new Chief Justice, like his predecessor, has
displayed great confidence in his own ability to draft a criminal code.[100]
And, even when the results produced by the Burger Court have differed
from those which might reasonably have been expected from the Warren
Court, the decisional approach has remained relatively constant. In
Rodriguez, for example, the court (1) continued the validity of two-level
equal protection analysis and (2) took judicial notice of current social
science research.[101] It should come as little surprise, therefore, that some
of the most thoughtful and scholarly Court-watchers have concluded
that the transition from Warren to Burger has produced less change than
had been anticipated, that the continuities have been more impressive
than the discontinuities.[102]

This continuity, though it was hardly what was advertised either by
President Nixon or by his more partisan critics—perhaps because it did
not make "good" news copy—, has been the result of both institutional
and individual factors; it is attributable both to the nature of the Supreme
Court and to the character of thought of some, if not all, of the "new"
Justices. Continuity is one of the most important contributions of the
Court to the mixed system of government practiced under the American
Constitution.[103] Unlike the other two branches of the federal government, the Supreme Court never starts "from scratch." It is never
renewed at a single blow. No one appointment to the Court, even the
appointment of a Chief Justice, is ever as consequential as a change in the
resident of the White House or the control of Congress. Moreover, "a
'new' court never starts de novo with a wholly new set of ideas."[104]

[98]Mason, *supra* note 94, at 35.

[99]*E.G., compare* Jenkins v. Georgia, 418 U.S. 153 (1974), *with* Miller v. California, 413 U.S. 15 (1973).

[100]*See, e.g.,* Miller v. California, 413 U.S. 15, 25 (1973) (Burger, C.J.); Bivens v. Six Unknown Named Agents, 403 U.S. 388, 422-23 (1971) (Burger, C.J., dissenting).

[101]San Antonio Independent School Dist. v. Rodriguez, 411 U.S. 1, 27 n. 64 (1973).

[102]*E.g.,* Mason, *supra* note 94; Kurland, *supra* note 61, at 91-92; Kalven, *supra* note 51, at 3-6; Gunther, *supra* note 41, at 1-5.

[103]*See* A. BICKEL, THE LEAST DANGEROUS BRANCH: THE SUPREME COURT AT THE BAR OF POLITICS 29-33 (1962).

[104]Kalven, *supra* note 51, at 5.

Judicial change is incremental not precipitate, a process not an event.[105] Each "new" Court carries with it the intellectual baggage of its predecessors, and this is particularly important to understanding the continuities between the Warren and Burger Courts. While political conservatives, the Nixon appointees have also been judicial conservatives. But one of the principal canons of judicial conservatism is adherence to the rule of *stare decisis*. Yet, in contemporary America, this means adherence to fifteen years of precedent established by the Warren Court. The new Justices, then, have been forced to choose between their political conservatism, which urges wholesale reversal of Warren Court policy, and their judicial conservatism, which counsels reliance upon established precedent. Thus far, with the possible exception of Mr. Justice Rehnquist, they have heeded their judicial conservatism. The result has been that the transition from the Warren to the Burger Court, like most previous judicial changes occasioned by political realignment, has involved "subtle shifts in style, direction, and momentum, falling far short of what the public . . . may have expected."[106]

It is no longer too early to chart such shifts. But, because they are subtle and the volume of Burger Court decision-making still affords "little for the Court's expert critics [if] too much for the dilettante Court watcher,"[107] it is treacherous cartography. It is possible to identify certain concerns or patterns underlying Burger Court decision-making. But can one be confident that an apparent trend will take root over the next several terms of Court and grow into a characteristic? It is often difficult to see the forest for the trees, no less so when the forest is enveloped in fog.

Nevertheless, privacy does appear to have become a value whose constitutional time has arrived. The Burger Court has rendered several significant decisions which could be interpreted as manifesting a growing judicial concern for privacy and a willingness to protect it, even if that may involve the sacrifice of other constitutional values. The record, of course, is not unambiguous.[108] In particular, the Burger majority's greater solicitude for law enforcement has produced some

---

[105]See Shapiro, *Stability and Change in Judicial Decision-Making: Incrementalism or Stare Decisis?* 2 LAW IN TRANS. Q. 134 (1965).

[106]Kalven, *supra* note 51, at 5.

[107]Kurland, *supra* note 61, at 91.

[108]See, e.g., California Bankers Assoc. v. Shultz, 416 U.S. 21 (1974); United States v. Kahn, 415 U.S. 143 (1974); Wyman v. James, 400 U.S. 309 (1971).

decisions in which the governmental interest has been sustained in the face of an individual claim to privacy.[109] But these cases "cannot be taken simply as a movement by the Court toward licensing police interference with individual privacy,"[110] for there have been conflicting decisions, even in the area of law enforcement.[111] And when the privacy interest has been interfered with not by the police but by the smut peddler the Burger Court has found the case easy indeed. Thus, in *Rowan v. United States Post Office Dept.*,[112] the Court unanimously upheld the constitutionality of Title III of the Postal Revenue and Federal Salary Act of 1967 which permits private citizens to terminate mailings from specified senders which the recipient, in his sole discretion, finds to be erotically provocative.[113] Failure to comply with the recipient's wishes subjects the sender to criminal penalties. Title III, thus, raises obvious First Amendment problems. But *Rowan* advanced the propositon that "the right of every person 'to be let alone' must be placed in the scales with the right of others to communicate."[114] Once placed in the balance, the privacy right was then found to be the weightier. Similarly, in *Moose Lodge No. 107 v. Irvis*,[115] the Court placed the right to privacy in the scales with the right of others not to be discriminated against on the basis of their race and struck the balance in favor of privacy, though the unanimity of *Rowan* dissipated. The majority, of course, made it clear that the decision was applicable only to truly private clubs and that it would not be fooled by labels.[116] But, if an association were truly private, *Moose Lodge* left little doubt of the majority's feelings about the right to be let alone.

The most significant Court endorsement of a right to privacy, however, has been the abortion decision.[117] In *Griswold*, the Warren court had moved to protect the privacy of the marital bedroom, but in *Eisenstadt v. Baird* the Burger Court reasoned that, if "the distribution of

---

[109]*E.g.*, Adams v. Williams, 407 U.S. 143 (1972); United States v. Biswell, 406 U.S. 311 (1972).

[110]Kurland, *supra* note 35, at 265.

[111]*E.g.*, United States v. United States District Court, 407 U.S. 297 (1972); Coolidge v. New Hampshire, 403 U.S. 443 (1971); Bivens v. Six Unknown Named Agents, 403 U.S. 388 (1971); Colonnade Catering Corp. v. United States, 397 U.S. 72 (1970).

[112]397 U.S. 728 (1970).

[113]39 U.S.C. §4009 (Supp. IV, 1969).

[114]397 U.S. at 736.

[115]407 U.S. 163 (1972).

[116]*Id.* at 177-78; *see e.g.*, Sullivan v. Little Hunting Park, Inc., 396 U.S. 229 (1969); Daniel v. Paul, 395 U.S. 298 (1969).

[117]Doe v. Bolton, 410 U.S. 179 (1973); Roe v. Wade, 410 U.S. 113 (1973).

contraceptives to married persons cannot be prohibited, a ban on distribution to unmarried persons would be equally impermissible."[118] The constitutional right to be let alone could not be predicated on marital status. *Roe* and *Doe* then further advanced the judicial concern for privacy by extending "the . . . right well beyond the limits suggested by prior decisions."[119] Indeed, despite its own efforts that very same term in *Rodriguez* to limit active equal protection analysis to situations in which the Bill of Rights guarantees were closely involved, the Burger Court in the abortion decisions "made no clear attempt to link the woman's interest in the abortion decision either to specific Bill of Rights guarantees or to the traditional concerns of American law."[120] The majority's spokesman, Mr. Justice Blackmun, did indicate that other governmental inhibitions upon the exercise of personal privacy might be acceptable, were they to reflect the predominant moral view of society. But, given the assertions in *Furman* of an ability on the part of some Justices to know what society's morality *would be* if society were just better informed, this need not represent a very significant limitation upon a judiciary determined to protect the right to be let alone.

In *Lloyd Corp., Ltd. v. Tanner*[121] and its companion case, *Central Hardware Co. v. N.L.R.B.*[122] this new appreciation of privacy translated itself into a renewed concern for *private property.*[123] In both cases, the Court permitted the restriction of First Amendment activites, anti-war leafletting and union organizational solicitation respectively, on the ground that the premises involved were not the functional equivalent of public forums.[124] Like *Irvis*, *Lloyd Corp.* and *Central Hardware* taught

[118]405 U.S. at 453.

[119]*The Supreme Court, 1972 Term*, 87 HARV L. REV. at 81 The *Review* argues that in their recognition of a constitutional right to privacy the abortion decisons go beyond both Griswold v. Connecticut, 381 U.S. 479 (1965), and Stanley v. Georgia, 394 U.S. 557 (1969), because both *Griswold* and *Stanley* emphasized the close relationship between the privacy interests endangered and some specific guarantee of the Bill of Rights. Since this was true only of *Stanley*, the *Review* is correct but for the wrong reason. *See* Dixon, *The* Griswold *Penumbra: Constitutional Charter for an Expanded Law of Privacy*, 64 MICH. L. REV. 197 (1965). *Doe* and *Roe* do advance the privacy right recognized in *Griswold*, since it turned either upon privacy in a place, the marital bedroom, or in the marital relationship itself. But the seeds of *Doe* and *Roe* had already been planted in the penumbral theory.

[120]*The Supreme Court, 1972 Term*, 87 HARV. L. REV. at 84.

[121]407 U.S. 551 (1972).

[122]407 U.S. 539 (1972).

[123]*See generally* Funston, *supra* note 21.

[124]*Cf.* Amalgamated Food Employees Local 590 v. Logan Valley Plaza, Inc., 391 U.S. 308 (1968); Marsh v. Alabama, 326 U.S. 501 (1946).

342   *Constitutional Counterrevolution*

the lesson that a corollary of an expanding right to privacy is a contracting doctrine of "state action." As such, the cases "may well mark a watershed in constitutional law.".[125] They have insulated a vast scope of personal choice and action from judicial control. If the discriminatory behavior of individuals is to be curtailed or prevented it will have to be done by legislatures.

Such a conclusion, however, dovetails nicely with a second trait of Burger Court jurisprudence, a greater deference to legislative judgment than characterized the Warren Court.[126] In fact, the Burger Court has displayed a more deferential attitude not only toward legislatures but also toward other governmental agencies. To be sure, the Court has on occasion retrogressed, as in *Furman* where at least some members of the majority thought it a valid judicial function to judge the propriety of the legislative purposes which might be served by capital punishment.[127] But in many other decisions the new Justices have exhibited a desire to transfer the burden of solving society's difficult problems from the judicial to the political process. The days when the Court would attempt to save us from ourselves may have ended. The Burger majority has exhibited little taste for effecting a solution simply because the legislature has failed to act. Rather, through its own modesty, the Court has challenged legislatures to act. In *Laird v. Tatum*, for example, a closely divided Court found that controlling the military surveillance of civilians was properly within the jurisdiction of Congress not that of the Court.[128] In *Branzburg v. Hayes*, the Court strongly suggested that it might be appropriate for legislatures to create statutory privileges to protect newsmen from revealing their sources of information, but it declined to find that such privileges were a matter of constitutional right.[129] Again, in *Environmental Protection Agency v. Mink*, the Burger Court refused to compel the release of documents relating to the Amchitka nuclear test.[130] Though importuned by thirty-eight members of Congress, the Court found that the materials, prepared to advise President Nixon, fell

[125]Kurland, *supra* note 35, at 239.
[126]Like the Warren Court, however, the Burger Court has not been overly receptive to the claims of *legislators* who were parties to litigation before the Court; *see, e.g.,* Environmental Protection Agency v. Mink, 410 U.S. 73 (1973); United States v. Brewster, 408 U.S. 501 (1972); Groppi v. Leslie, 404 U.S. 496 (1972).
[127]408 U.S. at 331 (Marshall, J.).
[128]408 U.S. 1 (1972).
[129]408 U.S. 665 (1972).
[130]410 U.S. 73 (1973).

within two exemptions to the Freedom of Information Act.[131] The Court concluded that Congress had intended the executive to exercise sole judgment as to whether documents should be classified in order to protect the national security or advance foreign policy and that an executive designation of "secret" or "top secret" precluded further inquiry by the judiciary. Congress, of course, if it did not like the situation was left free to repeal or amend the statute, but the Court seemed to be suggesting that Congresswoman Mink and her fellow litigants should address themselves to their congressional colleagues and not to the federal judiciary. And, again, in *Gravel v. United States*, while extending to congressional aides the constitutional protections afforded to Senators and Representatives,[132] the Court found that the protection would not preclude grand jury questioning concerning the gathering of information for a congressional hearing or the private publication of the information gathered.[133] While perhaps a harsh result, "given the fact that Congress still retains the power to eliminate criminal penalties for the release of executive documents . . ., the result reached in *Gravel* may [have been] proper."[134]

When, however, the legislature has acted, the Burger Court has exhibited a willingness to uphold the action, even if it might not have produced such a result itself. In *Lau v. Nichols*, for example, the Court unanimously ordered San Francisco school officials to provide special instruction for Chinese-speaking students.[135] Had the petitioners rested their claim to meaningful participation in the public school program on the Equal Protection Clause, it is doubtful that they would have prevailed, in light of the outcome in *Rodriguez*.[136] But the significant factor differentiating *Lau* from *Rodriguez* and explaining the result was the existence of a colorable statutory claim under the 1964 Civil Rights Act.[137]

Not only have legislatures been the beneficiaries of this new judicial

---

[131]5 U.S.C. § 552 (1966). *See generally* Note, *The Freedom of Information Act and the Exemption for Intra-Agency Memoranda*, 86 HARV. L. REV. 1047 (1973).

[132]U.S. Const. art. I, § 6: "The Senators and Representatives . . . for any speech or debate in either House . . . shall not be questioned in any other place."

[133]408 U.S. 606 (1972). The information in question was, of course, the "Pentagon Papers."

[134]*The Supreme Court, 1971 Term*, 86 HARV. L. REV. 1, 199 (1972).

[135]414 U.S. 563 (1974).

[136]San Antonio Independent School Dist. v. Rodriguez, 411 U.S. 1 (1973).

[137]*See* 42 U.S.C.A. § 2000d (1964).

modesty; other decision-making agencies have also found a more sympathetic judicial ear. In a significant series of cases concerning the regulation of broadcasting, the Burger Court has indicated a serious appreciation of its own lack of expertise in the area and a concomitant desire to leave the resolution of major communications problems in the hands of the F.C.C.[138] The Court has even deferred to the decision-making of an institution for which several of its members have no great enthusiasm, the petit jury. Mr. Chief Justice Burger, in particular, has had faint praise for the jury system in his speeches advocating reforms in judicial administration.[139] Yet, in his opinion for the Court in *Paris Adult Theatre*, the Chief Justice exhibited great confidence in the ability of trial jurors to recognize pornography, ruling that expert testimony as to the social value of a challenged work need not be admitted where the work itself was introduced into evidence.[140] Chief Justice Burger and his colleagues in the majority again expressed a firm trust in the wisdom and rationality of jurors in *Harris v. New York*, feeling that limiting instructions were sufficient to prevent the consideration of unwarned statements as anything other than evidence of the defendant's credibility.[141] *McGautha v. California*, approving standardless discretion for juries in the application of capital punishment,[142] and *Apodaca v. Oregon*, relying upon the presumptive reasonableness of jurors,[143] are yet other examples of a Burger Court confidence in trial juries.

But, if the extrajudicial statements of some of its members suggest that the Burger Court's confidence in the petit jury has been grudging at best, its faith in the grand jury has appeared to know no bounds. Both *Branzburg* and *Gravel* have vested very great power in grand juries to compel the disclosure of information. In *United States v. Dionisio*, the Court concluded that the Fourth Amendment was inapplicable to grand jury subpoenas,[144] and in the *Calandra* case the Court held that unlawfully obtained evidence could lawfully be used as the basis for grand jury questioning.[145] Whether the thrust of these decisions has been

[138]*E.g.*, Columbia Broadcasting Sytem v. Democratic Nat'l. Comm., 412 U.S. 94 (1973).

[139]The Chief Justice, for example, has urged the dropping of juries in most civil cases; Los Angeles Times, Nov. 15, 1970, § at 1, col. 4. *See generally* Zeisel, *And Then There Were None: Dimensions of the Federal Jury*, 38 U. CHI. L. REV. 710 (1971).

[140]Paris Adult Theatre I v. Slaton, 413 U.S. 49, 56 n.6 (1973).

[141]401 U.S. 222 (1971).

[142]402 U.S. 183 (1971).

[143]406 U.S. 404 (1972).

[144]410 U.S. 1 (1973).

[145]United States v. Calandra, 414 U.S. 338 (1974).

to convert the grand jury into an arm of the prosecution,[146] at a minimum they have sustained very far-reaching investigatory power.

This preference for allowing agencies other than courts to govern has been coupled with an apparent desire to shift the burden of decision back to the local level. Contrasted with the Warren Court's nationalization of American problems and problem-solving,[147] this may represent one of the major differences between the Warren and Burger Courts, though the impulses will have to become stronger and more consistent before the pattern is definitive. Nevertheless, even those who abhor such a trend have agreed that it is manifest.[148] Under the Burger Court "the states will be allowed more freedom of movement than in the past, perhaps with the hope that the national system can teach better by example than by precept."[149]

Indeed, the Burger Court's tendency toward decentralization has marked its decisions on reapportionment, obscenity, and school finance. In apportionment, both *Abate v. Mundt*[150] and *Mahan v. Howell*[151] have accorded greater flexibility and discretion to state legislatures in their electoral districting, and they have done so in order to allow for the preservation of the integrity of local political subdivisions. *Milliken v. Bradley*, in rejecting interdistrict remedies for segregated schools, also spoke of local boundaries as something more than mere matters of administrative convenience, the maintenance of which should occasion judicial respect.[152] What *Milliken* may augur for the future of reapportionment, however, remains uncertain. In obscenity, *Miller v. California* has, of course, approved the use of state standards of decency and sexual candor as measures for the obscene,[153] and in *California v. LaRue* the Burger Court made another, albeit disingenuous, bow to localism by resting upon the Twenty-First Amendment to sustain a state power to ban sexually explicit entertainment in bars.[154] But perhaps more graphically than any other case *San Antonio Independent School District v.*

[146]As long ago as 1827, Bentham had already declared that the grand jury, as a shield against unwarranted official prosecution, was obsolete. 2 J. BENTHAM, RATIONALE OF JUDICIAL EVIDENCE 313 (1827).

[147]*See* P. KURLAND, POLITICS, THE CONSTITUTION, AND THE WARREN COURT ch. 3 (1970).

[148]Dorsen, *supra* note 6, at 95.

[149]Kurland, *supra* note 35, at 307.

[150]403 U.S. 182 (1971).

[151]410 U.S. 315 (1973).

[152]418 U.S. 717 (1974).

[153]413 U.S. 15, 30-34 (1973).

[154]409 U.S. 109 (1972). *See generally* Note, *Economic Localism in State Alcoholic*

Rodriguez illustrates the Burger Court's wish to defer to local control.[155] In *Rodriguez*, the Court declined to invoke active equal protection review to test the constitutionality of the local property tax as a means for financing public education, on the grounds that no fundamental interest was involved. In its definition of a fundamental interest, the Court relied heavily upon the absence of any specific recognition of a right to education in the Constitution.[156] Almost all state constitutions, however, contain such provisions.[157] "By basing its decision on the absence of any explicit or implicit right to education in the Federal Constitution, the Court thus left open to state courts the opportunity to find that school finance systems violate state constitutions."[158] Many have done so.[159] In Michigan, for example, the State Supreme Court ruled that, given the existence of a clause in the state constitution providing for public education, education was a fundamental right in Michigan.[160] The state was, thus, required to justify its local property taxation system for financing public education by advancing some compelling state interest which the scheme served. Since no such interest could be found, the system was struck down. *Rodriguez* not merely allowed for such outcomes; it invited them.

There have been decisions which appear to run contrary to this trend, such as *Wright v. Emporia.*[161] There the Court, though impressed by the city's interest in improved educational quality and local control, refused to countenance the creation of a new school district because it would inhibit desegregation efforts. At one level, *Wright* would appear to be in conflict with the result in *Milliken v. Bradley*. But, if one's concern is to respect local political integrity, the two cases are reconcilable. Surely, there is a difference between the dissecting of existing school districts and the adherence to local governmental units of long standing.

Mr. Chief Justice Burger is on record, through his extrajudicial

---

Beverage Laws—Experience Under the Twenty-First Amendment, 72 HARV. L. REV. 1145 (1959).

[155] 411 U.S. 1 (1973).

[156] *Id.* at 33-34.

[157] *See The Supreme Court, 1972 Term,* 87 HARV. L. REV. at 111 n. 44.

[158] *Id.*

[159] *See, e.g.,* Serrano v. Priest, 5 Cal.3d 584 (1971); Milliken v. Green, 389 Mich. 1 (1972); Robinson v. Cahill, 118 N.J. Super. 223 (1972); Sweetwater County Planning Comm. v. Hinkle, 491 P.2d 1234 (Wyo. 1971).

[160] Milliken v. Green, 389 Mich. 1 (1972).

[161] 407 U.S. 451 (1972). *See also* Dunn v. Blumstein, 405 U.S. 330 (1972); Keyes v. School Dist., 413 U.S. 189, 217 (1973) (Powell, J., concurring).

remarks, as having "an abiding conviction that the strength of our entire system in this country and the essence of true federalism lies in diversity among the states."[162] In particular, he has praised the states for being an entire generation ahead of the federal system in the reform of judicial administration. Certainly, such remarks are a change from the days in which the Warren Court's substantive concerns led it to believe that the states were never ahead in anything. Whether the new Chief Justice will be able to lead a majority of his brethren consistently to embrace the proposition that "the states should make the final choices and the final decisions"[163] remains doubtful. But already there has been a "decisive shift in the Court's . . . attitude toward the proper distribution of power between the state and federal [judicial] systems."[164]

This transformation of approach has manifested itself in the resurrection of the abstention doctrine or, to put it more colorfully, "the chilling of *Dombrowski v. Pfister.*"[165] In *Dombrowski,* the Warren Court had permitted the federal courts to entertain challenges to state criminal statutes prior to their enforcement. Reasoning that the threat of prosecution under overly broad statutes affecting free expression would have a "chilling effect" upon the exercise of First Amendment rights,[166] the Court permitted federal judges to enjoin state court proceedings in order to effect a thaw. Motivated by its concern for federalism, however, the Burger Court has narrowed the breadth of *Dombrowski* itself and has done so "in a manner so emphatic as to indicate that the growth prospects of *Dombrowski* as a precedent . . . were being deliberately blunted."[167] It was no surprise that the abstention doctrine had become moribund during the Warren years. "No self-denying ordinance could be appropriate to a jurisprudence that regarded the federal courts as the curer of all ills of American society."[168] Its revival by the Burger Court has served

[162]Address by Chief Justice Warren E. Burger, National Conference on the Judiciary, Mar. 12, 1971, in 54 JUDICATURE 410, 412 (1971).

[163]*Id.* at 417.

[164]*The Supreme Court, 1970 Term,* 85 HARV. L. REV. at 42.

[165]Kalven, *supra* note 51, at 13; Dombrowski v. Pfister, 380 U.S. 479 (1965).

[166]*See generally* Note, *The First Amendment Overbreadth Doctrine,* 83 HARV. L. REV. 844 (1970); Note, *The Chilling Effect in Constitutional Law,* 69 COLUM. L. REV. 808 (1969).

[167]Kalven, *supra* note 51, at 13. *See* Socialist Labor Party v. Gilligan, 406 U.S. 583 (1972); Byrne v. Karalexis, 401 U.S. 216 (1971); Dyson v. Stein, 401 U.S. 200 (1971); Perez v. Ledesma, 401 U.S. 82 (1971); Boyle v. Landry, 401 U.S. 77 (1971); Samuels v. Mackell, 401 U.S. 66 (1971); Younger v. Harris, 401 U.S. 37 (1971); Reetz v. Bozanich, 397 U.S. 82 (1970).

[168]Kurland, *supra* note 61, at 80.

as confirmation of a "trend away from free and easy access to the federal courts for abstract declarations of constitutional invalidity."[169]

The demise of *Dombrowski*, however, has been but one facet of a related trend in Burger Court decision-making, the revival of the "passive virtues."[170] The Court has on several occasions and not without strong dissents aborted cases raising the most serious of constitutional issues.[171] At least three of the Nixon appointees have expressed a desire to narrow the scope of federal habeas corpus relief.[172] and most enticingly the Court has begun a re-examination of the doctrine of standing.[173] In *Broadrick v. Oklahoma*, the Court declined to consider an attack upon the state's "Hatch Act" on the grounds that, even were the legislation overbroad, it was clearly constitutional as applied to the appellants' conduct.[174] The litigants, the Court ruled, could not attack

---

[169]Kurland, *supra* note 35, at 210.

[170]*See generally* Bickel, *The Passive Virtues*, 75 HARV. L. REV. 40 (1961).

[171]*E.g.*, DeFunis v. Odegaard, __U.S.__, 94 S.Ct. 1704 (1974); Monks v. New Jersey, 398 U.S. 71 (1970); DeBacker v. Brainard, 396 U.S. 28 (1969).

The result in *DeFunis*, avoiding the difficult question of "reverse" or "benign" descrimination by invoking the doctrine of mootness, while understandable, is particularly difficult to accept as a logical matter in view of the fact that only a week before the doctrine of mootness had been given an entirely different interpretation in Super Tire Engineering Co. v. McCorkle, __U.S.__, 94 S.Ct. 1694 (1974). In *McCorkle*, the Court held that a dispute over welfare benefits for strikers was justiciable and not moot, even though the strikers had returned to work. In light of *McCorkle*, the dissenters' position in *DeFunis* seems unassailable as a matter of reason if not of judgment.

[172]Schneckloth v. Bustamonte, 412 U.S. 218, 250, 256-71 (1973) (Powell, J., Rehnquist, J., & Burger, C.J., concurring). Mr. Justice Blackmun, concurring separately, stated that he had not joined Justice Powell's opinion because he did not think it necessary to reach the habeas corpus issue, though he added enigmatically that he agreed "with nearly all that Mr. Justice Powell has to say." *Id.* at 249.

Brown v. Allen, 344 U.S. 443 (1953), was the first case in which the Supreme Court held that the federal judiciary might redetermine issues in habeas corpus proceedings which had been fully and fairly adjudicated in state courts. Since *Brown* and the subsequent decisions in Fay v. Noia, 372 U.S. 391 (1963), and Townsend v. Sain, 372 U.S. 293 (1963), the federal district courts have experienced a habeas corpus explosion. *See generally Developments in the Law—Federal Habeas Corpus*, 83 HARV. L. REV. 1038 (1970); Shapiro, *Federal Habeas Corpus: A Study in Massachusetts*, 87 HARV. L. REV. 321 (1973). It has been argued that this expansion of habeas corpus to attack state convictions has imposed too great a burden on the federal courts and has had a deleterious effect upon the state courts. *See, e.g.*, Friendly, *Is Innocence Irrelevant? Collateral Attack on Criminal Judgments*, 38 U. CHI. L. REV. 142 (1970). The Nixon appointees appear to have been persuaded by these arguments.

[173]*See generally* Jaffe, *Standing Again*, 84 HARV. L. REV. 633 (1971); Scott, *Standing in the Supreme Court—A Functional Analysis*, 86 HARV. L. REV. 645 (1973).

[174]413 U.S. 601 (1973).

the statute's overbreadth on the theory that it might be unconstitutionally applied to others. Only the most important countervailing
policies would permit a relaxation of the traditional rules of standing.
Similarly, in *Laird v. Tatum*, the Burger majority adjured an opportunity
to pass upon the military surveillance of civilians, concluding that the
plaintiffs were in no position to seek judicial relief since the exercise of
their First Amendment rights had obviously not been "chilled."[175] "In
short, all shudders are not caused by chills. But what the majority refused
to accept was the proposition that the surveillance was injury itself. . . ."[176] Perhaps most significantly, in *Sierra Club v. Morton*, the
Court refused to grant standing to an environmental protection group to
seek judicial review of an administrative action.[177] Concluding that
public actions had no place in the federal courts, the Court denied
"standing to plaintiffs basing their claims solely on their status as
'citizens.'"[178] Congress, of course, could open the federal judiciary to
such actions, a fact which the Court conceded,[179] again exhibiting a
preference for leaving things to the political processes rather than the
judicial. But the *Sierra Club* majority would not relax the rules of
standing on its own initiative.

Consistency, however, has not marked this constriction of the
standing requirement. Whether these cases should "be regarded as a
sport,"[180] it is true that "self-restraint [has] not yet [been] reinstated as a
governing principle."[181] In some cases, the Burger Court has actually
expanded the class of those qualified to maintain suits in the federal
courts.[182] Similarly, despite its invocation of the abstention doctrine, the
Burger Court has also approved federal court intervention in state
proceedings,[183] expanding the scope of two exceptions to a federal statute

[175]408 U.S. 1 (1972).
[176]Kurland, *supra* note 35, at 232.
[177]405 U.S. 727 (1972).
[178]*The Supreme Court, 1971 Term*, 86 HARV. L. REV. at 239. Undoubtedly the most
intriguing opinion in *Sierra Club* was the dissent of the Court's resident environmentalist,
Mr. Justice Douglas. 405 U.S. at 741. Although he had been one of the most adamant of the
Justices who would deny representation in the legislatures to natural objects, in *Sierra Club*
Justice Douglas would have granted them standing to maintain an action in the federal
courts.
[179]405 U.S. at 732 n. 3.
[180]Kurland, *supra* note 61, at 81.
[181]*Id.*
[182]Barlow v. Collins, 397 U.S. 159 (1970); Data Processing Service v. Camp, 397 U.S.
150 (1970).
[183]Mitchum v. Foster, 407 U.S. 225 (1972); N.L.R.B. v. Nash-Finch Co., 404 U.S. 138
(1971).

which prohibited federal court injunctions of state trials.[184] "However, the Court clearly indicated . . . that its loosening of the . . . prohibition [did] not signify a complete abandonment . . . of the principles of comity and the avoidance of unnecessary federal-state court tensions."[185] Reiterating its respect for the integrity of the state court systems, the Burger Court even in these apparently exceptional cases urged federal interference in state proceedings only under "exceptional circumstances."[186]

In spite of the byzantine contortions, Burger Court decision-making has seemed to display a greater attention to procedural and jurisdictional questions than characterized the Warren Court. There has been at least a tentative "return to the Brandeis-Frankfurter notions about the necessity for a real rather than an abstract case before the Court would indulge in the decision of constitutional issues,"[187] a desire to stay the hand.

These, then, have been the hallmarks of Burger Court decision-making after seven years under the new Chief Justice: a restrained, though unenthusiastic, continuity with Warren Court precedent; a heightened appreciation for privacy, which may yet replace equality as the pre-eminent constitutional value; a new deference to the wisdom of other governmental agencies; a willingness to permit decisional responsibility at the state or even the community level; and a revivification of the doctrines of restraint and self-abnegation. At times, these traits have been but barely discernible at best, but even this faltering has been characteristic of the Court since Richard Nixon replaced Earl Warren with Warren Earl Burger. It has been a Court of prudence and caution, willing to consolidate its ground, unwilling to advance or retreat with abandon. Perhaps its approach to the apportionment cases has been most typical.[188] In those decisions, the Burger Court has asserted a greater tolerance for population deviations than the Warren Court would have, presumably on the theory that this would serve to minimize federal judicial interference with the states' political processes. The Warren

---

[184]28 U.S.C. § 2283. *See also* Lynch v. Household Finance Corp., 405 U.S. 538 (1972) (prejudgment wage garnishments may be enjoined by federal courts because not "proceedings" within the meaning of § 2283); Fuentes v. Shevin, 407 U.S. 67 (1972) (repossession of goods purchased under installment sales contracts held to be extrajudicial procedures not covered by § 2283).

[185]*The Supreme Court, 1971 Term*, 86 HARV. L. REV. at 216.

[186]Younger v. Harris, 401 U.S. 37, 46 (1971).

[187]Kurland, *supra* note 35, at 209.

[188]*E.g.*, Gaffney v. Cummings, 412 U.S. 735 (1973); Mahan v. Howell, 410 U.S. 315 (1973).

Court, of course, found such considerations insufficient to divert it from its self-appointed mission.[189] But the Burger Court, with its greater deference to legislatures and its greater concern for the principle of federalism, has taken a less ambitious concept for the role of the Court and, thus, has sought to lower the federal judicial profile generally. It has, for example, been quick to reprimand federal judges who have continued enchanted with the pursuit of mathematical equality and with their own power.[190] So, too, the Burger Court's withdrawal from fundamental interest analysis,[191] its attempts to avoid decisions based upon active equal protection review,[192] and its narrower position on the right to travel interstate have all betokened a reassessment of the Court's role in the American political process.[193] Burger Court decision-making has quite accurately been characterized as an attempt "to move the Court forward just an inch without committing it to starting down the road to a small social revolution."[194] It is this incrementalism, this prudence and caution, contrasting as it does with the style of Warren Court decision-making, rather than differences in the substance of decision, which has given rise to the popular perception of a Court quite distinct from its predecessor.

Thanks largely to impressions created by the news media, the nation has come to believe that the Supreme Court under Mr. Chief Justice Burger has executed a sharp departure from the paths marked out by its predecessor. This impression has been abetted by some unfortunate rhetorical flourishes on the part not only of Justices Douglas, Brennan, and Marshall, who have found themselves in an uncomfortable minority position, but also of the Nixon appointees. The differences between the Warren and Burger Courts, however, have been more matters of rhetoric than of reality, of degree rather than of substance. This discrepancy between reality and perception merely serves, of course, to emphasize again the importance of the Court as symbol and of symbols to political discussion. The public believes that the Court has changed, and this has been sufficient to reverse the trend toward ever-decreasing public

---

[189]*See, e.g.*, Reynolds v. Sims, 377 U.S. 533, 566 (1964).

[190]Sixty-seventh Minnesota State Senate v. Beens, 406 U.S. 187 (1972).

[191]*E.g.*, San Antonio Independent School Dist. v. Rodriguez, 411 U.S. 1 (1973); Eisenstadt v. Baird, 405 U.S. 438 (1972).

[192]*E.g.*, Vlandis v. Kline, 412 U.S. 441 (1973); Frontiero v. Richardson, 411 U.S. 677 (1973).

[193]Vlandis v. Kline, 412 U.S. 441 (1973).

[194]Kalven, *supra* note 51, at 19-20.

confidence in the Court which was reported in the public opinion polls during the latter years of Mr. Chief Justice Warren's tenure. The polls now find increasing popular approval for the Court. In the summer of 1973, for example, after the abortion, death penalty, and school busing decisions, decisions which if anything represented advances on Warren Court policy and certainly were continuations of Warren Court method, the Gallup Poll found that public reaction to the Burger Court was more favorable than it had been to the Warren Court.[195] An Institute for Survey Research survey conducted some months later, asking Americans to rate fifteen of the nation's major institutions in terms of how well they were serving the country, found the Court outranking the other two branches of the federal government as well as state and local government. And, while the Court ranked only seventh of the fifteen rated institutions, it was seen as the institution with the highest integrity.[196]

This era of good feelings which the Burger Court has enjoyed during its first half decade, however, cannot continue without some positive contribution from the Court itself. Like its predecessor, the Burger Court must eventually face up to the necessity of opinion craftsmanship and provide reasoned and reasonable explanations for its policy choices. After a period of suspended judgment, legal scholars and other opinion leaders have now begun to assess the Burger Court's intellectual powers.[197] While they have necessarily been qualified, the assessments have not been favorable.

Burger Court decision-making has seemed to be clearer about where it does not want to go than about where it does. While it has displayed little constitutional creativity, it has set limits to the growth of Warren Court doctrine. Often, however, this has been accomplished through "the most crabbed handling of precedents and the most inarticulate reasoning."[198] In part, of course, the Warren Court's own failures of logical coherence have invited this. The Burger majority has shown no desire to overrule or

[195]Los Angeles Times, July 29, 1973, § I-A, at 1, col. 1.

[196]I.S.R. Newsletter, Winter, 1974, at 8. On a scale of 0 to 8 (from very poor job to very good job), the Court rated 4.82. The institution receiving the highest rating, 5.50, was the military; the lowest-rated institution was the presidency, 3.30.

[197]*See, e.g.*, Symposium, *The Burger Court: New Directions in Judicial Policy-Making*, 23 EMORY L.J. 641 (1974); Howard, *Mr. Justice Powell and the Emerging Nixon Majority*, 70 MICH. L. REV. 445 (1972); Bickel, *The New Supreme Court: Prospects and Problems*, 45 TULANE L. REV. 229 (1971); Mason, *supra* note 94; Tribe, *supra* note 75; Kalven, *supra* note 51; Gunther, *supra* note 41, Mendelson, *supra* note 18; Kurland, *supra* notes 35, 38, and 61.

[198]Gunther, *supra* note 41, at 4.

even to restrict the expansion of precedent firmly founded in clear and careful explanation. But there's the rub! "The Warren Court's errors are coming home to roost: the widely criticized deficiencies in articulating adequate reasons, and the occasional preference for the tortured, evasive response to basic constitutional issues make the Warren Court philosophical legacy a fragile one."[199] But the new Court will not be able to remain content with confining the jurisprudence of the Warren Court and marking time. Eventually, it must either follow the logical imperative of precedent or "explain the reasons for departure from it and . . . justify, again by reason rather than personal predilection, the results reached in every case."[200] In its first half decade, the Burger Court has proven itself unwilling to do the former and apparently incapable of doing the latter. The result has been to introduce into its opinions an intellectually confused quality which reflects the practice of the Warren Court even when rejecting its precedent. Perhaps a few examples may suffice.

In its war upon the obscene, the Burger Court has continued the two-level theory of the First Amendment.[201] The use of this scheme of analysis has not been unique to obscenity cases. Earlier Courts used it to sustain the regulation of "fighting words"[202] and to justify the prohibition of libel.[203] But the Burger Court has actually extended the Warren Court's position on the First Amendment law of libel,[204] rejecting the "public figure" rule for determining the scope of the constitutional protection and taking "a significant step toward the absolute immunization of the news media from libel judgments."[205] Had the libel cases been decided before *Roth*, "the Court would have been unable to use the two-level theory in the obscenity area, or at least been without any precedent to support such use."[206] Nevertheless, the Burger Court has persisted in

---

[199]*Id.* at 3-4

[200]Kurland, *supra* note 35, at 329.

[201]*See generally* T. EMERSON, THE SYSTEM OF FREEDOM OF EXPRESSION 485-95 (1970).

[202]Chaplinsky v. New Hampshire, 315 U.S. 568 (1942).

[203]Beauharnais v. Illinois, 343 U.S. 250 (1952).

[204]*Compare* Rosenbloom v. Metromedia, Inc., 403 U.S. 29 (1971), *and* Ocala Star-Banner Co. v. Damron, 401 U.S. 295 (1971), *and* Time, Inc. v. Pape, 401 U.S. 279 (1971), *and* Monitor Patriot Co. v. Roy, 401 U.S. 265 (1971), *with* Curtis Publishing Co. v. Butts, 388 U.S. 130 (1967), *and* Associated Press v. Walker, 388 U.S. 130 (1967), *and* New York Times Co. v. Sullivan, 376 U.S. 254 (1964). *But cf.* Gertz v. Robert Welch, Inc., 418 U.S. 323 (1974).

[205]*The Supreme Court, 1970 Term*, 85 HARV. L. REV. at 222.

[206]*The Supreme Court, 1972 Term*, 87 HARV. L. REV. at 163; *see also* Kalven, *The*

nurturing the two-level theory in its obscenity decisions, while eroding the rule's philosophic base in its libel cases.

This doctrinal dualism has appeared again in the equal protection litigation,[207] where the Court has at times endorsed two-level equal protection analysis,[208] while on other occasions the Justices have attempted to create a single standard of intermediate vigor.[209] But the Burger Court's inability to articulate a coherent theory of equal protection review has been most troubling when contrasted with the standard of review under the Due Process Clause adopted in the abortion cases. In *Rodriguez*,[210] the Court rested its rejection of the equal protection claim on the principle that "it is not the province of this Court to create substantive constitutional rights."[211] Yet four of the Justices who signed that statement, including three of the Nixon appointees, had in *Doe* and *Roe* adopted a position clearly related and relatable to the open-ended, fundamental rights reasoning of *Griswold*.[212] In an attempt to buttress its creation of a substantive right to decide whether to bear a child, the *Roe* majority emphasized the practical importance of the abortion decision for the pregnant woman.[213] But if, as *Rodriguez* would have it, the determination of whether the abortion decision is constitutionally protected must rest solely upon the explicit wording of the Constitution, the importance of the individual's decision is itself irrelevant to the Justices decision. Surely the educational decisions involved in *Rodriguez* were of some consequence for the affected children.

Moreover, the abortion decisions' concern for the protection of possibly odious private choice in matters sexual could not be comfort-

---

New York Times Case: A Note on "The Central Meaning of the First Amendment," 1964 SUP. CT. REV. 191, 204-05, 217-18.

[207]*See* Gunther, *supra* note 41.

[208]*E.g.*, San Antonio Independent School Dist. v. Rodriguez, 411 U.S. 1 (1973).

[209]*E.g.*, Reed v. Reed, 404 U.S. 71 (1971).

[210]San Antonio Independent School Dist. v. Rodriguez, 411 U.S. 1 (1973).

[211]*Id.* at 33.

[212]Mr. Chief Justice Burger and Justices Blackmun, Powell, and Stewart were in the majorities in both *Rodriguez* and the abortion cases. They were, however, not the only "switchers;" Mr. Justice White, who opposed the creation of unenumerated, fundamental rights in *Doe* and *Roe*, would have had the judiciary create a right to education and, thus, wound up in the minority in *Rodriguez* as well as in the abortion cases. On the other hand, Justices Douglas, Brennan, and Marshall, ever ready to expand the law to reach the "right" result, dissented in *Rodriguez* but helped to form the majority in *Doe* and *Roe*. With equal consistency, Mr. Justice Rehnquist rejected substantive due process in the abortion cases and substantive equal protection in the school finance decision, dissenting in the former and providing the critical, fifth vote in the latter.

[213]Roe v. Wade, 410 U.S. 113, 153 (1973).

ably squared with the Court's position in the obscenity cases.[214] If a woman's right to seek an abortion creates in a physician an immunity from prosecution under criminal abortion statutes, why doesn't an individual's decision to examine pornographic materials, itself protected under *Stanley*,[215] create a right of access to secure such materials?

The reapportionment cases have fared little better. *Gordon v. Lance*,[216] by approving a state constitutional requirement of extraordinary majorities for the approval of bond issues, has undermined "majoritarianism as a rule of decision."[217] The Warren Court, in the teeth of overwhelming countervailing evidence in the American constitutional tradition, had appeared to shape simple majoritarianism into a Fourteenth Amendment principle. While the Burger Court was probably correct in abandoning this alleged basis for the reapportionment cases, *Gordon* and its companion cases[218] make it necessary, as a vindicated Harlan cautioned in concurrence,[219] for the Court to supply some alternative rationale on which to rest reapportionment doctrine. Subsequent cases, however, have suggested that "the Court is not likely openly to 'recognize the error of its ways' for some time to come."[220] Indeed, one of the Burger Court's attempts to escape from the morass has involved the drawing of distinctions between congressional and state legislative districting.[221] Reduced to its essence, the position rests upon the bare statement that in the future the two will be treated differently because they are different. (It is a position which parallels the effort to distinguish between public aid to parochial higher education and aid to church-related elementary and secondary schools).[222] "One man, one vote," thus, has continued as the rule under the Burger Court, "although whatever doctrinal base it might have had [has taken] a bad beating."[223]

[214]Paris Adult Theatre I v. Slaton, 413 U.S. 49 (1973); Miller v. California, 413 U.S. 15 (1973); United States v. Thirty-seven Photographs, 402 U.S. 363 (1971); United States v. Reidel, 402 U.S. 351 (1971).

[215]Stanley v. Georgia, 394 U.S. 557 (1969).

[216]403 U.S. 1 (1971).

[217]*Id.* at 167 (Harlan, J., concurring).

[218]Abate v. Mundt, 403 U.S. 182 (1971); Whitcomb v. Chavis, 403 U.S. 124 (1971).

[219]*Id.* at 165.

[220]Kurland, *supra* note 38, at 283.

[221]*Compare* White v. Weiser, 412 U.S. 783 (1973), *with* White v. Regester, 412 U.S. 755 (1973), *and* Gaffney v. Cummings, 412 U.S. 735 (1973).

[222]*E.g., compare* Hunt v. McNair, 413 U.S. 734 (1973), *and* Tilton v. Richardson, 403 U.S. 672 (1971), *with* Committee for Public Education and Religious Liberty v. Nyquist, 413 U.S. 756 (1973), *and* Lemon v. Kurtzman, 403 U.S. 602 (1971).

[223]Kurland, *supra* note 38, at 284.

In the area of law enforcement policy, the Burger Court's pronouncements have been no less—though no more—*ad hoc* than its predecessors. When it has not, as in *Harris*[224] or *Kirby*[225] or *Russell*,[226] been continuing rules without engaging in any analysis of their theoretical or practical defects, it has persisted "in its role as a court of errors and appeals, deciding individual cases while affording little guidance to the other courts that have to administer the rule."[227] The result has been that the law of criminal defendants' rights, if it does not resemble the proverbial one-way railroad ticket, has remained in considerable flux.

But perhaps no area has been as characterized by *ad hoc* decisionmaking as racial discrimination policy. In *Wright v. Emporia*,[228] for example, the majority was considerably influenced by the possibility that "white flight" from the county school system would create schools with substantially disproportionate racial compositions. The likelihood of such schools developing was thought a fit predicate for recognizing broad powers in a lower federal court to achieve desegregation. But in *Milliken v. Bradley* the manifest reality of "white flight" was thought to be a factor of negligible importance.[229] In *DeFunis v. Odegaard* a majority could not be found ready even to confront the issue of "reverse racial discrimination" let alone to resolve it.[230] But when a related issue arose in the context of sexual discrimination the Court not ony decided the case on its merits but upheld a Florida statute favoring women at the expense of men.[231] The only feature the two cases held in common was the paucity of explanation.

This should not be taken to mean that mediocrity has uniformly characterized Burger Court opinions. Rather, their quality has been uneven. This differential quality has apparently been conditioned by the new Justices' response to Warren precedent. Where they have grappled "with those Warren era values which they find most congenial,"[232] they have produced some very carefully reasoned opinions.[233] With the glaring exception of the obscenity cases, this has been particularly true of

[224]Harris v. New York, 401 U.S. 222 (1971).
[225]Kirby v. Illinois, 406 U.S. 682 (1971).
[226]United States v. Russell, 411 U.S. 423 (1973).
[227]Kurland, *supra* note 61, at 28.
[228]407 U.S. 451 (1972).
[229]418 U.S. 717 (1974).
[230]416 U.S. 312 (1974).
[231]Kahn v. Shevin, 416 U.S. 351 (1974).
[232]Gunther, *supra* note 41, at 4.
[233]*E.g.*, Griggs v. Duke Power Co., 401 U.S. 424 (1971).

the Burger Court's First Amendment interpretation, both of the speech and press clauses and of the religion clauses.[234] These decisions have often been supported by lucid statements demonstrating a grasp of the issues' complexities. But, when confronted with policy directions with which it disagrees, the new majority's logic and its reading of precedent have been disingenuous. Unfortunately, what this has meant in practice has been that the Burger Court's clearest and most craftsmanlike contributions to constitutional exegesis have come in the field of church-state relations which, while not unimportant, has not been a subject of great social moment.

Especially has this been true of the decisions of the new Chief Justice himself. At times he has displayed flashes of great ingenuity. His remarks in *Swann* on the origin of segregated residential patterns and his position in *Walz* that tax exemptions actually promoted the separation of church and state suggest a Madisonian mentality, the solution to a problem is to be found in the problem itself.[235] But at other times, when the limits of the judicial process have felt too confining, the Chief Justice has manifested a penchant for statute drafting, advising the nation's legislators on how to control pornography and secure the overthrow of the exclusionary rule.[236] Such opinions differ not at all from the Warren Court's ill-fated efforts in *Miranda* and *Schmerber*.[237]

It has been almost touching to find those who applauded the Warren Court and turned a deaf ear to criticisms of its opinion drafting now complaining about "decisions that pronounce rather than persuade."[238] Those who ignored warnings about the dangers inherent in fundamental interest analysis now object that 5-4 votes are merely reflections of "numerical power."[239] But it has not been and will not be enough for the Burger Court to adopt Warren Court methodology and turn it to other ends. "What is a vice in a liberal . . . is not necessarily a virtue in a

---

[234]*E.g.*, Wisconsin v. Yoder, 406 U.S. 205 (1972); Coates v. Cincinnati, 402 U.S. 611 (1971); Walz v. Tax Commission, 397 U.S. 664 (1970).

[235]Swann v. Charlotte-Mecklenburg, 402 U.S. 1, 20-21 (1971); Walz v. Tax Commission, 397 U.S. 664, 674-76 (1970).

[236]Miller v. California, 413 U.S. 15, 25 (1973) (Burger, C.J.); Bivens v. Six Unknown Named Agents, 403 U.S. 388, 411 (1971) (Burger, C.J., dissenting).

[237]Miranda v. Arizona, 384 U.S. 436 (1966); Schmerber v. California, 384 U.S. 757 (1966).

[238]*The Supreme Court, 1971 Term*, 86 HARV. L. REV. at 164.

[239]Dershowitz & Ely, Harris v. New York: *Some Anxious Observations on the Candor and Logic of the Emerging Nixon Majority*, 80 YALE L.J. 1198, 1226 (1971).

conservative."[240] What is necessary is a renewed judicial appreciation for craftsmanship. Warren Court precedent should be no more sacrosanct than any other prior conclusions reached by the Supreme Court, perhaps even less so. But, if they are to be laid to rest, they should "not be denied the modest rite of a funeral oration."[241]

At least in its early years, the Burger Court has seemed to represent the triumph of Potter Stewart. If not as opinion leader, as dominant vote, Mr. Justice Stewart has been a central figure on the Court. In this role, of course, he has been joined by Mr. Justice White. But, in symbolic terms, Mr. Justice Stewart has at times seemed almost to personify the Burger Court's decisional mode and direction. Throughout his tenure, Justice Stewart has often relied upon *ad hoc* judgment; his "I-know-it-when-I-see-it" approach has surfaced in areas other than obscenity, if never quite so explicitly.[242] The Burger Court, of course, through its confident endorsement of the perceptual powers of trial jurors, has elevated this approach to the status constitutional doctrine in obscenity trials.[243] Its more modest view of the scope of the Establishment Clause has seemed to echo Mr. Justice Stewart's position in *Engel v. Vitale*.[244] In reapportionment, the greater flexibility of the Burger Court in measuring permissible population deviations between districts has been reminiscent of Stewart's concern in *Lucas* for overall fairness.[245] The trend in criminal law policy has also seemed to signal a return to Stewart's position in *Escobedo* regarding when the right to counsel becomes operative.[246] And, as for desegregation of the schools, the apparent disjunction between *Wright v. Emporia*[247] and *Milliken v. Bradley*[248] may be accounted for, if not explained by, the fact that it was Potter Stewart who

---

[240]*Id.* at 1227.

[241]McCloskey, *Economic Due Process and the Supreme Court: An Exhumation and Reburial,* 1962 SUP. CT. REV. 34, 40.

[242]*See* Jacobellis v. Ohio, 378 U.S. 184, 197 (1964) (Stewart, J., concurring).

[243]Paris Adult Theatre I v. Slaton, 413 U.S. 49, 56 n.6 (1973).

[244]370 U.S. 421, 444 (1962) (Stewart, J., dissenting); *see, e.g.,* Tilton v. Richardson, 403 U.S. 672 (1971); Walz v. Tax Commission, 397 U.S. 664 (1970).

[245]Lucas v. Forty-fourth Gen'l Assembly of Colorado, 377 U.S. 713, 744 (1964) (Stewart, J. dissenting); *see, e.g.,* Gaffney v. Cummings, 412 U.S. 735 (1973); Mahan v. Howell, 410 U.S. 315 (1973); Abate v. Mundt, 403 U.S. 182 (1971). *See generally* Baker, *One Man, One Vote, and "Political Fairness"—Or, How the Burger Court Found Happiness by Rediscovering* Reynolds v. Sims, 23 EMORY L. J. 701 (1974).

[246]Escobedo v. Illinois, 378 U.S. 478, 493 (1964) (Stewart, J., dissenting); *see* Kirby v. Illinois, 406 U.S. 682 (1972).

[247]407 U.S. 451 (1972).

[248]418 U.S. 717 (1974).

cast the fifth and majority vote in both cases. Stewart, then, may come to play the role for the new Court which Mr. Justice Black played for the old. It was Black's constitutional theories that were effectuated by the Warren Court's decisions. It may yet be Stewart's ideology which will be vindicated by the votes of the Burger majority. Unfortunately, however, for the Court as an institution, while Mr. Justice Black had a carefully thought out judicial philosophy, Mr. Justice Stewart has not. Upon his appointment to the Court, when asked by reporters what was his judicial philosophy, Stewart replied, "I really don't know what it is."[249] At times since he took his seat, Mr. Justice Stewart's career has suggested a conscious effort to provide documentation of the veracity of that remark.[250] The result has been that a Court which mirrors his approach has been a Court adrift.

As is so often the case, statistical data about the Burger Court have tended to substantiate the conclusions reached without their assistance by more "impressionistic" observers, relying upon the analysis of decisional substance.[251] After an interim period in which there was little or no pattern to the voting, the Court has settled into a trifurcated state. Unlike the latter Warren Court, which was split into two relatively stable wings, the new Court consists of a left, a right, and an uncohesive center. On the left, with Douglas gone, are Justices Brennan and Marshall, the champions of the old era. On the right are Mr. Chief Justice Burger and Mr. Justive Blackmun,[252] joined by Mr. Justice Rehnquist. In the middle, one finds Stewart, White and Powell. This middle group, then, has been the "swing" group. But, if that term is taken to mean that they have been as likely to vote with the Douglas-Brennan-Marshall troika as with the

---

[249]N.Y. Times, Oct. 8, 1958, § 1, at 1, col. 1.

[250]*See* Israel, *Potter Stewart*, in 4 THE JUSTICES OF THE SUPREME COURT 1789-1969: THEIR LIVES AND MAJOR OPINIONS 2921 (L. Fiedman & F. Israel eds. 1969).

[251]The statistical data is collected and presented in *The Supreme Court, 1972 Term*, 87 HARV. L. REV. 1, 303-14 (1973); *The Supreme Court, 1971 Term*, 86 HARV. L. REV. 1, 297-306 (1972); *The Supreme Court, 1970 Term*, 85 HARV. L. REV. 3, 344-53 (1971); *The Supreme Court, 1969 Term*, 84 HARV. L. REV. 1, 247-53 (1970); Kurland, *supra* note 35, at 182-87; Kurland, *supra* note 38, at 268-72; Kurland, *supra* note 61, at 2-5.

[252]The Washington press corps was quick to label the Chief Justice and Mr. Justice Blackmun the "Minnesota Twins" due to their high levels of interagreement. While conceding the humor of the appellation, it should be noted that, in their unyielding efforts to over-simplify the complex, the reporters ignored the fact that during the very same terms the levels of interagreement between Justices Douglas, Brennan, and Marshall were at least as high if not higher, as also was the level of interagreement between Mr. Justice Brennan and Mr. Chief Justice Warren during the last *six terms* of the latter's tenure. Kurland, *supra* note 38, at 268; *The Supreme Court, 1970 Term*, 85 HARV. L. REV. at 345.

Burger-Blackmun-Rehnquist triumvirate, it must be conceded that the centrists have not swung much. Rather, they have tended to vote much more consistently with the right wing. For a time, it did appear that Mr. Justice Stewart was moving toward a more liberal position in response to the shifting center of gravity on the Burger Court.[253] But his subsequent performance has suggested that this was at most a short-term phenomenon which has now terminated. This voting pattern, however, may suggest why, in its first half decade, the Burger Court has done so little to reverse Warren Court precedent. Even when Mr. Justice Powell has joined the other Nixon appointees, "the lack of an assured 'fifth' vote means that concessions must be made, bargains struck, and wholesale repudiation of the legacy of the Warren Court postponed."[254] Moreover, such a conclusion assumes that the new Justices, as a monolithic bloc, have desired to reject Warren Court doctrine. But there has been evidence in the opinions themselves that only Mr. Justice Rehnquist and perhaps Mr. Chief Justice Burger have that sort of uncompromising philosophic hostility toward the Warren Court. But whatever assumption one grants, the ironic conclusion suggested by the statistical data is that the fate of Warren Court decision-making rests with two Justices, Stewart and White, who were among its least enthusiastic supporters.

The appointment of a Nixon quartet has not, then, transformed a slim liberal majority into a slim conservative majority. Instead, in the mid-1970s America has been confronted with a Supreme Court "perhaps more fragmented than at any time in its history."[255] The commentary upon the Burger Court's work has been replete with such adjectives as "divided,"[256] "ambivalent,"[257] "uncertain,"[258] and "indecisive."[259] The Court has been seen—correctly—as being in "disarray"[260] and "in search of a role."[261] The absence of a stable majority has been evidenced by the extraordinary number of cases in which the Burger Court has been so

---

[253]*See* Dorsen, *supra* note 6, at 85.

[254]Grossman & Wells, *Introduction: The Burger Court in Search of a Role*, in SUPPLEMENTAL CASES FOR CONSTITUTIONAL LAW AND JUDICIAL POLICY MAKING 6 (J. Grossman & R. Wells eds. 1973).

[255]*The Supreme Court, 1970 Term*, 85 HARV. L. REV. at 345.

[256]Gunther, *supra* note 41, at 1.

[257]TIME, July 22, 1974, at 15.

[258]Gunther, *supra* note 41, at 1.

[259]TIME, July 22, 1974, at 15.

[260]Kurland, *supra* note 38, at 298.

[261]Grossman & Wells, *supra* note 254.

split that there has been no majority opinion[262] as well as by the relatively numerous instances in which decisions have been affirmed by an equally divided Court.[263] And perhaps the most distressing aspect of this development has been the unusually acerbic tone of some of the opinions.[264] While the Burger Court's internal divisions may be no more serious than those of earlier courts, they have certainly seemed to be more bitter. Nor have the differences between Justices often been made so painfully public. In the long run, this personal rancor cannot enhance the Court's image.

Such performance, however, may become the norm, unless the Burger Court develops a coherent judicial philosophy. But for the decisional trends identified earlier to be molded into a set of constitutional principles will require that one or more of the Justices assume the role of intellectual leader of the Court. The deaths of Justices Black and Harlan seriously deprived the Burger Court of this intellectual leadership.[265] Though these two men differed in their premises, philosophies, and conclusions, they were alike in their insistence upon thinking through the constitutional problems, rather than simply resolving cases on an *ad hoc* basis. With their departure, the Court is threatened with disintegration, unless someone "emerge(s) from the shadows to lead the Court in justifying its conclusions by adequate reason."[266] Both Mr.

[262]*E.g.*, Furman v. Georgia, 408 U.S. 238 (1972); Kirby v. Illinois, 406 U.S. 682 (1972); New York Times Co. v. United States, 403 U.S. 713 (1971); Tilton v. Richardson, 403 U.S. 672 (1971); United States v. Harris, 403 U.S. 573 (1971); McKiever v. Pennsylvania, 403 U.S. 528 (1971); Coolidge v. New Hampshire, 403 U.S. 443 (1971); Rosenbloom v. Metromedia, Inc., 403 U.S. 29 (1971); California v. Byers, 402 U.S. 424 (1971); United States v. Thirty-seven Photographs, 402 U.S. 363 (1971); United States v. White, 401 U.S. 745 (1971); Mackey v. United States, 401 U.S. 667 (1971); Williams v. United States, 401 U.S. 646 (1971); *In re* Stolar, 401 U.S. 23 (1971); Baird v. State Bar, 401 U.S. 1 (1971); United States v. Jorn, 400 U.S. 470 (1971); Oregon v. Mitchell, 400 U.S. 112 (1970); Dutton v. Evans, 400 U.S. 74 (1970).
See generally The Supreme Court, 1970 Term, 85 HARV. L. REV. at 352-53.
[263]*E.g.*, School Board of Richmond v. State Board of Education, 412 U.S. 92 (1973); Grove Press, Inc. v. Maryland State Board of Censors, 401 U.S. 480 (1971); California v. Pinkus, 400 U.S. 922 (1970). *See generally The Supreme Court, 1970 Term*, 85 HARV. L. REV. at 353.
[264]*E.g.*, Coolidge v. New Hampshire, 403 U.S. 443, 493 (1971) (Burger, C.J. dissenting); Rogers v. Bellei, 401 U.S. 815, 845 (1971) (Brennan, J., dissenting); Labine v. Vincent, 401 U.S. 532, 541 (1971) (Brennan, J., dissenting). *See generally* Los Angeles Times, April 11, 1971, § A, at 2, col. 1.
[265]*See* Kurland, *supra* note 38, at 319-22.
[266]*Id.* at 321.

Justice Stewart and Mr. Justice White may have the potential, but nether has exhibited any desire for the role. Neither Mr. Chief Justice Burger nor Mr. Justice Blackmun may have the intellectual capacities. It is unlikely that either member of the Warren duo will do so. The Court and the country, thus, have been left with Mr. Justice Rehnquist and Mr. Justice Powell. Rehnquist is unquestionably a superior legal technocrat, though hardly a "strict constuctionist," if that term is taken to mean opposition to expanded governmental power vis-à-vis the individual.[267] But in his first terms, Rehnquist has given every appearance of desiring to become a right-wing reflection of Mr. Justice Douglas, and like his counter-part on the left it is doubtful that he could secure the confidence of his colleagues necessary to become the Court's dominant spokesman. In time, Mr. Justice Powell could become the Court's professional conscience. His age would appear to be the chief obstacle. But he has the mental ability, and in his early career he "has cast himself in the role of heir to the Frankfurter-Harlan mantle."[268]

How the Burger Court and its Chief Justice are remembered will hinge largely upon whom, if anyone, emerges to marshall and direct its intellectual energies. Mr. Chief Justice Burger is "closer to Chief Justice Warren's jurisprudence and talents than he is to those of a Frankfurter or a Jackson. It is possible that the new Chief Justice, like the old one, instead of molding the court in his own image will instead be made over in the image of the Court."[269] Potential analogies abound. The Burger Court's sharp divisions and its failure to develop any clear pattern of decision have reminded some of the Court under Stone and Vinson.[270] Others, influenced by Mr. Chief Justice Burger's concern for administration and his extrajudicial activity, have suggested a resemblance to Mr. Chief Justice Taft, a similarity heightened by the parallel between the teamwork of Burger and Blackmun and the voting record of Taft and Van Devanter as well as the role played by both Chief Justices in the selection of their closest colleague.[271] But the most optimistic analogy would be to the Taney Court. During the Warren years, the Court's

[267]Miller, *Rehnquist Hardly a "Strict Constructionist,"* Los Angeles Times, Nov. 7, 1971, §G, at 1, col. 1.

[268]Kurland, *supra* note 35, at 181. *See also* Gunther, *In Search of Judicial Quality on a Changing Court: The Case of Justice Powell,* 24 STAN. L. REV. 1001 (1972).

[269]Kurland, *supra* note 61, at 91.

[270]E.g., Dorsen, *supra* note 6, at 83; Kurland, *supra* note 38, at 320.

[271]*See, e.g.,* Swindler, *The Chief Justice and Law Reform, 1921-1971,* 1971 SUP. CT. REV. 241; Kurland, *supra* note 38, at 271.

defenders were, of course, quick to draw parallels with the Marshall Court.[272] "Perhaps the analogy may prove more insightful than intended. After the Marshall era, a period of great constitutional creativity, the Court experienced a period characterized by limitation and modification but not by major departure from established precedent. Under Mr. Chief Justice Taney . . ., the Court sought to answer the difficult, if minor, questions left open by Marshall's sweeping declarations of policy and did so with great success. The Burger Court may yet play Taney to Warren's Marshall."[273]

But, if that is to happen, the Burger Court must strive for the highest standards of constitutional adjudication. The Taney example, of course, suggests that this is an attainable goal. Even a caretaker Court "more concerned with the state of the law than the state of the country"[274] can creatively consolidate the past with the present so as to limit the expansion of old doctrines without creating new ones. "Reconciliation of the impacts of personnel changes with the demands of judicial craftsmanship is a challenge that confronts any Court in transition. Can the Burger Court meet that challenge with distinction, or is it doomed to drift for years?"[275] Some early assessments have been optimistic.[276] But other analysts have expressed serious doubt that the present panel possesses the necessary reservoir of talent.[277] For them, the Burger Court's continuity has been stale and arid, deriving largely from the similarity between the unsatisfying character of its opinions and those of its predecessor.

In short, the popularly postulated schism between the Burger Court and the Warren Court has neither been as great as claimed nor perhaps as great as it should have been. In terms of results, even thoroughgoing civil libertarians have been forced to admit that a Court which has outlawed the death penalty, validated busing, refused to reverse *Reynolds*, rendered the abortion decisions, and extended the right to counsel "is not a complete loss."[278] In terms of the reasoning offered to support those

[272]E.g., Black, *The Unfinished Business of the Warren Court*, 46 WASH. L. REV. 3, 10-12 (1970). *See generally* P. KURLAND, *supra* note 147, at 10-15 (1970).

[273]Funston, *The Burger Court: New Directions in Judicial Policy-Making*, 23 EMORY L.J. 643, 656 (1974).

[274]Grossman & Wells, *supra* note 254, at 12.

[275]*Gunther*, supra note 41, at 5.

[276]*See, e.g., id.* at 7; Kalven, *supra* note 51, at 3-6, 36.

[277]*See, e.g.*, Kurland, *supra* note 38, at 319-22.

[278]Dorsen, *supra* note 6, at 103.

results, the Burger Court's rationales have been as ill thought through and often as *ad hoc* as those of the Warren Court. Unable to define its own identity and uncertain of what, if any, new philosophical direction it should ultimately take, the Burger Court's thinking has been largely derivative. It has displayed some limited creativity, as in the area of privacy, but that creativity has been chiefly characterized by a reluctance to take the bold stroke. Even in its integrative decisions, however, it has often failed to provide "adequate reason and doctrine on which those conclusions could be properly based. As is evident from the ease with which some of the jerry-built Warren Court opinions are threatened with extinction, so, too, will those that replace them be judgments for the moment unless some strong intelligence with a sense of institutional function explains why the answers are what the answers are."[279]

No President since Franklin Delano Roosevelt, perhaps no President in history, made such an election issue of the Supreme Court of the United States as did Richard M. Nixon. No presidential candidate ever created such public expectation that he could and would redirect the course and style of judicial policy-making. "But because these expectations were created to meet the needs of the President they were not necessarily realistic in terms of how the Supreme Court operates."[280] In the past, successful nominees to the Court have often proven independent and unpredictable; and, even when they have not, certain institutional factors have precluded radical transformations. While judicial interpretation can be changed and does change over time, the inherent incrementalism of the judicial process dictates that such change occur slowly and within the intellectual framework established by preceding Courts. In spite of Nixon promises, therefore, the Warren Court's work has not yet been threatened with wholesale reversals, especially by "strict constructionists" dedicated to the doctrine of *stare decisis*.

Nevertheless, it may prove tempting for some new Justices who will take their seats in the '70's to adopt the model of the Warren Court in the service of different goals, even to emulate its methodology while reversing its policies. Warren Court precedent, after all, is far from firmly entrenched and would seem ripe for eradication and removal by a Court willing to copy the Warren Court's own blithe regard for *stare decisis*. Indeed, in a cruel moment, one might even feel that no less would

---

[279]Kurland, *supra* note 38, at 320.
[280]Grossman & Wells, *supra* note 254, at 2.

be deserved by those who saw "no point in querulous admonitions that the Court should restrain itself. . . ."[281]

Shortly before his death, Mr. Justice Black replied to those who minimized the importance of institutional restraint and process in favor of a result-oriented jurisprudence.

> To the people who have such faith in our nine Justices, I say that I have known a different Court from the one today.[282]

But one might still feel that something more than the back of the Black hand would be appropriate for those who shortsightedly sought to revive substantive due process[283] and adhered to the "fashionable theory that administrative agencies [could not] be trusted to take important initiatives altering the status quo, whereas the courts [were] far more dependably 'with it.' "[284] And, in truth, President Nixon sought to provide them with that sort of medicine. The Haynsworth and Carswell nominations were, in more ways than one, the direct result of the Warren Court's extreme politicization of itself. But a petty and mean spirit will not preserve our institutions. The Senate's rejection of Judges Haynsworth and Carswell was of great importance, for it not only represented a significant step in redressing the balance of the separation of powers which had been knocked askew in recent years but also illustrated that the system of mixed government envisioned by the Founding Fathers was not totally without relevance for mid-twentieth century America.

It is to be hoped that the Justices of the Supreme Court in the coming years, many of them not Nixon appointees, will have learned from the difficulties and failures, as well as from the successes, of the Warren Court and from the Fortas, Haynsworth, and Carswell incidents and that they will apply these lessons in such a way as to regain public and scholarly confidence and restore the Court to its appropriate role in the American system of government. What is called for is not a rejection of judicial policy-making but rather a recognition that it is *judicial* policy-

---

[281]Wright, *Professor Bickel, the Scholarly Tradition, and the Supreme Court,* 84 HARV. L. REV. 769, 804 (1971).

[282]H. BLACK, A CONSTITUTIONAL FAITH II (1968). *See also* Frank, Book Review, 85 POL. SCI. Q. 640 (1970).

[283]*See, e.g.,* J. SAX, DEFENDING THE ENVIRONMENT: A STRATEGY FOR CITIZEN ACTION (1971); J. COONS, W. CLUNE & S. SUGARMAN, PRIVATE WEALTH AND PUBLIC EDUCATION (1970).

[284]Jaffee, Book Review, 84 HARV. L. REV. 1562, 1565 (1971).

making and as such suffers from certain political and structural limitations. The whole history of the Supreme Court stands for the proposition that the Court can make a contribution to the policy-making process in America, but only a contribution. It cannot for long be the major component in that process. It can (and should) make policy, but due to its institutional character it must make policy only in a certain way. The procedures through which the Court makes policy have been adopted not out of caprice but because thay have proven to be functional. The Justices who have made the greatest contributions to the development of American law have been those who have most appreciated this fact.[285] Thus, what will be needed in the coming decade will not be a wholesale reversal of Warren Court decisions, though some may be discarded, but a refinement of them, a renewal of respect on the part of the Justices for the Court's limitations and traditional processes, a rebirth of craftsmanship in the construction of opinions, a return to prudence, and retreat from the advanced and untenable position the Warren Court had staked out for itself in the policy-making process.

It is too early to predict that what is needed will be what is delivered. But, in the wake of Watergate and the Viet Nam war, there is some evidence of a new awakening to the realization that the old saw about ends not justifying means may have had more than a kernel of truth in it. As regards the Supreme Court, this new awakening has suggested to many that those critics who agreed with the Warren Court's policies but voiced serious reservations about its policy-making were not necessarily reactionary but may have been right.[286] Hopefully, the successors to the

---

[285]Critics will immediately cry, "Aha! What about Marshall?" But note that Marshall exercised the power of judicial review only once, Marbury v. Madison, 1 Cranch 137 (1803), and in his major encounters with the states, which were in those days much more formidable political adversaries for the Court, he either allied himself with the other branches of the federal government or resolved the case in such a way as to leave the state no opportunity to circumvent the decision, McCulloch v. Maryland, 4 Wheat. 316 (1819), Cohens v. Virginia, 6 Wheat, 264 (1821). *See also* Barron v. Baltimore, 7 Pet. 243 (1833); Willson v. Black-Bird Creek Marsh Co., 2 Pet. 245 (1829).

[286]*E.g.*, Goodwin, *The Shape of American Politics*, 43 COMMENTARY 25, 26-27 (June 1967):

> [T]he nine justices of the Supreme Court make major political decisions, unresponsive to the democratic process, in secret meetings on Friday afternoons. Both the number and the scope of such decisions steadily mount. Liberal critics have generally approved this development, because they approve the content of the decisions, while the fundamental reshaping of an important institution seems not to trouble them. But it is a transformation which almost certainly will come back to

Warren Court will appreciate that the Rule of Law is not synonymous with rule by the Court. If not, "the time of the plague may well have arrived."[287]

plague us as judicial personnel and social attitudes change, and as an institution which has become more and more political develops an even greater sensitivity to transitory shifts in political temper.

[287] P. KURLAND, *supra* note 147, at 18.

Postscript

One of the frustrations of writing about the contemporary Court is that one is shooting at a moving target. Individually and collectively, the Justices will not stand still, enabling the scholar to contemplate them at his leisure and to draw appropriate conclusions. Today's sanguine assertion may be seriously qualified, if not demolished, by next week's events. Indeed, shortly after the finished manuscript of this book went to the publisher, tragedy struck the Court. Its longest sitting Justice, William O. Douglas, suffered a debilitating stroke. But, refusing to recognize the gravity of his situation, he did not give up easily. Motivated no doubt by memories of past personality clashes with Gerald Ford as well as by philosophic differences with the President, Douglas resisted resignation until his unseemly stubbornness began to raise questions about his mental as well as his physical capacity. While his courage was to be admired, it was feared that his continued presence on the bench might seriously damage the institution of the Court itself. To his credit, Mr. Justice Douglas removed himself with good grace before these fears were realized.

To succeed Douglas President Ford named federal judge John Paul Stevens. It is perhaps a measure of the extent to which the modern Supreme Court has politicized itself that the Stevens nomination, based as it was upon considerations of judicial merit rather than partisan or ideological qualification, was met with virtually unanimous and unmitigated surprise. The Senate, dumbfounded, confirmed Justice Stevens with ease.

Even before Mr. Justice Douglas's retirement, however, his brethren had taken steps to moot the great liberal activist by unofficially discounting his vote. An informal consensus was reached according to which no 5-4 decisions would be rendered in which Douglas's vote would determine the outcome.[1] This arrangement, coupled with the failing Justice's inability to shoulder his full share of the burden of the Court's workload, resulted in a sharp decline in the number of cases disposed of with full opinion, even though the 1974 Term experienced the latest regular session adjournment in history. Moreover, despite a larger than normal last-minute caseload, an unusually high number of cases, eleven, were held over for reargument and decision at the 1975

Term which itself opened a week earlier than had any previous term. As a result, the 1974 Term was not only the Court's longest regular session but also one of its dullest, and the 1975 Term promised little more. Even with the cases held over, the absence of significant litigation prompted one of the Justices to characterize the docket as one of "the least interesting" in recent memory.[2]

Nevertheless, the two terms did witness a second development of consequence, the emergence of Mr. Justice Blackmun as his own man. The Justice's assertion of intellectual independence, which may be said to have begun with his opinion for the majority in the abortion cases,[3] was neither dramatic nor consistent, and it was clear that he was struggling to develop a coherent judicial philosophy.[4] Yet his increasing confidence and individualism were sufficiently marked to occasion comment.[5] No longer could Justice Blackmun's position be easily categorized; nor his vote readily predicted.

These events — the removal of Mr. Justice Douglas from the Court scene, his replacement by Mr. Justice Stevens, and the emergence of Mr. Justice Blackmun — have exacerbated some of the decisional trends noted in the preceding pages. They have attenuated others. But the broad outlines traced in the foregoing have remained generally accurate, if for no other reason owing to the brief respite in judicial business necessitated by Douglas's illness. In the area of race relations, the general public mood continues to be one of a relaxation of concern for integration for integration's sake,[6] and Burger Court decision-making has reflected this trend. Though it has not retreated from its commitment to desegration to achieve equal educational opportunity, the Court has made no further contribution to an understanding of the substantive content of that goal; nor, since *Milliken v. Bradley*, has the Court rendered any major decision on the techniques which may be employed to achieve it.[7] It has, however, continued to take a very narrow approach to the concept of "state action," in *Jackson v. Metropolitan Edison Company* going even beyond *Moose Lodge's* restrictive definition of the degree of state involvement necessary to bring the Fourteenth Amendment into play.[8]

The record in the constitutional law of criminal procedure remains mixed. *Miranda* has been further confined,[9] but the Court has unanimously refused to countenance a police effort to convert the giving of the warnings into a simple expedient for evading the Fourth

Amendment.[10] The scope of the search which may be conducted incident to a lawful investigation is broad,[11] but the Court has unanimously taken a sceptical approach to the power of law enforcement to initiate an investigatory stop.[12] And, where trial rather than law enforcement procedures have been concerned, the Burger Court has often found for the defendant.[13] The exclusionary rule may yet be qualified by the creation of a constitutional harmless error rule.[14] But Mr. Chief Justice Burger, speaking extrajudicially, has asserted that neither the exclusionary rule nor *Miranda* will be wholly abandoned.[15]

In *Meek v. Pittenger,* the Burger Court has thrown the law of state aid to religious instruction into yet more confusion.[16] Relying upon *Board of Education v. Allen,* the Court upheld a Pennsylvania program for the loan of textbooks to students but struck down, as violations of the Establishment Clause, the direct loan of other instructionally related materials, such as films and laboratory equipment, and the provision of testing and counselling services. Only Justices Stewart, Blackmun, and Powell concurred in all parts of the judgment, however. Justices Brennan, Marshall, and Douglas thought the entire state program unconstitutional, while Rehnquist, White, and Burger would have declared the programs fully constitutional, except for those materials which might be easily diverted to religious purposes. To reach this result, the Court abandoned both the "excessive entanglement" rule relied upon in *Walz v. Tax Commission* and the "primary purpose and effect" test used in *Committee for Public Education v. Nyquist* in favor of a new "aid-to-the-enterprise" theory, thereby lending credence to the judgment that in this area the Court is "incapable of evolving a coherent constitutional theory."[17]

Similarly, as of this writing, the law of obscenity regulation remains a muddle.[18] The law of legislative apportionment, however, having witnessed no doctrinal development of note, is reasonably stable, and the Burger Court continues to claim and exercise a power to limit the retrospectivity of its constitutional rulings.[19]

The general themes of Burger Court policy-making identified in Chapter IX have also persisted. Although some decisions suggest that the Court may not be as solicitous of the value of privacy as was thought,[20] the reformation of the First Amendment law of libel does indicate that the Burger Court remains more sensitive to this value than was the Warren Court.[21] Likewise, a concern for localizing the solution of social and political problems and for the preservation of community integrity has continued to characterize the Court's decisions.[22] Indeed, one of the more important cases of the 1974 Term, *Hicks v. Miranda,* interestingly enough an obscenity prosecution, represented an effort to redistribute the power to enforce constitutional rights between the federal and state judiciaries, limiting the power of the lower federal courts to oversee the actions of state officials.[23] *Hicks,* too, was but another manifestation of the Burger Court's resurrection of the "passive virtues."[24] In particular, the mootness doctrine has been invoked with a vigor that belies its name,[25] and the time may yet come that the Great Writ, habeas corpus, will be returned to its original purposes.[26] The Court's attention to the maintenance of procedural safeguards in non-criminal settings, a decisional trait noted elsewhere,[27] has been expanded to embrace both public school students and mental patients.[28] But the most pronounced characteristic of Burger Court decision-making has come to be deference to the judgment of other governmental entities. The Court has reduced civilian jurisdiction over military courts-martial,[29] allowed broad investigatory powers to administrative agencies,[30] upheld state residency requirements in divorce proceedings,[31] given a sweeping endorsement to the authority of congressional committees,[32] and embraced an expansive concept of the pardoning power of the President.[33]

Thus, speaking generally, the conclusions reached in the foregoing text about the Burger Court and its relation to the Warren Court appear to be still warranted. Supreme Court nominees are not always what they seem, and the "Nixon bloc" has not proven to be nearly as united as many predicted or as some still claim. Nor has the change from Warren to Burger been as great as was anticipated; except in the areas of the criminal law and the censorship of obscenity, the work of the Warren Court remains intact; and even in those areas the Burger Court's approach has been one of qualification rather than of outright reversal. In part, this has been attributable to the mutability of societal concerns. Many of those issues which confronted the Warren Court no longer present themselves before the Burger Court, or they appear in vastly different guises. But it would also seem to be true that, under Mr. Chief Justice Burger, the high court intends to maintain a lower profile. The recent diminution of the judicial presence in American policy-making has been only partially attributable to the aberration caused by Justice Douglas's absence. The Burger Court has and pre-sumably will continue to abjure the hallmark of the Warren Court, the sweeping pronouncement of principle enunciating broad concepts of constitutional right—often ill thought out and requiring redefinition at the next term of Court. The present Justices have given evidence of a desire to apply their power sparingly, coupled with the healthy scepti-cism about the practical limits of the law as a vehicle for social change.

There remains, nevertheless, the need for intellectual coherence in the drafting of judicial policy, for the Supreme Court of the United States cannot escape policy-making. That need has gone largely unful-filled during the past decade or more. Mr. Justice Stevens is reputed to be the craftsman who will supply what has been missing.[34] At the very least, Stevens may add a crucial vote to the Court's center, if he turns out to be the moderate he has been reported to be. In view of Mr. Justice Blackmun's growing independence, a centrist coalition of Jus-tices Blackmun, Stevens, Powell, Stewart, and White could emerge which would control the direction of the Court for the next several years. But without the development of a principled set of rules to guide judicial decision, such a coalition could make for some very poor constitutional law. Reducing the public's expectations of the Court and the Court's expectations of itself will not be enough. It is intelligence that marks the difference between judicial restraint and a do-nothing Court.

NOTES

[1]TIME, July 7, 1975, at 44.

[2] TIME, Oct. 13, 1975, at 83. The only major litigation facing the Court at the 1975 Term were the challenge to the constitutionality of the 1971 Federal Election Campaign Act, as amended in 1974, and yet another effort to raise the issue of the inherent constitutionality or unconstitutionality of the death pen-alty. In Buckely v. Valeo, _____ U.S. _____, 96 S.Ct. 612 (1976), the Court sustained most of the campaign spending reform law, but it found that the expenditure limitation provisions of the act violated the First Amendment and held that the composition of the Federal Elections Commission was con-stitutionally impermissible. The capital punishment case, Fowler v. North Carolina, *cert. granted,* _____ U.S. _____, 95 S.Ct. 223 (1974) (No. 73-7031) was still pending at the time of this writing. *See also* Gregg v. Georgia, *cert. granted,* _____ U.S. _____, 96 S.Ct. 1090 (1976) (No. 74-6257); Lurek v. Texas, *cert. granted,* _____ U.S. _____, 96 S.Ct. 1090 (1976) (No. 75-5394).

75-5394).

3 Roe v. Wade, 410 U.S. 113 (1973); Doe v. Bolton, 410 U.S. 179 (1973).

4 E.g., United States v. ITT Continental Baking Co., _____ U.S. _____, 95 S.Ct. 926 (1975); Southeastern Promotions, Ltd. v. Conrad, _____ U.S. _____, 95 S.Ct. 1239 (1975); Blue Chip Stamps v. Manor Drug Stores, _____ U.S. _____, 95 S.Ct. 1917, 1937 (1975) (dissenting opinion); United States v. American Building Maintenance Industries, _____ U.S. _____, 95 S.Ct. 2150, 2160 (1975) (dissenting opinion); Rizzo v. Goode, _____ U.S. _____, 96 S.Ct. 598, 609 (1976) (dissenting opinion).

5 *See, e.g.,* Wall Street Journal, Mar. 10, 1976, at 1, col. 1.

6 *See, e.g.,* TIME, Feb. 17, 1975, at 77; Los Angeles Times, Mar. 11, 1975, § A, at 1, col. 4.

7 Indeed, in DeFunis v. Odegaard, 416 U.S. 312 (1974), the Court went out of its way to avoid such a decision. *See generally* Posner, *The DeFunis Case and the Constitutionality of Preferential Treatment of Racial Minorities,* 1974 SUP. CT. REV. 1.

8 419 U.S. 345 (1974), *noted in The Supreme Court, 1974 Term,* 89 HARV. L. REV. 47, 139 (1975).

9 *See* Oregon v. Hass, _____ U.S. _____, 95 S.Ct. 1215 (1975) (where defendant was in custody and was given *Miranda* warnings and stated he wished to obtain counsel but was unable to do so until arrival at station house, inculpatory information provided by defendant in interim period held admissible for impeachment purposes); Michigan v. Moseley, _____ U.S. _____, 96 S.Ct. 321 (1975) (*Miranda* does not require that once a person has indicated a desire to remain silent any subsequent interrogation may be undertaken only in presence of counsel.)

10 Brown v. Illinois, _____ U.S. _____, 95 S.Ct. 2254 (1975), *noted in The Supreme Court, 1974 Term,* 89 HARV. L. REV. at 68.

11 United States v. Robinson, 414 U.S. 218 (1973); Gustafson v. Florida, 414 U.S. 260 (1973). *See generally* LaFave, *"Case-by-Case Adjudication" versus "Standardized Procedures": The Robinson Dilemma,* 1974 SUP. CT. REV. 127; White, *The Fourth Amendment as a Way of Talking About People: A Study of Robinson and Matlock,* 1974 SUP. CT. REV. 165.

12 United States v. Brignoni-Ponce, _____ U.S. _____, 95 S.Ct. 2574 (1975); United States v. Ortiz, _____ U.S. _____, 95 S.Ct. 2585 (1975).

13 *E.g.,* Faretta v. California, _____ U.S. _____, 95 S.Ct. 2525 (1975) (defendant has a constitutional right to make his own defense without assistance of counsel, where he voluntarily and intelligently elects to do so); Mullaney v. Wilbur, _____ U.S. _____, 95 S.Ct. 1881 (1975) (placing burden of proof of mitigating factors on homicide defendant violates due process).

14 *See* Stone v. Powell, *cert. granted,* _____ U.S. _____, 95 S.Ct. 2676 (1975) (No. 74-1055); Wolff v. Rice, *cert. granted,* _____ U.S. _____, 95 S.Ct. 2677 (1975) (No. 74-1222). *See generally* Note, *Harmless Constitutional Error,* 20 STAN. L. REV. 83 (1967); Note, *Harmless Constitutional Error: A Reappraisal,*

83 HARV. L. REV. 814 (1970).

¹⁵ TIME, April 19, 1976, at 89. Scholarly assessments of the desirability of Mr. Chief Justice Burger's efforts to improve the administration of justice and to build support for the judiciary through exhortation as well as by example have varied. *Compare* Swindler, *The Chief Justice and Law Reform, 1921-1971,* 1971 SUP. CT. REV. 241, *with* Kurland, *1970 Term: Notes on the Emergence of the Burger Court,* 1971 SUP. CT. REV. 265, 271-272. While it may or may not be appropriate for the Chief Justice to hold press conferences, however, it is rather more difficult to defend his discussing with the media issues involved in cases still pending before the Court.

¹⁶ _____ U.S. _____, 95 S.Ct. 1753 (1975), *noted in The Supreme Court, 1974 Term,* 89 HARV. L. REV. at 104-110. In the reports, the defendant's name is incorrectly spelled as "Pittinger."

¹⁷ Wilson, *The School Aid Decisions: A Chronicle of Dashed Expectations,* 3 J. LAW & EDUC. 101, 101 (1974).

¹⁸ *See, e.g.,* Erznoznik v. City of Jacksonville, _____ U.S. _____, 95 S.Ct. 2268 (1975) (permitting drive-in theatres to show nude movies, no matter what the distraction to drivers on nearby roads), *noted in The Supreme Court, 1974 Term,* 89 HARV. L. REV. at 123.

¹⁹ *E.g.,* United States v. Peltier, _____ U.S. _____, 95 S.Ct. 2313 (1975); Bowen v. United States, _____ U.S. _____, 95 S.Ct. 2569 (1975).

²⁰ *E.g.,* United States v. Bisceglia, _____ U.S. _____, 95 S.Ct. 915 (1975). *See also* Doe v. Commonwealth's Attorney, _____ F. Supp. _____, 44 LW 2230 (E.D. Va 1975), *cert. denied,* 44 LW _____ (1976).

²¹ *See* Gertz v. Robert Welch, Inc., 418 U.S. 323 (1974); Time, Inc. v. Firestone, _____ U.S. _____, 96 S.Ct. 958 (1976).

²² E.g., Village of Belle Terre v. Boraas, 416 U.S. 1 (1974). *See also* Construction Industry Association of Sonoma County v. City of Petaluma, 522 F.2d 897 (9th Cir. 1975), *cert. denied,* _____ U.S. _____, 96 S.Ct. 1148 (1976) (No. 75-923).

²³ _____ U.S. _____, 95. S.Ct. 2281 (1975), *noted in The Supreme Court, 1974 Term,* 89 HARV. L. REV. at 151.

²⁴ *See* Bickel, *The Passive Virtues,* 75 HARV. L. REV. 40 (1961).

²⁵ *E.g.,* Board of School Commissioners v. Jacobs, _____ U.S. _____, 95 S.Ct. 848 (1975).

²⁶ *See* Stone v. Powell, *cert. granted,* _____ U.S. _____, 95 S.Ct. 2676 (1975) (no. 74-1055).

²⁷ O'Neil, *Of Justice Delayed and Justice Denied: The Welfare Prior Hearing Cases,* 1970 SUP. CT. REV. 161; Funston, *Judicialization of the Administrative Process,* 2 AM POL. Q. 38 (1974). *See generally* Sarat & Grossman, *Courts and Conflict Resolution: Problems in the Mobilization of Adjudication,* 69 AM. POL. SCI. Q. 1200 (1975).

²⁸ Goss v. Lopez, 419 U.S. 565 (1975) (suspension of public school students); O'Connor v. Donaldson, _____ U.S. _____, 95 S.Ct. 2486 (1975) (civil confinement of the nondangerous mentally ill). *But cf.* Arnett v. Kennedy, 416

U.S. 134 (1974).

²⁹ Schlesinger v. Councilman, _____ U.S. _____, 95 S.Ct. 1300 (1975).

³⁰ United States v. Bisceglia, _____ U.S. _____, 95 S.Ct. 915 (1975).

³¹ Sosna v. Iowa, 419 U.S. 393 (1975), *noted in The Supreme Court, 1974 Term,* 89 HARV. L. REV. at 87.

³² Eastland v. United States Servicemen's Fund, _____ U.S. _____, 95 S.Ct. 1813 (1975), *noted in The Supreme Court, 1974 Term,* 89 HARV. L. REV. at 131.

³³ Schick v. Reed, 419 U.S. 256 (1974), *noted in The Supreme Court, 1974 Term,* 89 HARV. L. REV. at 59.

³⁴ *See* TIME, Dec. 8, 1975, at 58.

Bibliography

The extensive footnoting of the preceding text should already have given the careful reader a fairly complete and accurate picture of the sources consulted in preparing this manuscript. The following remarks, therefore, are intended to be not so much a bibliographic compilation as an evaluative note upon some of the more important sources, in order to direct the interested reader to the most valuable commentaries. I have also included some suggestions for further reading. Throughout the text, standard legal citation has been used; if the reader is unfamiliar with this citational form or desires clarification of a particular note, he should consult *A Uniform System of Citation: Forms of Citation and Abbreviations* (11th ed.; Cambridge, Mass.: The Harvard Law Review Association, 1967). In these bibliographic comments, however, a somewhat more complete style has been adopted to assist the reader in consulting or purchasing the materials cited.

GENERAL WORKS

Robert G. McCloskey, *The American Supreme Court* (Chicago: The University of Chicago Press, 1960), is a brief and eminently readable historical summary especially valuable for the beginning student who is approaching an evaluation of the contemporary Court without a firm foundation in constitutional history. More detailed and more scholarly, although a somewhat dreary narrative, is Alfred H. Kelly and Winfred A. Harbison, *The American Constitution: Its Origins and Development* (4th ed.; New York: W. W. Norton & Co., 1970). The classic work is Charles Warren, *The Supreme Court in United States History* (2 vols.; Boston: Little, Brown and Co., 1922), but it covers only the period from the founding to 1918. Similarly, Carl Brent Swisher, *The Growth of Constitutional Power in the United States* (Chicago: The University of Chicago Press, 1946), is a good, systematic analysis but only through the New Deal Period. For the modern developments, Alpheus T. Mason,

The Supreme Court from Taft to Warren (New York: W.W. Norton & Co., 1964), is a fairly simple treatment, as is G. Theodore Mitau, *Decade of Decision: The Supreme Court and The Constitutional Revolution 1954-1964* (New York: Charles Scribner's Sons, 1967). Much better for style, substance, and scholarship is Paul L. Murphy, *The Constitution in Crisis Times, 1918-1969* (New York: Harper & Row, 1972). Perhaps the best of all would have been Robert G. McCloskey, *The Modern Supreme Court* (Cambridge, Mass.: Harvard University Press, 1972). Unfortunately, Professor McCloskey died before he had completed the manuscript. But even as printed, with McCloskey's chapters on the Stone and Vinson Courts and the inclusion of seven previously published articles on the Warren Court, it is an extremely valuable work with which all serious students should be familiar.

Henry J. Abraham, *Freedom and the Court: Civil Rights and Liberties in the United States* (2d. ed.; New York: Oxford University Press, 1972), is an excellent overview of precedent in areas which have been especially important for the modern Supreme Court. Also focusing upon substantive law rather than constitutional history is Norman Dorsen, ed., *The Rights of Americans: What They Are—What They Should Be* (New York: Random House, 1970). Jonathan D. Casper, *The Politics of Civil Liberties* (New York: Harper & Row, 1972), approaches the same subject and material from a somewhat different but no less important perspective.

For the serious student of the Court, the most difficult task is simply keeping up to date. Even during the Burger years, rapid development has been a characteristic of many of the areas of law dealt with in this book. Apart from regularly reading *United States Law Week* or the Advance Sheets of *The Supreme Court Reporter*, the non-professional may find it sufficient to keep abreast with *The Supreme Court Review* and each November's issue of the *Harvard Law Review*. *The Supreme Court Review* provides an annual running commentary by leading legal scholars on selected aspects of the Supreme Court. The *Harvard Law Review* each November publishes a critical survey of the Court's work during the preceding term. Close attention to these two sources is a quick and relatively easy way of following the Court's progress. But, at base, there is no substitute for reading the Court's own opinions as made available in the pages of the *United States Reports*.

CHAPTER ONE: THE NEED FOR REASONS

Harold J. Spaeth, *An Introduction to Supreme Court Decision Making* (San Francisco: Chandler Publishing Co., 1972), is a very good, brief beginning treatise. Also worthwhile are Paul Freund, *The Supreme Court of the United States: Its Business, Purposes, and Performance* (Cleveland, Ohio: The World Publishing Co., 1961), which takes a traditional, lawyerly approach, and Glendon Schubert, *Judicial Policy Making: The Political Role of the Courts* (Glenview, Ill.: Scott, Foresman and Co., 1974), which utilizes a more behaviorally oriented, social science methodology.

Paul M. Bator, Paul J. Mishkin, David L. Shapiro, and Herbert Wechsler, eds., *Hart and Wechsler's The Federal Courts and the Federal System* (2d ed.; Mineola, N.Y.: The Foundation Press, Inc., 1973) must be considered definitive on questions of procedure and jurisdiction. But also useful is Henry J. Friendly, *Federal Jurisdiction: A General View* (New York: Columbia University Press, 1973); and Alexander M. Bickel, *The Caseload of the Supreme Court—And What, If Anything, To Do About It* (Washington, D.C.: American Enterprise Institute for Public Policy Research, 1973), may serve as a somber, if not unwelcome, representative of the reality principle in this significant but seemingly esoteric field.

The classic treatment of the doctrines and devices of judicial limitation and avoidance is Alexander M. Bickel, "The Passive Virtues," *Harvard Law Review*, 75 (November 1961), 40-79. This essay is incorporated into Alexander M. Bickel, *The Least Dangerous Branch: The Supreme Court at the Bar of Politics* (Indianapolis, Ind.: The Bobbs-Merrill Co., Inc., 1962), which is itself an improtant contribution to the almost infinite literature on the subject of judicial review in America. Excellent introductions to the on-going debate over the origins, scope, purpose, and worth of this institution are Leonard Levy, ed., *Judicial Review and the Supreme Court: Selected Essays* (New York: Harper & Row, 1967), and David F. Forte, ed., *The Supreme Court in American Politics: Judicial Activism vs. Judicial Restraint* (Lexington, Mass.: D.C. Heath and Co., 1972). Among the more cogent statements by practitioners are Robert H. Jackson, *The Supreme Court in the American System of Government* (New York: Harper & Row, 1963); Learned Hand, *The Bill of Rights* (Cambridge, Mass.: Harvard University Press, 1958); Hugo L. Black, "The Bill of Rights," *New York University Law Review*, 35 (April 1965), 865-81, and *A Constitutional Faith* (New York: Alfred A. Knopf, Inc., 1968); and Felix Frankfurter, "John Marshall and the Judicial Function," *Harvard Law Review*, 69 (December 1955), 217-38. In particular, the differences between Black and Frankfurter are carefully charted in Wallace Mendelson, *Justices Black and Frankfurter: Conflict In the Court* (2d. ed.: Chicago: The University of Chicago Press, 1966). Herbert Wechsler, "Toward Neutral Principles of Constitutional Law," *Harvard Law Review*, 73 (November 1959), 1-35, is one of the best known and respected scholarly contributions to the debate, as also is Robert A. Dahl, "Decision-Making in a Democracy: The Supreme Court as a National Policy-Maker," *Journal of Public Law*, 6 (Fall 1957), 279-95. Eugene V. Rostow, *The Sovereign Prerogative: The Supreme Court and the Quest for Law* (New Haven, Conn.: Yale University Press, 1962), should not be overlooked, but it should be read in connection with George Mace, "The Antidemocratic Character of Judicial Review," *California Law Review*, 60 (June 1972), 1140-49. And a spirited, if not particularly substantial, recent entry is Sam J. Ervin, Jr., and Ramsey Clark, *Role of the Supreme Court: Policymaker or Adjudicator?* (Washington, D.C.: American Enterprise Institute for Public Policy Research, 1970).

CHAPTER TWO: WITH LIBERTY AND JUSTICE FOR ALL

The historical materials on American law and racial discrimination are catalogued in Harold W. Horowitz and Kenneth L. Karst, eds., *Law, Lawyers and Social Change* (Indianapolis, Ind.: The Bobbs-Merrill Co., Inc., 1969), and Richard Bardolph, ed., *The Civil Rights Record: Black Americans and the Law, 1849-1970* (New York: Thomas Y. Crowell Co., 1970). Jacobus tenBroek, *Equal Under Law* (New York: The Macmillan Co., 1965), deals with the anti-slavery origins of the Fourteenth Amendment, while C. Van Woodward, *The Strange Career of Jim Crow* (New York: Oxford University Press, 1966), discusses the evolution of the doctrine of "separate but equal" after the ratification of that amendment. The demise of the doctrine of "separate but equal" is dramatically treated in a case study, Daniel M. Breman, *It Is So Ordered* (New York: W. W. Norton & Co., 1966). The difficulties of implementing that decision are dealt with in J. W. Peltason, *Fifty-eight Lonely Men: Southern Federal Judges and School Desegregation* (Urbana, Ill.: University of Illinois Press, 1971). Clement E. Vose, *Caucasians Only* (Berkeley, Calif.: University of California Press, 1959), and Lois B. Moreland, *White Racism and the Law* (Columbus, Ohio: Charles E. Merrill, 1970) examine the difficult problems posed by public enforcement of private, racially discriminatory choices. Federal protection of civil rights is ably discussed by Laurent B. Frantz, "Congressional Power to Enforce the Fourteenth Amendment Against Private Acts," *Yale Law Journal*, 73 (July 1964), 1353-84, and Harrell R. Rodgers, Jr., and Charles S. Bullock, III, *Law and Social Change: Civil Rights Laws and Their Consequences* (New York: McGraw-Hill, Inc., 1972). A useful retrospective is Robert L. Carter, "The Warren Court and Desegregation," *Michigan Law Review*, 67 (December 1968), 237-48, while Symposium, "The Nixon Court: Requiem for Judicial Activism?," *Black Law Journal*, 2 (Winter 1972), 195-254, looks to the future with trepidation.

Questions of economic discrimination and the law are the subject of inquiry in Frank I. Michelman, "On Protecting the Poor Through the Fourteenth Amendment," *Harvard Law Review*, 83 (November 1969), 7-59, and Ralph K. Winter, Jr., "Poverty, Economic Equality, and the Equal Protection Clause," *1972: The Supreme Court Review* (Chicago: The University of Chicago Press, 1973), 41-102. The materials on equal educational opportunity and school finance are pulled together in an excellent essay by Judith Areen and Leonard Ross, "The Rodriguez Case: Judicial Oversight of School Finance," *1973: The Supreme Court Review* (Chicago: The University of Chicago Press, 1974), 33-55. Robert M. O'Neil, *The Price of Dependency: Civil Liberties in the Welfare State* (New York: E. P. Dutton & Co., Inc., 1970), is an original and far-ranging work which analyzes in depth many of the issues dealt with in this book, as well as a host of others.

The doctrinal ramifications of the Court's work in these areas are parsed in "Developments in the Law—Equal Protection," *Harvard Law Review*, 82 (March 1969), 1065-1192, and Gerald Gunther, "In Search of Evolving Doctrine on a Changing Court: A Model for A Newer Equal Procection," *Harvard Law Review*, 86 (November 1972), 1-48. Also worthwhile is Wallace Mendelson, "From Warren to Burger: The Rise and Decline of Substantive Equal Protection," *American Political Science Review*, 66 (December 1972), 1226-33.

CHAPTER THREE: THE NEW MATH

The political background of the reapportionment rulings is traced in Gordon E. Baker, *The Reapportionment Revolution* (New York: Random House, 1967); their place in the history of constitutional development is treated in William M. Wiecek, *The Guarantee Clause of the Constitution* (Ithaca, N.Y.: Cornell University Press, 1972), and Richard Claude, *The Supreme Court and the Electoral Process* (Baltimore: The Johns Hopkins University Press, 1970). Each succeeding reapportionment ruling has been the subject of numerous law review articles; some of the classics are cited in footnote number one of chapter three. Among the best, recent essays are Note, "Reapportionment—Nine Years Into the 'Revolution' and Still Struggling," *Michigan Law Review*, 70 (January 1972), 586-616, and Gerhard Casper, "Apportionment and the Right to Vote: Standards of Judicial Scrutiny," *1973: The Supreme Court Review* (Chicago: The University of Chicago Press, 1974), 1-32. However, of the three areas of decision-making which have been the most significant for the modern Supreme Court (race relations, legislative apportionment, and criminal defendants' rights), reapportionment is the only one which has been the subject of a definitive scholarly treatment; it is Robert G. Dixon, Jr., *Democratic Representation: Reapportionment in Law and Politics* (New York: Oxford University Press, 1968).

CHAPTER FOUR: COURTHOUSE AND STATION HOUSE

The literature on the Supreme Court and criminal defendants' rights is virtually limitless. The volumes by Abraham, Casper, and Dorsen which have previously been mentioned are good starting points, as is the book-length discussion of the subject by Fred P. Graham, *The Due Process Revolution: The Warren Court's Impact on Criminal Law* (New York: Hayden Books Co., Inc., 1970). The Symposium, "The Supreme Court and the Police," *Journal of Criminal Law, Criminology, and Police Science*, 57 (September & December 1966), 238-311, 379-425, is a concise, if critical, review, available in reprint form from the International Association of Chiefs of Police. A more indulgent attitude toward the Warren Court is displayed by A. Kenneth Pye, "The Warren Court and Criminal Procedure," *Michigan Law Review*, 67 (December 1968), 249-68. Essays by three of America's leading jurists, however, are less laudatory and are among the classics in this field: Roger J. Traynor, "The Devils of Due Process in Criminal Detection, Detention, and

Trial," *Catholic University Law Review*, 16 (September 1966), 1-22; Walter V. Schaefer, "Police Interrogation and the Privilege Against Self-Incrimination," *Northwestern University Law Review*, 61 (December 1966), 506-26; Henry J. Friendly, "The Bill of Rights as a Code of Criminal Procedure," *California Law Review*, 53 (October 1965), 929-56. Also good are Charles A. O'Brien, "Dilemmas of Criminal Justice in a Democratic Society," *University of San Francisco Law Review*, 3 (October 1968), 1-12, and Alexander M. Bickel, "Judicial Review of Police Methods in Law Enforcement: The Role of the Supreme Court of the United States," *Texas Law Review*, 44 (April 1966), 954-64. John Galloway, ed., *The Supreme Court and The Rights of The Accused* (Washington, D.C.: Facts on File, Inc., 1973) is a comprehensive, contemporary collection on the subject. Also recent, Otis H. Stephens, *The Supreme Court and Confessions of Guilt* (Knoxville, Tenn.: University of Tennessee Press, 1973), is a good survey of evolving judicial interpretation.

Surprisingly, the liberal outcry over the Burger Court's alleged revision of the Warren Court's codification of the constitutional rights of the criminally accused has translated itself into only limited and relatively random commentary in the professional and scholarly journals. At this writing, the best critical essay is Alan M. Dershowitz and John Hart Ely, "*Harris v. New York*: Some Anxious Observations on the Candor and Logic of the Emerging Nixon Majority," *Yale Law Journal*, 80 (May 1971), 1198-1227. But Note, "Warrantless Searches and Seizures of Automobiles," *Harvard Law Review*, 87 (February 1974), 835-53, is also worth examination.

The reader interested in a summary statement of the law should consult Hazel B. Kerper, *Introduction to the Criminal Justice System* (St. Paul, Minn.: West Publishing Co., 1972). More analytic and more detailed are Livingston Hall, Yale Kamisar, Wayne R. LaFave, and Jerold H. Israel, eds., *Basic Criminal Procedure* (3rd ed.; St. Paul, Minn.: West Publishing Co., 1969), and Frank J. Remington, *et al.*, eds., *Criminal Justice Administration* (Indianapolis, Ind.: The Bobbs-Merrill Co., 1969).

CHAPTER FIVE: OF CHIMERAS AND COURTS AND CONSTERNATIONS

Unlike the material on the Court and crime, the literature on prospective overruling is reasonably confined. The student familiar with

Phillip Johnson, "Retroactivity in Retrospect," *California Law Review*, 56 (November 1968), 1612-32; Herman Schwartz, "Retroactivity, Reliability, and Due Process: A Reply to Professor Mishkin," *University of Chicago Law Review*, 33 (Summer 1966), 719-68; Paul J. Mishkin, "The High Court, the Great Writ, and the Due Process of Time and Law," *Harvard Law Review*, 79 (November 1965), 56-102; and Paul Bender, "The Retroactive Effect of an Overruling Constitutional Decision: *Mapp v. Ohio*," *University of Pennsylvania Law Review*, 110 (March 1962), 650-83, could be said to be conversant on the subject. Also relevant is "Developments in the Law—Federal Habeas Corpus," *Harvard Law Review*, 83 (March 1970), 1038-1280.

CHAPTER SIX: MUCH ADO ABOUT NOTHING

Leo Pfeffer, *Church, State and Freedom* (Rev. ed.; Boston: Beacon Press, 1967) is an exhaustive treatment of almost every sort of church-state relationship in American law. Another fine volume, though focusing upon the establishment issue only, is Philip B. Kurland, *Religion and the Law: Of Church and State and the Supreme Court* (New York: Aldine Publishing Co., 1962), and Paul G. Kauper, *Religion and the Constitution* (Baton Rouge, La.: Louisiana State University Press, 1964), is equally worthy of mention. Dallin H. Oaks, ed., *The Wall Between Church and State* (Chicago: The University of Chicago Press, 1963), is also valuable as a collection presenting a number of divergent positions.

The origin and development of the law of church and state are surveyed by William H. Marnell, *The First Amendment* (Garden City, N.Y.: Doubleday & Co., Inc., 1964), and John F. Wilson, ed., *Church and State in American History* (Boston: D.C. Heath and Co., 1965).

Paul G. Kauper, "Prayer, Public Schools and the Supreme Court," *Michigan Law Review*, 61 (April 1963), 1031-68, would have to be included in any compilation of the classic articles in this area of constitutional jurisprudence, as would Louis H. Pollack, "Public Prayers in Public Schools," *Harvard Law Review*, 77 (November 1963), 62-78. Arthur E. Sutherland, Jr., "Establishment According to *Engel*," *Harvard Law Review*, 76 (November 1962), 25-52, is also highly regarded. Philip B. Kurland, "The Regents' Prayer Case: 'Full of Sound and Fury, Signifying . . . ,'," *1962: The Supreme Court Review* (Chicago: The University of Chicago Press, 1963), 1-33, is a trenchant charting of the first school prayer case, and it was ably followed by Ernest J. Brown,

"Quis Custodiet Ipsos Custodes?—The School Prayer Cases," *1963: The Supreme Court Review* (Chicago: The University of Chicago Press, 1964), 1-33.

Among the more substantial recent contributions have been Wilbur G. Katz, "Radiations From Church Tax Exemption," *1970: The Supreme Court Review* (Chicago: The University of Chicago Press, 1970), 93-108; Donald A. Gianella, "Lemon and Tilton: The Bitter and the Sweet of Church-State Entanglement," *1971: The Supreme Court Review* (Chicago: The University of Chicago Press, 1971), 147-200; and Richard E. Morgan, "The Establishment Clause and Sectarian Schools: A Final Installment?," *1973: The Supreme Court Review* (Chicago: The University of Chicago Press, 1974). But perhaps the most original analysis has been Wilbur G. Katz and Harold P. Southerland, "Religious Pluralism and the Supreme Court," *Daedalus*, 96 (Winter 1967), 180-92.

Essential to a complete understanding of the subject is Richard E. Morgan, *The Politics of Religious Conflict* (New York: Western Publishing Co., Inc., 1968), which analyzes the interest group pressures involved. Frank J. Sorauf, "Zorach v. Clauson: The Impact of a Supreme Court Decision," *American Political Science Review*, 53 (September 1959), 777-91, and Robert H. Birkby, "The Supreme Court and the Bible Belt: Tennessee Reaction to the 'Schempp' Decision," *Midwest Journal of Political Science*, 10 (August 1966), 304-15, should also be read.

CHAPTER SEVEN: NINE OLD MEN AND A FEW DIRTY BOOKS

The interested reader should begin with *The Report of the Commission on Obscenity and Pornography* (Washington, D.C.: United States Government Printing Office, 1970), but he should not stop there. The classic works of legal analysis in this field are William B. Lockhart and Robert C. McClure, "Literature, the Law of Obscenity, and the Constitution," *Minnesota Law Reivew*, 38 (March 1954), 295-395; Harry Kalven, Jr., "The Metaphysics of the Law of Obscenity," *1960: The Supreme Court Review* (Chicago: The University of Chicago Press, 1960), 1-45; C. Peter Magrath, "The Obscenity Cases: Grapes of Roth," *1966: The Supreme Court Review* (Chicago: The University of Chicago Press, 1966), 7-77; and Louis Henkin, "Morals and the Constitution: The Sin of Obscenity," *Columbia Law Review*, 63 (March 1963), 391-414. The results of these and other analyses are synthesized by Richard Funston, "Pornography and Politics: The Court, the Constitution, and the Commission," *Western Political Quarterly,* 24 (December 1971), 635-52.

An historical perspective on the problem is provided by Morris L. Ernst and Alan U. Schwartz, *Censorship: The Search for the Obscene* (New York: The Macmillan Co., 1966). In this context, Eberhard and Phyllis Kronhausen, *Pornography and the Law: The Psychology of Erotic Realism and Hard Core Pornography* (New York: Ballantine Books, Inc., 1959), is also useful, but it is cheapened by the extensive quotation of the most erotic passages of the works which the authors discuss, leaving the attentive reader questioning whether they were more interested in scholarship or sales.

General questions of free speech theory are competently dealt with by Martin Shapiro, *Freedom of Speech: The Supreme Court and Judicial Review* (Englewood Cliffs, N.J.: Prentice Hall, Inc. 1966), and Thomas I. Emerson, *The System of Freedom of Expression* (New York: Random House, 1970).

CHAPTER EIGHT: THE WARREN COURT IN RETROSPECT

Richard H. Sayler, Barry B. Boyer, and Robert E. Gooding, Jr., eds., *The Warren Court: A Critical Analysis* (New York: Chelsea House, 1969), is a valuable compilation of essays, most of them laudatory. Perhaps the best of the scholarly volumes praising the Warren Court is Archibald Cox, *The Warren Court: Constitutional Decision as an Instrument of Reform* (Cambridge, Mass.: Harvard University Press, 1968). More critical of the Court are two volumes by Alexander M. Bickel, *Politics and the Warren Court* (New York: Harper & Row, 1965), and the especially pithy *The Supreme Court and the Idea of Progress* (New York: Harper & Row, 1970). Also critical and somewhat more readable than Professor Bickel's prose is Philip B. Kurland, *Politics, the Constitution, and the Warren Court* (Chicago: The University of Chicago Press, 1970). J. Skelly Wright, "Professor Bickel, the Scholarly Tradition, and the Supreme Court," *Harvard Law Review,* 84 (February 1971), 769-805, criticizes the critics. The less scholarly but politically better muscled critics are discussed in a brief, specialized, but intereting study, Clifford M. Lytle, *The Warren Court and Its Critics* (Tucson, Arizona: The University of Arizona Press, 1968). Charles L. Black, Jr., "The Unfinished Business of the Warren Court," *Washington Law Review,* 46 (October 1970), 3-45, is useful as a concluding summation on

the Warren era and as an essay with which to begin one's consideration
of the new Court.

CHAPTER NINE: THE BURGER COURT IN PERSPECTIVE

The book-length discussions of the Burger Court have, thus far,
tended to be journalistic rather than scholarly, more simple than subtle,
and characterized by errors of fact, logic, and occasionally taste. Louis M.
Kohlmeier, Jr., *"God Save This Honorable Court!,"* (New York: Charles
Scribner's Sons, 1972), attempts to analyze the Burger Court within the
context of a general theory about the role of the Supreme Court in
American politics. James F. Simon, *In His Own Image: The Supreme
Court in Richard Nixon's America* (New York: David McKay Co.,
1973), is less ambitious and more balanced. Neither should be read
without also considering the review by D. Grier Stephenson, Jr., in the
Political Science Quarterly, 89 (Fall 1974), 652-54. Richard Harris,
Decision (New York: E. P. Dutton & Co., Inc., 1971), is another
journalistic—and mean-spirited—account of the Haynsworth-Carswell
fiasco.

Among the better scholarly analyses, Symposium, "The Burger
Court: New Directions in Judicial Policy-Making," *Emory Law Journal,*
23 (Summer 1974), 641-779, presents the thoughts and remarks of
several distinguished political scientists. Philip B. Kurland, "Enter the
Burger Court: The Constitutional Business of the Supreme Court, O.T.
1969," *1970: The Supreme Court Review* (Chicago: The University of
Chicago Press, 1970), 1-92, and "1971 Term: The Year of the Stewart-
White Court," *1972: The Supreme Court Review* (Chicago: The
University of Chicago Press, 1973), 181-329, are lengthy, albeit some-
times witty, catalogues; better and more analytic is Kurland's "1970
Term: Notes on the Emergence of the Burger Court," *1971: The
Supreme Court Review* (Chicago: The University of Chicago Press,
1971), 265-322. Alpheus T. Mason, "The Burger Court in Historical
Perspective," *Political Science Quarterly,* 89 (March 1974), 27-45,
presents a broader portrait. Also worthwhile are A. E. Dick Howard,
"Mr. Justice Powell and the Emerging Nixon Majority," *Michigan Law
Review,* 70 (January 1972), 445-68, and Alexander M. Bickel, "The New
Supreme Court: Prospects and Problems," *Tulane Law Review,* 45
(February 1971), 229-44.

There are several excellent essays dealing with particular facets of

Burger Court decision-making. The articles previously cited by Wallace Mendelson and Gerald Gunther are fine surveys of the changing topography of equal protection interpretation. The consequences this developing doctrine may have for the reappraisal of property as a constitutional value are discussed in Richard Funston, "The Double Standard of Constitutional Protection in the Era of the Welfare State," *Political Science Quarterly*, 90 (Summer 1975), 261-87. Julius G. Getman, "The Emerging Constitutional Principle of Sexual Equality," *1972: The Supreme Court Review* (Chicago: the University of Chicago Press, 1973), 157-80, is a fine treatment of a facet of equal protection analysis not dealt with by this text. Related to the problem of the legal status of women is the discussion of the abortion decisions in Laurence Tribe, "Toward a Model of Roles in the Due Process of Life and Law," *Harvard Law Review*, 87 (November 1973), 1-53. Less congratulatory of the Court is Richard A. Epstein, "Substantive Due Process by Any Other Name: The Abortion Cases," *1973: The Supreme Court Review* (Chicago: The University of Chicago Press, 1974), 159-85. Another feature of the evolving definition of due process is dealt with by Richard Funston, "Judicialization of the Administrative Process," *American Politics Quarterly*, 2 (January 1974), 38-60. Harry Kalven, "Even When a Nation Is at War," *Harvard Law Review*, 85 (November 1971), 3-36, contains some intriguing observations on First Amendment interpretation. Finally, two very significant decisions which could not be dealt with at length in the present study are carefully examined in Daniel D. Polsby, "The Death of Capital Punishment? Furman v. Georgia," *1972: The Supreme Court Review* (Chicago: The University of Chicago Press, 1973), 1-40, and Symposium, "United States v. Nixon," *U.C.L.A. Law Review*, 22 (October 1974), 4-140.

TABLE OF CASES

INDEX OF NAMES

SUBJECT INDEX